French Prose and Criticism, 1790 to World War II

Titles in the CRITICAL COSMOS series include

THE CRITICAL COSMOS SERIES

French Prose and Criticism, 1790 to World War II

Edited and with an introduction
by *HAROLD BLOOM*
Sterling Professor of the Humanities
Yale University

CHELSEA HOUSE PUBLISHERS
New York ◇ Philadelphia

© 1990 by Chelsea House Publishers, a division of
Main Line Book Co.

Introduction © 1990 by Harold Bloom

Printed and bound in the United States of America

10 9 8 7 6 5 4 3 2 1

Library of Congress Cataloging-in-Publication Data

French prose and criticism, 1790 to World War II / edited
and with an introduction by Harold Bloom.
    p.   cm. — (The Critical cosmos series)
  Bibliography: p.
  Includes index.
  Summary: A collection of twenty-six critical essays on
French prose and criticism from 1790 to World War II.
  ISBN 1-555-46081-X
  1. French prose literature—19th century—History and
criticism. 2. French prose literature—20th century—History
and criticism. 3. Criticism—France—History—19th century.
4. Criticism—France—History—20th century. [1. French
literature—19th century—History and criticism. 2. French
literature—20th century—History and criticism.
3. Criticism—France—History—19th century. 4. Criticism—
France—History—20th century.] I. Bloom, Harold.
II. Series: Critical cosmos.
PQ621.F74   1988
848'.08—dc19   87-28432
                                                    CIP
                                                     AC

Contents

Editor's Note

This book gathers together a representative selection of the best critical essays available in English on the major writers of French nonfictional prose and criticism from 1790 to the onset of World War II. I am grateful to Chantal McCoy for her erudition and judgment in helping me edit this volume.

My introduction centers upon Paul Valéry, probably the crucial French literary intellectual of this century, and considers his relation to his precursors in the context of his own ideas of influence and originality.

The historical sequence begins with Brian William Head's consideration of Destutt de Tracy, theorist of scientific method and of a "science" of ideology, and a pioneering critic of idealist metaphysics. Lilian R. Furst, writing on Mme de Staël's *De l'Allemagne*, judges it to have been both an illuminating and a misleading intermediary between German and French Romanticism.

Benjamin Constant is seen by Stephen Holmes as a theorist who taught his fellow citizens that "civil liberty and political liberty are mutually interdependent." Andrew Martin, studying Chateaubriand, presents him as a visionary of a primordial world that nevertheless excludes any possibility of a fresh beginning.

Fourier's language is deconstructed by the eminent critic Roland Barthes, who charmingly compares the erotic utopias of Sade and Fourier. The equally eminent theoretician of eros and civilization, Herbert Marcuse, relates the positivism of Saint-Simon and Comte to the advent of the modern discipline of sociology. Michelet, mythological prose-poet of history, is studied in his thematics of death by Linda Orr.

Ceri Crossley situates Edgar Quinet's vision of architecture within the contexts of his philosophy of history and of religion. The critical art of Sainte-Beuve, one of imaginative portraiture of authors, receives an appreciation from Emerson R. Marks. De Tocqueville's inability to work out

ix

the specific dynamics of the French Revolution is the subject of François Furet, while Aaron Noland charts the ironic confrontation of Proudhon and Rousseau, who influenced Proudhon despite every effort made to exorcise him.

Susan Blood finds in Baudelaire's reaction to the advent of photography an allegory or irony of personal resistance, presumably on behalf of a waning Romanticism. Our foremost critic of Orientalism, Edward W. Said, considers the reactions of Renan (and his younger contemporary Massignon) to Islam as having been emblems of French culture.

The critic Taine and the linguist Saussure are brought together by Hans Aarsleff, who finds in Taine a crucial extralinguistic influence upon Saussure. Mallarmé as prose speculator is analyzed both by Maurice Blanchot, seer of literary space, and by Barbara Johnson, deconstructor of poetic theory. We return to Saussure with Sylvère Lotringer's overview, and then pass to Terry F. Godlove, Jr.'s investigation of the role of theory of knowledge in Durkheim's sociology of religious existence.

Bergson, the central figure in modern perplexities over temporality and duration, is analyzed by the philosopher Gilles Deleuze. An antithesis to the humane Bergson, the French proto-Fascist Maurras, is incisively contemplated by Michael Sutton, who concludes that the essence of Maurras is a Catholicism without Christianity.

In an essay published here for the first time, Kevin Newmark brilliantly uncovers in Gide's profuse multiplication of genres an implicit theory of literature. The equally intricate and dialectical relation between Proust and Ruskin is explicated with great skill by David R. Ellison. Valéry's highly problematic relationship to his sources is deconstructed by Jacques Derrida with his customary inventiveness.

Margaret R. Higgonet sets forth the pervasive effect of the Romantic theory of the imagination upon the work of Gaston Bachelard, after which Jean-Pierre Morel charts the uneasy but crucial relation of the Surrealism of Breton to the speculations of Freud. This book concludes with A. Smock's study of Simone Weil, whose problematic stature (in my own judgment) is not enhanced by Smock's shrewd attempt to domesticate Weil's psychic and spiritual realities in the world of Kafka's *The Castle*.

Introduction

In the preface to his *Leonardo, Poe, Mallarmé*, Valéry calls these precursors "three masters of the art of abstraction." "Man fabricates by abstraction" is a famous Valérian formula, reminding us that this sense of abstraction is Latin: "withdrawn, taken out from, removed." "It Must be Abstract," the first part of Stevens's *Notes toward a Supreme Fiction*, moves in the atmosphere of an American version of Valéry's insight, but the American is Walt Whitman and not Edgar Poe:

> The weather and the giant of the weather,
> Say the weather, the mere weather, the mere air:
> An abstraction blooded, as a man by thought.

Valéry fabricates by withdrawing from a stale reality, which he refuses to associate with the imaginings of his masters. These "enchanted, dominated me, and—as was only fitting—tormented me as well; the beautiful is that which fills us with despair." Had Valéry spoken of pain rather than despair, he would have been more Nietzschean. The genealogy of imagination is not truly Valéry's subject. Despair is not a staleness in reality, or an absence of it; it is the overwhelming presence of reality, of the reality principle, or the necessity of death-in-life, or simply of dying. Valéry's beautiful "Palme" concludes with a metaphor that seems central to all of his poetry:

> Pareille à celui qui pense
> Et dont l'âme se dépense
> A s'accoutre de ses dons!

The palm is the image of a mind so rich in thinking that the gifts of its own soul augment it constantly. That may be one of the origins of Stevens's death-poem, "Of Mere Being," but Valéry's palm is less pure and less flickering than Stevens's final emblem. The two poets and poetic thinkers do not much resemble one another, despite Stevens's yearning regard for Valéry. Perhaps the largest difference is the attitudes towards precursors. Valéry is lucid and candid, and confronts Mallarmé. Stevens insists that he does not read Whitman, condemns Whitman for his tramp *persona*, and yet he cannot cease revising Whitman's poems in his own poems. But then that is how Whitman came to discuss his relation to Ralph Waldo Emerson, so clearly they order these matters differently in America.

In a meditation of 1919 on ''The Intellectual Crisis,'' Valéry memorably depicted the European Hamlet staring at millions of ghosts:

> But he is an intellectual Hamlet. He meditates on the life and death of truths. For phantoms he has all the subjects of our controversies; for regrets he has all our titles to glory; he bows under the weight of discoveries and learning, unable to renounce and unable to resume this limitless activity. He reflects on the boredom of recommencing the past, on the folly of always striving to be original. He wavers between one abyss and the other, for two dangers still threaten the world: order and disorder.

This retains its force nearly seventy years later, just as it would baffle us if its subject were the American Hamlet. Valéry's fear was that Europe might ''become *what she is in reality:* that is, a little cape of the Asiatic continent.'' The fear was prophetic, though the prophecy fortunately is not yet wholly fulfilled. When Valéry writes in this mode, he is principally of interest to editorial writers and newspaper columnists of the weightier variety. Yet his concern for European culture, perhaps a touch too custodial, is a crucial element in all his prose writing. Meditating upon Descartes, the archetypal French intellect, Valéry states the law of his own nature: ''Descartes is above all, a man of intentional action.'' Consciousness was for Valéry an intentional adventure, and this sense of deliberate quest in the cultivation of consciousness is partly what makes Valéry a central figure of the Western literary intellect.

Valéry deprecated originality, but his critical insights are among the most original of our century. His *Analects* are crowded with the darker truths concerning literary originality:

> The value of men's works is not in the works themselves but in their later development by others, in other circumstances.

> Nothing is more ''original,'' nothing more ''oneself'' than to feed on others. But one has to digest them. A lion is made of assimilated sheep.

> The hallmark of the greatest art is that imitations of it are legitimate, worthwhile, tolerable; that it is not demolished or devoured by them, or they by it.

Any production of the mind is important when its existence resolves, summons up, or cancels other works, whether previous to it or not.

An artist wants to inspire jealousy till the end of time.

Valéry's central text on originality is his "Letter about Mallarmé" of 1927 where his relation to his authentic precursor inspired dialectical ironies of great beauty;

> We say that an author is *original* when we cannot trace the hidden transformations that others underwent in his mind; we mean to say that the dependence of *what he does* on *what others have done* is excessively complex and irregular. There are works in the likeness of others, and works that are the reverse of others, but there are also works of which the relation with earlier productions is so intricate that we become confused and attribute them to the direct intervention of the gods.

> (To go deeper into the subject, we should also have to discuss the influence of a mind on itself and of a work on its author. But this is not the place.)

Everywhere else in Valéry, in prose and verse, is the place, because that was Valéry's true topos, the influence of Paul Valéry's mind upon itself. Is that not the true subject of Descartes and of Montaigne, and of all French men and women of sensibility and intellect? What never ceases to engage Valéry is the effect of his thought and writings upon himself. Creative misunderstandings induced in others were not without interest, but Valéry's creative misunderstandings of Valéry ravished his heart away. Texts of this ravishment abound, but I choose one of the subtlest and most evasive, the dialogue "On Dance and the Soul." Socrates is made by Valéry to speak of "that poison of poisons, that venom which is opposed to all nature," the reduction of life to things as they are that Stevens called the First Idea:

> PHAEDRUS: What venom?
> SOCRATES: Which is called: the tedium of living? I mean,
>   understand me, not the passing ennui, the tedium that
>   comes of fatigue, or the tedium of which we can see the
>   germ or of which we know the limits; but that perfect
>   tedium, that pure tedium that is not caused by
>   misfortune or infirmity, that is compatible with
>   apparently the happiest of all conditions—that tedium,
>   in short, the stuff of which is nothing else than life
>   itself, and which has no other second cause than the
>   clear-sightedness of the living man. This absolute tedium

Destutt de Tracy: Ideology, Language, and the Critique of Metaphysics

Brian William Head

THE CONCEPT OF IDEOLOGIE

Destutt de Tracy presented his colleagues in the Class of moral and political sciences on 20 June 1796 with a problem of nomenclature: what would be the most appropriate name for the "new" science of ideas? ("Mémoire sur la faculté de penser"). Inspired by Lavoisier and Condillac on the importance of nomenclature and conceptual reform, Tracy was keen to find a suitable name for a science which, he claimed, "is so new that it does not yet have a name." The birth of a new science evidently required a baptism; and the best place for this was in the presence of that section of the Class devoted to *Analyse des sensations et des idées*, whose task was precisely the further development of this science. In seeking a new name, Tracy was not yet proposing a thorough overhaul of all the working concepts of the science of thought: the desire to reform its whole nomenclature would only become widely felt when the science itself had been more systematically studied by *savants*. The first step was to find a suitable name to mark off the scientific study of ideas from the prescientific "metaphysics" of the past, just as it had been necessary for astronomy to separate itself from astrology.

Condillac had been content to use the term *métaphysique*, albeit with the qualification that scientific or observational procedures should be used in the gathering and analysis of facts. Tracy regarded this term as quite misleading and discredited. The common meaning of *métaphysique*, said Tracy, is

> a science which treats the nature of beings, spirits (*esprits*), different orders of intelligence, the origin of things and their first cause.

From *Ideology and Social Science: Destutt de Tracy and French Liberalism.* © 1985 by Martinus Nijhoff Publishers, Dordrecht.

Now these are certainly not the objects of your research. . . . More-over, metaphysics strictly means something other than physics: yet the knowledge of the faculties of man, as Locke believed, is certainly a part—an important part—of physics, whatever (ulti-mate) cause one wants to ascribe to these faculties.

The legislators establishing the Institut had wisely refrained from using the term "metaphysics." But the term which they had used was not very sat-isfactory; "analysis of sensations and ideas" was hardly a suitable name for the new science; it was rather like saying "analysis of the sources of wealth in a society" instead of "political economy." Another possibility was the term *psycologie,* which Condillac had sometimes used along with Charles Bonnet. However, Tracy argued that psychology literally meant "science of the soul"; it would not only be presumptuous to claim a knowl-edge of such an entity, but it would give the false impression that the *savants* of the Institut were investigating first causes. On the contrary, insisted Tracy, "the goal of all your works is the knowledge of effects and their practical consequences." What, then, was to be the name for this behavioural science to which Tracy and his colleagues were devoting their attention?

Tracy recommended his own neologism: "idéologie, ou la science des idées." Idéologie, he said, had a very clear etymological meaning, based on the Greek *eidos* and *logos,* and it made no presuppositions about the causes. Hence, it was a suitable word to express "the science of ideas which treats ideas or perceptions, and the faculty of thinking or perceiving." This formulation of the content of idéologie was by no means neutral, however. Tracy had not only defined the content in behaviouralist terms as knowl-edge of "effects" and "consequences," but he had also imported a whole epistemological doctrine by his equation of ideas with perceptions and of thinking with perceiving. This perspective was reinforced and extended in the following passage:

This word has still another advantage—namely, that in giving the name idéologie to the science resulting from the analysis of sen-sations, you at once indicate the goal and the method; and if your doctrine is found to differ from that of certain other philosophers who pursue the same science, the reason is already given— namely, that you seek knowledge of man only through the analysis of his faculties; you agree to ignore everything which it does not uncover for you.

Here we find not only statements which define the procedures and content of idéologie in terms of "analysis of sensations" and "analysis of (intellec-tual) faculties," but we also find sharp limits placed upon what is knowable, or what is to be taken as reliable knowledge. Such knowledge, according to Tracy, must be derived from analysing man's faculties, i.e. from investigating the operations of the mind in forming and expressing ideas. Let us examine more closely some of the main themes in Tracy's conception of idéologie.

First, we will take his view that the science of ideas is the fundamental science, necessary for guaranteeing reliable knowledge in all the other sciences. Tracy's reasoning seems to be as follows. All knowledge, regardless of subject-matter, consists of ideas, and their accuracy depends on our capacity for making a series of precise judgements. Knowledge of the processes by which errors arise and by which correct judgements may be formed, is the only basis available for ensuring the reliability of knowledge. The primacy of idéologie over the other sciences arises from the fact that in explaining the general operations of our intellectual faculties, it points out the methods for attaining certainty and avoiding error. Or, as Tracy succinctly wrote: "it is necessary to know our intellectual faculties in order to be sure we are using them well" (*Elémens d'idéologie, troisième partie: Logique*). In his early mémoires on idéologie, Tracy asserted that it was "the first of all the sciences in the genealogical order." Indeed, he went even further, suggesting that

> knowledge of the human understanding is really the only science (*la science unique*); all the others, without exception, are only applications of this knowledge to the diverse objects of our curiosity, and it must be their guiding light.
>
> ("Mémoire")

Tracy gives two main kinds of reasons for the primacy of *idéologie:* one relating to scientific method, and the other concerning the nature of human experience. The first argument is straightforward: he asserts that all the sciences require a guarantee of their truth-content; that scientific methods of observation and analysis are the best procedural guarantees of reliable knowledge; that all the sciences should adopt such methods; and that *idéologie* is central because it clarifies and recommends the logic of scientific method and explanation. The second argument, however, is more contentious and surprising. Here, Tracy argues that the science of ideas is fundamental to all our knowledge because the ideas of an individual are constitutive of his experience of the world and of his self.

> In fact, since nothing exists *for us* except through the ideas we have, since our ideas are our whole being, our very existence, the examination of the manner in which we perceive and combine them is alone able to show us in what consists our knowledge, what it encompasses, what are its limits, and what method we must follow in the pursuit of truths in every field. [emphasis added].

This doctrine of the primacy of ideas-as-experience is rather anomalous in what is otherwise a philosophy of monist materialism. The doctrine plays little role in Tracy's overall conception of idéologie and the human sciences, but it does suggest the overwhelming residual influence of the Cartesian *cogito* in French philosophy.

Tracy's view of idéologie as analytically and logically prior to all the other sciences led him to describe it as *la théorie des théories,* and to suggest that the "examination of our intellectual operations is the natural introduction to all the branches of studies." Knowledge of our means of knowing is *la véritable philosophie première ou science première.* But it is quite different from "that first philosophy of which all our ancient authors have spoken so much," for the latter had assumed the truth of their general principles and built their systems on shifting sands. The modern *philosophie première,* the "first of the sciences in their order of mutual dependence," is simply "the history of our intelligence considered in relation to its means of knowing" (*Logique*).

Tracy's assumptions about the genealogical and analytical priority of idéologie led him to reconsider the traditional classification of the branches of learning, propounded by Bacon and by d'Alembert Bacon's classification, said Tracy, was confused and fallacious, and d'Alembert had erred in following Bacon so closely. Not only was it wrong that theology had been accorded the primary place as a general ontology; but the major categories of memory (history), reason (philosophy, including theology and science), and imagination (poetry) showed a faulty understanding of our intellectual faculties. The proper way to classify the sciences, wrote Tracy, was to distribute them in accordance with "the order in which they are derived from one another and through which they are fortified and interrelated." The science of the formation of our ideas "incontestably" came first, closely followed by the science of their expression and of their deduction.[*Logique;* these three areas corresponded to the first three volumes of his *Elémens d'idéologie* (1801–5)]. *Idéologie* was to form "the trunk of the tree."

At the end of his *Logique* in 1805, Tracy drew up a plan which summarised the ambitious and ever-broadening scope of his conception of idéologie, as the new *prima philosophia* providing the epistemological groundwork for all the sciences. The scheme was divided into nine parts and an appendix as follows:

Elements of Idéologie

First Section: History of our means of knowing. In three parts.
1st part: On the formation of our ideas, or Ideology strictly defined.
2nd part: On the expression of our ideas, or Grammar.
3rd part: On the combination of our ideas, or Logic.
Second Section: Application of our means of knowing to the study of the will and its effects. In three parts.
1st part: On our actions, of Economics.
2nd part: On our sentiments, or Morality.
3rd part: On the rule of some by others, or Government.

Third Section: Application of our means of knowing to the study of beings other than ourselves. In three parts.
1st part: On bodies and their properties, or Physics.
2nd part: On the properties of extension, or Geometry.
3rd part: On the properties of quantity, or Calculus.
Appendix: On the false sciences, which are abolished by knowledge of our means of knowing and their proper use.

Taken together, these sciences would form "the totality of the trunk of the encyclopedic tree of our real knowledge."

Despite the enormous breadth of his ambitions, it should be evident that Tracy's intention was not to summarise all existing knowledge about man and nature, but to recommend and demonstrate the superiority of a particular method of enquiry: *analyse*. According to this method, as elaborated by Condillac (and adopted by Condorcet, Garat, and Tracy), all phenomena are susceptible to explication in terms of their location in an ordered progression from simple to complex facts; this approach is equally applicable to the study of animate and inanimate nature, and to mathematics. Any idea or concept can be "decomposed" by analysis into its constituent simple ideas which are anchored in sense-experience. Analysis demonstrates how complex ideas are built up from simple elements. The programmatic aspect of this doctrine implies that any ideas which cannot, in this way, be melted down and reconstituted on the basis of simple sense-experience must be expelled from scientific discourse as ambiguous or meaningless, and propositions based on such ideas are false or at least unprovable. Tracy asserts that analysis and idéologie are based upon scrupulous observation of the facts, drawing only those conclusions fully warranted by the evidence and always preferring "absolute ignorance" to any claim which merely appears to be plausible ("De la métaphysique de Kant," "Mémoire").

The study of the formation of ideas, based on observation of facts and the analysis of their relationships, was for Tracy *une science expérimentale*. The implication was that there were two kinds of "knowledge": that modelled on the physical sciences, and that which could hardly be called reliable knowledge at all. Condillac had claimed that there was really only one *science*—the history of nature—which could be subdivided into two, interdependent, parts: that dealing with facts or experience (*physique*), and that dealing with abstraction or reasoning upon these facts (*Art de raisonner*). Tracy, in similar fashion, claimed that there are two kinds of "truths," namely those of "experience or fact," and those of "reasoning and deduction." The deductive or abstract truths, however, had no validity independently of the facts from which they were abstracted. Idéologie, like all positive sciences, required both types of truths. The scientific genius, wrote Tracy, is one who is able to "discover in the facts those important and very general truths which have not yet been detected—but it can never be a question of creating them out of his own head." When idéologie and the human sciences had become more highly developed, he believed, they would be closer to the positive sciences of nature, especially physiology, than to any purely abstract science such as mathematics whose truths are entirely a deductive system abstracted from the objective world. In idéologie and the human sciences, claimed Tracy, "perfection is not proportional to the number of facts observed, but to the knowledge of the laws which govern these facts" ("Mémoire").

The problem, in Tracy's conception, was to find a starting-point for structuring "the facts" in accordance with the laws governing their inter-relationships. What kind of starting point was appropriate? Would it be a truth of observation or a truth of deduction? Tracy chose the latter, on the analogy of astronomy, which explained all its phenomena "by starting from this single truth, that attraction acts in direct proportion to mass and in inverse proportion to the square of the distance." Once such a secure starting-point had been found, the rest of the scientific system would be unfolded in a series of rigorous deductions. If this were accomplished, the system of truths would be complete and entirely "certain." On the foundation of *idéologie*, according to Tracy, the human sciences were capable of certainty in the same manner as the sciences of inanimate nature. A whole system of truths about man and society would follow:

> now that we are certain of the formation and filiation of our ideas, all that will be subsequently said—on the manner of expressing, combining and teaching these ideas, on regulating our sentiments and actions, and directing those of others—will be only the consequences of these preliminaries, and will rest on a constant and invariable base, consistent with the very nature of our being. Now these preliminaries constitute what is strictly designated as *idéologie*; and all the consequences derived from it are the object of grammar, logic, instruction, private morality, public morality (or the *art social*), education and legislation. . . . We will go astray in all these sciences only to the extent that we lose sight of the fundamental observations on which they rest.
>
> (*Elémens d'idéologie*, vol. 1)

The secure starting point for idéologie, the fundamental building block on which all the "ideological, moral and political sciences" rested, was sense perception. The methods of empirical observation and analysis (pioneered by Locke and Condillac in particular) had demonstrated to Tracy's satisfaction the truth of the ancient adage "nihil est in intellectu quin prius fuerit in sensu" (literally: there is nothing in the mind which was not previously in the senses). Idéologie was therefore

> a system of truths closely tied together, all stemming from this first indubitable fact, that we know nothing except through our

sensations, and that all our ideas are the product of the various combinations we make from these sensations.

("Mémoire")

Tracy's insistence on sense perceptions was a materialised form of the Cartesian *cogito*. Having assumed that the only fact of which we can initially be certain is our own existence as a sensing being, Tracy's whole system is erected upon this *être sensible*. The proposition that "man is a sentient being," is the *première vérité générale* from which he elaborates his entire theory of man and society. Tracy's disingenuous remark that his theories were devoid of presuppositions and that he had elaborated his idéologie purely by observation of man's thinking processes (*Logique*), is clearly misleading. Tracy had accepted the sensationalist paradigm of what constitutes knowledge and what procedures had to be followed to reach the truth, to the exclusion of all other conceptions and procedures.

In Tracy's view, the study of mental phenomena had wrongly been separated in the past from the study of physical phenomena. Descartes, for example, had separated the two spheres, and had concluded that our thinking faculty owed nothing to sense perceptions and that general principles were the foundation of knowledge. Tracy, following Locke and Condillac, argued that all ideas stem from sense perceptions or simple ideas which are transformed into complex ideas; and that knowledge must be based on particular facts, not upon *a priori* or axiomatic principles. The "artificial" separation of the mental and the physical had been bridged by empiricist writers like Locke, who, according to Tracy, was "the first man to try to observe and describe the human intelligence just as one observes and describes a property of a mineral or a vegetable, or a noteworthy aspect of the life of an animal: he also made this study a part of *la physique*" (*Elémens d'idéologie*, vol. 1). The study of the human intelligence, as of the human body, is part of natural history: hence Tracy's well-known claim that "idéologie is a part of zoology."

Tracy's epistemology assumes, then that sense-experience is primary; and indeed, Tracy goes beyond Locke in asserting that sense perception and thinking are absolutely identical terms. Locke had allowed the mind a certain independent activity in ordering and recalling ideas from among the materials provided by sense experience. Condillac virtually eliminated such independent reflectiveness of the mind by attempting to demonstrate that memory, comparison and desire consist in nothing but modifications of sense impressions (*Extrait raisonné du Traité des sensations*). However, Condillac wished to allow that mind was an entity not entirely reducible to physical operations, and spoke of "l'âme oisive." Tracy, noting the redundance of such an entity in a thoroughly reductionist sensationalism, obliterated the distinction between the mind itself and the activities of rearranging sense perceptions by which it was constituted. His purpose was to deny any independent reality to a mental or moral realm, and to assert a naturalistic monism of consciousness and physical environment. Thought (or perceiving and sensing) consisted of four basic faculties or modes of operation: simple sensibility, memory, judgement and desire. "This manner of envisaging it in these (four) elements unveils for us the whole mechanism" ("Mémoire"). All mental phenomena were produced by these modes. Where Condillac had shown that one faculty of the mind gave rise to the next in a generative manner, Tracy collapsed all such operations into aspects of the general sensibility of living creatures, all being "the results of our organisation."

Here, Tracy's physiological emphasis becomes very important. Tracy takes as pre-given the physical structure and operations of the body, including all the sensibilities involved in consciousness. Whereas the *content* of ideas was largely determined by experience, education and environment, the *structure* of the mind itself was stable and predictable owing to its physiological foundation. Even though the innate ideas hypothesis in its Cartesian, Kantian, and other versions was incompatible with Tracy's sensationalism, his theory appears to assume that the mind is so structured that its capacities are universally shared throughout the species, owing to a biological or physiological uniformity. Physiology provided, for Tracy, the stable and certain basis which guaranteed that simple sensations were perceived in the same way by men of all ages and epochs. The "certitude of all we know" depended on the physiological necessity that when we perceived simple objects X and Y, they are necessarily perceived as such and not as A and B. The same is true for "all beings who are organised like us."

An important question arises concerning the character of the physiological determinism implied by Tracy's doctrine and the extent to which the physiological substructure is modified by the social-environmental superstructure. This is an area where contradictory elements emerged in Tracy's writings, and he never discussed these problems at sufficient length to become aware of the inconsistencies. . . . despite Tracy's voluntarist doctrine of *motilité*, his general reductionism allows no role for genuinely independent volition. On the other hand, his educational doctrines . . . claim that changes in patterns of ideas and behaviour are made possible through a rational system of public instruction and legislation. Tracy was deeply influenced by the views of Cabanis on the interaction between the physical and moral aspects of man (*Rapports du physique et du moral de l'homme*), but these doctrines were largely taken for granted rather than argued or elaborated.

Tracy's professions of belief in the physiological basis of the intellect, and in the capacity of the physiologists to resolve many of the outstanding problems in the science of ideas, became quite marked in the years after 1796 when he had first argued that *idéologie* should be divided into two parts. *Idéologie physiologique* would deal with the physical and biochemical dimensions of human sensibility, and *idéologie rationnelle* would examine the psychological and logical aspects of the intellectual faculties. Tracy claimed he would confine himself to the latter aspects: "I take our faculties such as they are, and concern myself only with their effects" ("Mémoire"). Nevertheless, a "complete" account of the operations of these faculties would require a unified approach, including the knowledge of a physiologist, mathematician, grammarian, and *algébriste philosophe* ("De la métaphysique de Kant"). That the human sciences would require the co-operation of *savants* of various kinds was partly recognised in the organisation of the Institut, where Tracy and Cabanis were both in the section on "Analysis of Sensations and Ideas." However, the grammarians had, to Tracy's regret, been placed in a different Class; a more strictly "ideological" structure would have united them with the physiologists and idéologistes, for in Tracy's doctrine, the study of how ideas are expressed (grammar) is merely one aspect of the general study of the origin and communication of ideas.

Tracy plainly believed that intellectual and moral ideas were dependent upon physical faculties, but the claim remained ambiguous. It could have meant only that sense perceptions are necessary materials for the mind and that without the senses there can be no human consciousness. However, Tracy no doubt intended a stronger relation of dependence than the claim that bodies and brains are preconditions of minds and thoughts. Tracy argued, against theories which posited the existence of innate or intuitive ideas, that ideas have no autonomy, independence, or innate existence in the mind. Further, he asserted that all ideas are nothing but transformed and modified sensations, whose content derives entirely from data provided by the senses. Tracy, however, never attempted to demonstrate how the supposed physiological basis of mind shapes and interacts with the processes involved in reflection, judgement or desire. Tracy's reductionist language (idea = sense perception, thinking = perceiving sensations, idéologie = part of zoology and physics) was partly a methodological polemic against what he saw as "metaphysical" systems of ideas, which had misled men about nature and liberty, and which had asserted a dualism between the natural and moral, the physical and intellectual. Tracy's reductionism was also a confused doctrine, asserting a physiological base of human behaviour, without specifying the exact relationship between physiology and mind.

Tracy and Cabanis were rapidly identified as promoting the same materialist monism as La Mettrie and d'Holbach. The only new thing about *idéologie*, wrote a hostile reviewer in 1802, is the title itself. Idéologie "substitutes the movement of the brute for human reason, and sees in man nothing but muscles and nerves." Fortunately, opined the critic, the human heart and the passage of time would leave such demented systems behind, as so much flotsam left on the river bank after a storm. In obliterating reflective reason, claimed the critic, "the idéologues saw in man nothing more than Condillac's statue," man being analysed purely in terms of his physical needs. The ideological analysis of mind, wrote another critic, was just like a "treatise on mechanics" where all one can see are "actions and reactions, moving forces and inertia." The denial of a separate realm for human morality and reason, was to place man in the family of the monkeys. Those who espoused such a view wanted "to lead the moral man to the cemetery."

Tracy's views on the physiological basis of human thought and action remained undeveloped. He did not ask *why* the mind operated in the ways it did: this was a matter for the physiologists to determine (and in any case, they could do little more than re-describe the processes in physical terms, unless they trespassed into the forbidden area of first causes). Tracy focussed his attention on behavioural effects or operations of the mind, and especially upon the connections between thought and language, ideas and words, the signified and the sign. Here was a field where he expected idéologie to make great progress. Idéologie, as the *science des sciences* (*Elémens d'idéologie, deuxième partie: Grammaire*), was particularly suited to the task of clarifying ideas, making concepts more precise, and thereby promoting scientific understanding of phenomena in every field. The logical priority of idéologie over the positive sciences of man and nature depended on a view of language as a conventionalized set of signs which express our ideas; and a view of scientific advance as dependent on clarification of concepts and the rejection of those not validated by sense experience. The scientific language of "elements" and "compounds" also had the eminent advantage, for the philosophe and idéologiste, of lending itself to what Gillispie has called a "naturalistic pedagogy" (*The Edge of Objectivity*). *Idéologie* was seen to provide a grammar and syntax of *nature*, and a set of procedural rules for finding the basic elements (signs, concepts) of any language. The analysis of *language* was thus of critical importance for the *idéologiste* in his role both as scientific observer and as educator of mankind.

A language, for Tracy, is a system of signs whose meanings have been fixed or formalised by the attribution of conventional meanings to each symbol (*Logique*; "Mémoire"; *Elémens d'idéologie*, vol. 1). Some languages or sign-systems are more specialised than others (algebraic notation, for example, or the symbols of chemistry), but all share certain characteristics. First, language is created and sustained as a social phenomenon: it is a kind of collective network through which individuals share experiences and perhaps even contribute to the enlargement of knowledge. Secondly, a mastery of language involves a mastery of knowledge, of which the words are signifiers. In Tracy's view, the ability to manipulate an appropriate language was the avenue to understanding man and nature. The problem was to ensure that the words actually designated precise and observable facts, and that general ideas were squarely based on such facts.

THE SCIENCE OF SIGNS

The analytical method of idéologie was invoked to perform the function of making language more precise and scientific: to ensure that the vocabulary and syntax of languages were consistent with the facts discovered by observation, and with a rigorous interrelationship of concepts. As Gillispie has aptly remarked, the Baconian project of a renovation of learning became, in Condillac's work, identified with a "linguistic reform, redesignating words where necessary to make them speak facts, recombining them in a syntax of experience, lending reality to the expression used of the ancient atomists that theirs was an alphabet of nature." Tracy's inspiration was the same, and his model of language was no less atomistic and naturalistic. In the generation of ideas, he claimed, a small number of basic elements, combined in various ways, produce "an almost infinite multitude of ideas, just as a small number of letters variously arranged suffice to represent those ideas. Here as elsewhere, nature shows a remarkable economy of means and profusion of effects."

Tracy's interest in theories of language and the usage of signs was quite different from that of historical philology or pure linguistics. His purpose was far more practical. Ideological analysis was designed primarily to clarify our existing stock of ideas, eliminate vague concepts and false propositions, and provide criteria for rebuilding the human sciences. Tracy rejected all theories which attributed the form or content of language to any divine or supernatural agency. Rousseau had seen language as a divine spark planted in the mind, though its forms were developed by the passions; Maistre and Bonald had proposed a theory of innate ideas, and ridiculed the Locke-Condillac account of the development of language through association of simple perceptions. In his desire to establish idéologie as an empirical science, Tracy believed it necessary to overthrow the "innatist" theories, and to base the principle of language on its instrumental functions for satisfying human needs. Having established in this way how language evolved and functioned, it would become possible to improve its value as a precise instrument for codifying, communicating and enlarging our knowledge. Tracy's model of language was derived primarily from Condillac, whom Tracy therefore praised as the founder and creator of idéologie.

Condillac had argued that all animate beings have sense impressions or perceptions, and are attracted or repelled by them. But only human beings have the capacity to reflect upon these simple ideas, to compare, combine and judge them (*Essai sur l'origine des connaissances humaines*). The human faculties of reflection and judgement evolved very slowly over time, but rapidly outstripped those of the animal world when men began to invent and manipulate artificial signs to designate their ideas. The earliest signs were gestural and verbal, closely connected with immediate desires or passions. Gradually, various graphic forms of communication were developed, of which modern written languages are the highest form. The earliest signs designated sensible objects; gradually more general terms were derived or abstracted from the particular terms. Condillac regarded the use of language as a process which assigned conventional meanings to given signs or words. The use of concrete particular terms was unambiguous because the objects designated were immediately apparent. But the use of more abstract terms was bound to involve confusion and imprecision, because the objects designated were not immediately obvious, and because clear meanings for general ideas depended on a rigorous chain of conceptual relationships founded upon simple ideas. Finally, Condillac noted the importance of repetition and habit, which not only strengthen our intellectual operations, but also unfortunately confirm us just as much in our badly formed judgements as in our properly formed judgements.

Tracy took up these four points concerning the origins of language, the usage of signs, the role of habitual judgements, and the problems of making language more precise. In the first place, Tracy was little concerned to assemble fresh historical evidence on the origin of language, or to engage in any detailed comparative studies of living languages. He was generally content to rely on the research of Gébelin and others in regard to the ancient non-European languages, and on the large number of grammarians who had considered the development of the European languages. The earliest form of communication, Tracy surmised, was a "language of action" by which one's desires were made known. Gestures and movements would usually be complemented by articulated sounds of various kinds. Many animals could rightly be seen to have reached this level of communication ("Mémoire").

Wherein lay the distinction between men and other animate creatures? Was this not a major difficulty for sensationalist philosophy, given that all animate creatures were defined by their sensibility? Was not Tracy's definition of man as *l'homme sensible* a denial of a qualitative leap between human and other creatures? Certainly Tracy's critics believed that his emphasis upon sensibility (rather than morality and reason) was to condemn mankind to a search for purely material satisfactions and a life without the consolations and inspirations of religion (Bernardin de Saint-Pierre, *Harmonies de la nature*, in *Oeuvres*, vol. 9). As Aimé-Martin wrote:

> To reduce man to his body, is to reduce him to his senses. It results from this idea that the brute would have an intelligence superior to his own, because the senses of a great number of animals are more perfect than those of man. This single objection destroys the system of the materialists.
>
> ("Préambule" to Bernardin de Saint-Pierre's *Oeuvres*, vol. 8)

Tracy had anticipated this line of criticism in his earliest *mémoires* at the Institut. Man is superior even at the level of communication through gestures or movements: "the organisation of man is so superior to all others that even his language of action can become much more advanced than that of any animal"("Mémoire"). It was true that ideas, understood as sense perceptions, were experienced by all animate species; perceptions or thinking exist before language, insisted Tracy. But although animals rapidly attain the degree of intellectual development they require for their survival, they seldom surpass that level: their instinct is fixed and limited (*Elémens d'idéologie*, vol. 1). No doubt there are many animals whose physical sensibilities are more highly developed in certain fields than human sensibilities. This, however, does not confer a general superiority among such animals over the human species, for the animals have only very limited means of communication with their own species. The fact that our ideas originate in our sense perception, in no way proves that intelligence is the same thing as a refined capacity to perceive sensations: "the perfection of the senses is very far from being the measure of our intellectual capacity."

The superiority of the human species consisted in the ability to make use of conventional and durable signs, to give permanent form to ideas, enabling men to combine and multiply their ideas in a variety of ways in cooperation with their fellows. Tracy no doubt believed that there was a physiological basis for this human capacity to create and manipulate signs representing ideas. He assumed, as a given feature of our physical organisation, the capacity of the brain to deal with complex operations: comparison, recollection, judgement, desire, etc. More immediately, however, he pointed out the importance of the human ability to vocalise a vast range of distinctive sounds (a kind of oral-aural alphabet) which made available a more flexible and extensive system of signs than those given by gesture or movement (*Grammaire*).

Tracy claimed that Condillac was the first philosopher to have clearly demonstrated our dependence on signs in developing and communicating our ideas. Hobbes was also praised for having understood the difficulties and the importance of establishing clear connections between words and meanings (*Logique*). Signs are necessary to fix in our memory the meanings of and the relations between our ideas; without signs, says Tracy, we could hardly remember our ideas nor combine them. The use of consciously developed language sets man apart from the beast, and makes it possible for him to emerge from that historical stage where he was dominated by his immediate needs. Language, the symbolic embodiment of rationality, is the instrument of man's perfectibility. Having begun in total ignorance, the human species profited by shared experience and knowledge, and eventually reached a point where the desire to increase and propagate knowledge developed its own dynamic. Knowledge becomes a cultural possession only by virtue of sign-systems or languages, which are entirely a product of social interaction over many centuries. It is a slow process: our means of knowledge require considerable exercise before they are developed more fully.

> And so we are entirely the product of art (rather than nature), that
> is, of our work; and we resemble the natural man, or our original

whose meanings are fixed by conventional usage. However, while familiarity with the ideas contained in a language is the source of our cultural progress, there are certain inherent defects in the use of signs, said Tracy, which prevent us from ever achieving perfect communication, the implicit goal of idéologie.

There is a major problem in ensuring that the same meaning is always given to a sign by different people. Constancy in meanings is impossible to guarantee, said Tracy. On the contrary, it is strictly true that the exact meaning of a sign is known only to the first user; and even for him, only on the first occasion, because he may be mistaken in believing that later circumstances correspond exactly with the first situation. Few people are inventors of signs and of meanings. Language is generally learned as part of our education in a particular society. Tracy assumes that there is always a degree of uncertainty and vagueness in using conventional signs, especially in ordinary language where the sign system is more subject to individual variability in usage. To some extent, we can overcome the difficulty by gaining personal experience of the idea represented by the sign, especially in the case of simple sensations. But this becomes very difficult with complex ideas, for it would be necessary for each individual to analyse all the elements composing such ideas, examining their relations step by step, to be sure that the idea had the same content for that person as it had for others. Condillac and Tracy believed that brute facts, immediately striking the senses, are unambiguous and given directly to man by nature, so to speak. A simple sensation, they assumed, would be experienced in the same way by all individuals owing to their identical organic faculties, and presumably owing to the passivity of the perception.

Complex ideas allowed more possibilities for vagueness, error, or variability in meaning, and for the intrusion of faulty memory. Language in use, therefore, is necessarily individualised to some extent, owing to the improbability of each individual attaching exactly the same meanings to the same words (*Logique*). This, thought Tracy, was an inherent problem in complex communications and the use of abstract ideas. Ambiguity could never be eliminated; but idéologie could do much to reduce the problem by showing how to avoid precipitate judgements, at least in those specialised languages claiming to be systems of scientific knowledge. Fortunately, the defects of language are not all *inherent* in complex communication. Some defects are caused by ignorance and by habitual errors of judgement: these could be overcome by education and by correcting certain anomalies in the written language.

In searching out the possibilities for improving the accuracy of concepts and knowledge, Tracy considered the difference between language in general and algebraic analysis in particular. In 1796, he had confidently urged his colleagues to "imitate the mathematicians," since the latter had achieved a rigorous system of certain knowledge, beginning from a "palpable" first truth and proceeding slowly "from the know to the unknown" ("Mémoire"). Before long, Tracy recognised that the analogy was misleading, and in so doing rejected Condillac's tendency to posit algebraic equations as the epitome of linguistic exactitude. Tracy's comparison of language and algebra throws light upon the ideals of his reformist enterprise in conceptual reform, and also upon the impossibility of attaining a perfect language for expressing truths about man and society.

Tracy began by asserting:

> . . . we can regard as proven that the general effect of signs is, in summing up prior judgements, to make easier the subsequent analyses; that this effect is exactly that of the symbols and formulae of algebra; and that, consequently, languages are true instruments of analysis, and algebra is simply a language which directs the mind with more certainty that others, because it expresses only very precise relations of a single type. Grammatical rules have just the same effect as the rules of calculus; in both cases, it is only the signs which we combine; and, without our being aware of it, we are guided by words just as by algebraic symbols.
>
> (*Elémens d'idéologie*, vol. 1)

Tracy immediately qualified his analogy, by insisting on the distinctive characteristics of algebra. It is confined to ideas of quantity, which are invariable and distinct units whose relations are very precise and certain: providing one follows the rules, one always reaches a correct conclusion. But, he pointed out, most of our ideas are not quantitative, and it would be mistaken to take algebra as the desired model in our reforms of ordinary language, whose signs and relationships can never have the simplicity and precision of quantitative signs. Algebraic signs are a particularly clear and limited group of precise symbols; ordinary language is relatively untidy and imprecise.

> Words are . . . formulae which depict in an abridged way the results of previous combinations and which relieve our memory of the obligation of having these combinations presented ceaselessly in all their details. . . . (B)ut the results which these words express are not of a kind as simple or precise as those represented by algebraic symbols; and the modifications which we make them undergo in discourse . . . are much more varied and much less measurable than those undergone by algebraic symbols . . . (which) are all perceptible in numerical terms; those of words are not so, and that is an immense difference.

In rejecting the model of algebra for a perfected language, Tracy rejected Condillac's notion that correct judgements are nothing but statements of identity between the two terms of a judgement (*Art de penser*). Tracy also unwittingly cast doubt upon the very possibility of a deductivist science of man, and upon his own assumption that the human sciences could be brought to the same degree of certainty as the mathematical sciences.

Tracy was determined, above all, to show how the study of intellectual faculties could throw light on the correct operation of our judgements. The problem was to understand the mind sufficiently to enable us to make correct judgements. Given Tracy's view that language consists of signs and the combinations we make of them, the reform of language consisted in making our ideas (and their signs) more precise, and in making the links between them more certain. His ultimate practical objective was "ideological" education: "to make correct judgements habitual." This would be a substantial and long-term project of public instruction, which would never be completely successful, given the inherent defects of signs. However, some progress could be made.

> . . . a complete reform (of words and syntax) is almost impossible, for too many habits resist it. To change completely a usage which is tied at so many points to all our social institutions, would require a unanimous consent which cannot even be conjectured, and would be a real revolution in society. (But) . . . while letting this usage subsist, since it cannot be destroyed, it would be very useful to point out properly its defects, their causes and consequences, and to place alongside our existing written language a perfected model of what it should be.
>
> (*Grammaire*)

Tracy assumes that, for maximum clarity, the written language should represent as exactly as possible the *sounds* of the spoken language. The latter should be examined carefully by a learned body of experts who would draw up a *phonetic* alphabet, containing all the sounds and inflections of spoken discourse, and would publish extracts from local and foreign literature in the new phonetic form for the edification of the public. This would fix the pronunciation and prose form of languages as precisely as possible, while leaving their everyday variations" in the grip of routine and (customary) usage." At least the *savants* of every nation might wish to consult with profit such an *écriture universelle*. Tracy also hoped that a learned group from within the Institut might desire to take up the matter of perfecting the spelling, pronunciation, and syntax of the French language.

Tracy's hopes in these areas were neither unfounded nor ignored. Indeed, many of the problems of language raised by Tracy had been examined by grammarians and idéologistes towards the end of the eighteenth century. Discussions at the Institut on questions concerning the development and reform of language were very common between 1796 and 1803, and some of the idéologistes were involved in revising the *Dictionnaire de l'Académie française*. One of the most notable initiatives was the series of prize essay topics proposed by the Class of moral and political sciences, including three concerned with language. The first, proposed in 1796, was addressed to the question of determining "the influence of signs on the formation of ideas." The second, in 1799, asked candidates to "determine the influence of habit on the faculty of thinking, or in other words, clarify the effects on each of our intellectual faculties produced by the frequent repetition of the same operations." The third such competition, announced in 1802, sought essays on the topic: "Determine how one should de-compose the faculty of thinking, and what are the elementary faculties which are to be recognised?" Tracy himself was also active at the Institut pursuing related questions. For example, he was a member of a commission of the Institut appointed to examine the merits of a lexicological system devised by a M. Buttet, who sought to devise rules for giving exact meanings to words by the perfecting of our language. He was also appointed to a commission investigating the systems of *pasigraphie*, invented by de Maimeux and others, who sought to discover a "universal language" in which ideas were directly represented in symbolic forms other than the verbal forms of conventional languages. Tracy in 1800 presented to the Institut his own critical assessment of pasigraphy. Such a system, he claimed, had all the defects of hieroglyphic languages, and thus could not resolve the problems it set out to overcome ("Réfléxions sur les projets de pasigraphie").

Tracy had argued earlier, in his "Mémoire sur la faculté de penser," that a perfect language of any type was "a chimera, like perfection in any field." Existing languages had developed in a haphazard manner over many centuries; they were far from methodical or systematic. For a perfect language to be created, it would have to be composed all at once, by a genius with universal knowledge, and devoid of all particular passions but love of truth. A perfected language would in principle be able to represent our ideas precisely in a way which prevented misunderstanding, and might impart to our deductions the same certainty which exists in the languages of quantity (*Grammaire*). There would be no way, however, that such a language would be widely adopted, by other than a few *savants*. Moreover, even if it were adopted, it would immediately become disfigured by the conventional usages of spoken language and by the inherent weakness or limitations of our intellectual faculties.

A less ambitious series of reforms would try to improve spelling and pronunciation; make syntax follow more closely the "natural progression of ideas in deductions"; eliminate vague and euphemistic expressions; encourage the adoption of new terms wherever needed; formulate properly methodical nomenclatures in all the sciences; and correct our ideas by the discovery of new truths, especially in idéologie. All these things could be done to the French language, making it the nearest approximation to the needs of *savants* for precise expression. But while some such reforms could be made in each conventional language, Tracy concluded that a universal perfected language (*la langue universelle*) is bound to remain a "dream": indeed, it is "as impossible as perpetual motion."

The idéologistes of the 1790s had placed great faith in the progressive consequences of conceptual reform; it was central to their public instruction and the production of enlightened and virtuous citizens. This explains why the *écoles centrales*, created in the law of October 1795, included a course on *grammaire générale*, a subject which, according to Tracy, would demonstrate that "all languages have common rules which are derived from the nature of our intellectual faculties," and that this knowledge is necessary "not simply for the study of languages but is also the only solid basis of the moral and political sciences, (on which . . .) all citizens should have sound ideas." The science of language was intended to have important and beneficial consequences for social and moral behaviour.

While Tracy believed that great improvements could be made by linguistic and conceptual reforms introduced into the education system by enlightened teachers and administrators, the other side of the problem was to combat the sources of error and mystification which were institutionalised in positions of influence. The major source of illusions in France, according to Tracy, was the Catholic Church. In the following section, we therefore examine Tracy's view on religion and theological metaphysics, in terms of his desire to reduce the influence of "metaphysical" and "unscientific" thought.

METAPHYSICS AND RELIGION

Tracy wanted to establish a clear separation between sciences based upon observations and analysis, and bodies of doctrine whose object was

> not to discover the sources of our knowledge, their certitude and their limits, but to determine the principle and the purpose of all things, to divine the origin and destiny of the world. That is the object of metaphysics. We place it among the arts of imagination, designed to satisfy us and not to inform us.
>
> (*Elémens d'idéologie,* vol. 1)

There could be nothing more different in approach, insisted Tracy, between the "old theological metaphysics, or metaphysics strictly defined," and the "modern philosophical metaphysics or idéologie." The latter was the "remedy for all these infirmities" of the mind ("Dissertation sur l'existence"). *Idéologistes* and *métaphysiciens* were engaged in distinct enterprises. As an "experimental" science dealing with facts and observation, idéologie avoided the "metaphysical" error of believing that general ideas gave meaning to particular ideas, instead of vice versa. Metaphysics tended to separate the mental and material worlds, whereas they should be studied in their essential unity. Metaphysics tended to derogate the reality of man's natural objectivity, and see him as moving in a world of pure thought ("De la métaphysique chez Kant"). Condillac wrote that:

Nature itself points out the order we ought to follow in the communication of truth; for if all our knowledge comes from the senses, it is evident that the perception of abstract notions must be prepared by sensible ideas. . . . If philosophers do not care to acknowledge this truth, it is because they are prejudiced in favour either of innate ideas, or of a customary usage which seems to have been consecrated by time.

("Mémoires")

The "metaphysics" of Descartes and others who located the origins of ideas in pre-given categories of the mind, was thus contrasted by Tracy with idéologie, whose basic assumption was that a scientific epistemology could demonstrate the unity of mind and body, of the physical and moral realms, and could prove that all ideas were derived from our sense perceptions. Tracy did not attempt to refute in detail the various theories of innate and intuitive ideas. His procedure was to assert fundamental differences of principle between *a priori* "metaphysics" (in which Plato and Aristotle rubbed shoulders with Descartes, Malebranche, Leibniz, Berkeley, and Kant) and the philosophy of sensations and experience (whose key figures included Bacon, Hobbes, Locke, Helvétius, and Condillac). As a behavioural science, concerned with effects and not ultimate causes, idéologie was utterly opposed to pronouncements by philosophers and theologians claiming to know the purpose of creation or the destiny of man. Such matters could not be resolved by science; they could only be answered in accordance with revealed religion or private faith. The idéologiste's faith in the benevolent powers of reason in social life was contrasted to the mystifications inherent in acceptance of unverifiable dogmas about man, nature, and God. Tracy likened the difference between the old metaphysics and the new science of ideas, to that between astrology and astronomy, or between alchemy and chemistry (*Logique*).

The idéologues, like the philosophes before them, were involved in a bitter contest with Catholic orthodoxy for political and cultural influence. The Church had been a rich and powerful institution, supported by state authority and the censorship system, until it was disestablished from its official status and priests were obligated to swear loyalty to the civil constitution in 1790. In the following years, the goods of the Church were confiscated, convents were closed, and refractory priests were forced to emigrate or face execution. After the Terror and its forcible de-christianisation, there was a slight return toward religious toleration in 1795–97, before the Directory moved against "royalists" and anti-republicans in its efforts to bolster its precarious authority. The separation of Church and State had been formalised in a decree of February 1795. Tracy and the idéologues strongly supported such moves to reduce the influence of the Church, not only in politics but especially in education. However, as opponents of clerical influence and as sensationalist philosophers, they were accused by orthodox believers of destroying the moral stature of the human species by degrading it to the level of animal sensations and appetites. Idéologie was accused of being materialist, atheist, and destructive of morality. These critical claims, however, require certain qualifications.

In the first place, the idéologues, like most utilitarian social theorists, did not want to destroy morality as such, but sought to reduce the authority of the Church in prescribing moral rules and sought to found morality upon a rational consideration of human desires and interests. For Volney and others, moral behaviour was based on natural laws, or rational principles inherent in social life. The moral injunctions of the idéologues were indeed not very distant from certain principles in the Sermon on the Mount.

Secondly, most of the idéologues were deists or agnostics rather than atheists. They occasionally spoke of a divine providence which had ordered the universe; and some were active supporters of deist cults such as *théo-philanthropie* which flourished briefly under the Directory. Tracy and his colleagues were predisposed, by their scientific outlook and by their Voltairian ancestry, to be sceptical and agnostic towards theological revelations about the nature of the universe and the moral duties of man, and to be distrustful of claims by the Church to have privileged knowledge of the forms of authority and moral virtue prescribed by God for mankind.

Thirdly, the idéologues' view of man as anchored in natural history may be understood not so much as a denial of man's paramount place in the hierarchy of animal life, but more as a methodological strategy for a positivist science of human behaviour (*Traité de la volonté*). The idéologues were perfectly willing to agree that the human species had a unique capacity for reason, sentiment and morality. But they wished to demonstrate that these qualities had a physiological dimension (bordering on determinism, in one or two cases), and that these qualities were historically developed through language and social interaction (rather than being a divine gift). There would seem to be a clear line of continuity between the idéologues and Auguste Comte, not only in regard to a thorough-going scientism in their methodological pronouncements, but also in regard to the three stages theory of knowledge.

Tracy argued in his *Commentaire* (1806–7) that there have been three main stages in the development of reason and civilisation. The first was typified by despotism, force and ignorance; the second, aristocratic rule buttressed by religious opinions; and the third, representative government and the full flowering of reason. Comte's three stages were the theological, metaphysical and positive stages. The pattern of evolutionary progress is similar; both systems obviously owe a great deal to Condorcet's ten-stage *Esquisse* of 1793 (and the conception can be traced back even to Turgot). What is common to Condorcet and his successors is a view of religion, theology and abstract ontology as obsolete and pre-scientific explanations of man. Moreover, such systems of belief are seen as institutional obstacles to the development of scientific reason. Condillac had therefore been wrong, in Tracy's view, to retain "natural theology" among the philosophical principles needed to explain man's place in society and history. Indeed, Tracy completely excluded theology from the hierarchy of sciences, where it had traditionally occupied a pivotal position.

In considering theology and institutionalised religion in their dual aspect, as systems of knowledge/belief and systems of authority, Tracy made three kinds of criticism. Firstly, he asserted that many of the doctrines of revealed religion were not merely unverifiable, but had actually been disproved and exposed by science as mystifications and illusions about the operations of natural phenomena. Secondly, he criticised the Church for having resisted and obstructed the search for scientific knowledge about nature, and for attempting to impose a dogmatic and illiberal view of morality and the social order. Thirdly, he argued for a separation of Church and State, and in favour of religious tolerance, claiming that no religious beliefs should have the status of official doctrine, supported by public authority. Religious beliefs, in his view, should be essentially matters of private conscience and faith, not matters of orthodoxy and authority. Taken together, Tracy's criticisms led him to support policies designed to reduce the influence of the Catholic Church in France; and especially in public education, where so many impressionable young minds could be distorted by unscientific dogmas and superstitions.

The anticlericalism of the 1790s changed after the Consulate was established by Bonaparte, who decided that the traditional religion was a necessary basis for the social order. Catholicism was recognised as the official religion of France by the Concordat of 1802, and Chateaubriand's *Génie du christianisme* simultaneously provided a spiritual defence of the Church. The idéologues were outraged by Bonaparte's policies whereby the Church regained a great deal of its erstwhile influence. It was not possible to mount a strong attack upon the Concordat and the revival of Catholicism (owing to censorship), although Chateaubriand's work was ridiculed in the pages of *La Décade philosophique* and oblique criticisms of the Church and the Concordat were made in articles defending "la philosophie rationnelle" and "la saine morale."

Tracy had observed the changing fortunes of the Church with a watchful eye; he adopted a staunchly and sometimes bitterly anti-clerical position. He had welcomed in 1795 the publication of Charles Dupuis' voluminous *L'Origine de tous les cultes*, which attempted to reduce religious doctrines to allegories or myths about nature, and especially about astronomical phenomena. Tracy was so impressed by the thrust of Dupuis' erudite volumes, that he wrote some articles for the *Mercure français* giving a concise summary of the main arguments. The journal ceased publication in January 1798 before all of Tracy's remarks had appeared. Soon afterwards, Dupuis published a 600-page *Abrégé* of the multi-volume work (1798); but Tracy was not satisfied that Dupuis' summary was sufficiently analytical and didactic to serve the purpose of enlightening the wider reading public. Tracy therefore published, as an anonymous pamphlet, his summary of Dupuis: *Analyse de "l'Origine de tous les cultes."* A second and expanded edition, also anonymous, appeared in 1804: in the light of the revived influence of Catholicism, it was a veritable political tract (*Analyse raisonnée de "l'Origine de tous les cultes ou religion universelle"*).

Dupuis' main argument, wrote Tracy, was that the ancient fables had never been properly understood, because it was not recognised that "all religions are never anything but the worship of nature and its main agents, the stars, fire, and other elements; and because it was not seen that myths are only the allegorical and symbolic expressions of that first religion and its celestial aspects." Christianity could be understood, in these terms, as essentially the worship of nature and of the sun, under a variety of different names and symbols.

The perspective adopted by Tracy and Dupuis was that religious dogmas were a product of a non-scientific world-view, a product of ignorance, and had been propagated by priests who preached servility and fear. The empirical methods of science were foreign to the priests and theologians, who set themselves up as authorities on the moral and the natural world.

> Let us conclude, then, that every religious system is, at the theoretical level, a supposition without proof, a veritable lapse of reason; and, at the practical level, it is a powerful force for making men follow certain rules of conduct but a sure means of giving them false rules, and emanating from an illegitimate authority; hence, that all religion may be defined as an obstacle to good logic and to sound morality both private and public.

In some lines added to the 1804 edition, implicitly referring to Bonaparte, Tracy said that a man "convinced of the utility and the sanctity of religion, if he wanted to be just and did not aspire to become domineering and oppressive," would desire that no religion be taught in the public education system, for that would impose a uniform doctrine on people of contrary views. In writing his *Commentaire* on Montesquieu two years later, Tracy asserted that "any government which wants to oppress, is attached to priests and works to make them powerful enough to serve it." These critical references to Bonaparte are unmistakable. Tracy concluded his pamphlet in 1804 by asserting that

> theology is the philosophy of the infancy of the world, (but) it is time that it gave way to the philosophy of its age of reason; theology is the work of the imagination, like the bad physics or poor metaphysics which are born with it in times of ignorance and serve as its base; whereas the other philosophy is founded on observation and experience, and is closely tied to true physics and rational logic, which are all the product of the work of enlightened centuries; finally, a theologian is nothing but a bad philosopher

who is rash enough to dogmatise on things he does not and cannot know.

Tracy's identification of religion with speculative metaphysics and imagination was joined to an explanation of the historical origins of religious beliefs. Despite the apparent diversity and mutual antagonism of religious cults and sects, they all had a common basis, namely, that they were

> founded on the same idea—fear of invisible forces. Saint-Lambert said with good reason: *superstition is fear of invisible forces.* That is how he defined it; he could have added: *and it is the source of all religions.*

In seeking the causes of natural phenomena, primitive societies invented various spirits whose task was to ensure that the sun and planets, the rivers and the winds, continued to be activated in their customary way. The worship by men of these multitudinous spirits who presided over everyday life was inevitable for primitive men, with their unsophisticated knowledge of the processes of nature. Later, they imagined a superior being who supervised all the lesser spirits and gave an overarching order to the whole universe. But it was only ignorance of the real causes of phenomena which led man to explain events without a known cause as the product of the will of an unseen being.

Dupuis had especially emphasised the religious significance of primitive astronomy and the mythology of the constellations and signs of the zodiac. "The adventures of all these gods are only allegorical tales about the movements of celestial bodies and their various relations; and thus it is in the heavens that we must find the source and application of all the mythological and theological fables." These myths should not be dismissed without first seeking out their symbolic meanings. Dupuis had claimed that the key to decoding such myths lay in astronomical and physical phenomena. Analysis of these myths showed that the two main sources of human unreason are the personification of abstractions, and the use of metaphorical and metaphysical terminology. In such cases, wrote Tracy, ignorance is preferable to false ideas.

Tracy also elaborated a critique of religion as a social institution in terms of the historical development of a priesthood. In each primitive society there emerged people claiming to recognise more powerful spirits than those currently worshipped, or to know the best means of influencing such spirits, and who thus held sway over credulous people in their locality. Insofar as they did not join with other priests in founding a total religious system and theology, their social effect was relatively harmless. Tracy took a different view of a more powerful priesthood which emerged with the growth of societies: religious doctrines became more systematic and the priesthood became an organised and hierarchical body. Priests then became "an integrating and important part of the constitution of the state" (*Analyse*; and see *Commentaire* on religion as a form of social control).

At the height of their power, the priests made their doctrines into a "science" which stifled all other forms of inquiry (in his *Grammaire* Tracy condemns "the despotism of religious opinions"). They propounded that *mauvaise philosophie* which is based on imagination rather than observation, conjecture rather than doubt, and which endowed abstraction and essences with reality instead of studying the actual operation of our intellectual faculties (*Analyse*; and see "Sur les letters de Descartes"). Theologians began to assert the complete spiritualisation of the gods and of souls, depriving them of all material attributes. They could then attribute to these "purely imaginary beings" whatever qualities they chose, without fear of contradiction. The only way to disagree would be to deny the very existence of spiritual powers, and to do so would invite severe punishment. Theologians established a complete separation of the realm of ideas and judgements, from the realm of nature and material existence. Hence, they concluded that all our ideas and sentiments have their source not in our sensibilities but in another immaterial being, the universal spirit of God. By giving free rein to their favourite errors (belief in the real existence of abstract ideas, and belief in the reality of being deprived of all its sensible qualities) the theologians generated "a host of shocking absurdities," in which the Christian religion is especially prolific.

The early Christian religion, claimed Tracy, consisted largely of practices and precepts; not dogmas, mysteries and sacraments. But by the thirteenth century, and throughout the "barbaric" Middle Ages, Christianity suffered an "excess of theological delirium," full of "far-fetched dogmas which are truly *non-sense*" and sustained by a sophistical language. Such a system of beliefs began to lose ground, however, when the spirit of observation, experience, and doubt emerged alongside that of credulity and supposition. The truths based on observation and on the questioning of received opinion, began to replace the mass of accumulated errors. Once the facts of man and nature have been properly explained, Tracy asserted with more hope than conviction, the human mind would not abandon them again. Theology is like a child's imagination, destined to give way to a mature reason. Tracy expressed a desire to be rid of

> this multitude of different religious systems, which have done so much harm in the world, caused so often the spilling of men's blood, divided people into what amounts to hostile groups, prevented commercial and social interaction among them, especially the communication of knowledge, made some people into objects of aversion and malediction for others, and prescribed so many duties so contrary to their happiness and to reason, particularly that of hating and detesting those who think differently from themselves.

Dupuis' work had shown, to Tracy's satisfaction, that all the ancient and modern religions of Asia and Europe, which denounced one another so fiercely, were exactly the same apart from some changes in nomenclature. There could be no more bitter truth for the priests than this underlying unity of doctrine, for their great passion, he wrote, was hatred of their competitors. In that respect, said Tracy, priests are more like charlatans than thieves: for thieves keep a strong loyalty among themselves for their common security, whereas charlatans denigrate their fellows in trying to attract the crowd exclusively to themselves.

Tracy noted that it would be easier for modern Europeans to see that the ancient religions and myths were based on the worship of nature and the stars, than to see that Christianity was in the same mould.

> Christianity is so close to us, it still rules over *the least enlightened part of* our surroundings, it seems to have so little relationship to these brilliant fictions: how are we to be persuaded that Christ too is only a fantastic being, just one of a thousand versions of the sun-god?

Tracy further agreed with Dupuis that Christ was no more a historical figure than were Hercules, Bacchus or Osiris. Nevertheless, Tracy surmised, it would require a great deal of scientific analysis and demystification to destroy the influence of religious illusions "for the absurdities have a very strong hold on the human mind when they have an ancient priority over reason." How could this "ancient mass of prejudices and errors" be overturned? The exact analysis of our intellectual operations could demonstrate to educated men that we only truly know whatever falls under our senses, and that all other supposed beings are nothing but "personified abstractions, creations of our imagination." It was necessary to open the eyes of the common man by tracing the origin and evolution of these myths, showing their fundamental similarity and basis in astronomical allegories.

Tracy's ultimate objections to established religions were moral. Priests who claimed authority over the people, prescribing rules of belief and conduct, demanded blind faith in their own pronouncements. But it was a grave moral error, according to Tracy, to "make a virtue of stupid servility," and it was even greater error to "accustom men to seek their rules of conduct in the will of an unknown being" instead of finding them in a rational understanding of their own human needs. Priests hindered men from recognising the inherent link between virtue and happiness, and thus deprived men of the strongest motives for seeking out the good ("Quels sont les moyens de fonder la morale chez un peuple?").

> When I see religious men proclaiming almost unanimously that detestable maxim—that without the idea of the life to come, man has no motive for being good—I wonder in dread if they really want to degrade virtue, if they have sworn to pervert all moral ideas, and if their very devil could invent a principle better able to cover the world in misery and crime.
>
> (*Analyse*)

In the place of religion, a defective moral system based on false assumption and reasoning, Tracy advocated what he termed a morality "guided by reason" and based on the observation of man's intellectual faculties. In such a rational morality, we would rouse a man's personal interest in fulfilling his "true" duties instead of employing fear to induce him to fulfil his "imaginary" duties.

Finally, Tracy argued that religions are "essentially subversive of true principles of social order or of public morality," for it is the responsibility of the *civil* legislature to prescribe the duties of citizens. When priests claim for themselves this right, they usurp the sovereignty of the legislature and are often in conflict with it. So they are necessarily the enemies of all governments which they do not already control; and where the clergy does control the state, the liberty of all other citizens is violated, and equity and social equality are destroyed.

Theologians should not, then, be accorded special privileges; the truth of their doctrines should not be protected from criticism by authority; they should not have special rights to exercise public authority or to form a collective body. Their false doctrines, wrote Tracy, deserved to perish along with the false physics and logic which had so long supported them. Science, believed Tracy, would spell the demise of illusions about man and nature. All the "subtleties of the old theological metaphysics will vanish as soon as we specify the proper meaning of the word, to *exist*" ("Dissertation sur quelques questions d'idéologie"). As soon as the unity of man and nature was fully appreciated, the influence of supernatural explanations of reality would decline, and it would become possible to educate people in the ideological art of forming correct judgements about reality on the basis of observation.

Tracy, despite his fierce condemnation of priests and supernatural doctrines, wanted to avoid being taken for a "materialist" and "atheist." When Cabanis was accused of holding such positions by Mme de Staël, Tracy replied that such terms were not appropriate to describe

> men who loudly proclaim not to know what is spirit, nor what is matter, and who often repeat that they have never been, and never will be, occupied in determining the (ultimate) character of the principle of thought, for that is irrelevant to everything they have to say about it.
>
> (Tracy to Mme de Staël, February 23, 1805)

The behavioural scientist of mental operations did not wish to be seen as propounding a materialist ontology; that would also have been a false metaphysics, for it dealt with the "first causes" of the universe. On the other hand, he could not resist making anticlerical jibes whenever the occasion arose, as in his remark that "the religion of the Court of Rome . . . is a commodity for export and not for consumption" (*Commentaire*; repeated in *Traité de la volonté*).

Mme de Staël's *De l'Allemagne:*
A Misleading Intermediary

Lilian R. Furst

De l'Allemagne has long been established as one of the major intermediaries between France and Germany, a pillar of Franco-German literary relations. Goethe already recognised it "als ein mächtiges Rüstzeug . . . , das in die chinesische Mauer antiquierter Vorurteile, die uns von Frankreich trennte, sogleich eine breite Lücke durchbrach, so dass man über den Rhein und, in Gefolge dessen, über den Kanal endlich von uns nähere Kenntnis nahm" ("as a mighty weapon . . . , which immediately made a wide breach in the Chinese wall of antiquated prejudices that separated us from France, so that across the Rhine and thence across the Channel Germany at last came to be better known"). Subsequently *De l'Allemagne* became "un guide littéraire," often nicknamed the Bible of the Romantics, while Mme de Staël herself has been called "essentiellement une inspiratrice du romantisme," "une prophétesse," "that fascinating old queen of Romanticism," "institutrice de toute une génération" ("teacher to a whole generation"), and "Mistress to an Age." There would seem to be some truth in the witticism attributed to the Duc de Berry, that there were at that time three great powers in Europe: England, Russia, and Mme de Staël.

The intrinsic importance of *De l'Allemagne* resides not so much in either the quality or the quantity of its reportage on German literature as in the fundamental changes of attitude which it implied and induced. These pertain to the relationship of the French to their own literary heritage as well as to their evaluation of the Germans as a cultural force. In both these areas *De l'Allemagne* marks a crucial turning-point. In the history of French poetry, as Margaret Gilman has pointed out in *The Idea of Poetry in France* "with Mme de Staël and *De l'Allemagne* the idea of a poetry different from that

From *The Contours of European Romanticism.* © 1979 by Lilian R. Furst. University of Nebraska Press, 1979.

of the 'great tradition' comes to the fore." Gilman defines it further as "a poetry fraught with emotion, enthusiasm, and imagery, possessed of a mysterious, even mystical quality." The kind of writing which *De l'Allemagne* revealed to the French was certainly very far from the Neoclassical manner to which they were accustomed. There in lay one of the sources of its attraction to an age uneasily aware of the need to reform a pattern that was degenerating into a stale stereotype. In helping to provide a stimulus for a creative renewal of French poetry by showing fresh paths and possibilities, *De l'Allemagne* is of far-reaching significance. Moreover, its suggestion of Germany as a model for France was in itself a revolutionary reversal of the trend dominant until then. Throughout the seventeenth and eighteenth centuries Germany had looked to France for a cultural lead, its small courts admiring and aping Versailles. The French, on the other hand, barely disguised their contempt for their barbarian neighbour, whose literature they largely ignored, with the exception of a few idylls. Attempts had been made to improve and redress the current image of Germany as a boorish backwater; for instance, by Elie Fréron and Michael Huber in Paris in the mid-eighteenth century, and in the accounts of such travellers as Catteau-Calleville, Charles Villers and Benjamin Constant. But their earnest efforts to disseminate information had relatively little effect. It was not until Mme de Staël's demonstrative applause that a real change of attitude toward Germany occurred. Suddenly and startlingly, the despised laggard was held up not only as a daring innovator, but even as a potential teacher. In this respect, too, the importance of *De l'Allemagne* in the history of Franco-German literary relations can hardly be overestimated: quite simply, it denotes the beginning of a new epoch.

It is indeed its prominent position as one of the cornerstones of the nineteenth century that prompts and justifies this further analysis of its role as an intermediary. Partly because of the novelty of its content and partly because of the sensational circumstances of its publication in England following the ban by Napoleonic censure, *De l'Allemagne* made a tremendous impact. Six complete French editions appeared between 1814 and 1819 besides sundry extracts, reviews and five critical studies, and the years 1820 to 1870 witnessed fifteen further reprints. For long *De l'Allemagne* reigned supreme as the standard source of knowledge about German literature, not only in France, but also in England and the United States, where Mme de Staël's image of Germany was propagated by Carlyle and Ticknor respectively. This prompt acceptance, wide diffusion and lasting effect of the notions expounded in *De l'Allemagne* makes it all the more imperative that we should attain clarity about its nature and efficacy as an intermediary. And it is no diminution of Mme de Staël's total achievement to point out some of the misconceptions she harboured and their curious consequences.

De l'Allemagne is generally reputed to contain an account of German Romanticism which inspired the nascent French Romantic movement. The latter part of that proposition, viz. that *De l'Allemagne* inspired the French

Romantics, is certainly true, but not, as is frequently supposed, by its revelation of German Romanticism. Herein lies a cardinal fallacy common in critical discussions of *De l'Allemagne* and its influence. Mme de Staël does indeed present German literature as an essentially Romantic literature in contrast to the Classical heritage of France. In this she is following the distinction she had made in *De la littérature* between the literatures of the North and those of the South. Germany clearly belongs to the North with its aura of mists, melancholy, chivalry, in short the paraphernalia of Romanticism. This does not mean, however, that Mme de Staël actually writes about the German Romantic poets and thinkers. A glance at the contents of Part II ("De la littérature et des arts") of *De l'Allemagne* confirms this contention: there are sections on Wieland, Klopstock, Lessing, Winckelmann, Goethe, Schiller, and Herder as well as separate appraisals of Goethe's and Schiller's main plays. Other writers discussed in some detail include Bürger, Kotzebue, Klinger, Matthias Claudius, Iffland, Voss, Jacobi, Matthison, Tieck, Jean-Paul, Zacharias Werner and August Wilhelm Schlegel. With the exception of the last four, these are *not* the German Romantics. It becomes increasingly apparent on close analysis that while *De l'Allemagne* gives excellent coverage to various facets of the *Sturm und Drang*, it hardly touches the fringe of German Romanticism. The major poets of the *Frühromantik*, Novalis and Wackenroder, are not even mentioned in her survey of German literature, although reference is made to Novalis as a mystical thinker in Part IV (under the heading "La religion et l'enthousiasme"). Nor is there any true appreciation of Friedrich Schlegel's significance as an aesthetician and experimenter.

It can of course be argued that the *Sturm und Drang* represents a prefiguration of Romanticism. The line of continuity between the two movements is very evident in their rejection of the *status quo*, their common thrust towards a creative renewal of imaginative writing, their emphasis on the subjective, and their aesthetic credo of freedom in self-expression. But it would be wrong to overlook the differences, and simply to equate the *Sturm und Drang* with Romanticism. The *Sturm und Drang*'s preoccupation with immediate social problems as against the inward orientation of Romanticism with its primacy of the imagination; the political aims of the *Stürmer und Dränger* in their assertion of liberty in contrast to the Romantics' mystical tendencies and metaphysical inclinations; the preference in the *Sturm und Drang* for drama as opposed to the *Roman* in all its variants favoured by the *Frühromantiker*: these differences go beyond a mere matter of intensity; they are sufficiently deep to give rise to a really fallacious picture when the *Sturm und Drang* is taken for Romanticism, as Mme de Staël did.

Her treatment of German prose fiction in *De l'Allemagne* can serve as a concrete example of the misleading effect of her fusion of the two movements. Prose fiction was not only the genre to which the *Frühromantiker* gave the greatest importance, but also that in which they were the most innovative. Of this Mme de Staël conveys little or no inkling. Even though she significantly advanced French acquaintance with German prose fiction, her coverage of this vital segment nonetheless has severe limitations, and shows beyond dispute that she did not in fact introduce the salient works of German Romanticism into France.

Of the thirty-two sections that make up Part II of *De l'Allemagne* only one (xxviii) treats the narrative, whereas no less than thirteen deal with drama, and five with lyric poetry. The imbalance within the section "Des romans" is equally serious. After a peremptory dismissal of the many love-stories published in Germany, Mme de Staël devotes almost half of the section to Goethe. *Werther* is praised as "sans égal et sans pareil" ("un-equalled and unparalleled"), an example of Goethe's genius at its most passionate. For this novel, already popular at the time when she was writ-ing, Mme de Staël shows a deep understanding; as its two cardinal features, she underlines first Goethe's portrayal of "les maladies de l'imagination de notre siècle" ("the ills of the imagination in our century"), and secondly the letter form, appealing to her age in its focus on inner feelings rather than outer happenings. Thus, in a couple of brief paragraphs, Mme de Staël has shrewdly brought out the historical importance of *Werther*. Goethe's other novels, however, fare less well: *Wilhelm Meister*, "plein de discussions ingénieuses et spirituelles" ("full of clever and sprightly dis-cussions") that overshadow an uninteresting, quasi-superfluous hero, is deemed not "très-attachant" ("very engaging") with the exception of the beautiful episode of Mignon that won Mme de Staël's heart and that is recounted in some detail. Of *Die Wahlverwandtschaften* (The Elective Affin-ities) she is highly critical, faulting the novel's pessimistic implications, its avoidance of overt emotion, and above all, what she terms its vacillating stance, which she contrasts with the "confiance" and "enthousiasme" that a work of art should inspire. This is a clear example of her rejection of a work because it did not fulfil *her* expectations of the novel. Tieck's *Sternbald*, on the other hand, is most sympathetically reviewed; here, as with *Werther*, Mme de Staël is astute, indeed daring, in her appreciation of its imagina-tive, poetic organisation. After a brief tribute to Claudius, the last third of the chapter consists of an attempt to assess Jean-Paul Richter. Though intrigued by "des productions si extraordinaires" ("such extraordinary works"), Mme de Staël is at a loss for anything other than a paradoxical judgement: she praises the "beautés admirables," the "finesse," the "gaieté," the originality of his genius, but to her "l'ordonnance et le cadre de ses tableaux sont si défectueux, que les traits de génie les plus lumineux se perdent dans la confusion de l'ensemble" ("the disposition and the framework of his pictures is so faulty that the brightest strokes of genius are lost in the confusedness of the whole"). She is obviously disorientated by Jean-Paul's writing and unable to place him within her experience or conception of the novel. Yet it is a measure of her fascination with Jean-Paul's "sombre talent") that she not only summarises two episodes (that of Lord Horion and his son from the beginning of *Hesperus*, and from *Titan* Emmanuel's description of the sunset), but also risks "la traduction d'un morceau très-bizarre" ("the translation of a highly bizarre piece"), the so-called "Songe," the first piece of the *Blumen-Frucht-und Dornenstücke* (*Flowers, Fruits, and Thorns Pieces*). And there, apart from a passing mention of August Lafontaine, the section "Des romans" ends, with the tantalising remark: "On n'en finirait point, si l'on voulait analyser la foule de romans spirituels et touchants que l'Allemagne possède" ("One would never finish if one wanted to analyse the host of clever and moving novels that Germany has"); the study of these novels would surely inspire "le mouvement d'émulation" ("the urge to emulate").

Faced with this teasing conclusion, the contemporary French reader of *De l'Allemagne* might well have wished for more. His curiosity would certainly have been aroused about German prose fiction, yet after a few pages he is left with an appetite whetted but unsatisfied. For when we ask dispassionately, how adequate is "Des romans" as a presentation of German prose fiction at the turn of the century, the answer must be largely in the negative. In spite of Mme de Staël's pioneering exploration and her penetrating insight at various points, taken as a whole, as an introduction to German prose fiction, this section of *De l'Allemagne* is disappointingly scant. While it would be unfair to expect a comprehensive survey of the field, nevertheless the ommissions are numerous and glaring. The outstanding narratives of the *Frühromantik*—Friedrich Schlegel's *Lucinde*, Wackenroder's *Herzensergiessungen eines kunstliebenden Klosterbruders*, Novalis's *Heinrich von Ofterdingen*, the *Märchen* as genre—all these are totally withheld from the French reader.

In the face of this textual evidence, it is time to revise the accepted view of *De l'Allemagne* as the work that brought German Romanticism into France. Mme de Staël herself is to some extent responsible for this misconception in that she presented the literature of Germany to her readers as an essentially Romantic literature in antithesis to the Classical heritage of France. In a wider sense this may be true, insofar as Germany's tradition tended towards irrationalism. But in the specific literary meaning, as pertaining to the Romantic movement of the late 1790s and early 1800s, the assumption must be refuted. Even the editors of the critical edition of *De l'Allemagne*, staunch *Staëliens* though they are, concede that "Sous le nom de 'Nouvelle école' elle mélange constamment le *Sturm und Drang*, le *Classicisme* et le *Romantisme* naissant" ("Under the name of 'New School' she constantly mingles *Sturm und Drang*, *Classicism* and nascent *Romanticism*"). In that mixture the *Sturm und Drang* was the dominant element. The aesthetic that emerges from Mme de Staël's account of German literature is unmistakably that of the *Sturm und Drang*. Repeatedly throughout *De l'Allemagne*, *De la littérature*, the *Carnets de voyage* and her letters the prime emphasis is on enthusiasm which she, like the *Stürmer und Dränger*, glorifies as the salient, divine quality of the genius. Mme de Staël subscribes to the

Sturm und Drang conception of art as a spontaneous outpouring of enthusiasm. On the other hand, she does not share the German Romantics' preoccupation with the transcendental dimension, i.e. the transforming power of the imagination and the elevation of art to a religion. She appears to have had little awareness of the crucial importance of these facets when she impetuously presented—or rather, misrepresented—the *Sturm und Drang* as German Romanticism. But as a result of the picture proffered in *De l'Allemagne* it was the *Sturm und Drang* that came for long to be regarded in France as German Romanticism, much to the detriment of the *Frühromantik* that was overlooked and neglected.

How did this substitution of the *Sturm und Drang* for Romanticism come about? It was certainly not the outcome of ignorance on Mme de Staël's part. Though it has been argued that the book was dated even on its publication, springing as it did from impressions gathered some ten years earlier, there is little to suggest that this holds true for the sections on literature which appear to have been thoroughly re-worked in 1809. One of her collaborators then was August Wilhelm Schlegel, for years her close friend and tutor to her children, from whom she would surely have heard of the most recent German writing. With Friedrich Schlegel, whom she had met in Berlin, she corresponded: he gave her three volumes of *Athenäum* and his novel, *Lucinde*. She also had works by Novalis, Schelling, Schleiermacher, Tieck, Chamisso, Jean-Paul, Fouqué, Fichte, Werner, and Wackenroder, in fact a good repertoire of German Romantic literature in her library at Coppet. So it is in real puzzlement that one comes to investigate the reasons for her omission of the *Frühromantik* in favour of the *Sturm und Drang*.

The cause would seem to lie in a complex of outer and inner factors: the genesis and intent of *De l'Allemagne*; Mme de Staël's working method; her language problems; her own background, personality and prejudices. All these combined to make *De l'Allemagne* what it is: a misleading intermediary.

To take first the outer factors. It is well to bear in mind that *De l'Allemagne* was not originally and primarily a book about literature; indeed, it came to be written almost by chance. Prior to 1803, oriented rather toward England or Italy, Mme de Staël had shown little interest in Germany. The sections of *De la littérature* that deal with Germany betray her scant acquaintance with the country and its literature at that time. She had read *Werther*, but when Goethe sent her a copy of *Wilhelm Meister* in 1797 she could only admire its binding! Between 1800 and 1803 she took a few German lessons, met some *émigrés* recently returned from Germany, as well as Charles Villers, who had published a series of articles on German literature and thought. But by and large she may be said to have shared the contemporary French indifference to Germany. Nor was her journey in 1803–4 inspired by any thirst for knowledge. It was not of her own volition as a learned investigator, but as an exile banished by Napoleonic decree that she crossed the Rhine in November 1803, with reluctance, mis-givings and hesitations. Her initial unfavourable impressions of the coun-try, recorded in the recently published *Carnets de voyage*, gradually changed during her stay in Weimar, and it was there in February 1804 that she conceived the idea of a book to reveal Germany to the French. "J'ai passé des jours si heureux dans ce séjour [i.e. Weimar] que mon jugement sur tous les objets se ressent des impressions que j'y ai éprouvées." ("I have spent such happy days here [i.e. Weimar] that my judgement of everything is affected by my impressions here.") With these words Mme de Staël virtually admits the idealising trend that increasingly overlaid her earlier contradictory view of Germany. This idealisation was quickly fused with her ulterior political motives to turn *De l'Allemagne* from its very inception into an act of opposition to Napoleon. Still burning with resentment against the tyrant, she wanted to portray Germany, by contrast with France, as the land of liberty. As Heine so astutely realised, "Der Hass gegen den Kaiser ist die Seele dieses Buches *De l'Allemagne*, und obgleich sein Name nirgends darin genannt wird, sieht man doch, wie die Verfasserin bei jeder Zeile nach den Tuilerien schielt." ("Hatred of the Emperor is at the heart of this book, *De l'Allemagne*, and although his name is nowhere mentioned, one sees nonetheless how the author has her eye on the Tuileries in every line.") The obvious parallel with Tacitus' *De Germania* has often been made. What has not so far been underlined is the effect of this political bias on Mme de Staël's literary predilections. Her emphasis on the freedom in Germany naturally drew her towards the *Sturm und Drang*, particularly the dramas of rebellion which supported the rights of the individual against a repressive social order. The ethos and aesthetics of the *Sturm und Drang* fitted perfectly into her picture of Germany as the home of political idealism. Her focus on the *Sturm und Drang* thus served her practical purpose far more readily than a portrayal of the *Frühromantik* with its metaphysical emphasis could have done.

But this may suggest a greater degree of deliberate choice on Mme de Staël's part than was actually the case. Reading accounts of her travels and of the genesis of *De l'Allemagne*, one is constantly struck by the haphaz-ardness of the whole enterprise. Even the decision to go to Germany was a last-minute improvisation, prompted by her desire to see Villers, who was then in Metz. As for her study of German literature, it was unsystem-atic, to say the least. She was gifted with a lively mind, shrewd insight and an astonishingly, perspicacious instinctive judgement, but nothing was more alien to her than the scholar's slow, patient gathering of information. She relied on conversations, often rapid reading, samples, extracts, or the reports of friends. Heine's description "wie dieser Sturmwind in Weibs-kleidern durch unser ruhiges Deutschland fegte" ("how this whirlwind in woman's clothing swept through our tranquil Germany") is more than a mere witticism. Whirlwind impressions, however, are not the soundest basis for a balanced assessment of a country and its literature. A fair amount was, indeed, left to chance: she met those writers who happened to cross her path, read those books that were thrust at her (as in the case of Jean-Paul, whose *Briefe und bevorstehender Lebenslauf* were given to her by Villers to read in her carriage on the way). In Weimar, where she spent four out of her six months in Germany, she tended to meet the older generation, the former *Stürmer und Dränger*. The timing of her subsequent visit to Berlin, a centre of the *Romantik*, was, as Christopher Herold has pointed out, "unfortunate. Novalis was dead; Tieck was absent; Brentano, Arnim, and Hoffmann had not yet arrived; Kleist was there, but unknown; Schelling was teaching at Wurzburg, Schleiermacher at Halle, Hegel at Jena" (*Mistress to an Age*). This "unfortunate" timing is in many ways typical, and revealing of her adventitious approach to her subject. There is ample evidence to support Monchoux's contention that "le caprice de l'auteur est la principale loi de cet ouvrage décousu" ("the author's caprices were the main guidelines to this disjointed work") (*L'Allemagne devant les lettre françaises*).

This capriciousness was to some extent determined and also furthered by Mme de Staël's linguistic shortcomings. In her attempt to grasp German literature she was handicapped by her inadequate command of the language. In spite of her German lessons—first from Gerlach, her children's tutor, and later from Wilhelm Humboldt—she could not converse in German with any ease. As Jacobi wrote to her in November 1803: "il y a un mal auquel ni votre célébrité, ni votre beau génie, et bien encore moins mes bons offices ne sauraient rémédier: c'est que vous ne savez pas vous exprimer en allemand, et que nos gens de lettres ne savent pas s'exprimer en français" ("there is one difficulty which neither your fame, nor your brilliance, much less my good offices could remove: that is, that you cannot express yourself in German, and our men of letters cannot express themselves in French"). It is hard to assess how serious a barrier this was because of the conflicting evidence. On the one hand, Schiller, overcoming his reluctance to speak French, wrote to Goethe that he had managed tolerably well. On the other hand, Mme de Staël, referring to the same conversation, complained to her father that Schiller "parle très difficilement le français" ("speaks French with great difficulty"), while she reported to Villers: "nous nous sommes déjà disputés sans savoir nos langues mutuelles" ("we have already engaged in lively discussion without knowing each other's languages"). Her stay in Weimar is punctuated by repeated references to language problems. Wieland, for example, cautiously asked: "Oserais-je vous demander, Madame, si Fichte parle assez facilement le français pour pouvoir s'entretenir avec vous sur des objets de spéculation?" ("Might I venture to enquire, Madame, whether Fichte speaks French with sufficient ease to be able to discuss speculative topics with you?")—a pertinent question indeed. In January 1804 already she was recruiting Jacobi's assistance with these words: "Votre esprit est si clair et votre connaissance du français si parfaite que vous achèverez pour moi tous les commencements d'idées dont j'ai la tête remplie" ("Your mind is so clear and your knowledge of French so excellent that you will complete for me all the incipient ideas that fill my head"). Nor was Jacobi the only one to be pressed into service. With her customary ingenuity, Mme de Staël hit on the idea of using English, which she knew well, as the medium for her study of German thought when she met Henry Crabb Robinson. He was, as he put it, "commanded . . . to draw up for her Dissertations on the new philosophy"; he adds that she "paid me for the trouble in loud praise, and promises or threatens me (whatever you will) with incorporating them in her great work on the German nation and literature she is now writing." There is thus little doubt that, as she herself confessed in *De l'Allemagne*, it was only "á travers l'obstacle des mots" ("across the obstacle of the words") that she gained access to German literature. The insidious effect of these problems of communication was to bring her closer to those most proficient in French, specifically Wieland, who could hardly be said to represent the newest and most interesting in the German literature of the turn of the century.

Nevertheless, these outer factors alone would not in themselves have sufficed to focus Mme de Staël's attention on the *Sturm und Drang*. At a decisive level, inner factors too come into play, namely her own preferences and prejudices, which recent scholarship, notably that of Roland Mortier, André Monchoux, and Robert de Luppé, has shown to be more complex than was previously assumed. Mme de Staël has commonly been portrayed as the harbinger of Romanticism, the electrifying apostle of enthusiasm. While this popular image undoubtedly contains a good deal of truth, it is somewhat simplistic, and needs to be corrected by a consideration of other elements in her personality. In background and upbringing she was very clearly a product of the eighteenth century, "l'héritière la plus intelligente et la plus fidèle de l'esprit des lumières" ("the most intelligent and most faithful inheritrix of the spirit of the Enlightenment"), as Mortier has—with perhaps a touch of exaggeration—called her. Though disenchanted with the Neo-classical French heritage and, therefore, more open to new ideas than many of her compatriots, in the last resort she still retained a certain caution, indeed ambivalence. Robert de Luppé has even gone so far as to brand her a "prisonnière du passé" ("a prisoner of the past"), while Jean Gibelin maintains that "il ne lui est pas possible de sortir des limites élargies du goût français" ("she is not able to go beyond the expanded limits of French taste"). These statements seem to be an over-correction of the previous tendency to envisage Mme de Staël as wholly forward-looking. The truth lies between the extremes: she did espouse "l'enthousiasme," she did welcome the freshness of German literature, and she did want to see some of its innovations introduced into France; on the other hand, she did not hesitate to criticise Germany for its lack of elegance and *bon goût*, nor was she averse to appeals to "les anciens" in her literary judgements.

Her subconscious impregnation with French standards certainly affected her attitude to German Romanticism. Its radical break with traditional aesthetics and its experimentation with accepted forms were too outrageous for the child of the Enlightenment that lurked beneath her tempestuous surface. The amount as well as the nature of the innovations practised by the *Sturm und Drang* were more in consonance with her own inclinations and ideas than those of the *Frühromantik*. Genius and enthusiasm, the essential tenets of the *Sturm und Drang*, aroused a more positive response in Mme de Staël than the metaphysics and imagination fundamental to the *Frühromantik*. As Schiller commented to Goethe:

> ihr Naturell und Gefühl ist besser als ihre Metaphysik, und ihr schöner Verstand erhebt sich zu einem genialischen Vermögen. Sie will alles erklären, einsehen, ausmessen, sie statuiert nichts Dunkles, Unzugängliches, und wohin sie nicht mit ihrer Fackel leuchten kann, da ist nichts für sie vorhanden. Darum hat sie eine horrible Scheu vor der Idealphilosophie, welche nach ihrer Meinung zur Mystik und zum Aberglauben führt, und das ist eine Stickluft, wo sie umkommt.

> (her instinct and feeling are better than her capacity for metaphysics, and her fine understanding reaches the level of genius. She wants to explain, grasp, measure everything; she admits nothing dark and impenetrable, and those areas that she cannot illuminate with her torch do not exist for her. For this reason she has a terrible repugnance to idealistic philosophy, which in her view leads to mysticism and superstition, and that is a fatally poisonous atmosphere for her).

This perceptive diagnosis is confirmed by Mme de Staël's letters from Germany which abound in whimsical, faintly derogatory references to the "bizarre métaphysique" in which Goethe, Schiller and their circle were absorbed, and which was evidently alien and suspect to her.

In prose fiction too, to return to our specific example, her judgements show signs of being determined by her heritage. It is in keeping with the Neoclassical ranking of genres to place drama in prime position, lyric poetry second, and prose narrative a poor third, as Mme de Staël does. Some of her comments hint at a certain contempt for the novel, specially for those features which "les ancients n'auraient jamais fait" ("the ancients would never have done"). Her conception of the novel, as Robert de Luppé has pointed out, stood clearly in the lineage of Marmontel and La Harpe. Here, as in other parallel instances, her literary conservatism is in striking contrast to her dynamic belief in perfectibility. Her affiliations to the past made her wary of extremes, particularly in regard to form. Goethe is reputed to have faulted her lack of interest in form, while Heine called her "die Sultanin des Gedankens" ("the Sultana of thought") because of her concentration on substance, idea, and thought in preference to shape. This mental bias of hers may help to explain her avoidance of such works as *Lucinde, Heinrich von Ofterdingen* or the *Herzensergiessungen,* all of which would no doubt have struck her as too eccentric in form in contrast to the recognisable *roman épistolaire, Werther,* and the picaresque outline of *Sternbald.*

Through her turn of mind then, as well as her background and personality, Mme de Staël was thus more disposed to an innate sympathy with the ideals of the *Sturm und Drang* than with those of the *Frühromantik.* In these latent psychological and intellectual inclinations, even more than in such outer factors as her ulterior political motives and language problems, lie the deeper reasons for her preference for the *Sturm und Drang.* It is as strange a combination of circumstances as any in literary history that brought the acceptance of the *Sturm und Drang* in France as German Romanticism. Only the consequences of this misconception are as astonishing as its origins.

Mme de Staël's presentation of the *Sturm und Drang* as German Romanticism had both immediate and lasting after-effects. *De l'Allemagne* was immensely influential as an intermediary through its wide dissemination, its prodigious esteem and its almost unquestioned authority over many years. It was the standard primer for the French Romantics, few of whom knew enough German to attempt to read for themselves. What is more, *De l'Allemagne* was instrumental in sending a whole chain of eminent Frenchmen—Quinet, Ampère, Michelet, Philarète Chasles, Xavier Marmier, Taine, Lerminier, Blaze de Bury, Saint-René Taillandier, to name only the most prominent—on pilgrimage to Germany. The extraordinary persistence of Mme de Staël's image of Germany is too well known and too fully documented to require any further elaboration. Suffice it to say that the dissenting protests, such as those of Quinet, Heine, and Börne, were relatively sparse and little heeded. By and large, the vision of Germany projected by *De l'Allemagne* reigned supreme for a major part of the nineteenth century.

This holds true in the literary field too. Mme de Staël's views were accepted as virtually sacrosanct and her judgements repeated, often albeit in simplified fashion. Those German works and writers championed by her were the ones best received in France. The genres, periods and styles she recommended—the elegiac, the medieval, the Biblical—were adopted with alacrity. Goethe and Schiller were long—one might plausibly argue, still are—regarded in France as the foremost German Romantics. Again the fate of German prose fiction may serve as a paradigm. The continued dominance of Mme de Staël's preferences can be traced in the French reception of German prose for more than fifty years. *Werther,* for instance, the favourite of many of the French Romantics, completely overshadowed both *Wilhelm Meister* and *Die Wahlverwandtschaften.* Tieck's *Sternbald* was translated in 1823 by the baroness of Montolieu and was well received by *Le Globe* (iv [1828] and vii [1829]), the *Revue de Paris* (xliii [1841]) and the *Revue des Deux Mondes* (iv [1835]). The infiltration of Jean-Paul into France has been thoroughly traced by Claude Pichois who has shown that *bizarrerie*, Mme de Staël's term, became "le leit-motiv des jugements sur Jean-Paul" (*L'Image de Jean-Paul Richter dans les lettres françaises*), and who also maintains that the "Songe," which she translated, was to haunt three generations of French poets and thinkers from Vigny, Michelet, Balzac and Hugo, through Musset, Gautier and Nerval, on to Baudelaire, Flaubert and Renan. Even August Lafontaine enjoyed considerable popularity: he was avidly read by Lamartine, and familiar to Stendhal and Balzac, who referred to him (alongside *Faust!*) in *Eugénie Grandet*. The first more systematic account of German literature, Loève-Weimars' *Résumé de l'histoire de la littérature allemande*, published in 1826, also followed Mme de Staël closely in its choice and assessment of writers, including for example Jean-Paul and Tieck, and excluding Friedrich Schlegel and Novalis. Thereby Mme de Staël's image of German literature was further perpetuated.

The most serious consequences for the French in the long run arose, however, less from Mme de Staël's pronouncements on German literature than from her silences. Just as her judgements re-echoed through the nineteenth century, so her omissions left glaring gaps. Wackenroder, for instance, hardly receives any mention other than a brief comment by Amédée Prévost in the *Revue de Paris* (xliii [1841]) in an article on Tieck and his generation. Friedrich Schlegel, in line with Mme de Staël's approach, is known as a thinker, an Orientalist and a Catholic, but of *Lucinde* only a few fragments are translated and published in the *Nouvelle Revue Germanique* (3 série, ii [1835]). Similarly Novalis, again in accordance with Mme de Staël's projection, exists for the French as the proponent of a kind of mystical scientific thought and not, virtually until the end of the nineteenth century, as an imaginative poet.

This adds up to more than a mere catalogue of certain German writers known to the French in the nineteenth century and others not known. What it means in the final analysis is that for most of the century the French remained in ignorance of the *Frühromantik*. The *Hochromantik*—E. T. A. Hoffman, Heine, Uhland—penetrated into France earlier and more easily to stand alongside the *Sturm und Drang*. It was not until the middle of the century that the poets of the *Frühromantik* began to infiltrate into France, and it was really only the Symbolists who first appreciated the full import of *Frühromantik* aesthetics. France awoke to the *Frühromantik* through the intermediacy of Nerval, Baudelaire and Wagner whose operas embodied Friedrich Schlegel's ideal of a progressive universal poetry, as he called it in the 116th *Athenäum* Fragment, in the form of the *Gesamtkunstwerk*. The exaltation of the imagination as "la reine des facultés" ("the queen of the faculties") (Baudelaire), the systematic use of symbolic images as the carriers of meaning, the delving into the mysteries of the subconscious, the stress on the musical, associative qualities of poetry—all these aspects of the *Frühromantik* did not come into their own in France until the Symbolist movement.

It would obviously be an exaggeration to ascribe to Mme de Staël the full responsibility for these literary developments, and even for certain political consequences, as Alexander Gillies tried to do when he maintained that the collapse of France in 1940 sprang ultimately from the intellectual confusion resulting from the "series of legends" about Germany propagated by *De l'Allemagne* ("Some Thoughts on Comparative Literature," in *Yearbook of Comparative and General Literature* [1952]). Nevertheless, the seeds of many strange features of Franco-German literary relations were undeniably sown in this intermediary that was at one and the same time so illuminating and so misleading. For *De l'Allemagne* set off a chain reaction. It stands at the fountain-head not only of a newly respectful attitude of the French towards their neighbours across the Rhine, but also of a perplexing time-lag of some fifty years between literary developments in the two countries. Just as the French Symbolists are the true counterparts to the German *Frühromantiker*, so French Romanticism corresponds in fact to the *Sturm und Drang*. In the primacy of enthusiasm, genius, freedom and spontaneity as the kernel of its aesthetics, in the unfettered drama of rebellion, in the emotional vehemence of its personal poetry, in the lyrical autobiographical novel, in the worship of nature, in the social involvement: in all these vital aspects French *romantisme* has a strong kinship to the *Sturm und Drang*. Though other forces inevitably came into play, Mme de Staël's establishment of the *Sturm und Drang qua* Romanticism in France was decisive in shaping the particular character of the French Romantic movement. Perhaps even more important in the long run was the corollary to her championship of the *Sturm und Drang*, namely her neglect of the *Frühromantik* which was thus effectively blocked from the consciousness of the French for half a century. Epoch-making though *De l'Allemagne* was as an intermediary, it was as much to mislead as to guide the nineteenth century.

Benjamin Constant: Ancient and Modern Freedom in Context

Stephen Holmes

Les anciens n'avaient aucune notion de ce genre de liberté.
—CONDORCET

What cultural and organizational transformations have caused radically different kinds of freedom to flourish in the ancient city and the modern state? Why did subjective rights, difficult to imagine in antiquity, become self-evident in modern European societies? Constant believed that modern liberty was a normative counterpart to the sharp disjunction between state and society, a distinction which emerged in Europe after the Reformation. That is the sociological basis of what Max Weber himself called "Constant's brilliant construction."

A CONTEXTUAL THEORY OF INDIVIDUAL RIGHTS

One of the major obstacles to a historically oriented approach to constitutional rights is a dim but widespread conviction that rights somehow inhere in the human personality. Yet this mysterious "inherence" is as impervious to theoretical analysis as the related and equally obfuscatory notion of a "presocial" individual. According to Constant, rights to freedom, dignity, equality, and property do not have as their object an inborn quality discoverable in discrete individuals. Constitutional rights are valued not because they mirror human nature, but because they help to solve one of the fundamental problems of modern society. Rights counter the threat posed by the expansionistic tendency of the modern political sphere. Historically, they developed as a response to the danger that political officials might destroy the newly emergent autonomy of multiple channels of social cooperation. Not indestructible human nature but a relatively fragile and distinctively modern communicative order was the object of rights. Modern

From *Benjamin Constant and the Making of Modern Liberalism.* © 1984 by Yale University. Yale University Press, 1984.

liberty cannot be interpreted as a purely negative principle, as a quest to desocialize man or to eject him from social life. Constant associated modern liberty with the option of freedom from politics, but not with anything so unthinkable as freedom from society.

Constant also believed that "commerce," irrationally stigmatized under the old regime, was "one of the principal bases of liberty" (*Fragmens d'un ouvrage abandonné*). But this did not mean that his liberalism was a form of bourgeois ideology.

DEROMANTICIZING THE ANCIENT CITY

Rousseau whitewashed many cruel aspects of the classical city. To rectify this romantic falsification, Constant echoed Volney's description of the Spartans, the Romans, and even the Athenians as "half-savage peoples, destitute and piratical" ("Leçons d'histoire"). Daily contact with slaves had anesthetized ancient citizens to that "sympathy for pain" which modern men perceive as a natural moral sentiment. This Graeco-Roman numbness was to be expected since "the pain of a slave is a means for his master." Slavery enhanced the slaveowner's appreciation of his own freedom precisely because "slaves . . . were counted as nothing in the social system of antiquity." The brutality and lack of compassion resulting from slaveholding were not transcended when citizens entered the public forum. Indeed, an atmosphere of violence (immortalized in the Melian dialogue) pervaded political life. In sum, Constant subscribed to Hume's view that slaveholding had a decisive impact on the tone of Greek and Roman life: "a cruel and severe turn was given to their morals."

But Constant explained Condorcet's dictum that "the ancients had no idea of individual rights" without relying too heavily on postulates about the backwardness of ancient morality. He concentrated on institutional factors that prevented the concept of individual rights from flourishing in antiquity. He did not view ancient liberty as a context-free alternative. Instead, he depicted it as the parochial counterpart to a historically obsolete social organization. Because of the small size and the restricted population of their cities, "each citizen . . . had politically a great personal importance." Participation in the exercise of public sovereignty was a palpable joy to ancient citizens not so much because their *moeurs* were glory-directed and Homeric, but for the banal reason that their cities were tiny. The immediate pleasure of being a large fish in a small pond was so intense that it could console citizens when their lives were otherwise regimented by the all-embracing power of the collectivity (in Etienne Hofmann, ed. *Les "Principes de politique" de Benjamin Constant*). They were lured into ranking politics as the noblest human activity by a curious fusion of individual and group pride and by a sense of their own personal importance in this field ("De la liberté des anciens comparées à celle des modernes," *Cours de politique*; hereafter cited as "Anciens et modernes"). They were willing to sacrifice their undistinguished private lives to the public good, not because they were disinterested saints, but because they saw in politics a chance to leave a personal imprint on the course of history.

Besides size, there was another peculiar characteristic of the *polis* that prevented the Greeks from anticipating the modern ideal of freedom from politics. Once again, the crucial variable was not moral belief but institutional structure. Speaking of the ancients, Constant said: "Their *social organization* led them to desire a liberty utterly different from that guaranteed us by our system." The most striking thing about the organization of the ancient city was the way each individual's existence was "englobed within political existence." It was not just a matter of cramped quarters and nosy neighbors, although Constant was not prone to dismiss such factors as irrelevant. More important to him was that most spheres of life seemed to have political connotations or overtones. Man was a political animal because his total status was encapsulated within a relatively homogenous political sphere. Art, religion, and even sports were integrated into civic life. They offered adornments, not alternatives, to citizenship. Commerce and industry presented clearly demarcated, extrapolitical opportunities for action; but the moral code of a slaveholding society attached considerable disrepute to economic activity. As a result, freedom *from* politics *to* engage in productive tasks never seemed an attractive possibility to Greek citizens. It was a genuine alternative, but it could not be formulated as a publicly defensible ideal. The only nonpolitical but still respectable activity which the Greeks perceived as existing outside politics (and which thus was thought to set a limit on the omnicompetence of political authority) was philosophy. But classical philosophy, based on an ascetic moral code, was associated with a sanctimoniously aloof *vita contemplativa* and contrasted to all forms of *vita activa*. With this rarefied experience available to so few, it is not surprising that the ancients never developed the modern ideal of freedom from politics in order to engage in a rich variety of social opportunities, challenges, and *jouissances*.

Constant's argument drew heavily on the Greek political theorists' failure to develop the modern distinction between state and society. Talk of "the political" and "the extrapolitical" as distinct spheres of social interaction was a historical innovation of modern theory. The modern constitutional doctrine of individual rights was not meant to protect the atomized individual. Rights were calculated to defend the "line" between state and society. The contract myth long concealed this fact by encouraging theorists to conceive rights as shields behind which presocial individuals might escape from the influence of society. According to Constant's theory, by contrast, private rights shelter forms and channels of social communication from arbitrary encroachment by political officials; they contribute to the protection of society against the state, not to the defense of isolated individuals against society. Even though the ancients were well acquainted with contractarian theories, they had no idea of rights in Constant's or

Condorcet's sense because they lacked any systematic conception of freedom from politics. They lacked it because they had no idea of any "line" separating state from society. What they did not perceive to exist, they could not have perceived as a potential object of transgression. The Greeks did not conceive of individual rights because they did not acknowledge any sharply demarcated boundaries of the political which citizens might consider worth defending.

This was what Constant meant by his seemingly radical claims that, in antiquity, "the individual was entirely sacrificed to the collectivity" and that "all the Greek republics except Athens subjected individuals to a social jurisdiction of an almost unlimited scope." Certainly, ancient citizens were placed under enormous pressures by the "severe surveillance" of moralistic neighbors. "Each citizen was on view." Everyone was "circumscribed, observed, repressed in all his movements." Although a citizen could participate in punishing others, "he could, in turn, be deprived of his estate, despoiled of his rank, banished and put to death at the discretion of the group of which he was a part." Constant emphasized diffuse social pressure to conform, the tradition of rule by unpredictable popular decrees, and the custom of ostracism in order to explain the ancient claim that the city was "prior" to its citizens. The general absence of individual rights or personal independence in antiquity was due less to moral primitivism than to the social organization of the *polis*. No healthy extrapolitical institutions existed to shelter individuals from the encroachments of officials or neighbors. The part could not be defended against the whole because, by modern standards, the necessary partitions were lacking. The striking lack (to us) of social compartmentalization was not even perceived by the Greeks or Romans as a problem in their polities.

The ancients believed that everything of human value, except that marginal and otherworldly affair called philosophy, took place within the political sphere. Nothing to speak of lay beyond politics. This belief was due to the centripetal and relatively undifferentiated character of the ancient city. Because the political sphere was so all-pervasive and because trade and industry were considered more or less defiling, the choices accessible to most individuals outside politics appeared meager. The res publica "contained everything that a man held dear." Citizens found their happiness in citizenship because they had no place else to go. Just as there were no reliable *shelters* against political authority, so there were no attractive *alternatives* to political participation. That, in a nutshell, was Constant's sociology of ancient freedom.

But Constant did not restrict his attention to internal factors. Equally important for explaining the total engulfment of the ancient citizen in his city was the peculiarly belligerent international scene in which cities had to eke out of their survival:

> As an inevitable consequence of their small size, the spirit of these
> republics was bellicose: each people chafed continuously against

its neighbors and was irritated and menaced by them. Driven by necessity against one another, they endlessly fought or threatened to fight. Those who did not want to be conquerers could not lay down their arms under pain of being conquered. All purchased their security, their independence, their entire existence at the price of war. Thus, war was the unfailing interest, the almost habitual occupation, of the free states of antiquity.

("Conquête et usurpation," *Cours de politique*)

It was no accident that the ancients identified civic virtue with military valor and individual liberty with the independence of their cities. If a *polis* lost a war, its citizens might well be sold into slavery or perfunctorily butchered. A general willingness to subordinate private concerns to public safety, to see the city as prior to the citizen, was encouraged by this state of affairs: "Among the ancient nations, each citizen saw not only his affections but also his interests and his destiny enveloped in the fate of his country. If the enemy won a battle, his patrimony was ravaged. A public defeat precipitated him from the rank of a free man and condemned him to slavery" (*Les "Principes de politique"*). Being free meant owning slaves. Military defeat and spoliation of slaveowners posed an immediate threat to liberty. A man's material well-being and honor, as well as his survival, depended on his community's success in war. It is hardly surprising that uncooperative individualism was discouraged. In an obvious sense, "free riders" seemed like traitors.

This brings us to a *third* concept of liberty, distinct from both private independence and public participation: the freedom of a city from the hegemonic ambitions of its neighbors. Constant sometimes described the community's search for autonomy and grandeur in the international arena as the essence of ancient freedom. The classical Greeks and Romans were often willing to sacrifice personal influence on the outcome of public debate for the sake of the international independence and envy-provoking stature of their city. The freedom of the whole was prior to the freedom of the parts.

THE DELUSIONS OF TELEOLOGY

Early modern critics of ancient teleology expressed skepticism about the possibility of knowing nature's intentions. In politics, teleological arguments ordinarily justified normative conclusions on the basis of factual premises. Because certain inborn capacities (for example, language or reason) are unique to man, man is morally obliged to develop these capacities to the greatest possible extent. Hobbes, the archenemy of teleological politics, mocked this form of argument: man is the only creature capable of absurdity, yet men are not ethically required to maximize their potential in this regard.

Central to Constant's theoretical project was a similar attempt to demystify Aristotle's teleological theory of ancient politics. He followed Hobbes and Montesquieu here, but (because he wrote *after* Rousseau) he did so in his own way. In "Ancient and Modern Liberty," Constant made clear that he could not accept Aristotle's view of total citizenship as a glorious triumph of the best in man over a sniveling desire for mere life. He granted that the ancients offered noble examples of political liberty. But he did not think that this nobility was produced by heroic efforts. It was caused, rather, by a bizarre set of institutional and cultural factors reinforced by a perilous international situation.

The ancients preferred political participation to individual independence not because they were political animals or had higher standards than their modern counterparts, but simply because in the ancient city firsthand participation was the most efficient way to further particular (that is to say, not particularly noble) interests. Politics was the only interesting thing ancient citizens had to do. Constant mischievously reduced their participatory preference to a mean-spirited cost/benefit calculation. If modern individuals have come to have different goals than the ancients, that is because, for reasons of social organization, their payoff schedules have been reversed: "The ancients, when they sacrificed [individual] independence to political rights, sacrificed less to obtain more; while in making the same sacrifice, we would be giving up more to obtain less." The ancient ethics of collectivism and democratic participation did not represent the victory of duty over interest. Rather, the idealization of group solidarity resulted automatically from the meager human possibilities available in the ancient city. In modern Europe, as a plethora of new possibilities became accessible to citizens, ethical commitments began to shift. This moral transformation was a personal response to an unplanned and uncontrollable change in social structure.

Consider in this light one of Constant's blandest accounts of classical republicanism. Ancient liberty "consisted in exercising collectively, but directly, many parts of sovereignty as a whole; in deliberating on the public square about war and peace; in concluding treaties of alliance with foreigners; in voting laws; in pronouncing judgments; in examining the accounts, the act of the administration of magistrates; in making them appear before the people as a whole; in condemning them or absolving them." Described in this way, ancient politics sounds like the self-management of a genteel debating club. No wonder that "the exercise of political rights constituted the amusement and occupation of everyone." This amusement, however, was less innocuously delightful than it first appears. It, too, was colored by the cruel and severe turn of ancient morality: "As a member of the collectivity," the ancient citizen "interrogates, destitutes, condemns, despoils, exiles, and executes his magistrates and his superiors." The outrageous trial and summary execution of the generals in command at Arginusae was a prime example here. It shows what sort of "live and repeated pleasure" political participation must have been.

It bears repeating: as an inevitable result of their bellicose way of life, all ancient cities had to have slaves. Slavery, in turn, led to a sense of cultural disgrace being attached to productive work as well as to trade. The importance of slavelabor to *polis* life provides the setting for one of Constant's most humorous attempts at a demystification of ancient politics. Because of the episodic nature of ancient warfare and the stigma attached to economic chores, citizen-soldiers were constantly faced with great "intervals of inactivity." Politics was dull business compared with combat and pillage, but it was the only reputable way in which ancient citizens could kill time. Bored and nervously afraid of boredom, they filled up the intervals between wars (Constant wrote here of a *remplissage obligé*) with council meetings, debates, deliberations, legislation, scrutinies of ex-magistrates, trials, and the machinations of party faction. "Without this resource, the free peoples of antiquity would have languished under the weight of painful inaction." In other words, contrary to Aristotle, politics was not desired for its own sake. Participatory self-government in the *polis* cannot be explained teleologically. It was neither an expression of man's political nature nor a fulfillment of his highest inborn potential. Less nobly, it was an improvised solution to the hoplite's awful problem: a surfeit of leisure time and the terrifying threat of ennui.

Constant deliberately aimed to set Aristotle back on his feet, to replace the flattering teleological explanation of the Greek commitment to political life with a mundane and nonteleological analysis. Aristotle had argued that the *polis* was prior to the individual, that political science studied everything of human value, and that citizenship was man's highest good: "we must not suppose any one of the citizens to belong to himself, for they all belong to the *polis*, and the care of each is inseparable from the care of the whole" (*Politics*). Politics is the only realm where men can perform beautiful or memorable deeds and where they can make full use of *logos* (reason and speech), given by nature to man alone. Constant rejected this analysis: ancient politics was not a realization of man's innermost essence but rather an ad hoc strategy for soothing his nagging uneasiness. "Uneasiness" was Locke's word, translated by Constant's *inquiétude*, which had its own peculiarly nineteenth-century connotations.

No acorn-to-oak teleology is invoked in "Ancient and Modern Liberty." From a post-Copernican perspective, it is less cogent to conceive nature as a preprogrammed seed or Aristotelian *entelechia* than as a threat or a problem. Institutions are valued not because they allow a seed to grow, but rather because they counter a threat or solve a problem. Instead of mirroring nature, such institutions thwart it. A negative orientation toward nature is already implicit in Hume's classical discussion of justice and the right to private property. Property does not express nature's dearest wishes; but it does help to solve the social problem of insecurity about the future. That is why we need the institution. That *is* its justification. Writing under the influence of Hume and Montesquieu, Constant tried to explain the origin and self-perpetuation of classical citizenship in a strictly nonteleological and thus anti-Aristotelian fashion. Ancient liberty was prized not because it expressed human nature but because it solved a dire social problem.

Having witnessed the antics of Napoleon, Constant was unimpressed by the ancient ideal of martial glory. In modern societies, "the idea of citizen-soldiers is especially dangerous" because it contaminates civic life with the military spirit. In his "Sketch of a Constitution" of 1814, he made an energetic case against the republican glorification of citizen-soldiers. The ancients were driven toward the code of military valor by dint of circumstances. The warrior's ethic also had a sleazy side; it encouraged citizen-soldiers to plunder the innocent and seize property. Among the ancients, "a successful war added in slaves, tribute, and lands to both public and private wealth." Material gain and self-interest may have been the prime motivation for ancient political participation in general. Constant scrupulously avoided any mention of noble deeds.

The habit of war reinforced the political esprit de corps characteristic of the ancients. It also made a teleological account of ancient politics plausible in the first place: "In order to succeed, war requires common action. . . . A people profits from the fruits of war only as a collective being. . . . The aim of war is perfectly precise. It is victory or conquest. This aim is always before the eyes of those concerned. It unites them and chains them together. It forges their efforts, their projects and their wills into an indivisible whole." Mobilization for combat created political unity out of individual diversity. It channeled private energies toward an overriding common purpose. Social teleology was thus a philosophy of war. Aristotle had claimed that the aim of the individual citizen should conform to the aim of the whole political community. A shared *telos*, Constant added, was originally imposed upon ancient citizens by military discipline.

Another example of Constant's attempt to turn Aristotle right side up is his covert reference to the statement, also found in the *Politics*, that citizens with sufficient wealth will naturally hire stewards and, released from demeaning chores, occupy themselves with politics. Constant mockingly agreed: "Poor men handle their own affairs; rich men hire agents. This is the story of the ancient and modern nations" ("Anciens et modernes"). His meaning was exactly the opposite of Aristotle's. Because modern society is so wealthy, citizens can now deputize agents to handle their political "affairs" (the word itself is freighted with connotations of drudgery and small-minded connivance) while they pursue their economic "speculations" (which is meant to sound lofty). Constant did not simply invert the ancient subordination of economic to political life. He identified one of the main impulses behind the classical republican commitment to firsthand, full-time participation in politics as the cruel poverty of the ancient city. Here, again, men were not drawn into politics by some uplifting final cause; they were shoved onto the Pynx from behind.

Another piece of evidence that Constant was trying to demystify the teleological conception of ancient politics and thereby deromanticize the classical city, was his vaguely Hobbesian, mechanistic description of citizenship in a *polis*: "Men were, so the speak, nothing but machines. The laws regulated their springs and directed their wheels." This emphasis on the nakedly constraining elements in ancient political life undercut attempts to interpret the ancient/modern distinction on the basis of Aristotle's own good life/mere life dichotomy. The propelling motives Constant detected at the source of ancient politics were bodily fear, interest, uneasiness, vanity, avarice, and unreasoning patriotism—all combined with moral obtuseness toward the plight of slaves.

Constant spoke about ancient citizenship as "a vast career in which men were flushed with their own force and filled with a feeling of energy and dignity." But he was careful to qualify this assertion by adding that antiquity was an age in which the faculties of men developed in a direction "traced in advance." The Greeks and Romans noticed the preprogrammed nature of their freedom. But since antiquity was an age of illusions, they misinterpreted their lack of autonomy as a sign that destiny was calling or that their unique *telos* was unfolding. Constant dispelled this ancient mirage. The final cause inwardly felt by ancient citizens was in reality an exogenous compulsion: a combined effect of poverty, the exigencies of war, the lack of shelter from political surveillance, the paucity of attractive alternatives to political life, and the need to discipline slaves. The Aristotelian interpretation of this external compulsion as a message from nature testified to the comforting self-intoxication of the most sober of the Greeks.

To deglamorize the ancient city, Hume emphasized its susceptibility to bloody factional strife. Madison echoed this point: "such democracies have ever been spectacles of turbulence and contention" (*The Federalist Papers*). Constant touched upon factionalism and internecine conflict in his early manuscripts of 1800–06, but he made no mention of it in the lecture. The reasons for this omission are not difficult to discover. In 1819, Constant was being assaulted by the ultras as a wanton factionalist. He was repeatedly accused of seeking to introduce discord into the state. Since he believed the right of opposition to be the essence of representative government, he carefully avoided any censorious commentary on ancient factionalism. To evoke the traditional association of political participation with civic disorder could only abet the cause of his opponents.

THE SOCIAL BASIS OF MODERN FREEDOM

According to Thomas Hobbes, "there was never any thing so deerly bought, as these Western parts have bought the learning of the Greek and Latine tongues" (*Leviathan*). He was thinking chiefly of the republican doctrines of Aristotle and Cicero that, in his eyes, fired the English civil wars. Constant deliberately echoed Hobbes's claim, but he did so with a characteristic difference: "As a necessary result of the education they received, the men whom the flood of revolutionary events brought to power were imbued with opinions that had become false" ("Anciens et modernes"). The crucial innovation lies in the word *become*. The massive and irreversible process of historical change dominated Constant's thinking as it never had that of his contractarian predecessors.

What characteristics of modern, post-Reformation Europe gave birth to a new concept of freedom and made classical freedom obsolete? First of all, no modern nation is "surveyable at a glance," as Aristotle insisted all good polities must be. Nor is it possible for all modern citizens to look at one another and know each others' characters intimately. These are trite observations. Yet changes in scale and population had an immense impact on the firsthand experience of democratic citizenship. Even in the freest modern societies, the marginal contribution of the average individual to political decision-making is infinitesimally small: "The political importance that befalls each individual diminishes in proportion to the size of a country. The most obscure republican of Rome or Sparta was a power. The same is not true of the simple citizen of Great Britain or the United States. His personal influence is an imperceptible fraction of the social will that imparts a direction to the government." Given this new situation, the incentive for modern individuals to devote their time to politics is remarkably feeble. Each citizen's "part of sovereignty" has evaporated into "an abstract supposition." Today "the mass of citizens" is called upon to exercise sovereignty largely "in an illusory manner" (Les "Principes de politique").

Described in this derogatory fashion, modern citizenship seems signally unattractive. But large size and dense population also allow for anonymity. In an ancient republic, the most obscure citizen was a power with which everyone had to reckon—that is to say, he was not obscure. Ancient citizens were on perpetual display. This had now changed: "In our day, large states have created a new guarantee, that of obscurity." The value of obscurity was in fact integral to Constant's picture of liberal freedom. To evade professional and amateur spies, modern citizens must be able to come and go unobtrusively. Consider the original formulation of this point in the *Circonstances actuelles qui peuvent terminer la Révolution:*

> celebrity was as dangerous [in antiquity] as it is in our day. But the guarantee of obscurity did not exist. . . . There was not then, as there is in our large states, a mass of men, peaceable egoists who, mocking those poor fools who get themselves talked about, are able with the help of their individual means, the size of the country and the current organization of commerce and property, to carve out their destinies at a distance from public events.
>
> (Mme de Staël)

In antiquity, freedom (at least in theory) was associated with political visibility and with each citizen's readiness to serve the public safety at a moment's notice. In revolutionary France, freedom was associated with shelters, hideouts, disguises, and escape routes—anything that might interfere with the power over citizens exercised by grudge-bearing neighbors or by governmental spies and their potential informants. Thick walls symbolized the freedom which Montesquieu had defined as security. Security, in turn, hinged upon guarantees made to individuals and subgroups of noninterference by other persons, that is, on the establishment of a "free space" within which they might act as they chose. This "space" would be neutral with regard to content. It would permit pleasure, friendship, self-sacrifice, self-indulgence, creative thought, bizarre whims, religious devotion, or material acquisition. It was meant to exclude only those acts which obviously violated the "free space" of others.

Constant viewed barriers separating people not merely as signs of entrepreneurial self-reliance, but also and more importantly as barricades against *l'esprit de délation*. Emergent French individualism had at least as much to do with the all-corrosive distrust characteristic of civil wars as with the spirit of capitalism. Indeed, individualism and anticapitalism were quite compatible, though this was not a position Constant himself chose to adopt.

The spatial metaphors of "barriers," "walls," "spheres," and "separate domains" are essential to the modern understanding of freedom and individual rights. These images have a long, complex genealogy. It would be simplistic to reduce them to parochial correlates of the capitalist economy. The Greeks and Romans made a primitive but significant contribution to the modern idea of subjective rights against the state with their noting of the household as a sort of private enclave split off from the general political domain. The opportunities this inclosure contained, however, were not honorable or various enough to encourage many to see freedom from politics as a particularly attractive ideal. Another important source for the idea of an inviolable zone, shielded by rights, was the Christian contrast between the *imperium* and the *sacerdotium*. This dualism carried the implication (fully exploited only after the Reformation) that secular officials must stay out of all questions concerning personal salvation. As free cities arose in medieval Europe, free citizens saw liberty from baronial control symbolized by and embodied in town walls. The lesser magnates of Europe, in turn, fought tenaciously to preserve their privileges, immunities, and exemptions against the steady advance of the consolidating monarchies. They, too, helped promulgate the ideal of unassailable redoubts, barriers to fend off invasions of power-wielders into the "private" sphere.

Taken in isolation, neither increase in size nor the rise of capitalism can explain the emergence of a new concept of freedom in modern Europe. What must be studied is the social organization of modern states in all its complexity. When Constant referred to the "increased complexity of social relations" ("Anciens et modernes"), he meant the proliferation in modern society of two types of institution: walls, partitions, and shelters that enabled citizens to escape from (or to deflect) diffuse social pressure and the harassments of officials; and nonpolitical organizations that could engender new chances for individual and cooperative goal-seeking, opportunities more alluring than those available within the narrowly defined political domain itself. The idea of freedom from politics became widespread against a background of institutions that made such freedom plausible and enticing. Such institutions gave citizens "the possibility to exist isolated from public affairs." If politics was conceived primarily as authority, then sheltering institutions were crucial. If politics was conceived primarily as participation, then opportunity-generating institutions were required. Modern citizens are less dependent on their states for these two organizational reasons: they get less relative satisfaction from political involvement, and they have an easier time eluding the police. The crucial point is that modern liberty cannot be described in a privative fashion. It is not freedom *from* society, but rather freedom *in* society.

Liberal freedom cannot be adequately defined, in the Hobbesian manner, as a mere absence of obstacles. ["Liberty, or Freedome, signifieth (properly) the absence of Opposition; (by Opposition I mean externall impediments of motion;)." Hobbes, *Leviathan*, pt. 2, chap. 21. The shocking radicalness of this redefinition of freedom can best be appreciated against the background of the traditional English "liberties," a bundle of owned privileges or powers allocated according to birthrank.] Equally essential is the presence of possibilities. Possibilities, in turn, are creatures of social institutions; they cannot be generated out of the prodigality of the individual soul. Institutions prepattern the horizon of possible experiences and actions. Hobbes located freedom in an empty space, beyond law and the interference of other men. It is unconvincing, however, to conceive laws and fellow men simply as obstructions to freedom. Rules (such as grammar) often *create* social possibilites that would not otherwise exist. Similarly, social interdependence can increase freedom, can give men otherwise unavailable chances not only to secure cooperation for preexistent ends, but also to learn and acquire new ends. The Hobbesian claim that freedom is nothing but the absence of obstacles engendered the following mythology: without language, institutions, rules, and social interdependence, freedom is unbounded; for the sake of "order," we sacrifice some of our freedom. But this is an unsatisfactory approach to the problem. Accessible possibilities are constitutive of freedom. Freedom expands and contracts as does the horizon of those accessible possibilities which are important culturally and personally. Institutions, language, and rules for social cooperation, do not represent mere obstacles to freedom that must be accepted for the sake of self-preservation. They are enabling, not disabling. They are *creative* of possibilities and thus generative of freedom as well.

To cross the frontier from the public into the private does not entail forfeiting possibilities created within society. Constitutional rights do not protect the presocial individual but, rather, social pluralism and the "line" between state and society. The possibilities to which Constant's modern liberty refers are life chances made available within and by modern European societies. In these societies, it has become an anachronism to identify human self-determination in general with democratic self-government, for the simple reason that the polity and civil society are no longer coextensive. Autonomy must be *both* political *and* extrapolitical.

POLITICAL USES OF PROPERTY AND COMMERCE

The ideal of individual rights, as Constant described it, could arise only within the cultural and institutional context of modern society. To see in greater detail that Constant did not view "rights" in the contractarian manner, as timeless ideals, we need only consider his most frequently cited definition of modern liberty:

> [Modern liberty] is, for each individual, the right not to be subjected to anything but the law, not to be arrested, or detained, or put to death, or mistreated in any manner, as a result of the arbitrary will of one or several individuals. It is each man's right to express his opinions, to choose and exercise his profession, to dispose of his property and even abuse it, to come and to go without obtaining permission and without having to give an account of either his motives or his itinerary. It is the right to associate with other individuals, either to confer about mutual interests or to profess the cult that he and his associates prefer or simply to fill his days and hours in the manner most conforming to his inclinations and fantasies. Finally, it is each man's right to exert influence on the administration of government, either through the election of some or all of its public functionaries, or through remonstrances, petitions, and demands which authorities are more or less obliged to take into account.
>
> ("Anciens et modernes")

The right to dispose of one's own property is only one aspect of modern freedom. Behind the plausibility and utility of this right lies a massive and irreversible change in the structure of the economy. While Constant did not view commercialization as the sole factor behind the emergence of modern liberty, he considered economic modernization an indispensable stimulant to its development.

Only after slavery and serfdom were abolished did it become true that "free men must exercise all the professions and must supply all the needs of society." It is no great mystery that, in a caste-free age, all professions have come to seem honorable, and that the traditional disgrace associated with productive work has been dispelled. Deprived of breathing robots, free men necessarily began to view economic life as a culturally respectable alternative to politics.

Tocqueville thought that the spirit of commerce not only diverted individuals from taking part in public affairs but also made them more dependent on government (*De la démocratie en Amérique*). Constant adopted the more standard Smithian view that commercial life universalizes the ideal of the masterless man and helps accustom men to shifting for themselves. It habituates people to providing for their own needs without the intervention of political officials, creating citizens impatient with the meddling and bungling of their government. When the state tries to conduct or supervise our affairs, it often does so less intelligently and more expensively than people would have done themselves. Distrust of fatherly commands is natural among individuals trained by commerce in self-reliance. Modern commerce provided a barrier against political regimentation. To reinforce this point, Constant drew a sharp distinction between the modern institution of moveable stocks and the traditional institution of landed property.

Modern pluralism, providing the social basis for liberal politics, is quite distinct from the corporatism that underlay the illiberal politics of the feudal regime. After 1789, France ceased to be segmented legally into estates, guilds, towns, monasteries, and other closed communities: "The Revolution had this advantage: its violence broke down the artificial compartments where men had been enclosed in order to make them easier to govern" (Article of 20 August, 1818 in *Recueil d'articles: Le Mercure, la Minerve, la Renommée*). Economic stratification remained. But vying with class structure was a new set of fundamental divisions, not between corporations, but between activities. Politics, science, family relations, religion, and the market became a series of disjoined, though interrelated, realms. No individual was encapsulated inside any single sphere of activity. In this increasingly open and mobile society, everyone began to participate in a variety of dissociated "roles." It was this structural transformation that ushered in the egalitarian revolution. In contrast to the old pluralism of corporations, the new pluralism of abstract sectors made it increasingly difficult to ascribe unique social niches to individuals on the basis of birth.

Paradoxically, the radical transition from medieval to liberal pluralism occurred by virtue of an intermediate stage of political centralization. As every textbook informs us, centralizing powers broke down feudal barriers to commerce. It was only after the consolidation of modern European states that individual rights became a widespread political idea. Earlier, the only universally recognized rights were "status rights," rights attributable to individuals on the basis of their family's inherited location in a social hierarchy.

Constant's discussion of moveable stocks and landed property throws light on the political consequences of modern pluralism. Each form of wealth provided the basis for a different kind of citizenship. Land cannot be conveniently expatriated. By a skillful deployment of soldiers and threats of confiscation, political officials can put irresistible pressure on landowners. On the other hand, moveable stocks, *la richesse mobilière*, can be smuggled out of the country. Modern commerce and the circulation of goods thus erected "an invisible and invincible obstacle to that unlimited action of the social power." When citizen-merchants are threatened, "they transport their treasures far away." As a result, liquid assets build a wall against governmental coercion: the transactions of merchants "cannot be penetrated by authority" (*Les "Principes de politique"*).

Moveable stocks and bills of exchange not only provide a shelter behind which citizens may successfully hide. They also serve as a source of power, because governments are reluctant to embitter generous sources of credit. If "money is hidden and sent away," a government will not be able to raise the loans it needs. In Constant's view, "commerce is favorable to individual liberty" because it allows citizens to control officials by threatening to withdraw financial cooperation. If Athens was the one ancient city that tolerated at least some elements of modern freedom, this was because the Athenians used bills of exchange and other "antisocial" devices usually associated with advanced economies.

In the wake of the industrial revolution, the coupling of liberal politics with capitalist economies brought liberalism into disrepute. Marxists have repeatedly argued that a commitment to liberal political ideas was simply a mask for prior class interests generated in the economy. This accusation is historically implausible. What made the nascent capitalist economy seem a source of hope to early modern theorists was a *prior and independent* commitment to liberal political ideals. Liberals viewed trade and industry as effective means for their pursuit of noneconomic ends. During the Restoration, the political meaning of ownership was self-evident: "The purchasers of national lands represent the most important of the [interests] created by the Revolution. They are less defenders of completed sales and laws that have been passed than defenders of the division of properties. This division provides the foundation for the new organization of France. In the near future, within this century, it will be the foundation stone of the European order" (*Mémoires sur les Cent-Jours*). Far from being a mere economic good, serving material interests, property was charged with political significance. Purchasers of national lands were precommitted to opposing the illiberal politics of the émigrés.

Anticlerical and antimilitaristic reformers naturally sought allies among the commercial classes. Constant's own strategic alliances, in any case, were secondary to his political aims. Under the Consulate, for example, he fiercely attacked Bonaparte for suppressing freedom of debate and jury trials even though most businessmen supported the government's repressive policies. Neither brigands nor the leaders of popular uprisings should ever be brought before military courts. Liberal proceduralism must never be sacrificed for the protection of property. It was crucial, however, to forbid confiscation. This was the most obvious political dimension of private economic rights. "Confiscation was a habitual practice under the old monarchy" (*Ecrits et discours*). It was a very pernicious form of punishment because it provided an irresistible incentive for false accusations. To outlaw spoliation was to enforce popular sovereignty against the self-serving schemes of public officials. Constant even defined arbitrary government by reference to confiscation: "Here is arbitrary government: a man wishes to take the property of another; he denounces him to a minister (an accomplice or a dupe), has him indicted and condemned, his fortune confiscated, and a part of it given to him. What is known as theft under a legal regime is called a salary under arbitrary rule. The thief, rather than being hanged, is rewarded" (*Recueil d'articles 1820–24*). Property rights are politically motivated: they provide a barrier against a certain style of governance. Rulers who are forced to respect private property will find it somewhat more difficult to act as ravenous predators.

Cooperation in the marketplace can have a cordializing effect: it can teach religious sectaries how to avoid irrational bloodshed and even how to pool resources in common ventures. Commerce can be considered antisocial only if civil war is the essence of social life. In early modern Europe, a man's concern for his neighbor's salvation might lead him to slit his neighbor's throat. Indifference to certain aspects of one's neighbor's life, the deeroticizing of some communal bonds, actually increase the available chances for creative social interdependence.

De la conquête is an extended elaboration on the psychological contrast between commerce and war. Only advocates of the martial virtues can denigrate commerce as a form of base corruption. According to the "civic virtue" tradition, earning one's living by trade was dishonorable in comparison with invasions and cannonades, rape and plunder. Constant dissented from the civic virtue tradition: commerce was not the worst thing men can do to one another. A nation of shopkeepers, however tawdry, was preferable to a nation of warriors.

The importance of the concept "self-interest" in liberal thought should be understood in relation to the problems plaguing modern European states. The chief antonyms of "interest" were religious passions, hereditary privileges, and martial reflexes. Seen in this context, "self-interest" did not appear particularly mean-spirited or egoistical. Commercial habits, as well as commercial classes, were enlisted as recruits in an ongoing liberal campaign against rapine, revenge, tyranny, and general social insecurity.

Writing before the industrial transformation of Europe, Constant did not live to see "commerce" lose its progressive connotations and become associated with misery and massive social dislocation. Nevertheless, he was careful to distinguish the right to property, which he called "a social convention," from rights to religious toleration, freedom of opinion, and freedom from arbitrary arrest, which he considered more fundamental. In the seventeenth century, Locke had ascribed quasi-sacral attributes and a presocial origin to private property. With this countersacralization he hoped to outbid the prestige of divine-right kingship. No longer facing an authority rooted in a living religious tradition, Constant explicitly repudiated this mythical view of ownership. It was absurd to "represent property as something mysterious, anterior to society." Property law is a creation of social life and can be justified only by its beneficial consequences. In the present stage of economic development, the abolition of property would not have created a perfect society, as Babeuf believed. It would instead have led to a cataclysmic shortage of food. Private property allowed for social cooperation without legal castes. There was no obvious alternative. Only if "our discoveries in mechanics" could create "a total exemption from manual labor" would the erasure of all distinction between ownership and nonownership be compatible with the maintenance of civilized life. As a result, Constant hoped for a diffusion, not an abolition, of property. In the meantime, constitutional arrangements must prevent the state from adopting radically confiscatory policies.

Despite this warning, Constant was anxious to stress the contingent character of property rights: "Property, in its character as a social convention, falls under the competence and jurisdiction of society. Society possesses over it rights that it does not possess over the freedom, the life and the opinions of its members." Among all the rights of man, in other words, the right to property was the only one Constant held to be discussable. Economic liberalism was primarily a useful weapon in the arsenal of political liberalism. Political freedom might also serve the cause of economic freedom. But the principal relation was the inverse: limited government was a pre-condition for self-government.

ESCAPE ROUTES

The identification of freedom with asylums and escape routes was part of the unintended legacy of the revolutionary age. Constant's idea of modern freedom gave this bequest a systematic form. Not only merchandise but threatened individuals could learn to vanish at the appropriate time. They too could slip across the border. In antiquity, a war-ravaged international scene made such escapes difficult if not impossible. Expatriation was a brutal punishment in classical times; in modern times it has become a pleasure, a grand tour. The Latin word *hostis* meant both "stranger" and "enemy," which suggests how uninviting trips abroad once were. The attractiveness and easy accessibility of neighboring countries limits the power of the modern European state over its citizens. Like the monetization of economic life, international escape routes "offer to victims of injustice a sanctuary within reach," making the abstract split between state and society into a palpable experience (*Fragmens d'un ouvrage abandonné*).

Escape routes were creative, not merely protective. The marvelous achievements of late eighteenth-century Germany in philosophy and literature were made possible by competition among principalities offering asylum: "The division of Germany into a multitude of tiny sovereignties has, for more than a century, served as a guarantee of civil liberty in that country where, in other respects, almost all the institutions were feudal and despotic. The most unlimited freedom of thought and expression concerning matters of religion and politics fled from one principality into another, and found everywhere compensation and protection." The border between sovereign states, although only one sort of boundary, may well have been the prototype for Constant's idea of liberating escape routes, of partitions that fostered social creativity by providing citizens a sanctuary from fear and persecution.

To summarize: beside size, the most important difference between the ancient city and the modern nation is the emergence in the latter of a sharp state/society distinction. Both institutional and cultural changes have contributed to this general transformation. The boundaries of the political are now part of every citizen's daily experience. Politics can no longer pretend to contain everything a man holds dear. It is no longer plausible to stigmatize freedom from politics as a form of utter deprivation. The possibilities available inside the narrowly political sector of society have dwindled considerably. They cannot sustain the total life-engagement of the mass of citizens. Simultaneously, options accessible in extrapolitical spheres of society have been "infinitely multiplied and varied."

But the state/society distinction not only provides new forms of *vita activa* alongside politics. It also gives citizens a set of instruments with which to fend off the pretensions of powerful officials. This double function makes the state/society distinction an indispensable precondition for the emergence of modern freedom. Such freedom includes the liberty to be "distracted from political liberty," the freedom of citizens to stray off on unsupervised itineraries. Social coordination is possible, but not obligatory. A citizen's concern with the public good, however important, is likely to be intermittent and must remain voluntary.

Another important feature of modern liberty is reflected in an individual's right "to come and go without obtaining permission and without having to give an account of either his motives or his itinerary." Adolphe complained bitterly about the petty despotism of Ellénore, who always demanded a detailed account of his comings and goings. When she died, however, and he finally became independent, he was forlorn. The liberal guarantee of freedom did not entail a guarantee of happiness. Perfect independence may leave a citizen writhing in agony. To escape is not to arrive. In one of his more revealing letters, Constant admitted that he had been "agitated" and excruciatingly unhappy even "in the midst of the most profound repose." Despite this unhappiness, he consistently praised constitutional government because it guaranteed repose.

THE POLITICAL DIMENSION OF INDIVIDUAL FREEDOM

In modern societies, freedom from politics is a positive good, not a mere deprivation or lack. Constant absorbed this insight and went beyond it. He did not give a dogmatically apolitical definition of the freedom available in modern societies. Politics should no longer be mandatory as it had to some extent been in classical Greece and under the Terror; but it *should be* possible, and it *is* desirable. Constant concluded his catalogue of rights with a sentence worth repeating. He did so in a completely natural way, not as if he were groping with an awkward afterthought: "Finally, it is each man's right to exert influence on the administration of government, either through the election of some or all of its functionaries, or through remonstrances, petitions, and demands which authorities are more or less obliged to take into account" ("Anciens et modernes"). To those whose knowledge of Constant is confined to the stylized distinction between positive and negative liberty ("Constant . . . prized negative liberty beyond any modern writer" [Isaiah Berlin, *Four Essays on Liberty*]), it must come as a surprise to read his reiterated assertions that "political liberty is indispensable" and that "France knows that political liberty is as necessary as civil liberty." Even more emphatically: "Citizens will interest themselves in their institutions only if they are called to cooperate within them by voting. Now, this interest is indispensable for the formation of a public spirit, a power without which no liberty can endure." As such statements demonstrate, the idea of a deep wedge between liberalism and democracy does little to illuminate Constant's position. He did not banish the notion of liberty from the political realm. His position on this matter should have been difficult to misunderstand: "Those who wish to sacrifice political liberty in order to enjoy civil [or private] liberty with greater tranquillity are no less absurd than those who wish to sacrifice civil liberty in the hope of assuring political liberty and extending it further" (Les "Principes de politique"). Political rights were constituent of, not merely a precondition for, the liberty to be pursued in modern society. Important offices cannot be widely shared among all the citizenry, but the function of shaping policy through public discussion and elections can be. Indifference to citizenship is undesirable not because civic life is beautiful, but because solutions to common problems can only be discovered and implemented politically. In modern societies, democratic citizenship is not the only kind of freedom available to most people most of the time. It remains, however, an essential component of freedom as well as one that is an indispensable precondition for most other forms of freedom. In sum, the mythical opposition between liberalism and democracy cannot be established on the basis of Constant's contrast between ancient and modern liberty. On the contrary, he drew the distinction sharply in order to emphasize the tight interdependence of public influence and private security.

TWO FUNCTIONS OF REPRESENTATION

On the trail of both Montesquieu and Rousseau, Constant claimed that the representative system was "a discovery of the moderns." One of the aims of the 1819 lecture was to explain why representative government "was almost entirely unknown to the free states of antiquity." That British-style representation was unanticipated in republican antiquity is not altogether surprising. Modern citizens treasure representation for a modern reason: it provides an institutional framework for satisfying their desire not to participate continuously and exclusively in politics. Representative government is the political acknowledgment of the modern split between state and society. It extends the division of labor into government. Eighteenth-century proponents of representation, such as Tom Paine, invoked territorial expanse and the size of populations in its defense. Constant preferred to focus on time. Just as ancient participatory democracy was the improvised response to a surfeit of free time, so modern representative democracy is an answer to the scarcity of time:

> Just as the liberty we now require is distinct from that of the ancients, so this new liberty itself requires an organization different from that suitable for ancient liberty. For the latter, the more time and energy a man consecrated to the exercise of his political rights, the more free he believed himself to be. Given the type of liberty to which we are now susceptible, the more the exercise of our political rights leaves us time for our private interests, the more precious we find liberty to be. From this, Gentlemen, stems the necessity of the representative system. The representative system is nothing else than an organization through which a nation unloads on several individuals what it cannot and will not do for itself. Poor men handle their own affairs; rich men hire managers. This is the story of ancient and modern nations. The representative system is the power of attorney given to certain men by the mass of the people who want their interests defended but who nevertheless do not always have the time to defend these interests themselves.

> ("Anciens et modernes")

Unlike commercial agents, elected deputies represent the unity of the nation, and they must do so in public, not behind closed doors. But the commercial analogy, false to this extent, allowed Constant another provocative reversal of Aristotelian theory. According to the *Politics*, democracy was one of the perverted constitutions, since it granted the franchise to unworthy individuals. The best form of this inherently mediocre regime was a democracy of farmers: "being poor, they have no leisure, and therefore do not often attend the assembly." Constant inverted this idea. Not having to attend the assembly because we are absorbed in private interests has become a privilege and a sign of wealth.

Constant praised representative government for disencumbering citizens from time-consuming political chores. In a complex commercial civilization, in which all individuals depend on people they can never know, the concept of "autonomy" must be defined with care. If autonomy requires individuals to have a personal say in every decision that affects them, there can be no autonomy in modern society. Indeed, to live effective lives, individuals must now more than ever husband their resources, including time, and focus on specialized tasks. They must permit important decisions to be made for them and without their direct participation. That is an unavoidable consequence of the division of labor. Indeed, liberal freedom is the only kind of autonomy possible in a society based on the division of labor, a society that has created a permanent scarcity of time by generating more possibilities than anyone can successfully exploit or enjoy. The division of labor, however, allows independence and interdependence to increase simultaneously. Citizenship in a modern society cannot be the center of an individual's life. But it does not vanish into thin air.

Constant also had political reasons for stressing the limited and voluntary nature of popular participation. Modern states will never be popular states, "because there is nothing less popular, that is to say, nothing that puts the mass of the people less into action than representative government, which accords to the people only the right to vote, a right exercised for a few days and followed by a period of inactivity that is always rather long" (*Commentaire sur Filangieri*). In passages such as this, modern citizenship seems exiguous indeed. But a first impression is deceptive. During certain phases of the Restoration, Constant wrote in this manner, but only for strategic reasons. He had to calm the fears of moderate conservatives opposed to a widening of the franchise. In the same book from which the above passage is drawn, Constant also stressed the way representation mobilizes the cooperation of citizens in determining their collective fate: "the representative government is nothing but the admission of the people to participation in public affairs." In fact, Constant always insisted upon *both* dimensions of representative government. Representation simultaneously includes citizens in political life and frees them from political life. It enhances both independence and involvement: that is its utility and its strength. On different occasions, Constant emphasized one function and deemphasized the other; but his balanced view was that representation served both purposes at once.

THE ECONOMIC BASIS OF POLITICAL FREEDOM

One of the most disruptive and therefore attractive aspects of Constant's thought is the way in which it questions the association of liberalism with a hysterical fear of civic activism. Constant listed "the right for each citizen to exert influence on the administration of government" as an essential component of liberty in modern society. Citizens should not be coerced, but they should be willing to keep abreast of political events and to exercise "a constant and active surveillance" of their deputized representatives. Reconsider, in this context, Constant's argument that commerce provides an effective barrier against misgovernment.

Of all imaginable countervailing mechanisms, commerce seems to be the most suspiciously in tune with the fiscal interests of the middle class. Constant was probably as naive about the future of commerce as he was about the future of nationalism. He certainly did not foresee the politically troublesome consequences of capital flight. But his theory cannot be reduced to bourgeois ideology.

Most recent treatments of liberal freedom neglect the right to exercise influence on the government through the election of representatives as well as through the traditional method of petitioning and resisting. Such voluntary influence is quite different from involuntary conscription. It is nothing like being dragooned unwillingly into civic responsibility and having one's total status engulfed in the political sphere. Modern citizenship can never offer the same intense everyday enjoyment as did participation in an ancient republic. Nevertheless, public influence on political decisions is a crucial part of modern liberty, if only because it is a guarantee against the emergence of an authority so powerful that it can eventually violate individual independence when and where it wishes. Commerce was a useful weapon in the politics of *guarantisme*. To the extent that political participation is a countervailing power, it is in principle replaceable. Commerce was a force that might aid public opinion in one of its main tasks. It was another mechanism for controlling the government. In modern contexts, public opinion needs to be buttressed in a way that ancient public opinion did not. The same factors that permit the obscurity of modern citizens, the private screens that block the prying eyes of police informants, also inhibit surveillance of government officials by the public. Obscurity cuts both ways:

> In a republic where all citizens were maintained by poverty in an extreme simplicity of manners, where they inhabited the same city, where they did not exercise any profession which deflected their attention from the affairs of state and where they found themselves constantly spectators or judges of the employment of public power . . . the arbitrary authority of the censors was contained by a type of moral surveillance exercised against them.
>
> ("Anciens et modernes")

In small, relatively partition-free societies, "morality found support in an immediate public, spectator and judge of all actions in their tiniest details and most delicate nuances" ("Conquête et usurpation," *Cours de politique*). In modern societies, men are busy in their nonpolitical hideouts and unapprised of events unfolding on the public scene. When modern governments are granted discretionary powers analogous to those possessed by the Roman censors, they inevitably run wild, unlimited as they are by the pressure of public scrutiny.

Public surveillance of modern officials is insufficient and Montesquieu's intermediary bodies have been destroyed. It is thus necessary to introduce auxiliary mechanisms, such as the separation of powers, to inhibit excessive state authority. *Commerce is just another one of these auxiliary counterweights.* It can obstruct abuses of power by political authorities because it is nothing like a feudal corporation. Industry enchains the enemies of political liberty. Credit is incompatible with arbitrary power. Constant's underlying argument was this: the abolition of private property and the placing of all commercial activities under the control of the state could only benefit the unpropertied classes if the enfranchised poor could, in turn, control political authorities through full-time public surveillance. But that is impossible under modern conditions, in societies based on a far-reaching division of labor.

Meaningful participation in politics is itself dependent upon the state/society distinction. Privacy is a support for publicity. In the industrial-bureaucratic age, there can be no democracy without individual rights, no political liberty without civil liberty. To detach men from their economic independence by offering them "total" citizenship is but a shrewd demagogical ploy. When private independence has been destroyed, rulers will hasten to despoil citizens of their political rights as well. If a government annihilates private property, it can do anything it desires to its defenseless citizens: "the arbitrary treatment of property is soon followed by the arbitrary treatment of persons" ("Principes de politique," *Cours de politique*). Under modern conditions, the only guarantee of political influence is a sure foothold or bankbook out of the reach of the state. The ultra attack on the purchasers of national lands was a direct threat to representative government. The possibility of meaningful discussion depends upon the right of opposition, and the right of opposition (in turn) can only be guaranteed if the livelihood of citizens is independent of political officials. Furthermore, creative debate in the political arena can only occur if a unanimity of goals is not imposed upon individuals by their community. Constant wanted to limit politics in order to create a certain kind of politics: a politics of dissent and disagreement. His argument for capitalism was not acquisitive but democratic: only a decentralized economy will enable modern citizens to discuss political issues freely and exert influence on their elected officials.

This thesis brings us full circle. At the end of the 1819 lecture, Constant asserted that private independence can be guaranteed only by political participation. In the body of the lecture, he made the inverse claim: individual independence is not an alternative to self-rule, but a precondition for self-rule. The modern distinction between state and society makes democracy possible even in a large country. Viewed as a whole, Constant's argument was this: civil liberty and political liberty are mutually interdependent. The abolition of one will eventuate in the abrogation of the other. Contrariwise, an increase in one form of freedom does not logically imply a decrease in the other. Indeed, each presupposes and vitalizes the other, and neither can survive in isolation. That is why Constant, in summarizing his position, urged his fellow citizens to integrate public action and private independence in a new pattern. Ancient and modern liberty should not be merely balanced but *combined*.

The Occidental Orient:
Chateaubriand

Andrew Martin

Napoleon Bonaparte is one of a trio of legendary figures who populate the most reverential and the most censorious pages of Chateaubriand's *oeuvre*; the other two are God and Chateaubriand. His detailed study of the Emperor in the *Mémoires d'outre-tombe,* although less hostile than *De Buonaparté et des Bourbons,* still distances its author from its subject by the acccumulation of adverse judgements. But Chateaubriand is an inveterate contriver of rapprochements. And, like Hugo (like Lamartine, like Balzac), he cannot resist the temptation to detect frequent parallels and affinities between Napoleon's career and his own: Chateaubriand sees himself as the Napoleon of literature; he sees Napoleon, in turn, as the Chateaubriand of politics.

Their *oeuvres* display demonstrable similarities of language. Thematically considered, Chateaubriand's *Itinéraire de Paris à Jérusalem et de Jérusalem à Paris* often reads like a recapitulation of imperialist dogmas. Thus, for example, Chateaubriand's defence of the Crusades is reminiscent of Napoleon's comparison of the Christian and Islamic religions. Chateaubriand, rebutting the attitude of fashionable scepticism about Christian motives, affirms that:

> Il s'agissait, non seulement de la délivrance de ce Tombeau sacré, mais encore de savoir qui devait l'emporter sur la terre, ou d'un culte ennemi de la civilisation, favorable par système à l'ignorance, au despotisme, à l'esclavage, ou d'un culte qui a fait revivre chez les modernes le génie de la docte antiquité, et aboli la servitude?
> . . . L'esprit du Mahometisme est la persécution et la conquête; l'Evangile au contraire ne prêche que la tolérance et la paix.

[It was a matter not only of delivering the sacred tomb, but also of determining which should triumph on earth, a cult hostile to civilization, systematically favourable to ignorance, despotism, slavery, or a religion which had revived in the moderns the genius of learned antiquity, and abolished servitude. . . . The spirit of Mohammedanism is persecution and conquest; the Gospel, on the contrary, preaches only tolerance and peace.]

(*Itinéraire*)

Again, East and West are divided along an artistic, moral, and intellectual frontier whose very existence requires that it be crossed (from West to East) by an altruistic, Christian army charged with rehabilitating and re-educating a race of malevolent heathens. Presumably this worthy objective was not wholly achieved since the process must be repeated by Napoleon's army. Thus, while arguing (in the chapter of the *Mémoires* devoted to the subject) that the Egyptian expedition was a pointless sideshow, and admitting that its main result was massacre, rape, pillage, Chateaubriand nevertheless maintains that the Orient must have benefited from the salutary presence of the senior Western power. Echoing Napoleon (who is, however, denounced as an insincere imperialist, bent on mere self-glorification), he claims that the French sowed the germs of civilization, brightened the Islamic darkness with Christian light, and breached the wall of Barbarism.

The anxiety of the reader familiar with even a small number of French texts of the period purporting to describe the East for the edification of the West, is that the Orientalist seems doomed to repeat a sequence of scarcely permutated *idées fixes* articulated by a set of automatic metaphors. But in this case precisely the same anxiety is shared by the writer. The dilemma for Chateaubriand is that although (and because) the Orient is an irresistible topic, it has already been exhaustively treated by those that have gone before him. He suspects that there is nothing more to be said on the subject, nothing to be added to the mass of pre-existing material; or that, if there is, he is not competent to say it. At the same time, one of his most intransigent aesthetic imperatives concerns originality, which alone can bear witness to the existence of an individual soul. Aesthetic, linguistic originality, and temperamental, psychic individuality, are interdependent: individuality without originality is doomed; originality without individuality is inconceivable. Thus ego and text are mutually supportive (or destructive).

The *Itinéraire* is steeped (like all Chateaubriand's work) in an enviable erudition. Chateaubriand, not without pride, reminds us that he has had "la patience de lire à peu près deux cents relations modernes de la Terre Sainte, les compilations rabbiniques, et les passages des anciens sur la Judée [the patience to read about two hundred modern accounts of the Holy Land, the rabbinic compilations, and the passages of the ancients on Judaea]." He is fully equipped with all the necessary information about the countries he visits before he sets foot out of France. Increasingly, he suspects that his own trip is redundant. Wherever he travels, he cannot help stumbling across the literary or physical traces of his predecessors. Not only is he conscious of following in the footsteps of illustrious men; he is equally conscious of a predetermined discourse, an unavoidable library of encyclopedic descriptions, antiquated metaphors and motifs, scholarly analyses, travellers' stories, and more or less imaginative expositions all clustered round the subject of the Orient, and to whose definitive collective doctrine he is duly subservient. His route is bestrewn with his reading.

Moreau has argued that "son imagination a besoin de se sentir soutenue par des anciens textes" (*Chateaubriand, l'homme et l'oeuvre*). Support for this view can be drawn from Chateaubriand's favourable evaluation of the same trait in other writers:

> je vois que tous les poètes épiques ont été des hommes très instruits; surtout ils étaient nourris des ouvrages de ceux qui les avaient précédés dans la carrière de l'épopée: Virgile traduit Homère; le Tasse imite à chaque stance quelque passage d'Homère, de Virgile, de Lucain, de Stace; Milton prend partout, et joint à ses propres trésors les trésors de ses devanciers.

> [I see that all the epic poets were very learned men: they were especially nourished by the works of those who had preceded them in the path of the epic: Virgil translated Homer; in each stanza, Tasso imitates some passage of Homer, Virgil, Lucian, Statius; Milton takes from everywhere, and adds to his own treasures the treasures of his predecessors.]

This sounds like an unequivocal advocacy of imitation, of the Renaissance principle of erudite poetry, of intertextuality: Chateaubriand appears content to subsume himself in a community of like-minded (and suitably elevated) authors. And, in practice, it is indeed from the established corpus of Oriental scholarship that he derives his authority; he invests his predecessors with such prestige that he holds the falsity of a statement to be less important than its conformity to a tradition: "il me suffit d'être à l'abri sous leur autorité: je consens à avoir tort avec eux [it suffices me to be sheltered beneath their authority; I consent to being wrong with them]." In the last analysis, poetic, literary truth overrides scientific objectivity, good faith with the past outweighs fidelity to the present; thus contradiction is rejected, with contempt, as mere perversity: "Que dirait-on d'un homme qui, parcourant la Grèce et l'Italie, ne s'occuperait qu'à contredire Homère et Virgile? [What would one say of a man who, travelling through Greece and Italy, took as his sole task to contradict Homer and Virgil?]."

Books are Chateaubriand's most constant companions on his travels ("c'est en effet la Bible et l'Evangile à la main que l'on doit parcourir la Terre Sainte [it is indeed with the Bible and the Gospel in one's hand that one must travel the Holy Land]"), and yet the sense of a tradition is far from being an undiluted source of comfort, security, and inspiration for this writer. A trivial but emblematic event reveals ambivalent feelings towards the literary canon. The better to savour his view of the (ruined) Temple, Chateaubriand produces a copy of *Athalie* from his pocket and proceeds to reread the text with special attention to the passages related to that same (still intact) edifice. The rapture afforded him by Racine gives way, in the present, to a paralysing revulsion from writing: "La plume tombe des mains: on est honteux de barbouiller encore du papier après qu'un homme a écrit de pareils vers [The pen falls from my grip: one is ashamed to be still blackening paper after a man has written such verses]." The paralysis is, of course, only temporary: Chateaubriand's nerveless fingers recover in time to record his inability to write: writer's block is good for a couple of lines. But the feeling of inferiority, uncharacteristic of Chateaubriand, will recur, for it is not simply the unsurpassable quality of some of his predecessors' writing that is the cause of his anxiety and problematic aesthetic: it is its sheer quantity. The weight of documentary matter wearies the writer overburdened with books, who carries not only the Bible in his hand but Racine in his pocket.

The genre of the travel book proposes the adequate translation of a perception into a description. The problem for the Oriental traveller is that any perception he may enjoy is certain to be preceded, and to that extent conditioned by, a superabundance of prior descriptions, which his own description is constrained to replicate, thereby producing that copy of a copy denounced by Plato as third-hand mimesis. Berkeley resolved the being of an object into its being perceived; the being of an Oriental object is resolvable into its being described, and, moreover, its being already described. Description is not the externalization of perception; rather, perception is the internalization of description: cognition consists in recognition. The major difficulty confronting the travel writer in the mysterious East is that it is no longer sufficiently mysterious. The trouble with the Orient, Chateaubriand realizes with apprehension, is that it is a cliché.

Thus he arrives in Egypt (or at the Egyptian stage of his exposition), fearful that he will be unable to write, or at least write much, because unable to write anything that has not already been written:

> Que dirais-je de l'Egypte? Qui ne l'a point vue aujourd'hui? Le *Voyage* de M. de Volney en Egypte est un véritable chef-d'œuvre dans tout ce qui n'est pas érudition: l'érudition a été épuisée par Sicard, Norden, Pococke, Shaw, Niebhur et quelques autres. . . . j'ai moi-même dit ailleurs tout ce que j'avais à dire sur l'Egypte.

> [What could I say of Egypt? Who has not seen it today? The *Voyage* of M. de Volney in Egypt is a genuine masterpiece in every respect other than erudition: erudition has been exhausted by Sicard, Norden, Pococke, Shaw, Niebhur and a few others. . . . I myself have already said elsewhere all that I had to say on Egypt.]

Chateaubriand's admiration for his predecessors (including himself) cannot conceal an admixture of exasperation, even of antipathy; he is dependent for his facts upon their judgements, but resents the condition of dependence. The writer's perception of his aesthetic predicament receives its clearest expression with regard to his visit to Jerusalem:

> Ici j'éprouve un véritable embarras. Dois-je offrir la peinture exacte des Lieux Saints? Mais alor je ne puis que répéter ce que l'on a dit avant moi: jamais sujet ne fut peut-être moins connu des lecteurs modernes, et toutefois jamais sujet ne fut plus complètement épuisé.

> [Here I encounter a genuine difficulty. Must I offer an exact portrayal of the Holy Places? But then I can only repeat what others have said before me: never was a subject less known to modern readers, and yet never was a subject so completely exhausted.]

The account that follows unavoidably comprises a mosaic of annotated extracts from prior accounts cemented by occasional observations from the author. Thus the *Itinéraire* is exegetical in construction. The writer is condemned, it seems, either to reiterate or distort; but neither alternative is satisfactory since he cannot bring himself to forgo either the essential information given by previous writers or the freedom of the creative spirit that they threaten to take away in exchange. A prisoner of his precursors, Chateaubriand dreams of escape.

Thus there is a felt sense of relief, mingled with the opposite apprehension of error, occasioned by a relatively unstudied subject:

> Si la multitude des récits fatigue l'écrivain qui veut parler aujourdui de l'Egypte et de la Judée, il éprouve, au sujet des antiquités de l'Afrique, un embarras tout contraire par la disette des documents.

> [If the multitude of accounts wearies the writer who wishes to speak today of Egypt and Judaea, he experiences, when it comes to the antiquities of Africa, a quite contrary difficulty owing to the dearth of documents.]

The "disette" consists in there being, to Chateaubriand's knowledge, a mere thirty or so accounts of the area, which, however quantitatively abundant, fail (for once) to exhaust the matter of the "antiquities." Thus Chateaubriand can licitly, and proudly, declare his originality: "On peut donc dire que le sujet que je vais traiter est neuf, j'ouvrirai la route: les habiles viendront après moi [One can therefore say that the subject that I am about to consider is new; I will show the way: the clever will come after me]." The author's task is to blaze a trail: he is an advance scout to be succeeded by a troop of scholars. For once, the tables are turned (a claim qualified in the third preface by his discovery of a document already covering the field).

The metaphor underlines an analogy (persistent in the work of Rousseau, another of Chateaubriand's precursors and idols) between the process of writing and the experience of travelling. Literal displacements reappear transposed into figurative vehicles of the author's progress; thus the *Itinéraire* presents a certain itinerary of composition. The frequent sliding from the past historic (of action) to the present (of contemplation) and back again, blurring the distinction between *now* and *then,* reflects and reinforces the interplay between the journey and its narration. All Chateaubriand's texts in which the writer is also the traveller present an ambiguous assessment of travel, which reflects the pervasive ambivalence towards the writing of his literate predecessors. In the preface to *Voyage en Amérique,* the author depicts travellers ancient and modern as the discoverers to whom we owe our knowledge of the world. They are creators, giving substance and shape to the unknown, clothing with reality the bones of our theoretical speculations:

> Christophe Colomb dut éprouver quelque chose de ce sentiment que l'Ecriture donne au Créateur, quand, après avoir tiré la terre au néant, il vit que son ouvrage était bon: *vidit Deus quod esset bonum.* Colomb créait un monde.

> [Christopher Columbus must have felt something of that feeling Scripture attributes to the Creator when after producing the earth out of nothingness, he saw that his work was good: *and God saw that it was good.* Columbus created a world.]

But the golden age of discovery is past: nothing, fears Chateaubriand, remains to be discovered; our knowledge of the world is complete. Drake and the rest of his ilk "ne laissent plus un écueil inconnu." Again, praise is charged with regret: the panegyric on past achievement is also a lament on the impossibility of present emulation:

> Je viens me ranger dans la foule des voyageurs obscurs qui n'ont vu que ce que tout le monde a vu, qui n'ont fait faire aucun progrès aux sciences, qui n'ont rien ajouté au trésor des connaissances humaines.

> [I come to join the crowd of obscure travellers who have seen only what everyone has seen, who have not advanced the sciences an inch, who have added nothing to the treasure of human knowledge.]

Chateaubriand's evaluation of his own humble status on his journey West could equally apply to his journey East: the literary thesaurus is already complete and can no longer be added to, only subtracted from.

On the one hand, Chateaubriand is compulsively drawn to a kaleidoscopic variety of landscape. On the other, his attitude is not devoid of hostility or scepticism towards travelling and travellers (common to Pascal, Hugo, and Lévi-Strauss). Reality rarely fails, in the end, to disappoint, while the Oriental traveller in particular must carry with him, like Aeneas setting out from Troy with a past generation on his back, the burden of antecedent accounts of the Orient. In these circumstances, the text is bound to become introverted.

In the *Itinéraire*, the journey is relatively painless, fraught only with the occasional party of marauding bandits or fleet of pirates of some crazed and avaricious Turk or Arab (all disdainfully out-generalled by the seemingly invulnerable Frenchman). Travel becomes almost tediously effortless: nothing is inaccessible (unless rendered so by the cunning manoeuvres of some devious native guide, who thereby incurs Chateaubriand's just wrath and indignation). All the traditional hazards, difficulties, and excitements of the journey are transferred to the act of recording the journey. And the element of risk involved elevates the writer in place of the traveller to the status of hero of the story. Thus the *Itinéraire* effectively relates an arduous tour through a variety of exotic texts in which the heroic author encounters and recruits or conquers other writers. The last page, for example, recalls the persistent valour beyond the call of duty that has distinguished the writer's enterprise:

> un grand nombre de feuilles de mes livres ont été tracées sous la tente, dans les déserts, au milieu des flots; j'ai souvent tenu la plume sans savoir comment je prolongerais de quelques instants mon existence.

> [a great number of the pages of my books have been written beneath a tent, in deserts, at sea: I have often held the pen without knowing how I would prolong my existence for a few moments more.]

The *Itinéraire*, then, is in part the self-congratulatory record of how it came to be written.

The reasons for Chateaubriand's itinerancy may be political, religious, or psychological; his justifications are literary. A journey, in his view, is only ever as good as the narrative it gives rise to. Once overcome, the difficulties encountered by the writer en route—at once practical (how to write in a storm?) and theoretical (the proliferation and apparent sufficiency of prior narratives)—can only add to the (evanescent) satisfaction of arriving at a destination: the last page. Thus the reflexivity of the text contributes to the dramatization of the author.

The writer proclaims his subjectivity as the fundamental subject of all his writing: "Je parle éternellement de moi." [The first sentence of the *Essai sur les révolutions* does not concern revolutions; it asks: "Qui suis-je?".] And he recommends that the *Itinéraire* be considered more in the nature of an autobiography than a geographical or cultural dissertation. He is not a travel writer but rather a travelling writer. Chateaubriand's textual egocentricity is epitomized by his habit of defining the meaning of a place for him in terms of his meaning for it, which issues in the curious stylistic mannerism of the description of a hitherto unvisited place or thing bent magnetically towards his previous absence from the place or thing described. Thus: "Asie, partie du monde qui n'avait pas encore vu la trace de mes pas, hélas! ni ces chagrins que je partage avec tous les hommes [Asia, a part of the world which had not yet seen the trace of my steps, alas! nor those sorrows that I share with all men]." The interjection "hélas" is so placed that Chateaubriand may be regretting his "chagrins," the fact that he shares them with all men, or, more probably, that Asia has not yet had the opportunity to witness them.

The prominence of the Chateaubrianesque *moi* is conceived as a partial solution to the problem of the conflict between exhaustive antecedent scholarship and the unoriginal craving for originality. The genre of the *voyage* necessarily contains at least two constituents: *le voyageur* and *l'étranger*. In the case of the Orient, says Chateaubriand, the latter is already excessively annotated; therefore he undertakes to write about the former, namely, himself. The emphasis on the subject as subject-matter, the introversion of Chateaubriand's writing, is ostensibly vindicated by the suspicion that there is nothing else left to write about. If the individual is a unique being then it follows that any account of self, assuming it is adequate to its subject, must be original. But originality is the condition of adequacy.

It is by way of metaphor, suggests Chateaubriand, that originality might be attained. Thus Chateaubriand envisages himself as a crusading *chevalier errant* doing battle, on behalf of art, with the pre-existing "army of metaphors, metonyms and anthropomorphisms" that already confronts him like an enemy. Of the purpose of his trip, Chateaubriand writes that "j'allais chercher des images, voilà tout [I went in search of some images, that's all]"; and he records, with satisfaction, that he "revient à ses foyers avec quelques images nouvelles dans la tête et quelques sentiments de plus dans le coeur [returns to his home with a few new images in his head and a few more feelings in his heart]." "Sentiments" succeed "images": the novelty of the image seems to be less the means of expressing feelings than the prerequisite of their release. Thus the literary ambition of the *Itinéraire*, which translates into a pilgrimage the theory developed in *Génie du christianisme* of a literature renovated by belief (following the philosophical impieties of the eighteenth century), is implicated in a programme of emotional renewal.

The image of the *désert* which dominates Chateaubriand's conception of the Orient is an improbable candidate for the rank of *trouvaille*. Lévi-Strauss remarks that "le survol de l'Arabie propose une série de variations sur un seul thème: le désert [flying over Arabia offers a series of variations on a single theme: the desert]" (*Tristes Tropiques*). And given its prominence even in those of Chateaubriand's works quite unconnected with the Orient, the *désert* scarcely constitutes an *image nouvelle*. Rather, it appears as the precondition of novelty, the ground of metaphorical originality.

Napoleon perceived an incongruity between the potential riches of the country of Egypt and the actual indigence, material and intellectual, of its inhabitants: while the land is "belle," "fertile," and so on, the people are "laids," "misérables," and so on. He posits an antithesis between an inanimate and almost immaculate milieu and its animate and defective tenants. The same structure of opposition recurs in Chateaubriand, who supplements Napoleon's observation by the addition of his own reaction: one of indignation (one of the most frequently performed in his repertoire of emotions), almost of outrage. The apparent discrepancy between Orient and Orientals dismays him, as though paradise had been invaded by alien beings (which according to Chateaubriand is precisely what has happened):

> quand on songe que ces campagnes n'ont été habitées autrefois que par des Grecs du Bas-Empire, et qu'elles sont occupées aujourd'hui par des Turcs, on est choqué du contraste entre les peuples et les lieux; il semble que des esclaves aussi vils et des tyrans aussi cruels n'auraient jamais dû déshonorer un séjour aussi magnifique.

> [when one thinks that once these lands were inhabited only by Greeks of the late Empire, and that they are occupied today by Turks, one is shocked at the contrast between the peoples and the places; it seems that such vile slaves and such cruel tyrants should never have disgraced such a magnificent abode.]

Chateaubriand's abhorrence of what he perceives as an anomaly testifies to a theory of the environment: he requires that there exist a correspondence between place and populace, a visible congruity such that each would be an adequate expression of the other.

The Nile episode gives expression both to Chateaubriand's patriotic nostalgia and the intimate liaison he postulates between landscape and society. Observing an orderly, symmetrically arranged grove of palm-trees, on the bank of the river, he reflects:

> Les palmiers paraissaient alignés sur la rive, comme ces avenues dont les châteaux de France sont décorés: la nature se plaît ainsi à rappeler les idées de la civilisation, dans le pays où cette civilisation prit naissance et où règnent aujourd'hui l'ignorance et la barbarie.

> [The palm trees appeared aligned on the bank like those avenues with which the *châteaux* of France are decorated; nature is thus pleased to recall the ideas of civilization, in the country where this civilization had its birth and where today ignorance and barbarity reign.]

On the one hand, nature, imitating art, evokes a cultured society; the society, on the other, is entirely uncultivated. Thus a gap has opened up between the beauty of mother nature and the ugliness of human nature. But the palm-trees also indicate the solution to the problem they pose, by duplicating the French vocation of recalling civilization to its source. [Curiously, palm-trees invariably make Chateaubriand think of home: this may be because one of the redemptive gestures of the French army (recorded in *Description de l'Egypte,* and *Mémoires*) was to have demolished numerous unsightly buildings (occupied by Arabs) and planted palm trees in their place.] Chateaubriand is a perfect embodiment of the French role: a mobile extension of the *Château* (his name recalls an ancestor's home: [Baron] Brien's castle), a noble vehicle of it seigneurial values. His ideal space, his *locus amoenus,* would similarly eliminate any discrepancy between form and content.

The perceptible discontinuity of *milieu* and *peuple* in the Orient reflects the conflict which permeates the text between past and present. Chateaubriand's chronological schema admits three ages of man, to which the stages of a civilization correspond: *enfance/jeunesse*; *maturité*; and *décadence.* The Orient he perceives and reviles has attained a state of advanced senility, almost of moribundity: it prefigures its imminent condition of carrion by being fed upon by vulturine Turks. The Orient he imagines and admires has at least two things in common with France: that it is absent; and that (like himself) it is, or was, mature: that is, at the peak of its cultural productivity. Both the present (but absent) France and the lost (but recoverable) Orient are the apotheoses of the values of civilization, while the present (insupportable) Orient vividly embodies a decline.

Thus while the classical Orient and modern France coincide, the modern Arab, by infringing the aesthetic law of Chateaubriand's environmental logic, appears preposterously out of place:

> Nous passâmes par le canal de Menouf, ce qui m'empêcha de voir le beau bois de palmiers qui se trouve sur la grande branche de l'ouest; mais les Arabes infestaient alors le bord occidental de cette branche qui touche au désert libyque.

> [We passed through the Menouf canal, which prevented me from seeing the beautiful wood of palm trees that is situated on the main western branch; but the Arabs were then infesting the western bank of this branch which borders the Libyan desert.]

The intelligibility of the conjunction *mais* depends on our understanding that the invisible palm-trees, potentially beautiful, even supposing they had not been blocked from view, would in any case be deprived of all beauty by the proximity of disharmonious Arabs. The verb *infester* denotes the illicit, provisional character of the Arab presence: they do not belong by right to the area which they choose to inhabit: they are mere interlopers, destined to be expelled just as the French are destined to return, trespassers on the banks of the Nile, who have wandered away from the territory allotted in accordance with their uncultivated nature, and designated in the closing phrase: the "désert libyque." An earlier passage (whose opening line places the East under Western surveillance) recalls that:

> j'avais sous les yeux les descendants de la race primitive des hommes, je les voyais avec les mêmes mœurs qu'ils ont conservées depuis les jours d'Agar et d'Ismaël: je les voyais dans le même désert qui leur fut assigné par Dieu en héritage . . . l'Arabe, pour ainsi dire jeté sur le grand chemin du monde, entre l'Afrique et l'Asie, erre dans les brillantes régions de l'aurore, sur un sol sans arbre et sans eau.

> [I had under my gaze the descendants of the primitive race of men, I saw them with the same manners they have preserved since the days of Agar and Ismaël: I saw them in the same desert which was assigned to them by God as their heritage . . . the Arab, thrust, so to speak, onto the great highway of the world, between Africa and Asia, wanders in the shimmering regions of the dawn, on a ground devoid of trees and water.]

In this case, the rationale of secret harmonies is endorsed by divine fiat: the desert is the predestined habitat of the Arab, who is doomed to wander in search of trees and water (but is prohibited from ever legally attaining either).

The hierarchy of moral absolutes in which ethical and ethnic categories overlap, providing for the assured enunciation of *sententiae* about a collective soul or psychology (all Turks are corrupt, all Arabs stupid), interlocks with a relative aesthetic schema linking man's identity and destiny to his native surroundings. Man and his environment are bound by mutual sympathy: while the human subject is reducible to the sum of his ecological correlatives, geography is charged with moral and psychological connotations. It is enough to observe the landscape in which a people is set in order to acquire knowledge of its true character: the eminently fathomable inner nature, the collective essence of the Arab population, is visibly displayed in the outer nature to which Chateaubriand's God has eternally consigned it. The Arab is turned inside out, his mind externalized for inspection, projected outwards upon his environment. Intangible qualities of mind, emotion, morality, are no longer imagined to reside, inaccessibly, within the individual: they are publicly engraved upon a physical terrain: Chateaubriand's Arab shares with Hugo's the property of being all surface.

But the chief attribute of the Egyptian desert is its emptiness: it is the negative landscape par excellence: devoid of content, stripped bare, denuded. And the same is metaphorically true of the Arab: he is bereft (as the desert is of soil, vegetation, water) of rational thought, a moral code, political ideas of justice, liberty, democracy. He professes "une religion qui a brûlé la bibliothèque d'Alexandrie, qui se fait un mérite de mépriser souverainement les lettres et les arts [a religion which razed the library of Alexandria, which prides itself on its supreme contempt for literature and the arts]." Systematically philistine, the only book he has neglected to destroy is the Koran, perhaps because "il n'y a dans le livre de Mahomet ni principe de civilisation, ni précepte qui puisse élever le caractère: ce livre ne prêche ni la haine de la tyrannie, ni l'amour de la liberté [in Mahomet's book there is neither a principle of civilization, nor a precept capable of elevating the character: this book preaches neither the hatred of tyranny nor the love of liberty]." Motivated only by animal self-interest, he presents, in short, a negative mental landscape that finds its exact equivalent in the form of the desert. What the Arab and the desert have most in common is vacancy: the Orient is characterized by a dual geographical and human barrenness; the Arab is an intellectual Sahara. The Arab's lack of culture is reflected in the uncultivated nature of the land he inhabits. Chateaubriand thus exploits an agricultural etymology to provide a visible counterpart of educational underdevelopment or decay, to encode ignorance. Hence the mission of the cultured and cultivating French: to scatter the good seed. The Oriental stands in need of fertilization.

In contrast to the Arab, Chateaubriand himself retains an inexhaustible interiority which is the prerogative of the European. His identity is shaped by his childhood environment of Brittany, but he remains nonetheless a free agent, ecologically speaking, whose indeterminacy is mirrored in his endless travelling: he is never *chez lui* ("presque un étranger dans mon pays"), only a detached spectator in any territory. The Chateaubrianesque *je* is as limitless as the world. And while the hollow, superficial, infertile Arab mind is symmetrical with the desert, a flat, wide, empty plain, Chateaubrianesque immanence and profundity appear to find an objective correlative, a system of common denominators, in the *ruine.*

The vocabulary of ruins is extensive and ubiquitous in the *Itinéraire:* the travelling author is incessantly drawn to *débris, vestiges, remnants, décombres,* and more particularly to symbols of death, the *tombe, tombeau, cimetière,* or *sépulcre.* The crumbling edifice, the evocative remains of an ancient architecture, the grave: each allows for the expression of melancholy and the operation of the retrospective mode of thought and feeling to which the *Itinéraire* gives priority; and each offers an exact image of the pervasive mutability, the rise and fall of civilizations, which is a central theme of the book. The writer's sense of personal affinity with ruins springs from the perception not only that both are presently endangered and ultimately doomed to disappear, but also that both are laden with culture and history: both, in short, are *plena,* distinguished by their labyrinthine complexity, their wealth of irrecoverable meaning, their indecipherability. The secrets of the self are buried deep within the individual: hence the frequency of the verb *ensevelir:* René "s'ensevelit" in the depths of a forest, his memories and emotions are "ensevelis" within him (just as "palais" are "ensevelis" in "poudre"). Similarly, the meaning of the *grotte,* which is the privileged space of the ruin, is essentially subterranean and, chronologically, buried in the past, requiring excavation or evocation by the erudite observer.

Structurally, plenitude implies the contrast of vacancy. It is this juxtaposition of an inner cornucopia of feeling and an outer vacuity that inspires René's *ennui:* in *René,* a "coeur plein" meets a "monde vide." An analogous disposition of forces is evident in the *Itinéraire:* the inward, vertical, vertiginous fullness of the ruin is foregrounded against the outward, horizontal horizon of the desert. Likewise, the aristocratic French pilgrim stands out from the crowd of Oriental humanity. The time-spans of civilizations and citizens are condensed in an architectural image: the monument—temple, *château,* Chateaubriand—which becomes a ruin which is then engulfed in the desert.

Richard asserts that "l'imagination de Chateaubriand se livre donc à une grande mise en scène de l'absence. Autour du moi elle étend un désert de négativité [Chateaubriand's imagination abandons itself to a great dramatization of absence. It extends around the self a desert of negativity]." The hero of the *Itinéraire,* unlike the Arab, is never the mere reflection of an environment. Chateaubriand's elaborate network of analogies entails a real or imagined rapprochement of the self and a shifting milieu. Hence the affinity of the author with ruins does not exclude a sense of sympathy with their setting. Thus he concludes his recapitulation (in the *Mémoires*) of his Oriental adventures with this coda: "Je n'ai devant les yeux, des sites de la Syrie, de l'Egypte, et de la terre punique, que les endroits en rapport avec ma nature solitaire; ils me plaisent indépendamment de l'antiquité, de l'art et de l'histoire [I have before my eyes, of the sites of Syria, Egypt, and the Punic country, only the places having an affinity with my solitary nature; they please me independently of antiquity, art, or history]." He identifies these timeless, artless places quite specifically: "Les pyramides me frappaient moins par leur grandeur que par le désert contre lequel elles étaient appliquées [The pyramids struck me less by their size than by the desert they were set against]." The *Itinéraire* depicts Chateaubriand as a Christ-like figure wandering in the wilderness. His contempt of the Arab conceals a clandestine envy which finds expression in his unconcealed admiration for the Frenchmen, the residue of Napoleon's expeditionary force, who have become Mamelukes (the guardians of the old regime they were supposed to depose) and have "vécu longtemps dans le désert avec les Bédouins." The dual passion for the crumbling edifice and the immortal desert reflects an ambiguity of commitment.

In the *Itinéraire,* Chateaubriand parades his allegiance to the values of a *civilisation* which is conterminous with France; but he nevertheless senses and declares his kinship with an uncivilized past: hence his self-description: "Moi, Barbare civilisé." Chateaubriand's consciousness of a hybrid self, a dual personality, issues in the image he reserves for himself of the "androgyne bizarre" and induces both Thibaudet and Butor to affirm that there are "two Chateaubriands." His symmetrical journeys westwards and eastwards, tabulating the rise and fall, the birth and the decay of new and old cultures, enable him to find an outlet for the antinomial poles of his personality and give expression to the antagonistic values of civilization and barbarism whose respective emblems are plenitude and vacuity, erudition and ignorance.

Thus Chateaubriand's Oriental travels involve a process of exchange: like Napoleon, he is a European (but above all, a Frenchman, a patriot, championing France versus England and the rest of the world) exporting Western culture to the East; at the same time, he tries on the identities of the lands he visits, enacting the destinies of Egypt and Greece: "peut-être le génie des nations s'épuise-t-il; et quand il a tout produit, tout parcouru, tout goûté, rassasié de ses propres chefs-d'oeuvre, et incapable d'en produire de nouveaux, il s'abrutit, et retourne aux sensations purement physiques [perhaps the genius of nations can be exhausted; and when it has produced everything, travelled everywhere, tasted everything, sated with its own masterpieces, and incapable of producing new ones, it becomes mindless and reverts to purely physical sensations]." The *Itinéraire* merges the fate of civilizations with the evolution of an individual: the growth to maturity, the full flowering of genius, inevitably entails exhaustion and decay; but decline, in turn, implies a cyclical return to an original state of pure sensation, the recovery of a lost childhood (thus Chateaubriand's progress through space coincides with his regress through time). In Chateaubriand's literary epistemology, books are conceived of as foods feeding the literate mind: the fertilizers of culture. But the *Itinéraire* shows that the author's surfeit of erudition can give rise to a state of congestion, of intellectual indigestion or creative constipation. Chateaubriand, cursed by excess, is too crammed with potential material to make any use of it. Trapped in the labyrinth of his own learning, he seeks to free himself of the accretions that surround and stifle the self: to eliminate overabundant knowledge.

The desert seems to represent precisely such a deliverance because its transcendent emptiness calls up, in accordance with Chateaubriand's ecologic, its concomitant in the observer of an immanent evacuation. His fascination with the desert springs from an urge to relinquish the tradition of which he is ambassador, the ambition of inner, mental *déracinement* (an uprooting both of *racines* and Racine) corresponding to his physical exile. The desert purifies the world of its descriptions: it is the Orient minus Orientalism. Thus the primal condition of nescience—the negation of a cultural archive, the incineration of libraries—censoriously ascribed to the Arab, also constitutes the secret consummation of Chateaubriand's aesthetic. His plenitude may be a satiety that causes the suspension of creativity; the desert, by voiding, regenerates the jaded spirit.

Chateaubriand has alleged the search for new Muses as one reason for his journey East; later he admits that "naturellement un peu sauvage, ce n'était pas ce qu'on appelle la société que j'étais venu chercher en Orient: il me tardait de voir des chameaux et d'entendre le cri du cornac [naturally on the savage side, it was not what is called society that I came to seek in the Orient: I was impatient to see camels and to hear the cry of the elephant driver]." Both programmes are fulfilled in the contemplation of the desert: "L'Egypte m'a paru le plus beau pays de la terre: j'aime jusqu'aux déserts qui la bordent, et qui ouvrent à l'imagination les champs de l'immensité [Egypt seemed to me the most beautiful country on earth: I love even the deserts which surround it and which open up to the imagination the fields of immensity]." The arid, empty sands are a fertile source of inspiration: the *désert*, aesthetically, is adjacent to the measureless *champs* of the literary imagination; both literally and analogically, it is the ground of the novel, the *nouveau:* the camel, the cornac, and the freshly-minted metaphor.

Thus the *désert* is not exclusive to the Orient: it appears rather as a universal constant in Chateaubriand's work, a permanent companion of the author, conjured up on all his travels. Visiting the mausoleums of the Pharaohs, Chateaubriand recalls the tombs of Ohio:

> je commençais alors le voyage, et maintenant je le finis. Le monde, à ces deux époques de ma vie, s'est présenté à moi précisément sous l'image des deux déserts où j'ai vu ces deux espèces de tombeaux: des solitudes riantes, des sables arides.

> [then I was beginning the journey, and now I am finishing it. The world, at these two periods of my life, presented itself to me precisely in the form of these two deserts where I saw two types of tomb: cheerful solitudes and arid sands.]

Semantically, *désert* is not reducible to the geographical sense of a mere expanse of sand or rock; it is sometimes indistinguishable from Rousseau's primitive forest, inhabited by *sauvages*. The *désert* of the New World, writes Butor, is "l'équivalent de l'anglais *wilderness*. Il n'évoque nullement la stérilité, le Sahara; au contraire ce désert est caractérisé par la splendeur de sa flore. Il s'agit d'un lieu que la société humaine a laissé intact [the equivalent of the English *wilderness*. It in no way evokes sterility, the Sahara; on the contrary, this desert is characterized by the splendour of its flora. It signifies a place left intact by human society]" (Repertoire, II). Thus the remote phases of civilization, the nascent and the moribund, together and in parallel with the phases (recollected or projected) of Chateaubriand's childhood and senility, are united by the single ambiguous image of the *désert* [The Atlantic of the Brittany coast, which Chateaubriand regards as his *patrie*, is also "ce désert d'océan"]. The desert, then, making the absence of culture and the pre-eminence of nature, is ubiquitous, at once empty and full, sterile and fertile: a cornucopian void.

Chateaubriand traces the ancestry of solitude and nescience to biblical sources; he discerns their coincidence in the myth of the Garden of Eden to which allusions are scattered throughout his work. Chateaubriand's desert, which is also a garden, is, like Adam's pre-lapsarian paradise, blissfully purified of the nomenclatorial anxiety that is sinful, literate man's secular, sublunary malediction. Here the writer can finally achieve his ambition of absolute originality: only in the Edenesque *désert* is he able not only to "voir à nu" (like the first Western travellers in the East), but also to summon "la parole primitive que Dieu a donné à l'homme avec l'existence," the ideal language postulated and refuted by Rousseau, which closes the rift between sign and object. Thus the new world of the imagination seeks an origin in the old.

The *désert*, metonym of the Orient (with which it is contiguous), and metaphor of the Arab (to whom it corresponds), thus stands as the symbol of originality. "Où y a-t-il du nouveau? Est-ce en Orient? [Where is there something new? Is it in the East? . . . Let us go there]." Chateaubriand asks, and answers by the imperative "Marchons-y." But there is nothing new under the sun: the sun (the West, civilization, the knowledge enshrined in discourse) is the symbol of the old: its canonical *lumières* threaten to deprive language of its access to novelty. Chateaubriand's literary pilgrimage therefore imposes further conditions: "puisque nous cherchons de nouveaux soleils, je me précipiterai au-devant de leur splendeur et n'attendrai plus le lever naturel de l'aurore [since we are seeking new suns, I will rush before their splendour and will no longer await the natural appearance of the dawn]." Chateaubriand heads eastwards towards the benighted Orient to escape the rising of the sun; the desert can only achieve the complete negation of obsolete culture at night: Chateaubriand's ideal landscape would be sunless. Writing accordingly becomes a nocturnal enterprise: Chateaubriand describes himself as "courant le jour et écrivant la nuit." Symmetrically, in the American forest, with the rumble of Niagara echoing "de désert en désert," he discovers inspiration at night: "c'est dans ces nuits que m'apparut une muse inconnue [it is in those nights that an unknown muse appeared to me]." Chateaubriand's muse, like Hugo's, operates under cover of night.

Genette has noted that "l'imagination poétique s'intéresse davantage à la nuit qu'au jour [the poetic imagination is more interested in night than day]" and that the explicit preference for night over day constitutes "un choix coupable, un parti pris de l'interdit, une transgression [a guilty choice, a bias in favour of the forbidden, a transgression]" ("Le Jour, La nuit." In *Figures* II). In Chateaubriand, it represents an inversion of the Orientalist project, an attempt to infiltrate the East into the West: to incorporate the Oriental *nuit* into the Occidental *jour*. Genette has also noted that the antithesis of day and night is "un paradigme défectif" since "la relation entre jour et nuit n'est pas seulement d'opposition, donc d'exclusion réciproque mais aussi d'inclusion: en un de ses sens, le jour exclut la nuit, en l'autre, il la comprend [the relation between day and night is not only one of opposition, and thus of mutual exclusion, but also of inclusion: in one of its senses, day excludes night, in the other, it contains it]." Semantically, at least, Chateaubriand's anti-Orientalist intention seems eminently capable of fulfilment, since day already incorporates night.

But, conversely, as Blanchot remarks, "la nuit ne parle que du jour." If the day cannot exclude the night, neither can night exclude day, since it is a fraction of the diurnal cycle. Even when the sun is absent from Chateaubriand's desert, it is supplanted by the moon. The writer is nocturnal, and therefore (according to Nicholas's classifications) a lunatic, an owl who cannot tolerate the sun. The narrator of *Les Natchez* apostrophizes the moon, calling on it to "découvrir à ta lumière les secrets ravissants de ces déserts [reveal in your light the delightful secrets of these deserts]." But of course the moon does not emit light, it is only a pale reflector of the sun: its light is derivative. Thus the Chateaubrianesque desert, the scene of original writing, the primordial metaphor, cannot escape solar reflection.

Language then, even as it appears in its raw, metaphorical, Oriental state, is already irradiated by the Occidental sun of culture. And the Oriental desert, the chief exemplar of the *désert*, in which all its senses overlap, itself reflects the destructive effects of the sun. The *désert* is not distinct from the *ruines* it accommodates but is itself a vast ecological ruin, the remnant of an indeterminate process of dissolution. The desert (of Greece as well as of Egypt) is not a pure negation, a primitive state of nature, but the residue of a fertile, civilized past. The desert is not just the location of tombs but the paradigm case of the *tombeau*. Thus writing reverts from the ambition of originality to the recognition of mortality. The metaphor is a ruin of language, not a fresh construction but the destruction of inherited forms, a monument to the past, the wreck of an irrecoverable originality: the text, in turn, seems to Chateaubriand like a tomb, "un temple de la mort." In the introduction to the *Mémoires* (whose full title suggests less an autobiography than a post-mortem), Chateaubriand declares that he always imagines himself, while writing, to be seated in his coffin. The writer (as Nietzsche said of himself) is born posthumously, deprived of a birth.

But the writer seems equally deprived of a definitive death. Just as Chateaubriand regrets the derivativeness of his own writing, so, symmetrically, he fears its duplication. He realizes (reflecting on the ruins of the Parthenon) that "je passerai à mon tour: d'autres hommes aussi fugitifs que moi viendront faire les mêmes réflexions sur les mêmes ruines [I will pass away in my turn: other men as evanescent as I will come to make the same reflections on the same ruins]." He laments not so much the brevity of life as its prolongation in others: the prospect of individuality is debased by the eternal recurrence of the author's preoccupations and expressions. Chateaubriand cannot be a pioneer, the first to discover and describe the Orient; neither can he be the last, "le dernier historien" or "le dernier Français" to make the pilgrimage to the Holy Land: hordes of literary tourists are already following in his tracks.

The *Essai sur les révolutions* bemoans the severance from a past (because it severs authority). All Chateaubriand's writing confirms the condition of exile from a point of origin. However, in *Génie du christianisme*, Chateaubriand advances historical proofs upholding the validity of the Biblical account of Genesis, arguing that man and the world are relatively recent inventions, that the preponderance of ruins does not demonstrate the antiquity of civilization but only the speed at which it decays. In order to refute the paleontological objection involving the apparent age of the earth, he resorts to a theory of "vieillesse originaire" (*La Génie du christianisme*). If the Creation occurred recently but the earth is ancient, then "Dieu a dû créer, et a sans doute créé le monde avec toutes les marques de vétusté et de complément que nous lui voyons [God must have created, and undoubtedly did create the world with all the marks of old age and complementarity that we see in it]." The Creator creates a mature universe of ancient forests, aging animals, a reef-filled ocean, and a man thirty years old, eliminating an "insipide enfance" on apparently aesthetic grounds, since "la nature, dans son innocence, eût été moins belle qu'elle ne l'est aujourd'hui dans sa corruption [nature, in its innocence, would have been less beautiful than it is today in its corruption]." The primordial world is "à la fois jeune et vieux"; the beginning incorporates an infinite past; everything which is now has always been. Thus Chateaubriand preserves Genesis only at the cost of abolishing genesis, condemning youth, innocence, novelty, in short, the negative moment of a pure origin, as artistically intolerable. The logos emerges *in medias res*; such is, *a fortiori*, the case of discourse. The writer, born amid the ruins of culture and language, is the image of the Creator because he only creates what is already old.

Fourier

Roland Barthes

BEGINNINGS

I.   One day, I was invited to eat a couscous with rancid butter; the rancid butter was customary; in certain regions it is an integral part of the couscous code. However, be it prejudice, or unfamiliarity, or digestive intolerance, I don't like rancidity. What to do? Eat it, of course, so as not to offend my host, but gingerly, in order not to offend the conscience of my disgust (since for disgust *per se* one needs some stoicism). In this difficult meal, Fourier would have helped me. On the one hand, intellectually, he would have persuaded me of three things: the first is that the rancidness of couscous is in no way an idle, futile, or trivial question, and that debating it is no more futile than debating Transubstantiation ("First we will deal with the puerility of these battles over the superiority of sweet cream or little pies; we might reply that the debate will be no more ridiculous than our Religious Wars over Transubstantiation" [*Le Nouveau Monde amoureux*]); the second is that by forcing me to lie about my likes (or dislikes), society is manifesting its *falseness*, i.e., not only its hypocrisy (which is banal) but also the vice of the social mechanism whose gearing is faulty; the third, that this same society cannot rest until it has guaranteed (how? Fourier has clearly explained it, but it must be admitted that it hasn't worked) the exercise of my manias, whether "bizarre" or "minor," like those of people who like old chickens, the eater of horrid things (like the astronomer Lalande, who liked to eat live spiders), the fanatics about butter, pears, bergamots, Ankles, or "Baby Dolls." ("Ankles" are men who like to scratch their mistress's ankle; the "Baby Doll" is a sixty-year-old man who, desirous

From *Sade, Fourier, Loyola*. © 1976 by Farrar, Straus & Giroux, Inc. Hill & Wang Publishers, 1976.

of being treated like a spoiled child, wants the soubrette to punish him by "gently patting his patriarchal buttocks.") On the other hand, practically, Fourier would at once have put an end to my embarrassment (being torn between my good manners and my lack of taste for rancid things) by taking me from my meal (where, in addition, I was stuck for hours, a barely tolerable situation against which Fourier protested) and sending me to the Anti-Rancid group, where I would be allowed to eat fresh couscous as I liked without bothering anyone—which would not have kept me from preserving the best of relations with the Rancid group, whom I would henceforth consider as not at all "ethnic," foreign, strange, at for example a great couscous tournament, at which couscous would be the "theme," and where a jury of gastrosophers would decide on the superiority of rancid over fresh (I almost said: *normal,* but for Fourier, and this is his victory, there is no normality).

II.   Fourier likes compotes, fine weather, perfect melons, the little spiced pastries known as *mirlitons,* and the company of lesbians. Society and nature hinder these tastes a bit: sugar is (or was) expensive (more expensive than bread), the French climate is insupportable except in May, September, and October, we know no sure method of detecting a melon's quality, in Civilization little pastries bring on indigestion, lesbians are proscribed and, blind for a long time as far as he himself was concerned, Fourier did not know until very late in life that he liked them. Thus the world must be remade for my pleasure: my pleasure will be simultaneously the ends and the means: in organizing it, distributing it, I shall overwhelm it.

III.   Everywhere we travel, on every occasion on which we feel a desire, a longing, a lassitude, a vexation, it is possible to ask Fourier, to wonder: What would he have said about it? What would he make of this place, this adventure? Here am I one evening in southern Moroccan hotel: some hundred meters outside the populous, tattered, dusty town, a park filled with rare scents, a blue pool, flowers, quiet bungalows, hordes of discreet servants. In Harmony, what would that give? First of all, this: there would come to this place all who have this strange liking, this low mania for dim lights in the woods, candle-lit dinners, a staff of native servants, night frogs, and a camel in a meadow beneath the window. Then this rectification: the Harmonians would scarcely have need of this place, luxurious owing to its temperature (spring in mid-winter), because, by acting on the atmosphere, by modifying the polar cap, this exotic climate could be transported to Jouy-en-Josas or Gif-sur-Yvette. Finally, this compromise: at certain times during the year, hordes of people, driven by a taste for travel and adventure, would descend upon the idyllic motel and there hold their councils of love and gastronomy (it would be just the place for our couscous investigations). From which, once again, it emerges: that Fourierist pleasure is the end of the tablecloth: pull the slightest futile incident, provided it concerns your happiness, and all the rest of the world will follow: its organization, its limits, its values; this sequence, this fatal induction which ties the most tenuous inflection of our desire to the broadest sociality, this unique space in which fantasy and the social combinative are trapped, this is very precisely *systematics* (but not, as we shall see, the system); with Fourier, impossible to relax without constructing a theory about it. And this: in Fourier's day none of the Fourierist system had been achieved, but today? Caravans, crowds, the collective search for fine climate, pleasure trips, exist: in a derisory and rather atrocious form, the organized tour, the planting of a vacation club (with its classed population, its planned pleasures) is there in some fairy-tale site; in the Fourierist utopia there is a twofold reality, realized as a farce by mass society: *tourism*—the just ransom of a fantasmatic system which has "forgotten" politics, whereas politics pays it back by "forgetting" no less systematically to "calculate" for our pleasure. It is in the grip of these two forgettings, whose confrontation determines total futility, insupportable emptiness, that we are still floundering.

THE CALCULATION OF PLEASURE

The motive behind all Fourierist construction (all combination) is not justice, equality, liberty, etc., it is pleasure. Fourierism is not a radical eudaemonism. Fourierist pleasure (*positive happiness*) is very easy to define: it is sensual pleasure: "amorous freedom, good food, insouciance, and the other delights that the Civilized do not even dream of coveting because philosophy has taught them to treat the desire for true pleasures as vice." (Let us briefly recall that in the Fourierist lexicon, *Civilization* has a precise (numbered) meaning: the word designates the 5th period of the 1st phase (Infancy of Mankind), which comes between the period of the federal patriarchate (the birth of large agriculture and manufacturing industry) and that of guaranteeism or demi-association (industry by association). Whence a broader meaning: in Fourier, *Civilization* is synonymous with wretched barbarism and designates the state of his own day (and ours); it contrasts with universal Harmony (2nd and 3rd phases of mankind). Fourier believed himself to be at the axis of Barbaric Civilization and Harmony.) Fourierist sensuality is, above all, oral. Of course, the two major sources of pleasure are equally Love and Food, always in tandem; however, although Fourier pushes the claims of erotic freedom, he does not describe it sensually; whereas food is lovingly fantasized in detail (compotes, *mirlitons*, melons, pears, lemonades); and Fourier's speech itself is sensual, it progresses in effusiveness, enthusiasm, throngs of words, verbal gourmandise (neologism is an erotic act, which is why he never fails to arouse the censure of pedants).

This Fourierist pleasure is commodious, *it stands out:* easily isolated from the heteroclite hotchpotch of causes, effects, values, protocols, habits, alibis, it appears throughout in its sovereign purity: mania (the ankle scratcher, the filth eater, the "Baby Doll") is never captured save through the pleasure it procures for its partners, and this pleasure is never encumbered with other images (absurdities, inconveniences, difficulties); in short, there is no metonymy attached to it: pleasure is what it is, nothing more. The emblematic ceremony of this isolation of essence would be a *museum orgy:* it consists of a simple exposition of the desirable, "a séance wherein notable lovers lay bare the most remarkable thing they have. A woman whose only beautiful feature is her bosom exposes only the bosom and is covered elsewhere" (we refrain from commenting on the fetishist character of this framework, evident enough; his intention not analytical but merely ethical, Fourier would not deign to take fetishism into a symbolic, reductive system: that would be merely a mania *along with* others, and not inferior or superior to them).

Fourierist pleasure is free from evil: it does not include vexation, in the Sadian manner, but on the contrary dissipates it; his discourse is one of "general well-being": for example, in the war of love (game and theater), out of delicacy, in order not to disturb, no flags or leaders are captured. If, however, in Harmony, one chances to suffer, the entire society will attempt to divert you: have you had some failure in love, have you been turned down, the Bacchantes, Adventuresses, and other pleasure corporations will surround you and lead you off, instantly efface the harm that has befallen you (they exercise, Fourier says, philanthropy). But if someone has a mania to harass? Should they be allowed? The pleasure of harassing is due to a congestion; Harmony will decongest the passions, sadism will be reabsorbed: Dame Strogonoff had the unpleasant habit of harassing her beautiful slave by piercing her breast with pins; in fact, it was counter-passion: Dame Strogonoff was in love with her victim without knowing it: Harmony, by authorizing and favoring Sapphic loves, would have relieved her of her sadism. Yet a final threat: satiety: how to *sustain* pleasure? "How act so as to have a continually renewed appetite? Here lies the secret of Harmonian politics." This secret is twofold: on the one hand, change the race and, through the overall benefits of the societal diet (based on meats and fruits, with very little bread), form physiologically stronger men, fit for the renewal of pleasures, capable of digesting more quickly, of being hungry more frequently; and on the other hand, vary pleasures incessantly (never more than two hours at the same task), and from all these successive pleasures make one sole continual pleasure.

Here we have pleasure alone and triumphant, it reigns over all. Pleasure cannot be measured, it is not subject to quantification, its nature is the *overmuch* ("Our fault is not, as has been believed, to desire *overmuch*, but to desire *too little*"); it is itself the measurement: "feeling" depends on pleasure: "The privation of the sensual need degrades feeling" and "full satisfaction in material things is the only way to elevate the feelings": counter-Freudianism: "feeling" is not the sublimating transformation of a lack, but on the contrary the panic effusion of an acme of satiety. Pleasure overcomes Death (pleasures will be sensual in the afterlife), it is the Federator, what operates the solidarity of the living and the dead (the happiness of the defunct will begin only with that of the living, they having in a way to *await* the others: no happy dead so long as on earth the living are not happy; a view of a generosity, a "charity" that no religious eschatology has dared). Pleasure is, lastly, the everlasting principle of social organization: whether, negatively, it induces a condemnation of all society, however progressive, that neglects it (such as Owen's experiment at New Lamarck, denounced as "too severe" because the societaries went barefoot), whether, positively, pleasures are made *affairs of State* (*pleasures* and not *leisure:* this is what separates—fortunately—the Fourierist Harmony from the modern State, where the pious organization of leisure time corresponds to a relentless censure of pleasure); pleasure results, in fact, from a *calculation*, an operation that for Fourier is the highest form of social organization and mastery; this calculation is the same as that of all societal theory, whose practice is to transform work into pleasure (and not to suspend work for the sake of leisure time): the barrier that separates work from pleasure in Civilization crumbles, there is a paradigmatic fall, philosophical conversion of the unpleasant into the attractive (taxes will be paid "as readily as the busy mother sees to those foul but attractive duties her infant demands"), and pleasure itself becomes an exchange value, since Harmony recognizes and honors, by the name of *Angelicate*, collective prostitution: it is in a way the monad of energy which in its thrust and scope ensures the advance of society.

Since pleasure is the Unique, to reveal pleasure is itself a unique duty: Fourier stands alone against everyone (especially against all the Philosophers, against all Libraries), he alone is right, and being right is the desirable thing: "Is it not to be desired that I alone am right, against everyone?" From the Unique derives the incendiary character of pleasure: it burns, shocks, frightens to speak of it: how many are the statements about the mortal shock brought on by the overabrupt revelation of pleasure! What precautions, what preparations of writing! Fourier experiences a kind of prophylactic obligation for dispassion (poorly observed, by the way: he imagines his "calculations" are boring and that reassures him, whereas they are delightful); whence an incessant restraint of the discourse: "fearing to allow you to glimpse the vastness of these pleasures, I have only dissertated on . . . " etc.: Fourier's discourse is never just propaedeutic, so blazing with splendor is its object, its center: articulated on pleasure, the sectarian world is *dazzling*. ("If we could suddenly see this arranged Order, this work of God as it will be seen in its full functioning . . . it is not to be doubted that many of the Civilized would be struck dead by the violence of their ecstasy. The description [of the 8th Society] alone could inspire in many of them, the women in particular, an enthusiasm that would approach frenzy; it could render them indifferent to amusements, unsuited to the labors of Civilization" [*Théorie des quatre mouvements et des destinées générales*].)

The area of Need is *Politics*, the area of Desire is what Fourier calls

Domestics. Fourier has chosen Domestics over Politics, he has constructed a domestic utopia (but can a utopia be otherwise? can a utopia ever be political? isn't politics: *every language less one,* that of Desire? In May 1968, there was a proposal to one of the groups that were spontaneously formed at the Sorbonne to study *Domestic Utopia*—they were obviously thinking of Fourier; to which the reply was made that the expression was too "studied," *ergo* "bourgeois"; politics is what forecloses desire, save to achieve it in the form of neurosis: political neurosis or, more exactly: the neurosis of politicizing).

MONEY CREATES HAPPINESS

In Harmony, not only is wealth redeemed, but it is also magnified, it participates in a play of felicitous metaphors, lending the Fourierist demonstrations either the ceremonial brio of jewels ("the diamond star in a radiant triangle," the decoration of amatory sainthood, i.e., widespread prostitution) or the modesty of the sou ("20 sous to Racine for his tragedy *Phèdre*": multiplied, true, by all the cantons that have chosen to honor the poet); the operations connected with money are themselves motifs in a delectable game: in the game of love, that of the redemption (repurchase) of captives. Money participates in the brilliance of pleasure ("The senses cannot have their full indirect scope without the intervention of money"): money is desirable, as in the best days of civilized corruption, beyond which it perpetuates itself by virtue of a splendid and "incorruptible" fantasy.

Curiously detached from commerce, from exchange, from the economy, Fourierist money is an analogic (poetic) metal, the sum of happiness. Its exaltation is obviously a countermeasure: it is because all (civilized) Philosophy has condemned money that Fourier, destroyer of Philosophy and critic of Civilization, rehabilitates it: *the love of wealth* being a pejorative *topos* (at the price of a constant hypocrisy: Seneca, the man who possessed 80 million sesterces, declared that one must instantly rid oneself of wealth), Fourier turns contempt into praise: marriage, for example, is a ridiculous ceremony, save "when a man marries a very rich woman; then there is occasion for rejoicing"; everything, where money is concerned, seems to be conceived in view of this counterdiscourse, frankly scandalous in relation to the literary constraints of the admonition: "Search out the tangible wealth, gold, silver, precious metals, jewels, and objects of luxury despised by philosophers." (Since the coming of Harmony was imminent, Fourier counseled the Civilized to profit at once from the few goods of Civilization; this is the age-old theme (reversed, i.e., positive): Live to the full now, tomorrow is another day, it is futile to save, to keep, to transmit.)

However, this fact of discourse is not rhetorical: it has that energy of language that in writing makes the discourse waver, it forms the basis for the major transgression against which *everyone*—Christians, Marxists, Freudians—for whom money continues to be an accursed matter, fetish, excrement, has spoken out: who would dare defend money? There is *no discourse* with which money can be compatible. Because it is completely solitary (Fourier does not find on this point among his colleagues, "literary agitators," any co-maniac), Fourierist transgression lays bare the most secret area of the Civilized conscience. Fourier exalted money because for him the image of happiness was properly furnished with the mode of life of the wealthy: a shocking view today, in the eyes of the contestants themselves, who condemn all pleasure induced from the bourgeois model. We know that metonymy (contagion) is the purview of Error (of religion); Fourier's radical materialism stems from his constant, vigilant refusal of any metonymy. For him, money is not a conductor of sickness but merely the dry, pure element in a combinative to be reordered.

INVENTOR, NOT WRITER

To remake the world (including Nature), Fourier mobilized: an intolerance (for Civilization), a form (classification), a standard (pleasure), an imagination (the "scene"), a discourse (his book). All of which pretty well defines the action of the signifier—or the signifier in action. This action continually makes visible on the page a glaring lack, that of science and politics, that is, of the signified. What Fourier lacks (for that matter voluntarily) points in return to what we ourselves lack when we reject Fourier: to be ironic about Fourier is always—even from the scientific point of view—to censure the signifier. Political and Domestic (the name of Fourier's system), science and utopia, Marxism and Fourierism, are like two nets whose meshes are of different sizes. On the one hand, Fourier allows to pass through all the science that Marx collects and develops; from the political point of view (and above all since Marxism has given an indelible name to its shortcomings), Fourier is completely *off to one side*, unrealistic and immoral. However, the other, facing, net allows pleasure, which Fourier collects, to pass through. Desire and Need pass through, as though the two nets were alternatively superimposed, playing at topping hands. However, the relationship of Desire and Need is not *complementary* (were they fitted one into the other, everything would be perfect), but *supplementary*: each is the *excess* of the other. The *excess*: what does not pass through. For example, seen from today (i.e., *after* Marx), politics is a necessary purge; Fourier is the child who avoids the purge, who vomits it up.

The vomiting of politics is what Fourier calls Invention. Fourierist invention ("For me, I am an inventor, and not an orator") addresses the absolutely new, that about which nothing has yet been said. The rule of invention is a rule of refusal: to doubt absolutely (more than did Descartes, who, Fourier thought, never made more than a partial and misplaced use of doubt), to be in opposition with everything being done, to treat only of what has not been treated, to stand apart from "literary agitators," Book People, to preach what Opinion holds to be *impossible*. It is in sum for this purely structural reason (*old/new*) and through a simple constraint of the discourse (to speak only where there has not yet been speech) that Fourier is silent about politics. Fourierist invention is a fact of writing, a deploying of the signifier. These words should be understood in the modern sense: Fourier repudiates *the writer*, i.e., the certified manager of good writing, of literature, he who guarantees decorative union and thus the fundamental separation of substance and form; in calling himself an inventor ("I am not a writer, but an inventor"), he places himself at the limit of meaning, what we today call Text. Perhaps, following Fourier, we should henceforth call *inventor* (and not *writer* or *philosopher*) he who proposes new formulae and thereby invests, by fragments, *immensely and in detail*, the space of the signifier.

THE META-BOOK

The meta-book is the book that talks about the book. Fourier spends his time talking about his book in such a way that the work of Fourier that we read, indissolubly blending the two discourses, finally forms an autonomous book, in which form incessantly states form.

Fourier escorts his book a long way. For example, he imagines a dialogue between bookseller and client. Or elsewhere, knowing his book will be brought into court, he establishes a whole institutional system of defense (judge, jury, lawyers) and diffusion (the rich reader who wants to clear up some doubts for himself will call in the author to give lessons, as in sciences and the arts: "a kind of relationship without consequences, as with a merchant from whom one buys": after all, it is something like what a writer does today, going off on lecture tours to repeat words he has stated in writing).

As for the book itself, he posits rhetoric, i.e., the adaptation of types of discourse to types of readers: the *exposition* is addressed to the "Curious" (that is, to studious men); the *descriptions* (insights into the delights of private Destinies) are addressed to Voluptuaries or Sybarites; the *confirmation*, pointing up the blunders of the Civilized in thrall to the Spirit of Commerce, is addressed to the Critics. We can distinguish bits of *perspective* and bits of *theory*; there will be *insights* (abstract), *summaries* (half concrete), *elaborate dissertations* (bodies of doctrine). It follows that the book (a somewhat Mallarméan view) is not only pieced out, articulated (a banal structure), but, further, mobile, subject to a rule of *intermittent* actualization: the chapters will be inverted, the reading will be speeded up (expedited movement) or slowed down, according to the class of readers we want to reach; at its limit, the book is composed of nothing but jumps, full of holes like Fourier's manuscripts (especially *Le Nouveau Monde amoureux*), whose words are constantly missing, eaten by mice, and which therefore have the dimensions of an infinite cryptogram whose key will be given later.

This reminds us of reading in the Middle Ages, based on the work's legal discontinuity: not only was the ancient text (subject of medieval reading) *broken up* and its fragments then capable of being diversely combined, but, further, it was normal to conduct on any subject two independent and concurrent discourses, shamelessly put in a redundant relationship: Donatus's *ars minor* (abridged) and *ars major* (extended), the Modistes' *modi minores* and *modi majores*; this is the Fourierist opposition of insight-abridgment and dissertation. Yet the effect of this doubling up is twisted, paradoxical. We would expect that like any redundancy it would completely cover the subject, fill it out and end it (what can be added to a discourse that essentializes its purpose in résumé form and develops it in the form of an elaborate dissertation?). Now the contrary: the duplicity of the discourse produces an *interstice* through which the subject leaks away: Fourier spends his time in withholding the decisive utterance of his doctrine, concerning it he gives us only examples, seductions, "appetizers"; the message of his book is the announcement of a forthcoming message: *wait a little longer, I will tell you the essential very soon.* This method of writing could be called *counter-paralypse* (the paralypse is the rhetorical figure that consists in stating what one is not going to say and thus stating what one pretends not to say: *I shall not speak of* . . . followed by three pages). The paralypse implies the conviction that the indirect is a profitable mode of language; however, Fourier's countermarch, other than that it obviously translates the neurotic fear of failure (like that of a man afraid to jump—which Fourier, transferring to the reader, utters as the mortal fear of pleasure), points out the vacuum of language: caught in the toils of the meta-book, his book is *without subject*: its signified is dilatory, incessantly withdrawn further away: only the signifier remains, stretching out of sight, *in the book's future.*

THE OLD SHOE ABLAZE

Somewhere, Fourier speaks of "nocturnal furnishings." What do I care that this expression is the trace of an earth-shaking transport? I am carried away, dazzled, convinced by a kind of *charm* in the expression, which is its delight. Fourier is crammed full of these delights: no discourse was ever *happier.* With Fourier, the expression derives its felicity (and ours) from a kind of upheaval: it is excentric, displaced, it lives on its own, outside its context (the context, the semanticists' puzzler, has all the ingratitude of law: it reduces polysemy, clips the wings of the signifier: doesn't all poetry consist in liberating the word from its context? doesn't all philosophy consist in putting it back?). I do not resist these pleasures, they seem "true" to me: I have been "taken in" by the form.

Of what do these charms consist: of a counter-rhetoric, that is, a way of contriving figures by introducing into their code a "grain" (of sand, of madness). Let us here, once again (after many centuries of rhetorical classification), distinguish tropes (or simple metaboles) and figures (or ornaments that act upon an entire syntagm). Fourier's metaphorical vein is the path of truth; it supplies him with simple metaphors of a definitive precision ("from delivery vans we derive *fatigue dress*, the gray cloak and trousers"), it clarifies meaning (monological function), but at the same time and contradictorily it clarifies *ad infinitum* (poetical function), not only because the metaphor is drawn out, orchestrated ("Nocturnal furnishings will be considerably assorted and composed of our vivid and variously colored moons, next to which Phoebe will appear as what she is, a pale ghost, a sepulchral lamp, a Swiss cheese. One would have to have as bad taste as the Civilized do to admire this pallid mummy"), but further and above all because the Fourierist syntagm simultaneously produces a sonorous pleasure and a logical vertigo. Fourier's enumerations (for his verbal "delirium," based on calculation, is basically enumerative) always contain a preposterous point, a twist, a wrinkle: "the ostrich, the deer, the jerboa": why the jerboa, unless for the sonorous flourish at the end, for the sound? "And what can Hell in its fury invent worse than the rattlesnake, the bug, the legion of insects and reptiles, the sea monsters, poisons, plague, rabies, leprosy, venereal disease, gout, and all the morbiferous virulences?": the bug and the sea monster? Rattlesnakes and venereal disease? This string of nonsense derives a final savor from the *morbiferous*, plump and brilliant, more alimentary than funereal, both sensual and ridiculous (Molièresque), that crowns it; for the enumerative *cumulus*, in Fourier, is as abrupt as the movement of the head of an animal, a bird, a child who has heard "something else": "There will remain only the useful strains, like the whiting, the herring, the mackerel, sole, tuna, tortoise, in short, all those that do not attack swimmers": what charms us is not the content (after all, there is no question that these fish are beneficent), but a certain turn that makes the affirmation vibrate toward its opposite region: mischievously, through an irresistible metonymy seizing the words, a vague image becomes detached which, across the denegation, reveals the whiting and the mackerel in the process of attacking a swimmer (a properly surrealist mechanism). Paradoxical, for it is always in the name of the "concrete" that Civilization claims to teach the "mad," it is always through the "concrete" that Fourier becomes absurd and charming at once: the "concrete" is constructed in a scene, the substance calls upon the practices metonymically attached to it; the coffee break refers to the whole of civilized bureaucracy: "Isn't it shocking to see thirty-year-old athletes crouched over desks and transporting a cup of coffee with their hairy arms, as though there weren't women and children to attend to the finicky functioning of offices and households?" This vivid representation provokes laughter because it is out of proportion with its signified; hypotypose usually serves to illustrate intense and noble passions (Racine: "Imagine, Céphise . . . "); in Fourier, it is demonstrative; a kind of anacoluthon intervenes between the domestic detail of the example and the scope of the utopian plan. This is the secret of these amusing syntagms frequent in Fourier (in Sade too) that join in a single sentence a very ambitious thought and a very futile object; starting from the notion of the culinary contests in Harmony ("thesis meals"), Fourier continues to concoct strange and delicious, ridiculous and decisive syntagms, in which the tiny pastries (which he so liked, *mirlitons*) are associated with highly abstract terms ("the 44 systems of tiny pastries," "the batches of tiny pastries anathemized by the council," "the tiny pastries adopted by the Council of Babylon," etc.). Very precisely, this is what we can now call *paragrammatics:* namely, the superimpression (in dual hearing) of two languages that are ordinarily foreclosed to each other, the braid formed by two classes of words whose traditional hierarchy is not annulled, balanced, but—what is more subversive—disoriented: Council and System lend their nobility to tiny pastries; tiny pastries lend their futility to Anathema, a sudden contagion *deranges* the institution of language.

The transgression Fourier commits goes even further. The frivolous object he promotes to demonstrative rank is very often a *base* object. This conversion is justified because Harmony recuperates what Civilization disdains and transforms it into a delightful good ("If the Vaucluse phalanstery harvests 50,000 melons or watermelons, almost 10,000 of them will be set aside for its own consumption, 30,000 for exportation and 10,000 will be of inferior grade and divided among horses, cats, and for fertilizer": here we find that art of enumerative cadence we have just mentioned: Fourierist enumeration is always reverse conundrum: what is the difference between a horse, a cat, and fertilizer? None, for the function of all three is to reabsorb inferior-grade melons). Thus a poetics of rubbish is constructed, magnified by the societary economy (e.g., the old marinated chickens). Fourier knows this poetics well: he knows the emblems of rubbish, the old shoe, the rag, the sewer: an entire episode in *Le Nouveau Monde amoureux* hymns the exploits of the new crusaders, dealers in old shoes and boot cleaners, whose arrival at the Euphrates crossing is greeted by a magnificent display of fireworks "ending with an old shoe ablaze, beneath which is the legend: Long live pious cobblers."

Naturally, Fourier was aware of the "ridiculousness" of his demonstrative objects (of his rhetoric) ("This respectable convoy of cobblers marches after them in pomp and the finest boat is loaded with their baggage and this is the arm upon which they lean to win the palms of true glory. Bah! glory in old shoes, our Civilized will say; I was expecting this stupid response. And what fruit have they gleaned from the trophies of St. Louis and Bonaparte who have led immense armies vast distances only to have them drown in their trophies after having ravaged the country and been execrated by it?"); he was well aware that the bourgeoisie is devoted to the hierarchical division of languages, objects, and usages as strongly as it is to those of class, that nothing is worse in their eyes than the crime of lèse-language, and that one has only to join a noble (abstract) word and a base (denoting a sensual or repulsive object) term to be sure of loosing their zeal as proprietors (of "fine" language); he knew that people made fun of his faithful melons, of the triumph of his leathery fowl, of the English debt paid off in hens' eggs. Yet he assumed the incongruity of his demonstrations with a certain martyred air (the martyrdom of the inventor). Thus to the paragrammaticism of his examples (interweaving two exclusive languages, one noble, one outcast), must be added a final, infinitely dizzier, ambiguity: that of their utterance. Where is Fourier? in the invention of the example (old marinated chickens)? in the indignation he feels at the laughter of others? In our reading, which simultaneously encompasses the ridicule and his defense? The loss of the subject in the writing has never been more complete (the subject becoming totally irreparable) than in these utterances where the disconnection of the utterance occurs *ad infinitum*, without a brake, on the model of the game of topping hands or the game of "rock, scissors, paper": texts whose "ridiculousness" or "stupidity" is based on no certain utterance and over which, consequently, the reader can never gain any advantage (Fourier, Flaubert). "God," Fourier says, "displays a subtle and judicious irony in creating certain products that are enigmatic in quality, like the melon, made for the innocent mystification of banquets ill suited to divine methods, without in any way deceiving the gastronomes who cleave to the divine or societary diet" [allusion to the difficulty that exists in choosing a good melon, "such a perfidious fruit for the Civilized"]. "I do not mean to say that God created the melon solely for the sake of this jest, but it is part of that fruit's many uses. Irony is never overlooked in the calculations of nature. . . . The melon has among its properties that of *ironic harmony*" (in short, the melon is an element of a *writing*). What reader can hope to *dominate* such an utterance—adopt it as a laughable or a critical object, *dictate to it*, in a word?—in the name of *what other language?*

HIEROGLYPHICS

Fourier wants to decipher the world in order to remake it (for how remake it without deciphering it?).

Fourierist deciphering starts from the most difficult of situations, which is not so much the latency of signs as their content. There is a saying of Voltaire that Fourier refers to in this regard: "But what obscure night still enveileth nature?"; now, in this veil finally there is less the notion of mask than of a cloth. Once again, the task of the logothete, of the founder of language, is an endless cutting up of the text: the primary operation is to "grab" the cloth in order then to pull on it (to pull it off).

We must therefore in some measure make a distinction between deciphering and cutting up. Deciphering refers to a pregnant depth, to an area of relationships, to a distribution. In Fourier, deciphering is postulated, but in a completely minor way: it concerns the lies and pretenses of the Civilized classes: thus the "secret principles" of the bourgeois "who begins by debiting a hundred lies in his shop by virtue of the principles of free trade. Hence a bourgeois goes to hear Mass and returns to debit three to four hundred lies, to trick and steal from thirty or so buyers in line with the secret principle of businessmen: we are not working for glory, we want money." Quite another thing, and of quite another order of importance, is cutting up—or systematization (putting to a system); this reading, an essential part of the Fourierist task, concerns all of Nature (societies, sentiments, forms, natural kingdoms) as it represents the total space of Harmony—Fourier's man being totally incorporated into the universe, including the stars; this is no longer a denunciatory, reductive reading (limited to the moral falsehoods of the bourgeoisie), but an exalting, integrating, restorative reading, extended to the plethora of universal forms.

Is the "real" the object of this second reading? We are accustomed to considering the "real" and the residue as identical: the "unreal," the fantasmatic, the ideological, the verbal, the proliferating, in short, the "marvelous," may conceal from us the "real," rational, infrastructural, schematic; from real to unreal there may be the (self-seeking) production of a screen of arabesques, whereas from unreal to real there may be critical reduction, an alethic, scientific movement, as though the real were at once more meager and more essential than the superstructions with which we have covered it. Obviously, Fourier is working on a conceptual material whose constitution denies this contrast and which is that of the *marvelous real*. This marvelous real is contrasted with the marvelous ideal of novels; it corresponds to what we might call, contrasting it directly with the novel, the novelesque. This marvelous real very precisely is the signifier, or if one prefers, "reality," characterized, relative to the scientific real, by its fantasmatic train. Now, the category under which this novelesque begins to be read is the *hieroglyphic*, different from the symbol as the signifier can be from the full, mystified sign.

The hieroglyph (the theory of which is set forth principally in the *Théorie des quatre mouvements*), postulates a formal and arbitrary correspondence (it depends on Fourier's free will: it is an idiolectal concept) between the various realms of the universe, for example between forms (circle, ellipse, parabola, hyperbola), colors, musical notes, passions (friendship, love, parental, ambition), the races of animals, the stars, and the periods of societal phylogenesis. The arbitrary obviously resides in the attribution: why is the ellipse the geometric hieroglyph for love? the parabola for parenthood? Yet this arbitrary is just as relative as is that of linguistic signs: we believe there to be an arbitrary correspondence between the signifier /pear tree/ and the signified "pear tree," between some Melanesian tribe and its totem (bear, god), because we spontaneously (i.e., by virtue of historical, ideological determinations) imagine the world in substitute, paradigmatic, analogical terms, and not in serial, associative, homological—in short, poetic—terms. Fourier has this second imagination; for him, the basis of meaning is not substitution, equivalence, but the proportional series; just as the signifier /pear tree/ or the signifier *bear* is *relatively* motivated if taken in the series *pear tree–plum tree–apple tree* or in the series *bear–dog–tiger*, so Fourierist hieroglyphics, detached from any univocity, accede to language, i.e., to a system both conventional and reasonable. The hieroglyphic, in fact, implies a complete theory of meaning (whereas only too often, relying on the presence of the dictionary, we reduce meaning to a substitution): hieroglyphics, says Fourier, can be explained in three ways: (1) *by contrast* (beehive/wasp's nest, elephant/rhinoceros): this is the paradigm: the beehive is *marked* with productivity, a characteristic absent in the wasp's nest; the elephant is marked with lengthy defenses, a trait reduced to a short horn in the rhinoceros; (2) *by alliance* (the dog and the sheep, the pig and the truffle, the donkey and the thistle): this is the syntagm, metonymy: these elements usually go together; (3) lastly, *by progression* (branches: giraffe, stag, buck, roebuck, reindeer, etc.): this, foreign to linguistic classification, is the *series*, a kind of extended paradigm, consisting of differences and proximities, out of which Fourier creates the very principle of societal organization, which basically consists in putting in a phalanstery contrasting groups of individuals, each group linked by an affinity: for example, the sectine of Flowerlets, amateurs of small, varied flowers, contrasted to but coexisting with the Rosist sectine: it might be said that the series is an actualized, syntagmatized paradigm, by virtue of the number of its terms, not only *livable* (whereas the semantic paradigm is subject to the law of rival, inexpiable opposites, which cannot cohabit), but even *felicitous*. Progression (the series) is undoubtedly what Fourier adds to meaning (as linguists describe it for us), and consequently, what frustrates its arbitrary nature. Why, for example, in Association, is the giraffe the hieroglyph for Truth? A farfetched notion and assuredly unjustifiable if we try, desperately, to discover some affinitive or even contrasting trait shared by Truth and this huge mammiferous ungulant. The explanation is that the giraffe is caught up in a system of homologies: Association having the beaver as its practical hieroglyph (because of its associative and constructive abilities) and the peacock as its visual hieroglyph (because of the spread of its nuances), we need, across from but yet in the same series, that of animals, a properly unfunctional element, a kind of neuter, a zero degree of zoological symbolism: this is the giraffe, as useless as the Truth is in Civilization; whence a counter-giraffe (complex term of contrast): this is the Reindeer, from which we derive every imaginable service (in the societary order there will be a new animal created, even more ecumenical than the Reindeer: the Anti-Giraffe).

So replaced in the history of the sign, the Fourierist construction posits the rights of a baroque semantics, i.e., open to the proliferation of the signifier, infinite and yet structured.

LIBERAL?

The combination of differences implies the respecting of the individuation of each term: there is no attempt to redress, to correct, to annul taste, whatever it may be (however "bizarre" it may be); quite the contrary, it is affirmed, it is emphasized, it is recognized, it is legalized, it is reinforced by associating everyone who wishes to indulge it: taste being thus incorporated, it is allowed to act in opposition to other tastes at once affinitive and different: a competitive game (of intrigue, but *coded*) is initiated between the amateurs of bergamot pears and the amateurs of butter pears: to the satisfaction of a simple taste (a liking for pears) is then added the exercise of other, formal, combinative passions: for example, *cabalistics*, or the passion for intrigues, and *butterfly*, if there are unstable Harmonians who take pleasure in switching from the bergamot pear to the butter pear.

From this semantic construction of the world it follows that, in Fourier's eyes, "association" is not a "humanist" principle: it is not a matter of bringing together everyone with the same mania ("co-maniacs") so that they can be comfortable together and can enchant each other by narcissistically gazing at one another; on the contrary, it is a matter of associating to combine, to contrast. The Fourierist coexistence of passions is not based on a liberal principle. There is no noble demand to "understand," to "admit" the passions of others (or to ignore them, indeed). The goal of Harmony is neither to further the conflict (by associating through similitude), nor to reduce it (by sublimating, sweetening, or normalizing the passions), nor yet to transcend it (by "understanding" the other person), but to exploit it for the greatest pleasure of all and without hindrance to anyone. How? By playing at it: by making a text of the conflictual.

PASSIONS

Passion (character, taste, mania) is the irreducible unity of the Fourierist combinative, the absolute grapheme of the utopian text. Passion is *natural* (nothing to be corrected about it, unless to produce a *contra-naturam*, which is what occurs in Civilization). Passion is *clean* (its being is pure, strong, shapely: only Civilized philosophy advises flaccid, apathetic passions, controls, and compromises). Passion is *happy* ("Happiness . . . consists in having many passions and ample means to satisfy them" [*Théorie des quatre mouvements*]).

Passion is not the idealized form of feeling, mania is not the monstrous form of passion. Mania (and even whim) is the very being of passion, the unit from which Attraction (attractive and attracting) is determined. Passion is neither deformable, nor transformable, nor reducible, nor measurable, nor substitutable: it is not a force, it is a number: there can be neither decomposition nor amalgamation of this happy, frank, natural monad, but only combination, up to the reunion of the *integral soul*, the trans-individual body of 1,620 characters.

THE TREE OF HAPPINESS

The passions (810 for each sex) spring, like the branches of a tree (the classifier's fetish tree) from three main trunks: *lustful–ness*, which includes the passions of feeling (one for each of the five senses), *group-ness* (four basic passions: honor, friendship, love and family), and *serial-ness* (three distributive passions). The entire combinative stems from these twelve passions (whose pre-eminence is not moral, merely structural).

The first nine passions are derived from classical psychology, but the latter, formal, three are a Fourierist invention. The Dissident (or Cabalistic) is a reflective enthusiasm, a passion for intrigue, a calculating mania, an art of exploiting differences, rivalries, conflicts (here there is no difficulty in recognizing the paranoid texture); it is the delight of courtesans, women, and philosophers (intellectuals), which is why it can also be called the Speculative. The Composite (actually less well defined than its fellows) is the passion for excess, for (sensual or sublime) exaltation, for multiplication; it can be called the Romantic. The Variating (or Alternating or Butterfly) is a need for periodic variety (changing occupation or pleasure every two hours); we might say that it is the disposition of the subject who does not devote himself to the "good object" in a stable manner: a passion whose mythical prototype is Don Juan: individuals who constantly change occupation, manias, affections, desires, "cruisers" who are incorrigible, unfaithful, renegade, subject to "moods," etc.: a passion disdained in Civilization, but one Fourier places very high: the one that permits ranging through many passions at once, and like an agile hand on a multiple keyboard, creating an *harmonious* (appropriately put) vibration throughout the integral soul; an agent of universal transition, it animates that type of happiness that is attributed to Parisian sybarites, *the art of living well and fast, the variety and interconnection of pleasures,* rapidity of movement (we recall that for Fourier the mode of life of the possessing class is the very model of happiness).

These three passions are formal: included in the classification, they ensure its functioning ("mechanics"), or more precisely still: its game. If we compare the aggregate of the passions to a deck of cards or a chess set (as did Fourier), the three distributive passions are in sum the rules of this game; they state how to conciliate, balance, set in motion, and permit the transformation of the other passions, each of which would be nugatory in isolation, into a series of "brilliant and countless combinations." These rules of the game (these formal, distributive passions) are precisely the ones society rejects: they produce (the very sign of their excellence) "the characters accused of corruption, called libertines, profligates, etc.": as in Sade, it is syntax and syntax alone that produces the supreme immorality.

Thus the twelve radical passions (like the twelve notes in the scale). Naturally, there is a thirteenth (every good classifier knows he must have a supernumber in his chart and that he must make adjustments for the outcome of his system), which is the very trunk of the tree of passions: Unity-ness (or Harmonism). Unity-ness is the passion for unity, "the individual's tendency to reconcile his happiness with that of everything around him, and with every human type"; this supplementary passion produces the Originals, people who appear to be ill at ease in this world and who cannot accommodate themselves to the ways of Civilization; it is thus the passion of Fourier himself. Unity-ness is in no way a moral, recommendable passion (*love each other, unite with each other*), since the societal unit is a combinative, a structural game of differences; Unity-ness is in direct contrast to simplism, the vice of the Civilized spirit, "the use of the mind without the marvelous, or of the marvelous without the mind"; simplism "made Newton miss out on the discovery of the system of nature and Bonaparte on the conquest of the world." Simplism (or totalitarianism, or monologism) would today be either the censure of Need or the censure of Desire; which, in Harmony (in Utopia), would be answered by the combined science of one and the other.

NUMBERS

Fourier's authority, the Reference, the Citation, the Science, the Anterior Discourse that enables him to speak and to have personal authority concerning the "carelessness of 25 learned centuries that failed to conceive of it," is *calculation* (as for us today it is formalization). This calculation need not be extensive or complicated: it is a *petty calculation*. Why petty? Because although important (the happiness of mankind depends upon it), this calculation is simple. Further, pettiness includes the notion of a certain affectionate complacence: Fourier's petty calculation is the simple lever that opens up the fantasmagory of adorable detail.

Everything occurs as though Fourier were searching for the very notion of detail, as though he had found it in a numeration or frantic subdivision of every object that came into his mind, as though this object instantly released in him a number or a classification: it is like a conditioned reflex that comes into play apropos a whole crazy total: "In Rome in the time of Varro there were 278 contradictory opinions concerning true happiness." A question of illicit liaisons (in Civilization)? They exist for Fourier only if he enumerates them: "During the twelve years of bachelorhood, man forms on the average 12 liaisons of illicit love, around 6 of fornication and 6 adulterous, etc." Everything is a pretext for numbering, from the age of the world (80,000 years) to the number of characters in it (1,620).

The Fourierist number is not rounded off, and in fact this is what gives it its insanity (a minor sociological problem: why does our society consider a decimal number "normal" and an intradecimal number "irrational"? At what point does normality occur?). This insanity is often justified by the even more insane reasons Fourier gives in denying the arbitrary constants in his accounts, or, which is even crazier still, displaces this arbitrary by justifying not the number given, but the standard for it: the height of societary man will be 84 thumbs or 7 feet; why? we will never know, but the unit of measurement is pompously justified: "I am not being arbitrary in indicating the foot of the King of Paris as a natural measurement; it has this property because it is equal to the 32nd part of the water level in suction pumps" (here we find that sudden twisting of the syntagm, the anacoluthon, the audacious metonymy that makes Fourier's "charm": in the space of a few words, we have suction pumps mingled with the height of societary man). The number exalts, it is an operator of glory, as is the triangular number of the Trinity in the Jesuit mode, not because it enlarges (which would destroy the fascination with detail), but because it demultiplies: "Consequently, if we divide by 810 the number of 36 million which the population of France has attained, we will find that in this Empire there exist 45,000 individuals capable of equaling Homer, 45,000 capable of equaling Demosthenes, etc." Fourier is like a child (or an adult: the author of these lines, never having studied mathematics, has been very late in experiencing this feeling) discovering with enchantment the exorbitant power of the combinatory analysis or geometrical progression. In the end, the number itself is not needed for this exaltation; one need only subdivide a class in order triumphantly to achieve this paradox: detail (literally: *minutia*) magnifies, like joy. It is a fury of expansion, of possession, and, in a word, of orgasm, by number, by classification: scarcely does an object appear than Fourier taxonomizes (we are tempted to say: sodomizes) it: is the husband unhappy in Civilized marriage? It is *immediately* for eight reasons (risk of unhappiness, expense, vigilance, monotony, sterility, widowhood, union, ignorance of his wife's infidelity). Does the word "harem" arise *currente calamo* into the sentence? *Immediately*, there are three classes of odalisks: honest women, petites bourgeoises, and courtesans. What happens to women over eighteen years of age in Harmony? nothing, save to be *classified: Wives* (themselves subdivided into *constant, doubtful,* and *unfaithful*), *Misses* or *Demi-dames* (they change protectors, but successively, having only one at a time), and *Galantes* (both further subdivided); for both terms in the series, two taxonomic embellishments: *Damsels* and *Independents*. Wealth? there are not only Rich and Poor, there are: the poor, those who scrape by, those who have just enough, the comfortable, and the rich. Of course, for anyone with the contrary mania, tolerant neither of number nor of classification nor of system (numerous in Civilization, jealous of "spontaneity," of "life," of "imagination," etc.), the Fourierist Harmony would be hell itself: at thesis meals (contest meals), every course would have two labels, written in large letters, visible from afar and set on pivots, in both directions, "so that one can be read from across the table and the other the length of the table" (the present author has experienced a minor hell of this sort—but the system came from a French brain: in the American college where he took his meals, in order that the students might converse profitably while eating, and that they might benefit equally from the professor's lively discourse, each diner was supposed to advance one place at each meal, moving closer to the professorial sun, "in a clockwise direction," as the rule stated; there is little need to say that no "conversation" resulted from this astral movement).

Perhaps the *imagination of detail* is what specifically defines Utopia (opposed to political science); this would be logical, since detail is fantasmatic and thereby achieves the very pleasure of Desire. In Fourier, the number is rarely statistical (designed to assert averages, probabilities); it is, through the apparent finesse of its precision, essentially quantitative. Nuance, the game being stalked in this taxonomic hunting expedition, is a guarantee of pleasure (of fulfillment), since it determines a *just* combinative (knowing with whom to group ourselves in order to achieve complementarity with our own differences). Harmony must thus admit the operators of nuances, just as a tapestry workshop has specialists who are detailed to knot the threads. These nuance makers are: either operations (in Fourierist erotics, the "simple salute" is a preambular bacchanalia, a scrimmage enabling the partners to test each other before making a choice; during it, "trial caresses or reconnoiterings of the terrain" are practiced; this takes about eight minutes), or they are agents: there are: either "confessors" (these confessors do not hear any Fault: they "psychoanalyze" in order to elicit sympathies, often hidden by the subjects' appearance and ignorance: they are the decipherers of complementary nuances) or "dissolvents" (dissolvents, introjected into a group that has not yet found its just combinative, its "harmony," produce tremendous effects on it: they undo erroneous couplings by revealing to each his passions, they are transferers, mutators: thus lesbians and pederasts, who, thrown into the scrimmage, first accost the "champions of their own ilk," "recognize their own kind and sunder a good number of couples whom chance had united").

Nuance, the acme of number and of classification, has the *integral soul* as its total field, a human space defined by its amplitude, since it is the combinative dimension within which meaning is possible; no man is self-sufficient, no one his own integral soul: we need 810 characters of both sexes, or 1,620, to which are added the omnititles (the complex degree of contrasts) and the infinitesimal nuances of passion. The integral soul, a tapestry in which each nuance finds utterance, is the great sentence being sung by the universe: it is, in sum, the Language of which each of us is but a word. The Language is immortal: "At the era of the planet's death, its great soul, and consequently ours, inherent in it, will pass on to another, new sphere, to a planet which will be implaned, concentrated, saturated."

THE NECTARINE

In any classification of Fourier, there is always a portion that is reserved. This portion has various names: passage, composite, transition, neuter, triviality, ambiguity (we might call it: *supplement*); naturally, it has a number: it is the ⅛ of any collection. First, this ⅛ has a function, familiar to scientists: it is the legal margin of error. ("Calculations of Attraction and Social Mobility are all subject to the ⅛ exception . . . it will always be understood.") Only, since in Fourier it is always a question of the *calculation of happiness*, error is at once ethical: when (abhorrent) Civilization "makes a mistake" (in its own system), it produces happiness: in Civilization, the ⅛ thus represents happy people. It is easy from this example to see that for Fourier the ⅛ portion does not derive from a liberal or statistical concession, from the vague recognition of a possible *deviation*, from a "human" failing in the system (to be taken philosophically); quite the contrary, it is a question of an important structural function, of a code constraint. Which one?

As a classifier (a taxonomist), what Fourier needs most are passages, special terms that permit making transitions (meshing) from one class to another ("Transitions are to passionate equilibrium what bolts and joints are to a framework"), the kind of lubricator the combinatory apparatus must use so as not to creak; the reserved portion is thus that of Transitions or Neuters (the neuter is what comes *between* the mark and the non-mark, this sort of buffer, damper, whose role is to muffle, to soften, to fluidify the semantic *tick-tock*, that metronome-like noise the paradigmatic alternative obsessively produces: *yes/no, yes/no, yes/no*, etc.). The nectarine, which is one of these Transitions, damps the opposition of prune and peach, as the quince damps that of pear and apple: they belong to the ⅛ of fruits. This portion (⅛) is shocking because it is contradictory: it is the class in which everything that attempts to escape classification is swallowed up; however, this portion is also superior: the space of the Neuter, of the *supplement of classification*, it joins realms, passions, characters; the art of employing Transitions is the major art of Harmonian calculation: the neuter principle is controlled by mathematics, the pure language of the combinative, of the composed, the very badge of the *game*.

There are ambiguities in every series: the sensitive, the bat, the flying fish, the amphibians, the zoophytes, sapphism, pederasty, incest, Chinese society (half barbaric, half civilized, with harems and courts of law and etiquette), lime (fire and water), the nervous system (body and soul), twilights, coffee (ignominiously ignored at Mocha for 4,000 years, then suddenly the subject of a mercantile craze, passing from abjection to the highest rank), children (the third passionate sex, neither men nor women). Transition (mixed, Ambiguous, Neuter) is everything that is contrary duplicity, junction of extremes, and hence it takes as its emblematic form the ellipse, which has a double focus.

In Harmony, Transitions have a beneficent role; for example, they prevent monotony in love, despotism in politics: the distributive passions (composite, cabalistic, and butterfly) have a transitional role (they "mesh," ensure changes of "objects"); Fourier always reasoned contrariwise, what is beneficent in Harmony necessarily proceeds from what is discredited or rejected in Civilization: thus Transitions are "trivialities," ignored by civilized scholars as unworthy subjects: the bat, the albino, ugly ambiguous race, the taste for feathered fowl. The prime example of Trivial Transition is Death: transition ascending between Harmonian life and the happiness of the other life (sensual happiness), it "will shed all its odiousness when philosophy deigns to consent to study the transitions it proscribes as trivial." Everything rejected in Civilization, from pederasty to Death, has in Harmony a value that is eminent (but not pre-eminent: nothing dominates anything else, everything combines, meshes, alternates, revolves). This functional *justness* (this *justice*) is ensured by the ⅛ error. Thus, the *Neuter* is in opposition to the *Median*; the latter is a quantitative, not a structural, notion; it is the amount of the oppression to which the large number subjects the small number; caught in a statistical calculation, the intermediate swells up and engulfs the system (thus the *middle* class): the neuter, on the other hand, is a purely qualitative, structural notion; it is what *confuses* meaning, the norm, normality. To enjoy the *neuter* is perforce to be disgusted by the *average*.

SYSTEM/SYSTEMATICS

"that the real content of these systems is hardly to be found in their systematic form is best proved by the orthodox Fourierists . . . who, despite their orthodoxy, are the exact antipodes of Fourier: doctrinaire bourgeois."
                                        —MARX AND ENGELS, *German Ideology*

Fourier perhaps enables us to restate the following opposition (which we lately stated by distinguishing the novelistic from the novel, poetry from the poem, the essay from the dissertation, the writing from the style, production from the product, structuration from the structure [in *S/Z*]): the *system* is a body of doctrine within which the elements (principles, facts, consequences) develop logically, i.e., from the point of view of the discourse, rhetorically. The system being a closed (or monosemic) one, it is always theological, dogmatic; it is nourished by illusions: an illusion of transparency (the language employed to express it is purportedly purely instrumental, it is not a writing) and an illusion of reality (the goal of the system is to be *applied*, i.e., that it leave the language in order to found a reality that is incorrectly defined as the exteriority of language); it is a strictly paranoid insanity whose path of transmission is insistence, repetition, cathechism, orthodoxy. Fourier's work does not constitute a *system*; only when we have tried to "realize" this work (in phalansteries) has it become, retrospectively, a "system" doomed to instant fiasco; system, in the terminology of Marx and Engels, is the "systematic form," i.e., pure ideology, ideological reflection; *systematics* is the play of the system; it is language that is open, infinite, free from any referential illusion (pretension); its mode of appearance, its constituency, is not "development" but pulverization, dissemination (the gold dust of the signifier); it is a discourse without "object" (it only speaks of a thing obliquely, by approaching it indirectly:

thus Civilization in Fourier) and without "subject" (in writing, the author does not allow himself to be involved in the imaginary subject, for he "performs" his enunciatory role in such a manner that we cannot decide whether it is serious or parody). It is a vast madness which does not end, but which permutates. In contrast to the system, monological, systematics is dialogical (it is the operation of ambiguities, it does not suffer contradictions); it is a writing, it has the latter's eternity (the perpetual permutation of meanings throughout History); systematics is not concerned with application (save as purist imagining, a theater of the discourse), but with transmission, (significant) circulation; further, it is transmittable only on condition it is *deformed* (by the reader); in the terminology of Marx and Engels, systematics would be the *real contents* (of Fourier). Here, we are not explaining Fourier's system (that portion of his systematics that plays with the system in an image-making way), we are talking solely about the several sites in his discourse that belong to systematics.

(Fourier puts the system to flight—cuts it adrift—by two operations: first, by incessantly delaying the definitive exposé until later: the doctrine is simultaneously highhanded and dilatory; next, by inscribing the system in the systematics, as dubious parody, shadow, game. For example, Fourier attacks the civilized [repressive] "system," he calls for an integral freedom [of tastes, passions, manias, whims]; thus, we would expect a spontaneistic philosophy, but we get quite the opposite: a wild system, whose very excess, whose fantastic tension, goes beyond system and attains systematics, i.e., writing: liberty is never the opposite of order, it is *order paragrammatized:* the writing must simultaneously mobilize an image and its opposite.)

THE PARTY

What is a "party"? (1) *a partitioning*, isolating one group from another, (2) an orgy, or *partouze*, as we say in French, wherein the participants are linked erotically, and (3) a hand, or *partie*, the regulated moment in a game, a collective diversion. In Sade, in Fourier, the party, the highest form of societary or Sadian happiness, has this threefold character: it is a worldly ceremony, an erotic practice, a social act.

Fourierist life is one immense party. At three-thirty in the morning on the summer solstice (little sleep is needed in Harmony), societary man is ready for the world: engaged in a succession of "roles" (each one being the naked affirmation of a passion) and subject to the combinative (meshing) rules of these roles: this very exactly is the definition of mundanity, which functions like a language: the mundane man is someone who spends his time *citing* (and in *weaving* what he cites). The citations Fourier employs in blissfully describing the worldly life of societary man are drawn paradoxically (paragrammatically) from the repressive lexicons of the Civilized regime: the Church, State, Army, Stock Exchange, Salons, the penitentiary

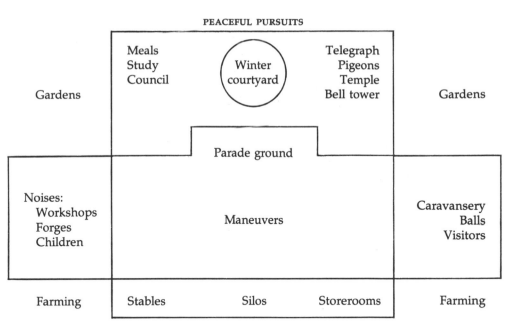

There are three stories, children on mezzanine

colony, and Scouting furnish the Fourierist party with its most felicitous images. (Innumerable locutions, such as: "Saints and Patrons beatified and canonized in the council of the Spheric Hierarchy." "Every pivotal sin is liable to a sevenfold reparation"—true, that this reparation is hardly penitential, consisting as it does of making love seven times with seven different people. "The Official Journal of Gastronomic Transactions of the Army of the Euphrates," etc. [*Le Nouveau Monde amoureux*].)

All mundanity is dissociative: it is a matter of isolating oneself in order to retreat and to trace out the area within which the rules of the game can function. The Fourierist party has two traditional enclosures, that of time and that of place.

The topography of the phalanstery traces an original site which is broadly that of palaces, monasteries, manors, and great blocks of buildings in which are mingled an organization of the building and an organization of territory, so that (a very modern viewpoint) architecture and urbanism reciprocally withdraw in favor of an overall science of human space, the primary characteristic of which is no longer protection, but movement: the phalanstery is a retreat within which one moves (however, trips are taken outside the phalanstery: great mass excursions, ambulatory "parties"). Obviously, this space is functionalized, as shown in the following reconstruction (very approximate, since Fourierist discourse, like all writing, is irreducible).

The greatest concern of this organization is communication. Like the adolescent groups who live together during their summer vacations with constant pleasure and regretfully return home in the evenings, the societaries have only a temporary place for undressing and sleeping, warmed only by a brazier. In contrast, Fourier describes with great predilection and insistence the covered, heated, ventilated galleries, sanded basements, and corridors raised on columns that connect the palaces or manors of neighboring Tribes. A private place is allowed solely for lovemaking, and even this is only so that the unions made during the bacchanalias, get-togethers, or meetings for the purpose of selecting a companion, can be consummated—or "sealed."

Corresponding to topographical delimitation is this apparatus for temporal enclosure called *timing*; since a passion (for investments, for objects) must be changed every two hours, the optimal time is a divided time (the function of *timing* is to demultiply duration, to superproduce time and thereby to augment life power: "The day will never be long enough for the intrigues and merry reunions produced by the new order": we might be listening to an adolescent who, on vacation, has discovered his "group"); for example, in the combined Order there are five meals (at 5 A.M., the matutinal or "eye opener," at 8 A.M., lunch, dinner at 1, snack at 6, and supper at 9), and two collations (at 10 and 4): reminiscent of the schedule in an old-fashioned sanatorium. Harmonian man—physiologically regenerated by a diet of happiness—sleeps only from 11 in the evening to 3:30 in the morning; he never makes love at night, a detestable Civilized habit.

Love (erotic happiness, including the sentimental *eros*) is the main business of the long Harmonian day: "In Harmony, where no one is poor and where everyone is acceptable for lovemaking until a very advanced age, everyone devotes a set part of the day to this passion and love thus becomes a principal business: it has its code, its tribunals [we already know that the penalties consist in new loves], its court, and its institutions:" Like the Sadian *eros*, Fourier's is a classifier, a distributor: the population is divided into amorous classes. In Sade, there are storytellers, fuckers, etc.; in Fourier there are troops of Vestals, Youths and Favorites of both sexes, Genitors, etc. From Sade to Fourier, only the *ethos* of the discourse changes: here jubilant, there euphoric. For the erotic fantasy remains the same; it is that of *availability:* that every love demand *at once* find a subject-object to be *at its disposal*, either by constraint or by association; this is the province of the ideal orgy, or in French, *partouze*, a fantasmatic site, contra-civilized, where no one refuses himself to anyone, the purpose not being to multiply partners (not a quantitative problem!) but to abolish the wound of denial; the abundance of erotic material, precisely because it is a matter of Desire and not of Need, is not intended to constitute a "consumer society" of love, but, paradox, truly utopian scandal, to make Desire function in its contradiction, namely: to fulfill *perpetually* (*perpetually* meaning simultaneously *always* and *never* fulfilled; or: *never and always:* that depends on the degree of enthusiasm or bitterness in which the fantasy is concluded). This is the sense of the supreme amorous institution of Fourierist society: the Angelicate (another ecclesiastical citation): in Harmony, the Angelicate is this handsome couple who, through "philanthropy," properly give themselves to any man or woman desiring them (including the deformed). The Angelicate has an additional function, not philanthropic but mediatory: it *conducts* desire: as though, left on his own, every man were incapable of knowing whom to desire, as though he were blind, powerless to invent his desire, as though it were always up to others to show us *where the desirable is* (clearly not the principal function of so-called erotic representations in mass culture: conduction, not substitution); the Angelic couple is the apex of the amorous triangle: it is the vanishing point without which there can be no erotic *perspective*. (Can a more Sadian classification be imagined than the following: the Angelicate is organized along three degrees of novitiate: (1) *cherubic* (the postulant must sacrifice an entire day to each member of the venerable choir); (2) *seraphic* (the sacrifice last several days and is offered to both sexes); (3) *sayidic* (the sacrifice is offered up to a chorus of patriarchs: probably even older!).)

The party, a ritual common in Sade and in Fourier, has as its "proof" a fact of the discourse which is to be found in both: the amorous practice cannot be uttered save in the form of a "scene," a "scenario," a "tableau vivant" (a strictly fantasmatic disposition): the Sadian "séances" which often even have a "setting": gardens, woods, colored veils, garlands of flowers, in Fourier the Cnidian novel. In fact, they are part of the very force of fantasy, of the destructive power it has over cultural models by using them *disrespectfully*, of "representing" the erotic scene in the most insipid colors and with the "proper" tone of petit-bourgeois art: Sade's most shocking scenes, Fourier's pro-Sapphic ravings, occur in a Folies-Bergères setting: a carnival-like conjunction of transgression and opera, the sober site of mad acts, where the *subject is swallowed up in its culture*, a decision that simultaneously sweeps away art and sex, denies transgression itself any gravity, prohibits its ritualization (by providing for widespread prostitution the stage setting of *The Pearl Fishers*), the headlong flight of the signified across the shifting of aesthetics or sex, which ordinary language tries to achieve in its fashion when it speaks (in French) of *ballets roses* and *ballets bleus* ("performances" by girls [pink] or boys [blue] "danced" before older men).

COMPOTES

An Eastern book says there is no better remedy for thirst than a little cold compote, well sweetened, followed by a few swallows of cool water. Fourier would have been doubly enchanted at this advice: first, because of the conjunction of solid and liquid (the exemplar of a Transition, a Mix, a Neuter, a Passage, a Twilight); next, because of its promotion of compotes to the status of a philosophical food (the *Compound*, not the Simple, slakes thirst, desire).

Harmony will be sweet. Why? For many reasons, constructed in superdetermination (the likely index of a fantasy). First because sugar is an *anti-bread*; since bread is a mystic object of Civilization, the symbol of labor and bitterness, the emblem of Need, Harmony will invert the use of bread and turn it into the colophon of Desire; bread will become a luxury food ("one of the most costly and most husbanded victuals"); in contrast, sugar will become wheat. ("Then Africa will cheaply furnish the commodities of its hot climate, cane sugar, which, pound for pound, will have the value of wheat, when it is cultivated by 70 million Africans and all the peoples of the Torrid Zone" [*Théorie de L'unité universelle*].) Next, because sugar, hereby promoted, mixed with fruit in a compote, will form the bread of Harmony, the basic nourishment of those who have become wealthy and happy. In a way, all Harmony has grown out of Fourier's taste for compotes, as a man's desire can grow of a child's dream (here the dream of Candyland, of lakes of jam, of chocolate mountains): the opus turns the far-off fantasy into sense: an entire construct with immense, subtle ramifications (the societary regime, the cosmogony of the new world) grows out of the etymological metaphor: the compote (*composita*) being a composite, a euphoric system of the Mixed is built up; for example: is a hyperglycemic diet dangerous to health? Fourier is quick to invent a counter-sugar, itself often highly sugared: "there will be no drawbacks to this abundance of sweets when we can counterbalance sugar's wormy influence with a great abundance of alcoholic wines for men, white wines for women and children, acid beverages like lemonade, tart cedar." Or rather: on the carrousel of the signifier, no one can say *what comes first*, Fourier's taste (for sugar, the negation of anything conflictual? for mixed fruits? for cooked food transformed into a semi-liquid consistency?) or the exaltation of a pure form, the composite-compote, the combinative. The signifier (Fourier is in full accord) is a non-originated, non-determined material, a text.

THE WEATHER

Antique rhetoric, especially the medieval, included a special topic, the *impossibilia* (*adunata* in Greek); the *adunaton* was a common site, a *topos*, based on the notion of an *overabundance*: two naturally opposite, enemy elements (vulture and dove) were presented as peacefully living together ("The fire burns within the ice / The sun grows dark / I see the moon about to fall / This tree moves from its place," wrote Théophile de Viau); the impossible image served to stigmatize a hateful tense, a shocking *contra-naturam* ("We will have seen everything!"). Once again, Fourier inverts the rhetorical site; he uses the *adunaton* to celebrate the marvels of Harmony, the conquest of Nature by contra-natural means; for example, nothing is more incontestably "natural" (eternal) than the brackishness of the sea, whose water is undrinkable; Fourier, by the aromal action of the North Polar cap, turns it to lemonade (tart cedar): a positive *adunaton*.

   Fourier's *adunata* are many. They can all be reduced to the (very modern) conviction that man's farming modifies the climate ("the air is a field, subject as is the earth to industrious exploitation"). For Fourier, human "nature" is not deformable (merely combinable), but "natural" nature is modifiable (the reason being that Fourier's cosmogony is *aromal*, tied to the notion of the sexual fluid, whereas his psychology is discontinuous, dedicated to arrangement, not to effluvium. This *topos* of the *impossible* abides by the categories of antique rhetoric:

I.   *Chronographies* (temporal impossibilities): "We shall be witness to a spectacle to be seen once on each globe: the sudden passage from incoherence to social combination. . . . During this metamorphosis, each year will equal a century of existence," etc.

II.   *Topographies:* Spatial impossibilities, very numerous, arise from what we call geography: (1) *Climatology:* (a) Fourier changes climates, makes the Pole into a new Andalusia and moves the pleasant temperature of Naples and Provence to the coast of Siberia; (b) Fourier improves the seasons, hateful in civilized France (theme: *Spring has fled!*): "1822 had no winter, 1823 no spring at all. This confusion, which has gone on for ten years, is the result of an aromal lesion the planet is suffering because of the undue duration of chaos, civilized, barbarous and savage" (theme: *It's because of the Bomb*); (c) Fourier orders micro-climates: "The atmosphere and its protection are an integral part of our clothing. . . . In Civilization, no one ever dreamed of improving that part of the clothing we call atmosphere, with which we are perpetually in contact" (the theme of the phalanstery's corridors, heated and ventilated). (2) *Podology:* "[Crusaders of old shoes] . . . are carried off en masse to Jerusalem and brought out to cover over with good soil and plantations that Calvary where the Christians come to recite useless Our Father's; in three days, a fertile mountain has been created. Thus their religion consists in usefulness and agreeableness toward those countries to which our stupid piety brought only ravage and superstition." (3) *Physical Geography:* Fourier subjects the map of the world to a veritable plastic surgery: he moves continents, grafts climates, "lifts" South America (as we lift breasts), "lowers" Africa, pierces isthmuses (Suez and Panama), permutates cities (Stockholm is put in the place of Bordeaux, St. Petersburg of Turin), makes Constantinople the capital of the Harmonian world. (4) *Astronomy:* "Man is called upon to displace and replace the stars."

III.   *Prosographies:* modifications of the human body: (a) *Stature:* "Mankind's height will increase 2 to 3 inches per generation, until it has attained the average of 84 inches or 7 feet for men." (b) *Age:* "Then the full span of life will be 144 years and vigor proportionate." (c) *Physiology:* "This multitude of meals is necessary for the ravenous appetite the New Order will create. . . . Children raised in this way will acquire iron temperaments and will be subject to a renewal of appetite every 2 or 3 hours, due to the speedy digestion that will result from the delicacy of the food" (here again we touch on a Sadian theme: what in Fourier is the regulation of indigestion by digestion becomes inverted [or set right] in Sade, where indigestion rules the digestion—coprophagy requires good fecal matter). (d) *Sex:* "In order to confound the tyranny of men there must have existed for a century a third sex, male and female, stronger than man."

It is nugatory to stress the reasonable nature of these ravings, because certain of them are being implemented (acceleration of History, the modification of climate through agriculture or urbanization, the piercing of isthmuses, the transformations of soils, the conversion of desert sites into cultivated sites, the conquest of the heavenly bodies, the increase in longevity, the physical improvement of the race). The most insane (the most resistant) *adunaton* is not the one that upsets the laws of "nature," but the one that upsets the laws of language. Neologisms are Fourier's *impossibilia*. It is easier to predict the subversion of "the weather" than to imagine, as does Fourier, a masculine form of a feminine word, *Fés* for *Fées:* the upheaval of a strange graphic configuration in which femininity has been sunk, there is the true *impossible:* the impossible garnered from sex and language: in *matrones* (feminine) and *matrons* (masculine)," a new, monstrous, transgressor *object* has come to mankind.

The Foundations of Positivism and the Rise of Sociology: Saint-Simon and Comte

Herbert Marcuse

In the decade following Hegel's death, European thought entered an era of "positivism." This positivism announced itself as the system of *positive philosophy*, taking a form quite different from that which later positivism assumed. We shall begin our discussion of the development of post-Hegelian social thought with a brief sketch of the main trends in Saint-Simon's work and in the critical social theory that developed in France. We shall then turn to an analysis of [one of the] most influential writings of the positivist social school: Comte's *Sociology*.

SAINT-SIMON

Saint-Simon, like Hegel, begins with the assertion that the social order engendered by the French Revolution proved that mankind had reached the adult stage. In contrast to Hegel, however, he described this stage primarily in terms of its economy; the industrial process was the sole integrating factor in the new social order. Like Hegel, again, Saint-Simon was convinced that this new order contains the reconciliation of the idea and reality. Human potentialities are no longer the concern of theory apart from practice; the content of theory has been transferred to a plane of rational activity carried on by individuals in direct association with one another. "Politics, morals, and philosophy, instead of terminating in leisurely contemplation detached from practice, have eventually arrived at their veritable occupation, namely, to create social happiness. In a word, they are ready to realize that liberty is no longer an abstraction, nor society a fiction." The process of realizing this is an economic one. The new era is that of industrialism, which brings with it a guarantee that it can fulfill all human potentialities. "Society as a whole is based on industry. Industry is the only guarantor of its existence, and the unique source of all wealth and prosperity. The state of affairs which is most favorable to industry is, therefore, most favorable to society. This is the starting point as well as the goal of all our efforts." The progress of economic conditions necessitates that philosophy pass into social theory; and the social theory is none other than political economy or "the science of production."

At first Saint-Simon contented himself with proclaiming the principles of radical liberalism. Individuals had been set free in order that they might work, while society was the natural integer that sewed their independent efforts into a harmonious whole. Government was an evil necessary to cope with the danger of anarchy and revolution that lurk behind the mechanisms of industrial capitalism. Saint-Simon began with a predominantly optimistic view of industrial society—the rapid progress of all productive forces, he thought, would soon blot out the growing antagonisms and the revolutionary upheavals within this social system. The new industrial order was above all a positive one, representing the affirmation and fruition of all human endeavor for a happy and abundant life. It was not necessary to go beyond the given; philosophy and social theory needed but to understand and organize the facts. Truth was to be derived from the facts and from them alone. Saint-Simon thus became the founder of modern positivism.

Social theory, Saint-Simon held, would use "the same method that is employed in the other sciences of observation. In other words, reasoning must be based upon the facts observed and discussed, instead of following the method adopted by the speculative sciences, which refer all facts to reasoning" (*Mémoire sur la science de l'homme*). Astronomy, physics, and chemistry had already been established on this "positive basis"; the time had now come for philosophy to join these special sciences and make itself entirely positive.

Saint-Simon promulgated this positivism as the ultimate principle of his philosophy: "In all portions of my work, I shall be occupied with establishing series of facts, for I am convinced that this is the only solid part of our knowledge." Theology and metaphysics, and, moreover, all transcendental concepts and values were to be tested by the positivistic method of exact science. "Once all our knowledge is uniformly founded on observations, the direction of our spiritual affairs must be trusted to [*conferée à*] the power of positive science."

The "science of man," another name for social theory, thus was launched on the pattern of a natural science; it had to be impressed with a positive "character, by founding it on observation and by treating it with the method employed by the other branches [!] of physics." Society was to be treated like nature. This attitude involved the sharpest deviation from and opposition to Hegel's philosophic theory. The interest of freedom was removed from the sphere of the individual's rational will and set in the objective laws of the social and economic process. Marx considered society to be irrational and hence evil, so long as it continued to be governed by inexorable objective laws. Progress to him was equivalent to upsetting these laws, an act that was to be consummated by man in his free development. The positivist theory of society followed the opposite tendency: the laws of society increasingly received the form of natural objective laws. "Men are mere instruments" before the omnipotent law of progress, incapable of changing or charting its course. The deification of progress into an independent natural law was completed in Comte's positive philosophy.

Saint-Simon's own work did contain elements that ran counter to the tendencies of industrial capitalism. According to him, the progress of the industrial system presupposed that the struggle between classes was first transformed and diverted into a struggle against nature, in which all the social classes joined. The form of government he envisaged was not one in which rulers command their subjects, but one in which the government exercises a technical administration over the work to be done. We might say that Saint-Simon's philosophy developed in just the reverse way to Hegel's. It began with the reconciliation of idea and reality and ended by viewing them as irreconcilable.

Economic crises and class struggles intensified in France as the revolution of 1830 approached. "By 1826 it was evident that the nation and the monarchy were moving in opposite directions; the monarch was preparing to establish a despotism while the nation was drifting toward revolution" (Frederick B. Artz, *Reaction and Revolution*). The lectures that Saint-Simon's pupil, Bazard, gave in these years on his master's doctrine turned it into a radical critique of the existing social order.

Bazard's presentation holds to the basic assumption that philosophy must be made identical with social theory, that society is conditioned by the structure of its economic process, and that rational social practice alone will eventually produce a genuine social form oriented to human needs. The given form of society is no longer adequate to progress and harmony as far as Bazard is concerned. He stigmatizes the industrial system as one of exploitation, as the last but by far not the least example of the "exploitation of man by man," which has run the gamut of civilization's history. In all its relations, the industrial system is molded by the inevitable struggle between the proletariat on the one hand and the owners of the instruments and machinery of production on the other.

> The whole mass of workers is today exploited by those whose property it utilizes. . . . The entire weight of this exploitation falls upon the working class, that is, upon the immense majority who are workers. Under such conditions, the worker has become the direct descendant of the slave and the serf. He is, as a person, free, and no longer attached to the soil, but this is all the freedom

he has got. He can exist in this state of legal freedom only under the conditions imposed upon him by that small class which a legislation born of the right to conquest has invested with the monopoly of wealth, with the power to command the instruments of labor at will and at leisure.

(*Doctrine Saint-Simonienne: Exposition*)

Saint-Simon's positivism was thus turned into its opposite. Its original conclusions had glorified liberalism, but it now knew that the system underlying this liberalism holds within it the seed of its own destruction. Bazard showed, as Sismondi had before him, that the accumulation of wealth and the spread of poverty, with their attendant crises and growing exploitations, follow from the economic organization in which "the capitalists and proprietors" are the ones to arrange the social distribution of labor. "Every individual is left to his own devices" in the process of production, and no common interest or collective effort exists to combine and administer the multitude of works. When "the instruments of labor are utilized by isolated individuals" subject to the rule of chance and the fact of power, industrial crises are made inevitable.

The social order, then, Bazard said, has become general disorder "as a result of the principle of unlimited competition." Progressive ideas like the ones with which capitalist society justified its social scheme at the beginning, ideas of general freedom and of the pursuit of happiness within a rational scheme of life, can reach fruition only with a new revolution "that will finally do away with the exploitation of man by man in all its insidious forms. That revolution is inevitable, and until it is consummated all the glowing phrases so oft repeated about the light of civilization and the glory of the century will remain mere language for the convenience of privileged egoists." The institution of private property will have to come to an end, for if exploitation is to disappear the scheme of property by which exploitation is perpetuated must also disappear.

The *Doctrine Saint-Simonienne* reflects the social upheavals caused by the progress of industrialism under the Restoration. During this period, machines were introduced on an ever larger scale (especially in the textile mills), and industry began to concentrate. However, France experienced not only the industrial and commercial growth which Saint-Simon's early writings extoll, but the reverse of this as well. Costly crises shook the entire system in 1816–17 and in 1825–27. Workers banded together to destroy the machines that caused them so much misery and unemployment. "There could be no doubt that the rise of large-scale industry had an unfavorable influence on the condition of the worker. Agrarian home labor suffered from factory competition. The introduction of machines rendered cheap female and child labor possible and these in turn served to depress wages. Migration to the cities created a scarcity of housing facilities, and this condition, together with a general lack of proper food, made for a breeding ground of rickets and tuberculosis. Epidemics like the cholera epidemic of 1832 took their toll particularly among workers. Misery fosters dipsomania and prostitution. Industrial centers have a mortality far above the average, especially among children (Henri Sée, *Französische Wirtschaftsgeschichte*, Jena 1936, vol. 2).

Government intervened—with repressive measures against workers. The Lex Le Chapelier of 1789 had prohibited organization of workers. Strikes were now answered with a call of the army. Leaders were given lengthy prison sentences. Increasing restrictions were placed on the freedom of workers. "While pledging the entire power of the state against the workers, the authorities are extremely lenient with the entrepreneurs." In 1829 the ship owners of Grenouillle associated themselves for the purpose of lowering the wages of their seamen. The judiciary and the ministry of the navy declared their procedure contrary to law, but refused any legal action because they feared "that the seamen could be driven to rebellion."

Occurrences like these made it obvious that the economic process, or factors in it, reached its tentacles into the totality of social relations and held them in grip. Smith and Ricardo had treated this economic process as a specialized science, where wealth, poverty, labor, value, property, and all its other paraphernalia appeared as strictly economic conditions and relations, to be derived from or explained by economic laws. Saint-Simon had made the economic laws the foundation of the whole process of society. Now, when his socialist successors in France were building social theory on an economic base, they were changing the conceptual character of political economy. It ceased to be a "pure" and specialized science, becoming instead an intellectual force for exposing the antagonisms of the modern social structure and for guiding action in the direction of resolving them. By the same token, the commodity world ceased to be conceived in terms of its own reification. When Sismondi, for instance, argued against Ricardo that "political economy is not a science of calculus but a moral science," he was not advocating a regress from scientific to moral criteria in reasoning, but was indicating that the focus of economic theory should be upon human wants and desires (*Nouveaux principes d'économie politique*). Sismondi's statement belongs in the last analysis with the tendency that operated in Hegel when he gave to social theory a philosophic construction. Hegel was getting at the point that society, which was the historical stage in the self-development of men, had to be interpreted as the totality of human relations, and this with an eye to its role in advancing the realization of reason and freedom. It was precisely this philosophic interpretation of social theory that turned the latter into a *critical* theory of political economy. For, as soon as it was viewed in the light of reason and freedom, the prevailing form of society appeared as a complex of economic contradictions that bred an irrational and enslaved order. Because the philosophic interpretation of society carried the critical implications that it did, any disjunction between philosophy and social theory was held to weaken these critical motives, which pushed philosophical concepts to see beyond and to go beyond the given state of affairs. Proudhon saw the reason for the apologetic conclusions of economic theory and its consequent frustration of any principle of action to consist in "the separation of philosophy from political economy." "Philosophy," he said, "is the algebra of society, and political economy is the application of this algebra." Philosophy to him, then, was "the theory of reason." Following out this beginning, Proudhon defined social theory as "the accord between reason and social practice," and in stating the subject matter of social theory he placed great stress on its comprehensive area of application; it deals with "the entire life of society," with "the ensemble of its successive manifestations" (*Système des contradictions économiques*), thus reaching far beyond the range of the special science of economics.

Emphasis on the philosophic nature of social theory, however, does not attenuate the importance of its economic foundation. Quite the contrary, such emphasis would expand the scope of economic theory beyond the limits of a specialized science. "The laws of economy are the laws of history," Proudhon says (*De la création de l'ordre dans l'humanité*).

The new political economy was quite different from the classical objective science of Adam Smith and Ricardo. It differed from this in that it showed the economy to be contradictory and irrational throughout its structure, with crisis as its natural state and revolution as its natural end. Sismondi's work, the first thoroughgoing immanent critique of capitalism, amply illustrates the contrast. It held to the criterion of a truly critical theory of society. "We shall take society in its actual organization, with its workers deprived of property, their wages fixed by competition, their labor dismissed by their masters as soon as they no longer have need of it—for it is to this very social organization that we object."

All forms of social organization, Sismondi declared, exist to gratify human wants. The prevailing economic system does so under continuous crisis and growing poverty amid accumulating wealth. Sismondi laid bare the mechanisms of early industrial capitalism that led to this result. The necessity of recurring crises, he stated, is a consequence of the impact of capital on the productive process. The increasing exploitation and the persistent disproportion between production and consumption are consequences of the system of commodity exchange. Sismondi went on to sketch the hidden relations behind exchange value and use-value and the various forms for appropriating surplus value. He demonstrated the connection between the concentration of capital, overproduction, and crisis. "Through the concentration of wealth among a small number of proprietors the internal market continues to shrink and industry is ever increasingly compelled to sell on external markets where even greater concussions threaten." Free competition falls far short of giving full development to all productive capacities and to the greatest satisfaction of human needs; it brings wholesale exploitation and repeated destruction of the sources of wealth. To be sure, capitalism brought immense progress to society, but the advance resulted in "a constant increase in the working population and in a labor supply that usually surpassed the demand" (*Nouveaux principes*). The economic mechanisms of commodity production is responsible for these antagonisms. Were the tendencies of the system given their full expression, the result would be "to transform the nation into a huge factory" that, "far from creating wealth, would cause general misery."

Only six years after Saint-Simon had inaugurated positivism, social theory gave this radical refutation to the social order by which he had justified his new philosophy. "The system of industry" was seen as the system of capitalist exploitation. The doctrine of harmonious equilibrium was replaced by the doctrine of inherent crisis. The idea of progress was given a new meaning: economic progress did not necessarily mean human progress—under capitalism, progress is made at the expense of freedom and reason. Sismondi repudiated the philosophy of progress together with the entire panoply of optimistic glorification. He called upon the state to exert its protective authority in the interest of the oppressed mass. "The fundamental dogma of free and general competition has made great strides in all civilized societies. It has resulted in a prodigious development of industrial power, but it has also brought terrifying distress for most classes of the population. Experience has taught us the need for the protective authority [of government], needed lest men be sacrificed for the advancement of a wealth from which they will derive no benefit."

Only a short decade after the publication of Sismondi's work, social philosophy fell back upon the dogma of progress, and, characteristically enough, relinquished political economy as foundational for social theory. Comte's positive philosophy ushered in this regress. We shall deal with it now.

THE POSITIVE PHILOSOPHY OF SOCIETY: AUGUSTE COMTE

Comte severed social theory from its connection with the negative philosophy and placed it in the orbit of positivism. At the same time he abandoned political economy as the root of social theory and made society the object of an independent science of *sociology*. Both steps are interconnected: sociology became a science by renouncing the transcendent point of view of the philosophical critique. Society now was taken as a more or less definite complex of facts governed by more or less general laws—a sphere to be treated like any other field of scientific investigation. The concepts that explain this realm were to be derived from the facts that constitute it, while the farther-reaching implications of philosophical concepts were to be excluded. The term "positive" was a polemical term that denoted this transformation from a philosophic theory to a scientific one. To be sure, Comte wished to elaborate an all-embracing *philosophy*, as the title of his principal work indicates, but it is readily visible that, in the context of positivism, philosophy means something quite different from what it meant previously, so much so that it repudiates the true content of philosophy. "Philosophie positive" is, in the last analysis, a contradiction *in adjecto*. It refers to the synthesis of all empirical knowledge ordered into a system of harmonious progress following an inexorable course. All opposition to social realities is obliterated from philosophic discussion.

Comte summarizes the contrast between the positivist and the philosophic theory as follows: positive sociology is to concern itself with the investigation of facts instead of with transcendental illusions, with useful knowledge instead of leisured contemplation, certainty instead of doubt and indecision, organization instead of negation and destruction (*Discours sur l'esprit positif*). In all these cases, the new sociology is to tie itself to the facts of the existing social order and, though it will not reject the need for correction and improvement, it will exclude any move to overthrow or negate that order. As a result, the conceptual interest of the positive sociology is to be apologetic and justificatory.

This has not been true of all positivist movements. At the beginning of modern philosophy, and again in the eighteenth century, positivism was militant and revolutionary. Its appeal to the facts then amounted to a direct attack on the religious and metaphysical conceptions that were the ideological support of the *ancien régime*. The positivist approach to history was developed then as proof positive that the right of man to alter the social and political forms of life accorded with the nature and progress of reason. Again, the principle of sense-perception as the basis of verification was used by the French Enlightenment philosophers to protest the prevailing absolutistic system. They held that since the senses are the organon of truth and since the gratification of the senses is the proper motivation of human action, the advancement of man's material happiness is the proper end that government and society should serve. The given form of government and society patently contradicted this end; in the last analysis, this was the "fact" to which the positivists of the Enlightenment made their appeal. They aimed not at a well-ordered science, but at a social and political practice, remaining rationalists in the genuine sense that they tested human practice by the standard of a truth transcendent to the given social order, the standard represented by a social ordering that did not exist as a fact but as a goal. The "truth" they saw, a society wherein free individuals could use their aptitudes and fulfill their needs, was not derived from any existing fact or facts but resulted from a philosophic analysis of the historical situation, which showed an oppressive social and political system to them. The Enlightenment affirmed that reason could rule the world and men change their obsolete forms of life if they acted on the basis of their liberated knowledge and capacities.

Comte's positive philosophy lays down the general framework of a social theory that is to counteract these "negative" tendencies of rationalism. It arrives at an ideological defense of middle-class society and, moreover, it bears the seeds of a philosophic justification of authoritarianism. The connection between positive philosophy and the irrationalism that characterized the later authoritarian ideology, ushered in with the decline of liberalism, is quite clear in Comte's writings. Hand in hand with the shackling of thought to immediate experience goes his constant widening of the realm of experience, so that it ceases to be restricted to the realm of scientific observation but claims also various types of supra-sensual power. In fact, the outcome of Comte's positivism turns out to be a religious system with an elaborate cult of names, symbols, and signs. He himself expounded a "positive theory of authority" and became the authoritative leader of a sect of blind followers. This was the first fruit of the defamation of reason in positive philosophy.

It had been the fundamental conviction of idealism that truth is not given to man from some external source but originates in the process of interaction between thought and reality, theory and practice. The function of thought was not merely to collect, comprehend, and order facts, but also to contribute a quality that rendered such activity possible, a quality that was thus *a priori* to facts. A decisive portion of the human world therefore consisted, the idealists held, of elements that could not be verified by observation. Positivism repudiated this doctrine, slowly replacing the free spontaneity of thought with predominantly receptive functions. This was not merely a matter of epistemology. The idealistic idea of reason, we recall, had been intrinsically connected with the idea of freedom and had opposed any notion of a natural necessity ruling over society. Positive philosophy tended instead to equate the study of society with the study of nature, so that natural science, particularly biology, became the archetype of social theory. Social study was to be a science seeking social laws, the validity of which was to be analogous to that of physical laws. Social practice, especially the matter of changing the social system, was herewith throttled by the inexorable. Society was viewed as governed by rational laws that moved with a natural necessity. This position directly contradicted the view held by the dialectical social theory, that society is irrational precisely in that it is governed by natural laws.

The "general dogma of the invariability of physical laws" Comte calls the "true spirit" of positivism. He proposes to apply this tenet to social theory as a means of freeing the latter from theology and metaphysics and giving it the status of a science. "Theological and metaphysical philosophy do not hold sway today except in the system of social study. They must be excluded from this final refuge. Mainly, this will be done through the basic interpretation that social movement is necessarily subject to invariant physical laws, instead of being governed by some kind of will" (*Cours de philosophie positive*). The positivist repudiation of metaphysics was thus coupled with a repudiation of man's claim to alter and reorganize his social institutions in accordance with his rational will. This is the element Comte's positivism shares with the original philosophies of counter-revolution sponsored by Bonald and De Maistre. Bonald wished to demonstrate that "man cannot give a constitution to religious or political society any more than he can give weight to a body or extension to matter," and that his intervention only prevents society from attaining its "natural constitution" ("Théorie du pouvoir"). De Maistre wished to show that "human reason, or what is called philosophy, adds nothing to the happiness of states or of individuals," that "*creation* is beyond the capacities of man" and that his reason "is completely ineffectual not only for creating but also for conserving any religious or political association" ("Etude sur la souveraineté"). The "revolutionary spirit" was to be checked by spreading another teaching, that society possesses an immutable natural order to which man's will must submit.

Comte also charged sociology to make secure this teaching as a means of establishing "the general limits of all political action" (*Cours*). Assent to the principle of invariant laws in society will prepare men for discipline and for obedience to the existing order and will promote their "resignation" to it.

"Resignation" is a keynote in Comte's writings, deriving directly from assent to invariable social laws. "True resignation, that is, a disposition to endure necessary evils steadfastly and without any hope of compensation therefor, can result only from a profound feeling for the invariable laws that govern the variety of natural phenomena." The "positive" politics that Comte advocates would tend, he declares, "of its very nature to consolidate public order," even as far as incurable political evils are concerned, by developing a "wise resignation."

There is no doubt as to the social groups and purposes in whose behalf resignation is adduced. Rarely in the past has any philosophy urged itself forward with so strong and so overt a recommendation that it be utilized for the maintenance of prevailing authority and for the protection of vested interest from any and all revolutionary onset. Comte begins his propaganda for positivism by declaring that genuine science has no other general aim than "constantly to establish and fortify the intellectual order which . . . is the indispensable basis of all veritable order." Order in science and order in society merge into an indivisible whole. The ultimate goal is to justify and fortify this social order. Positive philosophy is the only weapon able to combat "the anarchic force of purely revolutionary principles"; it alone can succeed in "absorbing the current revolutionary doctrine." "La cause de l'ordre," moreover, will bring even greater advantages. Positive politics will tend spontaneously "to divert from the various existing powers . . . and from all their delegates the greatly exaggerated attention accorded to them by public opinion." The consequence of this diversion will be to concentrate all social effort on primarily a "moral" renovation. Time and again, Comte stresses the "serious and threatening dangers" that attend "the predominance of purely material considerations" in social theory and practice. The innermost interests of his sociology are much more sharply antimaterialistic than Hegel's idealism. "The principal social difficulties are today essentially not political but moral ones," and their solution requires a change in "opinions and morals" rather than in institutions. Positivism is therefore urged to give aid "in transforming political agitation into a philosophical crusade, which would suppress radical tendencies as, after all, "incompatible with any sane conception of history" (*Discours*). The new philosophical movement will in due time teach men that their social order stands under eternal laws against which none may transgress without punishment. According to these laws all forms of government are "provisional," which means that they will painlessly adjust themselves to the irresistible progress of mankind. Revolution under such conditions is without sense.

The "provisional powers" that govern society, Comte argues, will no doubt find their security effectively increased through the influence of "positive politics which is alone able to imbue the people with the feeling that, in the present state of their ideas, no political change is of real importance" (*Cours*). The lords of earth will learn, also, that positivism inclines "to consolidate all power in the hands of those who possess this power—whoever they may be. Comte becomes even more outspoken. He denounces "the strange and extremely dangerous" theories and efforts that are directed against the prevailing property order. These erect an "absurd Utopia." Certainly, it is necessary to improve the condition of the lower classes, but this must be done without deranging class barriers and without "disturbing the indispensable economic order." On this point, too, positivism offers a testimonial to itself. It promises to "insure the ruling classes against every anarchistic invasion" and to show the way to a proper treatment of the mass. Outlining the meaning of the term "positive" in his philosophy, Comte summarizes the grounds for his recommendation of himself to the *cause de l'ordre* by stressing that his philosophy is of its very nature "destined not to destroy but to organize" and that it will "never pronounce an absolute negation."

We have devoted considerable space to the social and political role of Comte's sociology because the subsequent development of positivism has obliterated the strong connection between the social and methodological principles.

We now raise the question, Which of its principles makes positive philosophy the adequate guardian and defender of the existing order? In drawing our contrast between the positivist spirit of the Enlightenment and later positivist views, we have already pointed to the latter's negation of metaphysics and to "the subordination of imagination to observation," and we have shown that these signified a tendency to acquiesce in the given. All scientific concepts were to be subordinated to the facts. The former were merely to make manifest the real connections among the latter. Facts and their connections represented an inexorable order comprising social as well as natural phenomena. The laws positivist science discovered and that distinguish it from empiricism, were positive also in the sense that they affirmed the prevailing order as a basis for denying the need to construct a new one. Not that they excluded reform and change—on the contrary, the idea of progress loomed large in the sociology of Comte—but the laws of progress were part of the machinery of the given order, so that the latter progressed smoothly to a higher stage without having to be destroyed first.

Comte had little difficulty in arriving at this result, for he saw the different stages of historical development as stages of a "philosophic movement" rather than of a social process. Comte's law of three stages illustrates this quite clearly. History, he says, takes the inevitable path of first, theological rule, then, metaphysical rule, and finally, positivist rule. This conception permitted Comte to come forward as a brave warrior against the *ancien régime* at a time when the *ancien régime* had long been broken and the middle class had long consolidated its social and economic power. Comte interpreted the *ancien régime* primarily as the vestige of theological and metaphysical ideas in science.

Observation instead of speculation means, in Comte's sociology, an emphasis on order in place of any rupture in the order; it means the authority of natural laws in place of free action, unification in place of disorder. The idea of order, so basic to Comte's positivism, has a totalitarian content in its social as well as methodological meaning. The methodological emphasis was on the idea of a unified science, the same idea that dominates recent developments in positivism. Comte wanted to found his philosophy on a system of "universally recognized principles" that will draw their ultimate legitimacy solely from "the voluntary assent by which the public will confirm them to be the result of perfectly free discussion." "The public," just as in neopositivism, turns out to be a forum of scientists who have the necessary equipment of knowledge and training. Social questions, because of their complicated nature, must be handled "by a small group of an intellectual élite." In this way, the most vital issues that are of great moment to all are withdrawn from the arena of social struggle and bottled for investigation in some field of specialized scientific study. Unification is a matter of agreement among scientists whose efforts along this line will sooner or later yield "a permanent and definite state of intellectual unity." All the sciences will be poured into the same crucible and fused into a well-ordered scheme. All concepts will be put to the test of "one and the same fundamental method" until, in the end, they issue forth ordered in "a rational sequence of uniform laws." Positivism thus will "systematize the whole of our conceptions" (*Système de politique positive*).

The positivist idea of *order* refers to an ensemble of laws entirely different from the ensemble of dialectical laws. The former are essentially affirmatory and construct a stable order, the latter, essentially negative and destructive of stability. The former see society as a realm of natural harmony, the latter as a system of antagonisms. "The notion of natural laws entails at once the corresponding idea of a spontaneous order, which is always coupled with the notion of some harmony" (*Cours*). Positivist sociology is basically "social statics," quite in keeping with the positivist doctrine that there is a "true and permanent harmony between the various existential conditions in society." The harmony prevails, and, because it does so, the thing to do is "contemplate the order, for the purpose of correcting it conveniently, but not and nowhere to create it."

A closer scrutiny of Comte's laws of social statics discloses their amazing abstractness and poverty. They center about two propositions. First, men need to work for their happiness; second, all social actions show that they are overwhelmingly motivated by selfish interests. The principal task of positivist political science is to strike the right balance between the different kinds of work to be done and the skillful employment of self-interest for the common good. In this connection, Comte stresses the need for strong authority. "In the intellectual, no less than in the material order, men find above all the indispensable need for some supreme directing hand capable of sustaining their continuous activity by rallying and fixing their spontaneous efforts." When positivism reaches its dominant position in the world, in the last stage of human progress, it changes hitherto existing forms of authority, but it does not by any means abolish authority itself. Comte outlines a "positive theory of authority," envisaging a society with all its activity based on the consent of individual wills. The liberalist tinge of this picture is shaded over, however. The instinct to submit triumphs, as the founder of positivist sociology renders a paean to obedience and leadership. "How sweet it is to obey when we can enjoy the happiness . . . of being conveniently discharged, by sage and worthy leaders, from the pressing responsibility of a general direction of our conduct."

Happiness in the shelter of a strong arm—the attitude, so characteristic today in Fascist societies, makes juncture with the positivist ideal of certainty. Submission to an all-powerful authority provides the highest degree of security. Perfect certainty of theory and practice, Comte claims, is one of the basic attainments of positivist method.

The idea of certainty did not, of course, emerge with positive philosophy, but had been a strong feature of rationalism ever since Descartes. Positivism did, however, reinterpret its meaning and function. As we have indicated, rationalism asserted that the ground of theoretical and practical certainty was the freedom of the thinking subject. On this foundation it constructed a universe that was rational precisely to the extent that it was dominated by the intellectual and practical power of the individual. Truth sprang from the subject, and the imprint of subjectivity was upon it whatever objective form it took. The world was real to the extent that it conformed to the subject's rational autonomy.

Positivism shifts the source of certainty from the subject of thought to the subject of perception. Scientific observation yields certainty here. The spontaneous functions of thought recede, while its receptive and passive functions gain predominance.

Comte's sociology, by virtue of the concept of order, is essentially "social studies"; it is also "social dynamics" by virtue of the concept of *progress*. The relation between the two basic concepts Comte has often explained. Order is "the fundamental condition of progress" and "all progress ultimately tends to consolidate order." The principal reason for the fact that social antagonisms still prevail is that the idea of order and that of progress are still separated, a condition which has made it possible for anarchist revolutionaries to usurp the latter idea. Positive philosophy aims to reconcile order and progress, to achieve a "common satisfaction of the need for order and the need for progress." This it can do by showing that progress is in itself order—not revolution, but evolution.

His antimaterialistic interpretation of history facilitated Comte's undertaking. He retained the Enlightenment conception that progress is primarily intellectual progress, the continuous advance of positive knowledge. He removed from the Enlightenment conception as much of its material content as he could, thus adhering to his promise "to substitute an immense intellectual movement for a sterile political agitation." Servant of the preeminent need to safeguard the existing order, the idea of progress stands in the way of physical, moral, and intellectual development except along lines that the given "system of circumstances" permits. Comte's idea of progress excludes revolution, the total transformation of the given system of circumstances. Historical development becomes nothing more than a harmonious evolution of the social order under perennial "natural" laws.

"Dynamic sociology" is to present the mechanics of this evolution. Its outlook is essentially "to conceive each state of society as the necessary result of the preceding one and the indispensable motor of the succeeding one." Social dynamics deals with the laws governing this continuity; in other words, the "laws of succession," whereas social statics treats of the "laws of coexistence." The former makes for "the true theory of progress," the latter, "the true theory of order." Progress is equated with a persistent growth of intellectual culture in history. The fundamental law of social dynamics is that increasing power accrues to those organic faculties by which man is differentiated in nature from lower organic beings, namely, "intelligence and *sociabilité*." As civilization proceeds, it comes closer and closer to exhibiting the nature of mankind in the concrete; the highest grade of civilization is the one most in conformity with "nature." Historical progress is a natural process and is, as such, governed by natural laws. Progress *is* order.

The process of making social theory compatible with existing conditions is not complete as far as we have developed it. All elements that would transcend or point beyond the validity of the given matters of fact have yet to be excluded; this requires that social theory be made *relativistic*. The last decisive aspect of positivism, Comte states, as we would expect, is its tendency "everywhere to substitute the relative for the absolute." From this "irrevocable predominance of the relativist point of view" he derives his basic view that social development has a naturally harmonious character. Every historical stage of society is as perfect as the corresponding "age of humanity" and system of circumstance permit. A natural harmony prevails not only among the coexisting parts of the social scheme, but also between the potentialities of mankind revealed therein and the realization of these.

According to Comte, relativism is inseparable from the conception that sociology is an exact science dealing with the invariant laws of social statics and dynamics. These laws are to be discovered only by scientific observation, which, in turn, requires a constant progress in scientific technic to cope with the highly complicated phenomena it has to organize. The attainment of complete knowledge coincides with the completion of scientific progress itself; prior to such perfection, all knowledge and truth are inevitably partial and relative to the attained level of intellectual development.

So far, Comte's relativism is merely methodological, based on a necessary inadequacy in the methods of observation. Owing to the fact, however, that social development is interpreted primarily as intellectual development, his relativism posits a pre-established harmony between the subjective side of sociology (the method) and the objective (the content). All social forms and institutions, as we have mentioned, are provisional in the sense that, as intellectual culture advances, they will pass into others that will correspond with intellectual capacities of an advanced type. Their provisional character, though a sign of their imperfection, is at the same time the mark of their (relative) truth. The concepts of positivism are relativistic because all reality is relative.

Science, to Comte, is the field of theoretical relativism, and the latter the area from which "value judgments" are excluded. Positivist sociology "neither admires nor condemns political facts but looks upon them . . . as simple objects of observation." When sociology becomes a positivist science it is divorced from any concern with the "value" of a given social form. Man's quest for happiness is not a scientific problem, nor is the question of the best possible fulfillment for his desires and talents. Comte boasts that he can easily treat the whole realm of social physics "without once using the word 'perfection,' which is replaced forever by the purely scientific term 'development.' " Each historical level represents a higher stage of development than the one preceding, by force of the fact that the later is the necessary product of the earlier one and contains a plus of experience and new knowledge. Comte holds, however, that his concept of development does not exclude perfection. The essential conditions of men and their capacities have improved with social development; this is incontestable. But the improvement of capacities takes place primarily in science, art, morals, and such, all of which, like the improvement in social conditions, move "gradually, within convenient limits." Accordingly, revolutionary efforts for a new order of society have no place in the scheme. They can be dispensed with. "The vain search for better government" is not necessary, for each established governmental form has its relative right, to be disputed only by those taking an absolutist point of view, which is false *per definitionem*. Comte's relativism thus terminates in the "positive theory of authority."

Comte's reverence for established authority was easily compatible with all-around tolerance. Both attitudes hold equally in this brand of scientific relativism. There is no room for condemnation. "Without the slightest alteration of its proper principles" positivism can "do exact and philosophical justice to all prevalent doctrines"—a virtue that will make it acceptable "to all the different existing parties."

The idea of tolerance had changed its content and function as positivism developed. The French Enlighteners who fought the absolute state gave no relativist framework to their demand for tolerance, but asserted that demand as part of their general effort to establish a better form of government—"better" in precisely the sense Comte repudiates. Tolerance did not mean justice to all existing parties. It meant, in fact, the abolition of one of the most influential of parties, that of the clergy allied with the feudal nobility, which was using intolerance as an instrument for domination.

When Comte came on the scene, his "tolerance" was not a slogan for opponents of the existing order, but for the opponents of these. As the concept of progress was formalized, tolerance was detached from the standard that had given it content in the eighteenth century. Earlier, the positivist standard had been a new society, while tolerance had been equivalent to intolerance towards those who opposed that standard. The formalized concept of tolerance, on the other hand, amounted to tolerating the forces of reaction and regress as well. The need for this kind of toleration resulted from the fact that all standards that go beyond given realities had been renounced—standards that in Comte's eyes were akin to those seeking an absolute. In a philosophy that justified the prevailing social system, the cry of toleration became increasingly useful to the beneficiaries of the system.

Comte, however, does not treat all parties equally. He says many times that there is an essential affinity between positivism and one large social group, the proletariat. Proletarians have an ideal disposition to positivism. Comte has an entire section in the *Système de politique positive* dedicated to the proposition that "the new philosophers will find their most energetic allies among our proletarians."

The fact of the proletariat worried Comte's sociology as well as it did its antithesis, the Marxian critique. There could be no positive theory of civil society unless the fact of the proletariat could be reconciled with the harmonious order of progress it so patently contradicts. For, if the proletariat is the foundational class in civil society, the laws of this society's advance are the laws of its destruction, and the theory of society must be a negative one. Sociology must, in the face of this, present a refutation of the dialectical thesis that accumulation of wealth takes place alongside an intensification of poverty.

Comte regarded the latter thesis as a "sinister and immoral prejudice," one that positivism had to eradicate if it would maintain the "industrial discipline" the society needs in order to function. Comte held that the theory and practice of liberalism could not safeguard discipline. "The vain and irrational disposition to allow for only that degree of order that comes of itself" (that is, that comes through the free play of economic forces) amounts to a "solemn resignation" of social practice in the face of every real emergency in the social process.

Comte's belief in the necessary laws of progress did not exclude practical efforts in the direction of such social reform as would remove any obstacles in the path of these laws. The positivist program of social reform foreshadows liberalism's turn into authoritarianism. In contrast to Hegel, whose philosophy showed a similar tendency, Comte slurred over the fact that the turn is made necessary because of the antagonistic structure of civil society. Classes in conflict, he held, are but vestiges of an obsolete régime, soon to be removed by positivism, without any threat to the "fundamental institution of property."

The rule of positivism, Comte says, will improve the condition of the proletariat, first in education and second through "the creation of work." The vision entails an all-embracing hierarchic state, governed by a cultural elite composed of all social groups and permeated by a new morality that unites all diverse interests into a real whole. Notwithstanding the many declarations that this hierarchy will derive its authority from the free consent of its members, Comte's state resembles in many respects the modern authoritarian state. We find, for example, that there is to be a "spontaneous union of the brain and the hand." Obviously, regulation from above plays an important part in the establishment of such a union. Comte makes the matter more explicit. He states that industrial development has already reached a point at which it becomes necessary "to regulate the relation between entrepreneur and worker toward an indispensable harmony that is no longer sufficiently guaranteed in the free natural antagonism between them."

The act of combining entrepreneurs and workers, we are assured, is by no means intended as a step towards abolishing the inevitably inferior position of the worker. The latter's activity, Comte holds, is naturally less extensive and less responsible than that of the entrepreneur. Society is a "positive hierarchy," and submission to the social stratification is indispensable to the life of the whole. Consequently, the new morality is to be primarily one of "duty" to the whole. The justified claims of the proletariat become duties, too. The worker will receive "first education and then work." Comte does not elaborate on this "work creation program," but does speak of a system in which all private functions become public ones, so that every activity is organized and exercised as a public service.

This "nationalization" of labor has nothing to do, of course, with socialism. Comte stresses that in the "positive order," "the various public enterprises can, to an increasing extent, be entrusted to private industry," provided that such "administrative change" does not tamper with the necessary discipline. He refers in this connection to an agency that has become increasingly important in maintaining positive order—the army. His effort to do justice to all social groups alike prompts him to recommend his philosophy to the "military class," with the reminder that positivism, though it approves of the slow disappearance of military action, "directly justifies the important provisional function" of the army in the "necessary maintenance of the material order." Because of the grave disturbances to which the social system is prone, "the army has the increasingly essential task of participating actively . . . to maintain the constancy of public order." As national wars disappear, we shall witness that the army will more and more be entrusted with the "social mission" of a great political gendarmerie (*une grande maréchaussée politique*).

In one decisive aspect, however, Comte's system retains the emancipatory function of Western philosophy, for it tends to bridge the gulf between isolated individuals and to unite them in a real universal. We have attempted to show how the positivist method engendered the quest for unification, and we have stressed its negative implications. But the idea of a universal positive order drove Comte beyond the empty conception of a unified science and the oppressive vision of a government of positive high priests. There is still another universality prevalent in Comte's system, that of *society*. It emerges as the one arena in which man acts out his historical life, and, by the same token, it becomes the only object of social theory. The individual plays almost no part in Comte's sociology, he is entirely absorbed by society, and the state is a mere by-product of the inexorable laws that govern the social process.

On this point, Comte's sociology transcends the limits of Hegel's political philosophy. The positive theory of society sees no reason for confining human development within the boundaries of sovereign national states. Its idea of a universal order is consummated only through the union of all individuals in mankind, and the positivist destruction of obsolete theological and metaphysical standards comes to fruition in the recognition of *humanity* as the *être suprême*. Humanity, not the state, is the real universal, nay, it is the only reality. It is the only entity that, in the age of mankind's maturity, is worthy of religious reverence. "The great conception of Humanity will irrevocably eliminate that of God" (*Système de politique positive*).

It is as if Comte had tried, with this idea of humanity, to make amends for the oppressive atmosphere in which his positivist sociology moved.

A Sort of History:
Michelet's *La Sorcière*

Linda Orr

La Sorcière is a radical presentation of the problematics of Michelet's historiography; along with the introduction to the *Histoire de la Révolution
française,* it is the extreme model the rest of his work can be placed against.
The two parts of the book (the parthenogenesis and rise of the cosmic Witch
and her son-lover Satan; the dispersal and degradation of the commercial
nun-priest-inquisitioner triads) throw history back to back at the culmi-
nating moment of the Black Mass. On the one hand, there is the hypoth-
esized story of the speechless, the mute of history, the outsiders, their
rebellion of reversals; on the other hand, the archive-producing machine
of the inquisition writes what it wants to hear, what it forces to be said.
In our current critical parlance, we might say that, on the one hand, there
is the "un-history," the other history which is by definition excluded from
the system of definitions we have, on the other hand, learned to associate
with history: (1) real, events; (2) data, documents; (3) chronicle or narrative;
(4) philosophies or figures of developmental human time; (5) the study of
all the above, "the discipline." Self-reflective historians have recently reversed what looked like an order of logic so that either the social formation
of the discipline (Foucault) or the narrative or tropes (Louis Mink, Hayden
White) come "first" and the data, even the "real" or "truth" are produced
either as an effect, or perhaps more pertinently as a *fact* of this reversal.
For anything to be thought (said, read, known), for anyone to exist, it (he/
she) can only think or know itself in the linguistic and rhetorical "places"
allotted that in turn can only be thought as "history," are always already
"history" (cause/effect; part/whole) and this "history" grounds an arsenal
of effects-facts that reach from the coherence of fiction to the power of the
explanation and the totality of science, which finally, in another twist,

From *Yale French Studies* no. 59 (1980). © 1980 by *Yale French Studies.*

reground history. A double discourse characterizes therefore history: it seems to return to facts whose recounting transparently lets the real through, but it rearranges an always reordered fiction it brings into being as a "past" in order to effect a future it can never conceive of. One story (e.g. *l'énonciation*) appears to be repressed by another one (*l'énoncé*), but both are told in the techniques of repression itself: the problem, however, is to know which is witch.

In Book I, the fable of the genesis of historiography that opens *La Sorcière* is forgotten so that the total, transparent coincidence of potential differences can perform the text of the un-history, the Black Mass. Here Michelet's Romantic-realist project would fuse disparate functions so that all is one: *l'énonciation* and *l'énoncé*; the subject of the *énonciation* and the object of the *énoncé*; the word and act; the unconscious and the real; the body and read-ing-writing. Whereas the realistic historian would try to isolate the *énoncé* and present it alone (as history speaking itself), Michelet allows his "I" to be glimpsed the better to astound when it is eclipsed in both extremes of a kind of total subjectivity and total objectivity, both equally possessed by Michelet and possessing him. *La Sorcière* is Romantic irony, but not in the sense of a distance from one's own sentimentality (usually associated with German Romanticism), but in the sense of a double discourse telling mu-tually exclusive "stories"; history for Michelet is the telling of story 1 (the un-history: Part I) in the form of story 2 (History, Part II) or vice versa. *La Sorcière* is the Herculean effort to keep them apart though they insist on both generating one another and on coming out alike, both equally total-izing, both ecstatic and disgusting. The distinction is as important as the one between the Revolution and the History of France, or between the (other history of the) "Revolution" and the *History of the French Revolution*, but, although Michelet's entire work should be read through the extreme imperative of *La Sorcière*, his history is often produced, especially his natural history, by the ingenious attempt to make the impossible passage last be-tween extremes.

The first chapters of *La Sorcière* not only deal with a myth of origin, that is, with the fable of how the medieval church and society established their repressive economy, but also mime the mythical genesis of historiog-raphy. The witch, related to the old pagan gods and to the animals, is not simply repressed by the church and society; she is tricked by them. One of the earliest fables of *La Sorcière*, itself a collection of fables, dramatizes how the voice that would be heard in Michelet's history has already been usurped. If written history is missing its own object from the beginning, it has forced out that oral object: the fable of the Golden Legend elaborates history's one event.

From the hallucinations of the isolated family, from the child's imag-inings and the woman's dreams, a ballad grows that is sung or danced "under the oak by the fountain." Before the priest steals this story, sweeping it away in a verbal *tour de passe-passe*, saying *Vox populi, vox Dei!*, he asks the people for reliable sources; they reply by showing him "authentic witnesses, or unimpeachable veracity,—the tree, the rock" (*Satanism and Witchcraft: A Study in Medieval Superstition*; title of A. R. Allison's translation of Michelet's *La Sorcière*). Substituting God's voice for the people's initiates the first instance of possession, though this possession will not be named so until later when it is blamed on the devil. The metaphor accompanying this fable illustrates that the monk's rendition of the legend will never resemble the original; monuments of culture will never have any connection with what is natural: "The monks wrote them (the Saints' Lives), but it was the people who made them. This young vegetation may throw its luxuriance of leaf and blossom over the crumbling walls of the old Roman building converted into a monastery, but it does not grow out of it, we may be sure." Thereafter, the degradation is swift: "Recopied, loaded, overloaded with embellishments, often grotesque embellishments, it will descend from age to age, till at last it takes honourable rank and place in the *Golden Legend*." Ten years previously in 1851, Michelet had started a "popular book" tentatively intitled *La Légende d'or de la démocratie*, finally published as *Pologne et Russie, Légende de Kosciusko*.

By 1300 (the first date to which Michelet draws attention), the peasant woman has already exclaimed: "I am no longer my own woman now." Her possessed body begins to round out and turn "all gold" as the money market also comes into existence, but she will not sign the pact with the devil until she is violently raped, gang-bang style by the lord's petty courtesans on her own front doorstep (with her husband trembling within the house). This decides her conversion to the other Satanic alternative where she can effect a return to the (regressive?) mythic beginning. The witch's complete triumph is almost too good to be true. Her ego has dissipated into an interpenetration of all nature with her "rehabilitated" stomach and womb as center and circumference. She presides over a world where signs are not separate from things and where the old veracity of history is again revealed in trees and rocks. But above all, the need to argue about truth is superceded; Satan, the mythical advocate, need only appear to be believed; reality itself overcomes any lingering habit of resorting to words. Satan seduces his "fair adversary, woman . . . by an argument that is no mere play of words, but a living reality, entrancing and irresistible."

But has the story Michelet is recounting escaped the fate of the Golden Legend, or has he substituted his word for hers, his God-Historian's word for the people's? If only he, like Satan, merely had "to show himself" for history to be proved true. . . . "Michelet," his textual unconscious, if you prefer, was never under the illusion that the investigations of history dealt with the vestiges of a living being. Just as the vine does not grow out of the ruin, no metonymic analogy can be extended from the historical object to what we call the real thing. Documents are no imprint of her body, no container of the contained, no inversion, no mirror image, no residue, no more highly evolved part. This realization does not exclude the fact that another "Michelet" wanted to resurrect the dead of history, to deliver up their bodies as a book or at least to produce his book on their hot thighs in the same manner as the witch baked her *confarreatio*. Michelet would like for us to be able to eat his book, at least to bring it (like television) into the intimacy of our homes. . . .

If the link is cut between the historical object and its vestigial documents, then, as Michelet hoped, one might posit an ur-text that could be read in the palimpsest of modern materials: "Unfortunately we possess detailed accounts of such scenes only of quite late date, the reign of Henri IV. . . . But even in these descriptions of an institution so far gone in decay are to be found certain marks of extreme antiquity that bear witness to the successive periods and diverse forms through which it had already passed." Sometimes the ancient structure could be surmised from the remaining text, but just as often there was no more than a kind of unverifiable spirit haunting the ruins. "Even to-day, when we read these beautiful tales [Golden Legends] . . . we cannot but recognise a very real inspiration (*un grand souffle*) and bewail the irony of fate when we think what was to be their eventual lot (*on s'attendrit en songeant quel fut leur sort*). Only the *souffle* survives, that is, a metaphor for a something-that-survives nowhere, an "outside" that only exists in the gesture of its evocation. So that history is both the bewailing of the irony of this "eventual lot" and the sorceress's constant sorting of lots, the shifting of slots, the sifting out of *découpages* that produce by the shift a present/past and generate, logico-rhetorically from there, teleology, a future. History is reformulating the always-already formulaic: "The object of my book was purely to give, not a history of Sorcery, but a simple and impressive formula of the Sorceress's way of life." Michelet answers the familiar question—which formula fits—by the term (both scientific and pseudo-scientific), "historical psychology." But his "historical psychology" is essentially erotic: by entering into the body of the witch, he reports graphically how she feels. There is, then, a literal dramatization of letting the object of history speak for herself. But is her voice not strangely low, like Satan's inside her? Historians are not so fortunate as the journalists Woodward and Bernstein of *All the President's Men,* for they must double for their own Deep Throat.

Michel Serres sees Michelet's Black Mass as the ritualized totality, the allegory, of all history, coalescing into a final transgression: incest. For Alain Besançon, the Black Mass permits regression to an indistinct life within the mother, free love in either a sado-anal or oral mode, and father is banished from the scene, even his penis is magically annulled. It appears as if Michelet has met the occasion in which his deepest pathological needs correspond with his country. France is Michelet's Deep Throat and vice versa; History speaks him and he speaks her.

But the Sabbath is metaphorically indistinguishable from the "terrible chorus" of St. Vitus' Dance which suggests that perfect fusion can also reverse into a monolith of imposed consent or universal hysteria. To eliminate the very existence of distinction is to court pathology or to promote a dictatorial order (reminiscent of the bind in Rousseau). Besançon marks the depth or height of madness in *La Sorcière* as the Black Mass at the close of Book I: Book II is supposedly the cure.

For some reason a silence has reigned over Book II. Book I was to have trawled the "muddy under-regions of the soul" (*les fangeux souterrains*), was to have orchestrated a dream-like popular pageant of time. Book II is waking up with a hangover to the hammer (Sprenger's *Marteau*) of endless inquisitioners, of their razzle-dazzle erudition. The sublime Sorceress is replaced from one page to the next by a bourgeois vamp or a hysterical nun. A fat businessman slumps in the easy chair, where Satan's throne once stood, and he reviews the slapstick of the sabbath. Or, disguised as a Jesuit priest, Satan completely sells out and stages the street miracles for a living. Instead of chanting the *Credo*, everyone is mumbling *Ave*'s. From song to noise, from Revolution to the huge Baudelairean yawn of *Ennui*, so it goes.

Michelet himself announced that his structural analysis of the diabolical trilogy (Aix, Loudun, Louviers) would be repeated with no variation but a gradual decline from decent entertainment in Provence to an obscene re-run in Loudun and a fake in Louviers. "The three affairs are one and identical. In all of them the libertine Priest, in all the jealous Monk and the maniac Nun by whose mouth they make the Devil speak,—and all end in the same way, by the death of the Priest at the stake." Barthes focuses on the "theophanic moment" of the first *Sorcière-Sibylle*, and Serres slips in the aside: "the second (witch) is an anecdotal continuation" ("Traduction thèse à thèse: *La Sorcière*"). Jean-Pierre Richard has also published an article dealing only with Book I (*Littérature*, May 1976). It is true that most of Book II is taken verbatim from the *Histoire de France* (Chaps. II, IV–VIII); chapters I and III provide transition; IX was written as an afterthought with the Introduction and Epilogue. That leaves only the last three chapters, which deal with the trial of Charlotte Cadière: a trial, according to Mandrou, that is insignificant as far as progress in legal procedure is concerned unless it serves as an example of recidivism. But this trial, totally anachronistic in the Enlightenment, subsumes more space in *La Sorcière* than any one other incident.

There are obviously reasons for this blindspot in past readings of the "book of predilection" of most *michelétistes* (Barthes). The unconscious material uncovered by Book II is not easy to deal with; the "lowest depths" of Book I are nothing in comparison to the *in-pace* of the imagination that takes over Book II. And if Book II is to effect a cure, it demands an acceptance of truly brutal realities. The tone is hardly describable: both rage and sadness dominate.

Rhetorical snags in the previously seamless discourse (whose very seamlessness is, however, in itself, a snag) become evident and cross like a crack through the whole book. Moreover, Michelet commits the one and only sin that calls his text into question as historical discourse: he openly falsifies documents.

There is a concentration of these rhetorical snags in the chapters on La Cadière: a journalistic listing of dates, an excess of detail (Michelet said in a note already quoted he would avoid this), frequent recourse to parenthetical references naming the actual page of court records, a strange use of italics, and the repression of the first person. The problem is that one cannot tell whether the increased intensity comes from the need to take a stronger polemical stand than in Book I or from a different kind of uncontrolled ego absorption in highly charged materials.

After the first half of the book where history vaguely progresses from the ninth to the fourteenth century, turning around the hypothetical pivot date of 1300, Book II passes from "legend" (already "hagiographed") into historiography: the chapter titles are arranged according to chronological dates as in the *Histoire de France* and the years close in until 1730 when time stalls. It is as if the temporal perspective of the whole book is projected back from that "present," with years trailing into vaguer and vaguer centuries described in less and less detail. At one point Michelet moves day by day: 27 février, 1731; 28 février. He couples a rhetorical style of hypothesis ("probably," "perhaps," and the imperfect subjunctive) with a parenthetical documentation for almost every statement he must have deemed controversial. One particular passage, which is stylistically overdetermined by this cognitive nervousness, is central to the argument. Michelet has as his source only three lines of court proceedings, in which "something repugnant" is merely suggested. "Since the case began" according to La Cadière's brothers, Girard took liberties with their sister. With this "evidence," Michelet spins out a scenario in which Girard's female cohorts drug Charlotte so that she retracts her deposition against him and is then left in a five-day stupor (between the first and sixth of March). During this interval, Girard comes to her cell, and though she is suffering from painful *"petites infirmités"* (Michelet's reference), Girard "eut l'indignité . . . d'y porter la main" (Michelet's reference: "did the outrageous indignity of touching it"). This passage again points up the double-bind of Michelet's polemical position in Book II: he believed that La Cadière, whom other historians had ignored or mocked (Mandrou also treats her case in a chapter entitled "Faux Sorciers"), was dealt a profound injury, that she was tortured, driven to suicidal attempts, misrepresented, in short that her life was ruined because of petty Church and Parliamentary politics. He believed hers was an important example of social injustice. But the image of the woman, half-dead, shoved into a dark, filthy, damp cell, being raped by jailors or former lovers, has also been repeated in literature so often as to have lost its specificity. Michelet is obsessively rewriting not only Diderot's *La Religieuse,* but Sade. La Cadière and Madeleine Bavent of Louviers before her, both share the fate of Sade's Justine. Michelet's sadistic the-

matics are well known, but his striking images of rape in *La Sorcière* fix the
diabolical counterpart to the paradisiacal return to the womb. The undercurrent of violence against women in *La Sorcière,* which is supposed to be
a defense of women, represents the revenge that the boy of Book I must
take against the mother who so humiliated him because she exercised such
great power by luring him into a treacherous alliance against the father:
she offered him an illusory oversized penis. If incest is the culmination of
Book I, it is surely the *basso profundo* of Book II, and Michelet's recurrent
fantasy of resuscitating the *jolie morte* (his wife, mother, and France) has
as its taboo counterpart sexual union on the marriage-deathbed in the *in-
pace.* There was something both horrifying and pleasurable about each
description in *La Sorcière,* book 2, that drew Michelet into an ever deeper
abyss of his own impotence.

The case of La Cadière parallels a Kafkaesque trial: her voice was long
lost in the shambles of justice: first, the reader finds out that, because she
could not write, her brothers wrote her letters for her (Michelet tries to
determine whose words are whose . . .); next, we are told that Girard
gained possession of all the correspondence and falsified it; Michelet dis-
credits the Registrar of the hearings; the Commission that rendered the
verdict ordered all of La Cadière's documents of defense destroyed after
the trial; the dossier at the Toulon library is set up in La Cadière's disfavor.
Finally, no word in any of the texts can be taken at face value; every piece
must be re-read *á demi-mot.* When an abbess writes to Girard of her *liberté*
(Michelet's italics), it means she would allow herself to be seduced by him.
A whole new language composed uniquely of euphemisms (e.g. *petites
infirmités* . . .) grows up through the complexity of a metaphorical network
in which one tries to translate the double-entendre of sex, death, and repressive politics. But this linguistic phenomenon itself repeats the reversal
of which *La Sorcière* speaks: euphemisms were meant, etymologically, to
protect God and the sacred, to ward off evil curses, for euphemism suggests
"good speech." But like the Golden Legend this figurative use of speech
was manipulated by the social forces to insure their continuation in power;
it is a form of "pressure exercised by the collectivity over the individual"
(John Orr, "Le Rôle destructeur de l'euphémie," *Cahiers de l'Association
Internationale des Etudes Françaises* 3–5 [1953]). The nuances of euphemism
add the final barrier to a language far too complicated for a simple defendant
to understand. Even lawyers and historians get twisted up in their own
catachrestic codes.

In Book II Michelet witnesses how judicial and historical machinery
forces its object, the witch, into categories, into sorts, into cells of sense:
printing *in-pace.* Whereas Michelet was eager in Book I to speak as several
shifters and to join them all into the universal *I* of Satan's Witch, as it
becomes clear that La Cadière has no voice in her own defense, the historian
loses his or rather abdicates, almost in embarrassment, and denies responsibility for what follows. The sign of the *énonciation,* the first person singular,

surfaces in *La Sorcière* at different times and is almost given a persona: "I have abridged and omitted much"; "I have omitted from the above picture." Michelet's ability to speak for his object, to replace in fact his voice for hers, is enhanced by the growing legitimacy of the Satanic substitution; in Satan's argument, one hears the historian speaking of his own relationship to the French reader: "I have seen it, your soul, I know it by heart, every hour of the day and night,—and better than you do yourself." The witch, who finds her tongue through Satan, practices the same ventriloquism on her timid mute clients: "Dumb, little one? Yet, what need to speak,—and you would never find words to tell. I will say it for you." In Book I everyone's desire and subjectivity is the general will, one might say that the *énoncé* is constantly being converted into *énonciation:* there is no difference between the historian's speech as it is written and that of his object as she speaks it. But the opposite seems to be the case in Book II. The historian's shifter *we* appears for the sole reason of pointing to its disappearance, and this exit is called "history." *We* is supplanted by an abstract voice that can speak of sex and death with impunity and without the need for euphemism; it seems in fact to be beyond the controls of the collectivity.

> The shocking narrative you will read is lifted textually from her (La Cadière's) three depositions (so naïve, of obvious veracity). We would have liked to abridge it to make it less painful. But then it would have no importance or utility. History, justice commands. Let us obey. Here it goes."
>
> [L'histoire, la justice commandent. Obéissons. Le voici." My trans. The passage is censured from the first French edition and from the English translation.]

At this very place in the text when the historian leaves to let "history" (the *énoncé*) speak, the "subjective" interpretation is most strident and desperate. The connection between history and justice is particularly problematic. History, the cognitive responsibility of the discipline, dictated that Michelet report not only La Cadière's "naïve" defense but her ultimate acquittal: Parliament finally reversed the preposterous decisions of the ecclesiastical courts. But according to Justice, the irreparable damage was done. Michelet imagines an ending that coincides with the structural repetition (the formula) he set up in the preceding chapters: "Eventually she disappeared, probably imprisoned under a *lettre de cachet,* and cast for the rest of her days into a living tomb." He later softens the melodrama to say simply "But I dare affirm she was never suffered to come back to . . . her native town, which had so loudly declared itself in her favour." Here it seems that his own fantasies, rather than merging with history, are, by the attempt to hide behind history, only exacerbated by the manoeuvre. History seems to drag the historian into material he both would and would rather not say; we know by his exit that he feels trapped. It is as if in his haste to escape from having to speak history Michelet finds himself in his own nightmare-fantasy funneling automatically into the *in-pace*. History's possession of the historian in Part I is celebratory (ego and unconscious speak as one *I*), but in Part II it is troubling; the possessed subject (in some ways like schizophrenia, like irony) both knows, is horrified, and yet does not know, forgets that someone else's voice comes out in place of his or hers.

Was then *La Sorcière* the other of the History of France or an ever more subtle collaboration with the machine of culture, the institution of cognition? "Dread apparatus for crushing and annihilating souls, cruel press for breaking hearts. The screw turns, and turns, till breath fails and the very bones crack, and she [the Sorceress] springs from the horrid engine a mystery in an unknown world!" Or was she, like any counter-culture (or any Revolution), re-assimilated as quickly as she was born? Or was she worse? The illusion of freedom and escape. Of the two "sublime faculties" of the Sorceress, the first was "the power of believing in her own falsehoods"; the second, reproduction by parthenogenesis: she gives birth by herself to a second, identical self, a son, Satan, a "conception of the mind," who, nevertheless, "has every mark of actuality. He has been seen and heard, and everybody can describe him." Though history, like the sorceress, can only reproduce itself (*la sorcière fait le sort*), it looks real and everyone acts as if it is.

But when everyone describes history, like Satan (according to what he or she has seen or heard), each historian must write an ever more imposing tome to establish the authority of his reading. Michelet himself was an obsessive writer. Especially after 1851, when he refused allegiance to the Second Empire and loses both his teaching post and his position at the National Archives, he has no other form of expression. His books begin to engulf him like a mollusk or madrepore in their volumes; the *Histoire de France* is in its fourteenth tome and still growing, but Michelet feels more and more alone. How could he be sure he was not the biggest Del Rio of them all? "From monk to monk the snowball goes on, ever growing. About 1600, the compilers being themselves subject to compilation and supplemented by the later recruits, we arrive at an enormous book, the *Disquisitiones Magicae*, of the Spaniard Del Rio." Michelet only propagated the culture of scholastics he detested saying "Words! Words! this resumes all their history. Their whole meaning was a tongue; phrasing and phrases (*verbe et verbalité*), and nothing else. One name will be theirs forever—Talkmongers (*Parole*)." Like the homeopathic magic of witchcraft where a poisoned plant is also the remedy, Michelet can kill the word only with the word. And no scientifically verifiable notion will assure us which pregnancy is the hot air of the nun's hysterical pregnancy or the satanic *aura*, the divine *afflatus*. Michelet, historian of the mute and dead, both believed and did not believe in his own falsehoods: "And as for the dumb, it was discovered, alas! that the individual who played this part was a known and proved impostor, a woman who had been caught red-handed in cheatery."

But history is far from farce, and if you laugh, as Georges Bataille knew, having first read Michelet with terror: *c'est que tu as peur* (*Madame Edwarda*). I myself (though this shifter sounds strange here) could at first only deal with Book II of *La Sorcière* in ironic terms, for I did not want to hear its helplessness and grief. And yet therein lies the cure.

Two metaphorical representations of utter frustration keep returning as out of a nightmare. They are both as melodramatic as a B-rated horror film and as serious as are their political implications. In one, a man who attends the Sabbath is more than castrated; he is literally made into a vegetable and must witness his wife being raped:

> They would entice to the festival some ill-advised married man, whom they proceed to intoxicate with their deadly brews . . . till he was *spellbound* [*enchanté*] and lost all power of motion and speech, but not the use of his eyes. His wife, also *spellbound*, but in a different way, with erotic beverages and reduced to a deplorable state of self-abandonment, would then be shown him naked and unashamed, patiently enduring the caresses of another before the indignant eyes of her natural protector, who could not stir a finger to help her.
>
> His manifest despair, his unavailing efforts to speak, his violent struggles to move his torpid limbs, his dumb rage, his rolling eyes, all provided the spectators with a cruel pleasure.

The second little fable tells of a medieval landowner who wakes to find himself completely dispossessed as a result of the rhetorical tricks of a neighboring Count who establishes feudalism, like many of his similarly ambitious contemporaries, by redefining *vassal* to mean, not valiant but serf.

> One there was who, under so dire an outrage, fell into such a passion of fury he could find never a word to say. Twas like Roland betrayed at Roncesvaux. All the blood of his body rose to his throat and choked him . . . His eyes flashed fire, his poor dumb mouth, dumb but so fiercely eloquent, turned all the assemblage pale. . . . They shrank back, in terror. . . . He was dead. His veins had burst. . . . His arteries shot the red blood into the very faces of his murderers. [Michelet's suspension points]

Is this what happens when a man comes into conflict with the sociolinguistic machines? Michelet's intense feeling of rage seems to have weakened the case of La Cadière instead of helping it. And what could he do but sit and watch the injustices of the Second Empire, but sit and write yet another book? He was perhaps on the side of the murderers too; the act of faith he sought in history was an *auto da fé*. Collingwood used the metaphor of screws and torture when referring to the historian's task, and Hexter quotes him: "He [the historian] must find a means of compelling the record to answer, devising tortures under which it can no longer hold its tongue, twisting a passage ostensibly about something different into an answer to the question he has decided to ask" (*The History Primer*). Is Michel de Certeau being too melodramatic, too "Freudian" when time and again he equates the *découpage* of time into a past with murder?

> Such is history. A game of life and death plays itself out in the calm unfolding of a narrative, resurgence and denial of the origin, unveiling of a dead past and result of a present practice. It reiterates, on a different register, the myths that are built up from a murder or an ordinary death and make out of language the trace that always remains of a beginning as impossible to recover as it is to forget.
>
> (*L'Ecriture de l'histoire*)

Michelet could not, after all, resurrect his dead until they were good and dead, until their bodies had been severed into historical periods which are, unfortunately for him, not natural like the woman's menstrual periods that he would imitate.

As a good liberal, Michelet wanted to show compassion and further justice; as a good anarchist, he wanted to jam the machine (see Hayden White, *Metahistory*: "Although Michelet thought of himself as a Liberal, . . . in reality the ideological implications of his conception of history are Anarchist"); as a writer and historian who accepted, in the course of *La Sorcière*, the implications of his trade, he invited a temporary cure by allowing the return in Book II of the banished fear of castration, of a feeling of impotence, and of a strong sense of guilt. At the same time, however, he understood the possibilities of subverting the system, of perhaps having it say what would outrage other historians.

Finally, cure meant not only accepting either reconciliation or repression of the separate ego within historical discourse, it meant accepting one's own death in the text of history. The thematics of death in Michelet's works is complicated and ambiguous: he was fascinated by the idea of death and considered he lived his life in an archival tomb. But accepting one's death within or in the margins of a text is not only signing it and allowing it to enter the marketplace, it is a return to something, that appeared to be one's possession, one's own body, as a reader or more specifically as a historian in order to cut it up and rearrange it in different sequences. Certain contemporary novelists try to protect themselves by incorporating a reading of themselves within their own text. Michelet simply quotes a whole block out of the *Histoire de France*. On the one hand, this gesture is simple, for Michelet often composed his different sorts of texts (natural history, history, *Journal*) as if they were a mutually inclusive *bricolage*; sometimes he copied a passage out by hand, sometimes he clipped a section and pasted it in. It is also obvious that his interpretation in Book II had so radically changed from the very short and mostly pejorative passages on witchcraft in the

Histoire de France that he had to rewrite that section. (The germ for an entirely new book seems most evident in a note added in 1860 to the *Histoire de France*, Book V, Chap. V, originally published in 1837: "The medieval sabbath is a nocturnal revolt of serfs against the God of the priests and seigneurs.") Still, the *Histoire de France* is completely banished from Book I of *La Sorcière* only to return simultaneously in the text with the inquisitioners and their tomes. And then: as both an undigested and digested morsel. Nor did Michelet duplicate anything the following year when he published a few pages on La Cadière in the *History of France*, Tome XV (1863). La Cadière as an individual appears in a note, referring the reader to *La Sorcière*, and the rest of the passage deals with the trial as the turning point in the struggle of secular over ecclesiastic justice. And yet Michelet never tells the reader of *La Sorcière* that he has reused whole chapters from himself. Clearly the chapters are to be read as integral to *La Sorcière* and not as foreign material. Quoting this mass of text has a double but contradictory result. Chapters already canonized in the *Histoire de France* secure *La Sorcière* literally in the middle of the text as if they form the ground of its history. From that monument a bridge can be built out over the dark "sea" of the medieval witch and back up again to a more controversial contemporary history. On the other hand, those chapters quoted verbatim are dead weight: Michelet wanted to use the energy of a fresh reading to dress up the corpse of his volumes, hoping thereby to resuscitate, by extension, the whole *Histoire de France*.

La Sorcière performs its possession either in the conciliatory mode of Book I or in the conflictual mode of Book II: centripetally, the woman-orphan-révoltée (*La Sorcière*) joins with the old pagan gods of the *Histoire de France*, and all converge in a central hoorah; centrifugally, the book of the Law-Church-Father, the *Histoire de France*, contaminates the outside chapters until the whole process is paralyzed or emptied out. The chapters from the *Histoire de France* speak in a bass voice from the mouth of a young woman (the body of *La Sorcière* surrounding the *Histoire de France*). Or a revolutionary discourse (*La Sorcière*) assumes power, while traditional history (*Histoire de France*) is captured and made into the alien other.

Michelet, the writer of 1861, also speaks the words of the dead self, sufficiently cut off from his present self so as to become a past. And even before he completes *La Sorcière* and signs it, he feels the same deadening and liberating process take over the "new" text, as fast as he can write it. Someone else, as from the dead, seems to be writing through him, if not his own voice from beyond the tomb. The last note of *La Sorcière* brings the book back to its tenuous origin and end as if history only extends between the writer's phrases, and then the historian launches his book in a compensatory gesture of cosmic confidence. He relates how he sits in a garden at Toulon watching dawn as did the former occupant of the same house where he is living, a man, recently dead, who was a doctor, i.e. the modern descendant, according to Michelet, of Satan and the Witch and who himself wrote a book entitled *Agony and Death*. Michelet (replacing now the dead doctor) sits in the garden filled with huge cactuses and suave African plants and looks across the bay to his future death; he looks to Hyères where, unknown to him then, he, Jules, will die in a dozen or so years. There is a last death the text does not tell: between the composition of the body of the text and its framework (epilogue, introduction, one chapter and notes) occurs the death of Michelet's only son whose funeral he did not attend.

The Treatment of Architecture in the Works of Edgar Quinet Published before 1851

Ceri Crossley

This article aims to provide a general description of the manner in which architecture is presented in those works which Quinet published prior to his departure into exile in December 1851. Our analysis does not claim to be exhaustive. We have for the most part limited our investigation to references to religious as opposed to secular architecture and our broad intention is to situate Quinet's attitude to architecture within the context of his understanding of the history of religions and the philosophy of history.

However, before we turn to a detailed discussion of the meaning which Quinet attributes to architectural creation we must first indicate briefly the main characteristics of his aesthetic theory. Fortunately for the reader Quinet's views on aesthetics are to be found conveniently summarised in his very short doctoral thesis entitled *Considérations philosophiques sur l'art* (1839). An examination of this thesis rapidly reveals that the author's prime concern is neither with the techniques involved in the production of great art, nor with the analysis of the reactions of a spectator contemplating a work of outstanding beauty. His aim is rather to assign to art a metaphysical meaning, in virtue of which he may proceed to both a classification of the different art forms and to a description of their historical development in relation to religion.

From the outset the writer makes abundantly clear his rejection of the doctrine of art for art's sake and his opposition to the theory that art is essentially an imitation of nature. He argues that the artist's goal should not be to produce a copy of the objects of the natural world since the latter are themselves symbols. The real task of the artist is to represent invisible, ideal beauty in sensuous form, to reveal the spiritual meaning of the uni-

From *Literature and Society: Studies in Nineteenth and Twentieth Century French Literature*, edited by C. A. Burns. © 1980 by Ceri Crossley. University of Birmingham, 1980.

verse. Quinet, nevertheless, does not deny the existence of natural beauty; nature is the creation of the divine artist and the objects of sense are already expressions of spirit in sensuous form. He is in no doubt, however, that artistic beauty belongs to a higher sphere than natural beauty. Moreover, like Goethe and Schelling, he stresses that the artist is the rival of nature. The artist transforms, recreates, perfects nature so as to reveal the presence of the divine, of the Idea. Natural beauty is incomplete because it is transient; art, which attains a higher level of reality, is capable of resisting the destructive power of the ravages of time.

Having put forward these general considerations Quinet moves on to develop a classification of the arts based upon a threefold division into Oriental, Greek and Christian art which is in some respects strongly reminiscent of the division into Symbolic, Classical and Romantic art proposed by Hegel. It is immediately apparent that Quinet's approach to the arts cannot be dissociated from his writings on the philosophy of history and the history of religions. For although the artist aspires to ideal beauty, this ideal generally takes the form of the idea of God as it is conceived by the collectivity of which the artist is a member. Consequently aesthetic questions cannot be resolved in isolation from the study of religion in its historical development.

Quinet identifies architecture with that first moment in the history of religions which he terms Oriental pantheism. Freedom and individuality barely existed at this early stage in the development of human consciousness. Man, far from seeking to impose his will upon nature, was content to reproduce the harmony of the universe. Nature was worshipped as divine. Architecture, according to Quinet, was well suited to give expression to the symbolic character of the religions of the East. Moreover, architecture has as its means of expression nature in its most material—hence its least free, least spiritual—form. In addition, it should be noted that Quinet shared the belief of so many of his contemporaries that architecture was essentially an anonymous, collective creation.

The next important stage after Oriental pantheism was the civilisation of ancient Greece. Man now became the measure of all things; freedom, individuality and consciousness of self all increased. This was the moment when, in Hegelian terms, the Absolute was conceived as concrete spirit; in Quinet's terms, man replaced nature as the symbol of the divine. The anthropomorphic character of the Greek idea of God resulted in that apotheosis of humanity which received its finest expression in statuary: in sculpture man represented himself as a demi-god, free from all that was contingent and transient. The serenity of classical Greek art was, however, destroyed by the coming of Christianity which signalled the birth of genuine individuality, of true subjectivity. Now painting came to the fore. In accord with the spirit of the Christian religion, it depicted men not as demi-gods, but as suffering individuals living in history.

In the light of the close link which we have seen Quinet make between

architecture and Oriental pantheism it comes as something of a surprise to
the reader to discover that nowhere does he undertake a detailed examination of the architecture of the East. Whilst attention is paid to the Greek
temple, to the mosque and particularly to the Gothic cathedral, we encounter only passing references to "les temples des Indiens et des Ara-
méens" or to the influence of planetary worship upon the form of the
seven-walled city of Ecbatana (*De la nature et de l'histoire dans leurs rapports
avec les traditions religieuses et épiques*). Indeed, insofar as the architecture of
the "Orient" is discussed at all it would appear to be largely synonymous
with the monuments of ancient Egypt. And yet, when Egyptian religion
is looked at in some detail in *Le Génie des religions* (1842) we learn disappointingly little on the subject of architecture. The truth of the matter is
that Quinet does not wish to adhere strictly to his historico-religious framework. The spacio-temporal location of a particular art form is in no way
absolute; each art possesses its own history. What is more, the arts can
also be said to form a hierarchy in virtue of their increasing spiritual content,
a hierarchy rising from architecture through sculpture and painting to music
and poetry.

Since architecture takes as the matter of its appearance inorganic nature
the first question which we must ask is: to what extent do the origins of
architectural form lie in an imitation of nature? Quinet's thesis provides an
answer:

> Presque toujours la géologie a décidé des formes primitives de
> l'architecture. La forme pyramidale des monuments égyptiens a
> des relations avec la nature granitique des terrains. Au contraire,
> les assises parallèles des temples grecs semblent être le prolonge-
> ment des couches calcaires des montagnes de la Grèce.
> (*Considerations philosophiques sur l'art*)

It is to be noted that this idea had already been developed in *De la
Grèce moderne et de ses rapports avec l'antiquité* (1830) where Quinet informs
us that the famous Cyclopean walls blend so well with their natural setting
that the spectator is at a loss to decide at which point the walls themselves
begin. In a like manner he asserts that the tiers of seats of the ancient
amphitheatres follow directly the shape of the curve formed by the mountains. The best illustration of the relationship between architecture and
nature is, however, provided by the Greek temple: "[les temples] bâtis sur
le plan de la contrée tout entière, faisaient en quelque manière partie de
l'édifice de la nature, achevée, couronnée par l'esprit et par la main de
l'homme" (*Le Génie des religions*).

Quinet was, of course, not alone in wishing to associate a certain
architectural style with a particular country, climate and scenery. Chateaubriand, drawing inspiration from Bernardin de Saint-Pierre's *Harmonies de
la nature* had had similar ambitions. In his *Itinéraire de Paris à Jérusalem* he
drew a close parallel between Greek art and its environment:

Les climats influent plus ou moins sur le goût des peuples. En Grèce, par exemple, tout est suave, tout est adouci, tout est plein de calme dans la nature comme dans les écrits des anciens. On conçoit presque comment l'architecture du Parthénon a des proportions si heureuses, comment la sculpture antique est si peu tourmentée, si paisible, si simple, lorsqu'on a vu le ciel pur et les paysages gracieux d'Athènes, de Corinthe et de l'Ionie. Dans cette patrie des Muses la nature ne conseille point les écarts; elle tend au contraire à ramener l'esprit à l'amour des choses uniformes et harmonieuses.

In the case of Quinet, however, we must also bear in mind the wider philosophical context within which his writings on art and aesthetics are set. In an essay which appeared in 1830 he argues that the Absolute which manifests itself as unconscious nature subsequently aspires to self-knowledge in and through the mind of man. The history of religions is envisaged as a westward movement of peoples; different natural environments are unconscious, objective representations of divine thoughts which are then given subjective, conscious expression by certain collectivities. The idea of God produced by each religion is the fullest realisation possible of the divine thought which is present in nature at that point. Man is the "parole vivante" of nature which speaks through him. This notion underlies much of Quinet's understanding of both art and of religion. For our purposes a convenient example is provided by the following reference to the frieze of a Greek temple:

De toutes parts les lignes, les formes, les harmonies errantes sur le penchant des monts, viennent à se rencontrer au sommet dans cet organe intelligent [le frise], et donner comme une figure éternelle à la pensée, qui végète ou scintille au soleil, ou s'écoule en grondant au fond des vallées.

(*De la Grèce moderne et de ses rapports avec l'antiquité*)

Art cannot be explained as an imitation of nature in any restricted sense. Art is the revelation of the idea which lies hidden in nature:

le temple, le théâtre, l'enceinte, et le mont diaphane, et la colline aux flancs ouverts, et les couches de marbre, mutuellement se mirent dans leurs formes et s'achèvent l'un l'autre. . . . Merveilleux types d'art, toute chose autour d'eux, dans l'ombre et la lumière, tend à s'en approcher sans pouvoir les atteindre; et nous touchons aux lieux où l'architecture n'est rien autre que le moule idéal de la nature, reproduit par l'humanité, et sur lequel se sont mystérieusement organisés, dans l'origine, la cosmogonie et le génie d'une contrée.

This method of interpretation is in fact analogous to that used by Quinet elsewhere, in his analysis of myth and religion. The two worlds of nature and history whose ideal identity is realised in myth also combine in architecture. Architecture becomes a silent epic, having its origins in nature but unfolding in history (*De la nature et de l'histoire*). An important conclusion follows from these remarks. If, despite obvious superficial differences, the architectural monuments of all periods can be interpreted as reflecting in various ways the relationship between nature and history, then the way is open to consider the history of architecture as a continuity: "des temples de Thèbes jusqu'à la cathédrale gothique il n'y a qu'une modification continuelle d'une forme primitive." Moreover, this continuity is the continuity of the history of religions. Architecture becomes a tangible expression of the stages through which the religious consciousness has evolved. The pyramids of Egypt, the temples of Greece, the Gothic cathedral are all visible milestones which mark stages along the road of mankind's quest for the Absolute (cf. Quinet's remarks on Voss and Heine in *Allemagne et Italie* [1838]).

It should be emphasised that the notion of continuity does not invalidate the threefold division which we have described above. Quinet never abandons the belief that the distance separating Greece from the Orient is also that which separates sculpture from architecture. Hence the significance which he attributes to the Lion Gate at Mycenae in which he finds evidence of the Greek achievement in the history of religions. The Lion Gate marks the first appearance of "l'esprit hellénique" still absent from the surrounding architecture. The monument hovers uncertainly between "le génie du symbole et la beauté de l'art," between architecture and sculpture, between Asia and Europe. No longer "purement égyptien" the forms depicted in the bas-relief take on "un commencement de vie." Here, for the first time, "[la Grèce] cherche à se mouvoir et à se dégager en groupes plastiques sur le seuil du monument sacerdotal de l'Asie" (*De la Grèce moderne*).

The foregoing example reinforces our view that in Quinet's eyes architecture, far from being identified with the East and with oriental pantheism in an exclusive manner, is in fact taken to be the art form which most adequately renders the symbolic character of periods of intense religious faith irrespective of time and place. And in point of fact the monument to which Quinet devotes most attention is the Gothic cathedral, the embodiment of the spirit of medieval Christianity:

> Cette vaste nef, avec ses deux chapelles latérales en forme de croix, et qui figure le corps du Christ dans le sépulcre, ce mystère, ces demi-ténèbres, cette tour principale, qui, image du pouvoir spirituel, monte dans la nue, n'est-ce pas là l'édifice, non de la chair, mais de l'esprit?
>
> (*Le Génie des religions*)

In *Ahasvérus* (1883) the voice of the cathedral rings out:

> Les nombres me sont sacrés: sur leur harmonie je m'appuie sans peur. Mes deux tours et ma nef font le nombre trois et la Trinité. Mes sept chapelles, liées à mon côté, sont mes sept mystères qui me serrent les flancs. Ah! que leur ombre est noire et muette et profonde! Mes douze colonnes dans le chœur de pierre d'Afrique sont mes douze apôtres, qui m'aident à porter ma croix; et moi je suis un grand chiffre lapidaire que l'Eternité trace, de sa main ridée, sur sa muraille, pour compter son âge.

As the Greek temple was related to its surroundings, so the Gothic cathedral incorporates into its structure elements drawn from nature:

> Tout ce qu'il [le christianisme] a trouvé sur sa route, et tout ce qui vit autour de lui, fleurs, eaux, formes, esprits cachés dans les montagnes, dans les forêts, dans les replis des rocs, pics aiguisés des Alpes, ombres des pins, pierres oubliées des druides, il recueille tout cela, comme l'oiseau fait son nid. Il s'en vêtit ainsi que d'un manteau contre les froids d'hiver, et, sentant que c'est le lieu où il doit s'arrêter, il se bâtit de ces objets épars des abris gigantesques, d'obscures cathédrales pour y passer sans remuer les siècles qui lui restent.
>
> ("De l'avenir des religions")

As early as the thirteenth century "une même architecture, la gothique, s'etait formée depuis les confins de l'Andalousie jusqu'aux extrémités de la Suède" (*Allemagne et Italie*). Gothic is not, therefore, the exclusive property of Northern Europe. It took on new aspects under the influence of different climates, environments and national geniuses. In Italy, for example, the religious architecture of the North was substantially modified as a new element of pagan sensuality manifested itself. This phenomenon, Quinet maintains, is clearly discernible in Milan cathedral:

> La voûte ténébreuse du Nord s'est changée en un marbre blanc d'un éclat presque païen. Sur cette terre de Saturne, le mysticisme de l'architecture gothique est dépaysé; le soleil ardent du Midi pénètre, avec une curiosité profane, jusqu'au fond de la nef. Le trèfle et la rose chrétienne ont fait place, dans les ornements, au laurier idolâtre. D'ailleurs il n'y a plus de flèche qui monte dans le ciel.

Turning to the subject of Venetian architecture, Quinet not surprisingly likens St. Mark's to St. Sophia. The strong Byzantine influence meant that the grandeur of the cathedrals of the North was absent: "[l'architecture de Venise] ne porte pas dans les nues la pensée religieuse d'une race nouvelle." Florence, on the other hand, marks the fusion of Christianity with pagan antiquity. The spirit of the Renaissance is embodied in Brunelleschi's cathedral dome. Having travelled to Rome, Quinet offers the following comment upon St. Peter's: "Plus de symboles de douleur comme dans l'architecture du Nord ou dans la byzantine; ni croix, ni sépulcre: c'est ici l'emblème du Christ régnant, ou plutôt le temple d'un Jupiter chrétien." He concludes the account of his Italian journey, by remarking that in Italy Gothic architecture extended no further south than Rome. In other words the genius of the Italian people developed between the twin poles of Milan cathedral and the ruins of Paestum which are taken respectively to stand as symbols of the Germanic and the Greek worlds. (Between 1848 and 1852 Quinet published in three volumes his long cultural history of the Italian people entitled *Les Révolutions d'Italie*. In this work he interprets the early development of architecture in Italy as follows: "Dans le dixième et le onzième siècle, toute l'Italie se couvre sans bruit d'églises, de tours, de dômes, de *palais du peuple*. Plus la langue de ces temps est stérile, plus ces chroniques de pierre parlent haut: peuplées de statues et de peintures, elles expriment ce que les lèvres ne pourraient encore dire. L'architecture de l'ogive et l'architecture à plein cintre se disputent le sol, à la suite du parti de l'Empire et du parti du Sacerdoce. Comme un enfant qui ne peut encore parler s'exprime par une foule de gestes, ainsi l'Italie moderne, déjà pleine de pensées et de factions, mais dont la langue n'est pas encore déliée, s'exprime en gestes de pierre par son architecture guelfe et gibeline.")

Quinet visited Italy in 1831. More than a decade later and by now a Professor at the Collège de France he undertook a journey to Spain and Portugal. Once again his attention was drawn to the Gothic monuments which he encountered. Thus Burgos cathedral provides an excellent illustration of the role played by climate and vegetation in the development of architectural form:

> Oserai-je dire que je retrouve l'aridité de la Castille sur la face de la cathédrale de Burgos? Des soleils séculaires ont tari la sève de la rose gothique; les deux clochers aigus armés de pointes rappellent les tiges hérissées de l'aloès. Quelques statues apparaissent de distance en distance, rares habitants de ces hauts murs gris de bruyères. [*Mes Vacances en Espagne* (1846). Many of the points made in this work are also discussed in *L'Ultramontanisme ou l'église romaine et la société moderne* (1844) and *Le Christianisme et la Révolution française* (1845).]

Having travelled as far as Toledo, Quinet tried to define the particular nature of Spanish Gothic. He remarks that, whereas elsewhere in Europe the cathedral was primarily a symbol of the Holy Sepulchre, in Spain it took on a new significance since it came to symbolise the victory of Christianity over the forces of Islam. A number of factors, however, come together to produce that which is unique in Spanish Gothic architecture:

> En France, en Allemagne, en Angleterre, l'Eglise du moyen âge, c'est le deuil éternel. En Italie, le luxe de l'art moderne va jusqu'à

effacer l'impression religieuse du passé; d'ailleurs le gothique n'a jamais pu y prendre profondément racine. L'Espagne est le seul pays qui ait concilié des nefs du Nord avec la splendeur païenne du Midi. Sur la face macérée du moyen âge elle a jeté le linceul de pourpre de la Renaissance. Imaginez Notre-Dame de Paris couverte de l'or des Incas et des Caciques, un mélange de religions et de dieux opposés, l'ascétisme de la cathédrale, les treillages et les jalousies de marbre de la mosquée, la magnificence du temple du Soleil, Cologne, Damas, Mexico, subitement rapprochés dans une légende de pierre.

A visit to the mosque of Cordova provided Quinet with an ideal opportunity to compare and contrast the Gothic cathedral directly with the mosque. Christian cathedrals, we are told, are always firmly rooted in the earth:

Dans nos cathédrales chrétiennes, les plus grandes hardiesses reposent toujours sur un fond de raison. On est rassuré aussitôt qu'étonné. Voyez comme les tours du catholicisme sont profondément enracinées, comme elles posent un large pied sur terre; elles ne tendent pas à renverser les lois de la gravité et les mathématiques éternelles.

The mosque, on the other hand, is described as the house of a capricious deity, far removed in character from the God worshipped in the cathedral:

Logique, expérience, principe, raison, nature, tout cela disparaît devant une fantaisie du sultan de l'univers; en sorte que la gloire de sa maison consiste à contrarier, à renverser toutes les habitudes de l'éternelle géométrie.

Even the manner in which the two types of monument were erected is contrasted. The building of the Gothic cathedral extended over a long period; the mosque, on the other hand, is an example of what Quinet terms spontaneous architecture. Its construction was completed, "comme le Coran, en une seule époque." Yet despite the fact that Quinet discerns such differences between the two styles he still asserts that each possesses a particular type of beauty deriving from the character of the religion concerned:

Dans nos cathédrales, la végétation divine plus resserrée monte, aspire de cimes en cimes. Le tronc plus vigoureux des piliers porte haut son branchage. Sa beauté est dans la nue, tandis que la sève arabe va s'épuisant dans la foule des rejetons et des colonnes. Mais, ce que cette architecture perd d'un côté, elle le regagne de l'autre; car le sublime de la mosquée, c'est de n'avoir pas de limites à l'horizon. Elle s'étend, en un moment, comme le royaume de l'Islam, sur une surface sans bornes. Dès que vous êtes engagé

dans les colonnes, vous perdez de vue l'enceinte. Point de mu-
railles; il reste l'immensité monotone d'Allah, partout semblable
à lui-même, beauté, majesté, solitude incommensurable, religion
du désert.

As long as faith remained unquestioned the Gothic spires continued
to climb towards the heavens. "Encore! encore! oh! je veux monter plus
haut" is the cry of the cathedral in *Ahasvérus*. But as the Middle Ages fell
into decline, so the building of the cathedrals ceased:

[l'architecture gothique] était arrivée à son faîte avec la société
qu'elle représentait. Elle n'avait pas la force de monter plus
haut. . . . La plupart des cathédrales allaient rester inachevées; un
vent froid avait souffleé sur ces plantes célestes et les avait étiolées
à leurs cimes.

(*Des arts de la Renaissance, et de l'église de Brou*)

The coming of the Reformation and the Renaissance signalled that the
religious aspiration of the age of faith had passed: "le dôme du seizième
siècle s'arrondissait déjà sur les ruines de l'architecture gothique et byzantine." In Quinet's eyes the cathedral at Brou stands as a highly charged
symbol of the last phase of the development of Gothic architecture. The
edifice is an example of an "architecture expirante" and it embodies "la
lassitude et l'affaissement" of the end of an epoch. The spirit of asceticism
which characterised the great cathedrals is absent from this church which
has become a monument to earthly love, to personal feeling and emotion.
Unlike the cathedrals, which were the creation of the collectivity over a
period of generations, Brou is the expression of "une pensée individuelle
et isolée"; here, continues Quinet, "l'individualité triomphante des modernes s'est divinisé."

In conclusion we should note that Quinet considers the present both
as a time of crisis marked by doubt and anxiety and as a period which may
presage a new religious rebirth (cf. Quinet's use of the theme of the ruined
church as symbol in *Allemagne et Italie* and *Ahasvérus*). Does this suggest
that a corresponding transformation of religious architecture will take place?
In 1831 he certainly points to the possibility of such a transformation: the
Gothic cathedral may yet grow and develop new forms (this transformation
needs to be envisaged in the light of Quinet's belief that a rebirth of religion
may take place in America). It should be emphasised, however, that this
is an isolated example. The lectures delivered at the Collège de France in
the 1840s represent an unambiguous call to action. In the modern world,
so Quinet maintains, Christianity becomes a reality by advancing the causes
of freedom, equality, fraternity and solidarity; the Christian message is
inextricably linked to the destiny of revolutionary France. Catholicism, in
comparison, stands condemned as the embodiment of sterility and reaction.
This hostility towards the Church of Rome means that Quinet cannot allow

the Gothic cathedral to play an important role in his vision of mankind's future. For what is the cathedral if not a symbol of the past, of the Middle Ages? Henceforth the encounter between the human and the divine will will take place within the spirit of the individual.

Sainte-Beuve's Literary Portraiture

Emerson R. Marks

For the literary criticism of Charles Augustin Sainte-Beuve the last half-century has been a long night of comparative disfavor and, in the English-speaking world at least, of neglect. Though the appearance of A. G. Lehmann's study in 1962 and of new English translations of selected essays since then may be signs of a revival of sorts, no important critic or school of critics today claims him as intellectual ancestor. During the years of unparalleled fascination with the subject, the most influential and historically conscious analyses of literary criticism made hardly more than passing reference to his work. Wimsatt and Brooks allow him in all a single page of their *Literary Criticism: A Short History.* Northrop Frye's *Anatomy of Criticism* contents itself with one reference, Wellek and Warren's *Theory of Literature* with two. On the face of it this would seem a strange fate for a man who between his death in 1869 and the first World War was often called the greatest of critics and whose manner and doctrine were widely copied in Britain and the United States. Certainly it is hard to think of any other critic whose reputation and influence suffered so complete a decline.

Yet as a fact of literary history Sainte-Beuve's case is more arresting than mysterious. It is a symptom, perhaps the most startling and dramatic of many, of that reorientation—revolution may be too strong a word for it—in the total function of criticism instituted by T. S. Eliot. Since Eliot's early essays the predominant view has been that the critic's business was with the literary work, not with the man or personality or mind that produced it, and the "biographical" soon took its place among a small group of well-defined critical heresies. In such a situation Sainte-Beuve could hardly escape the severe downgrading that ensued. Was he not the author of several collections of essays whose primary concern with the psychology

From *L'Esprit Créateur* 14, no. 1 (Spring 1974). © 1974 by *L'Esprit Créateur*.

of authors was advertised by the word *Portrait* appearing in the titles of three of them? And did he not late in life declare himself a natural historian of minds, for whom literary study was only a means to the end of moral study? The fact that Sainte-Beuve's varied practice includes a great deal of critical writing which is neither moral history nor biography, that he often focused on texts, and more than once protested against confusing a writer and his book—all this was generally overlooked. Lately, it would appear, it has been simply unknown. The persistent modern caricaturing of Sainte-Beuve as critic prompted A. G. Lehmann to wonder how much of his work his modern judges have actually read. He especially deplores "the standard approach which makes him out to be the founder of the *Personal Heresy.* Because even if he was that," Lehmann adds, "he was a great deal else besides" (*Sainte-Beuve: A Portrait of the Critic, 1804–1842*).

Postponing for a moment the question of the personal heresy, no defense of Sainte-Beuve against his modern detractors can deny that the literary portrait, however conceived or practiced, is the distinctive mark of his criticism. In fact, those who do take the trouble to read much of his voluminous prose will not easily find reason to challenge Ferdinand Brunetière's conclusion that Sainte-Beuve's peculiar contribution was "l'introduction du *portrait* dans la critique" (*L'Evolution des genres*). The real question, one that it will be enlightening and useful to pose now, is what the literary portrait in fact is at its best—and at its worst. Its worst was what Eliot had in mind when in 1929 he traced to Sainte-Beuve the critics' habit of neglecting novels or poems as works of art to examine instead the "personality" of the age they expressed ("Experiment in Criticism"). Considering the great vogue and influence of Sainte-Beuve's *Portraits* and *Lundis* among British and American men of letters during the half-century following his death, there is no reason to question Eliot's ascription. Lehmann's impression is that the French critic's reputation has suffered from the bad habits of later critics claiming to adopt his method; but even if it can be shown that these imitators did, by the dreary inverse alchemy of their kind, turn Sainte-Beuve's gold into lead, much of the base metal was patently of his own mining. In the *Portraits littéraires,* the *Portraits contemporains,* and the *Portraits de femmes,* as well as in the later-written *Lundis,* there are several critiques in which literary works are slighted in favor of painstakingly detailed and often prolix studies of the psychology of authors. Whatever the sins of his disciples, Sainte-Beuve's own example, often enough, would have been sufficient to diminish his standing in the eyes of a generation who, having learned to regard a close reading of texts as their proper business, was to interdict not only the Personal Heresy but, with equal rigor, the Intentional Fallacy.

The critical ideal implied by these principles and prohibitions is as sorely affronted by some of the older commentary on Sainte-Beuve as by his own bad example. For Gustave Michaut, writing eighty years ago, Sainte-Beuve's biographical preoccupations were a definite virtue because "la critique a pour but de donner un portrait vivant de l'homme, afin de comprendre et juger l'oeuvre où cet homme, même malgré lui, s'est révelé" (*Saint-Beuve avant les "Lundis"*). Such a conception of the critical function put forth by a leading *Beuvien* could only serve to confirm the worst suspicions about him in the minds of those taught by Eliot that "the poet has, not a 'personality' to express, but a particular medium" ("Tradition and the Individual Talent," in *Selected Essays*).

It was Eliot himself who once suggested that no critical doctrine is ever quite correct ("Matthew Arnold," in *The Use of Poetry and the Use of Criticism*), presumably not excluding his own. But of the two opposing views of the relation of the artist to his art represented by Michaut's words and by the celebrated phrase from "Tradition and the Individual Talent," it is Eliot's that is more fully supportable from critical history. If a fairer estimate of Sainte-Beuve's literary criticism than that now prevalent can be made, it will not be by appealing to the kind of naïve biographism which he himself often repudiated.

The better way is to admit that some of the objections to Sainte-Beuve's practice are justified. His substitutions of biography or "psychography" for a direct analysis of a work are not rare exceptions. In the piece on Madame de Staël in *Portraits de femmes*, one can still admire the combination of meticulous research with engaging critical analysis and sheer narrative charm. The analysis itself, however, is slim, and disproportionate attention is given to work of little intrinsic merit. Sainte-Beuve quotes and discusses at length de Staël's youthful poetry, mainly for what it reveals of the author. For the same reason, and only for that reason, *Delphine* and *Corinne* receive far more space than the *Allemagne*. Coming to *De la littérature*, he disappointingly turns from the book itself to the debate stirred up by its publication. It is much the same with the essay on Madame de Lafayette. There are some trenchant remarks on her narrative concision and a brief appreciative description of *La Princesse de Clèves*, its tone, style, and structure; but these are buried in a long account of her highly rational mind, her distaste for letter-writing, her relationship with Madame de Sévigné, her liaison with La Rochefoucauld, and her long final illness.

Similar examples can be found in the other series of *Portraits*. The Molière essay included in *Portraits littéraires* contains some dozen pages of excellent characterization of the playwright's comic art and dramatic genius, but they comprise only about a fifth of the total. Nor did Sainte-Beuve's mature years diminish his biographical penchant. Though less prodigal of anecdotes and sometimes more deft in the strokes of its portraiture, the typical *causerie* of the two great series contains if anything less direct explication of specific works than do the earlier *Portraits*.

This peculiarity of Sainte-Beuve's work has, I think, little or nothing to do with his alleged adoption of a so-called scientific method. True, he called himself a natural historian of minds and in certain aspects of his practice he anticipates the naturalist criticism which Hippolyte Taine tried to erect into an all-embracing system. But like his theory of the families of minds, conceived on an analogy with the classification of biological species, these notions seem now to have been largely obeisances to the prevailing scientism of his age. They are rarely applied to specific writers and then only in a crude and undeveloped manner. His actual procedure rather supports Victor Giraud, among others, in his view that Sainte-Beuve was no scientist dispassionately toiling in a literary laboratory of psychological natural history, but instead "un lettré, un littérateur," and if not in fact a dilettante certainly "un humaniste" (*La Critique littéraire*).

The humanist Sainte-Beuve had nonetheless his "flair psychologique" (in Philippe Van Tieghem's phrase) (*Histoire de la littérature française*) which, to judge from the whole tenor of his writings, including the novel *Volupté*, was an interest even more compelling than his fascination with history, human or natural. The roots of this psychologistic bent are probably beyond the knowing even of psychologists, but some of its manifestations in criticism are plain enough. One is the tendency to relish fact over fiction, even, curiously, to find it more dramatic than fiction. Samuel Johnson, another shrewd prober of the human psyche, whose literary biographies Sainte-Beuve warmly admired, confessed that biographical literature was his favorite. Mr. F. L. Lucas, a modern literary psychologist, goes so far as to declare that "novels in general, unless superlatively written, seem to me a feeble waste of time compared with biography and psychology" (*Literature and Psychology*). In an important part of his temperament Sainte-Beuve belongs in the company of these men. Commentators have often remarked on the large number of *causeries* given over to memoirs, letters, and histories, and some critics have acknowledged ruefully how frequently he gave precedence to generals and statesmen over genuine men of letters, and to second-raters over artists of the first rank. In a psychographer, however, these preferences are understandable and predictable: nonimaginative writings will serve as well as fictive productions to recreate the living man. Indeed, they may do better, if, as I shall argue is often Sainte-Beuve's case, that "re-creation" is itself an imaginative work, imbued with aesthetic qualities of its own.

Sainte-Beuve's preoccupation with diaries, letters, and recorded conversations goes beyond their obvious importance to the literary biographer. At times he takes a quasi-aesthetic delight in them, and the verve with which he sifts and interprets their contents enlivens many of his pages. In *Port-Royal*, for example, he dwells long and fondly on the letter in which Antoine Le Maître announced his decision to join the famous Jansenist community. This letter, Sainte-Beuve declares, is no less beautiful than *Polyeucte* or *Athalie*. The apparent indifference to the aesthetic mode which such an utterance betrays can only confirm some modern readers in their poor opinion of Sainte-Beuve as critic. It lends credence to the charge that criticism proper doesn't interest him because literature properly so-called doesn't especially attract him. What else can one conclude of a critic who in some forty pages on Stendhal confines his treatment of *Le Rouge et le noir* and *La Chartreuse de Parme* to a brief complaint about their morality? His very tone suggests not only misjudgment but even indifference: "Romancier, Beyle a eu un certain succès" (*Causeries du lundi*).

This restriction of his appreciative powers, however, beclouds only one facet of his total sensibility. So many-sided is Sainte-Beuve's performance that any generalization about it needs a qualification almost as weighty as the generalization itself. Unlike Lucas, Sainte-Beuve is not prone to invidious comparisons among literary genres. Receptive and tolerant to a fault, he was an omnivorous reader whose motto might have been *nihil scriptum mihi alienum*. Nor can there by any question of his having favored biographical and character studies because of an incapacity for critical analysis and evaluation. Few *Portraits* or *Causeries* are without some examination of specific works, and many contain passages of "pure" criticism that reveal an uncommon degree of sensitivity and appreciative talent. These occur at every period of his life from the earliest reviews in the *Globe* through the last *Lundis*.

What we have in the best pages of Sainte-Beuve, however, is something different from the kind of thing produced by mere critical acumen and good taste—something different and, if not better, at any rate rarer. Though one hesitates to evoke the rather discredited term *creative criticism*, the finest *Portraits* are works of imaginative appeal, of a quality not surprising in one for whom poetry was "mon premier et mon dernier amour," and who, unable quite to make his mark as poet, yet maintained to the end collateral relations with the muse. The early study of Madame de Charrière (1839) opens with the frank avowal that his literary portraits are not criticism at all in any strict sense. He employs the critical essay only as a "cadre . . . , une forme . . . pour produire nos propres sentiments sur le monde et sur la vie, pour exhaler avec détour une certaine poésie cachée. C'est un moyen quelquefois, au sein d'une Revue grave, de continuer peut-être l'élégie interrompue."

There is here, unmistakably, a touch rather too precious, the romantic attitudinizing of a not yet defunct Delorme. Yet to dismiss the statement, with a recent French critic, as a mere piece of "coquetterie" (Roger Fayolle, *Sainte-Beuve et le XVIIIe siècle*) too blandly overlooks the actual quality of the *Portraits* and *Lundis* themselves, those of them to which we most willingly return. Sainte-Beuve was obliged at last, after long struggle, to abandon his rash dream of being a poet who would on occasion raise his critical voice in the reviews. But the unique tone of that voice, the range of its sympathy and responsiveness, rather enforces Gérald Antoine's judgment that "parmi les cendres d'un poète téméraire Sainte-Beuve a su réchauffer la veine du critique le plus souple, et de poète-critique devenir . . . critique-poète" (*Sainte-Beuve: Vie, poésies et pensées de Joseph Delorme*). As critic he could savor, in Longinian terms, the most impassioned poetry, could celebrate in Musset, for example, "cette vertu d'ascension merveilleuse qui transporte en un clin d'oeil" (*Portraits contemporains*). In contrast, his own poetic leaning, as an admirer of the English "Lakists," favored a verse "cotoyant la prose," as he put it in a metrical epistle. When such "vers prosé" fails, as M. Antoine does not neglect to point out, it becomes a mere "vers prosaique." Though the judgment is no doubt presumptuous in any but a native French speaker, it seems fair to ask whether lines like these from "Le Suicide" are not an instance of this lapse:

> Ce n'est pas un regret, un espoir qui l'enchaine;
> C'est pur désir de voir, curiosité vaine,
> Qui le retarde encor.

Admittedly there is a kind of poetic prose as offensive to good taste as the most pedestrian verse, much of it perpetrated in the criticism written by poets *manqués*. With Sainte-Beuve, however, owing perhaps to his unusual intelligence, even the most casual incursion of the fanciful into the discursive, far from seeming an intrusion, is typically a metaphorical equivalent of some moral or aesthetic discrimination. "Respectons," he writes, "honorons donc la libéralité naturelle et raisonnée de Mme Geoffrin; mais reconnaissons toutefois qu'il manque à toute cette bonté et à cette bienfaisance une certaine flamme céleste, comme il manque à tout cet esprit et à cet art social du XVIIIᵉ siècle une fleur d'imagination et de poésie, un fond de lumière également céleste. Jamais on ne voit dans le lointain le bleu du ciel ni la clarté des étoiles" (*Causeries du lundi*). Needless to say, this passage is not Sainte-Beuve at his best. Yet read against the lines from "Le Suicide" it may suggest how a poetic talent too limited for the role of *poète-critique* could be turned to the account of the *critique-poète*.

Sainte-Beuve once told a correspondent that he took as his motto the English word *Truth*, a fact often misread to argue him a naturalist in revolt from earlier rhetorical criticism. Neither history nor biography, Beuvian portraiture is an art which employs the materials of both and shares with both their disciplined care for fact and detail. The portraits in Théophile Gautier's *Les Grotesques*, Sainte-Beuve complained, fell short in precisions of detail, whereas his own "procédé de *peintre*" in *Port-Royal*, he elsewhere insists, was not to reduce by a few bold strokes the unique features of his persons to "quelque grandes lignes principales," but instead by patient aggregation and revision to record every individualizing particular. The impulse to this scrupulosity came not from pedantry but from the artistic conviction (so passionately affirmed by William Blake) that "rien ne vit que par les détails: celui qui a l'ambition de peindre doit les chercher" (*Port-Royal*). Clearly, Sainte-Beuve's truth was moral and imaginative truth, not the truth of the historiographer or the naturalist. "Ce n'est pas l'histoire de Port-Royal que j'écris. . . . C'est le portrait."

Truth in this sense is opposed not to the imaginative or the fictive but to the false, the sham. In Sainte-Beuve's thinking truth so conceived becomes a criterion for artist and critic alike. He was never a naïve realist. As early as 1835 he saw the critical irrelevancy of guessing the identity of the real persons from whom Madame de Staël may have drawn the characters in *Delphine*. He expected no fidelity to any real original "chez les romanciers d'imagination féconde." His mature conception of the creative imagination, which is set forth in *Chateaubriand et son groupe*, liberates it from the shackles of the probable or the actual. Adopting the old figure of the mimetic mirror, he makes it a magic one, which heightens and rearranges the world it reflects. Yet, although he admits the distinction may be subtle, he sharply separates true artistic distortion from the morally fraudulent, the misleading. "Je voudrais qu'on peut dire du talent qu'il est un *enchanteur*, jamais un *imposteur*."

Sainte-Beuve's grasp of the vital difference between historical and imaginative truth is admirably demonstrated in the thoroughly Aristotelian conception of dramatic *mimesis* that informs his brilliant appreciation of Molière in *Port-Royal*. First comes the theory: "Chez Molière, plus que chez aucun auteur dramatique en France, le théâtre, si profondément vrai, n'est pas du tout, quant aux détails, une copie analysée, ni une imitation littéralement *vraisemblable* d'alentour; c'est une reproduction originale, une création, un monde." Then, from the scene in which Tartuffe throws his handkerchief to Dorine to cover her bare throat, comes the application: "Cela n'est pas vraisemblable, dira-t-on! mais cela parle, cela tranche; et la vérité du fond et de l'ensemble crée ici celle du détail. . . . Avec Molière, on serait tenté à tout instant et à la fois de s'écrier: *Quelle vérité! et quelle invraisemblance!*"

For Sainte-Beuve, quite unabashedly, the critical function, though centrally analytical and discursive, was an exercise of the total sensibility. Obligated like novelist, dramatist, or poet to the service of *Vérité*, the critic was nonetheless free to exploit to that end whatever resources of the imagination lay at his command. In this regard Sainte-Beuve was happily endowed. He has a poet's feel for language, noticing the perfect coalescence of thought and image in Joseph Joubert, for example, and delighting to find in his diction a mirror of the man's temperament. The recurrence of words denoting light (*lumineux, lumière*) "trahissent cette nature ailée, amie du ciel et des hauteurs." Cacophony is painful to Sainte-Beuve, as in the ear-wounding charge hurled at him by one hapless pedant: "il dé*ment* constam*ment* le juge*ment*" (*Nouveaux Lundis*).

The poet's character, John Keats once told us, consists in a "negative capability" which enables him to abandon his own identity for that of some other person or object. It is not without significance that Sainte-Beuve strove constantly to achieve precisely this kind of imaginative empathy in his critical composition. "Dans ma critique," he confided to his *Cahiers intimes*, "je tache d'appliquer mon âme à celle des autres; je me détache de moi; je les embrasse, je tache de les revêtir et de les égaler. Ai-je réussi?" Candor obliges us to reply that usually he did not succeed. But in his most memorable *Portraits* and *Lundis,* and above all in certain chapters of *Port-Royal,* he came as close to success as is possible in so exacting an endeavor.

In Sainte-Beuve's whole critical *oeuvre* one can discriminate kinds and degrees of this empathy. One kind, for which he might have found a model in William Hazlitt, whose criticism he admired, amounts to a critical Theophrastian "character" of the work under scrutiny, an attempt to render its unique essence. A notable example from late in his career occurs in the two-part *Lundi* on Bossuet. His express aim is to "bien saisir la forme particulière à son esprit," which he proceeds to do in a passage of portrayal sustained through almost three pages. Sainte-Beuve's prose takes on some of the eloquence and sweep of his celebrated subject: "Bossuet, dirai-je donc, c'est l'esprit qui embrasse le mieux, le plus lumineusement, le plus souverainement un corps, un ensemble de doctrines . . . "—and so on in a half-page sentence which rises to a climax of metaphorical intensity: "comme sous la voûte d'une nef les tonnerres d'une orgue immense"—and then descends through a gradual decrescendo to a close of quiet, abstract summation: "en un mot, c'est le plus magnifique et le plus souverain organe et interprète de ce qui est institué primordialement et établi" (*Nouveaux lundis*). Moments like these abound in Sainte-Beuve, and we may fairly suppose that it was by their persuasive force, and not as the inaugurator of a method, that he became, in Remy de Gourmont's arresting phrase, a "créateur de valeurs" (*Promenades philosophiques*).

So inclusive was the range of Sainte-Beuve's appreciative powers that one hesitates to pick out his best. With this reservation, however, I should name the third book of *Port-Royal,* the *Pascal.* It is for his achievement there, we might note, that another creator of values, T. S. Eliot, called Sainte-Beuve a critic of genius ("The *Pensées* of Pascal," in *Selected Essays*).

The final chapter of *Pascal,* dealing with the *Pensées,* is a superb example of imaginative portraiture. Sainte-Beuve recreates—better say *creates*—the conversation held (as he is forced to imagine) at Port-Royal in Paris, in which Pascal outlined to his Jansenist friends the great moral and apologetical treatise he was then planning. Sainte-Beuve conceives this exposition in dramatic terms: "C'est un premier acte. . . . C'est le ressort de son drame." It is a drama complete with prolegomena and successive acts which embody the burning "moments" of a relentless dialectic. A critical *examen* thus becomes, as it were, the scenario of an intellectual Christian tragedy, of which Pascal, surrogate of humanity, is the questing, agonizing hero. At crucial points we are not so much readers as witnesses to a grand spectacle. "On assiste à toutes les péripéties de ce drame du Prométhée chrétien." And the rising vehemence of the conflict is resolved for us less effectively by the theological abstractions of the dialectic than by the final image of "cet Archimède en pleurs au pied de la croix."

So ardent, in places, is Sainte-Beuve's style in this chapter that one is driven to reflect how easily it might have produced an impression of either sentimentality or brittle elegance. That it is rather a rhetoric which avoids both of these hazards owes much, perhaps everything, to the critic's having found in the *Pensées* a subject deeply congenial to his own nature, of which, before writing, he had made himself the intellectual master. The result is a piece of criticism that is also, within the proper limits of its kind, a work of art.

De Tocqueville and the Problem of the French Revolution

François Furet

Tocqueville's attachment to history did not spring from a love of the past but from his sensitivity to the present. He was not of that breed of historians who wander in the past, seeking the poetry of bygone ages or the diversions afforded by scholarship; he was totally committed to a different kind of historical curiosity, in which an examination of the present leads to the search for filiations. Unlike his contemporary Michelet, he was free of the obsessive passion for the past, the lugubrious and sublime fanaticism of a haunter of graveyards. The object of the lifelong search that gave his intellectual work its penetrating insight and its coherence was to find the meaning of his own time. He began his quest not in time, but in space, using geography as a kind of comparative history. To test his inspired reversal of the traditional hypothesis, he went to study the United States, not in order to recapture the childhood of Europe, but to gain a sense of its future. The history of Europe was but a second voyage for him, closely related to the first and subjected to the set of hypotheses that had resulted from sounding out the present.

Moreover, these two voyages—in space and in time—are linked not only by the intellectual meaning Tocqueville gave them, but also because he wrote about them very early in his career, between 1830 and 1840. The first two parts of *Democracy in America* appeared in 1835, the last two in 1840. In between, in 1836, Tocqueville published a short essay entitled "Political and Social Condition of France" in the *London and Westminster Review*. Tocqueville's first major creative period, which preceded his actual political career, thus shows the link between his two major intellectual concerns.

From *Interpreting the French Revolution*, translated by Elborg Forster. © 1981 by Maison des Sciences de l'Homme and Cambridge University Press. Cambridge University Press, 1981.

After retiring from politics, Tocqueville returned only to the historical part of his project, which he had simply outlined and shelved, as it were, in 1836; this time he locked himself up in the archives, read the primary sources, took copious notes and for several years practised the hard discipline demanded by the historian's craft. Yet the ultimate purpose of his research remained unchanged: he still wanted to understand, and thus foresee, where France's contemporary history was headed. History, for him, was not a resurrection of the past, even less a description or a narrative, it was a set of materials to be organised and interpreted. The similarity between Tocqueville's 1836 and 1856 writings is therefore not so much in his sources—which were infinitely better and more complete in *L'Ancien Régime*—as in his system of interpretation. In the spirit of the Tocquevillean method itself, this may well be the best approach to a history which openly acknowledges that it is inseparable from an explanatory theory.

I

Tocqueville's general interpretation of the French Revolution can thus already be found in a short essay published in England in 1836, after his visit to America. The full title of the original text was "Etat social et politique de la France avant et depuis 1789," a surprising anticipation of the title that Tocqueville was to give to his last book twenty years later. Strictly speaking, Tocqueville's essay corresponds only to the first part of the title, as it just deals with pre-revolutionary France. The sequel, referred to in a ten-line transition that gives this text a curious conclusion, never seems to have been written; it is not fully clear why Tocqueville interrupted his work on the subject at that date. In 1836, as he was to do twenty years later, Tocqueville concentrates on the Ancien Régime more than on the Revolution, on pre-1789 more than on post-1789 France. The article can be summarised as follows:

The introduction states the central idea of the essay: the Revolution was merely a local and particularly violent explosion of universally held ideas. The first part is mainly a description of French civil society at the end of the old monarchy. For Tocqueville, the Church had become a political institution cut off from the population, and the nobility a caste rather than an aristocracy (that is, an English-style ruling class). While the Church is dealt with rather summarily, the nobility is analysed in great detail. Politically, the nobility was cut off from power by the monarchy; deprived of its local administrative authority without having been compensated with a share in government power, it was powerless to oppose the king on behalf of the people or to exert any real influence on the king against the people. Hence the anachronistic character of noble privileges (the nobles were no longer loved or feared), notably economic and honorific ones.

Economic redistribution benefited the Third Estate, which controlled the country's non-landed wealth. Hence the fragmentation and changing ownership of noble estates, the breaking up of the nobility into a mass of moderately well-to-do individuals and the phenomenon that might be called the "democratisation of the nobility."

Finally, the author discusses the rise of the Third Estate, which took place independently of the nobility (here Tocqueville almost echoes Sieyès), for it "created a new people," with its own aristocracy. That rise accounts for the division within the ruling class and for the revolutionary spirit of the Third Estate. "The division among the various aristocratic elements had pitted the aristocracy against itself in a kind of civil war from which democracy alone was to profit in the end. Rebutted by the nobility, the leading members of the Third Estate could fight back only by adopting principles that served their purposes at the time, but were dangerous precisely because they were so effective. As one section of the aristocracy in revolt against the other, the Third Estate was therefore compelled to endorse the idea of equality for everyone in order to combat the specific idea of inequality that thwarted it."

Tocqueville emphasises the fact that the aristocratic principle rapidly lost ground, partly as a result of the influence of the intelligentsia on society and a kind of "egalitarian" fusion between the nobility and the intellectuals. This "imaginary democracy" in spirit was matched by a real democracy of wealth, brought about by the fragmentation of landed property; the consequent rise in the number of small-scale fortunes created favourable conditions for political democracy. Eighteenth-century France was thus marked by a discrepancy between its institutions (based on inequality) and its way of life, which already made it "the most truly democratic nation in Europe."

Tocqueville then proceeds to describe the *political* consequences of these social conditions: just as aristocratic societies tend toward local government, so democratic societies tend toward centralised government. Democratic society begins by wresting local government from the aristocracy, but since it is too weak and too fragmented to exercise power on its own, it entrusts it to the king—the only force that can hold it together despite its interests and its weaknesses—through the mediation of its natural leaders, the jurists.

In France the effects of these "general causes" were compounded by "accidental and secondary" factors: the dominant rôle of Paris, the need to maintain national unity among very diverse provinces, and the personal rather than parliamentary nature of power.

Yet governmental and administrative centralisation had by no means extinguished the spirit of liberty, which Tocqueville considers to be one of the characteristic traits of French national temperament. That is why, in the eighteenth century, the aristocratic notion of liberty (the protection of privilege at every level) was superseded by a democratic one, based on common law instead of privilege.

So the Revolution did not create a new people, nor a new France: "It regulated, coordinated, and put into law the effects of a great cause but it was not itself that cause." It was the end result of long-term trends in Ancien-Régime society, far more than a radical transformation of France and the French. These trends toward democracy, which Tocqueville analyses according to their impact on civil society, on attitudes, on government and on ideology, formed a kind of common rootstock for both the old and the new régime, and the Revolution simply appears as one stage in the development of their effects—a stage to which Tocqueville does not attribute a specific character. In his view, the continuity of French history has wiped out the traces of its discontinuities.

The main conceptual elements of this interpretation of the French Revolution in a long-term historical setting, an interpretation that stresses the weight of the past and reduces the significance of the change for which the Revolution wanted to take the credit, did not originate with Tocqueville. But since he was always so discreet about his readings—there are very few explicit references to other authors in his books, and relatively few in his correspondence—it is hard to identify his sources. One of them, however, is clear: he had obviously read Guizot, with whom he was engaged in a continuous intellectual and political exchange marked by a mixture of complicity and hostility, which is a most telling example of the ambiguities of French liberalism in the first half of the nineteenth century. His senior by eighteen years, Guizot had already written his most important works when Tocqueville was writing his 1836 essay. Although Guizot was more fundamentally a historian than Tocqueville, they shared the same basic political creed, liberalism, the same view of history as interpretation, and the same central frame of reference within which to structure a very long past, that is, the concept of the French Revolution as both the culmination of a universal (i.e. European) history and the mystery specific to French history. Given this common approach, it is interesting to find out to what extent Tocqueville followed, or learned from, Guizot and to analyse the differences between their interpretations.

Having gone back to teaching history after his fall from political power in 1820, Guizot published the essential parts of his explanatory system in his first major historical works, notably in his *Essais sur l'histoire de France* (1823). Charles Pouthas points out that in his 1828 lectures, later published as *Histoire de la civilisation en Europe et en France*, Guizot modified some of his judgments and above all corrected some factual errors, notably concerning early French history and the barbarian invasions (*Guizot pendant la Restauration*). Yet these are minor changes so far as the question discussed here is concerned, for between the 1823 *Essais* and the 1828 lectures, the main lines of Guizot's interpretation of French history remained the same. All of the great protagonists are already present in the *Essais:* the seigneurs, the Church, the king, the *communes* (free towns); and so are the societies and types of government—aristocratic, theocratic, monarchical, democratic—that are or should be embodied by those protagonists, along with the conflicts or periods of equilibrium with which they fill the history of France. In 1828 as in 1823, this history was merely the empirical confirmation of an intellectual schema that remained essentially unchanged.

Guizot sought to define the history of France as a march toward a "society," that is, toward an organised social whole all of whose strata are linked by a unifying principle. Feudalism, which emerged from chaos or non-society around the tenth century, under the Capetians, was the first form of organised society in French history. It was hard on the people, but its internal dialectic pointed to "a better future," for it rested both on the oppression of the people, "the nation as personal property," and on egalitarian relations within the dominant class, "the sovereign nation" of fiefholders: "Here I come upon a different sight; I see liberties, rights, and guarantees which not only bestowed honour and protection on those who enjoyed them, but by their nature and intent opened the subservient population a door to a better future." The complex hierarchy of fiefholders established a network of reciprocal relationships of relative equality among the seigneurs, from the least among them all the way up to the king; yet the fief consolidated its holder's individualism and his independence from the authorities. "Such a situation looked like war rather than a society; yet it preserved the energy and dignity of the individual; a society could arise from it."

Guizot was referring to the type of society that he saw as a culmination of history, and was founded on a redefinition of "individuals" and "public institutions," of the liberty and order that had been sacrificed to feudalism. As soon as feudalism had been established, it was attacked at both ends: from below in the name of liberty, and from above in the name of public order. "Such efforts were not made amidst the clash of diverse and ill-defined systems reducing each other to impotence and anarchy [as in the first five centuries of French history, according to Guizot]; they arose within a single system and were directed against it alone." And Guizot concludes his analysis with these admirable lines: "This monarchical system, which Charlemagne, despite his genius, had been unable to found, was gradually made to prevail by much lesser kings. The rights and guarantees that the Germanic warriors had been unable to preserve were recovered one by one by the *communes*. Only feudalism could be born of barbarism; but feudalism had hardly reached maturity when the monarchy and liberty began to take shape and grow within it" (italics mine).

In a detailed examination of those two processes, Guizot shows that both the monarchy and liberty were given a chance to develop by the political weakness of the feudal aristocracy. Isolated in its respective fiefs, disunited for lack of a collective organisation comparable to that of the Roman patriciate, the Venetian Senate, or the English barons (for the inequality of the feudal hierarchy precluded any such organisation), the aristocracy was not only worn down locally by the opposition of the population, but also held down by the most powerful overlord, the king.

It soon became clear that feudalism was useful only for guiding society's first steps out of barbarism, and was incompatible with the progress of civilisation; *it did not contain the seeds of any durable public institution*; it was lacking not only the principle of aristocratic government, but any other principle as well; and, once it had perished, it would leave behind it a nobility around the throne, aristocrats above the people, *but no aristocracy to govern the State* (italics mine).

The opposite development took place, according to Guizot, in medieval England, where kingship and feudalism were born together at the time of William the Conqueror: "England had two social forces, two public powers, neither of which existed in France at the time: an aristocracy and a king. These forces were too barbaric, too dominated by passion and personal interest to permit the development of either despotism or free government; yet they also needed each other and were often obliged to work together." Out of the struggle between the English barons *forming an aristocracy* and the king *embodying a monarchy* came the charters ("a beginning of public law"), followed by institutions, that is, "a free and national government."

For Guizot, the historical development of France was thus characterised by feudalism's failure to create an aristocracy, and by the *communes*' failure to create democracy. Hence the absence of free institutions, hence also the absolute monarchy, the end-result of a double impotence. It was the Revolution—the culmination of a centuries-long class struggle between feudalism and the *communes*—that finally created democracy, that is, both a society and free egalitarian institutions; it was the Revolution which rallied society round a single unifying principle.

The major features of Guizot's and Tocqueville's general interpretations have a number of points in common. First, both authors try to fit so-called "events" into a wide time-span and conceptual framework. Both feel that the Revolution was but the culmination of a very long historical process that had its roots in the formative stages of French society. In that sense, their history of France, though it implicitly contains the future it is supposed to explain, and is obsessed, as it were, by the French Revolution, was nonetheless bound to be not so much a history of the Revolution as a description of its origins.

For the fundamental dialectic that produced the revolutionary conflict and accounts for the course of history is the same in both authors; it is the dialectical relationship between civil society and institutions, between the state of society and government. Within this general approach to the problem, the two authors' conceptual framework for their historical analysis is also very similar. Both feel that, from the outset, French civil society was essentially composed of two rival groups, the nobility and the Third Estate, both of them existing since the Frankish conquest, and both potential bearers of a system of socio-political values, respectively aristocracy and democracy. Their relations with the central authority, the king, are the underlying pattern of French history—yet they also account for its *special nature* in comparison with the English model.

But Guizot, unlike Tocqueville, did not think that there had ever been a true aristocratic political society in French history. For him, as for Mably, the Middle Ages and feudalism were nothing more than a state of anarchy, unbearable for the people and incapable of building any genuine political institutions. And since the French—unlike their English contemporaries— were too weak to develop such institutions, the growth of royal power was an indispensable period of transition toward democracy and liberty.

Tocqueville, by contrast, felt that there had indeed been an aristocratic society, accompanied by a paternalist local government that protected individual liberty against encroachment from the central power. It was the gradual erosion of that aristocratic society under the impact of the royal administration and more general trends that opened the way, not to liberty, but to equality.

Both Tocqueville and Guizot, therefore, saw the fundamental dialectic of French history in socio-political terms, as centered on the growth of royal power supported from below by the mass of the democratic "people." Guizot, however, spoke of liberty where Tocqueville spoke of democracy or equality, because Guizot felt that aristocracy was an obstacle to liberty, while Tocqueville saw it as the foundation and bulwark of liberty. The fundamental disagreement in their interpretations concerns the rôle played in French history by the king and the aristocracy, and the political and moral values they embodied.

It is therefore tempting to compare the underlying political commitments of these two men—and to contrast Guizot's pride as a commoner ("I am of those who were raised by the tide of 1789 and who will never consent to step down") with Tocqueville's nostalgia ("Everywhere in the world, the societies that will always have the greatest difficulties in holding out against absolute government will be precisely those where aristocracy has been lost once and for all"). The contrast in their experiences and existential attitudes shows up even more clearly the similarities in the major conceptual elements of their historical analysis. The originality of Tocqueville's 1836 essay in relation to Guizot's work was due no doubt more to the insights accidentally afforded by his family background than to his intellectual imagination.

Twenty years later, on the other hand, *L'Ancien Régime* arrived at an infinitely more complex synthesis of Tocqueville's aristocratic inheritance. Tocqueville had brought to it not only many more years of thought and research, but also his experience as a politician.

II

L'Ancien Régime et la Révolution is written in an extremely brilliant and compact style. Tocqueville's notes and drafts, now published in full in the second volume of the Gallimard edition, testify to his great concern with form, and to the painstaking work he devoted to polishing and repolishing his expressions. Yet this apparently limpid prose is in fact infinitely less clear than the 1836 text, for neither the historical conceptualisation nor the steps in the demonstration are easy to identify.

Yet that must be done; for even in the later work Tocqueville deliberately refused to write in the classical style of contemporary "histories of the Revolution" and altogether shunned narrative. Moreover, he did not cite Thiers, Lamartine or Michelet, all of whom he had probably read (we know that he had read Thiers, whose historical works he comments on in his *Correspondence*) or at least skimmed; and if he broke with the historians' time-honoured tradition—which is still alive—of criticising or copying his predecessors, it was not so much from disdain as from a desire to place his work at a different level than that of narrative history. His history, which in this sense is extraordinarily modern, is an examination of selected problems for the purpose of constructing a general explanation and interpretation of the Revolution. Hence his exclusive reliance on manuscript or printed primary sources; hence also the general design of the book, which sacrifices chronology for the sake of logical coherence.

The book is divided into three major parts. The first defines the historical significance of the Revolution and its essential content, which was not religious (since religion was, in the medium term, actually "revived" by the Revolution) nor exclusively social or political, but indissolubly socio-political: the substitution of egalitarian institutions for the old "feudal" ones—and Tocqueville used the word "institutions" to refer to both the social and the political order, that is, to both equality of conditions and the modern administrative State. Hence the universal character of the Revolution, expressed in the almost religious form that democratic ideology gave it in France. Tocqueville thereby makes it clear from the outset that he was more interested in analysing the deeper significance and origins of events than the visible forms they took. He was convinced that by finding out how the dialectic between the State and civil society had evolved in France, how it was experienced, interpreted and retrospectively imagined in the last centuries, and especially the last decades, of the Ancien Régime, he would unlock the secret of the French Revolution and account for its chronological precedence and its intellectual impact on European history. Tocqueville thus went from comparative sociology to the sociological statement of a problem in French history.

The rest of the book is arranged according to two types of causal explanations: long-standing and general causes (Book 2) and specific and recent causes (Book 3). Tocqueville thus establishes a hierarchy of causes according to their time-scale. General causes are those that have been at work for a long time, deeply embedded in several centuries of history; their effects have arisen out of the remote past; unbeknownst to anyone, indeed beyond the reach of human memory, they were preparing new social and political conditions. Specific causes made themselves felt only in the eighteenth century, sometimes just in the last decades; they do not explain why change had become inevitable—those reasons are inherent in the long-term evolution—but why it took place at a specific date and in a specific manner.

Let us begin with the long-term causes, which are analysed in the twelve chapters of Book 2. For the most part, their treatment follows the theoretical premises outlined in Book 1, since Tocqueville first reviews the historical features of administrative centralisation (chaps. 2–7) and then of civil society (chaps. 8–12). Yet the first chapter, devoted to feudal rights and the peasantry, seems oddly out of place. Why did Tocqueville use it to introduce his description of the imbalances of the Ancien Régime, and why did he return to the study of the rural world in the last chapter of Book 2 (chap. 12), as if to say that this problem is important enough to frame the general analysis as a whole? I am unable to answer that question. Admittedly, the two chapters look at the peasant world from two different angles, since the first is devoted to the relation between peasant and seigneur, while the last deals with the relations between peasant and State. Nonetheless one would expect those two topics to have been created together at the end of Book 2, after the study of administrative centralisation and its effect on all levels of civil society.

Tocqueville, of course, may have wanted to begin his general analysis of the Ancien Régime with an examination of what the revolutionaries considered its most outrageous aspect, in order to present, at the very outset, by means of this special example, one of his fundamental ideas: the continuity between the Ancien Régime and the Revolution. Tocqueville was convinced that feudal rights had become hateful to the French not because they were particularly burdensome (they were more onerous in the rest of Europe) but because the French peasant was already, in many respects, a nineteenth-century peasant, that is, an independent owner in relation to his seigneur. Because feudal rights were no longer accompanied by an exchange of services, they had ceased to be institutions and had become survivals. Tocqueville thereby also accounts for an apparent paradox: given that, on the one hand, the Revolution was more than three-fourths accomplished before it even began and that, on the other hand, such vestiges of feudalism as did subsist in the countryside were particularly resented precisely for that reason, it becomes understandable why the Revolution attached such exaggerated importance to the liberation of the peasants.

By examining objectively the real content of the revolutionary break, Tocqueville shows the rôle played by ideological distortion. That was an exceptionally fruitful idea, considering how many of yesterday's and today's historians tend to take revolutionary discourse at face value, whereas probably no consciousness is more "ideological" (in the Marxist sense of the term) than that of the revolutionaries.

Having used the theme of feudal rights to characterise the dialectic between continuity and break (one might almost say: continuity in fact, yet perceived as a break) that marked the Revolution, Tocqueville turns to the crucial development that provided the historical continuity between the Ancien Régime and the Revolution: the growth of public power and administrative centralisation. It should be noted—and we shall return to this point later—that here Tocqueville reverses the logical or chronological order of his 1836 text and begins where he had left off twenty years earlier. Highly original as well—in comparison not only with his own 1836 article but also with his contemporaries—is his treatment of the classic theme of the growth of royal power, for he places the emphasis not on the purely political victories of the monarchy but on its increasingly firm administrative hold over society. For him, the administrative conquests of the king of France were the dominant feature of French history since the end of the Middle Ages, and the central power exerted its influence on civil society through the administration of the country's everyday affairs. The picture he presents is too well known to be summarised here; yet it involves a number of problems that deserve to be reviewed.

The first is that of its historical accuracy. Tocqueville was remarkably knowledgeable about administrative archival sources for the eighteenth century; moreover, he had the intelligence to look at them at both ends of the hierarchical ladder. On the one hand, he went through the documents in series F (central administration) of the Archives Nationales, and many of the complementary manuscripts preserved at the Bibliothèque Nationale. On the other hand, at the local level, he systematically explored the papers of the *intendant's* office at Tours and carefully studied Turgot's account of his experiences as *intendant* of the Limousin. He wanted to know how power really worked, how it reached down from the central bureaucracy to the smallest village community, through the all-important mediation of the royal *intendants*. In doing so, he came face to face with the contradiction familiar to every historian of the Ancien Régime: from above, extraordinarily minute regulations for everything were handed down; below, disobedience was chronic, a situation reflected in the fact that the same edicts or *arrèts* were promulgated every few years. Tocqueville's description takes that double reality into account. He begins by analysing the inroads of the royal administration in town and country (chaps. 2–5), only to show, from chapter 6 on, the limits of its reach: "rigid rules, lax practices; such is its character [i.e. of the Ancien Régime]" (chap. 6). To this he adds a lucid and unwittingly self-critical remark, considering that in the preceding chapters he has in a sense done what he now criticises: "Whoever would set out to judge the government of that time by its law codes would end up with the most preposterous errors." This statement is echoed in an even clearer sentence found in the appendix: "The administration of the Ancien Régime was so diverse and so heterogeneous that it would survive only so long as it *took very little action*" (italics mine). (Yet in other passages, for example, Book 2, chap. 6, Tocqueville notes the "prodigious activity" of government in the Ancien Régime. The solution to this apparent contradiction lies in the distinction—to be found throughout Tocqueville's work—between government and administration, even though the distinction, which is perfectly clear in certain passages of *Democracy in America*, becomes blurred in the chapters of *L'Ancien Régime* analysed here. At what level, for example, did the *intendant* operate? It is the contrast between the government's increased activity and its impotence in practice that accounts for the progressive loss of faith in the law.) Thus, it was not so much the administration's real power in the Ancien Régime that struck Tocqueville, as its disintegrating effect on the body politic, its annihilation of all intermediary power of recourse, whether seigneur, priest, communal syndic, or alderman. The State-as-Providence was not yet a reality, but it already existed in people's minds. By obliterating everything but arbitrary central power and the isolated individual, the Ancien Régime invented the *mould* which the Revolution used to shape its institutions. It presented all the political inconveniences of State control, without as yet providing any of its practical advantages.

Yet Tocqueville's dialectic between administrative and government power entails a number of difficulties. Some are related to his interpretation of the facts. For instance, despite his close attention to certain obstacles to the exercise of power under the Ancien Régime—resulting from the extraordinary diversity in customs and procedures, and in the legal status of persons and communities—Tocqueville tended on the whole to overestimate the extent of administrative centralisation in the Ancien Régime. His opinion is summarised in one of his preliminary notes, where he attempts to define that system of authority in a single phrase: "A very centralised and very preponderant royal power, deciding all important matters, and endowed with imprecisely defined but vast prerogatives which in fact *it exercises*" (italics mine, vol. 2). This fundamental belief, which ultimately contradicts other statements about the limits within which royal power had to operate, makes for some strange silences or unwarranted simplifications in Tocqueville's treatment of the real historical forces of centralisation. At this stage of his analysis, for example, he says nothing about the sale of public offices, a key factor in the formation of a monarchical bureaucracy, but ambiguous as far as his thesis is concerned, since the sale of public offices was both a means employed by the central power and an obstacle to its autonomy. But when Tocqueville does try to define the bureaucracy of the Ancien Régime, he writes (chap. 6): "The administrative officials, almost all of whom were commoners, already formed a class with its own particular attitudes, its own virtues, honour and pride. It was the aristocracy of the new society, which, already well-formed and alive, was only waiting for the Revolution to make room for it." For Tocqueville this type of analysis had the advantage of creating, above and, as it were, outside of society, a homogeneous social group, defined by its function, sharing a common set of values, and actively involved in centralisation. Unfortunately, this analysis is based throughout on mistaken assumptions. In the first place, the administrative officials of the eighteenth century—one has only to think of the *intendants*—were by no means "almost all . . . commoners." Secondly, they were deeply divided, not only by their personal ambitions and their networks of patronage, but also by their political and ideological choices— witness the sharp division between physiocrats and anti-physiocrats. More- over, the most "functional" administrators, i.e. those directly connected with the central power—the bureaucracy of Versailles, the *intendants* and their deputies (*subdélégués*)—would not survive the Revolution, not even its first phase, while those who owned their offices would, on the contrary, form one of its leading groups. Tocqueville's probably exaggerated view of governmental and administrative centralisation led him to deduce its pre- sumable agents from the process he had described.

Tocqueville was on even shakier ground when it came to chronology and causes; indeed he proceeded by allusions and by a succession of un- connected remarks, without ever advancing a general theory of political change. Here, no doubt, he was not in his field. Having come to history fairly late in life, and not being familiar with pre-eighteenth-century sources, he was visibly indebted to his predecessors, whose materials he rearranged according to his own intuitions and presuppositions. The broad historical picture in chapter 4 of Book 1 is faithful to the classic periodisation of French history: medieval political institutions broke down in the four- teenth and fifteenth century under the advancing administrative monarchy, which impinged upon the power of the nobles. Tocqueville is faithful not only to that traditional chronology but also—without having made a special study of the field—to his own 1836 interpretation: he retrospectively places great emphasis on the nobles' traditional power, which he views as a sort of local self-government based on an exchange of services or as an idyllic relationship of trust between the seigneur and the peasant community. But none of that is truly analysed in historical terms. Tocqueville seems to believe that between the fifteenth and eighteenth centuries centralisation developed in a regular manner, although he never discusses its causes or its phases: Louis XIV is not even mentioned. Nor are the wars of the monarchy, a crucial factor in the growth of the State, ever evoked. Con- cerning the eighteenth century, he writes (Book 2, chap. 5) these sibylline words: "The rapid progress of society constantly created new needs, each of which was a new source of power for it [the government], for it alone was in a position to satisfy them. While the administrative sphere of the law courts remained fixed, that of the government was moving, and con- stantly expanded at the same pace as civilisation itself." The progress of centralisation is thus simply and vaguely related to that of "civilisation." Tocqueville's way of sharing his contemporaries' belief in progress consists of using one of the most obscure words of historical vocabulary to express his deep and abiding feeling of inevitability. That is as much as we shall ever know.

Having described in the first seven chapters of Book 2 (with the exception of chapter 1) the functioning—or rather what would now be called the dysfunctions—of the eighteenth-century administrative monarchy, Tocqueville, from chapter 8 on, turns to the analysis of civil society. As was pointed out earlier, this arrangement reflects a reversal of his usual approach, by comparison not only with the 1836 essay but also with *Democracy in America*. In the latter, the broad picture of "the social state of the Anglo-American" (part 1, chap. 3) precedes the analysis of political institutions, and Tocqueville expressly notes at the end of the chapter: "The political consequences of such a state of society are easily deduced. One could not possibly expect that equality would fail to penetrate the political world as it had penetrated all others." Tocqueville emphasises the predominance of social factors (in the widest sense, including mental attitudes, mores, and the "public spirit") over political factors, but at the same time he implicitly formulates a global typological theory of society *à la* Montesquieu or Max Weber, which is clearly present in the 1836 article as well. It postulates that "aristocratic" societies tend toward local government, while "democratic" societies tend toward centralised government. In fact, in the earlier period, Tocqueville does not seem to have been hostile to civil equality (which is the essential feature of his definition of "democracy") or to governmental centralisation (so long as it went hand in hand with administrative decentralisation). That is the underlying meaning of his study of America.

Yet, twenty years later, the organisation of *L'Ancien Régime* very probably reflects a change in his judgment and his thinking. It has been pointed out, incidentally, that the word "democracy" is used much less frequently in *L'Ancien Régime* than in the 1836 text, as if Tocqueville had gradually abandoned that key concept of his earlier analysis without, however, completely striking it from his vocabulary. What had happened? Tocqueville had just experienced as a politician, not simply as an intellectual, the upheavals of the years 1848–51. In 1848, the popular and socialist explosion, a new French version of the "trend" towards democracy, clearly showed the outer limits of social democratisation, which Tocqueville had described as accomplished; moreover, the 1848 risings were a sight that filled him with horror. The well-reasoned optimism that had underlain his analysis of American society gave way to fear. The reformer of the days before the Revolution had become a conservative intent upon preserving the order restored at such great cost. Hence he was faced with a two-fold problem, the theoretical one of defining his terms and the existential one of making a value judgment. In 1851, the government of notables, which Tocqueville had supported and in which he had even participated, believing it to be the best of all French régimes since 1789 (as he put it in his *Souvenirs*), had come to an inglorious end on 2 December 1851, to be succeeded by the worst centralising despotism since 1789. It had now become difficult to explain a set of political institutions as diverse as the July Monarchy, the

Second Republic or the despotic rule of the second Napoleon in terms of a single state of society, a concept whose extreme flexibility was being demonstrated before Tocqueville's very eyes. The reversal in his approach and his new emphasis on the autonomy and the primacy of purely political factors—more specifically of political-administrative structures—are probably related to his experiences during those years.

Actually, one can find traces of this reversal in the notes for *L'Ancien Régime,* in which Tocqueville worked out his concepts more freely than in the final text. Here, for example, is a note about the meaning of the word "democracy" (vol. 2):

> The greatest intellectual confusion arises from the use of the words *democracy, democratic institutions, democratic government.* So long as we are unable to define these words clearly and to agree on their definition, we shall live with an inextricable confusion of ideas, to the great advantage of demagogues and despots.
>
> It will be possible to say that a country governed by an absolute prince is a *democracy,* because he governs by law or in the presence of institutions favourable to the welfare of the people. His government will be called a *democratic government.* He will be said to form a *democratic monarchy.*
>
> Now the words *democracy, democratic monarchy* or *democratic* government can mean only one thing when used in their true sense: a government in which the people participate in government to a greater or lesser extent. Its meaning is intimately related to the idea of political liberty. To call "democratic" a government in which political liberty is absent is to utter an obvious absurdity, if one considers the natural meaning of those words.

This note is rather perplexing, since Tocqueville here condemns precisely the meaning he had hitherto given to the word "democracy." In fact, his correction consists in transferring the concept from the social sphere (equality) to the political sphere (sharing in power, and liberty), as if the former were now conditioned by the latter.

Another telling indication of this shift can be found in an appendix to chapter 5 of Book 2, on centralisation. Here Tocqueville makes a remarkable comparison between French colonial rule in Canada and English colonial rule in America, noting that in the colonies the underlying character of the two administrations is magnified to the point of caricature. In Canada, there is no nobility, no "feudal tradition," no predominant church power, no set of old judicial institutions firmly rooted in the mores of the population, in short, nothing carried over from civil society in old Europe, nothing to oppose absolute government. "It already looks just like modern centralised administration, like Algeria." By contrast, in neighbouring English America, where social conditions were comparable, "the republican element, which is the basis, as it were, of the English constitution and way of life, expresses itself freely and flourishes. The administration proper did very little in England, and private citizens did a great deal; in America the administration practically did not take care of anything, and individuals, working together, did everything. Whereas the presence of upper classes made the inhabitant of Canada under French rule even more subservient to government than the inhabitant of France at the same period, the absence of upper classes in the English provinces made their inhabitants increasingly independent of authority. Both colonies eventually established an entirely democratic society; but in Canada, at least so long as it belonged to France, equality went hand in hand with absolute government, while in America it went hand in hand with liberty."

It seems to me that two striking ideas are expressed in this note, written at the same time as *L'Ancien Régime:*

1. Political liberty is not necessarily related to the presence of upper classes, an "aristocracy" in Tocqueville's sense. The contention that in English America "the absence of upper classes" made individuals "increasingly independent of governmental power" marks a clear break with the conceptual schema of 1836, in which aristocracy, local government and political liberty are equated.
2. The decisive factor in the development of these two societies is not, therefore, their social state—which in both cases is "democratic"—but their tradition and political-administrative practices.

And that is indeed the conclusion to be drawn from the analysis of the essential features of *L'Ancien Régime*. It is not, of course, that Tocqueville is carried away by any single-cause explanation, which is totally alien to his way of thinking. On the contrary, he continues to pay close attention to the tangled web of reasons and consequences that is empirically revealed to him by his sources. Nonetheless, in his last book, civil society is less a cause than a result of the political and moral environment. That is perhaps the most fundamental intellectual originality of *L'Ancien Régime* both in comparison with Tocqueville's earlier work and in relation to nineteenth-century political sociology as a whole.

Thus the central phenomenon and essential aspect of historical change in France is the growth of royal power and of government centralisation, both of which in turn are related to the development of direct taxation (the *taille*). This process both dislocated and unified civil society ("the division into classes was the crime of the old monarchy," Book 2, chap. 10), which was split up into increasingly rival groups composed of increasingly similar individuals. The upper classes' inability to preserve their traditional political power, or to unite in order to gain a new kind of power, gave free rein to administrative despotism, which in turn compounded the consequences of government centralisation.

In analysing French civil society in the second part of his book, Tocqueville, faithful to the legacy of Restoration historiography, speaks of "classes": "One can, of course, cite individual examples to the contrary, [but] I am speaking of classes, which alone have a place in history" (book 2, chapter 12). Yet his use of this fundamental concept is ambiguous throughout. At times he defines classes as the orders of the Ancien Régime, at other times he defines them by a combination of Ancien-Régime legal criteria and an extremely vague criterion of wealth and social status, which includes the well-to-do bourgeoisie in the upper classes. The real reason for this ambiguity and for the constant shift from one meaning to another is the central question that Tocqueville was trying to answer about eighteenth-century French society: why was it unable to move, without a revolution, from the rigid hierarchy of the society of orders to the modern dichotomy between the notables and the people, the upper classes and the lower classes? But if that is really, as I believe it is, the crucial question for him, then it also shows how far he had come since *Democracy in America*. Tocqueville's approach was no longer centered on social equality and political democracy, but on the rôle of the upper classes and the élites. It is true that, as he himself had intimated in *Democracy in America* (vol. 1, end of chap. 9), he was no longer dealing with a society formed *ex nihilo* by republican immigrants who believed in equality, but on the contrary with a world firmly rooted in aristocratic tradition; and it is also true that he could not subject the two societies to the same kind of analysis. Yet the fact remains that there is a marked difference in tone between the two books, and that the prose of *L'Ancien Régime* is suffused with an atmosphere of sadness: what had been a hope for the future in the 1830s has become a nostalgic longing for the past. Additional evidence for this change in tone, the shift from optimism to nostalgia between *Democracy in America* and *L'Ancien Régime*, is provided by two texts in which Tocqueville seeks to define the kind of person who thrives in democratic societies, and where he implicitly gives his opinion on the matter.

Democracy in America, vol. 1, chap. 14 (end of chapter): "We must first understand what is wanted of society and its government. Do you wish to give a certain elevation to the human mind and teach it to regard the things of this world with generous feelings, to inspire men with a scorn of mere temporal advantages, to form and nourish strong convictions and keep alive the spirit of honorable devotedness? Is it your object to refine . . . habits, embellish . . . manners, and cultivate the arts, to promote the love of poetry, beauty, and glory? Would you constitute a people fitted to act powerfully upon all other nations, and prepared for those high enterprises which, whatever be their results, will leave a name forever famous in history? If you believe such to be the principle object of society, avoid the government of democracy, for it would not lead you with certainty to the goal.

"But if you hold it expedient to divert the moral and intellectual activity of man to the production of comfort and the promotion of general well-being; if a clear understanding be more profitable to man than genius; if your object is not to stimulate the virtues of heroism but the habits of peace; if you had rather witness vices than crimes, and are content to meet with fewer noble deeds, provided offenses be diminished in the same proportion; if, instead of living in the midst of a brilliant society, you are contented to have prosperity around you; if, in short, you are of the opinion that the greatest object of a government is not to confer the greatest possible power and glory upon the body of the nation, but to ensure the greatest enjoyment and to avoid the most misery to each of the individuals who compose it—if such be your desire, then equalize the conditions of men and establish democratic institutions.''

L'Ancien Régime, Book 2, chap. 11: "The men of the eighteenth century hardly knew that passionate attachment to well-being which is like the mother of servitude, a temperate yet tenacious and unchangeable passion, which often goes along and indeed becomes intertwined with a number of private virtues, such as love of family, unimpeachable mores, respect for religious beliefs, and even a lukewarm and assiduous practice of the established religion. This passion permits honourable conduct and prohibits heroism, and is an excellent means of producing steady people and unspirited citizens. Our forebears were better and worse.

"In those days the French loved life and adored pleasure. Perhaps their manners were more dissolute, their passions and their ideas more reckless than they are today, but they were free of that tempered and well-mannered sensualism we see around us.'' Tocqueville is always looking back to the nobility, evoking the mythical image of its glorious past, when the rural communities were united under its wings, when civil society was relatively close-knit and held together by fraternal bonds and in any case free: such was the society that the monarchy had destroyed.

Yet this "existential" change in Tocqueville's attitude, however evident and indeed understandable for a man so attuned to his time—not many speculative thinkers have been so teleological and so clearly motivated by practical needs—naturally fitted into a conceptualisation of the history of the nobility which, on the whole, remained faithful to his 1836 arguments, even if it changed their effective connotation. *L'Ancien Régime*, being less schematic, makes it easier to understand Tocqueville's approach, with all its unresolved contradictions.

Parodying Bainville's dictum, one might summarise Tocqueville's dialectic as follows: eighteenth-century society had become too democratic for the residue of noble domination it preserved, and too noble-dominated for its democratic aspects. The "too democratic" aspect is treated in chapters 7–10 of Book 2—which describe the move toward intellectual unification and the gradual isolation of upper-class groups from one another—as well as in chapter 12, where Tocqueville treats the peasant problem separately, as he had done at the beginning of Book 1. The "too noble-dominated" aspect it treated in the curious chapter 11, where Tocqueville analyses, in order to celebrate it as the opposite of "democratic" mediocrity, the independent spirit and the sense of liberty with which the aristocratic traditions had imbued French society under the Ancien Régime; yet he emphasises that this spirit, being tied to the idea of privilege, was not suited to survive the advent of democratic institutions, much less to give rise to them.

Just where, then, are we to look for this contradictory development, which bore the seeds of the revolutionary explosion? Since the answer is never very clearly stated, it is important to elucidate this point. Tocqueville deals with economics, society and something one might call, for lack of a better term, ideology.

His economic analysis is always superficial and vague, but at least one can understand why certain factors are not mentioned. Economics was a dimension of human life that had interested him only for its interaction with social or intellectual life, but never in itself or as a basic mechanism of change. That is why he did not make a systematic study of the specifically economic documents of the Ancien Régime, even though he was thoroughly familiar with the sources for the social, administrative, political and intellectual history of the period. He noted the growth in industrial activity in Paris (Book 2, chap. 7) only in order to indicate that "industrial affairs" were attracted to the capital by the centralisation of "administrative affairs." Concerning the changing patterns in the distribution of wealth among classes (which is only partly a matter of economics), his approach is strangely simplistic: he speaks of the impoverishment of the nobility and the enrichment of the "bourgeois" (Book 2, chap. 8) without relating the alleged process to economic causes. Noting the kingdom's urbanisation through the massive migration of the "middle class" to the towns, he simply returns to his "administrative" explanation: "Two causes had been most important in producing this effect: the privileges of the *gentilshommes* and the *taille* [direct taxation]" (Book 2, chap. 9). Finally, his explanation for peasant misery remains extremely vague: "The progress of society, which made for the wealth of all other classes, brought despair to the peasant; civilisation turned against him alone" (Book 2, chap. 12). (This statement contradicts what Tocqueville says earlier about the impoverishment of the nobility. We now know that the notion of an impoverishment of "the" nobility as a social unit does not hold for the eighteenth century, since economic circumstances in fact favoured a steep rise in landed income of every kind (feudal dues, rents and direct management). Tocqueville's second statement thus seems more accurate than the first; but it is also less characteristic of Tocqueville's thinking, which requires him to *deduce* the nobility's economic decline from its political decline.) Moreover, his picture of peasant life as a whole is marked by a complete ignorance of the technical aspects of rural economy.

The economic development of French society is thus either simply deduced from another development (that of the political-administrative sphere) or reduced to vague abstractions ("progress of society," "civilisation"); in other words, it is ignored as a factor in its own right. Moreover, matters of economic doctrine are also similarly approached. Tocqueville has read the physiocrats, for example, but he never mentions their specifically economic analysis (which probably did not interest him), not even the crucial anti-mercantilist implications of the "laissez-faire, laissez-passer" doctrine; the one part of physiocratic thought he does mention, only to criticise it, is the theory of "legal despotism" (Book 3, chap. 3), which in fact is but the corollary of the definition of economic rationality (and moreover not even accepted by "marginal" physiocrats who, like Turgot, were rather Gournay's disciples). Tocqueville referred to the only aspect of physiocratic thought that squared with his analysis of the eighteenth century; but in restricting one's vision in this manner one is condemned to miss the extraordinary vogue of economic liberalism that pervaded the upper strata of society. And indeed Tocqueville does not breathe a word about it.

In his sociological description—in the narrow sense—Tocqueville is once again on familiar territory. Not that, as we have seen, the tools of his investigation were novel or even precise. But in this area it was easier for him to go back not only to his own history, which virtually obsessed him, but also to his fundamental discourse, for he was once again in an area that responds more directly to the effects of politics and administration. Society offers a vast field in which to document the consequences of legislation and government action. Yet how often does Tocqueville beg the question! Take the statement that the nobility became impoverished. Here is the explanation: "Yet the laws that protected the nobles' property were still the same; seemingly their economic condition remained the same. Nonetheless, they were becoming poorer everywhere in exact proportion to the rate at which they were losing power." And further on: "The French nobles were gradually becoming poorer as they came to lack the practice and the spirit of government" (Book 2, chap. 8). The fragmentation of noble property was thus itself only a sign and a consequence of that fundamental fact.

This type of analysis compounds its logical obscurity with disregard for established facts. The correlation between power and wealth, for each social group, is as dubious in Tocqueville as it is in Marx (where wealth comes *before* power). Moreover, Tocqueville establishes this correlation merely to give us a biological comparison that does nothing to satisfy the reader: political power, we seem to be told, is "that central and invisible force which is the very principle of life," the very heart of human society. Besides, it is all the more difficult to follow Tocqueville's analysis as he never reckons with the redistribution of wealth within society by the State, a study that might well have led him, for the eighteenth century, to opposite conclusions. Finally, as has already been pointed out, the eighteenth-century French nobility—at least a part of it, but Tocqueville never makes any distinction within the group—was by no means excluded from power. Of the eighteenth-century nobility that occupied, conquered, and crowded all the avenues to power in France, one might say that it had lost the "spirit of government," but certainly not its "practice."

Tocqueville, however, may be assuming more or less explicitly—more, if at all—that the recent nobility, ennobled and made wealthy by the king for its services to the State—men like Colbert or Louvois—were not part of the ideal model of the nobility and its traditional political values. This implicit exclusion would at least fit in with the idea that in the eighteenth century the machinery of the State was run exclusively by "bourgeois." But that merely moves the contradiction one step back, for Tocqueville criticises the French nobility for having become a "caste" defined by birth alone, and for having ceased to be an aristocracy, i.e. a *corps* that, although limited in numbers, is relatively open to citizens who wield political power. In fact, the French nobility never was that "aristocracy" of which Tocqueville dreams, in the sense in which sixteenth-century Venice, for example, governed by its Senate, was an aristocratic State. Yet the French nobility had been open throughout the Ancien Régime to the advancement of commoners, for by its end the old families who traced their lineage back to the Middle Ages had become a distinct minority within the order. It was as a result of the sale of offices and ennoblement by the king, in other words, *as a result of absolutism and consubstantially with it,* that the nobility ceased to be a closed *corps* of hereditary landowning seigneurs and incorporated into its ranks, in the name of service to the State, the sons of the wealthiest merchants and the most deserving of the king's servants. When Tocqueville writes, "The more the nobility ceased to be an aristocracy, the more it seemed to become a caste" (Book 2, chap. 9), one could reverse his statement and say that the more the nobility ceased to be a caste, the more it became an aristocracy.

Here we may well have reached the core of Tocqueville's system of interpretation and its ambiguities. For the entire sociological analysis of *L'Ancien Régime* is based on an opposition between aristocracy and nobility, a dialectic in which aristocracy is posited as the "should-be" of the nobility, as its very essence. But then Tocqueville, whose historical learning, except for the eighteenth century, was quite superficial, had a rather banal, indeed legend-like, notion of the history of the French nobility (and aristocracy). As for its origins, he never went beyond the classic argument that identified the nobles with the Frankish conquerors (cf. in particular the last chapter of volume 1 of *Democracy in America* ["The Present and Probable Future Condition of the Three Races That Inhabit the Territory of the United States"] or the beginning of chapter 9 of Book 2 of *L'Ancien Régime*. In the passage of *Democracy in America* Tocqueville curiously asserts that ever since human society began to exist, all aristocracies and the inequalities they imposed were the products of military conquest. One wonders how Tocqueville would fit into this schema, for example, Renaissance Italian republics or eighteenth-century England), making them an aristocracy created by the conquest. They soon lost this character ("during the Middle Ages," writes Tocqueville at the beginning of chapter 9 of Book 2, although this statement seems to contradict his description of medieval institutions in chapter 4 of Book 1) as a result of royal usurpations of power and became a "caste." A "caste," in the very unusual meaning Tocqueville attributes to the term, was not so much a group closed to all who were born outside it as a group deprived of all political power and therefore all the more fiercely determined to preserve its compensatory privileges. It thus becomes clear that this history provides the nobility with origins and at the same time sets its goals for the future. It implies that the nobility was ruining itself not because its real past and the historical mechanism by which it had renewed itself inextricably tied it to the absolute monarchy, but because it was unfaithful to its origins and to its aristocratic principle. This historical account also shows that the political aspect was always paramount in Tocqueville's interpretation. Tocqueville was ultimately no more interested in society *per se* than in economics *per se*. Despite his close attention to fiscal sources, census data, and seigneurial rent rolls (*terriers*), which is obvious from his notes, and despite some marvellous comments on specific points, he was quite indifferent to the history of that society. The actual process by which the French eighteenth-century nobility, with its groups and sub-groups, had come into being did not interest him. For him, classes, above all his own, the nobility, were the trustees of traditions and values they could betray or embody; and he felt very strongly that nobility was inseparable from the political principle of aristocracy and that the notion of a nobility consisting of the king's servants was a contradiction in terms, since a nobility defined by function was not a nobility at all. Tocqueville was therefore bound to see the king as Saint-Simon had seen Louis XIV, surrounded by bourgeois who were busily engaged in ousting the nobility from all its traditional positions. Here is the last and belated echo of a specific political conflict, as well as the reaffirmation of a principle.

Tocqueville's historical description in *L'Ancien Régime* is thus essentially not concerned with economics, nor even with the structures of society and the history of its classes. Rather, it is concerned with the frame of mind of the French, with what one might call their national temperament or character. To him this was the arena *par excellence* of the clash between democratic and aristocratic tendencies, between consent and opposition to centralisation. One would have to apologise for speaking in such vague terms if it were possible to define Tocqueville's thinking more clearly. In volume 2 of *Democracy in America*, where he studies the effects of "democracy" on the American mentality, Tocqueville successively defines the "intellectual movement," the "feelings" [of the Americans] and finally their "actual mores." It is not always easy to make a clear distinction between the levels of his study—notably between what he calls "sentiments" and "mores"—but at least a guiding thread is provided. *L'Ancien Régime* is totally different: Tocqueville not only modifies, as we have seen, the ranking of causes by shifting the emphasis to governmental and administrative centralisation, but he also fails to distinguish between types of effects. Actually, the notion of traditions (intellectual or emotional) or of mores fits in fairly well with the picture of French society in Book 2, for Tocqueville contends that centralisation had brought about the development of "democratic mores," which clashed with the aristocratic tradition, and that the two trends reinforced and exacerbated each other by dint of their very incompatibility. Eighteenth-century Frenchmen were becoming ever more similar yet ever more distinct, ever more subservient yet ever more independent-minded. The closing years of the Ancien Régime were marked by the judicial combat between two principles and their conflicting influence on public opinion. In *L'Ancien Régime* democracy is not so much a state of society as a state of mind.

This modification permits Tocqueville to bring into his analysis a revolutionary dialectic that is clearly indispensable for dealing with his subject. For "democracy," as he had studied it in the United States, was not only a state of society, but a founding principle, brought over and built-up *ex nihilo* by democratically minded men who never had to struggle against an opposing principle, an opposing history and opposing traditions. In such conditions, he argues, society as a whole develops in harmony, for its democratic principle, embodied in actual facts, pervades every area of life, notably mentalities and manners. France at the end of the Ancien Régime presented Tocqueville with a completely different problem, for it involved a *history*, a *change*, and a *revolution*. Democracy (equality of conditions) cannot characterise the state of society before the Revolution, since it defines the state of society after the Revolution. Hence his recourse to a different conceptualisation: what was common to "before" and "after" was centralisation, as the vehicle for change and for the spread of democratic attitudes in a society that clung to its aristocratic forms, emptied though they were of their content. Defined in historical terms, the contradiction that brought this society to revolution was thus not essentially of a social, but of an intellectual and moral order; it coincided only secondarily—and quite belatedly, i.e. in 1788—with an awareness of an internal conflict within civil society between the nobility and the Third Estate. It was thus the expression of a conflict of values deeply embedded in society as a whole, and notably in the mind of every "enlightened" individual: democratic individualism and the nobility's caste spirit, both equally degenerate forms of their respective models, but for that very reason all the more incompatible and hostile to each other. The only principle that ultimately brought them together was despotism.

III

This interpretation accounts for the content of Book 3 of *L'Ancien Régime*, which, unlike the earlier books, is not devoted to the long-term causes of the Revolution but to the "specific and more recent facts that finally determined its place in history, its birth and its character" (Book 3, chap. 1)—in other words, to the examination of what we would call its short-term causes.

Tocqueville feels that toward the middle of the eighteenth century, specifically in the 1750s, the phenomena he had studied and the contradictions they produced were rapidly gathering speed. The first change, understandably, involved mentalities and ideas. It is as if the long process of administrative centralisation and social disintegration that he had analysed in the preceding books culminated in a cultural revolution during these years: France, at least its élites, that is, the groups whose political impact was decisive, was massively won over by an abstract philosophy of the political and social order that was all the more incompatible with existing society as it arose precisely from the very lack of political experience that characterised the individual in that society, whether nobleman or bourgeois. Deprived of true liberty, Frenchmen turned to natural law; incapable of collective experience, unable to test the resistances of a political process, they unwittingly set their course toward a revolutionary utopia; without an aristocracy, without organised leadership, without the possibility of calling upon professional politicians, they turned toward men of letters. Literature took on the rôle of politics. This phenomenon was subsequently fostered and intensified by an internal dialectic, for the intellectuals were by nature, and not just by the force of circumstance alone, the social group most lacking in political experience. In destroying the aristocracy, the monarchy had turned writers into make-believe substitutes for a ruling class. France then went from a debate about how to run the country to the discussion of ultimate values, from politics to revolution.

It is not so much the ideas of the period that were completely new. In fact, Tocqueville stresses that they were old. What was new was their impact throughout society, their resonance, their reception and their rôle. Nor were these ideas specifically French: they were shared by the entire European Enlightenment, yet all of Europe did not move toward the same revolutionary future. By this outline of a sociology of the production and the consumption of ideas in France in the second half of the eighteenth century, Tocqueville suggests that the Revolution was above all a transformation in values and patterns of thought, and that this transformation encountered particularly favourable conditions and was already well under way in France during the 1750s, owing to the long process of monarchical centralisation. The cultural (or, if one prefers, intellectual and moral) revolution, which had been a minor factor in the long term, became the essential element in the revolutionary process in the short term, for it channelled religious sentiments toward the imaginary cult of the State-as-model, thereby neutralising from the outset any liberalising tendencies that might be stimulated by this new awareness. For Tocqueville the chief goal of the revolution was "democratic despotism," as prefigured and already developed in the physiocratic doctrine, rather than parliamentary liberalism; it was the "preparation" of 1793 much more than a working toward 1789.

Tocqueville sees this sudden change of pace in French history, which he had first analysed in the intellectual sphere, in the economy and in society as well: he points out that—notwithstanding the beliefs of the actors in the great drama, who were obsessed with the idea of "regeneration"—the Revolution did not strike a country in decline, but a prosperous one, which had experienced a great period of growth since 1750. Indeed the regions that were struck hardest were those that had responded most readily to the century's economic and social development, such as the Ile-de-France. That is the famous thesis of chapter 4, which, in a general sense, though not in every detail, has been largely confirmed by modern studies in eighteenth-century economic history. Unlike today's Marxist or Marxist-oriented historians, however, Tocqueville does not see that situation as a factor in the struggle between social classes with opposing interests, but diagnoses it instead as one more element that upset traditional attitudes and beliefs: the régime was too old to accommodate innovation, and the people were too liberated to tolerate the vestiges of their servitude, or rather their feeling of servitude. Reforms, which were incapable of overcoming the awareness that the situation was intolerable, only served to accelerate the disintegration of society: it was in 1787, not 1789, that Loménie de Brienne destroyed the Ancien Régime with his administrative reform, which replaced the *intendants* with elected assemblies. That, Tocqueville points out, was a more important revolution than all those France was to undergo after 1789, for the later ones affected only political institutions and not the "administrative constitution." The year 1787 marked the complete upheaval of the traditional relationship between the French people and the State, and of the very texture of social life. In short, the Ancien Régime was already dead in 1789, and the Revolution could kill it only in spirit, since that was the only place where it was still alive. Hence the extraordinary ease with which events followed their course. Was 1789, then, merely a hoax?

But if the actual content of the Revolution, thus defined, was indeed already secured before the outbreak of the Revolution, then the revolutionary phenomenon, in the narrow sense of the term, was circumscribed from the outset. It did not bring a political and social transformation—for that transformation either had already been accomplished or, to the extent that it was incomplete, would be accomplished as a matter of course. The revolutionary process merely expressed two modes of historical action, namely, the use of violence and the use of ideology (or intellectual illusion); and in reality these two modes are one. For violence and political radicalism are inherent in the eschatological ideology of a "before" and an "after," of the old and the new, that characterised the revolutionary endeavour. The formation of the centralised democratic State, which for Tocqueville is the very meaning of the French Revolution, was also the meaning of the Ancien

Régime. The Revolution only gave a new name to that process; but it was the Revolution *because it believed* that it had invented it. Here Tocqueville shows an admirable intuitive understanding of the discrepancy between the rôle objectively played by revolutions in historical change and the perception of that rôle by contemporaries or its intellectual fascination for succeeding generations. Unlike the many historians, who for almost 200 years now, don the costumes of the period when they recount the Revolution by means of a commentary on the Revolution's interpretation of itself, Tocqueville suggests that revolutionary times are precisely the most difficult to understand, since they are often periods when the veil of ideology hides most completely the real meaning of the events from the protagonists. That, no doubt, is the fundamental contribution of *L'Ancien Régime* to a theory of revolution.

Yet the central intuition of the book is never stated that explicitly. Tocqueville could only have done so had he written the history of the revolutionary events from the two-fold perspective he had announced in *L'Ancien Régime*; that is, if he had treated the events in themselves and then, above all, the ideology, or successive ideologies, that served to justify them. (Cf. his letter to Lewis of 6 October 1856: "Since my purpose is far more to depict the evolution of the sentiments and ideas that successively produced the events of the Revolution than to recount the events themselves.") But in 1856 he never did write the second volume of his book, thereby repeating—unintentionally this time—his silence in 1836. His death, eighteen months after the first volume appeared, may well not be the only explanation. Tocqueville, in his systematic approach, having finally succeeded in constructing a historical interpretation of the Ancien Régime, had yet to master the problems he saw in formulating a commensurate historical theory of the French Revolution.

The very history of the book, and the posthumous fragments that have come down to us, attest to that (*L'Ancien Régime et la Révolution*, vol. 2, "Fragments and Unpublished Notes about the Revolution"). We know that Tocqueville began the research that eventually led him to write *L'Ancien Régime* by studying the Consulate; in mid-1852 he wrote two chapters devoted to the public spirit at the end of the Directory (published as Book 3 of vol. 2), which he intended to use as the preamble to that study. Then, toward the end of 1852, he gave up the project in order to return to the analysis of the Ancien Régime. He spent the summer of 1853 studying the archives of the *intendance* of Tours, and so deliberately abandoned his initial line of research. These two successive projects clearly indicate his major preoccupation, which was to study administrative institutions and their continuity, beyond the Revolution, from the Ancien Régime to the Consulate settlement. He himself indirectly admitted as much when, in April 1853, he made the following comment on the Paris municipal archives: "These boxes contain few documents dating before 1787; from then on, the old administrative constitution was profoundly modified, and one comes

to a rather uninteresting period of transition that separates the administration of the Ancien Régime from the administrative system created by
the Consulate, which is the system that still governs us today."

In point of fact, that "rather uninteresting period of transition"—a
truly astounding phrase for a man who wanted to write a history of the
Revolution—has left few traces in his posthumous fragments. Most of his
reading notes are devoted to the Ancien Régime and the years just before
the Revolution, specifically to the administration of the Ancien Régime and
to pre-revolutionary ideology. They contain very little about the Constituent
Assembly, nothing at all about the Legislative Assembly or the Committee
of Public Safety, and practically nothing about the Convention: just a few
rather banal pages about the Terror. Yet one cannot explain this impressive
silence only by the reason Tocqueville had given in 1853. For we have seen
that although he had begun by examining administrative centralisation,
the underlying theme of his study of the Ancien Régime, Tocqueville had
become increasingly interested in the ideological aspect of the Revolution.
Why, then, did he so carefully read the pre-revolutionary pamphlets, but
not the speeches of the *conventionnels?* Why Mounier and not Brissot? Why
Sieyès and not Robespierre?

That is all the more puzzling as some of these fragmentary notes indicate that Tocqueville did perceive the dynamic character of revolutionary
ideology. At one point, for instance, he comments on a page of Burke as
follows:

> It is quite true that, almost on the eve of the Revolution, France
> was very far from the state of mind that was to be exhibited by
> the Revolution. It is only too true that the spirit of liberty was not
> yet present among the masses (and it never was found there).
> These people still lived by the ideas of a different order and of a
> different century.

> (Vol. 2)

He also repeatedly (vol. 2, Book 5, chap. 2) noted the rôle of the "uncivilized" lower classes in the revolutionary process. Moreover, it is well known
that in *L'Ancien Régime* he expressed his admiration for the men of 1789
and his loathing for those of 1793. The trouble is that those scattered remarks are difficult to reconcile with Tocqueville's detailed analyses of the
emergence of the "true spirit of the Revolution" (vol. 2, Book 1, chap. 5)
based on the pamphlets of 1788–89 and the *Cahiers de doléances*, for those
analyses convey the impression that revolutionary ideology, fully developed at this early stage, was already speaking "the final word of the Revolution." Even more extraordinary are some of Tocqueville's omissions: he
says almost nothing, except for the sentence quoted above, about intellectual and ideological differences within the French population. One simply
finds Enlightenment culture above, and a kind of cultural nothingness, a
noncivilisation, below. There is not a word, finally, about the messianic

mission of Jacobinism and ideological warfare as both an outgrowth and a tremendous intensification of revolutionary patriotism after 1792, despite its being, in terms of Tocqueville's own analysis, the most general ideological expression of the attachment of the masses to the new democratic State and their participation in it. Even in the only two completed chapters of volume 2, where he analyses the state of mind of the French at the end of the Directory, Tocqueville manages to avoid a discussion of the problem of war and peace, which, at that time, was probably the overriding issue in domestic politics and also precluded, for emotional and practical reasons, a liberal solution to the political crisis.

But if so great a thinker could remain blind to such overwhelming evidence, he must have suffered from a kind of conceptual block, which may well have been the price he paid for his penetrating insight. Tocqueville, basically, never ceased to waver between two major lines of research, two basic hypotheses about French history. One is the hypothesis of administrative centralisation. It almost naturally led him to write on the Ancien Régime, and it might have led him to write a similar account of the Consulate or the Empire, for it provided him with a guiding thread for the long-term continuity of French history. But while this hypothesis gave a content to the Revolution, it also deprived it of its special character as historical process or mode, that is, of its specificity. Moreover, if the Revolution crowned and completed the work of the Ancien Régime by producing the administrative "constitution" of the Consulate, then why 1830, why 1848, why all the additional revolutions that Tocqueville never ceased to study with passionate interest? Henceforth, the administrative constitution was established once and for all, and yet the political constitution was subject to sudden change every fifteen or twenty years.

It is probably this realisation that led Tocqueville to adopt his second major line of research, in which he defined revolution as a rapid transformation of the customs and mentalities of a society and as a radical ideological venture. This vast cultural split, which individuals desired all the more fervently as it was favoured, not thwarted, by the evolution of society, is analysed first as a consequence of centralisation and of the dislocation of traditional social groups. Tocqueville then endows it with a kind of autonomous force in 1788, which is meant to explain the outbreak of the Revolution; yet, imprisoned by his first hypothesis, he never carries the second one to its logical conclusion. The reason is, partly, that in this area he never clearly states just what he means by "mores," "frame of mind," "habits," "feelings," and "ideas." But, above all, once he had analysed the factors that touched off the Revolution as a cultural process, he seems to have failed to put together the elements needed for the history of that cultural dynamic.

Perhaps it can be said that Tocqueville has given us not so much the history of "The Ancien Régime and the Revolution" he had meant to write as an interpretative description of the Ancien Régime and some fragments of a projected history of the Revolution. The first text constitutes Books 1 and 2 of *L'Ancien Régime*; the second was never written, and the preparatory notes for it are all that has come down to us. In between, Book 3 of *L'Ancien Régime* acts as a very subtle yet necessary transition, for the two texts do not follow the same internal guidelines. The first, despite its hidden contradictions, is based throughout on a relatively static analysis of administrative centralisation and its effects on society. In the second, that is, starting with Book 3, history suddenly comes into play at the beginning of the 1750s; it is precisely the history of which Tocqueville had thorough and first-hand knowledge only from that date onward. In the second approach, therefore, cultural phenomena in the widest sense tend to become largely independent of the growth of administrative structures and are treated as determining factors of the revolutionary explosion. The Revolution is no longer defined as the building of the democratic State, since that was already accomplished by 1788, but rather as the application of an eschatological ideology: hence Tocqueville's detailed analysis of the 1788–89 pamphlets and the *Cahiers*.

Nonetheless, most of Tocqueville's notes on the revolutionary years show him to be locked into his first approach to the problem. That is not surprising, since they were taken at the time he was writing his book. There is no indication, then, that before his death Tocqueville ever clearly resolved the problem that had stymied him in 1836: how to work out a theory of the revolutionary dynamic. Yet in the last years of his life, unlike in 1836, he was able to chart the direction for further research. That is the real legacy of this great unfinished work.

By way of a postscript: after I had written this essay, a new text (new at least to me) came to my attention. It is a letter from Tocqueville to Louis de Kergolay (16 May 1858), which seems to confirm the cogency of my analysis.

Less than a year before his death, at the time when he was in the midst of his work on the second volume, that is, on the Revolution itself, Tocqueville spoke about his problems and the state of his research to his friend Kergolay. He complained about the enormous number of contemporary works to be read and then came to the interpretation itself: "There is moreover in this disease of the French Revolution something very strange that I can sense, though I cannot describe it properly or analyse its causes. It is a *virus* of a new and unknown kind. There have been violent Revolutions in the world before; but the immoderate, violent, radical, desperate, bold, almost crazed and yet powerful and effective character of these Revolutionaries has no precedents, it seems to me, in the great social agitations of past centuries. Where did this new race come from? What produced it? What made it so effective? What perpetuates it? [F]or the same men are still with us, even though the circumstances are different now; and they have a progeny everywhere in the civilised world. I am exhausting my mind trying to conceive a clear notion of this object and seeking a way to depict it properly. Independently of all that can be explained about the French Revolution, there is something unexplained in its spirit and in its acts. I can sense the presence of this unknown object, but despite all my efforts I cannot lift the veil that covers it. I can palpate it as through a foreign body that prevents me from grasping it or even seeing it."

Proudhon and Rousseau

Aaron Noland

The central rôle of Jean-Jacques Rousseau in nineteenth century European thought has long been recognized by scholars, and hence when Bertrand de Jouvenel, writing after World War II, declared that Rousseau has exercised "the greatest influence on the development of the political beliefs and institutions" in modern Europe ("An Essay on Rousseau's Politics," preface to *Du contrat social*) and, more recently, when Frank Manuel noted that Rousseau's influence "was all-pervasive in nineteenth-century social theory" (*The New World of Henri Saint-Simon*) both men were simply reaffirming a traditional view. But if there is a consensus concerning the preeminence of Rousseau in the last century, there is by no means a similar consensus as to the precise character and nature of Rousseau's impact and influence on the many and diversified streams of nineteenth century political and social thought. The relation of Rousseau to the radical reformist and revolutionary movements, particularly socialism, communism, and anarchism in their many varieties, is a case in point. Here high-level, sweeping, and often contradictory generalizations abound. Repeatedly, throughout the nineteenth century, Rousseau was identified as being the "master," "father," or "grandfather" of the socialists and the other radical reformers of the time, while almost all the latter were labeled the "disciples," "sons," or "grandsons" of Rousseau. Jules Barbey D'Aurevilly, writing in 1858, declared that the lineage was far from being a legitimate one, for all the utopian reformers of the age were "les bâtards du génie de Jean-Jacques" (quoted in Albert Schinz, *Etat présent des travaux sur J. J. Rousseau*). At the same time these views of Rousseau's influence have repeatedly been denied, as for example when Alfred Cobban asserted that "with one or

From *Journal of the History of Ideas* 28, no. 1 (January–March 1967). © 1967 by Journal of the History of Ideas, Inc.

two exceptions . . . the early socialists were consistently hostile to Rousseau'' (*Rousseau and the Modern State*).

To the serious student of nineteenth century social thought, however, the question of Rousseau's influence is not one to be resolved by simple generalizations. To call Rousseau the "master" of socialist and other radical reformers, or contrarily, to affirm that the latter were "hostile" to him does little to advance our appreciation of the precise relationship that existed between Rousseau's thought and the radical reformers of the time. The receptions accorded Rousseau's ideas by Charles Fourier, Louis Blanc, Etienne Cabet, Pierre-Joseph Proudhon, or Constantin Pecqueur—to select a few names at random—differed greatly; and in order to discover just how each of these and other thinkers responded to Rousseau, what aspects of his thought entered into their ideologies and in just what manner Rousseau's teachings were bent to serve the conceits or needs of each thinker, or, as the case may be, what aspects of Rousseau's thought were rejected outright—to discover this one must deal with each thinker as a separate case and not lump them together simply because many shared a common identity as socialist, or anarchist, or communist. This would seem to be simple common sense and self-evident; yet few indeed are the studies that have endeavored to relate Rousseau to the reformist movements of thought in this manner. No attempt will be made in this paper to fill even in a summary manner the lacunae in this field; rather, this paper will examine one case only: Proudhon's confrontation of Rousseau in the terms described above.

Judgments concerning the relation of Rousseau to Proudhon are not lacking. Barbey D'Aurevilly, in his review of one of Proudhon's many books, identified Proudhon as a *philosophe* and called him "the Jean-Jacques of the nineteenth century," a man who, like Rousseau himself, dreamed of the total reconstruction of a society (*Sensations d'art*). Alfred Fouillée, early in the twentieth century, asserted that Proudhon's efforts to work out a system of ethics independent of metaphysical or religious doctrines made him "one of the most important of Rousseau's continuers (*L'Idée moderne du droit*). On the other hand George Beaulavon, in his classic edition of *Du contrat social*, published in 1903, placed Proudhon alongside Benjamin Constant as "the most serious adversary of Rousseau" on the basis of Proudhon's violent criticism of *Du contrat social*. A few years later the Sorbonne sociologist Célestin Bouglé reaffirmed this judgment declaring that "Rousseau had no worst detractor than Proudhon" (*La Sociologie de Proudhon*, 1911).

What did Proudhon himself think of Rousseau? Proudhon was well aware of the presence of Jean-Jacques, and in the vast body of his work—the twenty-six volumes of the complete works, the twelve volumes of the posthumous works, and the fourteen volumes of correspondence—he gives ample evidence of his concern with Rousseau, "whose authority," he noted in 1851, "has ruled us for almost a century" (*Idée générale de la Révolution au XIXe siécle*). Proudhon, in his various writings, cites Rousseau more frequently by far than any other political theorist. Yet it is in vain that one seeks in these writings for any consistent attitude toward Rousseau and his work. On the one hand, Proudhon hailed Rousseau as "the apostle of liberty and equality," as a "great innovator," and as an "admirable dialectician" (*Deuxième mémoire sur la propriété*). On the title page of his first published work on social questions, *The Utility of the Celebration of Sunday as Regards Hygiene, Morality and Social and Political Relations* (1839), Proudhon quoted a passage from Rousseau's *Du contrat social* wherein Rousseau describes the sovereignty of the people in a democratic assembly, and in that same work Proudhon posed the fundamental problem concerning the social order—a problem that was to remain his preoccupation throughout his life—in a manner reminiscent of Rousseau's own formulation. Rousseau, in *Du contrat social*, had stated that "The problem is to find a form of association which will defend and protect with the whole common force the person and goods of each associate, and in which each, while uniting himself with all, may still obey himself alone, and remains as free as before." Proudhon posed the problem as follows: "To find a state of social equality which would not be a repressive community (*communauté*), nor a despotism, nor a fragmented or disordered grouping (*ni morcellement, ni anarchie*), but a state characterized by liberty in order and independence in unity." Moreover, Proudhon more than once in his rôle as social critic, identified himself with Rousseau, and in a letter, written in August 1843, in which he spoke of his hopes for the future, he declared that while he did not possess Rousseau's talent, he nevertheless hoped "to exercise no less an influence."

On the other hand, Proudhon again and again assailed Rousseau both as a man and as a thinker in language that was unusually brutal even for an age when polemicists were particularly resourceful in handling invective. Scattered throughout Proudhon's work are such descriptions of Rousseau as: he is a "rhetorician," a "charlatan," a "demagogue," a "perfidious declaimer," and a "scoundrel" (*Idée générale* and *De la capacité politique des classes ouvrières*). In his unpublished *carnets* Proudhon labeled Rousseau a "thief, idler, vagabond, liar, hypocrite"; he was a man "without dignity, impure, unfaithful, and an ingrate" ("Carnet"). Elsewhere Rousseau was depicted as possessing a "weak character," an "impassioned and effeminate spirit," and a "false judgment" (*De la Justice dans la Révolution et dans l'Eglise*). Writing in 1851, Proudhon, in the course of criticizing Rousseau's political theory, declared: "Never did a man unite to such a degree intellectual pride, aridity of soul, baseness of tastes, depravity of habits, ingratitude of heart: never did the eloquence of passion, the pretention of sensitiveness, the effrontery of paradox arouse such a fever of infatuation." Later Proudhon was to write (1858) that "the Revolution, the Republic, and the people have never had a greater enemy than Jean-Jacques" and that "Rousseau did not understand either philosophy or economics" (*De la Justice*). "The time is not far away," Proudhon wrote (in 1851), "when a quotation from Rousseau will suffice to render a writer suspect" (*Idée générale*).

What is one to make of all this? One may, of course, simply say what every student of Proudhon knows, that Proudhon's work is full of just such contrary judgments concerning the work of other social thinkers, his predecessors as well as his contemporaries, and that his treatment of Rousseau is an illustration of the contradictory, ambiguous, and paradoxical nature of Proudhon's writings. There is, indeed, some truth in this evaluation. But it would be wrong to let the matter rest at this point. It is the contention of this paper that an examination of Proudhon's criticism of Rousseau's political theory not only will show how one prominent socialist—or anarcho-socialist if you wish—of the nineteenth century responded to Rousseau, but also may contribute something to the clarification of a few of the central conceptions of Proudhon's own social theory, itself so much the subject of continuing controversy.

Parenthetically, it is noteworthy that Proudhon was familiar with only certain works of Rousseau, namely, *Du contrat social, Emile, La Nouvelle Héloïse, Les Confessions,* the *Discours,* and the *Lettre à d'Alembert.* In his own writings Proudhon cites these works and often quotes extensively from some of them, particularly *Du contrat social* and *Emile.* In his unpublished *cahiers de lectures,* numbering forty-one in all, many pages of notes are devoted to Rousseau, more than to any other political theorist, and in the yet unpublished *carnets* (eleven), too, Proudhon devotes a good deal of attention to Rousseau's works. There is no evidence, however, in Proudhon's published or unpublished writings that he read any works of Rousseau other than those listed here. This means, of course, that Proudhon's knowledge of Rousseau was far from complete. Moreover, it is apparent from Proudhon's critique of Rousseau that he did not always understand clearly just what Rousseau was trying to say—and this is not very surprising in view of the many difficult Rousseauean texts—and Proudhon's misreadings or misunderstandings sometimes leave one with the impression that Proudhon was fighting a straw man rather than the citizen of Geneva.

Proudhon initiated his attack on Rousseau's theory by challenging the latter's definition of the social contract, namely that it was a form of association "which will defend and protect with the whole common force the person and goods of each associate, and in which each, while uniting himself with all, may still obey himself alone, and remain as free as before" (*The Social Contract*). In Proudhon's view the contract was too narrowly defined, too vague in its terms, to serve as the basis for the structuring of civil society and establishing the rights, obligations, and duties of its constituents. To be sure Rousseau had given the conditions of the social pact "*as to that which concerns the protection and defense of goods and persons,*" but, Proudhon asserted, Rousseau left far too many essential matters out of account, for he "says not a word" about "the multitude of relations which, whether we like it or not, places man in perpetual association with his fellow man"—and here Proudhon referred specifically to economic relationships, such as "the mode of acquisition and transmission" of products, "labor, exchange, the value and price of products," as well as to education

(*Idée générale*). Rousseau, Proudhon affirmed, made no mention in the social contract "of the principles and laws which rule the fortunes of nations and individuals," not a word about labor or the industrial forces, "all of which it is the very object of a social contract to organize." Out of the multitude of relations which the social contract is called upon to define and regulate, Rousseau "saw only political relations," which were, as shall be indicated, of secondary importance to Proudhon. Rousseau simply did not know what economics meant: "His program speaks of political rights only; it does not mention economic rights." Rousseau's social contract could only, in Proudhon's eyes, serve as the basis for "a mutual insurance society for the protection of our persons and property," a society in which economic matters—to Proudhon "really the only matters of importance"—are left "to the chance of birth or speculation." Given its narrow base and limited concerns, this contract, in Proudhon's words "is nothing but the offensive and defensive alliance of those who possess against those who do not possess." Moreover, even within its own limited frame of reference, Rousseau's contract did not spell out precisely the commitments involved. Addressing Rousseau, Proudhon queried: "Where in your agreement are my rights and my duties? What have I promised to my fellow citizens? What have they promised to me?"

Proudhon found additional proof for his contention that Rousseau "understood nothing of the social contract" in the latter's comments on government. After having posited as a principle that the people alone are the sovereign, that the people can be represented only by themselves, and lastly, that the law should be the expression of the will of all, Rousseau, Proudhon contended, "quietly abandons and discards this principle." This, according to Proudhon, is done by substituting the will of the majority for the "general, collective, indivisible will." Now having done this, Rousseau then discovers, in his own words, that "it is unimaginable that the people should remain continually assembled to devote their time to public affairs," and subsequently he manages, in Proudhon's words, to get back "by way of elections, to the nomination of representatives or proxies, who shall legislate in the name of the people and whose decrees shall have the force of laws. Instead of a direct, personal transaction where his interests are involved, the citizen only has left the power of choosing his rulers by a plurality vote." To Proudhon, Rousseau's rejection of pure democracy (that is, the condition in which the whole people rules itself) as impractical and an ideal only—did not Rousseau state that "So perfect a government is not for men"?—opened the doors to tyranny and the destruction of liberties. This possibility is further enhanced by Rousseau's dictum that "if the general will is to be able to express itself . . . there should be no partial society within the State"—a statement which Proudhon re-formulated in the following manner: "That in a well-ordered Republic no association or special meeting of citizens can be permitted, because it would be a State within a State, a government within a government" (*Idée générale*)—for this ban would reinforce the "republic one and indivisible," and such a concentration of authority and power would constitute the basis for a tyranny of the most violent sort (*Contradictions politiques*). Freedom, equality, and justice could only be assured, in Proudhon's view, in a civil society in which a network of associations and private groupings flourished and in which "each individual would be equally and synonymously producer and consumer, citizen and prince, ruler and ruled" (*Carnets de P.-J. Proudhon*).

Another feature of Rousseau's *Du contrat social* which Proudhon rejected was its concern with civil religion. Rousseau's insistence that "it matters very much to the community that each citizen should have a religion" and that the Sovereign should fix the articles of "a purely civil profession of faith" so as to encourage those "social sentiments without which a man cannot be a good citizen or a faithful subject" and would be "incapable of truly loving the laws and justice"—those beliefs along with Rousseau's affirmation that "All justice comes from God, who is its sole source"—struck Proudhon as reactionary, dangerous, and absolutely erroneous ideas that must be opposed by every true lover of liberty and justice. Within the compass of this paper, however, it is not possible to do more than give the briefest indications of Proudhon's position on these matters, matters which he treated at length in a number of books and articles. Proudhon, drawing inspiration from one strain of the positivist thought of his day, maintained that the notion that God was the ultimate source of justice and right as well as the belief that religion was the necessary handmaid of government belonged to the childhood period of mankind, and that mankind had outgrown that period in displacing revelation and divine intervention by science and positive law and in displacing God by man as the source of morals and justice (*La Justice poursuivie par l'Eglise* and *De la création de l'ordre dans l'humanité ou Principes d'organisation politique*). Moreover, historically, religion had been "the eternal source" of tyranny and the "highway for authority" (*Les Confessions d'un révolutionnaire pour servir à l'histoire de la révolution de février*). As for justice and authority, they were, to Proudhon, "incompatible terms." Historically, too, "God and King, Church and State, have ever been the body and soul of reaction (*l'eternelle contre-révolution*)." Proudhon maintained that "the triumph of liberty" lay in separating them and in getting this separation accepted "as a principle." In reviving the old relationship between religion and government in his study of the social contract, Rousseau, in Proudhon's view, had done the cause of liberty and progress a disservice.

This examination and enumeration of the specific criticisms which Proudhon made of Rousseau's political theory as set forth in *Du contrat social* does not in itself, however, give the full measure of Proudhon's case against that theory. The overarching, fundamental reason why Proudhon rejected Rousseau's theory not only in its specifics but in its essential formulation—a reason implicit in the criticisms that have just been examined—must be made explicit at this point. Rousseau's theory was, in Proudhon's view, a metaphysical, artificial, and hence arbitrary construct, which therefore could contribute nothing of value to the problem of establishing a viable civil society characterized by liberty, equality, and justice. Proudhon contended that Rousseau conceived of the principle of order in civil society as an essentially *political* principle. Thus he devoted himself in *Du contrat social* to the description and analysis of the appropriate institutions and processes of government, for example, sovereignty, voting, legislation, forms of political organization, etc. What Rousseau had failed to understand was that government as such, any government at all, was "illegitimate and powerless" as "a principle of order" (*Idée générale*; see also *La Guerre et la paix*). Indeed, in itself the very idea of the social contract "excludes that of government," for what characterized the contract, in Proudhon's view, was an agreement for equal exchange between contracting parties, "and it is by virtue of this agreement that liberty and well-being increase"; while by the establishment of governmental authority, "both of these necessarily diminish."

Proudhon maintained that Rousseau had misconstrued the history of the idea of social contract since the sixteenth century. He had failed to see that "the revolutionary tradition of the sixteenth century gave us the idea of the Social Contract as an *antithesis* to the idea of Government." It was the French protestant theologian Pierre Jurieu (1636–1713), the adversary of Bishop Bossuet, who in direct opposition to the notion of the sovereignty of divine right, affirmed, Proudhon says, "the sovereignty of the people, which he [Jurieu] expressed with infinitely more precision, force, and profundity by the words *Social Contract* or *Pact*, in plain contradiction to such conceptions as authority and government. . . . " Authority and government had always been inextricably bound, for authority was to government "what the thought is to the word, the idea to the fact, and the soul to the body. Authority is government in principle, as government is authority in practice. To abolish either, if it is a real abolition, is to abolish both." In Proudhon's view the social contract posited by Jurieu was *not* an agreement of the citizen with the government, for this would have meant "but the continuation of the same idea." It was, rather, "an agreement of man with man," an "essentially reciprocal" pledge "from which must result what we call society." In this social contract all pretension of men to *govern* one another is abdicated entirely. In Proudhon's account of the history of the idea of the social contract, the seventeenth century, while not comprehending this notion clearly, did reaffirm it. The "great and decisive negation of government" envisioned by Jurieu lay at the heart of Morelly's thought, and the notion would have become explicit in the doctrines of Babeuf if the latter "had known how to reason and deduce his own principles." Proudhon noted that from the date of the controversy of Jurieu with Bossuet to the publication of Rousseau's *Du contrat social* almost a century had elapsed, and that when Rousseau's book appeared, "it was *not* to assert the idea, but rather to stifle it."

Thus, in Proudhon's final assessment of the matter, Rousseau really "understands nothing of the social contract," and his book is but "a masterpiece of oratorical jugglery" and "a code of capitalist and mercantilist tyranny" that called for the perpetuation of the proletariat, "the subordination of labor, a dictatorship, and for the Inquisition." Proudhon's indictment of Rousseau did not end, however, with this sweeping condemnation of *Du contrat social*. Proudhon certainly believed that "the evil that men do lives after them," and therefore, that the powerful influence of Rousseau's political theory on the generations that succeeded his own had to be taken into account in taking the measure of the man. In this respect, Proudhon, writing in 1851, ascribed to Rousseau a large measure of the responsibility and blame for the "fruitless disorder" and general confusion that had characterized French life since the French Revolution. In following the inspiration for Rousseau's teachings, France had indeed paid a terrible price, for "the vogue of Rousseau," Proudhon affirmed, had "cost France more gold, more blood, and more shame than the detested reign of the famous courtesans" of Louis XV "ever caused her to sacrifice."

Given the limits of this paper, only a few highpoints of Proudhon's anti-Rousseauean brief can be touched on here. Rousseau was the inspiration for the Constitution of 1793, "which promised everything to the people and gave them nothing," and he was the guiding light for the Jacobins who, in Proudhon's view, were terrorists, inquisitors, and "the Jesuits of the French Revolution" (*De la Justice*), and particularly the despotic Robespierre, whom Proudhon variously described as "the eternal denouncer, with an empty head and a viper's tongue," as "the exterminator," "the reptile," and as the "firm disciple of Rousseau"—the man who promoted the centralization of state authority, the destruction of liberty and freedom, and "the return to God by society" (*Idée générale*). Moreover, Rousseau served as the inspiration for Jacobin-Socialists like Louis Blanc and Communists like Etienne Cabet. Finally, casting his net wide, Proudhon declared that Rousseau, being "the father of constitutionalism," was the fundamental inspiration for most of those reformers and system builders in the nineteenth century, whether identified as socialists, democrats, or liberals, who endeavored to establish a more just order of society on the basis of some political principle or principles and who proposed as ameliorative measures one or another political mechanism, technique, or device—such as the sovereignty of the people, direct legislation and direct government, or universal suffrage (*Mélanges: Articles de journaux, 1848–1852;* see also the *Correspondance* and *Solution du problème social*). And like Rousseau himself, none of these individuals, in Proudhon's view, realized that "beneath the governmental machinery, in the shadow of political institutions, out of the sight of statesmen and priests, society is producing its own organism in a slow and silent manner; society is constructing a new order, the expression of its vitality and autonomy, and the negation of the old politics as well as the old religion." They did not see "that for a constitution of political powers should be substituted an organization of economic forces" (*Idée générale*).

One further consideration and this presentation of Proudhon's indict-ment of Rousseau will be complete. Here a shift of focus is required, for in this matter Proudhon confronted Rousseau more as a moralist than as a political theorist. Although Proudhon had confidence in mankind's future and believed in progress (*Philosophie du progrès*), he did feel, as did other perceptive social critics of his generation, quite uneasy, if not outright alarmed, about the state of health of the civilization of the France of his time. He was dismayed, particularly after the *coup d'état* of Louis Napoleon and the creation of the Second Empire, at the growing corruption and cynicism that permeated the society, and he denounced again and again, with the voice of an Old Testament prophet, the egoism and self-indul-gence, the moral indolence and apathy, the emotionalism, irrationality, and sentimentalism that were so widespread as to seem all but universal. In his unpublished *carnet*, on December 29, 1852, Proudhon noted that "Cow-ardice, corruption, egoism, and hypocrisy, all the base sentiments, the vile passions, and all the perverse ideas—these compose at the present moment the character, soul, and spirit of the nation." Three years later he wrote that "the epoch is bad, the generation is cowardly—upper class, middle class, and lower class are equally rotten" (*Correspondance*). France was now entering a period of decadence, with its moral sense "chloroformisé." "Dur-ing the past ten years," Proudhon wrote in April 1862, "decadence in France has made frightful progress," with corruption, stupidity, venality, and cowardice more entrenched than ever. An entire generation was "gangrenée."

Proudhon attributed this decadence, this degeneration of the moral fiber of Frenchmen, to a number of factors, the full examination of which lies beyond the scope of this paper. One of these factors, of fundamental importance, is, however, relative to our study and merits some consider-ation. Progress, to Proudhon, meant in essence the successive realization of the immanent ideal of justice in man and in the web of all the relationships into which he entered and which, in sum, constituted the social fabric or the social order. The ever more complete realization of justice—and with it liberty, equality, and fraternity—imposed on mankind the imperious necessity to move increasingly, as the basis for its actions, from instinct to reason, from intuition to reflection, and from spontaneity to deliberate choice. The progress of mankind, moral and other, could be measured by the extent to which reason prevailed over sentiment and ideas over feelings in the conduct of men. Proudhon put the matter another way in a discussion of decadence in literature and society. All progress in literature, as in so-ciety, was characterized by the preëminence of ideas, which he identified as "the masculine element," while decadence in both literature and society was characterized by the obscuration (*l'obscurcissement*) of ideas, by the predominance of passions, or sentiments, or purely literary devices and techniques—all of which he labeled as "the feminine element." "If in a society or a literature," Proudhon affirmed, "the feminine element comes to dominate or even to counterbalance the masculine element, there will be a cessation of the forward movement in that society and that literature, and soon decadence" (*De la Justice*).

Now in Proudhon's view, the cessation of this forward movement in French society and literature, and with it in the origin of the decadence and moral decay that Proudhon found so evident in the France of his day, began with Rousseau. Rousseau was, in Proudhon's words, "the first of the *femmelins de l'intelligence* [whose ranks included Lamartine and George Sand], in whom ideas became obscured, passion or affectivity prevailed over reason, and who, despite some qualities that were eminent, even virile, predisposed literature and society towards their decline." Long before Pierre Lasserre and Irving Babbitt, Proudhon had portrayed Rousseau as the father of romanticism, taking note of what he took to be Rousseau's glorification of the state of nature and the noble savage at the expense of modern man and the civil order and his pandering to feelings and sentiments at the expense of reason. Moreover, Rousseau initiated a direct attack on the moral foundations of society by preparing, in his *Nouvelle Héloïse*, the way for the dissolution of real love and the institution of marriage: "from the publication of this novel dates, in our country, the mollification or enervation of real feelings of the heart, a mollification that must follow closely on the heels of a cold and dismal lack of pudicity (*impudicité*)." Proudhon did not, in every case, find Rousseau's provocative evocation of feelings and emotions worthy of condemnation, and he recognized his rôle in preparing the ground for the French Revolution: "He put the flame to the power that during the preceding two centuries French letters had amassed. It is something to have kindled in the souls of men such conflagration. It is in this that the force and the virility of Rousseau consists; but for the rest, he is woman (*femme*)."

In view of the many-faceted attack by Proudhon on Rousseau that has just been presented, it would appear that there was little in common between the two men and that the early student of Proudhon's thought, Aimé Berthod, was apparently quite right when he declared, in 1909, that "It is a matter of fact that neither the moral ideas, religious theories, nor political conceptions of Proudhon derive in any way from Rousseau. Rather, they are the opposite" ("Les Tendances maîtresses de P.-J. Proudhon," in *La Revue socialiste*). It would, indeed, appear that this is the case, but appearances can be deceiving. Robert Derathé, one of the outstanding contemporary Rousseauean scholars, has remarked that "the big thinkers are themselves inclined to overestimate the originality of their own doctrines and to exaggerate the weaknesses or errors of earlier doctrines," and he goes on to point out that if these thinkers do recognize willingly their indebtedness to their counterparts of a remote epoch, "they are, in general, unjust concerning their immediate predecessors" (*Jean-Jacques Rousseau et la science politique de son temps*). Derathé had Rousseau specifically in mind; nevertheless, the observation, there is reason to believe, applies with equal force to Proudhon. Moreover, Proudhon's rhetoric, with its sarcasm and invective, tends often to divert attention from the beliefs which Proudhon in fact shares with his antagonist of the moment whoever he be, Saint-Simon, Fourier, or Rousseau. That rhetoric underscores differences. Proudhon did endeavor to affirm his indebtedness to others, as for example when he asserted that his "true masters" were "the Bible, first of all, then Adam Smith, and finally, Hegel," whose works, it may be noted parenthetically, Proudhon knew only secondhand and then rather superficially. But Proudhon was also aware that it was not always possible to be fully cognizant of indebtedness and that the "originality" of a thinker might well be more apparent than real. "I recognize," he once wrote, "that there are very few ideas concerning which a writer can say "these are my very own." All that really belongs to us is a certain way of stating that, *un à-propos*, and a relationship that we discover between these ideas and certain others" (quoted in the "Notice sur P.-J. Proudhon," *Correspondance*).

In any event, there are some interesting parallels in the stance and views of Rousseau and Proudhon, some that are basic and others that are merely marginal, that should be taken into account before a final judgment is made concerning the relations between the two thinkers. Briefly, Proudhon, like Rousseau, believed that the civil order or society was not an artificial construct, but rather that the possibility of creating a society was inherent in man and that, therefore, a society was a "natural" environment for man. Furthermore, both men held that it was only in a society that the rich potentials of human nature could possibly be realized—that it was only in a community of men that justice could flourish and liberty and equality be assured (*Qu'est-ce que la propriété?*). Both men also emphasized the idea of a social contract in the formation of society. Proudhon's basic difference with Rousseau on this point is that he did not think of the contract as a single act or as particularly political in character. Instead he thought in terms of many contracts, indeed of an all but endless multiplication of contracts among specific individuals for specific ends and purposes that would cover the entire spectrum of human desires and aspirations. "The idea of contract," Proudhon wrote in 1851, is "the only moral bond which free and equal beings can accept," and it was the social contract which Proudhon relied upon "to bind together all the members of a nation into one and the same interest" (*Idée générale*). To Proudhon, the contract was always reciprocal, "freely discussed and individually accepted," and should always "increase the well-being and liberty of every citizen." Indeed, society was to him another name for the sum total of these contracts. Proudhon called the contractual society that he envisioned "mutualism" (*la mutualitè*) (*Capacité politique de classes ouvrières*).

Rousseau and Proudhon both posited the sovereignty of the people as basic to a just social order. But to what he called the "artificial" and "abstract" sovereignty of Rousseau—artificial and abstract because it was conceived of only in political terms and manifested through governmental institutions, themselves not an organic expression or extension of a society—Proudhon opposed the "effective sovereignty" of the people, and this sovereignty he anchored in what he characterized as a "natural group." What did Proudhon mean by the term "natural group"? In a work published posthumously it was defined as follows: "Whenever men together with their wives and children assemble in some one place, link up their dwellings and holdings, develop in their midst diverse industries, create among themselves neighborly feelings and relations, and for better or worse impose upon themselves the conditions of solidarity, they form what I call a natural group. This group then takes on the form of a community or some other political organism, affirming in its unity its independence, a life or movement that is appropriate to itself, and affirms its autonomy." In this natural group, as Proudhon envisioned it, "the multitude that is governed would be at the same time the governing multitude; the society would be identical and adequate to the state, the people to the government, as in political economy producers and consumers are the same" (*Contradictions politiques*). Thus what Proudhon set forth is a state of affairs which satisfies Rousseau's own specification for the best form of constitution, namely, "that in which the executive and legislative powers are united." Proudhon contended that natural groups similar in character and not too removed from one another would have common interests; "and one can conceive that they would understand one another, associate themselves, and by this mutual assurance, form a superior group." Such groups might be organized on the level of the canton, commune, region, province, or department. These groups would link up, however, "only to guarantee their mutual interests and to develop their resources, never going so far as to abdicate their independence by a sort of immolation of themselves before this new Moloch." Each of these natural groups being essentially "indestructible organisms," there would, in Proudhon's theory, "exist between them a new bond of right (*droit*), a contract of mutuality; but this bond would no more be able to deprive them of their sovereign independence than a member of the community could, in his capacity as citizen, lose his prerogatives as a free man, producer, and proprietor." Thus Proudhon sought to make certain that the sovereignty of the people, which Rousseau held could never be alienated, would indeed never be alienated.

Furthermore, in these natural groups and in combinations of them on different levels, universal suffrage, which was, in the context of the centralized governments of his day, viewed by Proudhon as merely a catchword or gimmick, as "an enormous, mischievous platitude" (*Carnets*), would serve a useful and necessary purpose, for it would express the true wishes and interests of a people dealing in a direct manner with real problems and issues that arose naturally from an organic, not artificial, environment. In the future mutualist social order, as Proudhon envisioned it, universal suffrage would finally come into its own as "the democratic principle *par excellence*" (*Les Démocrates assermentés et les réfractaires*).

Finally, it is important to note that while Proudhon rejected Rousseau's general will as being a confused and ambiguous notion which, if taken seriously, could lead only to "tyranny" and "despotism," none the less Proudhon himself set forth a conception of a "collective reason" (or a "general reason" and a "public reason," as he called it at times) that occupies a position in his theory of society comparable to the general will in Rousseau's and, moreover, appears to have been modeled on Rousseau's notion. This collective reason is, in Proudhon's words, "the guardian of all truth and all justice," the source of all "public law and human rights," and the fount of "our morality and our progress." "It is different in quality and superior in power to the sum of all the particular reasons . . . which produce it" (*De la Justice*).

What, in Proudhon's view, is specifically the relation between the reason of the individual and the collective reason, in what manner is the latter "different in quality and superior in power" to the former, and what is the organ for its expression in society? Proudhon's description of the collective reason is somewhat more extensive and explicit than Rousseau's treatment of the notion of the general will; but like the latter it is not free from difficulties and consequently more than one reading of the relevant texts is possible. This affirmed, the following answers seem appropriate.

Proudhon maintained that in the reason of the individual there are always present beclouding elements introduced by self-interest or particularistic concerns, always a mixture of what Proudhon called "passionate, egotistical, and transcendental elements—in a word absolutist elements." Because these absolute elements in human reason seek to grasp the inner nature of things, things in themselves (*l'en soi des choses*)—something the human mind cannot do since it can deal only with "the relations of things" (*les rapports des choses*) or "the reason of things" (*la raison des choses*)—it, the absolute in human reason, is the cause, Proudhon asserted, "of our errors of judgment" and the "source of all the deceptions, illusions, lies . . . superstitions, utopias, frauds, and mystifications of which we are the victims." Driven by "the tyranny of the absolute," an "absolutism innate in his being," man seeks constantly "to raise himself above the law" and "to change the relations between things so as to modify their reality. Unceasingly the reason of the individual "modifies and tortures the facts" in order to bend them to its own absolutist conceit.

Now as long as each individual reasoned alone "the tendency of each particular reason towards absolutism encountered neither resistance nor check." With the coming into being of social groups and what Proudhon called "collectivities," the absolutisms of disparate individuals confronted one another. "Before a human being like himself, absolute like himself," Proudhon declared, "the absolutism of the individual is drawn up short—or to put it another way, the two absolutes in individual reason destroy one another, leaving as a residue of their respective reasons only pure reason, only the relations of things, *à propos* of which they struggled." For just as only a diamond can make an incision on a diamond, so too "only a free absolute is capable of balancing another free absolute, to neutralize and eliminate it in such a manner that as a consequence of their reciprocal annulment (*leur annulation réciproque*), there remains from the encounter only the objective reality which each one had tended to distort for his own profit." The proverb has it that from the clash of ideas comes illumination: Proudhon modified the proverb in saying that "it is from mutual contradiction that the spirit is purged of all ultra-phenomenal elements; it is the negation that a free absolute makes of its antagonist which produces, in moral sciences, adequate, sufficient ideas, free of all egotistical and transcendental dross—ideas, in a word, that conform to reality and to social reason." The collective reason is the legacy of the resultants of these clashes of absolute reasons which take place within the context of collectivities and social groups. "Opposing absolute to absolute in such a manner as to annul at all points this unintelligible element, and only considering as real and legitimate the product of antagonistic ends, the collective reason arrives at synthetic ideas, very different, often even the inverse, of the conclusions of the *moi individuel*." Thus the distinction between the individual reason and the collective reason is clear: "the former is essentially absolutist, the latter antipathetic to all absolutism," and while the ideas that are the product of individual reason are permeated with absolutes, those of the collective reason are synthetic, objective, and impersonal.

The collective reason achieves this objectivity not at the cost of repressing individual reason: quite the contrary, the collective reason necessarily presupposes the latter, since it is the product of the clash of individual reasons. Much more than did Rousseau in the case of his general will, Proudhon insisted on the need for deliberation among individuals, for the confrontation of contradictory individual reasons. As he put it: "This collective reason, truly practical and juridical, says to us: remain what you are, each of you . . . defend your interests and produce your thought . . . discuss and debate with one another, reserving always the respect that . . . intelligent beings owe one another. Reform and reproach yourselves: respect only the decrees of your common reason, whose judgments can only be yours, freed as it is of this absolute." Thus the very impersonality of the collective reason demands, in Proudhon's words, "as a principle, the greatest contradiction; as an organ, the greatest possible multiplicity." And the organ of the collective reason, in Proudhon's theory, is the social group or the collectivity that unites free individuals engaged in common pursuits and in the promotion of common interests—varied groups such as the workshop, mine, mill, and farm; schools and academies; organizations of artists and scholars; local, regional, and other kinds of assemblies; and clubs, juries, etc.

In the light of what has been presented in this paper, what judgment can properly be made concerning Proudhon's confrontation with Rousseau? That there would be sharp differences in the views of the two men was to be expected, for, leaving aside the contrasting temperaments and styles of life of these two most individualistic of men, they did, after all, live in eras and circumstances that were remote from one another—not indeed remote in terms of time but surely remote in terms of the changes in life and outlook occasioned by the momentous events, particularly the French Revolution and the beginnings of the Industrial Revolution, that had taken place in the years between the death of Rousseau and the coming of age of Proudhon. Proudhon's world simply was not Rousseau's. The surprising thing, particularly in view of the vituperation which Proudhon heaped upon Rousseau, is the extent to which the thought of Proudhon parallels that of Rousseau on many fundamental points. Rousseau did leave his mark on Proudhon, notwithstanding the latter's endeavor to exorcise him. Rousseau should properly be included, along with the Bible, Adam Smith, and Saint-Simon, as one of the "masters" of Pierre-Joseph Proudhon.

Baudelaire against Photography:
An Allegory of Old Age

Susan Blood

It is common critical practice to divide Baudelaire's life into two distinct phases: an optimistic youth and a premature, embittered old age. From a biographer's standpoint it is difficult to determine the moment of transition from one phase to the next, and many of Baudelaire's declarations create the impression that he experienced life as a perpetual verging on decrepitude: "Je ne suis pas positivement vieux," he wrote at the age of thirty-four, "mais je puis le devenir prochainement." For the critic who is strictly interested in Baudelaire's literary and critical production, however, an early and a late period can be easily distinguished. Between 1846 and 1857 Baudelaire developed his idiom, and certain of his attitudes—toward antiquity, the bourgeois reader, and the fate of the poet—are thoroughly revised. Whether this occurred for biographical reasons, or whether, as Paul Valéry suggests, because Baudelaire discovered Poe and adopted the American writer's fatalism, the later work is increasingly querulous and seems to reveal an aging and discouraged author.

Baudelaire's two major *Salons*, written in 1846 and 1859, fit nicely into this schema. The *Salon de 1846* opens with a dedication "Au bourgeois," and ends with the praise of modern life and its particular beauties. In between, Baudelaire pursues a definition of Romanticism as aesthetic modernism, that is as "l'expression la plus récente, la plus actuelle du beau." Although others in 1846 might consider Romanticism past its prime, Baudelaire thinks differently: "s'il est resté peu de romantiques, c'est que peu d'entre eux ont trouvé le romantisme; mais tous l'ont cherché sincèrement et loyalement." The scarcity of Romantics, then, must not be confused with the decadence of Romanticism, which remains a kind of Holy Grail—perhaps aging those who seek it, but itself untouched by time. Eugène De-

From *MLN* 101, no. 4 (September 1986). © 1986 by The Johns Hopkins University Press.

lacroix is described as "le chef de l'école *moderne*," that is, as Romantic par excellence, and his paintings merit this attribution because they are "de grands poèmes naïvement conçus" (my emphasis). Naïveté and Romanticism become the two criteria by which Baudelaire will criticize the paintings of the Salon.

All this faith in youth and the potential of the times is lost to the *Salon de 1859*. The old tolerance of aesthetic failure—"peu d'entre eux ont trouvé le romantisme, mais tous l'ont cherché sincèrement et loyalement"— has become a condemnation: "Que dans tous les temps, la médiocrité ait dominé, cela est indubitable; mais qu'elle règne plus que jamais, qu'elle devienne absolument triomphante et encombrante, c'est ce qui est aussi vrai qu'affligeant." The bourgeois consumer of art has been transformed from "la majorité,—nombre et intelligence" into a "Brute hyperboréenne des anciens jours, éternel Esquimau porte-lunettes ou plutôt porte-écailles, que toutes les visions de Damas, tous les tonnerres et les éclairs ne sauraient éclairer!" Romanticism itself is no longer spoken of as a fresh and timely expression, but as a memory: "Cette époque était si belle et si féconde," Baudelaire writes in 1859, "que les artistes en ces temps-là n'oubliaient aucun besoin de l'esprit." In contrast, "L'Artiste moderne," to whom Baudelaire devotes a chapter, is mainly interested in technical effects and popular success; like his scaly-eyed patrons, he is unappreciative of the spiritual difficulties involved in imaginative creation. Baudelaire calls him an *enfant gâté* who has profited from the noble reputation of his predecessors.

There is no doubt that the Salon of 1859 lent itself to Baudelaire's ill humor. For the most part, the paintings were of minimal interest—"Nulle explosion; pas de génies inconnus," Baudelaire reported. But his complaints went even further. This was to be Delacroix's last Salon, and the public had had over thirty years to examine the latter's prodigious *oeuvre*; yet his *Christ descendu au tombeau* elicited the same scandalized criticisms as had his first Salon painting, *Dante et Virgile,* in 1822. Only the explanation for his faults had changed: in 1822 he drew badly and abused color because of a youthful and undisciplined temperament; in 1859 he did the same things, but because his hand had grown palsied with age. Maxime du Camp went so far as to wonder: "Quelles sont ces peintures de revenant qu'on expose sous son nom?" Baudelaire, of course, decried this absurd, public injustice; but the image of a ghostly Delacroix seems to have lodged in his mind, and reinforced the nostalgic tone of the *Salon*. Typically, Baudelaire even recreated himself in the image of his idol: "cet homme [Delacroix] me donne quelquefois l'envie de durer autant qu'un partriarche, ou malgré tout ce qu'il faudrait de courage à un mort pour consentir à revivre . . . d'être ranimé à temps pour assister aux enchantements et aux louanges qu'il excitera dans l'âge futur." This self-casting as patriarch or as *revenant* was not a passing fancy on Baudelaire's part. He adopted the voice of a spectral old man throughout the *Salon de 1859*. Once again, it is difficult to decide how or why Baudelaire would adopt such a voice—was it for personal reasons, because he was embittered by illness and the recent trial of his poetry; did his defense of Delacroix simply disguise an immediate desire to avenge himself upon the bourgeois public; or was there something impersonal in the persona of the old man, and if so, how can one interpret that persona's utterances?

Since the answer to these questions is not simple and cannot be uncovered through direct inquiry, I would like to focus my attention on an incidental (or seemingly so) feature of the *Salon de 1859:* Baudelaire's denunciation of photography. Given the general tenor of the *Salon*, the denunciation comes as no surprise: it is part of Baudelaire's criticism of current trends in art and of his contention that popular opinion is wielding greater influence in the aesthetic domain. Moreover, the denunciation appears to "date" Baudelaire. His attitude may be characterized as reactionary, not only from a twentieth-century perspective, but according to the criteria Baudelaire himself established in the 1846 *Salon*. There he argued that reactionary artists, those who turn their backs on modern life, do so by confusing moral and aesthetic decadence. They pretend that painting cannot be renewed in a morally corrupt climate, and thus excuse their own lack of inventiveness and dependence upon past aesthetic modes: "Beaucoup de gens attribueront la décadence de la peinture à la décadence des moeurs. Ce préjugé d'atelier, qui a circulé dans le public, est une mauvaise excuse des artistes. Car ils étaient intéressés à représenter sans cesse le passé; la tâche est plus facile, et la paresse y trouvait son compte" ("De l'héroïsme de la vie moderne.") Baudelaire contended, against such prejudice, that moral and aesthetic decadence affect different spheres: "l'une concerne le public et ses sentiments, et l'autre ne regarde que les ateliers." In 1859, with "Le public moderne et la photographie," Baudelaire seems to disregard his earlier contention and collapses aesthetic issues into questions of public morality. The 1859 Salon saw the first exhibition of photographs, not yet included among, but adjoining the exhibition of paintings. Instead of assessing this phenomenon in terms of "les ateliers," Baudelaire concentrates on "le public et ses sentiments":

> S'il est permis à la photographie de suppléer l'art dans quelques-unes de ses fonctions, *elle l'aura bientôt supplanté ou corrompu tout à fait, grâce à l'alliance naturelle qu'elle trouvera dans la sottise de la multitude.* Il faut donc qu'elle rentre dans son véritable devoir, qui est d'être la servante des sciences et des arts, mais la trés humble servante, comme l'imprimerie et la sténographie, qui n'ont ni créé ni suppléé la littérature (my emphasis).

Permission, corruption, duty, humility: the language of this warning belongs, not to the aesthete, but to the moralist. Naturally, then, the warning is not limited to a small community of artists. "La multitude," the greater public is involved, as it both contributes to and suffers from aesthetic corruption: "s'il lui est permis [à la photographie] d'empiéter sur le domaine de l'impalpable et l'imaginaire . . . alors malheur à nous!" The "malheur" of aesthetic corruption is so extensive as to touch "nous tous," and Baudelaire leaves little room to imagine that some might escape its disastrous effects. In sum, the denunciation of photography presents all the features of a reactionary diatribe.

If we wish, however, to "date" Baudelaire on the basis of his reaction, that is, to claim that he could no longer greet "the new" with enthusiasm or that his modernist tendency had found its limit with the photograph, we run into certain critical difficulties. First we should realize that each interpretive option (that Baudelaire had become "old," or that "history" and its developments had simply outdistanced him) relies upon a particular notion of time. In the first instance, we may deem Baudelaire "aged" because of his moralist intonations and blatant use of categorical thinking. Presumably, a young Baudelaire would have readjusted his thoughts to entertain the aesthetic potential of photography. The Baudelaire of 1859 excludes photography from the aesthetic domain, "le domaine de l'impalpable et l'imaginaire," and consigns it to the domain of technology. Such a categorical exclusion is intimately tied to Baudelaire's moralist stance, as we may gather from the exhortation: "il faut donc qu'elle [la photographie] rentre dans son véritable devoir." The assignation of photography to a place, i.e. the categorical gesture, is simultaneously a moral imperative, a "devoir." Of course, this kind of imperative cannot be affected by historical contingencies; if photography happens to leave its proper place, that place is still its own, and the passage of time will not legitimize its pretensions to belonging elsewhere. In other words, Baudelaire's reaction to photography is thoroughly ahistorical. We may interpret his ahistorical moralizing as a sign of old age, but in so doing we eliminate our own possibilities of attaining to historical insight. This is because the view which sees moralizing as the portion of old age is itself firmly ensconced within the moralist tradition. That the elderly speak of duty because their charms have faded and their wits are slow is a classical topos. When we determine Baudelaire's age on the basis of his moralizing, we have not advanced beyond the wisdom of Molière's Célimène: "Il est une saison pour la galanterie,/Il en est une aussi propre à la pruderie." Such wisdom is ahistorical in that it describes only a cyclical temporality, that of the seasons of life. We may assign a season to Baudelaire's reaction, but our assignation remains as categorical as the reaction itself. History, then, lies outside our interpretation.

Our second interpretive option, that Baudelaire's reaction to photography merely marks the limits of his modernism, seems to avoid the hermeneutic circle of the first interpretation. When we no longer appeal to Baudelaire's interior experience of time, an experience which is subsumed by the human life cycle, then a purely external, linear temporality becomes possible. Our task becomes simply to locate Baudelaire and his views along a time line of aesthetic history. We may notice, for example, that Baudelaire advocates "modernism" in defense of the Romantic painters, but not with respect to the photograph; on these grounds we may conclude that Baudelaire's views *are* Romantic and that his "modernism" is meaningless outside the context of the Romantic movement. The difficulty with this method is that Baudelaire's views, both generally considered and in the *Salon de 1859*, defy linear periodization. True, the *Salon de 1859* is largely a discourse on the imagination, the most Romantic of shibboleths. But Baudelaire's imagination does not function like a canonic Romantic faculty. The Romantic imagination is typically set against classical conventions—rules of prosody, genre distinctions, etc. In the *Salon de 1859*, however, Baudelaire uses his own notion of the imagination to support the classical hierarchy of genres in painting. History painting, he argues, is to be privileged above *tableaux de genre* because the former requires "l'imagination la plus vigoureuse et les efforts les plus tendus" (see "Religion, histoire, fantaisie"). We are left, then, with a curious aesthetic anachronism—a Romantic classicism or a classical Romanticism—which resists location in a linear history of art. Since Baudelaire's reaction to photography partakes of this same anachronistic character (he uses a "classical," categorizing gesture to defend the "Romantic" imagination against photography), we must accept that our attempts to "date" that reaction inevitably raise questions as to the validity of our own historical suppositions.

In order to demonstrate this point in greater detail, I would like to examine Walter Benjamin's reading of Baudelaire's reaction to photography. Benjamin first cites the *Salon de 1859* in his 1931 essay, "Kleine Geschichte der Photographie." He contrasts Baudelaire's denunciation with Antoine Wiertz's enthused assertion that photography is "l'extrait de la peinture" and poses no threat to art and the productions of genius. Neither Baudelaire nor Wiertz, at least in Benjamin's estimation, is sensitive to the "authenticity" of the photograph. Leaving aside the more cryptic connotations Benjamin attaches to the word "authentic," we can still grasp some of his meaning: both Baudelaire's condemnation and Wiertz's approval are largely formulaic; that is, neither takes the shape of a specific response to photography. Wiertz no less than Baudelaire is tied to an aesthetics that derives its values from painting alone. Benjamin maintains that today, that is in 1931, one can only give meaning to either reaction by "displacing the accent" and reading the two together. In so doing we will see that each reaction mirrors the other and that both are *premature.* This is as far as Benjamin takes the historical view of the *Salon de 1859* in "Kleine Geschichte"; but he will return to the *Salon* eight years later, with a considerable development of the historical perspective.

In "On Some Motifs in Baudelaire," Benjamin analyzes the same *Salon* passage he had quoted in "Kleine Geschichte," and which I have quoted in part. The complete citation is as follows:

> Dans ces jours déplorables, une industrie nouvelle se produisit,
> qui ne contribua pas peu à confirmer la sottise dans sa foi . . . que

l'art est et ne peut être que la reproduction exacte de la nature. . . . Un dieu vengeur a exaucé les voeux de cette multitude. Daguerre fut son messie. . . . S'il est permis à la photographie de suppléer l'art dans quelques-unes de ses fonctions, elle l'aura bientôt supplanté ou corrompu tout à fait, grâce à l'alliance naturelle qu'elle trouvera dans la sottise de la multitude. Il faut donc qu'elle rentre dans son véritable devoir, qui est d'être la servante des sciences et des arts.

The second time Benjamin refers to this passage, he does not mention Baudelaire's failure to acknowledge some "authentic" character of photography. Instead he commends the accuracy of the poet's instincts: "To Baudelaire there was something profoundly unnerving and terrifying about daguerrotypy; he speaks of the fascination it exerted as 'startling and cruel.' Thus he must have sensed, though he certainly did not see through them, the connections of which we have spoken" ("On Some Motifs in Baudelaire," *Illuminations*). The connections Benjamin has in mind are those that link technological developments, such as photography, to "a society in which practice is in decline." Once these connections have been made it becomes difficult to argue for an authenticity of the photograph. An authentic object is one that bears the mark of the practiced hand that made it. This criterion is singularly lacking in the case of the photographic image, which remains untouched by the complex equipment that enters into its production. (In "The Work of Art in the Age of Mechanical Reproduction," Benjamin compares the cameraman to the painter. The cameraman's equipment "penetrates deeply" into the web of reality, but by this very token offers "an aspect of reality which is free of equipment." The painter, on the other hand, "maintains in his work a natural distance from reality" and this distance leaves its traces on the completed canvas. See *Illuminations*.) Clearly Benjamin has shifted the center of gravity of his argument. What interests him now is the opposition between two societies—industrial and preindustrial—and the *analogue* of that opposition in two forms of memory—voluntary and involuntary—which terms he has borrowed from Proust. Photography aligns itself both with industrial society and with the workings of voluntary memory, since the range of the latter is *extended* by the photograph. More of the world may be kept in a kind of permanent record, to which anyone may have access at any time; no detail need be forgotten or subject to the vagaries of involuntary memory. As Benjamin notes, Baudelaire's attempt to restore the distinction between "art and industry" confirms the connection between the photograph and voluntary memory: "Qu'elle [la photographie] enrichisse rapidement l'album du voyageur et rende à ses yeux la précision qui manquerait à sa mémoire . . . rien de mieux. Qu'elle sauve de l'oubli . . . les choses précieuses dont la forme va disparaître et qui demandent une place dans les archives de notre mémoire, elle sera remerciée et applaudie." Thus we have evidence of the connections that Baudelaire "sensed"; what he did not "see through," however, and what Benjamin hopes to reveal, is that art and industry are involved, not in a categorical opposition, but in a dialectical one. The region of art or "le domaine de l'impalpable et de l'imaginaire" (which Benjamin associates with involuntary memory) cannot remain distinct from the encroachments of industry. "The perpetual readiness of volitional, discursive memory, encouraged by the technique of mechanical reproduction, reduces the scope for the play of imagination." For Benjamin this dialectical necessity is mediated by the masses, and he finds his opinion seconded in Baudelaire's reference to "l'alliance naturelle qu'elle [la photographie] trouvera dans la sottise de la multitude." Of course Baudelaire did not credit the "natural alliance" between photography and the masses with any historical necessity, but in this he was showing "scarcely . . . Solomonian judgment." It is not possible to halt historical processes simply by claiming they are tasteless.

Benjamin's argument is compelling, and not only because time has legitimized the aesthetic pretensions of photography. Were we to forget the history of the photograph since 1859 and to remember only Baudelaire's denunciation, we might easily come to an identical conclusion. This is because Baudelaire, perhaps in his eagerness to sustain the case against photography, assigns not one but two limitations to its role. The first limitation is the categorical one: photography has it own domain, it preserves "les ruines pendantes, les livres, les estampes et les manuscrits que le temps dévore." The second limitation, which does not seem unrelated to the first, permits the transition from categorical to dialectical thinking: photography, like printing and stenography, is "la servante des sciences et des arts, mais la très humble servante." The complusive repetition, "mais la très humble servante," sounds a warning; there is no need for this servant to be humble, unless it is recognized that she may one day triumph over her master. Benjamin's dialectical reading seems to cut to the heart of "Le public moderne et la photographie," even explaining the stylistic peculiarities of the chapter: the pressures of the master/slave dialectic cause Baudelaire's categorical logic to stutter, thus occasioning his repeated emphases and anathemas ("La Fatuité moderne aura beau rugir, éructer tous les borborygmes de sa ronde personnalité, vomir tous les sophismes indigestes . . ." etc.) The historical forces that Benjamin will oppose to Baudelaire's denunciation are already inscribed within the latter's text.

These indications of a dialectical moment in Baudelaire's *Salon* do not, however, lend simple credence to Benjamin's reading. For one thing, they suggest that Baudelaire's assessment of photography and its possibilities may have been less naive than Benjamin imagined. For another, they require that greater emphasis be placed upon the *Salon* as text. Benjamin's reading is persuasive to the extent that it supplies the *Salon* with an "outside," an historical context. The dialectical interest of the reading occurs, not within the written work, but between the work and its context: to one side of the *Salon* we have the photograph as technological innovation; to the other, there is something more vague, which may correspond to history, or to the modern aesthetic sensibility, or to both. In any case, the *Salon* itself is seen as a moment of pure reaction, determined by its context, and not as a properly critical statement of its context. Once we notice an element of dialectical complexity within the *Salon,* however, the passage "outside" the work becomes less assured: if the text does not offer blind resistance to its context, then the distinction between inside and outside begins to break down; the negative gesture which should have returned us to the outside, may only implicate us further in the textual workings. This is, if one likes, the labyrinth of reading, and Benjamin does not avoid it despite his atextual treatment of the *Salon.* The inside/outside distinction becomes confused when Benjamin's effort to situate the *Salon* within an historical context becomes a self-reflexive one. In order to situate the *Salon,* Benjamin must claim to read the same photographic phenomenon as Baudelaire, only with the use of superior dialectical tools. These tools are superior because they coincide with historical processes; in other words, the dialectic is both a method of reading and the very substance of history. Thus, when Benjamin's reading situates Baudelaire's reaction, that reading doubles as history. This is why there is some confusion as to where the reading leads: if it finally points to what Benjamin calls "the open air of history," it only does so by means of a self-reflexive or aestheticizing moment. Once more we find all the ironies of the labyrinth: through self-reflexivity Benjamin hopes to reach the open air, through aesthetic activity he sets his sites on history. This "situation" has its own interest, but it does not guarantee the success of Benjamin's attempt to subordinate the *Salon* to an historical context. In fact, since his reading reduplicates so many of the terms and conceptual oppositions of the *Salon,* one might argue that the reading is largely situated by the *Salon,* and not vice versa. This is the possibility I would like to consider by examining the *Salon* in some of its textual complexity.

A first observation should be that Baudelaire does not conceive of his criticism as a *reaction* to the things he sees. On the contrary he writes, after noting the absence of vigorous and original painting: "Ne vous étonnez donc pas que la banalité dans le peintre ait engendré le *lieu commun* dans l'écrivain" ("L'Artiste moderne," in the *Salon de 1859*). Criticism thus appears as the close *offspring* of its context, almost as its context's reproduction. Moreover, criticism seems to reflect the mode of its own generation by taking on the form of verbal repetition—the *lieu commun.* Baudelaire does not imply that this need always be the case; he claims that a more innovative Salon "[aurait] nécessité dans la langue critique des catégories nouvelles." But under the circumstances, old, "classical" categories will do. The textual project that Baudelaire undertakes is to repeat these categories in such a way as to reveal their "nature . . . positivement excitante." Repetition, then, and not reaction will characterize the *Salon.*

If we are to accept Baudelaire's description of his project, we must at least question how it accounts for photography. The 1859 Salon may have been nothing new under the sun as far as its paintings were concerned, but this cannot be said of the photograph exhibition. Whether the photographs were of aesthetic interest or not, their very presence was a novelty. In Benjamin's eyes, and particularly from the materialist standpoint he takes here, such a novelty is of critical importance. For Baudelaire, however, the photograph exhibition is only symptomatic of a perennial flaw in the French temperament: "Le goût exclusif du Vrai (si noble quand il est limité à ses véritables applications) opprime ici [en France] et étouffe le goût de Beau. . . . [Le public francais] n'est pas artiste, naturellement artiste; philosophe peut-être, moraliste, ingénieur, amateur d'anecdotes instructives, tout ce qu'on voudra, mais jamais spontanément artiste" ("Le Public moderne et la photographie"). Baudelaire's categorical logic, which will assign photography to a limited domain, first creates distinctions in the area of taste. The opposition between art and industry must therefore be understood as a specific case of the *principal* opposition between the taste for the Beautiful and the taste for the True. When, as in the French temperament, the taste for the True becomes excessive and leaves its proper place, then one may deduce any number of consequences. It only follows that photography, with its power to produce a close likeness of its subject, may be hailed as more true and hence as aesthetically superior to painting. By the same token, the technical facility of a painter may be valued over any other talent. Although the invention of photography encourages an excessive taste for the True in matters of art, photography is not the condition of possibility of that taste. Instead, Baudelaire maintains that photography is the fulfillment of a misguided wish on the part of the French public. The public reasons: "Ainsi l'industrie qui nous donnerait un résultat identique à la nature serait l'art absolu." And Baudelaire adds: "Un Dieu vengeur a exaucé les voeux de cette multitude. Daguerre fut son messie."

Next to Benjamin's materialist interpretation of the relationship between photography and aesthetic taste, Baudelaire's suggestion of wish fulfillment may seem like a piece of magical thinking. This is largely a function, however, of his categorical logic, which allows him to deduce a place for photography without having to offer a causal explanation for its genesis. Given the existence of an aesthetics of natural imitation, one may posit the possibility of a perfect embodiment of that ideal. I want to insist that this is a categorical deduction as well as a rhetorical tactic; in other words, Baudelaire does not give a proleptic presentation of photography (providing the terms of its condemnation before he even mentions the technique) merely to convince readers to heed his warning. There is also a critical necessity involved in maintaining the distinction between what Baudelaire has called "les phénomènes du monde physique et du monde moral" (Exposition Universelle / 1855). By "previewing" the phenomenon of photography within the phenomenon of taste, Baudelaire is able to keep the moral world from collapsing into the physical world. This is a double imperative since the ability to make any kind of critical distinction is at stake in the effort to preserve the discrete character of the moral world. To use Baudelaire's terminology, critical distinctions number among moral phenomena. Although Baudelaire does not spell this out explicitly, it may be rapidly deduced from his statements on the nature of the physical world. As the public becomes increasingly occupied with physical phenomena, it loses the faculty of critical thinking:

> Demandez à tout bon Français qui lit tous les jours *son* journal dans son estaminent, ce qu'il entend par progrès, il répondra que c'est la vapeur, l'électricité et l'éclairage au gaz, miracles inconnus aux Romains, et que ces découvertes temoignent pleinement de notre supériorité sur les anciens; tant il s'est fait de tènébres dans ce malheureux cerveau et tant les choses de l'ordre matériel et de l'ordre spirituel s'y sont si bizarrement confondues!

The notion of progress introduced in this passage implies at one and the same time a confusion of categories and the ascendency of a materialist viewpoint: "j'entends par progrès la domination progressive de la matière," Baudelaire writes in the *Salon de 1859*. It is here that we may best seize his difference from Benjamin. For Baudelaire it is not possible to write a properly *critical* history from materialist premises. These premises can only exacerbate the confusion of categories, until we find ourselves in a situation where progress and decadence coincide. If belief in progress continues, Baudelaire warns, "les races amoindries . . . s'endormiront sur l'oreiller de la fatalité dans le sommeil radoteur de la décrépitude" (*Salon de 1859*). Thus, both progress and decadence, which we meant to use as historical concepts, become the dreams we dream on "l'oreiller de la fatalité"; and such dreams can only give a false picture of history for the same reasons that in Benjamin's words, fate is "temporal in a totally inauthentic way" ("Fate and Characters," in *Reflections*).

Curiously then, Baudelaire's position with respect to history seems to have come full circle; without leaving his original categories, since he promised he would only repeat himself, he now appears to argue in the name of true historical understanding. The condemnation of photography is no exception to his general argument: Baudelaire maintains that the photograph has contributed to a weakening of the historical imagination. On this point he invites us to consider that the new technique was immediately put, not to some thoroughly novel use, but to the taking of historical "scenes": "En associant et en groupant des drôles et des drêolesses, attifés comme les bouchers et les blanchisseuses dans le carnaval, en priant ces *héros* de vouloir bien continuer pour le temps nécessaire à l'opération, leur grimace de circonstance, on se flatta de rendre les scènes, tragiques ou gracieuses, de l'histoire ancienne" ("Le Public moderne"). It is hard to say whether this fashion did greater disservice to the ancients or to the moderns, but in either case historical understanding suffered. In Baudelaire's view such understanding characterizes "L'art sublime du comédien," an art that is disgraced and parodied by the taking of historical scenes. Although Baudelaire does not expound upon this opinion, the "grimace de circonstance" that he attributes to the costumed public gives us a clue to his meaning: the grimace is dictated by no other necessity than that of the moment and consequently bears only an accidental relationship to the costume, decor, etc. that surround it. It contains no temporal dimension and thus differs from the consummate theatrical gesture, which may resume an entire sequence of historical or fictional events. The historical photograph provides instead a neutral medium for the confused coexistence of old and new; hence Baudelaire's detection of a carnival-like atmosphere, in which his *drôles* and *drôlesses* stand time on its head.

Photography is not, however, the only medium in which the effects of a weakened historical understanding may be felt. Baudelaire criticizes on identical grounds what he calls "l'école des pointus" in painting. This school involves "la transposition des vulgarités de la vie dans le régime antique," as well as the calculated use of scumbling to give a time-worn appearance to canvases. Baudelaire suggests that painters aspiring to the school consult a newly released book by Edouard Fournier—*Le Vieux-Neuf: Histoire ancienne des inventions et découvertes modernes*—and himself adopts "le vieux-neuf" as an apt epithet for the paintings in question.

Although Baudelaire is well aware of the comic potential, both of historical photographs and of the "vieux-neuf" trend in painting, he refuses to grant either the full aesthetic dignity of the caricature. He says of "l'école des pointus": "Par sa manie d'habiller à l'antique la vie triviale moderne, elle commet sans cesse ce que j'appellerais volontier une caricature à l'inverse." In order to understand what Baudelaire means by an inverse caricature, we should first examine the qualities he attributes to caricature itself. The aesthetic value of caricature is intimately tied to history, and most spectacularly to revolution. As Baudelaire writes in *Quelques Caricaturistes français*: "La révolution de 1830 causa, comme toutes les révolutions, une fièvre caricaturale. . . . Dans cette guerre acharnée contre le gouvernement, et particulièrement contre le roi, on était tout coeur, tout feu." Thus caricature, through its critical power, constitutes a revolutionary force. This force, however, must be conceived primarily in aesthetic terms; that is, if the caricatural war of 1830 was led "particulièrement contre le roi," this was not because the political hierarchy made Louis Philippe the prime target of artists, but because his caricature by Philipon was a surpassing aesthetic success: "Cette fantastique épopée est dominée, couronnée par la pyramidale et olympienne *Poire* de processive mémoire." We may learn, too, from the exemplary pear-king that the critical or revolutionary potential of caricature resides in the power to sustain *likeness*. As Philipon demonstrated in "Le Charivari," his caricature of Louis Philippe could be linked by a series of like images to a "natural" portrait of the king. Were this not the case, the artist might have been charged with lack of talent rather than *lèse majesté*. Once again we come against the conundrum of Baudelaire's thoughts on history: the caricature partakes of revolution, not by bringing into being something radically new, but by reproducing likenesses.

Given that "le vieux-neuf," either in painting or in photography, also involves the reproduction of likeness, how can it be said that such reproduction *inverts* caricature? We might be more tempted to say that it simulates caricature or caricatural effects. And yet Baudelaire is clear that in some way the work of caricature is undone by "l'école des pointus." This may best be appreciated if we consider that the historicity of the caricature is not *given* to the caricaturist; i.e., he does not copy a revolutionary moment, but produces that moment as he copies. Otherwise his activity would not be an aesthetic one. In the case of "le vieux-neuf," however, "history" is presented to the painter or photographer as the jumble of old and new elements; this jumble need only be reproduced. Something, then, in the simple reproduction of "le vieux-neuf" undoes history as Baudelaire understands it. It should first be apparent that any dialectical tension is lost when old and new are immediately juxtaposed; and when a supposedly aesthetic activity does nothing to generate that tension, then even Benjamin would agree that history has been suspended.

Benjamin could only quibble, therefore, with a second contention that may be derived from Baudelaire's remarks on caricature and history. As we have observed, caricature is aesthetic, and hence historical in Baudelaire's sense, only if it is not fully dependent upon a particular moment in history; with *la Poire*, of course, this limited dependency may be difficult to discern, since the king of France is captured by the king of caricatures, and history and art seem to coincide. Baudelaire delights in this kind of coincidence, which he often gives as the figure of a Golden Age. Thus he says, in reference to Carle Vernet's engravings of fashionable folk under the Directory: "Telle était la mode, tel était l'être humain: les hommes ressemblaient aux peintures; le monde s'était moulé dans l'art." Such coincidence, however, implies no absolute determination, since sometimes history will do the work of caricature—"Souvent même les caricatures . . . deviennent plus caricaturales à mesure qu'elles sont plus démodées"—and sometimes a caricature, like Gavarni's *la Lorette*, will create history by spawning a generation in its image (see Baudelaire's discussion of the way in which Gavarni "a beaucoup agi sur les moeurs" in *Quelques Caricaturistes français*). In their mutual determination, neither history nor the caricature is grounded in real chronology. When Baudelaire attempts to organize recent French caricature into a history, he therefore claims that one must look to the style of the work and not to the date of its execution: "le mot moderne," he writes, "s'applique à la manière et non au temps." The modernity of caricature thus has little to do with the modernity of historical photographs and "l'école des pointus." The latter depends entirely upon real chronology; although the photographer who dresses his models in antique togas seems to enjoy freedom from chronology, his photograph is absolutely tied to the moment of its production. This is true of the "vieux-neuf" paintings as well, since Baudelaire views them as thoroughly *topical:* they belong to France in the mid-nineteenth century, and to no other time or place. For Benjamin such topicality should be the basis for a materialist dialectic; for Baudelaire it marks the end of dialectical possibilities, and hence, history. (I am speaking only of Benjamin's position in "On Some Motifs in Baudelaire." In the "Theses on the Philosophy of History," Benjamin is careful to distinguish between topical and dialectical transformations. See the fourteenth thesis, *Illuminations.*)

When we take stock of the preceding alignments between caricature and photography, it becomes apparent that any attempt to read the two dialectically will run aground. Either we follow Baudelaire's lead and see photography as suspending the dialectic of caricature, or we consider photography the caricature of caricature. Upon reflection, however, the second option proves to be no option at all: since caricature always already involves the production of difference through the reproduction of likeness, photography can only reproduce the caricatural process without making it differ from itself. In other words, photography either *is* caricature or suspends caricature; and this option remains categorical. That is, either photography may be classified as a kind of caricature, or it disrupts the category of caricature without opening a way to the latter's dialectical recovery. Baudelaire subscribes to the second possibility, which means that, for him, the dialectic can only function if categorical logic remains intact. As we have already seen, this makes it impossible to write the sort of materialist history Benjamin has in mind. The materialist moment and the dialectic cannot be made to fit together, one suspends the other, and vice versa, indefinitely.

The incompatibility of the materialist moment and the dialectic can be traced in Benjamin's two essays, despite the historical materialism propounded in "On Some Motifs in Baudelaire." This becomes apparent when we consider how the "authenticity" of photography changes from one essay to the next. In "Kleine Geschichte" that authenticity is opposed to the *inauthentic* reactions of Baudelaire and Wiertz, which fail to reach the "open air of history." These latter, then, are doomed to topicality. Benjamin underlines their historical inauthenticity by eliminating the difference between Wiertz's *progressive* attitude and Baudelaire's *reactionary* one: it does not matter that Wiertz projects his vision forward and Baudelaire backward, since neither attains to dialectical understanding. This analysis approaches Baudelaire's commentary on materialist ideology and "l'oreiller de la fatalité." When such an ideology holds sway, progress and decadence become mirror images of one another, false projections of temporality within the closed circle of fate. The *fatum* which presides over both Baudelaire and Wiertz is that of the homogeneous moment, the only temporality available to a materialist ideology. Somewhere beyond this enclosure Benjamin posits the "authenticity" of the photograph, which gives the promise of history.

The photograph's authenticity is tied to no specific moment, a fact we may deduce from Benjamin's assertion that "it will not always be possible to link this authenticity with reportage" ("Short History of Photography," in *Artforum* 15 [Feb. 1977]), in other words, reportage is only a moment in the dialectic of authenticity. Thus, in "Kleine Geschichte," the dialectic and the materialist moment are held apart by the distance that separates authenticity from inauthenticity. With this in mind, we should not be surprised by what transpires in "On Some Motifs in Baudelaire": Benjamin attempts to bring the materialist moment into a dialectical arena, and the authenticity of the photograph evaporates. When he associates photography with voluntary memory, Benjamin actually reinforces the link between the photograph's authenticity and reportage, and thereby short-circuits the dialectical possibilities he had earlier envisioned. If the photograph is only authentic by virtue of its ability to preserve positive information, and if the materialist dialectic is riveted to this moment of pure positivity, then sooner or later the materialist dialectic will be revealed as an *inauthentic* temporality, perhaps even as fate in a progressive-seeming mask. This is why the distinction between authentic and inauthentic appears to vanish in the later essay, why the photograph's authenticity is bound up in its inauthenticity, and why its fruits seem more fatal than epoch-making. Not only does Benjamin claim that photography banishes beauty from its reproducible sphere, he also maintains that it seals off "the womb of time" from which beauty had been drawn and puts an end to the hope for something new, which might have compensated beauty's loss. In view of such comments, Benjamin must have "seen through" the dialectic he proposed in the name of photography; a true dialectic would have freed beauty and time from the rule of fate. (It is interesting that Benjamin is not inclined, even here, to retrieve beauty by allying it to inauthenticity. This would have been a perfect opportunity to set Baudelaire against himself by citing, for example: "Tes yeux, illuminés ainsi que des boutiques, / Et des ifs flamboyants dans les fêtes publiques, / Usent insolemment d'un pouvoir emprunté, / Sans connaître jamais la loi de leur beauté" (*Tu mettrais l'univers entier dans ta ruelle*). When Benjamin *does* cite this passage later in his essay, he omits the last line and with it the possibility of an inauthentic beauty.)

The difference in Benjamin's treatment of photographic authenticity from one essay to the next should be sufficient to invalidate the historical materialist thesis that photography determines our perception of it. Moreover, photography appears in the second essay, not only as a technological fact, but also as a metaphor; that is, not only is the photograph an object upon which Benjamin may construct a history; photography also becomes the figure for that history. Although there is not time here to examine the figuration thoroughly, some details may be noted. Take Benjamin's contention that "The perpetual readiness of volitional, discursive memory, encouraged by the technique of mechanical reproduction, reduces the scope for the play of imagination" ("On Some Motifs"). If we compare Proust's and Baudelaire's remarks on voluntary memory with this statement, the metaphorical twist of the latter should become evident. For Proust, voluntary memory is not necessarily "perpetually ready"; the willful attempt to remember does not always yield results. And when Baudelaire speaks of the photograph as an archival memory, this is because voluntary memory is not ready enough with information and stands in need of supplementation. From this perspective it would seem as though voluntary, not involuntary memory would be most threatened by photography. Benjamin avoids this threat by changing the supplemental relationship between photography and voluntary memory into a metaphorical one: he makes voluntary memory *like* the camera, by transferring the latter's "perpetual readiness" to the former; this means that the camera no longer supplements a lack of memory, but "encourages" memory in one of its positive qualities. The transference of the quality of "readiness" is simultaneous with the photograph's encouragement of memory to reduce the scope for the play of imagination; in other words, the metaphorical process is simultaneous with the historical process Benjamin here describes. Thus, despite Benjamin's intentions, photography enters into history as metaphor and not as technological fact.

The photograph as metaphor should bring us back to Baudelaire's text, which, as I have argued, allows us to situate Benjamin's. If it is a metaphorical moment that inaugurates Benjamin's history, then that history confirms the "classical" categories of the *Salon de 1859,* and in particular the priority of the moral over the material world. One could say that Benjamin's history is governed by the imagination, which Baudelaire calls "La Reine des facultés": "C'est l'imagination qui a enseigné à l'homme le sens moral de la couleur, du contour, de son et du parfum. Elle a créé, au commencement du monde, l'analogie et la métaphore." Here metaphor is given its ontological priority as the first creation of the imagination and hence as the beginning of a history; this priority is moral, not material, since it is only their "sens moral" that allows color, contour and sound to participate in the metaphorical first moment. If it is true that Benjamin's history of the photograph fits this metaphorical model and thus presents a "classically" romantic physiognomy, how may its features be distinguished from those of Baudelaire's *Salon?* If the latter is in some sense to provide a reading of Benjamin's history, those features cannot be simply identical. We might begin to consider their differences by examining the metaphorical status of the photograph in Baudelaire's text.

Interestingly enough, despite Baudelaire's championing of the metaphor, his metaphorization of photography is limited. Even when he appears to give photography a persona, that of "la servante des sciences et des arts," he does not thereby transfer subjective qualities to the technique. Although we are justifiably afraid for the future of the arts, this is not because photography is "encouraging" their demise: "la sottise de la multitude" continues to be the agent of any aesthetic decadence. (Benjamin uses the verb *begünstigen*, "to encourage," or in the juridical sense, "to aid and abet" a criminal. The second meaning recalls Benjamin's description of Atget's photographs as scenes of a crime. Photography, then, would seem to possess guilty intentions, if only by assocation—it does not remain an innocent accessory in the conspiracy against art.) This is why Baudelaire, unlike Benjamin, does not make of photography's "perpetual readiness" a figure of historical necessity. We would be wrong to assume, however, that Baudelaire is not interested in the metaphorical possibilities of the photograph. When, for example, he describes Delacroix's clean and rapid execution of paintings, he evokes something like the photographic process: "Si une exécution très nette est nécessaire, c'est pour que le langage du rêve soit nettement traduit; qu'elle soit très rapide, c'est pour que rien ne se perde de l'impression extraordinaire qui accompagnait la conception." The notion of high fidelity developed here is one which belongs to techniques of mechanical reproduction and seems out of place next to the Romantic "langage de rêve." But it is precisely in this juxtaposition of the mechanical and the metaphorical that photography acquires a "sens moral" for the *Salon de 1859*. When this "sens moral" is applied to Delacroix, we are left with the unsettling image of the artist as machine: part of his subjective self, which presumably gave rise to the quality *sui generis* of his paintings, is subordinated to an impersonal, reproducing capacity. This may explain Baudelaire's description of his first encounter with Delacroix: "Evidemment il voulut être plein d'indulgence et de complaisance; car nous causâmes tout d'abord de lieux communs, c'est-à-dire des questions les plus vastes et les plus profondes." This breadth and depth of Delacroix's wisdom are contained within the most reproducible of verbal forms, the commonplace: " 'La nature n'est qu'un dictionnaire,' répétait-il fréquemment." Thus Baudelaire underlines the mechanical quality of Delacroix's instruction and recalls the project of his own *Salon*—to repeat the commonplaces of Romanticism.

Perhaps we are now in a position to appreciate the difference between such repetition and a truly reactionary attitude. Baudelaire has no illusions about the possibility of returning simply to Romanticism: that he chooses to present the movement as everyone's possession, "ce que tout le monde devrait savoir," indicates his understanding that the cliché can never coincide with what it repeats. Although the term *cliché* was not yet in usage, either for the photographic negative or as a synonym for the commonplace, Baudelaire's metaphorical allying of technique and verbal form seems to prefigure the word's current double meaning. In this sense one could argue that Baudelaire's insight is fundamentally historical, while Benjamin's is reactionary insofar as it seeks to coincide fully with an originary, metaphorical moment. It does not matter that Benjamin locates this moment in modern times, with the invention of photography; the origin is equivalent to itself no matter where it occurs in real chronology, and Benjamin's purely metaphorical treatment of the photograph does nothing to disturb that equivalence. Once the metaphor is subject to repetition, however, once it becomes cliché, then the temporal dimension is opened out and history becomes possible. It is noteworthy that Baudelaire's metaphorization of photography engages the cliché as a *departure* from metaphor and thus responds to the specificity of the photographic technique much more than does Benjamin's metaphorization. One might even want to attribute a materialist insight to Baudelaire, since the cliché/photograph relationship is not only metaphorical, but literal: i.e. the photograph is not only *like* a verbal cliché, it *is* a visual cliché. This slippage toward the literal determination of meaning seems consistent with Benjamin's case that photography "reduces the scope" for metaphorical determinations. But it does not imply that meaning is thereby determined *materially*. If we find a metaphorical-literal tension in the term "cliché," this is not because of the material invention of photography, but because the photograph and the commonplace existed in a metaphorical relationship prior to the term's coinage. The *literal* occurrence of the term "cliché," which permits simultaneously a literalization of the metaphorical relationship, is thus an *immaterial* occurrence. The oppositional structure that gives Benjamin's second essay its ideological framework—on the one hand there is metaphor, on the other there is materiality—is thus rendered inoperative.

With this opposition no longer in effect, it becomes possible to reassess the question of Baudelaire's "age." If Baudelaire did not use his considerable metaphorical powers to create a new critical language in the *Salon de 1859,* this is not necessarily an indication that those powers had materially diminished. We should recall the over-readiness of critics to explain Delacroix's late paintings by the artist's decrepitude. If we hesitate in dating Baudelaire on the basis of his chronological age, however, we should be equally wary of giving his "age" a purely metaphorical interpretation. Baudelaire does not become "like" an old man because of bitterness, shock, or horror; such an old age would consist solely of *affective* moments and lack any temporal dimension. Baudelaire's old age, on the contrary, involves nothing but acts of verbal repetition, which are grounded in the temporal and devoid of affect. This age, which lies in suspension between materiality and metaphoricity, is properly *allegorical*. Of course, it is Benjamin's accomplishment to have recognized the allegorical character of Baudelaire's aesthetics; if my analysis takes a somewhat different tack, it is only to question the alignment of allegory's literalizing tendency with the material. This alignment is not unique to Benjamin, but frequently underwrites the appearance of history in literary discourse as such.

Islam, Philology, and French Culture:
Renan and Massignon

Edward W. Said

Readers of Matthew Arnold may recall the exasperated and embarrassed way in which his catalogues of English provincialism in culture are compared with the maturity and finish of either French or German culture. A marvelous passage of classical English by Addison quickly reveals its triteness of thought to Arnold when he compares it with Joubert; and the orotund periods of Jeremy Taylor seem by the same token awkward when put alongside the simple grandeur of Bossuet's sentences. England never had a literary academy to watch over cultural effort, Arnold says, and this had been a blessing for the freedom of atmosphere it produced in English intellectual life, but also a drawback because it could not prevent vulgarity and triteness ("The Literary Influence of Academies").

A particularly striking point is made by Arnold in this connection during a discussion of what he calls English "habits of wilfulness and eccentricity." His instance is John William Donaldson, a philologist who in 1854 attempted to argue that the scriptures really derived from a mysterious book called *Jashar*. Arnold says, "I, who am not an Orientalist, do not pretend to judge *Jashar:* but let the reader observe the form which a foreign Orientalist's judgement of it naturally takes. M. Renan calls it a *tentative malheureuse*, a failure in short; this it may or may not be; I am no judge. But he goes on: 'It is astonishing that a recent article . . . should have brought forward . . . a work like this, composed by a doctor of the University of Cambridge, and universally condemned by German critics.' " Arnold goes to quote Renan again—this time on Charles Forster's *Mahometanism Unveiled* (1829), "which enchanted the English *révérends* to make out that Mahomet was the little horn of the he-goat that figures in the

From *The World, the Text, and the Critic.* © 1983 by Edward W. Said. Harvard University Press, 1983.

eighth chapter of Daniel, and that the Pope was the great horn." Arnold interprets Renan as also saying that since it is an Englishman who has written such things, one should not be surprised at any extravagance. Such assessments come "from a grave Orientalist, on his own subject, and they point to a real fact;—the absence, in this country, of any force of educated literary and scientific opinion, making aberrations . . . out of the question."

The least provincial of nineteenth-century English writers himself, Arnold envied French culture for the opportunities it presented to learned people for making statements that were authoritative and central at the same time. About the two fields on which Arnold deferred to Renan, oriental studies and philology, he had an especially good point. Even if according to Madame de Staël (in *De l'Allemagne*) France was very far behind Germany in wealth of academic institutions and methods of instruction, France was still considerably ahead of England. In his book *The Study of Language in England, 1780–1860* Hans van Aarsleff chronicles the extraordinary slowness with which England acquired the New Philology, a science that reigned unchallenged intellectually in France and Germany from the beginnings of the century. England was not only kept behind because of Horne Tooke's great influence, but the universities themselves provided no serious possibility for instruction in philology until well into the century. The result was that in England philology was confined to "dilettantes, mere antiquaries, and amateurs." When Bopp's *Conjugationssystem* was reviewed in the *London Magazine* in 1820, the writer noted that "England, with all her peculiar advantages has [not] done so much as was to be anticipated of her in this way." Any scholar seriously interested in philology seemed likely to have been more engaged in very peculiar research than in fulfilling a major national project of the sort represented by Renan in France, Rask in Denmark, Bopp in German. Aarsleff says that even as competent a philologist as Friedrich August Rosen—he had studied under Sacy in Paris and with Bopp in Berlin—could not have a proper career in England, where he had "to eke out an existence by writing articles on philology for the *Penny Cyclopedia*."

This state of affairs was roughly the same in specialized Oriental studies, which for its European success and prestige depended greatly on the systematic and organized advance of the New Philology. People like Donaldson and Forster seem interchangeable with fictional characters like George Eliot's Mr. Casaubon, who is engaged in the hopeless task of trying to compile a Key to all Mythology—in unconcerned ignorance of the latest in continental scholarship. And indeed it is worth remarking that when the Orient appears significantly in English literature of the early Victorian period it is usually as something eccentric and outré, never as important and central to organized European culture. Edward William Lane of course is the exception, but his work belonged at first not the world of high but to the world of useful culture. If in 1856 George Eilot could say that all "our" civilization (in a very general sense) came from the East, it is important to remember not only that Quinet in France had spoken of an Oriental Renaissance twenty-five years earlier and that Friedrich Schlegel had said much the same thing in Germany in 1800, but that for both of them their respective culture's access to the Orient was preeminently and strictly through the discipline of philology. Even Hugo in the preface to the *Orientales* in 1828 had intimated something of the sort.

Still, if we assume that Macaulay's famous 1835 denigration of literature in the Sanskrit and Arabic languages can be regarded as expressing a general European view of modern Oriental inferiority, it is nevertheless strikingly true that for the most part the Orient—in this case the Islamic Orient—was more regularly associated in England either with the problems of empire or with the corruptions of fancy than it was with the prestige of high culture, systematic learning, and philological discipline. Clearly Arnold implies this and of course regrets it, just as much as he also regrets what accompanies it, the general English failure to appreciate France, which in its turn seems often associated with frivolity and a corresponding lack of moral seriousness.

I can't resist mentioning a wonderfully neat and amusing example of this attitude, toward France and the Orient, that appears in Thackeray's *Vanity Fair*. Becky Sharp is half-French, a fact that stamps her in English society as being somewhat suspicious and definitely not in the best of taste. Her adventures are too well-known to require any summary here, but one scene in particular is telling for its way of indicating how far toward a thoroughly bad end her Frenchness, her social climbing, and her questionable taste are probably going to take her. This is the scene in Gaunt House when, still married to Rawdon Crawley, Becky takes part in charades organized around the theme of "Eastern revels." The climax of the charades is Becky's third-act appearance as Clytemnestra (a part that is socially inappropriate for her, to say nothing of its idiotic, untidy melodrama). Her appearance is prepared for by the following caricature of an Oriental fantasy:

> The second part of the charade takes place. It is still an Eastern scene. Hassan, in another dress, is in an attitude of Zuleikah, who is perfectly reconciled to him. The Kislar Aga has become a peaceful black slave. It is sunrise on the desert, and the Turks turn their heads eastward and bow to the sand. As there are no dromedaries at hand, the band facetiously plays "The Camels are coming." An enormous Egyptian head figures in the scene. It is a musical one, and, to the surprise of the Oriental travelers, sings a comic song, composed by Mr. Wagg. The Eastern voyagers go off dancing, like Papageno and the Moorish King, in the Magic Flute.

It is immediately after this that Becky flounces on stage as Clytemnestra "in a Grecian tent," a scene in which her extravagant costume and behavior compel her husband's relatives to condemn her "improper exhibitions."

As if to take the point as far as it can go, Thackeray later arranges for Amelia's reunion with William Dobbin to be celebrated in Pumpernickel, a German town where this proper and finally united couple watches a performance not of Eastern charades but of Beethoven's *Fidelio*. And it is in Pumpernickel—according to Thackeray's completely detailed description—that there stands a bridge built by Victor Aurelius XIV, "on which his own statue rises, surrounded by water nymphs and emblems of victory, peace, and plenty; he has his foot on the neck of a prostrate Turk."

Thackeray is no exception to what is a rather impressive view held by novelists and poets about the Islamic East. The Arabian Nights, for example, are regularly associated with the fantasies of childhood, beneficent fantasies, it is true, but ones occurring in a sense so that they may be left behind. Think of Wordsworth's account of this in *The Prelude*. Or consider Newman's evocation of his adolescent admiration for the Arabian tales, which in his case have the additional virtue of helping to prepare for his subsequent belief in miracles. Or then again take Jane Eyre, for whom the splendors and impossible romance of the Arabian Nights are her escape from the grimness of her early life in the Reed household and a little later during her ordeal at Lowood School. Even Arnold, whose own rather grave Oriental poems show that he took the material more seriously than others, was on occasion given to connecting aesthetic or stylistic excess with Oriental things in general, more particularly with immaturity and a shoddy lack of urbanity. The wittiest point about the Orient is made digressively by Byron in *Beppo:*

> On that I had the art of easy writing
> What should be the easy reading! could I scale
> Parnassus, where the Muses sit inditing
> Those pretty poems never known to fail,
> How quickly would I print (the world delighting)
> A Grecian, Syrian, or Assyrian tale:
> And sell you, mix'd with western sentimentalism,
> Some sample of the finest Orientalism!

In such a context Lane's philological efforts appear more prodigious and lonely than ever. For his compatriots the Orient was only a place where one worked, traveled, or fantasized. No less and no more than general philology, Oriental philology was in England a subject of eminently marginal interest. I suppose it would be true also to say that, for the cultivated Englishman, Islam and Arabian lore generally represented values, experiences, mores, and tendencies that were altogether too easily acquired, too quickly assimilable to a feverish imagination or by a capacity for elaborate fantasy, to be estimable. No special prestige was gained by Oriental knowledge in England until later in the century, and certainly much later than in France, not because no one knew anything about the Orient but because, unlike France, England's cultural formations drew less from the metropolis and the academy than they did from private scholarship, individual effort, and personal illumination. It is no accident that the origins of the modern English tradition of Arabic and Islamic scholarship should be found in so relatively unacademic and unmetropolitan an intellectual as Lane, whereas in France the tradition was not only begun but embodied in so institutional, literally monarchical, and central a figure as Silvestre de Sacy. The Duc de Broglie said about Sacy that "Ses grands ouvrages, ce sont les orientalistes qui se sont partagés, sous les yeux, l'Asie tout entière, et qu'il n'a cessé d'animer, en quelque sorte, du geste et de la voix" ("Eloge de Silvestre de Sacy," in Sacy, *Mélanges de littérature orientale*).

Let me try to suggest two or three hypotheses to explain this difference between France and Britain. One is that in postrevolutionary France the intellectuals were organized imperially, radiating out from and commanded almost entirely by Paris, based for the most part exclusively in state institutions whose purpose was to make knowledge depend upon officially certified sciences, scientific bodies, orthodox canons. Arnold makes a similar but much smaller-scaled observation. In England, on the other hand, "the new social grouping that grew up on the basis of modern industrialism shows a remarkable economic-corporate development but advances only gropingly in the intellectual-political field" (Antonio Gramsci, *Prison Notebooks*). What this means is that intellectual progress in England was not centralized, but took place in organic association with developments in the sociopolitical sphere (hence the prestige and authority of political economy); elsewhere in the culture the values of a traditional landowning class prevailed, which in such fields as philology and biblical studies meant the hegemony of traditional views unaffected (until at least the late 1830s) by revolutionary European developments.

Another hypothesis is one I have suggested elsewhere (in *Orientalism*) in connection with the difference between British and French Oriental studies: the British empire was an older and more extended one than the French, and its place in English cultural life as a fact and as a source or subject of knowledge was based on its difference and its distance from, as well as its moral use to, the home society. Think again of *Vanity Fair* or *Jane Eyre* and you will see what I am trying to suggest: how, for example, Josiah Sedley is always affiliated with India and later of course with Becky, as if, despite Sedley's colonial wealth, Thackeray wished to underline his moral and social unacceptability in polite English society. Rochester's wife, Bertha Morris, is a West Indian, a fact by no means incidental to her bestiality; yet she must be exorcised (or controlled) before Rochester can marry Jane. This is Brontë's way of telling us that denizens of the outlying Empire are useful as a source of wealth or as a moral ordeal for English men and women to experience, but never are they people to be accepted into the heart of metropolitan society. The pattern is repeated frequently in British writing. I do not mean to say, however, that French culture took a more charitable view of its imperial domains: rather it was a matter of approaching them differently.

My last hypothesis, which may be the most important of the three, is the most tenuous and the most tentatively proposed. It seems to me that in England the challenge of the New Philology to religion was not felt until at least after the middle of the century, that is, until roughly the appearance of *Essays and Reviews* in 1860. The English attitude to language, mainly among philologists and poets, was pretty much a religious or philosophical one. There did not yet occur that decisive rupture between the linguistic phenomenon and the Judeo-Christian theses about the origins of things (or for that matter between language and a philosophical theory of mind) that was the hallmark of European New Philology. Coleridge and Shelley, for example, understood the sheer workings of language as well as anyone in Europe, yet neither of them went beyond ideas about language that were common knowledge to Condillac, Herder, or Rousseau, a generation earlier; neither of them, in other words, had been able to separate language from mentalism or from religion. Neither of them, and certainly not English philology as a field, seems to have understood language in the secular, purely linguistic terms proposed by the New Philology.

I have proposed these cultural propositions as an introduction to my main subject, which is not only the work of Renan and Massignon but how their orientalism had the central cultural authority that it did in France, and how their work was better known and accepted by the French literate public than the work of comparable figures was known in England. What I want to show is that Renan and Massignon were so integral a part of the French culture of their epochs—Renan from 1850 to 1900, Massignon from 1900 to 1960—as to give their work on Islam and even Islam itself a far greater status and authority for the non-Orientalist cultural public than could have happened in England and perhaps elsewhere in the West. In other words, allowing even for their unique gifts as great prose stylists and important Islamic scholars, it is worth while to try to understand how Renan and Massignon could have happened only in France, and not—for some of the reasons I have so far given—in England. I do not mean to be saying that in Renan or Massignon French culture produced scholars of Islam necessarily superior to those in England or elsewhere. The comparison with England is simply a useful way of showing a dramatic difference in cultural production and style.

But there is something else to be said about such differences in style and production. The study of Islam in the West has been undergoing a profound crisis. For the first time in its history Western Orientalism confronts encroachments on its privileged domains of study that come from other disciplines (the social sciences, Marxism, psychoanalysis) and from the very region being studied. The net positive effect of such encroachments is that for the first time Orientalism is being asked critically to examine not only the truth or falseness of its methodology and its investigative results, but its relationship both to the culture from which it is derived and the historical period in which its main ideas were advanced. And this leads to the question: How capable is Orientalism of asking itself these critical questions, given the constitution of Orientalism as a field with a recognizable domain, traditions, and praxis? I think it is true to say that in France, where the study of Islam played a far more central role for its own sake than anywhere else in Europe, the links between orientalism broadly considered, the culture, and contemporary history are more articulated, more visible, more important to the discipline of Orientalism than elsewhere.

There is an enormous value therefore to studying such exemplary and inherently interesting figures as Renan and Massignon for what such a study might tell us about the visible cooperation between their work and their culture: by such historical and critical studies Orientalists, cultural and intellectual historians, and Third World critics of conventional Orientalism can better judge the less visible character of "area studies" like Orientalism in cultures (this one, for instance) whose claims for studying other societies are based on neither sympathy nor cultural prestige but on scientific objectivity and an impartial intellectual curiosity. My point will be that even if each in his own way Massignon and Renan was a genius very much at home in and acknowledged by the culture he addressed, neither man was able critically to examine the assumptions and principles on which his work depended. I shall argue implicitly that humanistic fields sustaining their coherence not by criticism or by intellectual discipline, but by the unexamined prestige of culture (as in France) or by science (as in the Anglo-Saxon world), eliminate the possibility of a valuable kind of radical self-criticism, which in the case of Orientalism has meant eliminating completely any possibility of admitting that the "Orient" as such is a constituted object, or by being willing to allow for the role of power in the production of knowledge. The result in the case of Orientalism has been a self-validating, hermetic occultation, with the chances of a humane understanding of other cultures, or of culture itself, considerably reduced.

Renan and Massignon, on the other hand, enable us to know a great deal about them not only as men who had erudite things to say about Islam, but as men who reveal the processes by which knowledge gets made. What is particularly interesting is that their personal problems, concerns, and predilections are very much a part of their public work and position as Orientalists. Not only will we see that the private man does not interfere with the scholar; on the contrary, French Orientalism culturally supported personality, not because the personality was easy to support but because its relation to culture was so significant.

So we must read in Massignon and Renan an account of the relationship between knowledge and the cultural, the personal, and certainly the historical circumstances in which it is produced—and it is no accident that both Renan and Massignon were especially sensitive to the problem, although they addressed it in quite different ways. Both men employ a special sort of comparative cultural anthropology, rather more than less nuanced and interesting, although in Renan's case the hierarchy he depends on for comparisons is much closer to the surface, and therefore more pronounced and unyielding, than in Massignon. Yet we shall note that exactly where they grasp Islam, they also lose it. One scholar understands the religion in secular terms but misses what in Islam still gives its adherents genuine nourishment. The other sees it in religious terms but largely ignores the secular differences that exist within the variegated Islamic world. In both instances, then, Orientalism perceives and is blinded by what it perceives.

One of the things that surely must have attracted Matthew Arnold to Ernest Renan is not only that Renan's writing is saturated with the experience of latecoming but that Renan gives every indication of having successfully surmounted it. For Arnold, however, latecoming means a deep sadness at living in an age neither like Periclean Athens nor like Elizabethan England, and this feeling runs everywhere through his prose. In poems like "Dover Beach," "Rugby Chapel," and the "Memorial Verses" of 1850, feelings of regret and gentle melancholy are additionally informed by the forlornness of having in the present age lost a great reassuring figure—his father, Wordsworth, Goethe. The modern predicament for Arnold is in having been born after the disappearance either of a major creative age or of a major creative moral personality.

For Renan there is a similar predicament, except that for him the potential acuteness of loss is transmuted quickly from what could be a crippling personal blow to a general, principally cultural access of power, happiness, and confidence. The *Souvenirs d'enfance et de jeunesse* tell simultaneously of the loss of his religious orthodoxy and of its happy replacement by philology, reason, and "la science critique." There is little morbid introspection in Renan—none of Arnold's insensate dialogue of the mind with itself—even when he speaks of himself in the *Souvenirs* as at war with himself, a romantic against romanticism, a tissue of contradictions, like the *hircocerf* spoken by the scholastics. Without the slightest twinge of embarrassment Renan said of himself that he thought like a man, felt like a woman, acted like a child; such a modus vivendi he says with no little vanity brought him the keenest possible "jouissances intellectuelles." Theological disputation in the young seminarian took a very concrete textual form and, thanks to Le Hir, his extraordinary teacher, Renan was helped to read the sacred texts in the original. "M. Le Hir fixed my life; I was a philologist by instinct. Everything that I am as a scholar, I am because of M. Le Hir." This also happened to include the fact, according to Renan himself, that both men were *arabisants médiocres*.

The intellectual pattern that Renan always seems to transcribe is one that makes it possible for him to admit: "In effect, I have changed very little throughout my life; destiny has after its fashion riveted me since my childhood to the role and function which I would have to accomplish." To express what it means to live after unitary religious faith has given way to the many inroads made on it by rationalism—this is Renan's professed vocation. But there is more to the vocation than that, as an attentive reading soon reveals. A great deal of what Renan wrote and researched is organized around a rather special temporal and psychological problematic. Like Vico and Rousseau, Renan accepted the idea that the origins of language and religion were inspired moments resembling a poetic, perhaps religious *raptus*, but unlike either of his predecessors Renan makes no real effort to reconstruct or even to understand what those moments were in terms of an outside cause. Revelation is something Renan repeatedly associates with an occurrence that took place once and for all in an inaccessible realm, a realm fundamentally both earlier and outside his own. When he came to tackle the origin of language in 1848 Renan was perfectly willing to grant that God may have started everything "in the sense in which God, having placed in man everything which is necessary for the invention of language, could be called the author of language." But to talk about God, Renan continues, is in this context to use "une expression detournée et singulière," especially when there are more natural and philosophical expressions to do the job.

Revelation may or may not have occurred; in any case it is not what Renan tries to recapture. What he always assumes is that he is on earth to show how other things can replace the primitive excitement or original revelation—so much so that for him history itself became entirely equivalent, interchangeable with, his writing of history. Renan's vocation is to say: you cannot reexperience the past; you cannot risk losing yourself in lamenting the loss of a primitive world of Edenic plenitude and revelation; don't view what in fact you have lost as a loss; take it instead as the virtue of encountering me, and my writing.

Rarely, however, is this general claim made to depend on Renan's mere person as a writer or scientist. For his writing is part of a transpersonal enterprise, which he calls "la science" or "la science critique" most of the time, whose reason for being is not only that it replaces revelation and the individuals who claim to have revelation, but that it has reorganized existence and any perception of existence in such a way as to make religious revelation unnecessary. Renan's confidence in what he does and his unhappiness about his vocation come not only from the vocation itself but also from its being mediated and legitimized by a great person or institution. What Renan very shrewdly and, I think, accurately saw was the extent to which such things as genius, inspiration, or revelation depended upon the vagaries or the innate gifts or the personal devotions of the individual. Unlike Arnold's scholar-gypsy who was waiting pointlessly for the spark from heaven to fall, Renan premised his serious activity as a scientist generally, and as a philologist particularly, on the notion that if there were a heaven or a spark, he would not be the one to benefit. His time was not the past—which is where one would locate the *sève originale* he referred to in speaking about the early days of revealed religion—but the present and, if he was careful, the future. Therefore it was necessary to invest in disciplines like philology that moved history away from the existential problems of revealed religion and toward what it was possible to study, toward those real things that mankind still had to worry about long before primitive excitement (or revelation for that matter) was definitely over. One's career took shape inside this accessible reality, which is modern culture of course as Renan defined it, and under the auspices of teachers like Le Hir who confirmed the young man's specifically cultural instincts.

But philology does not simply displace religion or the religious attitude as one goes about studying language. Rather, Renan says in *De l'origine du langage,* philology shifts one's attention away from the possibility that language was the result of some prior, exterior cause (such as God) to the certainty that language was "un tout organique, doué d'une vie propre," and hence to be studied by "une science de la vie." Thus philology takes the linguistic phenomenon and redisposes it from the past to the present, reorganizes it within its "veritable terrain," that is, *la conscience créatrice* that functions in the present and also in the future. The philologist's job must be to connect that postlapsarian moment just after language's birth with the present, then to show how the dense web of relationships between language users is a secular reality from which the future will emerge. To this project Renan remained extraordinarily faithful: all of his major religious and philological studies dealt with what we can call *the aftermath,* a postprimitive state whose sole form of existence, for the philologist, is not a believer's faith, or an apostolic succession, or a living community, but a set of texts permitting a clever philologist to discern in them all those faults and virtues hidden behind the protestations of devotion, the proclamations of faith, the sufferings of martyrs. Renan did his work with modern investigative instruments, and his standpoint was that of a secular professional whose judgments were based on the incontrovertible, largely ironic truth that, in spite of revelation, culture was moved forward by science, which left religion further and further behind. This view is specifically responsible for Renan's radically uncompromising view of Islam. But before I discuss that, I must say a few more things about Renan's views of culture and science.

The crucial text here is *L'Avenir de la science,* published in 1890 but originally written in 1848. I must confess at the outset that the book's rambunctious confidence and its air of self-esteem are somewhat repellent. But be that as it may, it is a very important book for Renan. In it he clearly means to be situating himself at the heart of modern culture—which he says is philological in spirit—and therefore speaking as much for that culture as about it. The title makes the point that science is the future; more, that science will change human life so much as even to reorganize God himself. "Organiser scientifiquement l'humanité tel est donc le dernier mot de la science moderne . . . et après avoir organiser l'humanité, organisera Dieu." The interesting thing is that Renan sees this happening as a result of a change of perspective caused by modern scientific discovery. Thus whereas the ancient (by which he meant the religious) world was closed and narrow, the new scientific world created by Humboldt is open, full of potentiality, rich. Here the past has been superseded entirely, transvaluated into what only a rationalistically investigative and daring mind can exploit, revel in, feel creative about. Though he does not say it outright, Renan clearly implies that the modern philological culture of which he is the accredited representative rules over the rational domain that emerged as a result of modern scientific discovery. Three concentric positions are thus legitimized. At the outer rim is the physical envelope whose earliest boundaries define the place from which the open postprimitive world springs; inside that is culture itself, historical, philological, dealing with all the products of human history; and inside that, at the center, is the philologist whose activity carries human history forward. Each of these positions and each of these places enforces the other; each makes all the others possible. "Moi étant là au centre, humant le parfum de toute chose, jugeant et comparant, combinant et induisant, j'arriverais au système des choses." Although that imperious "moi" seems lonely, it is in fact supported by all sorts of institutions and figures giving it authority and gravity: not only Humboldt, but Cousin, Burnouf, Le Hir, Cuvier, St. Hilaire—like Renan, central to the main activities of modern life.

A quick contrast with Arnold is instructive here. In *Culture and Anarchy* Arnold had said of the critic that if he is not to fall prey either to narrow class interest (Barbarians, Philistines, or Populace) and if he is to be truly a disinterested critic, he must belong to a small intrepid band formed by men of culture. These creatures are what we might call declassé intellectuals, and that is what Renan eminently is not. Everything about him exudes the authority of massive centralized institutions like schools, disciplines, missions, teams of cooperating but hierarchically arranged scientific workers. Far from such a smoothly running apparatus being merely what Arnold called machinery, it is for Renan the true plenitude of postlapsarian existence. Far from treating all this as a mere adjunct to the poverty of living without revelation, Renan judges the whole dense undertaking to be modern life itself, at its finest.

No wonder then that Islam comes off so badly. For Islam, as Renan said on so many occasions, is a religion whose founder never even pretended to divinity, much less to true originality. If Renan could treat organized religions like Judaism and Christianity as coming after their founders' encounter with the divine, how else could he treat Mohammed except as the latecomers' latercomer? No mystery, no miracles, no divinity, not even, he says in a remarkable passage near the end of "Mahomet et les origines de l'islamisme," women. Islam in other words is opened entirely onto the present, and it will not survive into the future; it offers nothing of interest to anyone trying to resurrect a distant, vaguely religious past. It is barren, incapable of truly regenerating itself, and it will disappear entirely under the influence of modern Occidental science.

To a certain extent, Islam's disappearance is what Renan undertook to hasten. And he did it with a consistency to his views about culture and science that is positively chilling. In 1883 he gave a speech at the Sorbonne entitled "L'Islamisme et la science" which serves as the opposing pendant to L' Avenir de la science: Islam in this instance is the very opposite of science and of the future. The most telling thing about the speech is Renan's insistence that Islamic culture properly speaking is neither science nor philosophy (as his book on Averroes had already asserted), but only language (his authority here is Abul-Faraj). Yet shorn of its roots in a past revelation, or even in an intimate relationship with divinity, Islam's language is not fit for science to nurture. On the contrary, Islam and its Arabic language represent hatred to reason, the end of rational philosophy, unremitting enmity to progress. Thus "pour la raison humaine, l'islamisme n'a été que nuisible." Why exactly? Because it made of the countries over which it ruled "un champ fermé." In other words Islam returned one to the closed world of the primitives and away from the open world of modern science. Because it came so long after Judaism and Christianity, however, Islam pertained exclusively to an earlier age of aborted, failed human effort with no memory of vivacious revelation to guide it. Its main service to the practitioner of modern European culture was a negative demonstration of the law of progress.

The paradox at the heart of Renan's view of Islam is resolved only when we understand him to be keeping Islam alive so that, in his philological writing, he might set about destroying it, treating it as a religion only to show the fundamental aridity of its religious spirit, reminding us that, even if all religions are essentially postscripts to permanently disappeared revelations, Islam was interesting to a philologist as the postscript to a postscript, the trace of a trace. As such it was a challenge to the philologist who, speaking for European culture, affirmed modern secularity in the space opened up not by the loss of religion, as Renan believed, but by the religious spirit itself in its continuing indifference to mere science and culture, a spirit to which he unwittingly returned in book after book, and left completely untouched.

Renan never really dealt with the secular fact of the enduring presence of religions like Islam, religions that could still exist and be powerful even in an age that culturally could prove beyond a shadow of a doubt that religion was a thing of the past. This is Renan's cultural predicament and its blind spot, however much he believed himself to have transcended religion.

Louis Massignon's whole massive work turns exactly on this issue, the survival of religion; he illuminates it, relives it, cherishes it, writes and rewrites it with unparalleled genius and insight. This is another way of saying that in Massignon the philological vocation adumbrated at the heart of French culture is transformed entirely. We are now dealing with a mind altogether of another sort of magnitude, with an experience so intense and remarkable that its only decent cultural analogies and supports are aesthetic and psychological, not, as in Renan's case, institutional and academic. To understand Massignon we would almost do better, that is, to read Mallarmé and Rimbaud than Sylvain Lévi. Yet no less than Renan, Massignon must be seen within the great structure of French cultural, political, and colonial domination of the Muslim world. Each of them, in very different ways, takes for granted that there is a peculiarly French mission to and in the Muslim world, in Renan's case to judge and finally to annihilate it, in Massignon's to understand and feel compassion for it, then finally to exist in harmony with its anguish, its needs, its divine dilemmas. Renan's epistemological attitude toward Islam, therefore, is one of divestiture and judgment, Massignon's of sympathetic assumption and rapprochement. Neither man doubts that Islam can in fact be an object of study for the European scholar, since both assume that scholarship dissolves all obstacles, makes all things acquirable, can represent anything, Renan by critical judgment and rejection, Massignon by sympathetic compassion.

What is most relevant for anyone trying critically to understand the nature of modern Orientalism is that in reading Renan one encounters a subtle mind, capable of making all sorts of fine distinctions, whose main project is to shut down Islam. In the end of course it is Renan, not Islam, who leaves one with the impression of something limited, superficial, and unenthusiastic. The reverse is true of Massignon, and in the rest of this essay I shall try to suggest some of the ways in which this great scholar defies routine analysis, but can still be apprehended as part of Orientalism. In his work, which spans roughly the first sixty years of this century, a reader finds embodied not only a daunting panorama of French intellectual culture (in its high Catholic variety), but also the great civilization and political problems of colonialism and decolonization. In addition Massignon treats such complex things as the reform movement in Islam, the relationship between Islam and Christianity, science confronting revelation, linguistics, anthropology, and psychoanalysis encountering philology, religion, and faith, and above all the struggles of one extremely powerful and refined mind to deal with most of the institutions of faith, and modern as well as traditional culture, in the midst of undiminishing activity in government, academy, and church.

Massignon is Renan's exact opposite on the matter of revelation. Whereas Renan speaks and writes *after* having already decided that revelation is no longer apposite to modernity, Massignon's entire career springs out of one moment of revelation in 1907. Here is how he describes it in quaint, incorrect, but somehow very moving English:

> Studying, after Sanskrit (and the inscriptions of Angkor), Arabic and the Moslem countries, travelling during years on the boundaries of the Arab desert in Africa and Asia, warrying [*sic*] many manlike struggles, I was suddenly struck by the lightning of revelation; disguised, taken prisoner on the frontier of the desert and the rice-fields, in Irak, I could not get rid of this midday sunstroke

as I had done with the reflected dawn light-glances of ancestral folk-tales. Furthermore, these folk-tales were reanimated in my memory, when I discovered in Islam religious symbols akin to the traditional culture of peasantry. Specially in the Islam of monsoon countries, from the Frankincense Arabia to the Spicy Indonesia.

(*Opera Minora*)

This is written in 1959, three years before his death. Massignon connects the experience with his father's sudden veneration for Japanese art in 1890, after which he felt a form of reverence for the very paper on which the images were printed. What paper was for the father, language became for the son. "La parole humaine . . . c'est un appel personnel poignant destiné à nous faire sortir de nous-mêmes, de notre pays, de notre parenté, à tout dépasser vers l'Amour" (quoted by Jacques Waardenburg in his *L'Islam dans le miroir de l'occident*). There is a kind of parallel for both aspects of this experience in Marcel's rediscovery of George Sand's *François le Champi* in the Guermantes library, near the end of Proust's *Le Temps retrouvé*. An involuntary conflation of two separate situations seems momentarily to eradicate the anguish of distance, of time, of identity. What the elder Massignon understands is the material identity of his work and Japanese art; he is a sculptor. What the son is given in revelation comes directly from the spoken word; since he is a philologist, his task is to see how texts in a foreign language contain, bear witness to, the divine Presence that in each utterance this language represents.

But Massignon is not interesting to a modern intellectual simply because he had a revelation and then recalled it in his work. Paraphrasing Sartre on Valéry, we can say that Massignon was a man who had a rich spiritual life, but not everyone who has a rich spiritual life is a Massignon. The question of what gives his career its sustained power and its unmistakable identity from beginning to end can be answered in intellectual terms. Without reducing or simplifying Massignon we can say that if, for Renan, language and culture were to be treated by philology in a temporal perspective, as aspects of a typology of historical periods, in Massignon the problems of language and of the philological vocation are considered within a *spatial* perspective, as aspects of a topography of distances, of geographical differentiation, of spirits of place separated from each other by a territory whose function for the scholar is that it must be charted as exactly as possible, and then in one way or another overcome. The underlying economy of Massignon's sprawling work is the ubiquitous fact of distance, the fact of how separate identities exist, even in a moment of revelation. At bottom, in other words, Massignon tries to experience the distance between Islam and Christianity, as a variant on the distance between man and God or between the word and spirit.

Thus he examined Islam not simply as a thing in itself, but as a differential phenomenon, as something felt in Arabia, Indonesia, and Morocco but not, say, in France or England. In much the same way, Mallarmé tried to understand language as the interplay of black and white, and Proust tried to devise a method for reducing the distance between past and present, having fully experienced the space between them and preserving the identity of both. Massignon's method derives not only from a Christian habit of witness and compassion, but from the aesthetics of late nineteenth-century *symbolisme*, in which an object is coexistent in language with its absence, in which the placing and displacing of things—their play of substitutions—are what language embodies.

There are numerous examples of this in Massignon's work; even a quick rehearsal of some gives a perfect idea of his procedures. His interest in al-Hallaj is surely one of the most obvious, since al-Hallaj is so powerfully the master figure of Massignon's oeuvre. Mansur al-Hallaj was a tenth-century Baghdad Muslim saint who was martyred because he dared not only to approach God directly but also to speak of himself as the truth, as a sort of pan-Christian incarnation. Not only did al-Hallaj himself represent an example of the substitution of one thing for another in the same man (the man and the divine, al-Hallaj's *ana'l haqq*); but al-Hallaj's Muslim experiences, although they occur at a great distance from them, correspond with the effusions of European Christian mystics. In this connection there is "L'Expérience mystique et les modes de stylisation littéraire" (1927), where Massignon compares the verbal techniques of European writers like Eckhart, John of the Cross, and Claudel with those of Muslim devotional poets. The point about these comparisons is not only that they demonstrate similarities in expression, but that they are precise despite the "differential" geographical circumstances separating them. But even in his analyses of European and Oriental mystical encounters with the divine, Massignon preserves what I have called his topographical problematic: he is less interested in man's complete identification with God than with the mystical struggle between man and God, and man and man, in which what man risks is the loss of his identity to God.

History, Massignon says, is made up of chains of individual witnesses scattered throughout Europe and the Orient, interceding with and substituting for one another. Substitution implies an endless chain of resubstitutions, in which there is a ceaseless movement of one thing always replacing another. For Massignon Islam was what, despite the occasional appearance of an al-Hallaj and despite its being an Abrahamanic religion, could be described as an imperfect substitute in the East for Christianity. He saw Islam displacing Christianity and Christianity displacing Islam. In Massignon's view Islam's identity is its resistance to and its final intransigence vis-à-vis the Christian incarnation. As such, therefore, the religion attracted and yet resisted the Christian in him, although—and here is the man's extraordinary stroke of genius—he conceived his own philological work as a science of compassion, as providing a place for Islam and Christianity to approach and substitute for each other, yet always remaining apart, one always substituting for the other. Moreover, the particular group of worship he founded was called Badaliya Sodality whose "texte d'engagement" noted that "*badaliya* requires a penetration in depth, which is the result of bringing together an attentive care for the life of families, and of past and present Muslim generations" ("Inédits de Massignon," in *Louis Massignon*).

Underlying the notion of substitution is the ever-present antithesis between the things that get substituted. Christ as sacrifice is obviously the prime substitute, since he is both sacrificial victim for all men and the son of God. Christianity as a system of faith, as a liturgy, as a language, is built out of that radical antithesis. The rigor of Massignon's method is to transfer this religious antithesis and substitution to the realm of languages and from there to Arabic and to Islam:

> For language is both a "pilgrimage" and a "spiritual displacement," since we only elaborate language in order to be able to go out from ourselves toward an other: and also to evoke with this other an absent One, the third person, *al-Ghayib* as He is called by Arab grammarians. And we do this so as to discover and identify all these entities with each other. This makes it possible to render our witness to Him, because He is the truth when we have accepted Him by virtue of the heart's fiat, this *Kun* [be] which is mentioned eight times in the Koran, and always for "the Word of God, Jesus son of Mary," and the Last Judgment.
> ("Valeur de la parole humaine en tant que témoignage")

Massignon goes still further, this time citing Mallarmé. In one sense, he says, words denote an absence (*manque*); but in Arabic the importance of the spoken language is that it is testimony (*shahada*), and carried to its ultimate grammatical form (*shahid*) it means martyr. To testify is to speak, and to speak is to move from yourself toward another, to displace self in order to accommodate another, your opposite and your guest, and also someone absent whose absence opposes your own presence. The irony of this is that you can never directly come together with another: your testimony can at best accommodate the other, and this of course is what language does and is, antithetically—presence and absence, unless in the case of the *shahid* (martyr) the self is obliterated for the sake of the other, who because of the martyr's love is more distant, more an Other than ever. This is the ultimate sacrifice, the ultimate grace, and of course the ultimate antithesis: it is human scandal and divine love, the *déchirante pureté* of Mansur al-Hallaj whose sacrilege is to have dared to reach beyond Islam toward Christianity and God. As Père de Foucauld put it, "When God chooses a witness, even in the humblest domains, God transforms that witness into somebody who for others is both unrecognizable and odious."

All of Massignon's writing forms a constellation of images around these notions. Arabic is a closed world with a certain number of stars in it; entering it, the scholar is both at home and repatriated from his own world. Thus a central pair of images is that of the guest and host. Note how there is always an antithesis to be confronted whose poles allow one to traverse the distance from language to religion and back again: from Arabic to French, from Islam to Christianity, then back again. And within each pole of the antithesis there are further antitheses—in Arabic, for example, there are differences expressed, and they accentuate separation. Massignon's characterization of Arabic, that it is essentially a language of compression and disjunction, in which consonants on the line are the body, vocalizations above or below the line its spirit, is part of the same thematic antithesis between alternating absence and presence. The religious experiences and rituals he was especially interested in (for example, the *mubhala*) also repeat the ritual of substitution and opposition. Similarly Massignon's style, as much as its subject matter, is a discontinuous, abrupt style—certainly one of the great French styles of the century—as if it wishes constantly to embody distance and the alternation of presence and absence, the paradox of sympathy and alienation, the motif of inclusion and exclusion, grace and disgrace, apotropaic prayer and compassionate love. Above all, we find in Massignon the continual alternation of distance and closeness between Islam and Christianity that always embodied in his work the basic idea of substitution, of attraction and repulsion itself. To the form of apotropaic prayer, therefore, Massignon assimilated in his philosophical work the notion of compassionate, substitutive sacrifical suffering, whose principle Christian form is of course the passion of Christ, whose early Greek form is the *pharmakos*, and whose Muslim form is the *abdal*.

It is probable that Massignon's ideas about sacrifice came to him from Joseph de Maistre and Alfred Loisy; yet he gave those ideas his own distinctive form. If a word is at once a presence and an absence, then one can say too that the person who suffers for the community, whose suffering is caused by what Massignon calls "le transfert de la douleur par la compassion," is at once all evil and all good, victim and hero, alien and citizen, outcast, guest and accepted host, presence and absence. Throughout his career Massignon was actively involved not only with Islam but also with sufferers, martyrs, refugees, convicts and expatriate workers in France, even as he remained a very great scholar of language, a great reader of difficult texts, a great interpreter of other religions, and a much-honored public figure. Together Islam and Arabic invoke in him Christian compassion which, unlike any other Orientalist of the century, he tried to convert into a meticulous understanding of both. He said on one occasion that most nineteenth-century philologists ended up by disliking the languages they studied. *His* philological vocation, unlike Renan's was premised on the wish not to repeat that dislike, but to transform alienation into love.

Still there is something odd about so heady a mixture in the man of an extraordinarily luxuriant, often overpowering mental fertility, fixated on martyrdom, on stigmatas, on gratuitous suffering, on hopeless pilgrimages, on death, on deserts, caves, prisons, on asceticism, on absence and night. The legacy of Huysmans, Massignon's godfather, is perhaps too obtrusive in him. Jacques Berque is right to say that Massignon took Orientalism as far as it could go, the way Hegel took philosophy to its absolute limits, and right also to suggest that Massignon's attachment to Abraham as ur-Semite ought to be counterbalanced by a strong dose of Heraclitus. Massignon himself was quite conscious of opening Orientalism out from the binds imposed on it by Renan. He made frequent reference to Renan's strictures, stated his disagreement with the man's hard-eyed ethnocentrism and rationalism, even carrying his antipathy as far as befriending Renan's grandson, Ernest Psichari, a mystic and anti-Renanian.

Renan and Massignon are polar opposites within Orientalism: Renan is the philologist as judge, the French scholar surveying lesser religions like Islam with disdain, speaking with the authority not only of a scientific European but of a great cultural institution; Massignon is the philologist as guest, as spiritual traveler extraordinary, as—to use Gerard Manley Hopkins' words for Duns Scotus—the rarest-veined unraveler of Islamic civilization the West has produced.

One last critical point must be made. Is it too much to say that as Orientalists Renan and Massignon, opposites and opponents in a way, can also be taken as substitutes for each other? The keynote to Renan's work is, of course, difference—Renan's differences with religion and with the Orient. The keynote of Massignon's work is also difference, but he added compassion to it—his Christian compassion for Islam which, Foucauld told him in 1915, came about "in confrontation with these Moslems toward whom God has given both of us special duties" (*Opera Minora*). But insofar as both men accept the barrier between East and West upon which Orientalism as a learned discipline is constructed, they can be considered as substitutes, *abdal*, different sides of the same coin. Both of them do their work within the edifice we call Oriental studies, which both men assumed that Franco-European culture had given them and which their work reinforced. The question raised by a juxtaposition of their works is the very question that Orientalism itself cannot really pose, must less answer—the question of the Orient. Its overwhelming reality for both Renan and Massignon was the source of one man's rejection and the other's ceaseless attempts to save Islam from itself. In neither case could the Orientalist be truly critical of himself or see his discipline critically and in a wholly secular perspective, where the other important questions—of human labor, of power, of men and women in society—might be posed and attended to.

To the situation of Massignon's and Renan's Orientalism as critical science, it is useful to apply Lukacs's ironic description: both are in "the situation of that legendary 'critic' in India who was confronted with the ancient story according to which the world rests on an elephant. He unleashed the 'critical' question: on what does the elephant rest? On receiving the answer that the elephant stands on a tortoise 'criticism' declares itself satisfied. It is obvious that even if he had continued to press apparently 'critical' questions he could only have elicited a third miraculous animal. He would not have been able to discover the solution to the real question" (*History and Class Consciousness*).

Taine and Saussure

Hans Aarsleff

Today Taine is so little known that it may be useful to say at the outset that he was a French critic, philosopher, and historian who by his contemporaries was considered the dominant intellectual figure during the last forty years of the nineteenth century. I shall give more information on that point later.

In a review of a book on modern German thought, Taine observed in 1869 that the author saw a difference between the German and French ideas of God. "He is right," said Taine, "all conceptions, among them that one, differ from one race to another. . . . unable to translate it, we have made it French; but becoming French, it has lost its true sense. By the same token, *God, Gott*, do not find their equivalent in our *Dieu*. With ideas that are so important, the nuance is everything; and to understand the full value of such a word in the speech of our neighbors, we must brave the risks of psychology" (review of Camille Selden, *L'Esprit moderne en Allemagne* published in *Le Journal de Débats* February 7, 1869). The following year saw a the publication of Taine's major philosophical work, which is also the key to his entire oeuvre, *De l'intelligence*. Here he made the same observation with new pairs of examples, arguing that their significations are not the same except in a limited way, owing to the dissimilarity of the objects and emotions in the speakers' minds. The full meaning of a word, including its value, is a function of the cultural system in which it occurs. In *De l'idéal dans l'art* (1867), Taine had already introduced and developed the concept of *valeur* as a feature that is characteristic of an epoch in the history of art; the historian must note the changes of value between epochs, for such changes create new systems. ("In the world of imagination as well as in the world of reality there are different levels because there are different values," and "I am speaking of historical epochs. The system of ideas and sentiments that filled a human head in the time of Louis XIV was altogether different from what it is today.") In Ferdinand de Saussure's *Cours de linguistique générale* (1916) *valeur* also plays an important role. English *sheep* and French *mouton* can have the same significations, but not the same *valeur*. Each word has its place in the system that determines its value (*Cours de linguistique générale*).

In the chapter on "La valeur linguistique," Saussure also made a statement that has now been cited so often that it has become a commonplace, like a key to his linguistic thought: "Language can also be compared to a sheet of paper: thought is the recto and sound the verso; we cannot cut one side without also cutting the other. So also in language, sound cannot be isolated from thought, or thought from sound." The linguistic sign is a psychic entity with two surfaces, intimately related and recalling one another. Everyone knows that he called them the *signifiant* and the *signifié*. This principle and the striking metaphor that illustrates it are also in Taine's great work.

In the opening book on "Les signes" in *De l'intelligence*, Taine argued that we think by means of signs, which for him are not only words but anything mental that goes into thinking; they are rarely full sensations, but usually faded or vague images of sensations. But we cannot think effectively unless these various kinds of images are linked to the signs we call words, which are themselves a special and privileged kind of images. This process Taine calls substitution. Thus "a general and abstract idea is a name, nothing but a name, the name that signifies and comprises a series of similar facts." Like Locke, Taine held that sensation does not reveal substances, but only the signs we take for facts. For Taine "the physical world is reduced to a system of signs," or in Saussure's words, "every material thing is already a sign for us." Taine, Saussure, and Wilhelm von Humboldt all dismissed the belief that language is a nomenclature. They agreed with Locke that words stand for ideas we form of things, not for things themselves as people generally believe by erroneously postulating a reliable "double conformity," as Locke called it, between thing-idea and idea-word (*An Essay concerning Human Understanding*).

Near the end of the first volume of *De l'intelligence* Taine came to the crucial point in his argument: how do physical and mental events connect? Many philosophers, he said, have argued that these two kinds of events are heterogeneous; they say that the image is internal while the sensation comes from the outside. Since they perpetually diverge, no common point can be found. Taine answers that they are not different events, but a single event known under two different aspects. This explanation satisfies Taine because it does not rely on any imaginary or unknown third element. He concludes that the two kinds of separate events previously postulated are always of necessity bound together, "for as soon as they are reduced to a single event with two aspects, it is clear that they are like the verso and recto of a surface, and that the presence or absence of one incontrovertibly entails that of the other. We have a single event with two faces, one mental, the other physical, one accessible to the understanding, the other to the senses." The sheet is his metaphor for the "central event" that "communicates its character to the rest."

But what, he asks, "is the value of each of the two points of view?" That of the understanding (*conscience*) is always direct, the image of the sensation within us, for Taine materially located in the constitution of the brain. But the other aspect, that of external perception, is indirect, for it never gives knowledge of the physical object itself: "In itself this physical and sensible object remains altogether unknown; we know nothing about it except the group of sensations it provokes in us . . . that is to say their constant effects on us, their fixed accompaniments, their signs, nothing but signs, *signs* and *tokens* of things *unknown*." Taine continued: "Thus there is a great difference between the two points of view. By the understanding I attain the fact in itself; by sense I attain only a sign. A sign of what? What is it that is always accompanied, denoted, *signified* by the internal motion of the nervous centers? . . . it is the sensation, the image, the internal mental event." Sharing Saussure's well-known fondness for dichotomies, Taine has analyzed the sign into the purely mental *signifié* and the invariably linked *signifiant* (a term Taine does not use), which, coming from the outside, to us appears physical. We now understand, "why the mental event, being single, must appear double to us; the sign and the event signified are two things that can neither become one nor be separated, and their distinction is as necessary as their connection. But in regard to this distinction and this connection, the advantage is entirely on the side of the mental event; it alone exists. The physical event is merely the manner in which it affects or could affect our senses."

It is evident that Taine's analysis contains all the elements of Saussure's doctrine of signs. For both Taine and Saussure the full range of signs included more than words, but both concentrated on words as the chief kind of mental images. As for Taine, Saussure's "images acoustiques" are only instruments of thought, but in themselves they are nothing until they become "des entités linguistiques" by being joined to concepts. At one point Saussure says that this "unité à deux faces" has been compared to "the unity of the human person, composed of body and soul,"—though he prefers to think of it as the union of hydrogen and oxygen in the chemical constitution of water. We may find this analogy unhappy, but it still shows that Saussure understood what Taine was talking about and that he sought a scientific image that falls into line with Taine's orientation. This preference for scientific illustrations—for crystallization, glaciers, moraines, geological layers, mineralogy, anatomy, spiral shapes, physiology, and "les formules de la science"—is a constant reminder that Saussure was working within the conceptual milieu of Taine's thought. When Saussure said that "without the aid of signs, we would be unable to distinguish two ideas in a clear and certain manner," that "there are no preestablished ideas, and nothing is distinct before the appearance of language," he was following Taine's argument—and as Taine acknowledged, Condillac's. For Taine, the joining of sound and concept formed what Saussure called "a complex unity, physiological and mental."

The two features I have dealt with bring Taine and Saussure so closely together that it would be implausible to argue that the young French-speaking Genevan did not know Taine's work. I shall show below that the similarities extend beyond the two I have discussed. On the question whether Saussure read Taine we have only circumstantial evidence, unless new material turns up. Saussure cites few names, and the records are sparse and cover only limited periods of his life. Records from the early 1890s show that he was then devoting much thought to problems of general linguistics in a manner that later emerged in the *Cours*, but since we have no records from the 1880s, we lack textual evidence for the inception, impulses, and growth of his thought. When he arrived in Paris in the fall of 1880 at the age of twenty-three he had spent three years at the universities of Leipzig and Berlin. He had already published brilliant work, but it gained only slow and grudging acceptance in German scholarship, of which Saussure later wrote privately in severely critical, even contemptuous, terms, especially in regard to its lack of method.

In Paris his work had already been accepted by prominent linguists. Only a year after his arrival he was, thanks to Michel Bréal, entrusted with courses in traditional philology at the Ecole des hautes études, where his teaching, extending to 1891, soon became legendary, not least for its close attention to method. When the *Cours* appeared, his student, colleague, and friend Antoine Meillet observed that he saw in it doctrines Saussure had already taught in Paris twenty years earlier (counting from 1907 when Saussure first gave the course at Geneva), such as the distinction between diachrony and synchrony. Among his closest friends was the linguist Louis Havet, whose father, also a linguist, had been Taine's teacher and later became his admirer and correspondent. There is good reason to think that the Parisian milieu strongly affected the young Saussure.

In this milieu Taine was the reigning intellectual influence. For this we have the clear testimony of at least two dozen contemporaries, speaking for sociology (Durkheim, Tarde), history and philosophy (Gabriel Monod, Emile Boutroux, François Picavet, Pierre Janet), experimental psychology (Thédodule Ribot), criticism, art, and literary history (Brunetière, Paul Bourget, Maurice Barrès, Gustave Lanson, and Anatole France), all of them areas in which Taine had applied his method. Taine was one of the founders of the Ecole libre des sciences politiques. He reshaped the study of history and extended its range, created experimental psychology, and gave primary impulses to naturalism in literature and to impressionism in painting. He was the first to call public attention to the work of Antoine-Augustin Cour-not, who contrasted his admiration for the eighteenth century and for Condillac to the philosophy of Victor Cousin. In the 1880s Nietzsche called Taine the greatest living historian, and it has been suggested that he found the concept of value in Taine. When Ribot started the successful *Revue Philosophique* in 1876, it opened with an article by Taine, soon to be followed by other articles by him as well as by detailed discussion of his philosophy. Among Taine's articles was one, based on personal observation, on language acquisition in the child, a subject that also plays a very large role in *De l'intelligence*. This article so greatly excited Charles Darwin that he dug out and published his own notes taken some thirty years earlier. Taine inspired a large literature on this subject, both in France and in other countries.

For the generation that gained maturity after 1865, Taine's achievement was this. He was the first popular and successful critic of the eclectic, spiritualist, and introspective philosophy which for a generation had ruled France, at times repressively, under the direction of Cousin. Taine proposed instead to apply the method of the natural sciences to the moral sciences. He found this method chiefly in the principles that Cuvier and Etienne Geoffroy Saint-Hilaire had developed in natural history. This method he expounded again and again, most prominently in the Introduction (1863) to *Histoire de la littérature anglaise* and in the prefaces (1858 and 1866) to *Essais de critique et d'histoire*. The Introduction to the *Histoire* outlines a program for what has later been called *histoire totale* or *histoire des mentalités*—a fact widely ignored by later historians, whose estimation of Taine has been determined largely by their rejection, itself ideological, of his *Origines de la France contemporaine*. Already in the 1858 preface to *Essais*, Taine had dismissed the sort of history that is a mass of details and anecdote, "man is not an assemblage of contiguous pieces, but a machine with ordered wheels; he is a system and not a heap." Or in other words, "history is a problem of psychological mechanics" (*Essais de critique et d'histoire*). A civilization observes Cuvier's anatomical *loi des dependences mutuelles*, "its parts interrelate like the parts of an organic body." Just as the comparative anatomist can reconstruct an animal if he has a tooth or bone, "similarly in any civilization we find that religion, philosophy, family life, literature and the arts form a system in which any isolated change entails a general change, so that an experienced historian who studies some limited portion of it discerns in advance and almost predicts the qualities of the rest" (*Histoire de la littérature anglaise*). The concepts of system and structure are fundamental, and the terms occur constantly in Taine's writing. For Taine history embraces all aspects of human life seen as social and collective manifestations. It was a naturalist rather than strictly positivist program—Taine never paid as much attention as is often believed to Auguste Comte, who had considered the study of mind entirely irrational except "through the medium of the brain—we might even say the skull," in Mill's felicitous phrase.

It was this program, this method, and the illustrations he gave that so greatly excited and inspired Taine's contemporaries. On his death in 1893, Anatole France wrote that Taine had inspired his generation around 1870 with "the dynamic cult of life. What he brought us was method and observation, it was a question of fact and idea, of philosophy and history, in short it was science. He set us free from the odious academic spiritualism, from the abominable Victor Cousin and his abominable school . . . he delivered us from hypocritical philosophism." For Durkheim, in a piece of high admiration, Taine had created "l'empirisme rationaliste."

Some of the quotations above show that the concept of system or structure which a later age has found in Saussure was fully developed by Taine with the same broad implications and application that have since been redeveloped from Saussure's linguistic thought. In this sense Taine is a true structuralist. Saussure is also known for his distinction between the social, collective *langue* that forms a structure "où tout se tient," and the individual manifestation that occurs in the *parole*. This parallels a methodological distinction that is also made by Taine and for which he, like Saussure, was criticized. In the second preface to *Essais* Taine noted that his critics had blamed him for neglecting the individual's role by dealing only with "national characteristics and general situations as the only great forces in history." He answered that they forgot that "the great forces are only the sum of inclinations and dispositions of individuals, that our general terms are collective expressions by means of which we, under one of our points of view, bring together twenty or thirty million souls inclined to act in the same way." For Saussure any change in the system of the *langue* is initiated in the *parole*, a contention that many have found paradoxical. But it agrees with Taine's view of culture and history that any change in the system comes from the outside, hence the mandatory attention to "les petits faits" that alert us to such changes. Only in this manner does it become possible to identify causes in history and to understand it.

The distinction between *langue* and *parole* follows from the insistence on structure and system. The same is true of Saussure's distinction between synchrony and diachrony, that is between the study of the material in a given state, "à un moment donné," and the study of features in time and change. Taine made the distinction in the Introduction to his *Histoire de la littérature anglaise* when he identified the three basic cultural forces as race, milieu, and moment. Race embraces the given "interior" force, the milieu the "exterior," and these two suffice for the description of a culture "à un moment donné." But to these two must be added a third, "le moment," "for in addition to the interior and exterior forces, there is the work those forces have already done together, and this work itself plays a role in the making of the one that follows; along with the permanent thrust and the given milieu there is the acquired speed." A few years later, in the 1866 preface to *Essais*, Taine became more explicit. Here he distinguished between the study of "la liaison des choses *simultanées*" and of "la liaison des choses *successives.*" Being a system, the former are governed by mutual dependencies (following Cuvier), while the latter is affected by the conditions supplied by the previous system (following Geoffroy Saint-Hilaire). It was Saussure who introduced the terms *synchronique* and *diachronique*, of which only the latter is strictly speaking new; the former is old and refers to the study of chronology and the simultaneity of events in history. But he introduced them only after he had observed that the sciences would be wise to pay attention to the axes on which the things they study are situated, "l'axe des *simultaneités*" and "l'axe des *successivités.*" The terminological agreements between Taine and Saussure (in this case as in several others also embracing Durkheim) can be extended, though they fall short of the more important conceptual similarities.

Taine was forced to make the distinction between simultaneity and successivity for this reason, often made clear in his writings. Cuvier's principles of comparative anatomy had supplied the method for the study of structural systems. Since Cuvier was totally committed to the fixity of species, his anatomy was entirely synchronic in regard to its objects of study. Though species can be annihilated by geological catastrophes, they are never transformed, and new ones never arise. To take account of change Taine turned to Geoffroy Saint-Hilaire's principles of anatomical connections and balance, developed within comparative embryology. Cuvier strongly opposed Geoffroy's diachrony (as he did Lamarck's), but Taine often expounded both in detail, contrasting Cuvier's "ahistorical" method to Geoffroy's "historical" method. Taine explained and illustrated these principles most fully perhaps in *De l'idéal dans l'art;* there are clear traces of his exposition in Saussure's discussion of synchrony and diachrony. This work also shows that for Taine the synchronic description of particular epochs must precede diachronic analysis, and that he, like Saussure, took language to be a fundamental cultural fact.

Among today's Saussurian commonplaces are also the linearity of speech and the arbitrariness of the linguistic sign. Taine never expressly discussed either one, but he obviously took both principles for granted—thus without the arbitrariness the principle of *valeur* would not arise, as Saussure pointed out. Both are, however, basic doctrines in the linguistic philosophy of the eighteenth century, prominent in Condillac and in his disciples late in the century, the *idéologues* with Destutt de Tracy as the most important figure. Since this work was soon, already by 1800, called the materialist and sensualist foundation of the French Revolution, it became the deliberate aim of the reaction to wash it off the record, as if there had been no respectable French philosophy since the seventeenth century and Descartes, who could so easily be—and was—made to serve the needs of the reaction.

Taine had opened his crusade for the eighteenth century long before the first pages of *De l'intelligence* credited the philosophy of signs to Condillac. Often calling him a follower of Condillac, contemporaries counted it one of Taine's greatest services to modern thought that he had restored respect for the philosophy that had been ridiculed, misrepresented, and repressed by the ruling and official academic philosophers. The result was a resurgence of interest in the eighteenth century, and especially in Condillac; it is amply illustrated in French publication during the later decades of the century. In this context the linguistic philosophy gained special prominence. Saussure's two principles of linearity and arbitrariness did not need to be discovered; they were old and could be found in available texts. It is also well known that Taine was the first important admirer of Stendhal, who revered Destutt de Tracy above all other philosophers.

I do not think than my analysis leaves room for doubt that Saussure, like many of his contemporaries, was deeply indebted to Taine—and much more evidence can be adduced than I have space for here. No other source contains all of Saussure's basic linguistic conceptions and methodological principles so tightly locked into a single, fully articulated system; and no set of separate sources presents these elements individually in a manner that so closely resembles Saussure's. What Ribot did for psychology and Durkheim for sociology, Saussure did for linguistics. My argument helps explain certain agreements between the linguistic thought of Saussure and Wilhelm von Humboldt, who was indebted to the linguistic philosophy of the *idéologues* and especially of Destutt de Tracy. My conclusion allows that the thought that found expression in the *Cours* took shape during the Paris years, when Saussure was still a very young man. Taine's writings were often reissued; when *De l'intelligence* in 1900 reached its ninth edition, 12,000 copies were in print, an astonishing number for a large and difficult two-volume work. This conclusion overrides many implausible, often ill-informed and conceptually weak arguments that have been presented in the extensive recent literature on Saussure's background. This background has been located almost exclusively in German philological work, often with disregard of obvious chronological problems and silence about Saussure's severe censure of German scholarship.

Among the arguments that have been seriously advanced are the opinions that Saussure owed a wholesale debt to a German book published as late as 1891, that this work in turn may have drawn its "Systembegriff" from eighteenth-century German pietistic theology and philosophy; that the concept of value comes from a German work published as late as 1902, and that the distinction between synchrony and diachrony is merely a restatement of the difference between descriptive and historical-genetic linguistics that had been noted by German philologists. This last opinion is conceptually inadmissible; it simply misses the point, as Hjelmslev forcefully pointed out in 1928.

The concept of system and structure was latent in comparative philology from the beginning, introduced around 1800 by Silvestre de Sacy on Cuvier's model. But it is implausible that Saussure would have recreated it from the source when Taine so fully and often expounded it with great clarity as the core of his method. Comparative philology had not taken account of Geoffroy Saint-Hilaire's diachronic principles. The often debated similarities between Durkheim and Saussure assume a new aspect, for they take their place within mutual indebtedness to Taine. At the same time the chronological problems vanish that are raised by the Durkheim relation. This is also true of Saussure's reputed debt to the Russian linguist Kruszewski and to the Austrian philosopher Heinrich Gomperz, who both cite Taine's *De l'intelligence* with approval, as well as John Stuart Mill and Alexander Bain to whom Taine also often acknowledged his debt. It was Destutt de Tracy, perhaps following Rousseau, who first gave a name to a prominent principle in Locke and Condillac when he said that language is "une institution sociale," a principle that is crucial in Saussure.

Today Taine is virtually forgotten, and the literature on Saussure has never sought to relate the two figures. But in Saussure's own time Taine was the ruling intellectual influence. It is not surprising that the innovative turn in linguistics should have an extra-linguistic impulse. Established systems are not likely to renew themselves by their own devices, especially not when those systems, then as today, are the jealously guarded pride and property of institutionalized academic hierarchies. The history of Taine's legacy to Saussure illustrates what both maintained: that only external factors change established systems.

Mallarmé and Literary Space

Maurice Blanchot

The poem or literary work seems to depend on a discourse that can never break off because it does not speak, but is. The poem is not this discourse—it is a genesis; the discourse never begins, only repeats itself over and over. But the poet is someone who has heard the discourse, has become its interpreter and mediator and has reduced it to silence as he speaks it. In this discourse the poem is on the verge of a beginning because all that begins is tested in the utter impotence of this reiteration, in this fruitless prolixity, this superfluity of helplessness, of what is not the poem and ruins the poem while consolidating its own endless inoperativeness through the poem. Though this discourse may be the poem's source, it is a source that has somehow run dry in order that it may become resource. No poet—no writer or "creator"—can extract his work from this essential inoperativeness. He cannot, unaided, make the pure speech of beginnings burst forth from that which is at the source. Therefore a poem is only a poem when it becomes the shared privacy of someone who writes and of someone who reads, the passionately unfurled space of a mutual conflict between speaker and hearer. And he who writes is equally he who has "heard" what is endless and ceaseless, who has heard it as discourse, penetrated its significance, submitted to its demands—he who has lost himself in its depth and yet, because he has endured it as it should be endured, has brought it to a halt, made it accessible in its discontinuity and, containing it forcefully within such limits, has uttered it and measuring it, has mastered it.

Mallarmé's account of the transformation he experienced when he began to appreciate the significance of the act of writing refers to this phe-

From *The Sirens' Song: Selected Essays by Maurice Blanchot*, edited by Gabriel Josipovici and translated by Sacha Rabinovitch. © 1982 by The Harvester Press Ltd. Indiana University Press, 1982.

nomenon. When he says, "I have experienced very disturbing symptoms provoked by the simple act of writing" it is the last words that matter, for they reveal something crucial, acknowledge something drastic whose sphere and substance is "the simple act of writing" (*Correspondence*). Writing thus becomes a life-and-death activity involving a radical upheaval. And it is to this same upheaval that he refers when he says: "Digging so deep into the poem I have unfortunately encountered two hopeless voids. One of them is nothingness" (ibid.), or the absence of gods; the other is his own death. Here again the restraint of this casual remark which could just as well refer to a simple manual craft, conveys a world of significance. "Digging so deep into the poem" the poet foregoes the security of being, encounters godlessness, dwells with this absence, becomes responsible for it and accepts both its risks and its advantages. He who digs so deep into the poem must renounce all idols, break with everything; reality is no longer his horizon nor the future his habitat since he has no right to hope—hopelessness is compulsory. He who digs deep into the poem confronts death, the void of his own death.

When Mallarmé tries to describe the language revealed to him in "the simple act of writing" he talks about "the twofold condition of speech, blunt or immediate here, there essential" ("Variations on a Subject"). This equally blunt distinction is none the less difficult to grasp since Mallarmé sees what he has so radically distinguished as cosubstantial and defines each in turn as silence. Thus for blunt speech it might suffice "for each one to exchange human thought, by taking or putting a coin silently in someone else's hand"; it is silent because it is worthless—simple wordlessness, a mere exchange where nothing is exchanged and where nothing is real but the process which is nothing. But the same applies to poetic discourse, the discourse whose power consists in not being, in evoking, in selflessness and total absence—the language of unreality, fictitious and fiction-making, emerging from silence to return to silence.

Blunt speech "refers to the reality of things." "To relate, to teach, even to describe" is to present objects as present, to "represent" them. Essential speech distances objects, makes them vanish, is always allusive and suggests or evokes. But if to distance a fact of nature, to perceive it through this distancing, to transpose it "in its quivering near-disappearance" is the function of essential speech, it is also the function of thought. Thought is pure speech; it is the supreme language, a language whose absence can only be perceived when we consider the infinite variety of idioms:

> to think being to write without accessories, or whispering but immortal speech being still silent, the diversity on earth of idioms stops anyone from uttering the words which, otherwise, would find themselves to be, at a stroke, in substance truth itself.
>
> (Ibid.)

(Which is Cratylus' ideal as well as the definition of automatic writing.) Thus one is tempted to say that the language of thought is preeminently the language of poetry and that meaning, pure concept and idea must be the poet's concern since they are the only means of shifting the load of matter and of evading its overwhelming shapelessness. "Poetry, near thought."

However, blunt speech is far from blunt. It does not represent what is present. Mallarmé does not want to "enclose in the subtle paper of the volume . . . the intrinsic dense wood of the trees" (ibid.). Yet nothing is more foreign to trees than the word trees as it is commonly used. It is a word that names nothing, represents nothing, survives in nothing, a word that hardly is a word and vanishes as if by magic when it has been said. What could be more like silence? Yet it "serves." And this, apparently, is what makes all the difference: it is used, usual, useful; it involves us in reality, refers to reality and real life where purpose is expressed and the need for a purpose is imperative. It is indeed a mere nothing, vacuity itself, yet active, operant, constructive—the pure silence of negation which gives rise to the feverish tumult of our activities.

Essential speech is the reverse. It is commanding—commands attention but commands nothing. Furthermore, it is quite foreign to thought, to the thought which seeks to dispel primal darkness. For poetry attracts no less than it releases, revives all the scattered, ignored and drifting flotsam; in it words are re-made "basic" and the word *nuit*, despite its brightness, merges with the night. (After deploring language's lack of "material truthfulness"—the fact that *jour* has a sombre ring to it and *nuit* a bright one—Mallarmé decides that it is precisely this lack which vindicates poetry: poetry is the word's "supreme complement," "it compensates, philosophically, for the penury of language." What is this penury? Languages do not possess the reality they express, being foreign to the reality of things, to the obscure, natural profundity that belongs to the imagined reality which is the human world, separate from being and a tool for beings.)

In blunt speech, immediate speech, although language as such is silent, beings talk and—as a consequence of the *use* to which it is put, because it serves as a link with reality, as a tool in a world of tools where value and utility are the speakers—it is an idiom in which beings express themselves as values, assume the stable aspect of independent objects and acquire the assurance of immutability.

Blunt speech is neither blunt nor immediate. But it gives the impression of being such. It is extremely considered, laden with history. But as a rule it is as though, in the ordinary process of living, we were unable to recognise ourselves as components of time and guardians of the future, so that we see speech as the means of unmediated vision, the symbol of immediate reality, always identical and always available. Immediate speech may indeed be a link with unmediated reality or with that which is immediately accessible, with our environment, but the immediacy conveyed by ordinary language is only dim, totally foreign distance clothed in familiarity: the unfamiliar seen as customary because of the veil language casts over it and because speech always creates illusions. Words contain the ingredient which conceals them and, in consequence, their mediation (which destroys immediacy) acquires the immediacy, novelty and innocence of originality. Moreover words, which communicate an impression of immediacy while providing only that to which we are accustomed, create the illusion that immediacy is familiar, so that it seems essentially to represent the happy security of natural harmonies, the familiarity of a native land, instead of that which is most terrible and disturbing: the fallacy of essential solitude.

In ordinary discourse language—in so far as it is the being of language and the language of being—maintains a silence which enables beings to speak and in which they find oblivion and comfort. When Mallarmé refers to essential discourse he either contrasts it to ordinary discourse, which is the illusion or promise of an immediacy that is in fact only familiarity, or else he assimilates it to the language of thought, that silent process which confirms our decision not to be, to be separated from being and, by making such a separation actual, to create the world—a silence which is the outcome and the expression of meaning itself. But this language of thought is nevertheless "current" discourse as well—it always refers us back to reality either as a purposeless task and a risky undertaking or as a stable position where we are entitled to assume that we are safe.

Thus the language of poetry is not merely opposed to ordinary language but to the language of thought too. Such language does not refer to reality—neither to reality as haven nor to reality as purpose. It distances reality and puts an end to purpose; it silences reality—it does not express human preoccupations, aims or activities but expresses human silence. But how does it do so? When beings are silent being becomes speech and speech strives to be. The language of poetry is not one person's idiom: nobody speaks it and nobody is what speaks it but it is as if speech talked to itself. Thus language acquires its full significance, becomes essential; language speaks as what is essential so that when the poet speaks it can be said that such speech is essential. This implies primarily that since words take the initiative they do not have to indicate objects or speak in somebody's name but are their own end. Henceforth it is not Mallarmé who speaks but language speaking to itself—language as poetry and the poetry of language.

In this perspective poetry emerges as a complex of words whose relationship, structure and authority consist of sounds, images and rhythms contained in an eminently autonomous and unified space. Thus the poet works with pure language and the language of such work reverts to its essence. He creates a language-object like the painter who, rather than reproducing with his colours that which exists, seeks the point where his colours become a creation. Or again—as Rilke maintained in the age of Expressionism, and as Ponge, perhaps, maintains today—he seeks to create a "poem-object" which will be the speech of the speechless, to turn the poem into form, existence, being: into a Creation.

And yet this powerful linguistic structure, this object from which chance has been carefully eliminated, whose survival depends on nothing but itself and which is based on itself alone, though we may call it a creation, something wrought, is from this point of view, neither. It is a creation in so far as it is structured, composed and premeditated, but in this respect it is a creation like any other, like any object fashioned with professional care and skill: not a work of art, a work which is the outcome of art, in which art emerges from an unfruitful timelessness as the single, over-whelming assertion of a genesis. And similarly the poem seen as an in-dependent, self-sufficient object, a language-object created for itself alone, a monad of words which reflects nothing but the nature of words, may well be a reality, a specific "being" of exceptional value and significance, but *a* "being" and therefore still very far from being, from that which evades every definition and every form of existence.

Mallarmé's personal experience seems to have begun at the precise moment when his interest shifted from the finished work, the work seen as a given poem or painting, to the work as quest for its own origins, merging with its origins—the "horrendous vision of a pure work." This became for him the whole significance and scope contained in the "simple act of writing." What is the poem? What is that language of the poem? When Mallarmé asks "Does something like Literature exist?" this question is already literature—literature in quest of its essence. Such a question cannot be ignored. What are the consequences involved in the fact that we possess a literature? If we say that "something like Literature exists" what effect will this have on existence?

Mallarmé was deeply troubled by the nature of literary creation. A work of art is something which exists. That is its purpose: to be, to make present "the word itself: *it is.*" "That is the whole mystery."

> That is what I tell myself, less articulately, in my random, solitary mutterings, which you none the less unravel, it is, yes, in respect to this precise statement: *it is*, I have some notes before me, and it pervades the furthest reaches of my mind. The whole mystery is there: to prove by two plus two, in view of a crucial purety, the hidden identities which consume and erode objects.
>
> (Letter to Vielé Griffin, 8 August 1891)

Yet neither can it be said that a work is part of existence, that it exists. On the contrary, it never exists in the manner of ordinary objects or beings. We should say, in reply to the above question, that Literature does not exist, or that if it occurs then it is something that does not occur like any existing object. Obviously language is contained in it, "displayed" in it, asserts itself with greater authority than in any other form of human ac-tivity. But in writing, language is wholly realised so that it has only the reality of the whole; it is the whole and nothing else, always on the verge of shifting from all to nothing. Such a shift is essential, is part of the essence of language, precisely because nothing is at work in words. As we know words have the power to make things vanish, make them appear as absence, assume the appearance of what is really a disappearance, a presence which, in its turn, becomes absence again through a process of erosion which is the life and soul of words, which makes them luminous when they are extinguished, scintillations of the dark. But words, having the power to make things "arise" from their absence and dominate this absence, are further able to vanish into things, to become wonderfully absent in the midst of all that they evoke, all that they proclaim while cancelling themselves out, all that they perpetually achieve through a process of self-immolation. In this they are like the mysterious act of suicide which is precisely what gives its full authority to the climactic moment of *igitur*.

Such is the crucial point to which Mallarmé returns again and again as to the heart of the danger to which the literary experience exposes us. It is the point at which the achievement of language coincides with its disappearance, at which everything is expressed (he says "nothing remains unexpressed") everything is speech, while speech is only the appearance of that which has disappeared—imaginary, unceasing and interminable.

This point is pure ambiguity. On the one hand, in the poem, it is that which the poem achieves, that in which it asserts itself; it is the point at which the poem must admit no other luminous evidence than that it is. In this respect it is the poem's actuality, and only the poem makes it actual. But on the other hand it is "a presence of Midnight," the other side, the point at which nothing ever begins, the vacant depth of the inoperativeness of being, the hopeless, sterile region where the writer's work becomes an endless quest for its origins.

Indeed, it is the crux and essence of ambiguity. Undoubtedly when we reach this point, through the impetus and power of the poem, only the poem and the poem's achievement make it possible. Let us take another look at the poem: what could be more real, more obvious—in it language becomes "luminous evidence." However, such evidence proves nothing, is based on nothing, is fluctuating elusiveness. It is limitless and timeless. What we take for words is "virtually like a trail of flashes," a quickening, a scintillation of excitement, a process of reciprocity which illuminates nonexistence, where nonexistence is reflected in the pure sinuosity of reflections that reflect nothing. Thus "all becomes suspense, a fragmentary arrangement with alternatives and contrasts." Thus, while the flame of unreality as language flares up only to subside, we are confronted with the unfamiliar presence of real things as absence, pure fiction, the site of celebrations where "solitary, unrestricted festivities" dazzle. One might be tempted to say that the poem oscillates mysteriously between its presence as language and the absence of real objects, like the pendulum in *Igitur* that, by keeping time, abolishes time; except that such a presence is itself oscillating perpetuity, oscillating between the successive unreality of limits that limit nothing, and the total achievement of this process—language as the essence of language in which its ability to refer to nothing and to become nothing is achieved as its essence, pervading every poem and disappearing in each "total rhythm," "with which is silence."

In the poem language is never real at any one stage of its progress, for language is all there is to the poem, and its essence consists in its having no other reality than this. However in this "all" which is its essence, in which it is essential, language is also eminently unreal—it is the total realisation of unreality (absolute fiction, and claiming to be such) which, having "consumed" and "eroded" all that exists and left every possible form of being in abeyance, encounters the ineliminable residue, that which is irreducible. And what is this residue? "The statement: it is," a statement which constitutes the basis of all words yet which is concealed by them, which, thus concealed, is their reality, their potentiality that only occurs when they cease, the flash where they flare and expire, swiftly, in a flower, on some ethereal transparency, a lightning flash, a flashing luminosity.

The lightning flash flares from the poem, as the poem's own flame, its total reality, its simultaneous vision. This is the instant at which the poem, so as to bestow being and existence on the "illusion" that "Literature exists," decrees total exclusion and thus excludes itself—so that the instant at which "all reality dissolves" in the power of the poem is also the instant at which the poem dissolves and is no sooner done than it is undone. This in itself is highly ambiguous. But ambiguity goes deeper. For this instant which is, as it were, the work's work, which apart from any significance, any historical or aesthetic assertion, expresses the work's existence, this instant is such only in so far as in it the work accepts the ordeal which always destroys the work beforehand and always reestablishes its excess of hopeless inoperativeness.

This is the most mysterious stage of the literary process. We can see why a poem must be the single clarity of that which is extinguished and through which everything is extinguished; why it can only exist when total negation is the proof of total assertion. So much we can understand. Even if it offends our need for peace, simplicity, and quiet we understand it in depth, like the profound determination which is ourselves and enables us to be only when we have risked our all to renounce its permanence and its privilege. Yes, we understand that in this respect the poem is pure genesis, the first and last moment when being emerges from the choice of freedom which enables us to finally exclude it without yet including it in the appearance of beings. But the poem's need to proclaim being precisely at the moment of interruption, "the statement: *it is,*" the point it illuminates while such illumination consumes it, we cannot fail to realise that this need is also the poem's impossibility because it is that which forbids access to the poem, the "beyond" where nothing comes of being, where nothing is accomplished, the depth of being's inoperativeness.

Thus it would seem that the point to which the poem leads is more than simply that at which it is realised in its glorious disappearance, at which it expresses a genesis, expresses being in a freedom which excludes it—for this is also the point to which it cannot lead because it is always the point at which there is no poem.

Are we perhaps over-simplifying when we reverse the process which is that of our active life, attempt no more than this reversal, and then think we have discovered the process we call art? Indeed such a simplification is no different from that which makes us perceive the image after the object, say: first there is the object, then the image, as if the image were merely a distancing, a refutation and transposition of the object. Likewise, we tend to say that art does not reproduce "reality" or copy it, that art is to be found where the artist, having abandoned the ordinary world, has gradually eliminated all that is serviceable, imitable and related to active life. Thus art is seen as the world's silence, the silence or neutralisation of what is familiar and actual in the world, just as the image is the object's absence.

The process thus described fails through over-simplification like all popular theories. Such theories imply that we can understand art since they enable us to imagine how artistic creativity begins. However the image they provide does not correspond to the psychology of creativity. No artist ever proceeds from the use to which he puts an object in reality to the canvas on which the object has become a painting; it is never enough for him to ignore an object's use, to neutralise the object so as to achieve the freedom of a painting. Indeed, it is because, by a basic inversion, he is already at one with the painting's requirements that, when considering a given object, he is not content with *seeing* it as it might be if it were obsolete, but makes the object the point of intersection of the work's requirements, and thus the point at which choices decrease, notions of value and utility vanish and the world dissolves. It is because he is already in a different time-scale—in the otherness of time, outside the process of time, exposed to the ordeal of essential solitude and under its spell—it is because he has ventured up to this "point" that, submitting to the work's demands, wholly possessed by it, he sees the objects of everyday life in a different perspective, deprived of their everyday utility, unadulterated and raised through a series of stylisations to that instant of delicate balance where they become paintings. In other words we cannot proceed from "reality" to art either by way of the process of refutation and resistance described above, nor in any other way. We always proceed from art towards what seems to be a neutralised semblance of reality—and which, in fact, only appears such to the conventionally conditioned eye of the inadequate beholder who is riveted to the world of purpose and capable, at best, of proceeding from reality to the painting.

He who does not belong to the work as genesis or to that other time-scale where the work is a quest for its essence, will never produce a work of art. But he who belongs to that time-scale also belongs to the great void of inoperativity where being is put to no positive use.

Or, to put this in yet another way, when an overfamiliar work seems to proclaim the poet's right "to purify the dialect of the tribe" does this imply that the poet is someone who has the ability or the creative skill to do no more than transpose "blunt and immediate" speech into essential speech, to raise the silent mediocrity of current speech to the accomplished

silence of a poem where, in a supreme disappearance, total absence becomes total presence? This simply is not possible. It makes no more sense
than to say that writing consists in merely using ordinary words with
consummate skill, in having a more than usually well stocked memory or
an exceptional ear for linguistic harmonies. Writing only begins where to
write consists in drawing close to the point at which nothing is revealed,
at which from the depth of concealment speaking is still only the shadow
of speech, a language which is an image of language, an imaginary language
and the language of imagery, the language nobody speaks, a whisper of
that what which is ceaseless and endless and must be *silenced* in order that
we may be heard.

When we observe Giacometti's sculptures there comes a point at which
they are no longer subjected to the fluctuations of appearance or the laws
of perspective. We see them absolutely: not cut down to size but abstracted
from size, sizeless and in space, dominating space through their ability to
replace it by an intractable, inexistent depth—the depth of imagery. This
point at which we see time as sizeless, involves us in infinity and is the
point where "here" coincides with "nowhere." To write is to discover this
point. Nobody writes who has not endowed language with the ability to
maintain or to establish contact with this point.

Mallarmé: Poetry and Syntax: What the Gypsy Knew

Barbara Johnson

PIVOTAL INTELLIGIBILITY

Syntax is somehow not an inherently exciting subject. But without it, no subject would ever be capable of exciting us. Ever present but often taken for granted, like skin—which, as everyone knows, is a thing that when you have it outside, it helps keep your insides in—, syntax is a thing that when you have it in your surface structure, it helps keep your deep structure deep. But what happens when you examine syntax as such? What can be said about this necessary but insufficient condition for saying anything at all?

Faced with this question, I did what any modern student of poetics would do: I went to see what Mallarmé said about it. In his essay on the uses of obscurity, *Le Mystère dans les lettres* (*The Mystery in Letters*), Mallarmé writes:

> Quel pivot, j'entends, dans ces contrastes, à l'intelligibilité? il faut une garantie—
>
> La Syntaxe—
>
> [What pivot, I understand, in these contrasts, for intelligibility?/ A guarantee is needed—/Syntax—]

It should be noted that Mallarmé does not say that syntax guarantees intelligibility. He says it guarantees the *pivoting* of intelligibility. Intelligibility, indeed, is not an entirely positive value in Mallarmé's essay. It plays a role analogous to that of the word *entertainment* in today's discussions of art or pedagogy: it is a bone thrown to those who will never understand and a necessary evil or necessary tease for those who will. Mallarmé contrasts ordinary writers with the manipulator of obscurity by saying that the former "puisent à quelque encrier sans Nuit la vaine couche suffisante d'intelligibilité que lui s'oblige, aussi, à observer, mais pas seule" ("draw from some Nightless inkwell the vain sufficient layer of intelligibility that he, too, obliges himself to observe, but not exclusively"). Using an almost Chomskyan distinction between depth and surface, he explains:

> Tout écrit, extérieurement à son trésor, doit, par égard envers ceux dont il emprunte, après tout, pour un objet autre, le langage, présenter, avec les mots, un sens même indifférent: on gagne de détourner l'oisif, charmé que rien ne l'y concerne, à première vue.
> Salut, exact, de part et d'autre—
> Si, tout de même, n'inquiétait je ne sais quel *miroitement, en dessous,* peu séparable de la *surface* concédée à la rétine—il attire le soupçon: les malins, entre le public, réclamant de couper court, opinent, avec sérieux, que, juste, la teneur est inintelligible. (emphasis mine here and passim)

> [Any piece of writing, outside of its treasures, ought, in deference to those from whom it borrows, after all, for a different purpose, language, to present, with words, a meaning however indifferent: one profits from thus turning away the idlers, charmed that nothing concerns them in it, at first sight.
> Greetings and just deserts on both sides—
> If, nevertheless, there were not I don't know what glimmering from underneath, hardly separable from the surface conceded to the retina—which awakens suspicion: the wise guys in the public, demanding that it be cut short, pronounce their seriously considered opinion that, precisely, the tenor is unintelligible.]

It is thus an obscure perception of the hidden possibility of obscurity that attracts the suspicions of the sly, casual reader, who would otherwise have been satisfied with whatever intelligibility the surface of the writing might present. Obscurity, in other words, is not encountered on the way to intelligibility, like an obstacle, but rather lies beyond it, as what prevents the reader from being satisfied with his own reading. Obscurity is an excess, not a deficiency, of meaning.

The poet does not seek to be unintelligible; his writing enacts the impossibility of a transparent, neutral style through its plays of depth and surface, darkness and light:

> Je partis d'intentions, comme on demande du style—neutre l'imagine-t-on—que son expression ne se fonce par le plongeon ni ne ruisselle d'éclaboussures jaillies: fermé à l'alternative qui est la loi.

[I began with intentions as one demands of style—neutral style, one imagines—that its expression not plunge down into darkness nor surge up with a stream of splashes: closed to the alternative that is the law.]

The opposition between *plonger* (plunge) and *jaillir* (surge up) here merges with the opposition between darkness and light through the use of the verb *se foncer*, which means both "to become darker" and "to dive deeper." In going on to say, after speaking of "the alternative that is the law," that syntax acts as a pivot "in these contrasts," Mallarmé is making the very *fact of alternation* into the fundamental law of writing. Writing becomes an alternation between obscurity and clarity rather than a pursuit of either, a rhythm of intelligibility and mystery, just as time is a rhythm of days and nights:

> Ce procédé, jumeau, intellectuel, notable dans les symphonies, qui le trouvèrent au répertoire de la nature et du ciel.

> [This procedure, twin and intellectual, notable in symphonies, which found it in the repertory of nature and the sky.]

It should not be forgotten that day and night, *jour* and *nuit*, are in themselves examples of the law of simultaneous contradictory alternatives, since Mallarmé complains elsewhere that their sounds and their meanings are directly opposed:

> A côté d'*ombre*, opaque, *ténèbres* se fonce peu; quelle déception, devant la perversité conférant à *jour* comme à *nuit*, contradictoirement, des timbres obscur ici, là clair. Le souhait d'un terme de splendeur brillant, ou qu'il s'éteigne, inverse; quant à des alternatives lumineuses simples—*Seulement, sachons n'existerait pas le vers*: lui, philosophiquement rémunère le défaut des langues, complément supérieur. (emphasis in original)

> [Alongside *ombre* (shade), which is opaque, *ténèbres* (shadows) is not particularly dark; what a disappointment to face the perversity that gives to *jour* (day) and *nuit* (night), contradictorily, a dark timbre here and a light one there. The hope of finding a term of splendor glowing, or else, inversely, being extinguished; as far as simple luminous alternatives are concerned—*Only*, let us note that *verse would not exist*: it is verse that philosophically compensates for the faults of languages, a superior complement.]

Verse, then, in its rhythms and rhymes, is a practice of pivoting, as its etymology (*versus*) indicates. It is an enactment of the alternative as law and of law as alternative, necessitated precisely by the perverse way language has of disappointing the search for simple alternatives. It is because language does *not* function as a perfect light meter, does not correspond to any "simple luminous alternatives," that constant alternation between clarity and obscurity becomes its law.

While pursuing this concept of syntax as a pivot for the turnings of darkness and light, I was startled to discover that the word *syntaxis* occurs in the title of a treatise by the second-century Greek astronomer, Ptolemy, whose geocentric view of the relations among the bodies in the solar system also deals with the question of what in the world turns around what. Could Ptolemy's outmoded *Syntaxis* tell us anything about syntax and modern poetry? Is there a relation between grammar and gravitation? Could the relations between clarity and obscurity really be as simple—or as complex—as night and day?

The question Ptolemy's work mis-answers is, of course, the question of a center. Ptolemy saw the universe revolving around the earth; Copernicus saw the earth revolving around the sun in a universe in which the sun turns out to be merely one of many stars. The displacement of the center from earth to sun is also a movement away from the centrality of man himself; the human observer is no longer the pivot of the universe but only a parasite on a satellite. Freud, another revolutionizer of the status of man, compared his discovery of the unconscious precisely to a Copernican revolution. As Lacan puts it:

> It was in fact the so-called Copernican revolution to which Freud himself compared his discovery, emphasizing that it was once again a question of the place man assigns to himself at the centre of a universe. . . . It is not a question of knowing whether I speak of myself in a way that conforms to what I am, but rather of knowing whether I am the same person as the one I am speaking of. . . . Is the place that I occupy as the subject of a signifier concentric or excentric, in relation to the place I occupy as subject of the signified?—That is the question.
>
> (*Ecrits*, "Agency of the Letter in the Unconscious")

For Lacan, this psychoanalytical Copernican revolution takes place as a rewriting of the Cartesian *cogito*. Instead of "I think, therefore I am," we have: "I think where I am not, therefore I am where I do not think. . . . I am not wherever I am the plaything of my thought; I think of what I am where I do not think to think."

This mention of Descartes brings us back to the question of syntax, not only because Lacan has syntactically strung out the *cogito* but also because the modern theorist of the concept of syntax, Chomsky, is a self-proclaimed Cartesian. After contrasting the rationalist view of knowledge proposed by Descartes and Leibniz with the empiricist views proposed by Hume and the modern behaviorists, Chomsky writes of his own project: "A general linguistic theory of the sort described earlier . . . must . . . be regarded as a specific hypothesis, of an essentially rationalist cast, as to the nature of mental structures and processes" (*Aspects of the Theory of Syntax*). But who is the syntaxer that will play Lacan to Chomsky's Descartes? Who is it that will revolutionize ratiocentric syntax?

The syntactical Copernicus we are seeking is, of course, none other than Mallarmé, who describes himself as "profondément et scrupuleusement syntaxier" ("profoundly and scrupulously a syntaxer") (Letter to Maurice Guillemot), and whose *cogito* could be not "I think, therefore I am," but "I write, therefore I disappear." Mallarmé, although he is historically prior to Chomsky, does indeed displace the verb-centered structures of Chomskyan grammars, putting a definitive crick in the syntax of what was once known as "la clarté française." In Mallarmé's syntax, there is often no central verb, or no verb at all, or a series of seemingly subordinate verbs with no main one. The sentences that conform to "le génie de la langue" are either semantically ambiguous or skeletons draped with conflicting interruptions. Mallarmé's syntax is never confused; it is, as he says, profound and scrupulous, as decentered as possible without being cut loose from the gravitational pull of incompatible grammatical possibilities.

Thus we can say that Mallarmé is to Chomsky as Copernicus is to Ptolemy as Freud is to Descartes, in that the former in each case works out a strategically rigorous decentering of the structure described by the latter, not by abandoning that structure but by multiplying the forces at work in the field of which that structure is a part. It is not by chance that Lacan, who makes much of Freud's discovery as a Copernican revolution, should also stylistically be one of the most important of Mallarmé's syntactic descendants. No one indeed in twentieth-century French literature is more "profondément et scrupuleusement syntaxier" than Lacan.

THE SYNTAX OF ASSERTION

> *If you do know that* here is one hand, *we'll grant you all the rest.*
> —WITTGENSTEIN, *On Certainty*

In order to analyze further the implications of the Mallarméan revolution in syntax, let us first consider two facets of Mallarmé's syntactic practices. While traditional syntax is what makes meaning decidable—what makes it impossible, for example, for "John kills Paul" to mean "Paul kills John"—, Mallarmé's syntax, as has often been noted, is precisely what makes the meaning of his poetry undecidable. In giving equal legitimacy to two contradictory syntactic arrangements in the same assertion, Mallarmé renders the very nature of assertion problematic.

In Mallarmé's critical prose, where his syntactical revolution is carried out with equal precision, a second type of problematization of the status of assertion is often manifest. To take just one example, consider the following remarks about "literary art":

> Son sortilège, à lui, si ce n'est libérer, hors d'une poignée de poussière ou réalité sans l'enclore, au livre, même comme text, la dispersion volatile soit l'esprit, qui n'a que faire de rien outre la muscialité de tout.

> [Its spellbinding power, if it is not the liberation, out of a handful of dust or reality without enclosing it, in the book, even as a text, of the volatile dispersal, that is, the mind—which has to do with nothing outside the musicality of all.]

In violation of one of the most fundamental rules of syntax, there is no main verb in this passage. Where we might expect "son sortilège est," we find "son sortilège, si ce n'est," The verb *to be* has become hypothetical, negative, and subordinate. The syntax of the description of the relations between literature and the world withdraws it from the possibility of affirmation. In other words, what at first looks like a statement that literature disperses rather than states is *itself* dispersed, not stated. Instead of affirming that literature does not state, Mallarmé's syntax *enacts* the very incapacity to state which it is incapable of stating.

It is not by chance that the verb *to be* should be the verb Mallarmé most often skips or conjugates otherwise. What Mallarmé's syntactical revolution amounts to is a decentering of the epistemological or ontological functioning of language. The syntax of polyvalent, decentered, or failed assertion reveals the unreliability of language as a conveyer of anything other than the functioning of its own structure, which is perhaps what Mallarmé is here calling "la musicalité de tout." This does not mean that language speaks only about itself, but that it is incapable of *saying* exactly what it is *doing*.

In the wake of Mallarmé, twentieth-century poetry has questioned the nature and possibility of assertion in a number of other ways. In surrealistic or automatic writing, effects of strangeness are often achieved by replacing normal semantic associations with bizarre incompatibilities within a syntax that remains relatively intact. "The earth is blue like an orange," for example, can only achieve its flash of impossibility through the tranquil assertiveness of its structure. Another modern phenomenon, pictorial or concrete poetry, suspends the syntax of assertion by transferring the reader's attention from the content of the signified to the typographical syntax of the signifier. It is through these and other poetic procedures that modern poetry makes explicit the problematizations enacted in Mallarmé's syntax. But must an assertion be—syntactically or semantically—manhandled in order to be problematic? Is there not something intrinsically enigmatic about the act of asserting as such?

All discourses, including poetry, make assertions. Assertions create referential effects. To assert is to appear to know, even if it is a knowledge of doubt. It would seem that the structure of knowledge and the syntax of assertion are inseparable. But it also seems necessary to cling to the belief that it makes a difference which comes first; the ground of everything seems to shift if we consider knowledge as an effect of language instead of language as an effect of knowledge.

The Swiss psychologist Jean Piaget, whose views of the development of operational thought in many ways parallel Chomskyan linguistics, concludes on the basis of certain tests that syntax acquisition in children can only occur when cognitive development is ready for it. He writes that "language serves to translate what is already understood. . . . The level of understanding seems to modify the language used rather than vice versa" (quoted in Ruth Tremaine, *Syntax and Piagetian Operational Thought*). While experimental science here seems to believe that syntax follows and translates prior understanding, I would like now to analyze how literature can be seen to say neither this nor the opposite, but to dramatize something quite different about the relations between syntax and knowledge. I shall turn to a poem by Apollinaire, "La Tzigane," in which obvious syntactic signals of the problematization of assertion are conspicuously absent:

LA TZIGANE

La tzigane savait d'avance
Nos deux vies barrées par les nuits
Nous lui dîmes adieu et puis
De ce puits sortit l'Espérance

L'amour lourd comme un ours privé
Dansa debout quand nous voulûmes
Et l'oiseau bleu perdit ses plumes
Et les mendiants leurs *Ave*

On sait bien que l'on se damne
Mais l'espoir d'aimer en chemin
Nous fait penser main dans la main
A ce qu'a prédit la tzigane

[*The Gypsy.* The gypsy knew in advance / Our two lives crossed by nights / We told her farewell and then / Out of that well sprang hope // Love as heavy as a private bear / Danced upright whenever we wanted / And the blue bird lost its feathers / And the beggars their *Ave*'s // Everyone knows that we are damned / But the hope of loving along the way / Makes us think, hand in hand, / Of what the gypsy once foretold.]

(*Alcools*)

The assertiveness of this poem is reinforced by the repetition of the verb *savoir* ("to know"): the poem begins with "La tzigane savait d'avance" and ends with "on sait bien." But what is the content of this knowledge? What is the poem affirming? In the first sentence—"La tzigane savait d'avance / Nos deux vies barrées par les nuits"—what the gypsy knew is not immediately intelligible. "Nos deux vies barrées par les nuits" could mean "our lives crisscrossed by nights of love," "our lives crossed out by darknesses," "our lives fettered by intimations of mortality," or "our lives ruined by our love." The prophecy would seem to be readable both positively and negatively, both as a prediction of love and as a prediction of loss. In the last stanza, the sentence "On sait bien que l'on se damne" reinforces the negative reading, yet in pivoting on a *mais*—"Mais l'espoir d'aimer en chemin / Nous fait penser main dans la main / A ce qu'a prédit la tzigane"— the poem returns to the gypsy's prediction in *opposition* to damnation. What then did the gypsy actually know? The answer seems both indicated and refused by the ambiguous word *barrées. Barrer*, which means both "to mark" and "to block," has thus itself marked out and blocked our very attempt to interpret the poem. The word *barré*, in other words, is enacting its meaning in its very refusal to mean. It is as though Apollinaire had made our interpretation turn on a crossed-out word instead of a word meaning "crossed out."

But this effectively displaces the poem's center of gravity. Instead of recounting the *content* of a prediction, the poem is recounting the *effects* of a prediction the content of which is never clear. The reader, like the consulters of the gypsy, is fooled into thinking he has been told something that can then turn out to be true or false. The syntax of affirmation causes him to forget that he has not really been told anything at all. If the gypsy's prediction is derived from a reading of the lines of the hand—which is also perhaps suggested by *barré*—then the final image of thinking of the gypsy while walking hand in hand, which casts the lines of the hand into total darkness, indicates that the message has become dark precisely because it has been embraced.

The fact of the gypsy's prediction, therefore, acts as the syntactical overdetermination of an unintelligible meaning that produces the same effects as knowledge. Life, love, death, happiness, deprivation, and damnation here revolve around the *syntax* of knowledge, not around knowledge itself. The same assertiveness that preserves outmoded knowledge in Ptolemy's writing produces anticipatory knowledge not in the gypsy but in her readers. Here, reading is believing that something has been predicted, as the poem's third and fourth lines suggest:

> Nous lui dîmes adieu et puis
> De ce puits sortit l'Espérance.

It is out of the well ("puits") of anticipation ("puis") that the hope of understanding arises. The juxtaposition of the homonyms *puits* and *puis* can be read as a figure for the relations between the syntactical and the semantic functions in the poem. The well is a traditional image for the locus of truth, for depth of meaning, while the linear, temporal seriality of syntax can be represented by the expression "and then." If the well of meaning is here bottomless, however, it is precisely because of its syntactical overdetermination: the *puits* of sense is both produced and emptied by the *puis* of syntax.

Thus, it is not the gypsy that knows in advance, but the syntax of assertion that is always in advance of knowledge. Knowledge is nothing other than an effect of syntax, not merely because any affirmation creates an illusion of knowledge, but precisely because syntax is what makes it possible for us to treat as *known* anything that we do not *know* we do not know. And this, in one form or another, is what poetry has always known.

Saussure: The Game of the Name

Sylvère Lotringer

> If Saussure didn't make public the anagrams he deciphered in Saturnian
> poetry, it was because they overthrow academic literature. Such critical
> chicanery didn't make him stupid: you see, he wasn't an analyst.
> —J. LACAN, *Radiophonie*

At the beginning of this century Ferdinand de Saussure pursued an astonishing, if not "insane" line of research, important fragments of which Jean
Starobinski has exhumed, discussed in various places and finally assembled
(*Les Mots sous les mots: Les Anagrammes de Ferdinand de Saussure*). Another
Saussure has been discovered, and his import must be recognized if it is
true, as Roman Jakobson has written, that we are in the presence of a major
discovery, a second Saussurian revolution.

This revolution, however, is second only in its mode of propagation:
the essential part of the anagrammatic studies precedes, in fact, the well-
known *Cours de linguistique générale*. The two "ways" of Saussure appear
so opposed, moreover, that one hesitates to attribute paternity of these two
enterprises to the same man: in one case, a discreet, quasi-secretive inquiry,
pursued pragmatically, accumulating concrete evidence; in the other, a
series of public lectures situated from the beginning on a theoretical level;
the first is a tenacious but perplexed intuition, perpetually in pursuit of its
own law, the second a *"clear idea,"* impatient with the reigning confusion,
which immediately finds its systematic formulation; on the one hand, inscribed in a hundred notebooks, stacks of notes, a work in *writing* that will
have to wait for half a century to arouse any interest, and on the other the
prestige of a *spoken word*, leaving no trace, that nevertheless immediately
wins disciples and a place in the foreground of Western thought. The two
Saussures are historically, systematically and philosophically opposed: the
"first" lays the scientific grounds for a discipline which constitutes the most
indisputable fruition of our culture, the "second" inaugurates a practice of
the text, the theory of which is at present attempting to constitute itself.

A two-faced Janus, Saussure situates himself, inescapably, at the cross-

---

From *Diacritics* 3, no. 2 (Summer 1973). © 1973 by Diacritics, Inc.

roads. Apostle of linearity, institutor of a systematics which will issue in the methods of "structuralism," here he turns about paradoxically and underwrites a series of polyphonic studies which thicken his famous sheet of paper and, bursting the tufts that were supposed to hold it together, consecrates the irruption of the signifier on the scene of writing. One could attempt to reconcile the two "ways" of the Geneva master by moving, as is indeed proper, over and beyond their differences. This madness, after all, will have served reason. No doubt, and we shall return to this point. Nevertheless, linguistics emerged from the anagram fully *armed* and, rather than "sublating" it in an expedient synthesis, it is important to sharpen the contradiction and to displace it onto what is still unsure ground, precisely there where reason strives to hold madness back to the limit of its own truth.

I propose here to locate the nodal points at which the course of Saussure's anagrammatic revolution deviated, bifurcated or simply stopped short, in order to restore to it its virtual—that is to say, present—import in its relation with psychoanalysis.

GENERALIZED ALLITERATION

ALLITERATION . . . touches on one of the sacred or perilous mysteries of Language.

—MALLARMÉ, *Les Mots anglais*

The first hazard that our "second" Saussure must avoid in his notebooks is a reduction of the "anagrammatic" instance (an inexact designation, as we shall see) to the all too inviting categories of Rhetoric. At the outset of his inquiry there thus ensues a characteristic interplay of approach and avoidance through which the contours of the phenomenon he intuits are outlined negatively. The rhetorical figures of similitude are thus one by one invoked and revoked, beginning with alliteration, "the play of certain letters or certain syllables" (Fontanier); but also rhyme, assonance and especially paronomasia (analogous signifiers, different signifieds) which might, moreover, have been specified as apophony, antanaclasis, etc. "Somewhere in the dictionary there is a thing called paronomasia, a figure of rhetoric which—paronomasia comes so close by its principle of." It is this proximity that brutally interrupts the enumeration. In each case it is a matter of emphasizing the correspondences of phonic elements at the core of the same syntagma, the return of the Same (sound) at the core of the Other (meaning). These procedures are ordinarily indexed and put to use in a line of poetry so as to produce a *perceptible* effect, intended for a virtual reader. Saussure deliberately abandons these "flourishes" to stylistics. He does not intend to isolate a specific rhetorical strategy, but what one might call a generalized alliteration, by which the contingency of the "ornament" would coincide with the rule of law.

The phonic symmetry that he pursues does not concern simply the initial alliteration or the final rhyme; it includes the whole line, from the first syllable to the last. In a "formula-line" such as the Saturnian, everything corresponds rigorously; yet this occurs independently of meter, which may be considered a secondary elaboration, destined to particularize, and thus to conceal in its specificity the "real phenomenon." The imperative of generality never ceases to guide Saussure's research. What will vary, and this is the key, is the way in which the elements involved in such an algebra of discourse are constituted and articulated.

These operations have in common the exclusion of the material of writing as such in favor of *speech*. Alliteration (*ad-littera*) must pay to generality the price of the letter. Right at the threshold of the subversion, Saussure unleashes the anathema which the *Cours* will pronounce upon writing, understood as an intolerable artifice, a travesty of language. Nevertheless—and this is a source of numerous ambiguities—he will continue to refer to "gram" (*gramma, grammatos*, written sign) to designate *phonè*. "In using the word *anagram*, I do not for a moment intend to bring writing into consideration." Why preserve, then, in the field of the phoneme, the trace of an order that he deliberately discards? "To replace *gram* by *phone* . . . would result precisely in suggesting that we are dealing with an unheard-of species of thing." But is this not precisely what compels him to reject any recourse to rhetoric? One may sense, in this awkward reticence and antiphrasis, a desire to repress the teaching (*enseignement*) of writing by retaining only its sign (*enseigne*). The problem nonetheless recurs in the letter of the statement which effects the contradictory restoration of the pertinence of that *unheard-of* thing which is in effect the gram. By a curious reversal, which is not the first since it is no longer a question, in this sentence, of replacing phone by gram, as one would expect, *but rather gram by phone*, the spoken word is inscribed in the space of writing (which is literally un-heard-of, *inaudible*) so as to be *heard*, in other words, to accede to understanding (*entendement*). Saussure's discovery will proceed in disguise, metaphorized by the recourse to the very letter whose return it prohibits.

Yet a new paradox is seen to overdetermine Saussure's reference to writing, for he effectively undertakes to treat the "*phone*" *as a* "*gram*." The distinctions he makes in effect wrest the phonic substance away from that logocentric tradition (Derrida) which elevated voice to the ideality of meaning. The phonetic gram will not be the presence to itself of a deferred absence, which it would have to re-present or signify for a subject (such as the *Fort-Da* of the infant for whom the bobbin takes the place of the absent mother). It cannot be enclosed in the concept of sign since it *consists* only in the reference back to another element which is not itself simply present. The gram never does more than *insist* (slide), in a line of poetry as in a dream, without however speaking to someone. It can only slide along the signifying chain by fracturing the syntax of meaning, by producing holes in it through which the elements of discourse can circulate, "as in the game called Alphabet where one disposes of wooden letters" (Marcel Proust). A poem presents itself as a "texture" of co-respondances, of cores responding to each other through the signifying material. In such a texture each element necessarily finds its phonic counterpart: counter-vowels, consonants of recall, occur in response to the expectation prepared by a first term, in a kind of exploded, disseminated, abstract echolalia which continually ties together the operations by a gain priming the numeration: "Every book contains the fusion of a few reiterated numerations"—"a parity in consonance" (Mallarmé). Thus, beneath the constraining line of discourse the profile of a counter-discourse takes shape, or rather a nondiscourse whose very parity dooms it to the disparate, to the extravagant. A fundamentally diversifying combination since it duplicates the line of verse with its inverse and uncovers a non-linear, extratemporal space where speech is lost in infinite disconnections.

The anagrammatical theory (very well named after all, as its literal inexactitude preserves the spirit of the letter) defines a domain which can no longer serve as an anchor-point for Western metaphysics: pairings, "regular balancing by numbers," formulas, itemizations, remainders—the space of the number: "The ideal poetic line would be one offering, for example, a total: 2 L's, 2 P's, 4 R's ($=2+2$), 6 A's, 2 O's, 4 U's, and so forth" ("Lettres de Ferdinand de Saussure à Antoine Meillet," *Cahiers Ferdinand de Saussure* 21 [1964]). The law of pairings initiated by Saussure inscribes a pre-verbal, translinguistic level in the order of discourse which contributes greatly to undermining its claims to universality. The number, in effect, is not simply the "historical" instrument of the word, as A. Leroi-Gourhan would have it (*Le Geste et la parole*), but a system of artificial notations irreducible to sign or to representation. Making the number reappear in language reactivates the subversive function that mathematical notation, like oriental writing, has continually brought to bear upon the ideology of the alphabet (cf. Jacques Derrida, *De la grammatologie*, and Julia Kristeva, "L'Engendrement de la formule," in *Sémiotike*). The signifying chain (the versified formula)—cadenced with abstract marks (themselves drawn out of an ensemble that can no longer be confined to them) that are purely operational since it is of little importance which vowel or which consonant is included in the counting here where everything is a matter of *differences*—reveals itself to be independent of a meaning which endeavors nevertheless to monopolize it.

It is at this point—a logical point and not a chronological one—that Saussure takes pause. What is to be done with the disturbing repetitions of the "pure" phonic datum, with the "regular distribution of vowels and consonants" glimpsed in the Saturnian and certain formula-lines of Homeric poetry? To which saint should they be dedicated—if not to a new

Saint-Axe (Ph. Sollers, *Lois*)? Here begins the circumvention of numbers, a virtual annulment, under the pretext of expansion, of Saussure's first hypothesis. The law of pairings appears "extremely difficult to verify," and the tallies almost impossible once he begins to hesitate in regard to the criteria of delimitation. If the versifier can regain control in the following line or even over the space of several lines, any verification becomes inoperative and any affirmation baseless. Especially since knowledge of the phonic material of the archaic texts remains difficult to grasp and since the Saturnian itself remains poorly defined (Françoise Rastier, "A Propos du Saturnien," *Latomus* 29 [1970]). Unless one gives up these very foundations and the positivism of an exact proof which depends on its closure in order to postulate that the alliterative phenomenon by which Language imperils itself is unlimited.

The outlines of such a transition might have been indicated in the letter of 1907 in which Saussure despairs of finding the sum of the different elements taken as monophones. It is then that he considers turning to the phonic groups (diphones, triphones): "One then encounters a more immediately distinguishable phenomenon, although more difficult on the other hand to reduce to a fixed formula" (*Cahiers*). Discarding the vowel/consonant distinction, far from promoting the establishment of another "logic," that of the signifier, actually sets aside all formulation—a confusion which satisfies the linguist's obvious desire for positivity while allowing him to skirt the fundamental issue: "Whether it is an approximation or a system that requires a definitive count is difficult to discern." Then, from an incidental remark, springs what is doubtless Saussure's most unsettling intuition, one which would have avoided the reversion of the anagrammatical theory toward the Logos (Saussure will later speak of a *logogramme*): "it is difficult to discern, especially when considering other texts where entire lines seem to be anagrams of preceding lines that may even be at a great distance in the text" (*Cahiers*). Here we can glimpse briefly the infinity of language, "the sacred mystery," a textual process without origin since it is caught in a ceaseless play of referral and reverberations, and without end inasmuch as it unfolds in a self-referential space, a perpetual refraction in a hall of mirrors where every site is a citation and every citation an *incitation* (a setting into motion). This insight will not be pursued, since at this point the train of thought bears upon the difficulty of deciding and not upon what would have made such a choice obsolete.

The halt occurs without delay, and substitutes a domesticated analogue—the anagram itself—for the scriptural advent which was in the offing: "What it can be worthwhile to take up without resolving either point 'a' or point 'b' concerning the precise count of monophones and polyphones is this *independent* fact—*one which may be considered in an independent manner, for I would not wish to go further than that*—that as soon as the occasion for it occurs, polyphones visibly reproduce the syllables of a word or of a name which is important for the text and thereby become *anagrammatical* polyphones." The good fortune of a timely detour, of a self-created op-portunity which seems to preserve the inquiry just when it is terminating it. For Saussure will never come back to this bifurcation, which he presents as contingent, independent, without, nevertheless, allowing himself to probe its articulation ("I would not wish to go any further than that"). Eventually he will explicitly distinguish two approaches to the phenome-non, one *internal* and *free* (the acoustic series—pairing of phonic elements), the other *external*, quick to seize the opportunity (the series of meaning—reproduction of a name). He will even refrain commendably from putting them into a definitive hierarchy, going so far as to envisage reversing the order of precedences. Nevertheless, these reservations only appear as a particularly acute form of denial: "Far from supposing that the question must necessarily begin with the word I call anagrammized, I would be delighted if someone would show me, for example, that there is not an anagram but only a repetition of the same syllables, or elements, in accord with laws of versification that have nothing to do with proper names, or with a determined word." The anagrammatical constraint which is more readily perceived wins out over generalized alliteration, marking a defin-itive exit from the realm of numbers. In fact, such a choice leads to placing the anagram at the origin (*archè:* commencement and commandment) or at the end of the play of phonemes—in short, to constituting the general law solely on the basis of the word.

THE MASTER-WORD

The thousands of words of a language are related to one another. Everything lies in knowing how to begin and end.
(MALLARMÉ, *Les Mots anglais*)

The transition from monophone to diphone (or syllable) takes places in the manuscript. In comparison to the letter of 1907, there has been a significant change in emphasis. The role of monophones is explicitly rejected as con-trary to the advent of the theme-word or hypogram toward which the phonic fragments will now be oriented: "I do not think that one could repeat too often that the *monophone* is non-existent for the hypogram." Isolated, "its value is nil." The monophone will no longer be seen except as the supplement of the diphone, a "minimal unit" itself moving toward integration. The connecting procedures will be all the more meticulous since the diphone, by definition, eludes any numerical count. Thus the number swerves toward the name. With the name, we have not yet settled accounts. The name (*nom*) is only the shadow (*ombre*) of the number (*nombre*), which is properly speaking the unnamable. Saussure, naming the number, calling (*appeler*) it names, will have to be content with spelling it out (*épeler*) through the text, citing it element by element, under the umbrella of the Sum which, from then on, only remains to be recited ("it suffices that nothing be missing from one end of the word to the other," *Cahiers*), like an incantatory formula.

Here, the *phonè* recovers its center, its preferred place, for in every name there is a certain coefficient of presence, a certain guarantee of identity. Every nomination *capitalizes* the meaning. All meaning goes to one's head. Thus, the hypogram is deliberately placed under the domination of the Logos, seat of the word and of reason, of reason as word. As Saussure proposes, it is a logogram, that is a gram "around a subject who inspires the whole of the passage and is more or less its *logos,* the reasonable unity, the intent (*propos*) of that passage." The unity of a subject (*propos*) refers back to the subject of the unity, to the supposedly knowing subject (the Cartesian ego) whose illusion of autonomy is grounded in reason. The heading of the Name tends to reintroduce, under the aegis of the Logos, a teleological structure at the core of phonic dissemination. One will not be surprised to see Saussure at this point undertake to squeeze the hypogram into a *mannequin-complex* which describes its contours. Initials and final letters, discarded by the law of pairings, are thus reinserted into the anagrammatical phenomenon. *Priamides* (Hector) is enclosed by Virgil in the limits of the syllabogram /PRIma quiES/. Likewise, in Lucretius, the Aphrodite mannequin, beginning with the A of *Aeneadum genetrix HOminum DIvomquE* forms "a unity moving toward the final E." The name is no longer simply dispersed throughout the text (a paragram) or gathered in a limited space (an anagram). That space itself is oriented. The mannequin may now attach itself to the hypogram according to various combinations, or even integrate it into that perfect—since overdetermined—form, the *paramorph.* Evidently enough, its intervention contributes greatly to reducing the phonic heterogeneity: "This internal ordering is a sign of the unity of the whole." It is Saussure who praises the presence in Claudius of the two *central* (and centering) principles of the diphone and the mannequin, "without a visible degeneration toward other, freer means" (*Cahiers*). Every "liberated," insane *generation* endangers reason, which can never expose it except as what it is not (de-generation). After a brief escape, the signifying production is duly *mastered* in the straitjacket of the name. The paramorph becomes a paramime (paronymic renewal/avoidance); anagrammatism, thus rendered powerless, is limited to imitating a word, to conferring to it "a second, factitious manner of being, added, so to speak, to the original." In the same way, Plato sees writing as a supplement to speech. The hypogram constitutes the (factitious) simulacrum of a full origin, a simulated fabrication ("disguise") which dis-simulates the natural aspect of the word and is thus illegitimate, inferior (from the Greek *hupo,* beneath, but also insufficient, diminished, lowered). Saussure will take cover behind this master-word.

The property of the name is to be a proper name, the name of the proper, of the absolute proximity of meaning, presence to itself of the divine. The play with phonemes becomes therefore a celebration of the name, a propitiatory sacrifice: "For a prayer to have its effect, the syllables of the divine name had to be indissolubly intermingled in it: God was riveted to the text, so to speak" (*Cahiers*). The Name of God was dismembered only in view of an ultimate reincarnation: to hypogrammatize a text is, in reality, to divinize it. Such an operation was inscribed from the beginning in the Saussurian approach. The pairing of phonic elements, the most abstract law and the one least apt to be subsumed under meaning (the subject-sign logic), was itself never conceived outside the context of an elaborating consciousness, a poetic intentionality which reproduced the name after having first decomposed it into its principal syllables. God is only riveted to the text inasmuch as the text, for Saussure, is always derived from a creator, from a thinking head. All ulterior hypotheses will be projected onto this fantasmatic screen—this myth of an originary inscription, which is absolutely constraining by virtue of its status, infinitely renewable in its particular substance (the occasion). Recourse to the master name is the inevitable outcome of an inquiry which remains bound within the problematics of a unitary, unsplit subject, of a subject who is the master of the name and the receptacle of meaning. "The pure work," wrote Mallarmé, "implies the elocutory disappearance of the poet, who yields the initiative to the words which are mobilized by the clash of their inequality." The words beneath the words appear, on the contrary, without initiative—at most, the result of an initiation.

It is exactly this fading of the subject in writing which poses a problem for the founder of modern linguistics. To be sure, it will occur to him to compare language to a game of chess where the player would be *unconscious* or unintelligent (*Cours de linguistique générale*)—a daring formulation, the scope of which, it should be noted, is strictly localized. Since the rules of the game of chess are explicit, for demonstrative purposes, we could postulate a paradoxical situation in which the player would be denied knowledge of the conventions without which the game is obviously impossible. On the other hand, in the linguistic game, the subject of the enunciation does not have to be unconscious—language is unconscious for him. More precisely, Saussure sees language as the locus of multiple contentions between the individual and the collectivity, nature (the faculty of language) and artifice (the social institution). The unpremeditated character of language does not in any way call into question the intentionality of the subject. Speech remains on the contrary, "an individual act of will and intelligence" (*Cours*), and the linguist scrupulously respects its privileged nature. From this silence with respect to factors of speech (*faits de parole*), we can infer that, being fully assumed by the subject, they are located outside the system. If the user is not the master of his language (*langue*—which he registers passively), he is the master of his discourse. The anagrammatical theory seems here to be curiously on the near side of the now classic hypotheses of the *Cours*. Saussure's impasse consists in envisaging the dispersion of phonemes as resembling a game of chess in which the players would be supremely conscious and intelligent. His inquiry stops short because he does not grant the anagram a status comparable at the very least to that of a fact of language (to do so would, of course, still be misleading)—although here again Saussure's position, already inviting us to go beyond his own intuitions, is nuanced. There is no doubt that, for Saussure, anagrams, imposed "naturally" by the contexture (the theme of the text, pressure stemming from the context) are knowingly put to use by the poet. The difficulties arising from such a constraint are, moreover, alternately minimized (the phenomenon is approximated to other processes of versification in order to be made credible) and magnified, since the imperfection of certain operations must be justified. Once the anagram is thus attributed to a fabricator, there is still a need to indicate the reasons for such a practice, for the maintenance of "this incredible relic from another age" in poets as different as Virgil, Lucretius, Horace—or Giovanni Pascali, their modern imitator—and especially to explain the surprising absence, over the centuries, of any proof of such a deliberate practice. All of which leads the Genevan master, on the one hand, naïvely to contact Pascali, in the vain hope of receiving from him the confirmation of his hypotheses, but on the other hand, and more boldly, to suspect in the implacable signifying activity a *second nature*, the result of an "inevitable and profound psychological sociation." Saussure never came closer to recognizing the dis-sociation of a subject inscribed in scriptural practice—the elocutory disappearance of the poet. The real proof (the "secret" of the anagram) did not lie in any acknowledgement from Pascali, but was to be found in circumstantial texts, (business) letters of Pliny or Cicero, short missives of Caesar, forms which are the least tainted with "literature" but just as subject to the phonematic logic.

That Saussure should have immediately equated sociation with a particular faculty of the writer's *attention*, "a preoccupation outside of which he perhaps does not believe he has the right to write a single line," without furnishing any other justification for such an injunction than some outmoded, religious practices, demonstrates the linguist's incapacity to fracture the enclosure of the subject. Saussure was decidedly not an analyst. If in his manuscripts he provides the material of psychoanalysis, and even the material subject to treatment, to paraphrase Lacan, he can only leave unwritten that which is operative, in other words, the object (a): "The unconscious may be as I said the condition of linguistics. However, this does not give linguistics the slightest hold over it" ("Radiophonie," *Scilicet* 2/3 [1970]).

Starobinski's suggestion that the linguist, assembler of orienting syllables, is the Isis of the hypogrammatical body now takes on a competely different perspective. Reuniting as he does the dismembered body of the signifier without occasioning thereby the splitting of the subject in language, Saussure cannot help but miss the lack which is operative there. The hypogram never allows for dismemberment except within the imaginary, in the "fantasy" of a total body from which the *little thing* (the penis) would not have fallen. The receptacle-coffin of Osiris is covered over by the trunk of a cedar with which the king of Biblos in turn will make a column, the support of his palace. The symbolic erection at the same time indicates and dissimulates the gap in which the meaning of power and the power of meaning are grounded. "La coupure bande," as Bataille said. Likewise, Isis will have to improvise a hasty replica, in place of the phallus which thwarts her collection, the ultimate effort to suture the cut and reestablish the unity of the body proper.

Just when the anagrams were turning into nonpublishable material, a work appeared which might have permitted Saussure to avoid his epistemological impasse, Freud's *Jokes and Their Relation to the Unconscious*. It is precisely the staging of this missed encounter between the words beneath the words and the jokes beneath the cogito which remains for us to sketch.

THE NAME OF DESIRE

One would find everywhere, either written out in huge letters, or hidden, or disguised . . . names which serve to designate a desire which itself does not have a real name.

(O. MANNONI, *Clefs pour l'imaginaire ou l'autre scène*)

We know that jokes belong to the formations of the unconscious in the same way as slips or dreams. Like them, they are elaborated on the Other Scene according to the constitutive laws of language: condensation, displacement, representability. However, the joke is produced as a *specific* meaning-effect (*effet de sens*) of the unconscious in the subject's speech and it is this which allows for comparing it with the hypogram.

The joke exploits phonic similarities but, unlike the slip, it does not *outplay* resistances—it *plays* them. The pun implies, as does the hypogram, that one word be used in two different ways, the original ("a first time in its entirety") and the factitious ("a second time decomposed into syllables as in a charade"). The name *Rousseau*, an anagram of Saussure, is dissected in the order of the signifier and is recathected for purposes of discharge in order to qualify one of the parents of the Geneva recluse as *roux* (red-headed) and *sot* (stupid). The technique of the joke consists in deferring the meaning in such a way as to permit the verbal material to space itself out, to be punctuated differently. As with certain Chinese ideograms, one must endeavor to erase the value assigned to a given character, reduce the latter merely to its signifying silhouette in order to engage it in another term. In both instances, however, the preliminary evacuation is only imperfectly effected and numerous reverberations remain, which contribute as much to the halo and ideographic multidimensionality as to the pleasure elicited by a play on words. Meaning has been set aside only in order to bring about a perceptible difference which is offered for consumption.

Already one detects what separates the joke and the anagram. In both cases, we have a word to be *imitated*. But while the joking "reply" (*replica*) aims at effecting an admissible shift in the meaning, the Saussurian simulacrum is content to introduce the master word in a syntagma whose only function is to paraphrase it. Saussure's is not a transformation but a travesty. These two operations are not necessarily mutually exclusive. Freud notes briefly the relation between jokes and *riddles*. In the first, the text is given but the technique is hidden while in the second the text must be guessed, the technique being simply imposed as a condition: "Guess a small number of syllables which when brought together in a single word, or assembled in one manner or another, give a different meaning" (*Le Mot d'esprit*). Since the text is given for Freud, his inquiry concerns the mind's mode of production; while, on the contrary, for Saussure the text itself must be found according to certain conditions.

The anagram takes after the riddle. The joke, on the contrary, must be grasped immediately; it is the most social of psychic activities for it always requires the presence of a third person. In spite of their apparent similarity, anagrams and jokes are opposite on every score. The former consists in choosing, according to various criteria, a word which will be made imperceptible by its dispersion in the text, while the latter, having momentary recourse to the unconscious in order to defer the meaning, allows a verbal perturbation to occur which implicates its recipient. Moreover, this necessity for communication exposes the joke (like literature in general) to the censorship of reason. In such cases, all the same, it is an effort to justify the operation of meaning and not, as with the hypogram, the meaning of the operation. Freud himself will be led to distinguish *good* puns where the approximate of the signifier brings together two analogous signifieds (*tradduttore / tradditore*) from *bad* ones which at most bring together two dissimilar representations. In that way, he reintroduces the circuit of value by assigning to a word its fair price. He does so, even as he recognizes that the *meaning* of a joke serves only to protect the pleasure produced from criticism, thus that the joke is inimical to evaluation. Although Saussure evidently seems fascinated by the decoding process to which his desire has led him, he suppresses at the outset in his pursuit of proof (the meaning of the operation) a ludic preoccupation which risked reopening sources of childish pleasure. For him, the anagram remains a sterile, puerile practice, and only the fact of such a constraint is judged worthy of investigation.

In Saussure the ascendency of meaning results, purely and simply, in concealing the work of the text. Even when he uncovers similar operations, such as in Vedic hymns dedicated to *Agni Arigiras* in which may be discerned "a series of puns like *girah* (chants), *anga* (conjunction), etc.," the technique is only seen as the condition of a general activity which aims at imitating the syllables of the sacred name. Teleology obliterates process. Hypograms, whose enigmatic character eludes all communication, should rather be compared to the dream text. Nevertheless, dreams do not fall under the rubric of meaning: the dream work doesn't think, it limits itself to transforming; anagrams think too much and don't transform enough. The status of the word for Saussure ought to have prepared us for this. Virtually detached from its signifying support, it appears as more than the sum of its constitutive elements: "The unity of the word . . . depends on characteristics other than its material quality" (*Cours*). The word owes its ability to transcend matter to its *unity*. Its "melodic" being necessarily escapes the various deformations which Freud indexed.

It is the "immaterial" quality of the "primitive" signified, subsequently buried in a screen-text, that allows it to be brought to light in its integrity. Its permanence is a function of its original identity. Between the poet-encoder and the reader-cryptanalyst is interposed an intersticial tissue devoid of any specificity (it registers the word by taking the form of its folds) through which the repressed word returns unchanged. The Saussurian *après-coup* (*Nachträglichkeit*) thus would restore intact the truth of the text beyond the oblivion of history (that the repressed name often figures explicitly in the screen-text changes nothing, for it is present in the unmarked mode: only the *vraisemblable* marks). We will posit, with Catherine Backès-Clément, that "the total return, without loss in the transition, without dismemberment, the perfect cycle of a regression to the rediscovered origin, is the menace with which idealism threatens the Freudian breakthrough . . . to return to an initial event in its reality, that is the myth; to construct a model-event, a fictive frame for events that are forever inaccessible, that is what Freud says" ("L'Evénement porté disparu," *Communications* 18 [1972]). Saussure remains dependent on the problem of origins, the matrix of idealism, and that is why he is constrained to suppress (*résorber*) the dismemberment he achieves through the fantasmatic unity of the proper name.

A signifying infinity for which the master-word should only present at most a partial and refractable configuration is, in the same movement, uncovered and inhibited in the constitutive reduplication of the unitary subject. Desire, writes O. Mannoni, always cloaks itself in false names—because there are no true ones. And once a name is articulated, desire never stops disarticulating it. Saussure is thus destined to defer perpetually the impossible confirmation of an inquiry which errs through consistency and perpetuates itself through insisting. It is true that the hypogram takes after the riddle, though after one which has no satisfactory solution. A cryptogram, Lacan suggests, has all its dimensions only when it is that of a lost language. *The Saussurian riddle has the dimensions of a language rediscovered.*

Anagrammatical functioning can enter into a theory of writing only by dispelling the obstacle of the name, by making it a model-event whose reality would be purely operative since it would permit an indication of the specific migrations of language. The Name is only the *fictive* framework of the germinative process, a "construction" by means of which the heterogeneous can be read at the risk of *being taken at its word*.

It is at this point that Saussure misses his second exit, one which might have been accomplished not through a lack (the law of pairings dispensed with the name) but through an excess, in an anagrammatical overabundance, an irrespressible riddling of the manifest text. Theme-words come *en masse* to saturate any given fragment: "One reaches the point of wondering whether all possible words could not actually be found in every text." Precisely. A vocable is retained only as a function of unexamined presuppositions arising from a plausibility in which scriptor and linguist would be "naturally" inscribed. Thus, Saussure traces in the *Cahiers* on Poliziano the absent name of *Leonora* Butti, mistress of Fra Filippo Lippi and the probable cause of his murder, a study which is all the more exemplary in that the linguist, hesitating between the "reality" and the "fantasmagoria" of the phenomenon, decides formally to abandon the hypogram if he cannot prove that its presence in Lippi's epigram was *intentional*. He has no trouble finding the cryptogram of Leonora, and even according to three distinct modes: 1) pairs (o-o, r-r, a-a-, ar-ar = RA);

2) accumulation:
"*Art*ifices potui digitis anim*are* co*L*or*E*"

$$
\begin{array}{c}
\text{l}\text{—}\text{e}\\
\text{o}\text{–}\text{o}\\
\text{n}\text{———}\text{o}\\
\text{r}\text{——}\text{r}\\
\text{a}\text{——}\text{a}
\end{array}
$$

or
3) Mannequin-complex: L——E

The only problem is that the painter's mistress never bore the name of Leonora, but rather that of Lucrezia! (Aldo Rossi, "Gli Anagrammi di Saussure," *Paragone* 218 [1968])—a demonstration by the absurd which shows that the name is not deliberate on the part of the scriptor, but rather generated through a de-scription. Saussure was not able to take advantage of such a slip, and he continues to be troubled by the sight of words offering themselves up *without his having looked for them*, outside of the individual motivation in which he strictly intends to contain them. This leads him to surround himself with guarantees and to exorcise coincidences, according to a neurotic protocol, evidence of which is often to be found in the manuscripts. A completely different conclusion might have imposed itself: not a panicky reclaiming of the whole, but a presentment of the productive function that devolves on any reading as soon as it escapes from the constraints of linearity and the snares of meaning. The recognition of other modes of significance alien to the subject-sign matrix could then be reached, and the semiotics freed from the tyranny of speech. Mathematics returns aptly at this point—to propose its model, but without any more success: "We are two steps away from a calculus of probabilities."

The hypogrammatical reconstitution fends off the shattering of the phonic by placing it before the mirror of the proper name. The Saussurian anagram constitutes, in other words, the imaginary dimension of all writing. The play on words, or rather *under* words, because it must pay a large debt to meaning—unity (immateriality, idealism), authority (master-word, word of the master), intentionality ("attention")—can only be the *vaccine* of a signifying economy which is still considered to be of a deplorable nature, an uncertain halt awaiting its consequences.

It is in fact in the *cahiers* that Saussure first perceives the fundamental principle of linearity. This principle is announced for the first time, moreover, *at the moment of the shift from monophone to diphone,* which is seen to be the turning point of anagrammatical research: "A first effect of the principle of the DIPHONE is tantamount to discarding the monophone as an element capable of expressing any position. But the former has a second significance. A diphone, simply by its presence before our eyes, *consecrates an order.* If P and I are given separately, nothing is determined as to the order IP or PI. Given PI, one possesses *outside of the data of the composition,* an element which it would be absolutely incorrect to think banal or simply—/ It is true that one would not find in any book on the—that *the fundamental condition of any word is to run on a linear—*" (unpublished text cited by Aldo Rossi; our italics). The inter-position of the diphone is a summons to the linear order which will have its consecration in the *Cours.* The *Anagrams* weren't published: linguistics was born of that exclusion. We would suggest that Saussure's reasoning unreason proposed in fact the suppressed foundation of all that he elaborated subsequently. Like Hegel, Saussure "reached an extreme. He was still young and believed that he was going mad. I even believe that he elaborated the system in order to escape ("each type of conquest, without a doubt, is the result of a man fleeing from a menace . . . the system is annulment") (Georges Bataille, *L'Expérience intérieure*). The *Cours de linguistique générale* appears therefore, by means of this reversal, as an escape forward, a grandiose *synthesis*—a pyramid erected on a fundamental repression.

The signifier mythically bound to its signified, and thus put at the disposition of meaning, can be delivered over to linguistic science—at the price of a small omission, which is precisely what is at stake in the psychoanalytic act. Freud had foreseen this in *Psychopathology of Everyday Life.* There he considers one by one verbal inversions, anticipations, post-positions, substitutions and contaminations, all of which are categories of Meringer and Meyer to which Otto Jespersen gave a more systematic turn ("Lapses and Blendings," in *Language,* 1922). In concluding his remarks on the insufficiencies of a purely linguistic study of slips of the tongue, he writes: "I do not doubt the laws whereby the sounds produce changes upon one another; but they alone do not appear to me sufficiently forcible to mar the correct execution of speech" ("Mistakes in Speech," chap. 5, *Psychopathology of Everyday Life*). Freud thereupon invokes a *foreign* factor, influences external to speech. There is no need to appeal to the anagrammatical intentions of the subject: this exterior of speech refers to the strangeness of the subject in relation to a language which does nothing but traverse him at the very moment he claims—through the linguistic apparatus—to have mastered it. To cleave the subject with a boundless anagrammatism is quite simply to subvert the system of the sign by restoring to the unconscious its place in language.

The Saussurian anagram inhibits the circulation of desire by constituting a nominal reserve in which the subject remains caught. In order for the subject to free himself from the name, the anagram would have to be exhaustively *spent* (*dé-pensé*), withdrawn from the specular functioning, from the speculations of thought, and restored to a signifying economy. This first attempt suffices nevertheless to unsettle that cultural product intended for communication (message), appreciation (value), and consumption (emotion), in short for the ideological entrapment of the subject, which is the function of *academic literature*—a doubly tautological formula, moreover, if one admits, with Roland Barthes, that "literature is what is taught" (*L'Enseignement de la littérature*) and what is taught has as its only function to seduce a class. By virtue of these anagrams, under whose pressure syntax is dislocated and the texts redistributed according to a logic which is no longer that of the sign or representation, even if it remains caught in the net of reason, literature appears for the first time as a secondary elaboration, a unifying, repetitive, fantasmatic activity which contrives to inhibit the textual process, to unite as best it can the transitory formulations destined to dissemination in order to constitute a smooth façade which forestalls the labor of meaning. The more a written work proclaims its homogeneity, the more a reworking, as in dreams, must be suspected. The poetic message becomes, as J. Starobinski emphasizes, a *useless luxury* of the hypogram. In the Saussuain breakthrough, it is this luxurious edifice which must now be torn down.

Epistemology in Durkheim's
Elementary Forms of Religious Life

Terry F. Godlove, Jr.

Where do categories such as space, time, quantity, quality, and relation purchase their peculiar necessity and universality? For Kant, the answer lies with the realization that objects of experience must conform to those conditions under which experience is possible. Thus, we explain the necessity and universality of our fundamental categories of experience not by a causal account of their origin, but by showing that we cannot help but presuppose them in all our empirical knowledge. I shall return to Kant's solution at the end of this paper, but until then I want to examine Emile Durkheim's answer in the *Elementary Forms of Religious Life* (1912). With Kant, Durkheim (1858–1917) argued that we cannot explain this peculiar necessity and universality so long as we view it as an effect caused by something in the spatio-temporal world. But against Kant, and based on this rejection of "empiricism," he went on to trace the modal structure of the categories to an ideal object *outside* the world, to an ideal object he called "society."

Durkheim's sociological idealism has never been well received, most critics offering empirical patches and apologies. Though I have no interest in defending Durkheim, I hope to show that his error lies at a deeper level than his critics allege. For he rightly saw that no empirical investigation can explain how it is that certain of our concepts are able to constrain any empirical investigation whatever. After some brief historical remarks, I shall argue that the idea of society as an ideal entity emerges, for Durkheim, from epistemological considerations which are not easily put off.

As an English critic has recently noted, "a rounded assessment of Durkheim's epistemology has yet to be undertaken" (John B. Allcock, "Ed-

From *Journal of the History of Philosophy* 24, no. 3 (July 1986). © 1985 by Journal of the History of Philosophy, Inc.

itorial Introduction" to Durkheim's *Pragmatism and Sociology*). Since epistemological considerations occupied Durkheim throughout his career, a rounded assessment would have to take up at least *The Rules of Sociological Method* (1895), *Sociology and Philosophy* (1898–1911), *Primitive Classification* (1903) (with Marcel Mauss), and *Pragmatism and Sociology* (1914). But though the present essay considers only a small part of Durkheim's epistemological writing, it treats, I think, his most sustained, mature, and philosophically significant statement. My aim is to throw Durkheim's theory into relief by holding it up against the Kantian approach to epistemology it was meant to supersede.

I

Between 1879 and 1882, Durkheim studied at the Ecole Normale Supérieure, where he was influenced by, among others, Comte, and two neo-Kantian teachers, Charles Bernard Renouvier and Emile Boutroux. Comte's influence was crucial; a recent biographer notes that, of all Comte's teaching, "its most important element was precisely the extension of the scientific attitude to the study of society" (Steven Lukes, *Emile Durkheim, His Life and Work: A Historical and Critical Study*). More specifically, Durkheim placed himself in the Comtean methodological tradition through his lifelong allegiance to a hypothetico-deductive method. From Renouvier, Durkheim absorbed a particular view of the Kantian categories. The categories, rather than given a priori—independent of all experience—are subject to practical forces of both an individual and societal nature; that is, they could be other than they are. From Boutroux came the idea that societal facts are irreducible to psychological facts, a hallmark of Durkheim's sociology. However, Durkheim soon rejected Boutroux's teleological mode of reasoning, substituting a "causalist" account relying on the method of concomitant variation.

As for Durkheim's own reading of Kant, his friend George Davy remarks that Durkheim the student was "suspicious" of the Kantian philosophy. We will see that his "suspicions" amounted to an outright rejection of the transcendental approach to epistemology. On the other hand, many of his writings reflect a deep respect for Kant's moral philosophy.

Whether from his own exposure to Kant, or through his neo-Kantian teachers, Durkheim the epistemologist took over a dichotomy between conceptual framework and incoming, uninterpreted content. Thus, midway through the Introduction to the *Elementary Forms*, Durkheim begins a discussion of the categories of experience with the following remarks:

> At the roots of all our judgments there are a certain number of essential ideas which dominate all our intellectual life; they are what philosophers since Aristotle have called the categories of the understanding: ideas of time, space, class, number, cause, substance, personality, etc. . . . [Thought] does not seem able to lib-

erate itself from them without destroying itself, for it seems that we cannot think of objects that are not in time and space, which have no number, etc. Other ideas are contingent and unsteady; we can conceive of their being unknown to a man, a society or an epoch; but these others . . . are like the framework of the intelligence.

That is, when we examine our experience, we find certain judgments and concepts which admit no possible exceptions—for example, that "every alteration must have a cause." Since thought cannot "liberate itself" from these judgments and concepts without "destroying itself," they represent features of experience which could not be otherwise. Furthermore, we can admit no possible exceptions either for ourselves or for any fellow human. As he puts it several pages later, "[the categories] are distinguished from all other knowledge by their necessity and universality." (I take Durkheim's claim for the strong necessity and universality of the categories to be his most consistently maintained and most plausible view. However, it is not difficult to find passages in the *Elementary Forms* in which these necessary and universal categories of thought are said, for example, to "vary incessantly" from place to place, and time to time. The idea of such categorial change—probably due to the influence of Renouvier—has been rightly criticized by Talcott Parsons as not only incompatible with Durkheim's "stronger" view, but as amounting to a self-refuting epistemological relativism. But whereas I see a glaring inconsistency, Parsons finds an "inextricable philosophical difficult[y]" (*The Structure of Social Action: A Study in Social Theory with Special Reference to a Group of Recent European Writers*, vol. I). I doubt whether the matter is resolvable through exegesis. As with other central doctrines of Durkheim's, there is no single, tidy "theory of the categories" in the *Elementary Forms*. I am reconstructing its central epistemological train of thought, that which is most philosophically important. Mine is not the only possible reconstruction; the book is too raw and too rambling for that.)

Durkheim apparently saw no need to argue for this picture of experience as containing necessary and universal features. It is apparently meant to follow from reflection on the character of his own experience, but to hold for beings fundamentally like himself. Durkheim writes in a phenomenological vein; the categories are "invested with an authority which we could not set aside even if we would. . . . They do not merely depend upon us, rather they impose themselves upon us." How to account for their necessity and universality then became a question of central importance for Durkheim.

With characteristic brevity he considers and rejects the answers supplied by both "classical empiricism" and "apriorism." The first holds that the categories "are constructed and made up of bits and pieces, and that the individual is the artisan of this construction." On this view, their peculiar hold over us is due to a certain "practical usefulness." Durkheim objects that in making the categories empirical and therefore contingent constructions, the empiricist doctrine bypasses, rather than explains their necessity and universality. Far from being in a position to construct their modal structure for ourselves, we find that all of our experience is constrained by and presupposes it. Thus, empiricism cannot account for what Durkheim calls our "surprising prerogative," namely, "that we can see certain relations in things which the examination of these things cannot reveal to us." That is, experience can teach us that every alteration has a cause, but not that the relation is one of necessity. Therefore, the origin of this necessity must lie elsewhere than in experience.

Given his rejection of empiricism, one might expect Durkheim to be sympathetic to apriorism, the doctrine that "the categories cannot be derived from experience [since] they are logically prior to and condition it." And in fact he does observe that, in admitting this much, the apriorist account is superior. He considers two versions of it. The first errs in making the categories "immanent in the nature of the human mind by virtue of its inborn constitution." Durkheim contends that this is merely to restate and not to resolve the problem, since one could as well ask how we came to have this subjective constitution and not some other.

A second apriorist explanation of the necessity and universality of the categories, that of "saying that only on this condition is experience itself possible changes the problem perhaps, but does not answer it. For the real question is to know how it comes that experience is not sufficient to itself, but presupposes certain conditions which are external and prior to it, and how it happens that these conditions are realized at the moment and in the manner that is desirable."

Durkheim complains that this, the Kantian or "transcendental" strategy, lacks "all experimental control; thus it does not satisfy the conditions demanded of a scientific hypothesis." A scientific hypothesis would specify "conditions which are external and prior" to experience, and which confer on the categories their necessary and universal status. Durkheim here voices the standard complaint that, in refusing to consider determining conditions antecedent to the spontaneity of thought itself, the transcendental point of view remains "suspended from nothing in heaven and supported by nothing on earth" (Lewis White Beck, *Essays on Kant and Hume*). Even admitting the transcendental strategy, the question recurs why our experience should have just these and not some other set of necessary and universal features.

The details of these criticisms, as well as the picture of experience as containing necessary and universal elements, remain, in Durkheim's hands, rather murky. He apparently felt that he had given them enough philosophical content to enable his audience to evaluate his argument, and in that he may have been right. But whatever the individual merits of these criticisms, when taken together they are clearly incompatible. According to Durkheim, empiricism fails because it falsely represents us as having the ability to stand outside the categories in constructing their necessary and universal structure from the successes and failures of everyday life. On the other hand, apriorism refuses to identify antecedent determinants of the categories' modal structure, and so offers no explanation at all. But how can we seek these antecedent causal conditions except as part of—on Durkheim's own terms—a futile attempt to adopt a standpoint outside of (antecedent to) our own categorial constraints?

So this was Durkheim's dilemma: if he was to escape both the errors of empiricism and apriorism, he had somehow to construe antecedent causes of the necessary and universal features of experience, and to construe them in such a way that they did not negate the very necessity and universality that he sought to explain. He interpreted the latter requirement to rule out any explanation of the categories' necessity and universality which made it a historical process. And adopting this ahistorical stance left him with no alternative, so he thought, except to assign causal efficacy to something without conceding it spatio-temporal location.

We can understand Durkheim's doctrine that society is an ideal entity as a response to these epistemological pressures. In contending that such concepts as time, space, class, number, cause, and substance reflect the earliest forms of social organization, Durkheim had already committed himself to the categories' social, though not ideal origin. (The thesis that the classification of things (categories) reproduces the classification of men (social organization) is generally regarded as a central theoretical contribution to the sociology of knowledge, and continues to find defenders and to spawn research programs. For example, Durkheim held that space is conceived in the form of an immense circle by some societies in Australia because their camp has a circular form. Again, the North American Zuni divide their pueblo into seven quarters, each representing a particular clan. He concludes, "Thus spatial organization is modeled after social organization and is a reproduction of it.") He turned to idealism as a way of overcoming what he perceived as the empiricist-apriorist deadlock. We can only understand the categories' necessity and universality, Durkheim insists, when we realize that

> society could not abandon the categories to the free choice of the individual without abandoning itself. If it is to live there is [need of a] minimum of logical conformity beyond which it cannot safely go. For this reason it uses all its authority upon its members to forestall such dissidences. Does a mind ostensibly free itself from these forms of thought? It is no longer considered a human mind in the full sense of the word, and is treated accordingly. That is why we feel that we are no longer completely free and that something resists, both within and outside ourselves, when we attempt to rid ourselves of these fundamental notions, even in our own conscience.

This is Durkheim's attempted middle way between empiricism and apriorism. As the unscientific apriorists cannot, he can point to the antecedent cause of our categorial framework, namely, society acting to insure its own survival. Unlike the hubristic empiricists, he seeks to represent its genesis as timeless, and so as independent of a constructing agent. Durkheim's is an argument to the best explanation: in order to account for the necessity and universality of the categories, we are forced to admit society—an ideal entity capable of imposing its requirements upon its members—into our ontology. (That is, for Durkheim, the hypothesis that the categories have a social (ideal) origin enjoyed greater explanatory scope and power, was more plausible and less ad hoc, and was disconfirmed by fewer accepted beliefs than any other incompatible hypothesis about the same subject.) "Thus," he concludes, "there is a realm of nature where the formula of idealism applies almost to the letter: that is the social realm." (Durkheim's idealism amounts not to the claim that the existence of objects in space is imaginary or even doubtful, but rather to the thesis that there exists a specifically social reality beyond what appears to common sense and ordinary sense experience.)

I want to make the transition from interpretation (section 1) to correction (section 3) by considering two of the most widespread and influential criticisms of Durkheim's sociological idealism. By recognizing their shortcomings we can see what is fundamentally right and wrong with Durkheim's line of argument.

II

In one of the most obvious broadsides, Talcott Parsons pointed out that no object without spatio-temporal location can produce an effect in the spatio-temporal world, and thus can carry no explanatory weight. In Parsons's words: "the effect of identifying society with the world of eternal objects is to eliminate the creative element of action altogether. Their defining characteristic is that neither the categories of time nor space apply to them. They 'exist' only 'in the mind.' Such entities cannot be the object of an explanatory science at all. For an explanatory science must be concerned with events, and events do not occur in the world of eternal objects. Durkheim's sociology in so far as it takes this direction, becomes, as Richard puts it, a 'work of pure interpretation' " (*La Sociologie générale*).

After having removed society from the natural world, Durkheim cannot then appeal to it in order to explain anything *in* the world, including the categorial structure of the mind.

Parsons and others have gone on to propose an empirical redeployment. They argue that a sociological epistemology need not appeal to shadowy objects existing outside the spatio-temporal world, but is free to trace the origin of any particular concept to a concrete historical cause. Thus, it is no coincidence that Robert Boyle and friends' "personal fortunes were deeply involved in the quest for stable social forms," and that they should propound a physics of inanimate matter. Similarly, there is more than an accidental connection between the need, on the part of Newton and his followers, to justify the Glorious Revolution of 1688, and their insistence on the passivity of matter. Echoing Durkheim's fundamental insight, David Bloor comments on these examples as follows: "The political context was used to construct different pictures of the physical world. . . . The effect in each case was to ensure that the classification of things reproduced the classifications of men" ("Durkheim and Mauss Revisited"). The suggestion is that we can then think of the sum of these concrete causes as "society." With this line of defense we limit our investigation to the world of ordinary sense experience, and so bypass the admitted force of Parsons's criticism.

The trouble with this strategy is that it also bypasses the object of Durkheim's investigations. Durkheim sought to explain not those concepts which we are free to construct for ourselves, but the universality and necessity of just those concepts which cannot fail to characterize human experience. In assigning them contingent, empirical causes we bypass the very universality and necessity which had set them apart for investigation.

So while Parsons's criticism is well-taken, his constructive proposal lacks Durkheim's depth of insight into the problem. Durkheim saw, as Parsons did not, that no causal (sociological) explanation could account for the necessity and universality of the categories, for the fact that "thought is impossible outside of them." He recognized that we cannot understand the peculiar necessity and universality of our conceptual framework so long as we view it as an effect caused by something in the spatio-temporal world. This recognition provided Durkheim's sociological idealism with a powerful philosophical motive. Parsons has not been alone in failing to appreciate its force.

On the other hand, Durkheim failed to see (or was unwilling to admit) that any investigation which takes the necessary and universal status of the categories as its object cannot be "scientific" in the only sense he recognized; that is, it cannot seek to identify their antecedent causal determinants. For he wrongly saw idealism as an alternative to empiricism which would yet allow him to speak meaningfully of antecedent causal conditions. But the investigation cannot be scientific in this sense, because, as Parsons points out, a commitment to locating the cause of *any* of our concepts must, if it is to make sense at all, be a commitment to its historical determination. And that approach, as Durkheim did realize (at least on occasion), cannot address, much less explain, their necessity and universality.

The idea that society, ideal or otherwise, could be the cause of the categories' necessity and universality has also been attacked for presupposing an agent able to recognize—that is, to *use*—the very concepts he is supposed to receive. An early commentator, William R. Dennes, put this second criticism with some force: "It is ridiculous to say that the categories of the mind are in any sense transferences from social organization. The categories of quantity would have to exist and to operate in order that an individual mind should ever recognize the one, the many, and the whole, of the divisions of his social group" ("Methods and Presuppositions of Group Psychology," *University of California Publications in Philosophy* 6 [1924]). And Dennes' assessment has been recently endorsed by Rodney Needham: "It is absurd to say that the categories originate in social organization: the notion of space has first to exist before social groups can be perceived to exhibit in their disposition any spatial relations which may then be applied to the universe" (Introduction to *Primitive Classification*).

Though their meaning is not entirely transparent, I take Dennes, Needham and others to be reasoning as follows. In order to make sense of Durkheim's theory we must be able to imagine a member of some primitive society going about his daily routine—trapping wild board, seeking shelter, etc.—without him possessing those categories the origin of which the theory purports to explain. For if it makes no sense to speak of anyone ever being without these categories, then it of course makes no sense to speak of their acquisition. Now the results of this little thought experiment do seem to come out squarely against Durkheim; whether for us or the primitive, it is nonsensical to speak of wild boars and shelters except as objects having locations in space and time, capable of causal interaction with other objects, and so on.

Because the object of Durkheim's theory is the origin of the categories in primitive society, it is natural to couch the present objection to it in the third person: anyone *back then* must have already been able to use the category of, say, plurality in order to be in a position to acquire it from society. Following Durkheim himself, his critics have uniformly adopted this third-person perspective. Dennes talks about "the individual" and "his social group," and Stephen Lukes, making the same point, writes that "the aboriginal must have the concept of class in order even to recognize the classifications of his society, let alone extend them to the universe."

But as any parent can testify, this is quite false. We *can* speak of anyone learning to make, for example, causal judgments, provided we catch him or her at an early enough age. Provided we take the child as an object interacting with other objects in the world, we can perfectly well identify a time during which he or she might come to acquire any of Durkheim's categories. So contrary to this line of criticism, Durkheim can quite well speak of the acquisition of necessary and universal categories, whether from society or elsewhere.

Unfortunately, Durkheim cannot avail himself of this defense, however convenient it may be. If the idea of concept-acquisition can be given sense only from within an empirical context, then, as we saw in discussing Parsons's criticism, Durkheim's entire project is misdirected. For if the investigation is empirical after all, then, as Durkheim himself (sometimes) realized, it bypasses its intended object, namely, the origin of the categories' necessity and universality. Viewed in this light, the scholarly dialogue assumes a somewhat farcical complexion. Durkheim's critics wrongly dispute something in which Durkheim cannot, in any event, allow himself to be interested, namely, the empirical acquisition of the categories. (Cf. Kant's "ludicrous spectacle" at A 58/B 83. Quotations from the *Critique of Pure Reason* are from the Norman Kemp Smith translation, 1929.)

Yet Durkheim and company do have the categories' necessity and universality in view, if not in focus. We *are* unable to picture any human being—primitive or not—locating himself in a world in which space is not three-dimensional, and time other than uni-directional. But in putting this point in the third person both Durkheim and his antagonists involve themselves in a subtle misrepresentation. While they make out that their observations are about what is and is not possible for another person, their conclusions are rather determined by their own inability to picture *themselves* acquiring, for example, the category of plurality without already possessing it. They rely not upon ethnographic reports about the mental capabilities of so-called primitive man, but upon what they know to be true of themselves, and then project these same capabilities and constraints back onto their aboriginal brothers.

There is of course neither point nor validity in alleging faulty methodology. Quite the opposite: if we wish to address ourselves to the necessity and universality of the categories at all, we must adopt this first-person perspective. The reason is that it is only when we speak of our own experience that we cannot admit exceptions to certain concepts and judgments which characterize it. And it is just these concepts and judgments in which we are interested. Thus, Durkheim's detractors are right to take our inevitable reliance on the categories as the clue to their universality and necessity, but only so long as each maintains the stance of one who reflects on the character of his or her own experience. For there *is* a sense in which it is question-begging for me to talk of my having acquired Durkheimian categories: it is question-begging for me to talk of that *experience*. (Thus, for the critics' objection to be valid, it has to assume a first-person orientation. But then of course it isn't an objection to Durkheim's third-person perspective at all.)

Lukes, one commentator who at times seems aware of this first-person requirement, generalizes by saying that "we cannot postulate a hypothetical situation in which individuals do *not* in general think by means of space, time, class, person, cause and according to the rules of logic, since this is what thinking *is*." Though I shall qualify it in the following section, Lukes's remark does hint at the thought-dependent nature of our inquiry. It hints that, quite apart from its idealist purport, Durkheim's argumentative strategy is self-defeating. Durkheim's theory of the social origin of the categories fails because it bypasses the very phenomenon it sought to investigate, their necessity and universality. In order to give sense to the idea of concept-acquisition—as he must do in order to avoid the charge of question-beg-ging—Durkheim must adopt the third-person point of view. But in so doing he turns his back on the very thing he was trying to understand.

III

Yet even as we reject Durkheim's sociological epistemology, a Durkheimian element seems to return when we reflect on the inescapability of our ca-tegorial constraints and ask to whom they belong. The peculiar thing, the point suggested by the quotation from Lukes, is that the very constraints we represent ourselves as holding up for inspection are operative in our act of self-examination. They are, in some sense, our possessions, but in a sense which leaves them unobjectifiable and in this respect unlike the details of our personalities and personal histories towards which we can hope to adopt a position of experimental detachment. Durkheim was right at least in this phenomenological sense: the categories are limitations not of our own creation. Rather, we find ourselves bound by them. Prompted by such considerations, we may be tempted to trace their coercive power to ourselves, to ourselves considered as impersonal agents lacking spatio-temporal location, but whose activities are nevertheless evident in the im-position of unavoidable constraints on our experience of the spatio-temporal world; not Durkheimian society, but something sharing an important func-tional property.

However, it is obvious that nothing is gained in the move from socio-logical idealism to transcendental psychology. In either case, we have only the illusion of explanation. Recalling Parsons, only something having a determinate location in space and time can serve as the cause of an effect having the same. Rather than turn to transcendental psychology, we do better to admit the results of the previous section: that however we derive the necessity and universality of certain of our categories of thought, our derivation cannot be causal in nature.

But if the necessity and universality of the categories could not have been determined by anything in or outside of the world, how *are* we to explain the modal structure which each in fact has? I think this question represents the philosophical high-water mark of the *Elementary Forms*, a level which Durkheim's own answer did not sustain. Indeed, it is easy to be sympathetic, for what sense *can* we give to the project of tracing the origin of the categories' necessity and universality when it has been stripped of all causal connotation?

Whatever the details of our investigative procedure turn out to be, we know from the last section that our object of study will come into view only from a first-person perspective. Indeed, Lukes's comment intimates just such a thought-dependent point of departure: "we cannot postulate a hypothetical situation in which individuals do *not* in general think by means of space, time, class, person, cause and according to the rules of logic, since this is what thinking *is*." If we take this first-person requirement seriously, we will have to begin with the categories, observe what ordering influence they have on the world of our experience, and infer their modal structure indirectly, "backwards" so to speak. Stealth is forced upon us; since we cannot make the categories themselves into objects of inspection without making use of them, we can only use objects of possible experience as informants.

Whatever its eventual usefulness, Lukes's remark about the nature of thought will require two major emendations. First, the remark is false as it stands, for we can easily conceive of beings whose thought and experience is constrained in ways very different from our own. For example, we do not contradict ourselves in conceiving of beings who make their escape through a fourth spatial dimension, or who work in the twentieth century and vacation in the fourth. The impossibility arises only when we try to picturre ourselves tagging along. Second, Lukes's observation, true or false, misses the point at hand. Whereas Lukes is (purportedly) telling us something about the nature of thought, we need a way of characterizing the relation between our necessary and universal categories of thought and *the world* which, in turn, will illuminate the origin of that very modal structure.

It has recently been pointed out that the problem in beginning our reflections with the nature of thought is how to coax objectivity out of a context which "seems unavoidably merely subjective." Writing of the truths of logic, Manley Thompson remarks that, "We show [their] objectivity not by showing [them] to be true of a subject matter, but by showing the necessity of presupposing logical principles in any thought, whatever the subject matter" ("On A Priori Truth," *The Journal of Philosophy* 78 [1981]).

We may ask whether this strategy can help us extend the results of the previous section. In the previous section we saw that we are unable to picture ourselves (or any fellow human) confronting a world which did not contain objects having definite spatio-temporal location, and about which we could not form judgments of, for example, quality, quantity, and relation. Just as Durkheim came to appreciate that certain features of our experience could not be otherwise, we can appreciate that these features thereby limit the form of any of our possible experiences. We might then apply Thompson's remark thusly: just as the objectivity of truths of logic are shown by exhibiting them as presuppositions of any thought whatever, so the necessity and universality of our fundamental categories of thought is shown by exhibiting them as presuppositions of any experience whatever. Just as all our thought (in order to be possibly thought by us) must conform to the principle of contradiction, so all objects (in order to be objects of possible experience) must conform to those conditions under which experience is possible.

In moving from thought to experience, we address the two problems with Lukes's observation. That is, we both confine our conclusions to beings fundamentally like ourselves (beings who must receive impressions through three spatial dimensions and one uni-directional temporal dimension, and who must connect them into judgments of experience), and we bring the world into the picture. In this first-person context, we get concepts which no possible experience could help us acquire, and which no possible experience could count against. We get the Kantian conception of apriority: necessary and universal concepts, knowledge of which is independent of all experience. We get transcendental knowledge (A 56 = B 81 [*Critique of Pure Reason*]).

We can now recognize the futility of trying to appeal to something in the natural world to explain something which, as Kant says, makes nature possible (B 160). We can also recognize the wisdom in Durkheim's sociological idealism: the Kantian epistemological subject, like Durkheimian society, is not a further object in the world. Like Durkheimian society, it finds its own content reflected in the world of experience. And like Durkheimian society, it is "collective" as opposed to "individual," for its properties are peculiar to no one in particular, but characterize the spontaneity of human thought, *überhaupt*. However, unlike Durkheimian society, the epistemological subject claims no shadowy existence outside the world, for its relation to the world is not causal, but epistemic. That is, it neither causes nor is caused by anything in the world of experience, but serves as a formal condition of its possibility.

IV

We may conclude that, while causal (sociological, historical) derivations can be given for *any* of our neighbor's concepts, the situation is more complex for those distinguished by a strict necessity and universality (those to which we admit no possible exception). If history is a true story told about the world of experience, then in addition to having an historical point of origin, our a priori concepts, to paraphrase Kant, make history possible. In justifying the use of our a priori concepts as unavoidable presuppositions of any experience capable of producing empirical knowledge, we do all that need or can be done to trace the origin of their necessity and universality. We trace it back to the possibility of experience.

This distinction between a causal and a justificatory account of our a priori concepts surfaces, in the *Elementary Forms,* as the distinction between the sociology of knowledge and epistemology. As the following passage makes clear, Durkheim was quite capable of making this distinction, though in the end he could not maintain it. After making his central sociological point—that the classification of things (categories) reproduces the classification of men (social organization)—Durkheim poses the resulting epistemological problem in an extremely vivid way: "But if the categories originally merely translate social states, does it not follow that they can be applied to the rest of nature only as metaphors? If they were made merely to express social conditions, it seems as though they could not be extended to other realms except in this sense. Thus in so far as they aid us in thinking of the physical or biological world, they have only the value of artificial symbols, useful practically perhaps, but having no connection with reality."

Durkheim is suggesting that the sociology of knowledge, however successful in its own right, raises a question of a different order. The sociology of knowledge asks, but cannot answer, how it is that we are able to represent reality *given* that our central categories have a social origin. If our fundamental categories of experience are forced upon us by an ideal entity, cannot they be applied to the material world "only as metaphors?" That was Durkheim's epistemological problem in the *Elementary Forms.* A recent gloss on Descartes' *First Meditation* captures Durkheim's worry as well: "All of our experience *could* be just the way it is now even if the external world were in fact very different from the way we believe it to be" (Barry Stroud, "The Significance of Skepticism," in *Transcendental Arguments and Science: Essays in Epistemology*). How do we know that Durkheimian society is a veracious God and not a *genie malign?*

Although Durkheim was keenly aware of the epistemological problem produced by his sociological theory, all his attempted solutions failed badly. In the most general sense, they failed because Durkheim could not break out of the third-person, naturalistic (sociological) point of view. From this point of view the categories are objects in the world, whose structure is explained by appeal to some other object in the world, perhaps society. On the other hand, the idea of an epistemic justification—legitimizing our use of the categories as unavoidable presuppositions of knowledge—makes sense only from the point of view of one who finds his or her own experience constrained a priori, and asks how that constraint is possible. For Durkheim, the idea of an epistemic, as opposed to a causal, derivation of necessary and universal features of experience, was therefore unavailable. Though he was able to articulate the subject matter of each, he was unable to pursue the distinction between a causal sociology of knowledge and a justificatory epistemology.

To sum up: Durkheim saw quite well the impossibility of giving a historical or sociological account of necessary and universal features of experience. This recognition is shown in his rejection of empiricism, in his contention that we cannot construct for ourselves what in fact constrains any act of construction whatever. However, his naturalistic standpoint left him with no choice but to posit determining antecedent causal conditions for our fundamental categories of thought, albeit causal conditions of an ahistorical variety. Thus, the valid insight that we cannot appeal to any object in space and time to explain the origin of the necessity and universality of our conceptual framework gave way to the error of supposing that some gain could be had by going outside the spatio-temporal world. Durkheim veered away from the insight that, when it comes to tracing the origin of the necessity and universality which marks certain of our concepts and judgments, the task of explanation is exhausted by that of justification.

In attributing causal efficacy to a world transcending that of possible experience, Durkheim's sociological idealism falls into what Kant called "transcendental illusion." From the Kantian point of view, society takes its place alongside world, God, and soul as an empirically empty concept which, nonetheless, resists dissolution even in the face of logical criticism. From the Kantian point of view, Durkheim's failed epistemology lends ironic confirmation to the second great contention of the *Elementary Forms:*

> At bottom, the concept of totality, of society, and of divinity are very likely only different aspects of the same notion.

Movement-Image: Commentaries on Bergson

Gilles Deleuze

THESES ON MOVEMENT: FIRST COMMENTARY ON BERGSON

First Thesis: Movement and Instant

Bergson does not just put forward one thesis on movement, but three. The first is the most famous, and threatens to obscure the other two. It is, however, only an introduction to the others. According to the first thesis, movement is distinct from the space covered. Space covered is past, movement is present, the act of covering. The space covered is divisible, indeed infinitely divisible, whilst movement is indivisible, or cannot be divided without changing qualitatively each time it is divided. This already presupposes a more complex idea: the spaces covered all belong to a single, identical, homogeneous space, while the movements are heterogeneous, irreducible among themselves.

But, before being developed, the first thesis contains another proposition: you cannot reconstitute movement with positions in space or instants in time: that is, with immobile sections [*coupes*]. You can only achieve this reconstitution by adding to the positions, or to the instants, the abstract idea of a succession, of a time which is mechanical, homogeneous, universal and copied from space, identical for all movements. And thus you miss the movement in two ways. On the one hand, you can bring two instants or two positions together to infinity; but movement will always occur in the interval between the two, in other words behind your back. On the other hand, however much you divide and subdivide time, movement will always occur in a concrete duration [*durée*]; thus each movement will have

From *Cinema 1: The Movement-Image,* translated by Hugh Tomlinson and Barbara Habberjam. © 1983 by Les Editions de Minuit, © 1986 by The Athlone Press. University of Minnesota Press, 1986.

315

its own qualitative duration. Hence we oppose two irreducible formulas: "real movement → concrete duration," and "immobile sections + abstract time."

In 1907, in *Creative Evolution*, Bergson gives the incorrect formula a name: the cinematographic illusion. Cinema, in fact, works with two complementary givens: instantaneous sections which are called images; and a movement or a time which is impersonal, uniform, abstract, invisible, or imperceptible, which is "in" the apparatus, and "with" which the images are made to pass consecutively. Cinema thus gives us a false movement— it is the typical example of false movement. But it is strange that Bergson should give the oldest illusion such a modern and recent name ("cinematographic"). In fact, says Bergson, when the cinema reconstitutes movement with mobile sections, it is merely doing what was already being done by the most ancient thought (Zeno's paradoxes), or what natural perception does. In this respect, Bergson's position differs from that of phenomenology, which instead saw the cinema as breaking with the conditions of natural perception. "We take snapshots, as it were, of the passing reality, and, as these are characteristics of the reality, we have only to string them on a becoming abstract, uniform and invisible, situated at the back of the apparatus of knowledge. . . . Perception, intellection, language so proceed in general. Whether we would think becoming, or express it, or even perceive it, we hardly do anything else than set going a kind of cinematograph inside us." Does this mean that for Bergson the cinema is only the projection, the reproduction of a constant, universal illusion? As though we had always had cinema without realising it? But then a whole range of problems arises.

Firstly, is not the reproduction of the illusion in a certain sense also its correction? Can we conclude that the result is artificial because the means are artificial? Cinema proceeds with photogrammes—that is, with immobile sections—twenty-four images per second (or eighteen at the outset). But it has often been noted that what it gives us is not the photogramme: it is an intermediate image, to which movement is not appended or added; the movement on the contrary belongs to the intermediate image as immediate given. It might be said that the position of natural perception is the same. But there the illusion is corrected "above" perception by the conditions which make perception possible in the subject. In the cinema, however, it is corrected at the same time as the image appears for a spectator without conditions (in this respect, as we will see, phenomenology is right in assuming that natural perception and cinematographic perception are qualitatively different). In short, cinema does not give us an image to which movement is added, it immediately gives us a movement-image. It does give us a section, but a section which is mobile, not an immobile section + abstract movement. Now what is again very odd is that Bergson was perfectly aware of the existence of mobile sections or movement-images. This happened before *Creative Evolution*, before the official birth of the cinema: it was set out in *Matter and Memory* in 1896. The discovery of the movement-image, beyond the conditions of natural perception, was the extraordinary invention of the first chapter of *Matter and Memory*. Had Bergson forgotten it ten years later?

Or did he fall victim to another illusion which affects everything in its initial stages? We know that things and people are always forced to conceal themselves, have to conceal themselves when they begin. What else could they do? They come into being within a set which no longer includes them and, in order not to be rejected, have to project the characteristics which they retain in common with the set. The essence of a thing never appears at the outset, but in the middle, in the course of its development, when its strength is assured. Having transformed philosophy by posing the question of the "new" instead of that of eternity (how are the production and appearance of something new possible?), Bergson knew this better than anyone. For example, he said that the novelty of life could not appear when it began, since when it began life was forced to imitate matter. . . . Is it not the same with the cinema? Is not cinema at the outset forced to imitate natural perception? And, what is more, what *was* cinema's position at the outset? On the one hand, the view point [*prise de vue*] was fixed, the shot was therefore spatial and strictly immobile; on the other hand, the apparatus for shooting [*appareil de prise de vue*] was combined with the apparatus for projection, endowed with a uniform abstract time. The evolution of the cinema, the conquest of its own essence or novelty, was to take place through montage, the mobile camera and the emancipation of the view point, which became separate from projection. The shot would then stop being a spatial category and become a temporal one, and the section would not longer be immobile, but mobile. The cinema would rediscover that very movement-image of the first chapter of *Matter and Memory*.

We must conclude that Bergson's first thesis on movement is more complex than it initially seemed. On the one hand there is a critique of all attempts to reconstitute movement with the space covered, that is, by adding together instantaneous immobile sections and abstract time. On the other hand there is the critique of the cinema, which is condemned as one of these illusory attempts, as the attempt which is the culmination of the illusion. But there is also the thesis of *Matter and Memory*, mobile sections, temporal planes [*plans*] which prefigure the future or the essence of the cinema.

Second Thesis: Privileged Instants and Any-Instant-Whatevers

Now *Creative Evolution* advances a second thesis, which, instead of reducing everything to the same illusion about movement, distinguishes at least two very different illusions. The error remains the same—that of reconstituting movement from instants or positions—but there are two ways of doing this: the ancient and the modern. For antiquity, movement refers to intelligible elements, Forms or Ideas which are themselves eternal and immobile.

Of course, in order to reconstitute movement, these forms will be grasped as close as possible to their actualisation in a matter-flux. These are potentialities which can only be acted out by being embodied in matter. But, conversely, movement merely expresses a "dialectic" of forms, an ideal synthesis which gives it order and measure. Movement, conceived in this way, will thus be the regulated transition from one form to another, that is, an order of *poses* or privileged instants, as in a dance. The forms or ideas

> are supposed . . . to characterise a period of which they express the quintessence, all the rest of this period being filled by the transition, of no interest in itself, from one form to another form. . . . They noted, then, the final term or culminating point (telos, acmè), and set it up as the essential moment: this moment, that language has retained in order to express the whole of the fact, sufficed also for science to characterise it.
>
> (*Creative Evolution*)

The modern scientific revolution has consisted in relating movement not to privileged instants but to any-instant-whatever. Although movement was still recomposed, *it was no longer recomposed from formal transcendental elements (poses), but from immanent material elements (sections).* Instead of producing an intelligible synthesis of movement, a sensible analysis was derived from it. In this way, modern astronomy was formed, by determining a relation between an orbit and the time needed to traverse it (Kepler); modern physics, by linking the space covered to the time taken by a body to fall (Galileo); modern geometry, by working out the equation of a flat curve, that is, the position of a point on a moving straight line at any moment in its course (Descartes); and lastly differential and integral calculus, once they had the idea of examining sections which could be brought infinitely closer together (Newton and Leibniz). Everywhere the mechanical succession of instants replaced the dialectical order of poses: "Modern science must be defined pre-eminently by its aspiration to take time as an independent variable."

Cinema seems to be the last descendant of this lineage which Bergson traced. One might conceive of a series of means of translation (train, car, aeroplane . . .) and, in parallel, a series of means of expression (diagram, photo, cinema). The camera would then appear as an exchanger or, rather, as a generalised equivalent of the movements of translation. And this is how it appears in Wenders's films. When we think about the prehistory of the cinema, we always end up confused, because we do not know where its technological lineage begins, or how to define this lineage. We can always refer to shadow puppets, or the very earliest projection systems. But, in fact, the determining conditions of the cinema are the following: not merely the photo, but the snapshot (the long-exposure photo [photo de pose] belongs to the other lineage); the equidistance of snapshots; the transfer of this equidistance on to a framework which constitutes the "film" (it was Edison and Dickson who perforated the film in the camera); a mechanism for moving on images (Lumière's claws). It is in this sense that the cinema is the system which reproduces movement as a function of any-instant-whatever that is, as a function of equidistant instants, selected so as to create an impression of continuity. Any other system which reproduces movement through an order of exposures [*poses*] projected in such a way that they pass into one another, or are "transformed," is foreign to the cinema. This is clear when one attempts to define the cartoon film; if it belongs fully to the cinema, this is because the drawing no longer constitutes a pose or a completed figure, but the description of a figure which is always in the process of being formed or dissolving through the movement of lines and points taken at any-instant-whatevers of their course. The cartoon film is related not to a Euclidean, but to a Cartesian geometry. It does not give us a figure described in a unique moment, but the continuity of the movement which describes the figure.

Nevertheless, the cinema seems to thrive on privileged instants. It is often said that Eisenstein extracted from movements or developments certain moments of crisis, which he made the subject of the cinema par excellence. This is precisely what he called the "pathetic": he picks out peaks and shouts, he pushes scenes to their climax and brings them into collision. But this is definitely not an objection. Let us return to the cinema's prehistory, and to the famous example of the horse's gallop: this could only be dissected exactly by Marey's graphic recordings and Muybridge's equidistant snapshots, which relate the organised whole of the canter to any-point-whatever. If the equidistant points are chosen well, one inevitably comes across remarkable occasions; that is, the moments when the horse has one hoof on the ground, then three, two, one. These may be called privileged instants, but not in the sense of the poses or generalised postures which marked the gallop in the old forms. These instants have nothing in common with long-exposures [*poses*], and would even be formally impossible as long-exposures. If these are privileged instants, it is as remarkable or singular points which belong to movement, and not as the moments of actualisation of a transcendent form. The meaning of the notion has completely changed. The privileged instants of Eisenstein, or of any other director, are still any-instant-whatevers: to put it simply, the any-instant-whatever can be regular *or* singular, ordinary *or* remarkable. If Eisenstein picks out remarkable instants, this does not prevent him deriving from them an immanent analysis of movement, and not a transcendental synthesis. The remarkable or singular instant remains any-instant-whatever among the others. This is indeed the difference between the modern dialectic, to which Eisenstein appeals, and the old dialectic. The latter is the order of transcendental forms which are actualised in a movement, while the former is the production and confrontation of the singular points which are immanent to movement. Now this production of singularities (the qualitative leap) is achieved by the accumulation of banalities (quantitative process), so that the singular is taken from the any-whatever, and is itself an any-whatever which is simply non-ordinary and non-regular. Eisenstein himself made it clear that "the pathetic" presupposed "the organic" as the organised set of any-instant-whatevers through which the cuts [*coupures*] have to pass.

The any-instant-whatever is the instant which is equidistant from another. We can therefore define the cinema as the system which reproduces movement by relating it to the any-instant-whatever. But it is here that the difficulty arises. What is the interest of such a system? From the point of view of science, it is very slight. For the scientific revolution was one of analysis. And, if movement had to be related to the any-instant-whatever in order to analyse it, it was hard to see any interest in a synthesis or reconstitution based on the same principle, except a vague interest of confirmation. This is why neither Marey nor Lumière held out much hope for the invention of the cinema. Did it at least have artistic interest? This did not seem likely either, since art seemed to uphold the claims of a higher synthesis of movement, and to remain linked to the poses and forms that science had rejected. We have reached the very heart of cinema's ambiguous position as "industrial art": it was neither an art nor a science.

Contemporaries, however, might have been sensitive to a development at work in the arts, which was changing the status of movement, even in painting. To an even greater degree, dance, ballet and mime were abandoning figures and poses to release values which were not posed, not measured, which related movement to the any-instant-whatever. In this way, art, ballet, and mime became actions capable of responding to accidents of the environment; that is, to the distribution of the points of a space, or of the moments of an event. All this served the same end as the cinema. From the time of the talkie, the cinema was able to make the musical comedy one of its principal genres, with Fred Astaire's "action dance" which takes place in any-location-whatever: in the street, surrounded by cars, along a pavement. But even in silent films, Chaplin had divorced mime from the art of poses to make it an action-mime. Mitry answered complaints that Charlie used the cinema, rather than serving it, by arguing that he gave mime a new model, a function of space and time, a continuity constructed at each instant, which now only allowed itself to be decomposed into its prominent immanent elements, instead of being related to prior forms which it was to embody (*Histoire du cinéma muet*).

Bergson forcefully demonstrates that the cinema fully belongs to this modern conception of movement. But, from this point, he seems to hesitate between two paths, one of which leads him back to his first thesis, the other instead opening up a new question. According to the first path, although the two conceptions may be different from the scientific point of view, they nevertheless have a more or less identical result. In fact, to recompose movement with *eternal poses* or with *immobile sections* comes to the same thing: in both cases, one misses the movement because one constructs a Whole, one assumes that "all is given," whilst movement only occurs if the whole is neither given nor giveable. As soon as a whole is given to one in the eternal order of forms or poses, or in the set of any-instant-whatevers, then either time is no more than the image of eternity, or it is the consequence of the set; there is no longer room for real movement. Another path, however, seemed open to Bergson. For, if the ancient conception corresponds closely to ancient philosophy, which aims to think the eternal, then the modern conception, modern science, calls upon *another* philosophy. When one relates movement to any-moment-whatevers, one must be capable of thinking the production of the new, that is, of the remarkable and the singular, at any one of these moments: this is a complete conversion of philosophy. It is what Bergson ultimately aims to do: to give modern science the metaphysic which corresponds to it, which it lacks as one half packs the other (*Creative Evolution*). But can we stop once we have set out on this path? Can we deny that the arts must also go through this conversion or that the cinema is an essential factor in this, and that it has a role to play in the birth and formation of this new thought, this new way of thinking? This is why Bergson is no longer content merely to corroborate his first thesis on movement. Bergson's second thesis—although it stops half way—makes possible another way of looking at the cinema, a way in which it would no longer be just the perfected apparatus of the oldest illusion, but, on the contrary, the organ for perfecting the new reality.

Third Thesis: Movement and Change

And this is Bergson's third thesis, which is also contained in *Creative Evolution*. If we tried to reduce it to a bare formula, it would be this: not only is the instant an immobile section of movement, but movement is a mobile section of duration, that is, of the Whole, or of a whole. Which implies that movement expresses something more profound, which is the change in duration or in the whole. To say that duration is change is part of its definition: it changes and does not stop changing. For example, matter moves, but does not change. Now movement expresses a change in duration or in the whole. What *is* a problem is on the one hand this expression, and on the other, this whole-duration identification.

Movement is a translation in space. Now each time there is a translation of parts in space, there is also a qualitative change in a whole. Bergson gave numerous examples of this in *Matter and Memory*. An animal moves, but this is for a purpose: to feed, migrate, etc. It might be said that movement presupposes a difference of potential, and aims to fill it. If I consider parts or places abstractly—A and B—I cannot understand the movement which goes from one to the other. But imagine I am starving at A, and at B there is something to eat. When I have reached B and had something to eat, what has changed is not only my state, but the state of the whole which encompassed B, A, and all that was between them. When Achilles overtakes the tortoise, what changes is the state of the whole which en-

compassed the tortoise, Achilles, and the distance between the two. Movement always relates to a change, migration to a seasonal variation. And
this is equally true of bodies: the fall of a body presupposes another one
which attracts it, and expresses a change in the whole which encompasses
them both. If we think of pure atoms, their movements, which testify to
a reciprocal action of all the parts of the substance, necessarily express
modifications, disturbances, changes of energy in the whole. What Bergson
discovers beyond translation is vibration, radiation. Our error lies in believing that it is the any-element-whatevers, external to qualities which
move. But the qualities themselves are pure vibrations which change at the
same time as the alleged elements move.

In *Creative Evolution*, Bergson gives an example which is so famous
that it no longer surprises us. Putting some sugar in a glass of water, he
says that "I must, willy-nilly, wait until the sugar melts." This is slightly
strange, since Bergson seems to have forgotten that stirring with a spoon
can help it to dissolve. But what is his main point? That the movement of
translation which detaches the sugar particles and suspends them in the
water itself expresses a change in the whole, that is, in the content of the
glass; a qualitative transition from water which contains a sugar lump to
the state of sugared water. If I stir with the spoon, I speed up the movement,
but I also change the whole, which now encompasses the spoon, and the
accelerated movement continues to express the change of the whole. "The
wholly superficial displacements of masses and molecules studied in physics and chemistry would become, by relation to that inner vital movement
(which is transformation and not translation) what the position of a moving
object is to the movement of that object in space." Thus, in this third thesis,
Bergson puts forward the following analogy:

$$\frac{\text{immobile sections}}{\text{movement}} = \frac{\text{movement as mobile section}}{\text{qualitative change}}$$

The only difference is this: the ratio on the left-hand side expresses an
illusion; and that on the right-hand side, a reality.

Above all, what Bergson wants to say using the glass of sugared water
is that my waiting, whatever it be, expresses a duration as mental, spiritual
reality. But why does this spiritual duration bear witness, not only for me
who waits, but for a whole which changes? According to Bergson the whole
is neither given nor giveable (and the error of modern science, like that of
ancient science, lay in taking the whole as given, in two different ways).
Many philosophers had already said that the whole was neither given nor
giveable: they simply concluded from this that the whole was a meaningless
notion. Bergson's conclusion is very different: if the whole is not giveable,
it is because it is the Open, and because its nature is to change constantly,
or to give rise to something new, in short, to endure. "The duration of the
universe must therefore be one with the latitude of creation which can find
place in it." So that each time we find ourselves confronted with a duration,

or in a duration, we may conclude that there exists somewhere a whole which is changing, and which is open somewhere. It is widely known that Bergson initially discovered duration as identical to consciousness. But further study of consciousness led him to demonstrate that it only existed in so far as it opened itself upon a whole, by coinciding with the opening up of a whole. Similarly for the living being: in comparing the living being to a whole, or to the whole of the universe, Bergson seems to be reviving the most ancient simile. However, he completely reverses its terms. For, if the living being is a whole and, therefore, comparable to the whole of the universe, this is not because it is a microcosm as closed as the whole is assumed to be, but, on the contrary, because it is open upon a world, and the world, the universe, is itself the Open. "Wherever anything lives, there is, open somewhere, a register in which time is being inscribed."

If one had to define the whole, it would be defined by Relation. Relation is not a property of objects, it is always external to its terms. It is also inseparable from the open, and displays a spiritual or mental existence. Relations do not belong to objects, but to the whole, on condition that this is not confused with a closed set of objects. (We raise the problems of relations at this point, although it was not raised explicitly by Bergson. We know that the relation between two things is not reducible to an attribute of one thing or the other, nor, indeed, to an attribute of the set [*ensemble*]. On the other hand, it is still quite possible to relate the relations to a whole [*tout*] if one conceives the whole as a continuum, and not as a given set.) By movement in space, the objects of a set change their respective positions. But, through relations, the whole is transformed or changes qualitatively. We can say of duration itself or of time, that it is the whole of relations.

The whole and the "wholes" must not be confused with *sets*. Sets are closed, and everything which is closed is artificially closed. Sets are always sets of parts. But a whole is not closed, it is open; and it has no parts except in a very special sense, since it cannot be divided without changing qualitatively at each stage of the division. "The real whole might well be, we conceive, an indivisible continuity." The whole is not a closed set, but on the contrary that by virtue of which the set is never absolutely closed, never completely sheltered, that which keeps it open somewhere as if by the finest thread which attaches it to the rest of the universe. The glass of water is indeed a closed set containing the parts, the water, the sugar, perhaps the spoon; but that is not the whole. The whole creates itself, and constantly creates itself in another dimension without parts—like that which carries along the set of one qualitative state to another, like the pure ceaseless becoming which passes through these states. It is in this sense that it is spiritual or mental. "The glass of water, the sugar, and the process of the sugar's melting in the water are abstractions and . . . the whole within which they have been cut out by my senses and understanding progresses, it may be, in the manner of a consciousness." In any case, this artificial division of a set or a closed system is not a pure illusion. It is well founded and, if it is impossible to break the link of each thing with the whole (this paradoxical link, which ties it to the open), it can at least be drawn out, stretched to infinity, made finer and finer. The organisation of matter makes possible the closed systems or the determinate sets of parts; and the deployment of space makes them necessary. But the point is that the sets are in space, and the whole, the wholes are in duration, are duration itself, in so far as it does not stop changing. So that the two formulas which corresponded to Bergson's first thesis now take on a much more rigorous status; "immobile sections + abstract time" refers to closed sets whose parts are in fact immobile sections, and whose successive states are calculated on an abstract time; while "real movement → concrete duration" refers to the opening up of a whole which endures, and whose movements are so many mobile sections crossing the closed systems.

The upshot of this third thesis is that we find ourselves on three levels: (1) the sets or closed systems which are defined by discernible objects or distinct parts; (2) the movement of translation which is established between these objects and modifies their respective positions; (3) the duration or the whole, a spiritual reality which constantly changes according to its own relations.

Thus in a sense movement has two aspects. On one hand, that which happens between objects or parts; on the other hand that which expresses the duration or the whole. The result is that duration, by changing qualitatively, is divided up in objects, and objects, by gaining depth, by losing their contours, are united in duration. We can therefore say that movement relates the objects of a closed system to open duration, and duration to the objects of the system which it forces to open up. Movement relates the objects between which it is established to the changing whole which it expresses, and vice versa. Through movement the whole is divided up into objects, and objects are reunited in the whole, and indeed between the two "the whole" changes. We can consider the objects or parts of a set as *immobile sections;* but movement is established between these sections, and relates the objects or parts to the duration of a whole which changes, and thus expresses the changing of the whole in relation to the objects and is itself a *mobile section* of duration. Now we are equipped to understand the profound thesis of the first chapter of *Matter and Memory:* (1) there are not only instantaneous images, that is, immobile sections of movement; (2) there are movement-images which are mobile sections of duration; (3) there are, finally, time-images, that is, duration-images, change-images, relation-images, volume-images which are beyond movement itself. . . .

THE MOVEMENT-IMAGE AND ITS THREE VARIETIES: SECOND COMMENTARY ON BERGSON

The Identity of the Image and the Movement

The historical crisis of psychology coincided with the moment at which it was no longer possible to hold a certain position. This position involved placing images in consciousness and movements in space. In consciousness there would only be images—these were qualitative and without extension. In space there would only be movements—these were extended and quantitative. But how is it possible to pass from one order to the other? How is it possible to explain that movements, all of a sudden, produce an image—as in perception—or that the image produces a movement—as in voluntary action? If we invoke the brain, we have to endow it with a miraculous power. And how can movement be prevented from already being at least a virtual image, and the image from already being at least possible movement? What appeared finally to be a dead end was the confrontation of materialism and idealism, the one wishing to reconstitute the order of consciousness with pure material movements, the other the order of the universe with pure images in consciousness. [This is the most general theme of the first chapter and the conclusion of *Matter and Memory*; all further references to this text will be abbreviated as *MM*.] It was necessary, at any cost, to overcome this duality of image and movement, of consciousness and thing. Two very different authors were to undertake this task at about the same time: Bergson and Husserl. Each had his own war cry: all consciousness is consciousness *of* something (Husserl), or more strongly, all consciousness *is* something (Bergson). Undoubtedly many factors external to philosophy explain why the old position had become impossible. These were social and scientific factors which placed more and more movement into conscious life, and more and more images into the material world. How therefore was it possible not to take account of the cinema, which was being developed at that very moment, and which would produced its own evidence of a *movement-image?*

It is true that Bergson, as we have seen, apparently found the cinema only a false ally. As for Husserl, as far as we know, he never mentions the cinema at all (it is noteworthy that Sartre too, much later, in making an inventory and analysis of all kinds of images in *The Imagination*, does not cite the cinematographic image). It is Merleau-Ponty who attempts, only incidentally, a confrontation between cinema and phenomenology, but he also sees the cinema as an ambiguous ally. It is simply that the reasons given by phenomenology and those of Bergson are so different that their very opposition should guide us. What phenomenology sets up as a norm is "natural perception" and its conditions. Now, these conditions are existential co-ordinates which define an "anchoring" of the perceiving subject in the world, a being in the world, an opening to the world which will be expressed in the famous "all consciousnes is consciousness of something." Hence movement, perceived or made, must be understood not of course in the sense of an intelligible form (Idea) which would be actualised in a content, but as a sensible form (Gestalt) which organises the perceptive field as a function of a situated intentional consciousness. The cinema can, with impunity, bring us close to things or take us away from them and revolve around them, it suppresses both the anchoring of the subject and the horizon of the world. Hence it substitutes an implicit knowledge and a second intentionality for the conditions of natural perception. It is not the same as the other arts, which aim rather at something unreal through the world, but makes the world itself something unreal or a tale [*récit*]. With the cinema, it is the world which becomes its own image, and not an image which becomes world. It will be noted that phenomenology, in certain respects, stops at pre-cinematographic conditions which explains its embarrassed attitude: it gives a privilege to natural perception which means that movement is still related to *poses* (simply existential instead of essential). As a result, cinematographic movement is both condemned as unfaithful to the conditions of perception and also exalted as the new story capable of "drawing close to" the perceived and the perceiver, the world and perception.

Bergson condemns the cinema as an ambiguous ally in a completely different way. For if the cinema misconceives movement, it does so in the same way as natural perception and for the same reasons: "We take snapshots, as it were, of passing reality. . . . Perception, intellection, language so proceed in general (*Creative Evolution*). For Bergson, that is to say, the model cannot be natural perception, which does not possess any privilege. The model would be rather a state of things which would constantly change, a flowing-matter in which no point of anchorage nor centre of reference would be assignable. On the basis of this state of things it would be necessary to show how, at any point, centres can be formed which would impose fixed instantaneous views. It would therefore be a question of "deducing" conscious, natural *or* cinematographic perception. [*MM*: "I say in consequence that conscious perception must be produced."] But the cinema perhaps has a great advantage: just because it lacks a centre of anchorage and of horizon, the sections which it makes would not prevent it from going back up the path that natural perception comes down. Instead of going from the acentred state of things to centred perception, it could go back up towards the acentred state of things, and get closer to it. Broadly speaking, this would be the opposite of what phenomenology put forward. Even in his critique of the cinema Bergson was in agreement with it, to a far greater degree than he thought. We see this in the brilliant first chapter of *Matter and Memory*.

We find ourselves in fact faced with the exposition of a world where IMAGE = MOVEMENT. Let us call the set of what appears "Image." We cannot even say that one image acts on another or reacts to another. There is no moving body [*mobile*] which is distinct from executed movement. There is nothing moved which is distinct from the received movement. Every thing, that is to say every image, is indistinguishable from its actions and reactions: this is universal variation. Every image is "merely a road by which pass, in every direction, the modifications propagated throughout the immensity of the universe." *Every image acts on others and reacts to others, on "all their facets at once" and "by all their elements."* "The truth is that the movements of matter are very clear, regarded as images, and that there is no need to look in movement for anything more than what we see in it." An atom is an image which extends to the point to which its actions and reactions extend. My body is an image, hence a set of actions and reactions. My eye, my brain, are images, parts of my body. How could my brain contain images since it is one image among others? External images act on me, transmit movement to me, and I return movement: how could images be in my consciousness since I am myself image, that is, movement? And can I even, at this level, speak of "ego," of eye, of brain and of body? Only for simple convenience; for nothing can yet be identified in this way. It is rather a gaseous state. Me, my body, are rather a set of molecules and atoms which are constantly renewed. Can I even speak of atoms? They are not distinct from worlds, from interatomic influences. It is a state of matter too hot for one to be able to distinguish solid bodies in it. It is a world of universal variation, of universal undulation, universal rippling: there are neither axes, nor centre, nor left, nor right, nor high, nor low. . . .

This infinite set of all images constitutes a kind of plane [*plan*] of immanence. The image exists in itself, on this plane. This in-itself of the image is matter: not something hidden behind the image, but on the contrary the absolute identity of the image and movement. The identity of the image and movement leads us to conclude immediately that the movement-image and matter are identical. "You may say that my body is matter or that it is an image." The *movement-image* and *flowing-matter* are strictly the same thing. Is this material universe the universe of mechanism? No, for (as *Creative Evolution* shows) mechanism involves closed systems, actions of contact, immobile instantaneous sections. Now, of course, closed systems, finite sets, are cut from this universe or on this plane; it makes them possible by the exteriority of its parts. But it is not one itself. It is a set, but an infinite set. The plane of immanence is the movement (the facet of movement) which is established between the parts of each system and between one system and another, which crosses them all, stirs them all up together and subjects them all to the condition which prevents them from being absolutely closed. It is therefore a section; but, despite some terminological ambiguities in Bergson, it is not an immobile and instantaneous section, it is a mobile section, a temporal section or perspective. It is a bloc of space-time, since the time of the movement which is at work within it is part of it every time. There is even an infinite series of such blocs or mobile sections which will be, as it were, so many presentations of the plane, corresponding to the succession of movements in the universe. (This notion of the plane of immanence and the characteristics which we give it, seem to be a long way from Bergson. Nevertheless, we believe that we are being faithful to him. Bergson does indeed present the plane of matter as an "instantaneous section" of becoming [*MM*]. But this is for ease of exposition for, as Bergson reminds us and will remind us later even more precisely, it is a plane where the movements which express the changes in becoming constantly appear and reproduce themselves. It therefore includes time. It has a time as variable of movement. Moreover, the plane is itself mobile, Bergson says. In fact to each set of movements which expresses a change there will correspond a presentation of the plane. The idea of blocs of space-time is therefore not at all contrary to Bergson's thesis.) And the plane is not distinct from this presentation of planes. This is not mechanism, it is machinism. The material universe, the plane of immanence, is the *machine assemblage* [*agencement machinique*] *of movement-images.* Here Bergson is startlingly ahead of his time: it is the universe as cinema in itself, a metacinema. This implies a view of the cinema itself which is totally different from that which Bergson proposed in his explicit critique.

But how is it possible to speak of images in themselves which are not for anyone and are not addressed to anyone? How is it possible to speak of an Appearing [*Apparaître*], since there is not even an eye? It is possible for at least two reasons. The first is in order to distinguish them from things conceived of as bodies. Indeed, our perception and our language distinguish bodies (nouns), qualities (adjectives) and actions (verbs). But actions, in precisely this sense, have already replaced movement with the idea of a provisional place towards which it is directed or that of a result that it secures. Quality has replaced movement with the idea of a state which persists whilst waiting for another to replace it. Body has replaced movement with the idea of a subject which would carry it out or of an object which would submit to it, of a vehicle which would carry it. We will see that such images *are* formed in the universe (action-images, affection-images, perception-images). But they depend on new conditions and certainly cannot appear for the moment. For the moment we only have movements, which are called images in order to distinguish them from everything that they have not yet become. However, this negative reason is not sufficient. The positive reason is that the plane of immanence is entirely made up of Light. The set of movements, of actions and reactions is light which diffuses, which is propagated "without resistance and without loss (*MM*)." The identity of the image and movement stems from the identity of matter and light. The image is movement, just as matter is light. Later on Bergson will show, in *Durée et simultanéité*, the importance of the theory of Relativity's reversal of "lines of light" and "rigid lines," luminous figures" and "solid or geometric figures": with Relativity "it is the figure of light which imposes its conditions on the rigid figure." (*Duration and Simultaneity*, chap. V. The importance and the ambiguity of this book, in which Bergson confronts the theory of relativity, is well known. But though Bergson had to forbid its republication, this was not because he realised that he might have made errors. The ambiguity came rather from readers who believed that Bergson was discussing the theories of Einstein themselves. This was obviously not the case (but Bergson was not able to dispel this misunderstanding). We have just seen that he completely accepted the primacy of light and blocs of space-time. The discussion bore on something else: do these blocs prevent the existence of a universal time conceived as becoming or duration? Bergson never believed that the theory of relativity was false, but only that it was incapable of constituting the philosophy of real time which ought to correspond to it.) If we recall Bergson's profound desire to produce a philosophy which would be that of modern science (not in the sense of a reflection on that science, that is an epistemology, but on the contrary in the sense of an invention of autonomous concepts capable of corresponding with the new symbols of science), we can understand that Bergson's confrontation with Einstein was inevitable. Now, the first aspect of this confrontation is the affirmation of a diffusion or propagation of light on the whole plane of immanence. In the movement-image there are not yet bodies or rigid lines, but only lines or figures of light. Blocs of space-time are such figures. They are images in themselves. If they do not appear to anyone, that is to an eye, this is because light is not yet reflected or stopped, and passing "on unopposed [is] never . . . revealed" (*MM*). In other words, the eye is in things, in luminous images in themselves. *"Photography, if there is photography, is already snapped, already shot, in the very interior of things and for all the points of space.*

This breaks with the whole philosophical tradition which placed light on the side of spirit and made consciousness a beam of light which drew things out of their native darkness. Phenomenology was still squarely within this ancient tradition: but, instead of making light an internal light, it simply opened it onto the exterior, rather as if the intentionality of consciousness was the ray of an electric lamp ("all consciousness is consciousness *of* something"). For Bergson, it is completely the opposite. Things are luminous by themselves without anything illuminating them: all consciousness *is* something, it is indistinguishable from the thing, that is from the image of light. But here it is a consciousness by right [*en droit*], which is diffused everywhere and yet does not reveal its source [*ne se révèle pas*]: it is indeed a photo which has already been taken and shot in all things and for all points, but which is "translucent." If, subsequently, a *de facto* consciousness is constituted in the universe, at a particular place on the plane of immanence, it is because very special images will have stopped or reflected the light, and will have provided the "black screen" which the plate lacked. In short, it is not consciousness which is light, it is the set of images, or the light, which is consciousness, immanent to matter. As for *our* consciousness of fact, it will merely be the opacity without which light "is always propagated without its source ever having been revealed." The opposition between Bergson and phenomenology is, in this respect, a radical one.

We may therefore say that the plane of immanence or the plane of matter is: a set of movement-images; a collection of lines or figures of light; a series of blocs of space-time.

From the Movement-image to Its Varieties

What happens and what can happen in this acentred universe where everything reacts on everything else? We must not introduce a different factor, a factor of another nature. So what can happen is this: at any point whatever of the plane an *interval* appears—a gap between the action and the reaction. All Bergson asks for are movements and intervals between movements which serve as units—it is also exactly what Dziga Vertov asked for, in his materialist conception of the cinema. Clearly, this phenomenon of the interval is only possible in so far as the plane of matter includes time. For Bergson, the gap, the interval, will be sufficient to define one type of image among others, but a very special type—living images or matters [*matières*]. Whereas the other images act and react on all their facets and in all their parts, here we have images which only receive actions on one facet or in certain parts and only execute reactions by and in other parts. These are, so to speak, "quartered" [*écartelées*] images. And from the outset their specialised facet, which will later be called receptive or sensorial, has a curious effect on the influencing images or the received excitations. It is as if this specialised facet isolated certain images from all those which compete and act together in the universe. It is here that closed systems, "tableaux," can be constituted. Living beings "allow to pass through them, so to speak, those external influences which are indifferent to them; the others isolated, become 'perceptions' by their very isolation" (*MM*). It is an operation which is exactly described as a *framing*: certain actions undergone are isolated by the frame and hence, as we will see, they are forestalled, anticipated. But, on the other hand, executed reactions are no longer immediately linked with the action which is undergone. By virtue of the interval, these are delayed reactions, which have the time to select their elements, to organise them or to integrate them into a new movement which is impossible to conclude by simply prolonging the received excitation. Such reactions which present something unpredictable or new will be called "action" strictly speaking. Thus the living image will be "an instrument of analysis in regard to the movement received, and an instrument of selection in regard to the movement executed." Because they only owe this privilege to the phenomenon of the gap, or interval between a received and an executed movement, living images will be "centres of indetermination," which are formed in the acentred universe of movement-images.

If we consider the other aspect, the luminous aspect of the plane of matter, one can say this time that the images or living matter provide the black screen which the plate lacked, and which prevented the influencing image (the photo) from being developed. This time, instead of diffusing and propagating in all directions "without resistance or dwindling," the line or image of light runs up against an obstacle, that is an opacity which will reflect it. The image reflected by a living image is precisely what will be called perception. And these two aspects are strictly complementary: the special image, the living image, is indissolubly the centre of indetermination or black screen. As essential consequence follows—*the existence of a double system, of a double régime of reference of images*. There is firstly a system in which each image varies for itself, and all the images act and react as a function of each other, on all their facets and in all their parts.

But to this is added another system where all vary principally for a single one, which receives the action of the other images on one of its facets and reacts to them on another facet.

We have not finished with the matter-movement-image. Bergson constantly says that we cannot understand anything unless we are first given the set of images. It is only on this plane that a simple interval of movements can be produced. And the brain is nothing but this—an interval, a gap between an action and a reaction. The brain is certainly not a centre of images from which one could begin, but itself constitutes one special image among the others. It constitutes a centre of indetermination in the acentred universe of images. But with the brain-image Bergson puts forward almost immediately, in *Matter and Memory*, a highly complex and organised state of life. This is because he is not considering life as a problem there (and indeed, in *Creative Evolution*, he will give serious consideration to life, but from another point of view). However, it is not difficult to fill in the gaps that Bergson has voluntarily left. Even at the level of the most elementary living beings one would have to imagine micro-intervals. Smaller and smaller intervals between more and more rapid movements. Moreover, biologists speak of "primeval soup," which made living beings possible, and where forms of matter known as dextrogyres and levogyres play an essential role. It is here that outlines of axes appear in an acentred universe, a left and a right, a high and a low. Once should therefore conceive of micro-intervals even in the primeval soup. Biologists say that these phenomena could not be produced when the earth was very hot. Therefore one should conceive of a cooling down of the plane of immanence, correlative to the first opacities, to the first screens obstructing the diffusion of light. It is here that the first outlines of solids or rigid and geometric bodies would be formed. Finally, as Bergson was to say, the same evolution which organises matter into solids will organise the image in more and more elaborate perception, which has solids as its objects.

The thing and the perception of the thing are one and the same thing, one and the same image, but related to one or other of two systems of reference. The thing is the image as it is in itself, as it is related to all the other images to whose action it completely submits and on which it reacts immediately. But the perception of the thing is the same image related to another special image which frames it, and which only retains a partial action from it, and only reacts to it mediately. In perception thus defined, there is never anything else or anything more than there is in the thing: on the contrary, there is "less." We perceive the thing, minus that which does not interest us as a function of our needs. By need or interest we mean the lines and points that we retain from the thing as a function of our receptive facet, and the actions that we select as a function of the delayed reactions of which we are capable. Which is a way of defining the first material moment of subjectivity: it is subtractive. It subtracts from the thing whatever does not interest it. But, conversely, the thing itself *must* then be presented in itself as a complete, immediate, diffuse perception. The thing is image and, in this respect, is perceived itself and perceives all the other things inasmuch as it is subject to their action and reacts to them on all its facets and in all its parts. An atom, for example, perceives infinitely more than we do and, at the limit perceives the whole universe—from the point where the actions which are exercised on it begin, to the point where the actions which it emits go. In short, things and perceptions of things are *prehensions*, but things are total objective prehensions, and perceptions of things are incomplete and prejudiced, partial, subjective prehensions.

If the cinema does *not* have natural subjective perception as its model, it is because the mobility of its centres and the variability of its framings always lead it to restore vast acentred and deframed zones. It then tends to return to the first régime of the movement-image; universal variation, total, objective and diffuse perception. In fact, it travels the route in both directions. From the point of view which occupies us for the moment, we go from total, objective perception which is indistinguishable from the thing, to a subjective perception which is distinguished from it by simple elimination or subtraction. It is this unicentred subjective perception that is called perception strictly speaking. And it is the first avatar of the movement-image: when it is related to a centre of indetermination, it becomes *perception-image*.

However, we should not think that the whole operation consists only of a subtraction. There is something else as well. When the universe of movement-images is related to one of these special images which forms a centre in it, the universe is incurved and organized to surround it. We continue to go from the world to the centre, but the world has taken on a curvature, it has become a periphery, it forms a horizon (a constant theme of the first chapter of *MM*: the circular formation of the world "around" the centre of indetermination). We are still in the perception-image, but we are already entering the action-image as well. In fact, perception is only one side of the gap, and action is the other side. What is called action, strictly speaking, is the delayed reaction of the centre of indetermination. Now, this centre is only capable of acting—in the sense of organising an unexpected response—because it perceives and has received the excitation on a privileged facet, eliminating the remainder. All this amounts to re-calling that all perception is primarily sensory-motor: perception "is no more in the sensory centres than in the motor centres; it measures the complexity of their relations." If the world is incurved around the perceptive centre, this is already from the point of view of action, from which perception is inseparable. By incurving, perceived things tender their unstable facet towards me, at the same time as my delayed reaction, which has become action, learns to use them.

Distance is in fact a radius [*rayon*] which goes from the periphery to the centre: perceiving things here where they are, I grasp the "virtual action" that they have on me, and simultaneously the "possible action" that I have on them, in order to associate me with them or to avoid them, by diminishing or increasing the distance. It is thus the same phenomenon of the gap which is expressed in terms of time in my action and in terms of space in my perception. The more the reaction ceases to be immediate and becomes truly possible action, the more the perception becomes distant and anticipatory and extracts the virtual action of things. "Perception is master of space in the exact measure in which action is master of time."

This is therefore the second avatar of the movement-image: it becomes *action-image*. One passes imperceptibly from perception to action. The operation under consideration is no longer elimination, selection or framing, but the incurving of the universe, which simultaneously causes the virtual action of things on us and our possible action on things. This is the second material aspect of subjectivity. And, just as perception relates movement to "bodies" (nouns), that is to rigid objects which will serve as moving bodies or as things moved, action relates movement to "acts" (verbs) which will be the design for an assumed end or result.

But the interval is not merely defined by the specialisation of the two limit-facets, perceptive and active. There is an in-between. Affection is what occupies the interval, what occupies it without filling it in or filling it up. It surges in the centre of indetermination, that is to say in the subject, between a perception which is troubling in certain respects and a hesitant action. It is a coincidence of subject and object, or the way in which the subject perceives itself, or rather experiences itself or feels itself "from the inside" (third material aspect of subjectivity). It relates movement to a "quality" as lived state (adjective). Indeed, it is not sufficient to think that perception—thanks to distance—retains or reflects what interests us by letting pass what is indifferent to us. There is inevitably a part of external movements that we "absorb," that we refract, and which does not transform itself into either objects of perception or acts of the subject; rather they mark the concidence of the subject and the object in a pure quality. This is the final avatar of the movement-image: *the affection-image*. It would be wrong to consider it a failure of the perception-action system. On the contrary, it is a third absolutely necessary given. For we, living matter or centres of indetermination, have specialised one of our facets or certain of our points into receptive organs at the price of condemning them to immobility, while delegating our activity to organs of reaction that we have consequently liberated. In these conditions, when our immobilised receptive facet absorbs a movement instead of reflecting it, our activity can only respond by a "tendency," an "effort" which replaces the action which has become momentarily or locally impossible. This is the origin of Bergson's wonderful definition of afffection as "a kind of motor tendency on a sensible nerve," that is, a motor effort on an immobilised receptive plate (*MM*).

There is therefore a relationship between affection and movement in general which might be expressed as follows: the movement of translation is not merely interrupted in its direct propagation by an interval which allocates on the one hand the received movement, and on the other the executed movement, and which might make them in a sense incommensurable. Between the two there is affection which reestablishes the relation. But, it is precisely in affection that the movement ceases to be that of translation in order to become movement of expression, that is to say quality, simple tendency stirring up an immobile element. It is not surprising that, in the image that we are, it is the face, with its relative immobility and its receptive organs, which brings to light these movements of expression while they remain most frequently buried in the rest of the body. All things considered, *movement-images divide into three sorts of images when they are related to a centre of indetermination as to a special image:* perception-images, action-images and affection-images. And each one of us, the special image or the contingent centre, is nothing but an assemblage [*agencement*] of three images, a consolidate [*consolidé*] of perception-images, action-images and affection-images.

Maurras's Genealogy of the Decline of France, and Proposed Remedies

Michael Sutton

THREE KEY WRITINGS

There are three works of Maurras that hold an important place in his published writings and that, when taken together, indicate both the rôle in his
political doctrine of his criticism of individualism and his notion of the
desirability of a political alliance between Positivists and Catholics. All three
were published at about the turn of the century, and, with another book
Le Dilemme de Marc Sangnier, they were to be the essential texts in the debate
in which Blondel and Laberthonnière took part.

The three works are *Trois idées politiques* (1898); . . . the article "Idées
françaises ou idées suisses," published as part of "Les Monod" in *L'Action
française* of 15 October 1899; and the book *L'Avenir de l'intelligence* (1905).

Trois Idées politiques: Chateaubriand, Michelet, Sainte-Beuve, to give this
small book of about eighty pages its full title, was a response to the public
speeches and writings in 1898 occasioned by the fiftieth anniversary of the
death of Chateaubriand, the centenary of the birth of Michelet, and the
erection of a bust of Sainte-Beuve in the Luxembourg Gardens. The subject
of the book, therefore, was not so much the political ideas of the three
writers as the political significance of their works judged from a contemporary standpoint—hence the headings of the three main sections of the
book, "Chateaubriand ou l'Anarchie," "Michelet ou la Démocratie" and
"Sainte-Beuve ou l'Empirisme organisateur," for such were the three political ideas the three men were portrayed as epitomizing. In addition, the
book contained a host of more general reflections. As Maurras wrote to
Barrès, it was his intention that "under the three pretexts of Chateaubriand,
Michelet and Sainte-Beuve," *Trois Idées politiques* should be "the outline of

From *Nationalism, Positivism, and Catholicism: The Politics of Charles Maurras and French Catholics
1890–1914.* © 1982 by Cambridge University Press.

335

a small treatise on Positive politics" (Maurice Barrès—Charles Maurras, *La République ou le roi: Correspondance inédite 1888–1923*).

It was indeed as such an outline that this slender book served to define Maurras's central ideas for the more reflective of those who formed the Action française in its early years. According to Louis Dimier, who had earned repute as an art historian of the French Renaissance before playing an active rôle in the young political movement, *Trois idées politiques* was a work that "we all knew by heart" (*Vingt Ans d'Action française*). Maurras himself made much the same point in a note to the 1912 edition: "my reflections at that time led to general conclusions that have not lost all their interest today, for these conclusions had some part in the launching of our *Action française* seven months later [after the publication of the first edition at the end of 1898], and I owe to them the establishing of my initial intellectual ties with some of my collaborators of these past fourteen years." At the end of the First World War Albert Thibaudet wrote of *Trois Idées politiques* as the pioneering work that had opened the way for Maurras's major political endeavour (*Les Idées de Charles Maurras*).

To turn to "Idées françaises ou idées suisses," it was certainly Maurras's most substantial contribution to *L'Action française* in its first years of existence, for it was not until 1904 that he again gave something both new and of pamphleteering force to the pugnacious little review, namely his comments and reflections on Sangnier's challenge to his positivism (most of the *Enquête sur la monarchie* appeared in the columns of *La Gazette de France* in 1900 and was first published in book form only in 1909). "Idées françaises ou idées suisses," as the editor's introduction to the article made clear, was a revisionist interpretation of "the revolutionary ideas that were called 'French ideas' or the maxims of 1789." From the standpoint of the author, who had made a certain idea of France his spiritual lodestar and yet viewed so gloomily the French past ever since Voltaire's return from England in 1729, few subjects were as important. And, in the article itself, this importance was underlined with some verve. That the article made at the time of publication a certain impression, at least on intellectual coteries within the orbit of the Ligue de la Patrie Française, is indicated by a circular for subscriptions to the review, dated 15 January 1900; therein especial attention was drawn to Maurras's talent, with the malevolent ideas he had described as Swiss being triumphantly castigated as responsible for France's servitude to "Protestant sectaries." Nearly fifty years later, the article was republished as the opening part of the book *Réflexions sur la révolution de 1789*, a collection of various writings by Maurras dealing with this cardinal concern of his.

The book *L'Avenir de l'intelligence* was composed of four essays. Three of them had originally appeared in the review *Minerva* in 1902 and 1903: the first gave its title to the book (it was to be published separately in book form in the 1920s); the second essay was "Auguste Comte"; . . . and the third was entitled "Le Romantisme féminin" (also published separately in the 1920s). The last essay, an expanded version of an article that had appeared in *La Gazette de France* in 1902, was called "Mademoiselle Monk"; after the First World War, Maurras saw fit to have this essay published as a small book with a preface by the young André Malraux.

In its design, the book of 1905 had two sections. The first, constituted by the essay "L'Avenir de l'intelligence," was partly a sombre consideration of the decline in the public stature of the man of letters ever since the Revolution and of the growing dominion over France of the power of high finance. Coupled with this consideration was the outline of a possible way in which France could be liberated from this oppression, not by the rise to political rule of the intelligentsia, but by the intelligentsia's own self-imposed reform and its successful championing, against the anonymous forces of financial capitalism, of the virtues of hereditary government—in other words, spiritual reform followed by institutional reform in the shape of the restoration of the monarchy. This essay was, in purpose and content, somewhat reminiscent of Renan's *La Réforme intellectuelle et morale de la France,* and of this similarity Maurras must have been aware.

The second section of the book was, as Maurras wrote, "a cahier of notes" relating to the execution of the desired changes. For the spiritual reform of those who found themselves incapable of the faith of Catholicism, the essay "Auguste Comte" was proffered as a résumé of "the magnificent discipline instituted by the genius of Auguste Comte under the name of Positivism." But the rigour of this intellectual remedy might appear daunting, and so the next essay, "Le Romantisme féminin," was presented as a caution against such faint-heartedness. It was a waspish study of the writings of Anna de Noailles (she and Barrès were lovers from 1903 to 1907) and of three other women contemporaries (Lucie Delarue-Mardrus, Renée Vivien and Gérard d'Houville—pseudonym of the wife of Henri de Régnier), all of whom were sirens beckoning towards "romantic and revolutionary ill." As the subtitle of this essay—"Allégorie du sentiment désordonné"—indicated, there was thus in the book a deliberate juxtaposition between the anti-individualism of Comte with his subjective synthesis and the anarchic individualism that was the essence of effeminate romanticism. It was in the philosophy of Comte, claimed Maurras, that the modern agnostic or atheist could find the elements of a workable alternative to a pernicious ordering of one's universe by a deification of the egoistic self. Unfortunately, though, the intellectual reform of an intelligentsia, necessary as it was, could not suffice for the restoration of the public weal. Therefore the final essay, "Mademoiselle Monk—ou la génération des événements," wherein Maurras reflected on the claim of the amorous Aimée de Coigny—*La Jeune Captive* of André Chénier—to have influenced Talleyrand to favour the return in 1814 of Louis XVIII, was presented to the reader as an allegory of the ability of determined people, alert for the favourable chance, to achieve the improbable—that is, for Maurras, as well as Aimée de Coigny, the return of the monarchy.

If there was one book published in the years before the First World War that best embodied the substance of Maurras's thought, it was *L'Avenir de l'intelligence*: important as the *Enquête sur la monarchie* was for the Action Française movement, Maurras's nationalism and anti-individualism, which were the ultimate concerns of *L'Avenir de l'intelligence*, were more fundamental to his own thought than his espousal of monarchy (the restoration of the monarchy being for him but a means, albeit the all-important one, of rescuing and safeguarding his true France). As Thibaudet justly remarked, *L'Avenir de l'intelligence* served in Maurras's total work as "his chosen Acropolis." Moreover, if *Trois Idées politiques* had helped secure Maurras's intellectual ascendancy within the group of contributors to the early *L'Action française*, it seems that *L'Avenir de l'intelligence* played a very important rôle in extending Maurras's influence beyond this narrow domain, especially to the younger generation that was to make its voice heard in the well-known survey of 1912, *Les Jeunes Gens d'aujourd'hui,* carried out by the young Henri Massis, together with Alfred de Tarde, under the joint pseudonym of Agathon. Evidence of this is a letter Maurras wrote to Barrès in 1909, thanking him for a notice of *L'Avenir de l'intelligence* on the occasion of its reissue that year. Although, he told Barrès, he was being virtually ignored by his fellow journalists and literary reviewers, this particular work was proving to be the first of his books to win little by little a largish audience; and, if the fruits of his efforts over the last ten years were now so ripening for the picking, this was largely because "the young generation is extraordinary."

That these three works—*Trois Idées politiques*, "Idées françaises ou idées suisses" and *L'Avenir de l'intelligence*—have, taken together, a certain unity was made clear by Maurras himself when in 1922 he published *Romantisme et révolution*, which was composed of the two books, *L'Avenir de l'intelligence* and *Trois Idées politiques,* and a long preface that drew heavily on "Idées françaises ou idées suisses." *Romantisme et révolution,* when it first appeared that year, was the third volume of the series *Les Ecrivains de la Renaissance française: l'Oeuvre de Charles Maurras,* published by the Nouvelle Librairie Nationale, and it had been originally intended that it should bear the title *L'Analyse des principes,* to indicate its place as the basic theoretical work in this collected edition of Maurras's major works. In the four-volume work *Oeuvres capitales,* produced by Flammarion under the guidance of Maurras (in the last year of this life) and published in 1954, the first part of the volume entitled *Essais politiques* was headed "Critique générale" and was constituted by the Preface to *Romantisme et révolution, Trois Idées politiques* in its entirety, the Preface (in a very truncated form) to the book *L'Avenir de l'intelligence,* and, finally, the essay of the same name. The essay "Auguste Comte" was also reproduced in *Oeuvres capitales,* but in the volume entitled *Essais littéraires* (under the heading of "Bons et mauvais maîtres").

Such then was the importance and unity of the three writings in question. To their design and content, when regarded as a whole, further attention is now given.

THE PAST AS TELEOLOGICAL DECLINE TO A DISMAL PRESENT

If one scrutinizes these three writings taken together, what one finds is basically a didactically inspired outline of the French past that leads directly to a certain view of Maurras's own present and the specification of remedial action. Moreover, as regards the balance of this effort, it is to the elaboration of this view of the past, rather than to the details of plans for the future, that Maurras's attention is mainly directed; it is in his diagnosis of the ill that afflicted France, rather than in his prescription for the same, that the substance of his thinking is primarily to be found.

The account by Maurras of a decline in France's fortunes to the nadir of his own day is, as in the case of *La France juive* of Drumont, a "practical past": the past, that is to say, is viewed in the light of immediate practical or existential interests. This style of thought has its own differentia. There is, for instance, on Maurras's part, an obvious and considerable concern with discrete origins (of France's decline), and such origins not only explain the extraordinary nature of what has occurred but actually facilitate the conception of events in the guise of a decline towards the final end of a dismal or miserable present. Furthermore, these writings are permeated with teleological judgements that pattern the march of events, and so most movements of events across the years are presented by Maurras as malign, though, in the initial period, before the introduction of the canker, such broad movements are necessarily of a favourable nature. This whole process of thought was made possible by Maurras's cavalier approach to the evidence of the past, for he used only that which substantiated or buttressed the preconceived framework of his account. And this, in turn, was related to his view's being primarily focused on the broad contours of the past, which was conducive to (though it need not necessarily have entailed) a lack of consistent attention to detail.

That Maurras's thought could carry force and conviction was due both to the fact that his account of the past was far from totally unfounded (that is, it was based on evidence of the past, however partially selected) and to the fact that the account, as a story of decline, was, with the aid of Maurras's fundamental ideas about Christianity and classical civilization, well-knit and told in a masterly fashion. Thus the distant age of bliss was given a vague and even ethereal shape, the narration of the fall from grace was suitably dramatic, while the darkness and shadows of the actual present had a certain reality even if they were exaggerated or distorted. Indeed, Maurras's account of the past can be seen as a clever story masquerading as history: therein was much of its power of persuasion, therein much of its strength as a mode of political thought promoting a reactionary frame of mind.

It is not to be supposed, of course, that Maurras's endeavour was particularly unusual. Comte, for example, embodied much of his political thought in what was effectively a "practical past," though it was set in the mould of the Enlightenment idea of progress.

More generally, France was the country where unfolded the foremost Revolution of the modern period and all that it entailed in the way of drama and trauma—the declaration of high ideals, the sweeping away of the privileges of the aristocracy and clergy, the purging of many of their members, and the rise and fall across Europe of the first great modern popular dictator and his invading armies. It was therefore the lot of the idea of Revolution to be conceived as a virtually sacred or satanic event, and as such it subsequently intruded into much of that country's writing of history and deeply marked, in diverse ways, its political life.

THE INCURSION OF INDIVIDUALISM AND THE DECLINE OF FRANCE

Maurras's story of France in the three works under consideration involved a backward reading of the past to the time preceding the onset of the ills that were to make for France's ruin. Thus, if the great and terrible year in the story was 1789, what he sought before then were the origins of this disaster and the fortunate situation of France before the seeds of disaster took root. In keeping with the polemical purpose of the story, Maurras either left this distant and happy past extremely vague, or else described it only briefly without tracing it further back than was required to show that once upon a time the place of France in the world had been truly blessed. To explain the main part of the story, the nature of France's fall, there was no need to follow the past back to the time of Clovis, and, indeed, an enthusiasm leading him to detail the millennium and more between the famous baptism of Rheims and the downfall of the eighteenth-century monarchy would have tended to encumber the purpose of the story, if not to confound it.

If, therefore, there was a beginning to Maurras's story of France as evinced in the three texts, it is best found in an impressionistic portrayal of the past honoured by those who still held fast to the values of an earlier time:

> Above all, I admire the waywardness of old France. The French State prior to 1789 . . . was monarchic, hierarchical, socialist and community-minded. . . . Old France had its own constitutions born of the races and territories that composed her. . . . Old France had the classical, juridical and philosophical frame of mind which is more concerned with the relations between things than with the things themselves, and her writers, even in the bawdiest of their tales, acknowledged the power of reason. . . . Old France professed that traditional Catholicism which, subordinating Jewish visions and Christian feeling to the discipline received from the Hellenic and Roman world, carries within itself the natural order of humanity.
>
> (*Trois Idées politiques*)

Here, then, at the outset, Maurras could draw a portrait of a France where individualism was properly bridled and the classical spirit or mind was completely at home, all this being facilitated by or promoted through the mediation of the Roman Church.

When Maurras chose to descend to a more clearly defined view of this past, it was not inappropriate that his backward reading of the centuries brought the beginning of the story to Ronsard, that ardent classicist and staunch anti-Protestant, who, like Maurras himself, had taken up a life of letters because of deafness: his name was the earliest in this story to be given noteworthy mention and accorded reverence.

Insofar, then, as the story had any definite beginning, it was in the century of the French Renaissance. Yet Maurras did not lavish attention on this period. Distinguished as much by Calvin as by Ronsard, and plagued by the wars of religion, it did not properly serve his polemical purpose. However much the greatness of France lay in the sixteenth century, it was but a prologue to the greatness of the seventeenth, the century that was truly the *grand siècle*—whatever Michelet's opinion about the eighteenth. When, though, Maurras touched upon the seventeenth century, the names emphasized were not Henri IV, Richelieu, Mazarin, Louis XIV or Colbert so much as Corneille, Descartes, La Fontaine, Racine and Bossuet. And, given the spiritual or intellectual nature of his nationalism, this was not surprising: the greatness of France was not to be found primarily in the personal craft of her rulers, but rather in ideas or states of mind, be they reified in literature, works of art or political and social institutions.

Looking at this golden age, mainly the seventeenth century, against which was to be measured the subsequent decline of France, Maurras portrayed the spiritual or mental outlook that constituted its greatness as one that partook of the virile "aesthetic of Harmony" that the Greeks had created and perfected—as such, it was fundamentally opposed to the effeminate "aesthetic of Character" that was to be a distinguishing mark of Romanticism. It was an outlook that was marked by a profound awareness of the order of reality external to the self, rather than by any misguided obsession with the aspirations and divagations of the individual ego.

Any suggestion, then, that Descartes was responsible for "the invention of revolutionary individualism" was ridiculous to Maurras's mind. Descartes's antipathy to individualism was proven beyond doubt by his rationalism. That the ontological or metaphysical nature of this rationalism was very foreign to the Comtian presuppositions of his own thought was something Maurras could gloss over. What was essential to the story was that the most renowned of all French philosophers should be shown to be no precursor of modern individualism: hence the plausible point that, whatever the apparent subjectivism of his fundamental axiom, the *cogito, ergo sum*, Descartes had really addressed himself to the power of reason present in all men, and had therefore been no advocate of any indiscriminate freedom of thought that gave an egalitarian right to individual fantasy and whimsy.

Other difficulties for Maurras's story, if they could not be gainsaid, could at least be explained away. Insofar as the notable literature of those fortunate times was at all contaminated by anarchic or individualistic tendencies, such contamination was either an extraordinary accident or else due to too close contact with the dangerous "Christian spirit," the spirit of the Bible:

> The little in our books of egalitarian or liberal spirit is to be explained either by a few historical accidents such as the character of Montaigne (yet whose peculiar bent of mind is not to be exaggerated and whose concern was perhaps just as much with man as with his own pitiful and delicate person), or else by the continuous reading and study of both Testaments by our clerical scholars. It is impossible to read indefinitely these sacred texts without breathing some miasmata of the prophetic and millenarian spirit. What is miraculous is rather the fact that this familiarity with the Bible did not wreak more havoc. If Calvin is left out of account, and a few pages of Fénelon, then Christianity in France appears as totally purged of evangelic and prophetic anarchism.
>
> ("Idées françaises ou idées suisses")

And indeed, continued Maurras, not only was it true that Christianity had formerly appeared in France free of its own worse elements, but one of the greatest of all Frenchmen, and a prelate to boot, had managed the seemingly impossible, namely, to put the Bible to use for the public good. So meritorious, Maurras went on to point out, was Bossuet's *Politique tirée des propres paroles de l'Ecriture sainte* that Comte had actually included it among the very limited number of works that were to constitute the Positivist Library.

However, it is clear that, whatever his admiration for Bossuet as a writer, Comte had had little regard for Bossuet's own Church in the seventeenth century: the Catholic Church, in Comte's view, had been a worthy or effective "spiritual power" for the West only during the period that extended from the pontificate of Gregory VII (1073–85) to, at the very latest, that of the overambitious Boniface VIII (1294–1303). But quite different was Maurras's judgement on the background to Bossuet's greatness: it was not just that Bossuet was a remarkable writer; of more significance was that Bossuet epitomized, as Aquinas had earlier, all that was best in the Roman Church. Moreover, Maurras deemed the Church to have been a most worthy "spiritual power" for France in the golden age that came finally to an end with the Revolution, with its Declaration of the Rights of Man and the Civil Constitution of the Clergy. And this high regard of Maurras for the Church clearly cut across his own personal considerations concerning the question of God's existence; his own lack of belief left untrammelled his appreciation of Catholicism as a religion in the traditionally ascribed etymological sense of something that binds men together. It was thus that, in the story evinced by these three works, the rôle of the Church in preserving for France the heritage of Graeco-Roman civilization was made vital to the picture of France as once having been pre-eminently the country where the values of order and harmony reigned supreme. There was, Maurras emphasized, to be no doubting the value of the Church's contribution to the spiritual or mental outlook that prevailed in France in the more fortunate days gone by:

> Before and after Bossuet, the doctrine of our best ecclesiastical authors remained very firmly subject to the Catholicism that had received from Rome and Athens the wisdom of the humankind. Tempering their Christian spirit with Greek knowledge and Roman empiricism, they reproved every revolutionary idea in the name of their twofold capacity as Catholic and Classicist. Even more than the Italians, who would seem nearer to the truth on account of their language and geographical situation but to whose permanent discredit there are the [Joachimite] *Eternal Evangel* and the Franciscan *laudi* [as composed, for instance, by Jacopone da Todi], our French clergy banished mysticism from their theory of public order. They resisted the Protestant contagion.

Outside France, so the story continued, even since the vernacular Bible of Wycliffe in England and—much more important—that of Luther in Germany, the peoples to the north and east of Europe had drunk deep of "Hebrew thought and all that it carried in the way of dreams of justice, beatitude, equality and inner revolt." Between these peoples and the posterity of Jacob there was indeed a secret affinity, and, once under the sway of this "Judaeo-Christian barbarism," the Germanic European, be he Saxon or Goth, soon threw off the only partially assimilated influences exerted by centuries of Catholicism, classicism and humanism:

> Isaiah and Jesus, David and Jeremiah, Ezekiel and Solomon, abruptly translated into his tongue, revealed to him the vanity of the effort of civilization. They taught him, with the accent of authority that is the mark of the divine, that he bore within his own heart a judge and master of all. And, lastly, by their example and their sayings, they provided him with models of the purest frenzy.

To support such contentions as these, which were never made very specific, Maurras was able to have recourse to his much loved point that Comte had thought of Protestantism as essentially individualistic. And, as proof of the actual political harm wrought by Protestantism, he pointed to the sixteenth-century civil wars in France, the Thirty Years War that tore Germany apart until the Treaty of Westphalia, civil war and revolution in seventeenth-century England, and, finally, the French Revolution itself.

The dramatic twist to Maurras's story, then, involved the successful introduction into France of the individualism that was, for him, at the core of Protestant Christianity. And it was with the breathtaking simplicity that can characterize good melodrama that Maurras presented such a tragic thwarting of the true destiny of France as having been brought about or initiated by but three persons. Two of them were dupes, namely, Voltaire and Montesquieu. The third, Rousseau, was not so much a dupe as the veritable villain of the story.

When Voltaire returned to France from England in 1729 and Montesquieu in 1731, this was the knell of France in her prime. Imbued with "constitutional anglomania" and the precepts of English liberalism—here Maurras had Locke in mind—they brought back ideas that were utterly incompatible with the political and social milieu in which the two of them had been raised. And these same ideas from Protestant England were imparted by them to the more gullible of their compatriots. Nonetheless, Maurras could at least say for them that their origins and upbringing had preserved their minds from total corruption, witness such masterpieces as *Candide* and *Les Considérations sur les causes de la grandeur des Romains et de leur décadence*, which stood in the best French tradition.

But the case of Rousseau was very different; the influence in France of his person and his writings was made out to be absolutely malign. For Rousseau, Maurras spared no invective. If this Genevan and occasional Calvinist was the story's arch-villain, he was properly portrayed as such. Not only was Rousseau's native city "a part of the world that had been overrun for two centuries by every blend of Judaeo-Christian anarchy," but, unlike the more normal of his fellow citizens, who were bound by ties of family and convention, he had seen fit to establish his own idiosyncratic rules for the finishing of his education and the gaining of experience of life. The result was lamentable: "folly, savagery, ignorance, singularity, solitude, arrogance and revolt—this is what this adventurer, nourished on the heart of the Bible, placed on the altar in the name of virtue."

Yet for Maurras to decry Rousseau as a mad egoist was not sufficient to explain why the Academy of Dijon and afterwards the Paris of 1750 were so ready to grant him their favour. It would have been no answer to suggest that the rather reactionary and idyllic *Discours sur les sciences et les arts* was in some tradition of liberalism fathered by Voltaire's *Lettres philosophiques* and Montesquieu's *De l'esprit des lois*, and Maurras did not go so far as to make such an implausible statement of affinities. Instead, to demystify a little the fabulous nature (within his story) of Rousseau's popularity, he stressed the lassitude of the society that so eagerly welcomed Rousseau and its decadent fascination with what was primitive.

Benefiting from the rightful prestige earned by the writers of the more glorious seventeenth century, Rousseau as well as Voltaire and the Encyclopaedists were able to use their popularity for installing a dictatorship over the written word, and, with the changes in attitude of mind that such a dictatorship engendered, the Revolution, said Maurras, was at hand. The Constituent Assembly, the Legislative Assembly and the Convention had indeed one common denominator, the obtrusive presence of men with literary pretensions in the line of the newly imposed wisdom. Such Rousseauesque notions as "the absolute respect due to individual consciences" and "the State's being constituted by the concourse of individual wills" had become the received ideas of the time, and, in terms of intellectual influence, the Genevan was the prime mover of the Revolution.

In so assigning some cardinal responsibility for the Revolution to Rousseau and—to a lesser extent—other eighteenth-century *philosophes*, Maurras was largely following the interpretation of the period put forward by Taine in the *Ancien Régime,* the first volume of his monumental work, *Les Origines de la France contemporaine.* It is true that the spiritual malefactor described by Taine as "classical reason" was, on the contrary, considered by Maurras as a "Christian spirit." Nonetheless, allowing for this difference of judgement about the precise nature and ultimate origin of the evil that had ruined France, Maurras's sketch of the intellectual dimensions of the Revolution was very close to the view of this great man of letters, whose successive volumes of a cautionary tale of France had first appeared during Maurras's childhood and youth, and from whom Maurras himself received a token of favour.

To return to the elucidation of the story evinced by the three works, the Revolution was not so much the expression of a struggle between ruler and ruled as a self-willed abdication of power in favour of a new style of politics by a monarch who was intellectually corrupted by the literary advocates of this same politics:

> Unless it be admitted that around 1789 a new range of feelings came into people's hearts and affected practical life, none of the public events that make up the web of modern history are comprehensible or credible. Many of those responsible for the conduct of public affairs regarded their law as mere prejudice; they seriously questioned the justice of their cause and the legitimacy of the administration and government for which they were publicly responsible. The sacrifice of Louis XVI is the perfect example of the type of fall from power that overtook the whole ruling class: before being cut down, they cut themselves down; it was unnecessary to overthrow them, for they collapsed of their own volition.
>
> (*L'Avenir de l'intelligence*)

And this failure of will Maurras did not limit to the eighteenth century; according to him, the spirit of the Revolution was not confined to 1789 and the several fateful years that followed, but had progressively manifested itself in new and still pernicious forms throughout the whole of the nineteenth century. Thus, as regards the monarchy, the rather robust Louis-Philippe was no more favourably disposed to resist revolution with force than the effete Louis XVI, and the manner of his abdication, together with the departure of his sons, the Duc d'Aumale and the Prince de Joinville, potentially masters of the army and navy, showed up the full extent of their lack of self-confidence.

It was the Corsican, Bonaparte, not the grandchildren of Philippe-Egalité, who personified "the ironical and harsh response of nineteenth-century military facts to eighteenth-century literary dreams." But in his domestic policy, Maurras pointed out, Bonaparte too partook of the spirit of the Revolution, giving, as he did through the Civil Code, the ideas of 1789 a more lasting form than hitherto realized. And by a good story-teller's sleight-of-hand—an oblique reference by Maurras to Bonaparte's associating at Ermenonville his own name with that of Rousseau—the latter was implicated in the "semblance of order" afforded by the Constitution of the Year VIII, the Concordat with Rome, and the national administration resulting from the creation of the prefectoral system, the University and the Bank of France. Yet this order, complained Maurras, proved perversely lasting: the political arrangements and institutions Napoleon imposed upon France, ill-founded as they were, endured for the whole century, whatever the apparent differences of succeeding regimes.

Thus it was the fortune of "the three Swiss ideas"—Liberty, Equality, Fraternity—to live on and plague France with their corruptive influences. Because of the perpetuation of these "mortal principles," the Revolutionary upheaval had not played itself out and so given way to "a viable order" as had occurred in seventeenth-century England.

The foremost of the trinity had greatly weakened the State:

> Of the three Swiss ideas that we have written on our walls, the first the principle of political liberty—constitutive of the Republican form of government—kills the submission of the citizen, not merely to the laws of the State, which he sees as the banal products of some provisional will (all wills being provisional), but even to those profound and august laws, *leges natae*, in which the wills of the citizen and of man count for nothing. Forgetful, negligent and disdainful of these natural and rational rules, the French State loses its prudence and so becomes liable to perish.

The middle member of the trinity had resulted in national energies being sapped by a bureaucracy of excessive proportions:

> The second of the Swiss ideas, the principle of equality—constitutive of the Democratic form of government—surrrenders power to the greatest number, that is to say to the inferior elements of the nation, to the least energetic producers and to the most voracious consumers, to those who produce least and need most. The Frenchman, discouraged by the vexatious interference of the Administration (the legal representative of the greatest number) if he is enterprising, and encouraged by the favours inevitably bestowed on his laziness by the same Administration if he is weak

or lacking in initiative, resigns himself to becoming a parasite on it. The result is that all the nation's activity soon slows down to the point of extinction.

As for the pneumatic binding force, it had tragically split the country into warring factions:

> The third Swiss idea, the principle of fraternity—constitutive of the Cosmopolitan form of government—enjoins, on the one hand, a boundless indulgence towards all men provided they live very far away from us, are completely unknown to us, speak quite another tongue, or, better still, have a different colour of skin; but, on the other hand, whosoever does not share all our slightest fits of philanthropic mania, be he our fellow citizen and our brother, is held on this principle to be evil and a monster. This principle of planetary fraternity, which would seek to establish peace between nations, is expressed in practice by the deflection of the rage and hostility that nature has secretly embedded in man—a political animal but a carnivorous one—into attacks on his own compatriots. Thus are the French led into civil war.

If "the three Swiss ideas" had reduced the political order of France to such a miserable pass—of which, in Maurras's mind, the conflict of the Dreyfus Affair was the supreme manifestation—it was, nonetheless, not the end of the matter. For, so the accusation continued, the author of *La Nouvelle Héloïse*, who had fathered the Revolution with the blind complicity of Voltaire and Montesquieu, had also opened the era of Romanticism. And not only, Maurras maintained, did Rousseau bewitch the France of his century with his sentimental tale of passion and virtue on the shores of Lake Geneva, but also he had made explicit the insinuating force that motivated such literary endeavour. There was a "morality of romanticism," and it was to be found in the opening pages of his *Confessions*: therein did Rousseau make his fundamental apology for "the sincere personality." Thus Maurras stressed that Romanticism, like the Revolution, was but an expression of Rousseauesque individualism. This romanticism had persistently betrayed, during the hundred years between the Revolution and his own day, what he took to be the true spiritual values of France. He blamed it, moreover, for having largely contributed to a sad decline in the prestige and influence of the intelligentsia.

Significantly enough for the main thesis of the story, Maurras could point out that the chief intermediaries between Rousseau and what has been termed "the romanticism of 1830" were Chateaubriand and Madame de Staël, one the author of *Le Génie du christianisme* and the other authoress of *De l'Allemagne*.

Also involved in this part of the story was a contention that the literary Romanticism of 1830 did not come to an end with the advent of the Parnassians: "just as the Consulate was the Revolution sobered up, so Parnassianism was a romantic art that had been trimmed, tidied up and given some semblance of order that impresses the vulgar." And the Symbolists and Decadents were but the third stage of the same romantic ill.

The individualism of this pan-Romanticism was not such that it could, of its nature, be confined to the purely aesthetic. "Individual revolt," wrote Maurras, "once recognized under the name of originality as an aesthetic principle, engendered an anarchy that was much more profound." What was encouraged was an attempted ordering of one's whole world from the standpoint of the particular self as dictated by mood and caprice.

The result of such a solipsistic view of the world was, in Maurras's judgement, an anarchical state of mind that was quite prone to manifest itself in politics and religion. Thus Chateaubriand could be described as "a shamefaced Protestant clothed in the purple of Rome" who had contributed "nearly as much as Lamennais, his fellow [Breton] countryman, to our religious anarchy," while underlying his political ideas had been a liberalism just as anarchical as his lyrical assessment of Christianity. Thus, too, the outpourings of George Sand, Lamartine, Michelet and Hugo, as well as Lamennais, were ascribed their full part in the political and social disturbances of the century, especially those of 1848. And here the romantics were no more than continuing the work of political anarchy started by their master, Rousseau, though the regimes whose stability was so disturbed were—whatever their appearance—impregnated with much the same ideas as these dissidents themselves held concerning the primacy of the individual.

To add to the tale of woe, a side-effect of this pan-Romanticism was that the philosophical doctrines of Kant, yet another admirer of Rousseau, came, as an emanation of "Judaeo-Germanic barbarism," to penetrate French intellectual life, this misfortune having been initiated by that seminal work, *De l'Allemagne*.

Because of their rebellious political attitudes, and because of their taste for the rare, the particular, the exotic and the foreign, which, Maurras maintained, could appeal little to the better educated, the romantics soon became distrusted in the more elevated reaches of society. Unlike the writers of the eighteenth century, who in any case had not been so totally deformed, the romantics, when faced with this distrust, had no capital of prestige to draw upon such as had been accumulated by the illustrious figures of the seventeenth century. Another ominous change, Maurras added, was that the rapid economic development of France during the nineteenth century had, by about the time of the Second Empire, brought about a situation in which the manner of living of the upper classes necessitated a very considerable degree of material wealth and where political and social power tended to be in the hands of a plutocracy; it was a world into which the professional man of letters could enter but not one to which he could belong. Thus, because of force of circumstances as well as its own proper faults, the intelligentsia had seen a grievous decline of its prestige and influence.

And this situation, Maurras went on to emphasize, witnessed the advent of the modern writer who, in a vain attempt to recover the happier social position of his predecessors, either pandered to the base tastes of the new reading public that was composed of the semi-literate masses, or else willingly served the newly ascendant plutocracy in manipulating public opinion, "the masses decorated with the title of public" being the nominal sovereign "as a result of one hundred years of Revolution." In either case it was prostitution, the proper rôle of the literary class being to guard and enrich the classical traditions of France.

So, in its main details, the story arrived at its appointed end, namely the France of the *fin de siècle* Paris of which Maurras himself was such an integral part. And, all in all, this view of the decline of a once perfect France wrought by an alien individualism was but an explanation by Maurras of the real and discordant France of his own day and of his place within it. Moreover, as a diagnosis of the nature of France's decline to such a sorry present, this practical past had implicit within itself a reactionary prescription for the future.

NECESSITY OF THE DESIRED ALLIANCE

All was not lost: remedial action was possible. Such names from the latter half of the nineteenth century as Comte, Le Play, Renan, Taine and Fustel de Coulanges, as Sainte-Beuve, Mistral, Anatole France and Moréas, were evidence for Maurras that the true identity of France had not been totally submerged. There was therefore a living tradition that could be put to good use. The ruling plutocracy, furthermore, was not unassailable, for a restoration of the monarchy—and, with it, an end to imported political ideas—was, in Maurras's view, quite feasible. It was thus within the power of the socially responsible members of the intelligentsia, if aware of the gravity of the situation and sufficiently strong-willed, to ally themselves with "the oldest elements of the nation" and promote a Counter-Revolution. In such a way could political order be saved and the intelligentsia redeemed, provided enough of the best minds were willing to mend their ways and restore discipline to their thought. Hence the necessity, in one shape or another, of moral and intellectual reform.

In the pursuit of this self-reform, wrote Maurras, those writers or publicists who were Catholic believers, and were anxious to purge their minds of all traces of anarchism or liberalism, were faced with really no problem: they had but to submit fully to the discipline flowing from Catholicism's own judicious presentation of doctrine. And they could also profit from the Church's position as the last autonomous corporate body in modern France whose concern was with matters purely spiritual or intellectual.

For those, on the other hand, who had been born into the French Catholic tradition but were so antipathetic to a theological explanation of the world and of man that they felt "an implacable need to experience the absence of God," there was the alternative of Comtian Positivism—and this was the alternative chosen by Maurras himself (as recounted in his allegorical pages about Comte's disciple, Jundzill).

The two alternatives—Catholic or Positivist—were the only viable ones. The efforts, for instance, of Desjardins and others in the Union pour l'Action Morale to overcome the anomie of the times with a Godless form of Christian morality were, Maurras contended, blatantly unsatisfactory: they had to gloss over the qustion of the ultimate foundations of the moralistic ethic they preached, yet they could not escape the fact that every ethic must be grounded on some sort of absolute value. Such moralists, in Maurras's judgement, were surreptitiously theistic, for the individual conscience they prized was nothing other than "an anonymous and shamefaced God." And, with such an identification of God and conscience, their moralism was permeated with the same individualism as that which underlay the anomie they wished to overcome.

Totally different, Maurras maintained, was the endeavour and accomplishment of Comte. It was the crowning idea of his system, Humanity, that anchored properly his various criticisms of individualism. If the God that was the centre and end of Catholicism was the foundation for the Catholic of the order in his thought, in his moral life and in his approach to politics, the positivist "Great Being," Maurras stressed, was intended by Comte to fulfil a similar rôle. Indeed, Maurras pointed out, the similarity was more than functional: the God of Aquinas's *Summa Theologiae* and the ruling construct of the *Système de politique positive* had, within their respective modes of reasoning, the same supreme grandeur:

> Catholic dogma puts at its centre the greatest being that can be conceived in thought, *id quo majus cogitari non potest*, the being *par excellence*, the being of beings, and the one that says: *sum qui sum*. Positivist dogma establishes at its centre the greatest being that can be known in the sense of "positively" known, which is to say independently of any theological or metaphysical approach.
>
> (*L'Avenir de l'intelligence*)

This Positivist apotheosis of "the entire body of men who have contributed to the great human edifice," Maurras went on to show, placed at the centre of human existence the interdependence of men, one with another, with the linkage between man past and man present becoming progressively more and more important over time than that between contemporaries.

Maurras thus reiterated, in terms that recalled Bonald's views on language and tradition, Comte's conviction of the immensity of the social and of the insignificance of the individual:

What thinks in us and is prior to us is the human language, which is not our own personal work but the work of humanity; it is also human reason, which precedes us, surrounds us and remains after us; it is human civilization, to which a personal contribution, however powerful it may be, is never more than a molecule of infinitesimal energy in the drop of water added by our contemporaries to the stream of the great river.

In Comte's design, so Maurras said "our own personal soul counts virtually for nothing."

Yet Maurras himself had no time for what he termed the "peace-loving dreams of the Religion of Humanity": whatever the substance of such dreams in the 1850s, there could be little doubt, he thought, of their irrelevance to a France that had suffered the disaster of 1870 and that was now confronted with a unified Italy and unified Germany as well as with the imperialisms of Britain and the United States. But, as has already been shown, this evident disunity of Humanity in no way prevented Maurras from holding on to the essential idea of a societal "Great Being." For, from Maurras's standpoint, Comte's great and unquestionable achievement had been to uphold, as the prime and most noble aspect of man's existence, his nature as but part of a human society whose present was dwarfed by its past and that consequently had a heritage to preserve for the future; by contrast, a notion of society limited to the immediate and personal interests of a particular present was not one that could provide a worthy axis or framework for the ordering of human life:

> Comte was profoundly aware of how anarchic and subversive it is to treat sociability as something limited to simultaneous human existences. This is to believe that it is only with our contemporaries that we form a society; it is to misunderstand the ineluctable weight of earlier generations, and to give solidarity in space priority over continuity—which is solidarity across time. In rejecting such a defective idea of social linkage by rendering to the dead and the yet unborn the pride of place in wise men's reflections, Comte truly founded his philosophy and his fame.

With such an appreciation of Comte's achievement, Maurras found it easy to substitute for Humanity his own idea of France, a notion of *la patrie* steeped in the past. Indeed, Maurras implied that Comte himself, if he had lived the hundred years of a Fontenelle, would have made some such substitution, since it was now clear that, for the foreseeable future, "the Country will represent humankind for any given group of men."

Positivism, therefore, was recommended by Maurras to his readers as "first and foremost a discipline." By subordinating experience, both theoretical and practical, to the interests of a human society or civilization, Positivism could provide to the atheistically disposed members of the intelligentsia a proper perspective for a successful tackling of France's needs. Positivism, in fact, was "a philosophy that was eminently French, classical and Romanic": more specifically, "reorganizing everything relatively and *subjectively* from the standpoint of man in society," it represented "the latest development and the latest perfecting of the 'humanism' of the Renaissance."

If it was in *L'Avenir de l'intelligence* that Maurras indicated the advantages of Positivism for the regeneration of the spirit or mind, it was in *Trois Idées politiques* that he stated most forcefully the necessity of a political alliance between Positivists and Catholics. This call to arms was made in one of the notes that constitute the last third of the small book, the note being entitled "Necessary Conjunction of Atheists and Catholics."

The note started with an allusion to the visit paid to Pope Leo XIII by Brunetière, the editor of *La Revue des Deux Mondes*, in 1894, and continued with a brief outline of Comte's overture to the Superior-General of the Jesuits thirty-seven years earlier:

> Contrary to what is so often repeated, the idea of bringing together in a league both atheists and Catholics is not something dreamt up by M. Brunetière.
>
> In the last year of his life (1857), Auguste Comte delegated one of his disciples, Alfred Sabatier, to go to the Gesù in Rome to negotiate with the Reverend Fr Beckx an alliance between Positivism and the Rule of the Jesuits against Deism, Protestantism and the other forms of modern anarchy "that keep society in a permanent state of unrest."
>
> The Frenchman was received by a dignitary of the order, who, from the very first words, lost the sense of the talk, for he took Auguste Comte to be Charles Comte, the economist. Without there having been any real contact, the two men took leave of one another after these final words of Alfred Sabatier: "When the political storms of the future reveal the whole intensity of the modern crisis, you will find young positivists ready to be killed for your sake in the same way as you are willing to be martyred for God.

Whatever Comte's failure, Maurras continued, the situation was now quite different:

> Since 1857 much has happened. From the Jesuits, now better informed, there has come an excellent analysis of Positivism, namely that of the Austrian, Gruber. Moreover, "the political storms of the future," of which Alfred Sabatier spoke, have virtualy become a present reality, and the intellectual crisis seems to deepen from day to day. Soon it will no longer be question of "free-thinkers" and "believers," but of anarchical minds and political minds, of *barbarians* and *citizens*. Commenting on the attempted enterprise

of Comte and Sabatier, Dr Audiffrent wrote a few years ago: "Positivism invites those who no longer believe in God and who wish to work for the regeneration of their kind to become Positivists, and it calls on those who believe in God to return to Catholicism." Atheists of a scientific turn of mind and Catholics of a theological turn of mind have, in the temporal realm and in the spiritual one, profound interests in common, notably the interests of tradition and the civilized world, which are threatened by both sudden collapse and imperceptible degeneration. If they range themselves behind one or other of these two systems, with each of the latter being forcefully presented, the defenders of the humankind will soon vanquish their adversary, the spirit of mystical anarchy. It is against this spirit, the born enemy of national groupings as well as of rational combinations, that the two Frances can positively conclude a political and moral agreement of great solidity.

I do not assume that this is happening; but, if it does not happen, then we are lost.

Now it is clear that, in spite of Maurras's pious invocation of Comte to justify his own designs, there are immediately obvious differences between his idea of an alliance as enunciated in this passage from *Trois Idées politiques* and Comte's idea, as formulated in his *Appel aux conservateurs*, of a "religious alliance" between "true conservatives" (Positivists) and "retrogrades" (Catholics).

Comte evidently understood a Positivist to be one who would accept intellectually or on trust the body of his teachings as developed within the ten volumes of the *Philosophie positive* and the *Politique positive* or as summarized in the *Catéchisme positiviste* and the *Appel aux conservateurs*. All these works were more like holy writ than books to be consulted eclectically or at will.

More important still, Comte's "religious alliance" was to be a positivist-directed one, and the Catholics whom he hoped would take part in it were to be primarily Catholic women and regenerated Jesuits (that is, regenerated into true "Ignatians") who had largely forsaken the adoration of God for "the worship of the Goddess of the crusaders" as a result of what Comte judged to be the favourable influence upon Catholicism of the ideas of Chivalry. To progress from "the special worship of the Virgin" to "the universal adoration of Humanity" was, in Comte's view, happily but a small step. The ultimate aim of his alliance was therefore the exclusive triumph of the Religion of Humanity, Catholics being induced to take part in the alliance only insofar as they felt their social aspirations and feelings at odds with the dogma and organization of Catholic officialdom—indeed only insofar as they were virtually ready to forgo orthodox Catholicism for a radically new spiritual discipline.

Clearly enough, then, if Maurras's desired alliance was a development of Comte's "religious alliance," it was a far-reaching one. His exhortation to his compatriots to stand by either Catholicism or Positivism was not the same as Comte's "appeal to conservatives," as is shown by a certain metamorphosis of terms on Maurras's part.

By "Catholics" Maurras evidently meant those who could profess to be believers and who, moreover, subscribed whole-heartedly to Catholic orthodoxy as it had been developed in the nineteenth century by such doctrinal formulations as the *Syllabus errorum* of 1864, the primacy of the Pope and his *ex cathedra* infallibility as enunciated at the First Vatican Council, and the papal encyclical *Aeterni Patris* of 1879 recommending the "wisdom" of Aquinas as a guide for philosophical speculation in the troubled intellectual climate of the time. Having himself grown up with an understanding of the Church that was no doubt much influenced by such recent developments as these, it was not difficult for Maurras to idealize the Church for the purposes of his own thought. "In the modern era," he could write with satisfaction, "Catholic philosophy has been modelled by preference on Aristotle, and Catholic politics has appropriated the methods of the politics of ancient Rome. Such is the character of the classical tradition." His enthusiasm for this image of Catholicism—and the corresponding Catholic—was quite genuine.

What Maurras meant by a "Positivist" is not so clear. He certainly did not limit the title to an adept of the Religion of Humanity. Nor, for that matter, did he limit it, after the fashion of Littré, to those who adhered only to Comte's philosophy of science and rejection of metaphysics and theology—this is evident, for instance, in that Maurras showed singularly little interest in Comte's reflections on mathematics, astronomy, physics, chemistry and biology, and, in addition, in that he did not even believe that sociology had been properly constituted as a science. What in fact he meant by a Positivist appears to have amounted to little more than a person who, for want of a metaphysical or theological justification of his place in the world, was disposed to eschew the temptation of individualism and to give a primacy in his life and thought to a past-orientated idea of France (effectively a "Great Being") that did not diverge widely—as regards the nature of France's greatness and the forces hostile to it—from Maurras's own. The Maurrassian Nationalist—to posit the existence of a type—together with kindred spirits were, that is, all Positivists.

To take an example: Maurras must have considered Barrès, at least from about the time of the publication of *Les Déracinés*, to have been a proper Positivist, and, indeed, Barrès himself, in the years around 1900, not only was fulsome in his praise of Comte but also drew attention to Maurras's idea of an alliance (for instance, at the launching of the Ligue de la Patrie Française). Another example is Renan: his *La Réforme intellectuelle et morale de la France* must have been deemed by Maurras to be the best sort of Positivist writing.

As for the aim of Maurras's alliance, it was simply the extirpation from

France of "the spirit of mystical anarchy," of individualism in all its perverse manifestations. It was agreement on a common struggle, rather than, as in Comte's case, a step in the preparation of a radically new politics and religion.

If, therefore, Comte's "religious alliance" had largely the nature of an association between professed believer and catechumen, Maurras's desired alliance was much more one of equals. Yet it would be a mistake to see in Maurras's idea a latitudinarian plan for the political and moral regeneration of society. While, at first glance, his idea that Positivists and Catholics have very much in common may appear somewhat startling, it is much less so when closely examined. For there is very little difference between the Maurrassian Positivist and the Maurrassian Catholic. Each is essentially the child of a past originating in ancient Greece and Rome and permeated with the classical values of order and harmony—two pasts that are confounded with one another. Each is the implacable foe of "the spirit of mystical anarchy," a product of Judaism and Protestant Christianity. Indeed, to Maurras's idea of Catholicism, at least as much as to Comte's Religion of Humanity—though for different reasons—T. H. Huxley's famous barb can be directed: Maurras's idea of Catholicism was, as he himself had effectively admitted, a "Catholicism *minus* Christianity" ("On the Physical Basis of Life"). It was, perhaps, because his admiration for Catholicism was without Christian faith that he could conceive it to be compatible with his brand of positivism, and so with the needs of his France.

The Duplicitous Genre
of André Gide

Kevin Newmark

Given the remarkable diversity of Gide's *oeuvre*—including as it does novels, *récits*, so-called "*soties*," lyrical prose pieces, theater, politico-anthropological essays, autobiographies, and the *Journal*—it comes as something of a surprise to note the relative absence in it of literary theoretical texts. Aside from a small number of occasional pieces he wrote for conferences and in response to journalistic inquiries around the turn of the century, some scattered considerations in the *Journal* he kept for over half a century, and perhaps *Le Journal des faux-monnayeurs*, the more abstruse and theoretical questions of literary practice seem to have concerned him little. Indeed, one of his more theoretically aware statements is his own admission, "It matters much less to me to theorize about texts than to write them." Unlike his early mentor Mallarmé or his immediate contemporary Valéry, whose sustained and often urgent reflections on the practice and even the possibility of poetic language occupy a large place in their work and account for a good deal of the interest they continue to elicit in contemporary criticism, Gide had a tendency to move in a different direction altogether. Rather than tracing the literary experience back to its theoretical conditions and complications, Gide preferred to look forward from the existence of literary texts toward their links with the outside world. One is not likely to confuse Mallarmé's definition of poetic figure, "l'idée même et suave, l'absente de tous bouquets," with Gide's liberating admonition, "Nathan-aël, à présent, jette mon livre." For this reason, Gide is more often classed along with French *moralistes* than with poeticians and theorists. But it is for the same reason that Gide's abundant considerations on psychology, sociolology, politics, and sexuality have not worn the test of time very well and appear today rather dated, since they always seemed governed by a

357

relation to a particular moment in a particular world that may no longer be our own.

Nonetheless, the very fact that Gide's work *is* so diffuse, so splintered, so shared between such a large number of genres among which no single form of writing is allowed to keep the upper hand for very long, should also alert us to the likelihood that this multiplication of genres is itself a self-consciously theoretical gesture of some interest. Thus, the "Envoi" at the end of *Les Nourritures terrestres*, "Jette mon livre; dis-toi bien que ce n'est là *qu'une des milles* postures possibles," could be taken just as easily to refer to Gide's own theoretical project of proliferating literary forms as it can to an encouragement toward existential availability. It cannot be *a priori* certain that the Gidian concept of personal and social *disponibilité* would be any less the effect of a fundamental, though implicit theory of genre than the other way around. What would it mean, for instance, to read Gide's well-known thematic and autobiographic duplicitousness in matters of sexuality, politics, and religion in terms of their relation to theoretical considerations of a primarily poetic, or linguistic nature? Were such considerations in Gide actually available to us, then their effect on our ordinary conception of his entire authorship would not be simply gratuitous, would not be a mere *acte gratuit*, since this effect would be a direct consequence of Gide's own principle of the *mise en abyme*; that is, an emblematic principle of self-reflection thanks to which it is always possible to read any text as the allegorical narrative of both the formal coming into being of the text itself and the resultant existential changes it produces in its author. It remains to be seen whether a genuine theory of duplicitous genre can actually be located among the texts of Gide or whether it must remain only a kind of *a posteriori* hypothesis used at best to justify the vagaries of an *oeuvre* that otherwise would be all too easy to criticize from an aesthetic point of view for being overly diffuse.

To some extent, Gide will broach the question in his famous refusal to consider *L'Immoraliste* and *La Porte étroite* as univocal statements that could be understood independently of their structural relationship to each other. It is in the particular excesses of the one, he says, that the excesses of the other are to be justified. But one does not have to wait for these and other rather meager comments Gide made in the period 1911–13 about the generic distinctions between *roman, récit,* and *sotie* to see how his work has been marked by a multiplicity of genres. The idea of a mixing of genres, of the *Gesamtwerk* or *l'oeuvre totale*, is in the air as Gide is coming of age in *fin-de-siècle* Paris, and could hardly have failed to come to his attention. The name that is on everyone's lips is Wagner, whose own attempts to consolidate different art forms implies the promise of an ultimate synthesis of each of the individual genres. For Gide, though, the reception of Wagner and his theory of the *Gesamtwerk* will be complicated by the fact that, as a musician of some expertise himself, he will be a less disinterested party than many of the other young literati who took part in discussions around the name of Wagner. On the one hand, Gide seems to have had no appreciation whatsoever for Wagner or his music, though on the other, as he hints in *Si le grain ne meurt*, he also realized that in Mallarmé's circle of initiates, the topic "Wagner" had very little to do with music and everything to do with a theory of literature. What would be the fundamental principle of such a theory of literature?

Writing about Wagner in 1885 for the *Revue Wagnerienne*, Mallarmé takes advantage of the occasion to sketch out his own theory of genres by way of a wholesale rejection of the hackneyed realism of the contemporary European theater: "Le Maître surgit au temps d'un théâtre, le seul qu'on peut appeler caduc, tant la Fiction en est fabriqué d'un élément grossier: puisqu'elle s'impose à même et tout d'un coup, commandant de croire à l'existence du *personnage* et de l'aventure—de croire, simplement, rien de plus." According to Mallarmé, the introduction of music to the scene is able to offset the crudeness of the fictional hero and his adventure by making them what he terms "allegorical." Later in the essay, Mallarmé makes it clear, or at least as clear as Mallarmé makes anything, that music *per se* is less important here than the function it performs of distracting the spectator from the realistic illusion set before him. The same effect that is realized by juxtaposing theater and music can be obtained equally well by juxtaposing "fable" and "ode." The clichés of literary history notwithstanding, it is the *interference* of genres rather than their fusion that is here being proposed by Mallarmé as the necessary condition of literature, since it is only in the circulation *between* the genres that something like "art" can be maintained in a state that is not *caduc, populaire, grossier*; in other words, that is not reduced to a sub-literary category by being a simple *copy* of real life. For Mallarmé, then, and this can easily be verified by having a look at his "Hérodiade" or "Après-Midi d'un faune," "theater" functions as a figure for literature itself, and it can become a genuine work only when it gives up the illusion of straightforward representation, that is, when it ceases being *mimetic*. The literary work ceases being mimetic when the irreducibility of a multiplicity of genres, that is, sources, pressures, and divisions, makes it *allegorical* in Mallarmé's sense; that is, when it becomes subject to the work of interpretation or reading rather than mere *belief*.

The first text that Gide published under his own name, *Le Traité du Narcisse (Théorie du symbole)* (1891), is not only an example of just such an "allegorical" work, it is also a narrative reflection on its own "genre" of allegory, and can thus legitimately be considered among Gide's most sustained attempts at producing something like a theoretical text. The very title of Gide's *Narcissus* points to the allegorical operation it performs by situating itself between two headings that depend for their power to signify on two irreducible genres: *Le Traité du Narcisse* and *Théorie du symbole*. Narcissus may be the myth that tells the story of the self as it constitutes itself as its own mirror image, but the two headings of Gide's text—which juxtapose a reference to classical *myth* with the question of a *theory* of linguistic symbols—do not relate to each other in a similarly specular way. Thus, being neither completely the same nor simply polar opposites, myth and theory cannot constitute themselves as a single head, or face, or self to which we might give the name "Narcissus." The text is neither a simple theoretical examination in purely discursive language of the "symbol" nor a wholly figural and narrative version of an archetypal myth. Rather, it is a hybrid genre that is simultaneously a representation of the symbol in the form of a myth *and* a theoretical representation of the way in which that myth is able to function symbolically. As such, it is a kind of *mise en scène* of the symbol and its symbolizing power and it opens up a curiously theatrical space between "myth" and "theory." It is and is not theater; it is not a representation *of* something, but it is theoretically *of* or *about* representation, it is something like the theater of the possibility of theater, or a meta-theatrical text of literary theory in the form of a mythical figure. Rather than theater, it would be the *mise en abyme* of theater by theory. It would be theater, but in the form of a theoretical representation of itself *as* theater rather than as a representation of something outside it, like reality.

Formally, we have little trouble noticing the *mise en abyme* dimension here, since the introduction to the text spells it out in no uncertain terms: "Toutes choses sont dites déjà; mais comme personne n'écoute, il faut toujours recommencer." Each of the episodes contains within itself this gesture of beginning all over again, but at the same time it is clearly marked that they do this from within a structure generated in a previous episode, so that the pictorial emblem for the *mise en abyme* (the Dutch cocoa box on which there is a picture of girl holding a Dutch cocoa box on which, and so on) is in this way transposed to a purely textual space: a text that recounts a new beginning that recounts a new beginning that recounts, and so on. And to the extent that this example *is* textual rather than mimetic, we might suggest that *Le Traité du Narcisse* is a more appropriate example of the *mise en abyme* as a literary device than are Gide's remarks about it two years later in the *Journal*. But the *mise en abyme* here is not only present in a formal sense, but also in a thematic sense. For precisely in the center of the text the operation of the symbol is compared to a descent into an "abyss": "et vienne un temps de nuit tacite, où les eaux plus denses descendent: dans les *abîmes* imperturbés fleuriront les trémies secrètes." What this means, of course, is that the *narration* of the "abyme," of the symbolic process of descending into the abyss, is told in the *form* of an abyss, in a structural *mise en abyme*. We could say that the form of this text represents, is a *mise en scène* of its theme, or that the theme is an unfolding, a *mise en scène* of its form. In either case, we seem to be dealing with a text in which form and theme are mirror images of each other, a simple text that represents its relationship to itself as text, that is, as an interweaving of structure and theme, theory and myth, in the form of the self-reflexive mythological hero Narcissus. The structure of this text relates to its theme in the same way that Narcissus gazes into his own eye. But can any text that involves the structure of the *mise en abyme* be that simple? And to the extent that the myth of Narcissus is as much the story of the undoing of the subject of self-reflection as it is of its constitution, is it not already somewhat misleading to take this particular myth as the theoretical symbol of the potential of symbolic language to signify adequation between theme and structure?

Le Traité du Narcisse, then, curiously enough for someone as self-conscious as Gide and despite the anecdotal background of an evening spent with Valéry near the tomb of Young's daughter in Montpellier, is *not* primarily an autobiographical text. Nor is it, at least not exclusively, a text that is about the self, self-consciousness, or subjectivity. Rather it is a theoretical dramatization, a *mise en scène* of the very *possibility* of autobiography based on different conceptions of symbolic language in general. For this reason, it makes theoretical use of the figure of the self as an emblem of the figural dimension of *all* poetic activity, and in particular as an emblem of the possibility of a specular relationship between what a text says (its theme) and the way that a text says it (its rhetorical structure), or between a subject's experience and the knowledge the subject himself can have of the experience. For the sake of convenience, and in order better to see the "dramatization" of the theory which this text is, we could even cut the narrative movement up into the five acts of classical French theater: there is the introduction that makes the classical reference and calls into question the necessity for a new version; the second act that recounts the search for a mirror and the beginning of Narcissus' dream of lost paradise; the third act that contains the story of Adam and the loss of paradise; the fourth act that introduces the possibility of regaining paradise thanks to poetic creativity; and the fifth act that echoes the first by asking again about the text's *raison d'être*.

The main narration of the text begins with Narcissus, who alone in the middle of a deserted landscape—"plus de berge ni de source; plus de métamorphose et plus de fleur mirée"—sets off in search of an appropriate *image*; that is, a phenomenal appearance or shape for his *soul*, in other words, his non-sensory interiority. This first conception of poetic language is easy enough to recognize as a more or less classical theory of the symbol: a structure in which there is some form of adequation between inside and outside; that is, a language that could synthesize perception and imagination with no great difficulty through the mediations of a metaphorical chain of substitutions by resemblance. For example, when the text says that, "[Narcisse] veut connaître enfin quelle forme a son âme; elle doit être, il sent, excessivement adorable, s'il en juge par ses longs frémissements," the metaphorical conception of language has already been put into place, since to describe the motion of the soul as a "frémissement" is to borrow the vocabulary of the sensory world in order to refer to the workings of a non-sensory region. In order to say that the soul can be subject to "*frémissements*" it is necessary to suppose the possibility of the soul's being compared with and eventually substituted by something like a leaf being blown about in the wind. The problem with this conception of poetic language is that the world of immediacy seems to have disappeared all too quickly under the weight of a subjectivity that borders on solipsism; that is, it finds no opposition strong enough to resist and therefore to support its own reflection. Narcissus requires a subject-object polarity in order to develop his self-consciousness, but without a third term against which to project both interior and exterior in order to determine their respective limits, he can never be sure he is looking at anything but himself. At this point in the text, Narcissus is impotent because he is all-powerful: "les images n'attendaient que lui pour être, et sous son regard se colorent." Such a state of indetermination—perhaps a critique of a romantic aesthetic—is characterized by "ennui"—are the objects real or merely projections of my own interiority? a question that appears in the text in the form "[Narcisse] ne comprend pas si son âme guide le flot, ou si c'est le flot qui la guide"—and so the text is forced to provide another view of the symbol that might rectify the "léthargique canal, presque horizontal miroir" of false antithesis of the inside/outside metaphor.

This move is made by way of a metonymic play on the signifier *élan*, which at first is used to characterize the varying crests in the watery mirror Narcissus uses to project his images, but which reappears two sentences later in the form "toutes les formes s'efforcent et *s'élancent* vers une forme première perdue, paradisiaque." The upward connotation suggested by the sheer proximity of these two words seems to be sufficient to turn the horizontal mirror of inside/outside metaphor upright, producing a vertical ladder of transcendental values in which it is no longer possible to communicate directly with an ideal state from which we have been separated. The figure for this second conception of poetic language is also contained in the key word *s'élancer*, which names the "throwing beyond" movement that characterizes *hyperbole*. Although still based on a relationship of analogy, the substitutions have now been temporalized, and rather than the inside/outside exchanges of metaphor they are composed of a steady process of *éloignement* from an origin. The hyperbolic division of the *"ici-bas"* and *"là-haut"* in this section is a form of the "sublime," both in the religious sense of lost paradise and the psychoanalytical "sublimation," or filtered recollection of a partially erased past. One of the models of this conception is undoubtedly the Mallarmé of early poems like "Les Fenêtres." But as we know, hyperbole runs a constant risk of falling from its sublime height into ridiculousness, and in this section this occurs when Adam modulates the psalm-like seriousness of the opening transcendental language into the colloquial tones of everyday street life. This is the language of *parody*, and it is clear that something is being mocked here. Adam subverts the tradition in which he finds himself by refusing to accept the place allotted him by God. The *acte gratuit* involved in breaking a limb from the sacred tree, which also results in tearing the sacred book in which the "truth" is to be read, is an act of literary blasphemy; it is the impatience of a young writer who, instead of accepting his derived status passively, decides to compete with God the father, who is merely a figure for the entire weight of a long literary heritage. And it is precisely this act of revolt that introduces the third and final theory of poetic language to be dramatized in this text.

The poet, then, who occupies the predominant position in the third part, is less like the Narcissus figure of metaphor in the first part than the Adam figure of parody in the second part. But whereas the parody of Adam, in order to be recognized as parody, still depends at least in a minimal way on the opening hyperbole that is constructed on a metaphorical wearing away of an original and now inaccessible paradise, the poet in the last part begins with a wholly delocalized and disembodied form of paradise: "Car le paradis est partout" states the virtual rather than definite or defined status of paradise and clears the way for a figural pattern that would no longer be based exclusively on the mimetic analogies of metaphor and hyperbole/parody. The crucial step in this regard is the comparison between the "savant" and the poet. The savant is representative of all modes of knowledge which proceed by way of "examples" through a gradual process of induction. No matter how complex, no matter how long the chain of substitutions here, the fact that each step is incremental and based on some logical tie with its precedent ensures the (analogical) continuity between origin and end required by scientific truth. For the poet, though, there is no question of such a continuity between analogical steps in a homogeneous process. The theoretical poetics of this last section operates a radical disjunction between appearance and essence; no longer a horizontal relationship of inside/outside, nor a vertical one of paradise lost/paradise recollected, the relationship between the world and its truth has become wholly empty and arbitrary here, as is always the case when the figure becomes vestmental: "[le poète] sait que l'apparence n'est que le prétexte de chaque chose, un *vêtement* qui la dérobe et où s'arrête l'oeil profane." By calling the phenomenon a mere article of "clothing," the poet seems to acquire a great measure of freedom by being able to discard and go beyond its empty externality at the whim of his subjective will. If the tropological models of the first two sections are both grounded in mimesis—metaphor and hyperbole—then the last model proposed would be a non-mimetic figure that holds all the world and the heavens at its own disposal—"car le paradis est partout" in fact names the capacity of the intellect to *use* the perceived world rather than simply to *imitate* it. The heady freedom of the poet who senses in himself this power suggests a figure something like "irony," but the concomitant risk involved with such freedom is a wild and aberrant creativity that threatens to escape any control whatsoever. And it is true that once the mimetic models have been dispensed with by making the ideal *infinitely* available, the text can give no indication of *how* the poet is to know what he is doing when he decides to bypass the metaphorical link of inside/outside or up/down and produce his own paradise by means of the caprice of "guesswork" (*deviner*).

The implications of this risk are inscribed in the text in an unavoidable though particularly complicated way at the very moment that the poet exercises his masterful freedom. Once the poet has moved past the phenomenal shape in order to descend into the "abyss" of the "*Idée*," he is ready to reassign the idea a form that is no longer subject to the vagaries of time or appearances. This is the truly linguistic moment of the treatise on theory, for the only poetic *acte gratuit* that could fulfill such conditions is the act of denomination, the positing moment of a non-phenomenal, non-temporal system of signification which has not yet begun to signify. Now the "crystalline" work of art, according to the treatise, will eventually be composed of "paroles, transparentes et révélatrices," but despite this rather hyperbolic claim in the last non-hyperbolic section, the traces of the originally wild act of denomination are still present in the persistent risk of something called "*l'orgueil du mot.*" The necessity of this transparency, along with the accompanying threat of pride, is also what organizes the famous "aesthetico-moral" note in this part of the treatise, and what generates the dictum "L'artiste doit avoir d'avance fait le sacrifice de soi-même." Where is it in this last section that we have anything like an example of the possible convergence of a sacrifice of the self with a transparency of the language, that is, of the non-subjective creation of a crystalline paradise that the text seems to be proposing as its own aesthetic model? It is the poetic act of denomination itself, but it takes place in a mode that is far removed from crystalline transparency: "et quand le Poète a perçu l'Idée, il la saisit, puis, insoucieux de cette forme transitoire qui la revêtait dans le temps, il sait lui redonner une forme éternelle, *sa* Forme véritable enfin, et fatale,—paradisiaque et cristalline." In the italicized possession of the pronoun *sa* it becomes impossible to determine whose *form* is being given to what: what is the genre of this form in which it is possible to read both "il sait lui redonner sa forme à elle" and "sa forme à lui"? The freedom of the poet—which in a more extended analysis of the text would have to include an examination of Gide's relationship to Schopenhauer and Novalis, and the entire question of romantic irony along with the absolute freedom often attributed to the infinitely ironic subject—is thus neither subjective nor transcendental, since it freezes the signifying movement that could take us with certainty either to the poet or to paradise. The form of this form, the genre of Gide's theory of the symbol, is the least transparent thing in the whole text, and it never makes it to the transparency of the sentence because it gets stuck in the "*orgueil*" of this one word "*sa*," or rather it gets stuck in the "*sa*" *as* word, as *signifiant*, as mode of signification prior to semantic product. The one place in the text where the linguistic moment— i.e. non-subjective, non-transcendental—is being theorized is also the spot where nothing can be manifested with clarity other than a knot of mutually exclusive "selves": subjective, transcendental, linguistic.

What this means, in an overly schematic way, is that the theoretical question of the subjective myth of Narcissus, the question of the self *as* symbolic language, at least the way that it has been dramatized in this text by Gide, is not the product of an existential or psychological situation, but results rather from a linguistic predicament, to wit, the *"orgueil"* of the word that always threatens to "prefer itself" and thus block the transparency of the meaningful sentence, or of incipient thought. It also means that the plurality of genres referred to earlier can perhaps be re-introduced here in a helpful way to characterize the two "Gides" of this text and potentially of all of Gide's texts: the mythological, subjective, self-conscious Gide of the *"phrases rythmiques et sûres"* who proposes a certain self-sacrifice only to rise again from it by glorifying it in the form of a *fin-de-siècle* aesthetics, and a darker, more theoretically aware Gide whose textual *"orgueil du mot"* performs a radically linguistic sacrifice of both the aesthetic and moral self that is more difficult to re-assimilate to a concept of subjectivity. And it would be in the form of this doubled and duplicitous identity, because never resolved, that the specularity of theme and structure that was obvious in the beginning would be disrupted at the end of the text. What this would mean for a reading of Gide's entire authorship is truly disruptive, for in the abyssal structure of the power of the *"sa"* to signify at the end of this text, we can read the impossible future of an *oeuvre* that will be constantly driven and thwarted by the (theoretical) challenge to reconstitute a self for itself in all the clarity of sincerity and authenticity.

Proust Reads Ruskin

David R. Ellison

In psychological terms, literary influence can be conceived as a struggle by a son to overcome the genius of a father figure, where the son, by the very fact of his chronological lateness, feels separated from the creative center his father had successfully discovered, exploited, exhausted. To write, the younger author must find a space of his own, a place belonging to him and no other; this he accomplishes by various strategies of confrontation and evasion whereby he attempts to render harmless the writings of his predecessor. Referring to the cultural context of Romanticism, Harold Bloom evokes the successor's "loss of reciprocity with the world, as compared to the precursor's sense of being a man to whom all things spoke" (*The Anxiety of Influence*). Although Bloom, like Ruskin, leaves room for Dante, Milton, and Shakespeare as exceptional figures whose creative energies seemed relatively untouched by the anxiety of influence, he sees in the Romantic agony and its modern inheritance an inward-turning movement that has affected all "strong poets," determining the path of their increasingly strained and conflictive relationship with what can be called "reality"—the immediate givens of sensual experience that provide metaphorical discourse with its objective correlative, its solidly fixed anchor in nature.

The same structure of increased innerness taken to the point of extreme solipsism characterizes the evolution of the contemporary novel. Loss of reciprocity with the world can be considered the major factor responsible for the transformations undergone by the fictional protagonist, whose increasing inability to control the social conditions of his existence leads, inexorably, to a defensive withdrawal. The path from Balzac through Flaubert and Huysmans to Proust, from the naïvely energetic hero to the bur-

From *The Reading of Proust.* © 1984 by The Johns Hopkins University Press.

lesque antihero to the isolated ambivalence of a nonpersonal "I" (with its apparently logical end point in the disembodied shadow voices of Beckett's universe), has the convincing (historical) rigor of a geometrical curve. Each successive step in the process challenges the individual writer to reinvent a language capable of moving farther away from the threats of the outside.

As Richard Terdiman has demonstrated in the best recent interpretation of Proust from the standpoint of historical determinism, Proust's creative response involves a turn away from the traditional temporality of successive actions oriented toward a dramatic finality (embodied, in nineteenth-century narrative, by the alternation of past definite and imperfect-descriptive tenses) (*The Dialectics of Isolation: Self and Society in the French Novel from the Realists to Proust*). With the elaboration of a fluid, indeterminate, imperfect modality that Genette has called the "iterative," the laws of memory recreate and reform temporal progression, subordinating it to the inner mechanism of subjectivity. According to Terdiman, the final result of this historical/technical development is a radical change in the subject matter of the novel: "An entire literature about the creation of literature will follow from the failures of life outside." Whereas Balzac's novels, in their adherence to the mimetic mode of representation, could be said to rivalize with nature, Proust concludes that art's only justification is its ability to justify itself *as* art. The *Recherche* uses the external trappings of the available social facts of its period, but bends them and subjects them to the overriding coherence of a highly personal vision.

At first sight, the intertextual relationship between Ruskin and Proust . . . would seem to fit this pattern perfectly. Whereas Ruskin subordinates his considerable talent as decipherer of iconographic and poetic symbols to an established, referentially grounded moral code, Proust plays with the ambiguities of this code in order to deepen a subjective meditation on the motivations of the linguistic sign. In Bardèche's view, such a reversal of priorities implies that Proust is able to overcome or neutralize the moral energy of his predecessor by an act of formal reconversion (*Marcel Proust romancier*). What Ruskin considered meaningful only through an appeal to experience and referential validity becomes, for his disciple, thematic material that can be voided of its concrete reality: thus guilt as existential pathos becomes the soil from which the *Recherche* can grow. But the question must be asked, Is the transition from realism to formalism made smoothly and unproblematically, according to the inevitable process that we call literary history, whose *telos* in the absolute of silence is now the hypothetical subject of postmodern fictional creation and criticism? Or, in the passage from moral force to novelistic form, is there some residue left behind that makes it difficult for the later author to master his master? Is the movement inward an easy shedding of superfluous and now outmoded representational *préjugés*, or can it be demonstrated that this movement itself has a rhetorical structure requiring independent analysis? Ultimately, we must leave open the possibility that literary history, far from being the abstract line of an inevitable geometric involution, may in fact arise from a misreading of its own logical premises. For our purposes, this would mean that in Proust's reconversion of Ruskin's imprisonment in common experience and morality we need to observe how referential *evidence* as such is made to function thematically, how it is enveloped by a fictional frame, so that a literary-historical interpretation of Proust's work can enjoy the rigor of a visible and understandable progression.

With these questions in mind we can examine . . . in greater detail . . . Proust's actual reading of Ruskin. I use the word "actual" here in contradistinction to the analytically demonstrable but somewhat hidden "reading" that was performed by Proust in his complication of Ruskinian "custom" and "association." We are fortunate to possess Proust's thoughts on Ruskin as they evolve from admiration to critical distance in the justifiably acclaimed translations of *The Bible of Amiens* and *Sesame and Lilies*. To see Proust read Ruskin is to study the series of repetitions, exchanges, contradictions, and strategic reworkings of ideas that link four stages of reflection in a complex unity: (1) the original Ruskinian opus and its translation; (2) Proust's notes, showing varying degrees of approbation and disagreement with the original text; (3) Proust's critical articles based upon *The Bible of Amiens* and *Sesame and Lilies*; and (4) the *Recherche* itself, insofar as its fictional forms and episodes elaborate the problems raised by Ruskin. In my analysis of Proust's three major articles on Ruskin—"Journées de pèlerinage," "John Ruskin," and "Journées de lecture"—I will examine the question of contextuality . . . : namely, in what way does the novel *A la recherche du temps perdu* relate to the "theme" of reading, or, in other words, how does the novel "swallow," "digest," or otherwise incorporate reading as one theme among others? The innerness of modern fiction consists of its capacity to speak about itself, or to place itself within itself and make of itself an object of (self-) understanding. How this occurs in the process of reading and how the act of reading relates rhetorically to the critical moment of self-understanding will be the focus of the present interpretations. ["Journées de pèlerinage" was first published in the *Mercure de France*, April 1900. "John Ruskin" appeared in the supplement to the *Gazette des Beaux-Arts* (*La Chronique des Arts et de la Curiosité*) in the issues of April and August 1900. Both articles combined to form the bulk of the translator's preface to *La Bible d'Amiens* (1904). Proust later included the two essays in *Pastiches et mélanges* (1919). The 1971 Pléiade edition of *Contre Sainte-Beuve*, to which I refer when quoting from all of Proust's critical work on Ruskin, contains the 1919 "definitive" versions of "Journées de pèlerinage," "John Ruskin," and also "Journées de lecture." "Journées de lecture" (the final title, adopted in *Pastiches et mélanges*) first appeared as "Sur la lecture" in *La Renaissance latine*, June 1905, and was later included as part of the translator's preface to *Sésame et les lys* (1906).]

THE BIBLE OF AMIENS AND "JOURNEES DE PELERINAGE"

The Bible of Amiens was written in spurts from 1880 to 1885. Characteristic of Ruskin's later style, it is a hodgepodge of digressions and idiosyncratic pronouncements on many tenuously related subjects. Its ostensible main theme is, however, never quite fully lost from view. After giving a short history of the Amiens cathedral, including the legends of Saints Martin, Geneviève, and Firmin, and after a fairly lengthy development on the passionate, warlike instincts of the Franks, Ruskin discusses the problems of scriptural interpretation, the career of Saint Jerome, and finally, elaborates his own allegorical reading of the Bible as represented in the stones of Amiens. We may assume that Proust's interest in *The Bible of Amiens* arose from his desire to penetrate the world of symbols that the Middle Ages had created to house its beliefs, and to examine, through Ruskin, the manner in which the literal appearance of the statuary related to the figurative meanings that we moderns, without a first-hand knowledge of the Bible, might not grasp immediately. But Ruskin's solid erudition is accompanied by a sense of humor, a playfulness, that also must have appealed to Proust. This lightness of touch is especially evident in Ruskin's interpretation of the personified abstractions Obedience, Rebellion, and Charity, and in the original, quasi-Heideggerian probing and stretching of etymological laws that Proust did not hesitate to qualify as a *"manie* étymologique*"* in his notes, but that surfaced in the *Recherche* as the private obsessions of Combray's curé and the demystifying scientific accuracy of Brichot.

As is well-established in the critical literature, Proust's knowledge of English was limited, though by no means as threadbare as his modesty compelled him to confess. His method of translation (which heralded the patchwork construction of his novel in a *palimpseste* of "paperoles") involved a double collaboration—with his mother for a literal rendition of the original, and with Marie Nordlinger for stylistic subtleties—thereby insuring a high degree of accuracy from which Proust could work to attain a smooth and elegant French version. Jean Autret has analyzed the two translations in painstaking detail, and has revealed a minimal tally of significant errors, concluding that the final result is faithful to and respectful of the Ruskinian text ("Les Travaux Ruskiniens de Proust," in *Influence de Ruskin*). Of primary interest to us is that the process of translation, among the most minute forms of word study, led Proust to meditate on the possibilities and limits of literary criticism as intellectual activity. Faithfulness to the translated author—that is, the perhaps impossible goal of avoiding the stigma *"traduttore, traditore"*—is the first obligation of the critic, who, in restating and clarifying the ideas of the author he studies, must take care lest he swerve from the letter of the text, lest he simplify or otherwise distort the original corpus of writings in an attempt at systematization.

The ideal of adherence to the set of intended meanings that constitutes *The Bible of Amiens* is thus the entire task of the translator and the first step in the commentator's work. But Proust was not satisfied to remain at this level, since the relatively short, late book of Ruskin is merely a part of a much larger whole within which it awakens, in the mind of the reader, textual correspondences or "echoes" of ideas he may have seen previously in other books of the same author. In his "Avant-propos" to *La Bible d'A-miens*, Proust justifies his extensive use of notes with an appeal to the reader's intuitive understanding of the thematic integrity that characterizes Ruskin's literary production as a whole. At the beginning of his introductory paragraph, the critic writes:

> Je donne ici une traduction de la *Bible d'Amiens*, de John Ruskin. Mais il m'a semblé que ce n'était pas assez pour le lecteur. Ne lire qu'un livre d'un auteur, c'est voir cet auteur une fois. Or, en causant une fois avec une personne, on peut discerner en elle des traits singuliers. Mais c'est seulement par leur répétition, dans des circonstances variées, qu'on peut les reconnaître pour caractéristiques et essentiels. Pour un écrivain, pour un musicien ou pour un peintre, cette variation des circonstances qui permet de discerner, par une sorte d'expérimentation, les traits permanents du caractère, c'est la variété des oeuvres. Nous retrouvons, dans un second livre, dans un autre tableau, les particularités dont la première fois nous aurions pu croire qu'elles appartenaient au sujet traité autant qu'à l'écrivain ou au peintre. Et du rapprochement des oeuvres différentes nous dégageons des traits communs dont l'assemblage compose la physionomie morale de l'artiste.

And later on in the same passage:

> Ainsi j'ai essayé de pourvoir le lecteur comme d'une memoire improvisée où j'ai disposé des souvenirs des autres livres de Ruskin—sorte de caisse de résonance, où les paroles de la *Bible d'A-miens* pourront prendre plus de retentissement en y éveillant des échos fraternels.

The *mémoire improvisée* that founds thematic criticism and, through Proust's critical intervention, contributes to a better understanding of the "symphonic" structure of Ruskin's works, is, of course, closely related to the specifically Proustian method of novelistic composition. But the difference between improvised (retrospectively schematized) memory and involuntary remembrance is that the latter is a lived process in which the mind measures the inner distances it traverses in thought and feels fully "la résistante douceur de cette atmosphère imposée qui a l'étendue même de notre vie" (*La Bible d'Amiens*). The act of writing can recreate what Proust calls the "poetry of memory"—the movement of remembrance in its essence—whereas reading can only reproduce by degrees the abstract form of this movement as it appears to the rational mind after the fact. Nevertheless, Proust does not insist upon the separateness or mutual exclusion of creation and criticism at this juncture; rather, he prefers to delineate their structural similarity and make of his own critical study the closest possible reflection of Ruskin's interpretive insights.

Proust's admiration for Ruskinian esthetics is especially evident in the first of the two essay-length developments of the translator's preface to *La Bible d'Amiens:* the article originally titled "Journées de pèlerinage." In it, Proust attempts to convince the reader to visit Amiens in "a kind of Ruskinian pilgrimage." In following Ruskin's text with a scrupulous attention to detail, in quoting long passages from its pages, in adding explanatory commentary, Proust abides by his program of interpretive faithfulness, to such an extent that it might appear he is renouncing his own personality in an act of total self-effacement. This is not quite true, as we shall see, but certainly the reader's first impression is that of a relative lack of critical intrusion. In allowing Ruskin to speak through him, however, Proust in no way refrains from what might be called a participatory enthusiasm. Indeed, "Journées de pèlerinage" is characterized by pleasure—physical, intellectual, esthetic—for it reproduces the joyful atmosphere of discovery through travel that permeates *The Bible of Amiens.* The exhilarating quality of Ruskin's writing derives, in part, from his theory of reading, which, as was evident in the ecstatic experiences of *Praeterita,* involves the interpenetration of observing subject and esthetic object in an act of transcendental revelation. The voyage to Amiens is already colored by the jubilant tone of the later interpretive experience; and conversely, the act of reading takes place in the open air, the beautiful natural context in which the voyage unfolds. Reading is the unveiling of truth in nature. The desire for knowledge is fulfilled as the previously enigmatic cathedral stones reveal their secrets at the call of Ruskin's voice.

At the beginning of his essay, Proust makes a distinction that subtends the entire logic of his further argumentation. He differentiates between the kind of pilgrimage that seeks in the referent the imprint of an author's intellectual presence (we visit Amiens in order to find, incorporated in the statues of its cathedral, the essence of Ruskin's thought) and the false adoration, or *fétichisme,* which consists of visiting the writer's tomb, where nothing remains of his thinking power. If this distinction is to hold and possess an unquestionable validity, it is necessary that the statuary of Amiens reveal with perfect clarity the message that Ruskin attached to its signifying surface: that is, between the book brought by the disciple in his mission of adoration and the building's meaning there can be no esthetic distance, no possibility of interpretive misunderstanding. In other words, if the stones became too interesting in themselves, there would be a danger of fetishistic contemplation inherent in the structure of the reading experience itself. Proust uses several rhetorical strategies to avoid just such a danger, and evokes, in the process, a conception of artistic creation and reception based upon transparency and unmediated communication. He begins by hypothesizing that intellectually sincere work, accomplished without the goal of pleasing others in a superficial way, will necessarily reach a wide group of readers, for we as individuals are part of a "trame universelle" that surpasses our egotistically limited perspectives. Readers of Ruskin can understand *The Bible of Amiens* because the physical/mental unit called "Ruskin" is composed of certain universal elements that all men have in common. Thus, the act of reading becomes contextualized within the higher enjoyments of the spirit:

> Quand on travaille pour plaire aux autres on peut ne pas réussir, mais les choses qu'on a faites pour se contenter soi-même ont toujours chance d'intéresser quelqu'un. Il est impossible qu'il n'e-xiste pas de gens qui prennent quelque plaisir à ce qui m'en a tant donné. Car personne n'est original et fort heureusement pour la sympathie et la compréhension qui sont de si grands plaisirs dans la vie, c'est dans une trame universelle que nos individualités sont taillées. Si l'on savait analyser l'âme comme la matière, on verrait que, sous l'apparente diversité des esprits aussi bien que sous celle des choses, il n'y a que peu de corps simples et d'éléments irré-ductibles et qu'il entre dans la composition de ce que nous croyons être notre personnalité, des substances fort communes et qui se retrouvent un peu partout dans l'Univers.

If Ruskin is not perceived as a threat at this point or as an energy to be overcome through the catharsis of an anxiety-ridden creative conscious-ness, it is because he has lost his identity and become abstracted in the general Laws of personality. This decomposition/dissemination of "Ruskin" into analyzable components allows "Journées de pèlerinage" to function as text of pleasure while giving us as readers the opportunity to participate in what Barthes has called the "pleasure of the text."

The ease with which Ruskin's thoughts penetrate and illuminate the referent derives from his literary creativity, which, Proust insists, does not involve conscious labor, but rather flows from the natural revelations of memory. Ruskin did not *write* his book, if the act of writing is conceived as taking place within the necessary separation of the author from the reality he seeks to transform. Ruskin merely opened his memory to us, and this process occurs without the interference of mediating steps, and even with-out the desire of the critic to influence his reader in any way. In absolute terms, then, *The Bible of Amiens* would not be a book. It is, instead, the chance recording of a disinterested remembrance that was not so much deliberately published as simply not prohibited from circulation. Proust would like us to believe that Ruskin's work is free from the rhetoric of persuasion, that it is simply a footnote, an afterthought of a great mind. These interesting but debatable conceptions are introduced in a discussion of the Vierge Dorée, one of the statues of the Amiens cathedral that Ruskin had mentioned casually in *The Two Paths* (1858) before analyzing its sym-bolical significance in 1885. As esthetic object, the statue had always in-terested Ruskin, so that when it becomes the center of a lengthy analysis, the critic is not engaged in an innovative interpretation, but in the kind of *resuscitation* that attains to the poetic dimension of Time. Proust explains:

J'ai pensé que vous aimeriez mieux *La Bible d'Amiens*, de sentir
qu'en la feuilletant ainsi, c'étaient des choses sur lesquelles Ruskin
a, de tout temps, médité, celles qui expriment par là le plus profondément sa pensée, que vous preniez connaissance; que le présent qu'il vous faisait était de ceux qui sont le plus précieux à ceux
qui aiment, et qui consistent dans les objets dont on s'est longtemps servi soi-même sans intention de les donner un jour, rien
que pour soi. En écrivant son livre, Ruskin n'a pas eu à travailler
pour vous, il n'a fait que publier sa mémoire et vous ouvrir son
coeur. J'ai pensé que la Vierge Dorée prendrait quelque importance
à vos yeux, quand vous verriez que, près de trente ans avant *La
Bible d'Amiens*, elle avait, dans la mémoire de Ruskin, sa place où,
quand il avait besoin de donner à ses auditeurs un exemple, il
savait la trouver, pleine de grâce et chargée de ces pensées graves
à qui il donnait souvent rendez-vous devant elle.

In these sentences and in the subsequent paragraphs devoted to the
Vierge Dorée, Proust is inaugurating the kind of meditation on the temporal
modality of artistic works that will be so prevalent in the *Recherche*. The
dialectic struggle between time as destructive force and the resurrecting
power of involuntary memory that structures the conclusion of *Le Temps
retrouvé* is already to be found in "Journées de pèlerinage," where the
interpretive-vivifying efforts of Ruskin must fight against the wind and
rain, whose repeated blasts will gradually render the features of the statue
unrecognizable. The meanings that Ruskin wrests from the cathedral's biblical text are more than successfully deciphered signs relating to an artifact;
they convey the transcendental purpose of the creative act, and as such,
provide the metaphysical justification for the artistic process.

Ultimately, it turns out that there are two mutually conflicting ways
to read "Journées de pèlerinage." On the one hand, if we adhere as closely
to Proust as he did to Ruskin, if we enter into the atmosphere of enthusiasm,
discovery, pleasure, and transparency that characterizes both *The Bible of
Amiens* and its Proustian commentary, the result is that we will share the
two writers' sentiments, we will be persuaded by the apparently disinterested tone of their prose, we will be made to believe in the poetry of Time
and the capacity of art to rise above and conquer its finite limits. In fact,
it is impossible to avoid performing this reading unless we are completely
insensitive to the pathos of temporal loss and recuperation. The question
which arises, however, and which leads to a second (deconstructive) reading, is, How does the logic of disinterest succeed in convincing us and
moving us to adopt given authorially intended beliefs—or, What is the
rhetoric of a "nonrhetoric"? We can gain some help in answering this
question if we remember that the origin of memory as poetry of time is in
a nonwriting that presumably results in a nonreading: Ruskin did not write,
but "opened" his remembrances to Proust, who, in turn, insists that *The*

Bible of Amiens is not a work of art, that the Vierge Dorée is not a symbol to be interpreted but a *person* with an individuality whose true significance resides in her ability to awaken in us "la mélancolie d'un souvenir." Ironically, the moments in "Journées de pèlerinage" that remind us most of the *Recherche* and foreshadow major themes of the novel are the consequence of a delusion or misreading. It is precisely because we do not read, because we, in superficial adherence to an author's thought, no longer examine the works he discussed *as* works, that the following poetry, the Proustian charm of persons and places, is made possible:

> Un jour sans doute aussi le sourire de la Vierge Dorée (qui a déjà pourtant duré plus que notre foi) cessera, par l'effritement des pierres qui'il écarte gracieusement, de répandre, pour nos enfants, de la beauté, comme à nos pères croyants, il a versé du courage. Je sens que j'avais tort de l'appeler une oeuvre d'art: une statue qui fait ainsi à tout jamais partie de tel lieu de la terre, d'une certaine ville, c'est-à-dire d'une chose qui porte un nom comme une personne, qui est un individu, dont on ne peut jamais trouver la toute pareille sur la face des continents, dont les employés de chemins de fer, en nous criant son nom, à l'endroit où il a fallu inévitablement venir pour la trouver, semblent nous dire, sans le savoir: "Aimez ce que jamais on ne verra deux fois,"—une telle statue a peut-être quelque chose de moins universel qu'une oeuvre d'art; elle nous retient, en tous cas, par un lien plus fort que celui de l'oeuvre d'art elle-même, un de ces liens comme en ont, pour nous garder, les personnes et les pays.

As the Vierge Dorée is transformed, in the mind of the observing subject, from a work of art to the equivalent of a person, there is both a loss of universality and a gain in affectivity. The rhetoric of Proust's argument sets out to convince us that the gain eliminates the loss, that our heightened awareness of the emotional aura surrounding the statue will compensate for whatever purely denotational value our interpretive efforts might have uncovered. In fact, the basis of Proust's logic here is that of Ruskinian *association:* we are interested in the esthetic object not for intrinsic reasons but because it is linked, in our minds, to a given city, to a given place with a specific name. The "personality" of the Vierge Dorée derives from the individuality of the city of Amiens, which, by the process of naming (railroad employees cry out the word "Amiens" as we arrive at the station, thus magically creating the place linguistically symbolized), assumes shape and the power of a sensual attraction. Indeed, the traveller, having shed all pretense at disinterested esthetic contemplation, relates to the city of Amiens and to the Vierge Dorée much as a lover relates to his mistress.

The Proustian motivation for travel can be described, in Ruskinian terms, as a *possession-taking*. Psychologically, the purpose of the voyage is

376   David R. Ellison

to realize an initial desire, to seize and penetrate in the real world, what had been merely imagined at an earlier moment. Thus, in the lyrical conclusion of his article, Proust describes the effect of Ruskin's knowledge upon the faithful disciple in the erotic imagery of the Song of Solomon, with emphasis on the metaphors of opening and penetration:

> Comprenant mal jusque-là la portée de l'art religieux au moyen âge, je m'étais dit, dans ma ferveur pour Ruskin: Il m'apprendra, car lui aussi, en quelques parcelles du moins, n'est-il pas la vérité? Il fera entrer mon esprit là où il n'avait pas accès, car il est la porte. Il me purifiera, car son inspiration est comme le lys de la vallée. Il m'enivrera et mevivifiera, car il est la vigne et la vie. Et j'ai senti en effet que la parfum mystique des rosiers de Saron n'était pas à tout jamais évanoui puisqu'on le respire encore, au moins dans ses paroles.

Initially, the follower, recognizing his own intellectual and spiritual limitations, must abandon himself, open himself to the truths of the master, thereby assuming the classical female role of a vessel waiting to be filled. But in a second phase, through the success of an initiation ritual, the disciple can enter with the master into the promised land, thereby obtaining by proxy the masculine attributes of domination and possession. "Journées de pèlerinage" terminates on a note of triumph, combining and intertwining in the best Ruskinian/thematic fashion the feminine beauty of lilies and the masculine promise of an Open Sesame. It seems as if the future author of the *Recherche*, in submitting first to the force of Ruskin, can then exercise his own creative energies and enter the sacred domain of art. Thus the passionate hope of Proust as formulated in 1904 would appear to express allegorically the transition from the secondary, weak position of critical work to the primary activity of authorial control that was later to be achieved in his novel. In this sense, the conclusion of "Journées de pèlerinage" is a prophetic statement, the unconsciously traced path of a career.

If we now ask the question, To what extent does Proust's novel realize or actualize this dream of authorial domination as possession of the personified esthetic object? we should keep in mind that the answer cannot be abstract or a mere matter of our critical conviction. Rather, we can assume that the *Recherche*, in emulating the Ruskinian voyage to Truth, will explicitly stage the dream of possession-taking in a fictional guise and will provide us with the clues necessary to locate its contextual development. It is not difficult to see that "Journées de pèlerinage" is the most evident textual origin of the young Marcel's reveries on names and that the voyage to Amiens commented on in the critical article is the early equivalent of the train ride to Balbec in the second part of *A l'ombre des jeunes filles en fleurs*. In both cases, the hope of attaining new knowledge orients the physical movement of travel; but in the novel there is a long separation between the Protean metamorphoses of subjective desire and the process of referential testing, which corresponds, in the book, to the three hundred pages that lie between "Noms de pays: le nom" and "Noms de pays: le pays."

Like Proust's adoration of the Vierge Dorée, Marcel's love of Balbec is impure, "mixed"; it is based upon an association of the cathedral with its town and with its supposed location on a precipice overlooking the fierce ocean of the Normandy coast. As a child the protagonist perceives the whistling of the wind in Combray as the harbinger of a project later to be carried out: "Alors, par les soirs orageux et doux de février, le vent—soufflant dans mon coeur, qu'il ne faisait pas trembler moins fort que la cheminée de ma chambre, le projet d'un voyage à Balbec—mêlait en moi le désir de l'architecture gothique avec celui d'une tempête sur la mer" (*Du côté de chez Swann*). Gradually, by a process of metaphorical fusion, the vague desire of Balbec with its panoply of erotic fantasies becomes subsumed within the monolithic power of its pronounced syllables. The word "Balbec" not only replaces the geographic place it represents, but, according to the rhetorical manipulation of the narrator, *encloses* and *absorbs* the city, and in so doing, grants it the attribute of particularity or individuality. (This was also the case for the Vierge Dorée, enclosed within the personified limits of "Amiens.") But the process whereby *contenant* and *contenu* exchange functions is accomplished in an act of subjective defiance of reality, thus raising the possibility, as Proust here foreshadows, of a later disillusionment:

> Mais si ces noms absorbèrent à tout jamais l'image que j'avais de ces villes, ce ne fut qu'en la transformant, qu'en soumettant sa réapparition en moi à leurs lois propres; ils eurent ainsi pour conséquence de la rendre plus belle, mais aussi plus différente de ce que les villes de Normandie . . . peuvent être en réalité, et, en accroissant les joies arbitraires de mon imagination, d'aggraver la déception future de mes voyages.

Using a technique that has been called, quite aptly, a "devaluation of suspense" (Richard Terdiman), Proust resumes in one sentence the future result of the protagonist's visit to Balbec. We know in advance, five pages after the beginning of the section on names, that the freely circulating *signifiant* owes its charm to its irresponsibility, that it is already inscribed in a movement of error that will be explained in "Noms de pays: le pays." Indeed, when Marcel arrives at Balbec, he finds that the presumed global unity of the dreamed word hides two radically different realities: Balbec-en-terre (or Balbec-le-vieux) and Balbec-plage (*A L'ombre des jeunes filles en fleurs*).

The two elements previously associated in the protagonist's mind—the cathedral and the ocean—are now revealed to exist in separate contexts. This means that the passage describing the progressive disillusionment that results from the encounter with reality will unfold from a disentanglement of the falsely constructed rhetorical associations in "Noms de pays: le nom." In a first step, the capacity of names to contain or enclose the "idea" of a city is shown to be impossible, since the one designation "Balbec" is not monosemic. Consequently, the individuality or personality conferred upon the imagined city by the evocative power of the name no longer exists: what remains for the observer to see is not a system of subjectively postulated, necessarily related elements, but an amalgam of pure contingency, a group of arbitrarily juxtaposed objects whose chief attribute is resistance to synthetic understanding. Rather than rise above the waves of a storm-battered coast, the cathedral's belltower "se dressait sur une place où était l'embranchement de deux lignes de tramway, en face d'un Café qui portait, écrit en lettres d'or, le mot 'Billard' "; and the church itself, "entrant dans mon attention avec le Café, avec le passant à qui il avait fallu demander mon chemin, avec la gare où j'allais retourner—faisait un tout avec le reste, semblait un accident, un produit de cette fin d'après-midi, dans laquelle la coupole moelleuse ou gonflée sur le ciel était comme un fruit dont la même lumière qui baignait les cheminées des maisons, mûrissait la peau rose, dorée et fondante."

It is significant that the accidental quality of the cathedral's presence on the town square, which indicates the unfounded nature of Marcel's dreams, is immediately negated and recuperated in the unified golden harmony of the afternoon. The deconstruction of a fragile metaphorical system of resemblances is superseded, in the brusque transition from "accident" to "*produit* de cette fin d'après-midi," by a metonymic system of juxtaposed illuminated objects, whose beauty is the result of a spatial or contextual totalization. It is as if, for Proust, even in a moment of heightened critical lucidity, the tendency of the mind were to continue constructing associative frameworks as a defense against the devastating threat of an absolute significant void.

The ironical relationship between these pages on Balbec-en-terre and the article "Journées de pèlerinage" becomes most obvious in the final paragraph of the passage. Here, the Vierge du Porche of Balbec can be read as the negative, inverted image of the Vierge Dorée at Amiens. Unlike its Ruskinian model, which possessed the resilient charm of a defined personality, the Vierge du Porche, as it stands in a cruelly dissonant city environment, "[est] . . . réduite maintenant à sa propre apparence de pierre, occupant par rapport à la portée de mon bras une place où elle avait pour rivales une affiche électorale et la pointe de ma canne, enchaînée à la Place, inséparable du débouché de la grand'rue, . . . soumise à la tyrannie du Particulier." Later in the same context, Proust contrasts the poetically imagined "oeuvre d'art immortelle et si longtemps désirée" to its real manifestation as "une petite vieille de pierre dont je pouvais mesurer la hauteur et compter les rides."

The degradation of universality to the tyranny of the Particular, the use of the travel experience as a vehicle for subjective demystification, the evident allusions to *The Bible of Amiens* in the inverted form of parody—all point to a conception of artistic creation radically opposed to Ruskinian *possession-taking* and imply, as well, that the transition from criticism to creation, from the contemplation of artistic forms to the self-composed energy of authorial force may be more difficult than the lyricism of "Journées de pèlerinage" seems to indicate. In the latter work, it was assumed that the "female" critical role of openness to the strength of the master would change to a "masculine" power once the act of mediation had been accomplished; then, the disciple turned new master could open his own doors with the magical commands of his will. But this smooth procedure can occur only if the mediator can be trusted, only if he incorporates the Truth. Significantly, in the ironical Proustian development of this Ruskinian scheme of transitions, the mediator, Swann, who had told the young Marcel that Balbec was "délicieux . . . aussi *beau* que Sienne" (my emphasis), cannot lay claim to any form of trust, since the episode as a whole renders problematic the very idea of beauty. It is logical, then, that the image of *opening* that structured Ruskin's ideas should now be reversed and complicated in the concluding sentence of Proust's description, where the play between *contenant* and *contenu* is evoked in a physically precise and witty manner:

> Pour Balbec, dès que j'y étais entré, ç'avait été comme si j'avais entr'ouvert un nom qu'il eût fallu tenir hermétiquement clos et où, profitant de l'issue que je leur avais imprudemment offerte, en chassant toutes les images qui y vivaient jusque-là, un tramway, un café, les gens qui passaient sur la place, la succursale du Comptoir d'Escompte, irrésistiblement poussés par une pression externe et une force pneumatique, s'étaient engouffrés à l'intérieur des syllabes qui, refermées sur eux, les laissaient maintenant encadrer le porche de l'église persane et ne cesseraient plus de les contenir.

Like Pandora's box, the name "Balbec" is the receptacle of illusory virtues and beliefs which, when released, can never be reappropriated; and yet the hope of a return to original harmony remains. The protagonist of the *Recherche* will continue to think that there are "d'autres villes encore intactes pour moi, que je pourrais prochainement peut-être pénétrer, comme au milieu d'une pluie de perles, dans le frais gazouillis des égouttements de Quimperlé"; but the inexorable negativity of the novel will continue to demonstrate the arbitrariness of the relationship between sign and referent, between the poetically evocative "perle" of Quim*perlé* and the actual appearance of the city in the particularity of its geographic prison. According to the semiology of Marcel Proust, there is no such thing as an "empty" sign that could exist in and for itself, detached from impure commerce with associated, interested desires. As soon as the name "Balbec" is emptied of its oceanic mythology, the referential pressure of metonymic relations (the cathedral in its immediate surroundings, suffused with the all-enveloping light of the sun) exerts itself upon the available nothingness of the sign and fills it with new meanings: *signum abhorret vacuum*. If, on an allegorical level, the protagonist of the *Recherche* is emblematic of the interpreter in general, then we see now that the process whereby he "reads" the world is not to be confused with an act of understanding and certainly not to be confused with the idea of authorial *possession*. Reading is based upon a potentially infinite series of erroneous, subjectively motivated transfers and substitutions. We can open the sign, but we will be condemned to do so with "imprudence," and we can only stand by as it closes itself immediately upon new illusions, which are our own creations.

The results of the Balbec-en-terre episode are paradoxical. If we understand that the text tells the story of the sign's arbitrariness and embeddedness in associative rhetoric, we can then conclude that the text is "about" the sign, that it manages to be the positive vehicle which assumes the responsibility of narrating a negative message. But if we respect the integrity of microtextual detail, we are compelled to see that this understanding of ours is the consequence of a delusion that the deconstruction of "naming" has forced into the open. One can say that the *Recherche* is "about" the inner structure of the linguistic sign, but in so doing we need to question the spatial metaphor of *aboutness* and its claims of comprehensiveness, control, mastery, and so forth. Such a questioning is precisely what the *entr'ouverture* of "Balbec" performs, its allegorical significance being that although the envelopment and imprisonment of reality in the sign is aberrant and illusory, it is also necessary and productive of the misreading without which what we call literature could not exist. The juxtaposition of microtext to macrotext, of episodic detail to thematic systematics, places the drama of Proustian textuality within the split of the sign, in the ambivalent, immediately closed opening of a promised meaning that our desire seeks to grasp.

"JOHN RUSKIN"

The second of Proust's critical articles based upon *The Bible of Amiens* is included in *Pastiches et mélanges* under the general title "John Ruskin." It consists of parts III and IV of the translator's preface to *La Bible d'Amiens*, the latter section being a "postscript" whose separateness from the main body of Proust's analyses is no longer visible in the version of *Pastiches et mélanges*. We must keep this in mind, because part IV is in many respects a refutation of part III: it shows with a high degree of explicitness specific areas of disagreement between Proust and Ruskin and serves as an interesting self-criticism of the French disciple, who accuses himself of an excessive "respect" for the ideas of his master. The final pages of "John Ruskin" can be read as a Proustian declaration of artistic independence, while the essay as a whole emphasizes the same close relationship of criticism to creativity that we observed in the intertextual links of "Journées de pèlerinage" to the Balbec-en-terre episode of the *Recherche*. But "John Ruskin" cannot be reduced to a series of themes or ideas: although the essay appears straightforward and logical (analytically rational), it has a rhetorical mechanism worth examining and an undercurrent of unresolved psychological tensions that combine to make of it a complex meditation on the nature and limits of literary influence. In the following analysis, I will be less concerned with restating or reformulating Proust's opinions of Ruskin's esthetics (these opinions are, in fact, well-argued and constitute a real contribution to Ruskin studies) than with an illumination of the more secret obsessive thoughts that cause the essay to repeat itself and hover around a central knot of preoccupations.

Proust begins "John Ruskin" with a long catalogue of those contradictions in Ruskin's thought which had caused readers of the nineteenth century to object that the theorist of Beauty and prophet of industrial times was in truth disorganized and incoherent. The first part of Proust's article is, in general terms, a refutation of this view. Following the lead of Robert de la Sizeranne, France's most intelligent disciple and critic of Ruskin, Proust demonstrates that all of Ruskin's writings were the manifestation of his "religion of beauty," but he immediately refines upon La Sizeranne's terminology, in an effort to eliminate from it all connotations of *dilettantisme* or *esthétisme*. Indeed, in a period of artistic hypersensitivity and excessive devotion to the self, it might appear that "un adorateur de la Beauté, c'est un homme qui, ne pratiquant d'autre culte que le sien et ne reconnaissant pas d'autre dieu qu'elle, passerait sa vie dans la jouissance que donne la contemplation voluptueuse des oeuvres d'art" ("John Ruskin"). Proust contends that "la principale religion de Ruskin fut la religion tout court" and that if Ruskin searched for truth in the varied guises of Beauty, one needs to understand that "cette Beauté à laquelle il se trouva ainsi consacrer sa vie ne fut pas conçue par lui comme un objet de jouissance fait pour la charmer, mais comme une réalité infiniment plus importante, pour laquelle il aurait donné la sienne."

The first few pages of Proust's *défense et illustration* of Ruskinian esthetic theory have a familiar ring to the reader of the *Recherche*. In demonstrating the superiority of his master's ideas over those professed by the adherents of *l'art pour l'art*, Proust is already suggesting certain key notions of his own theory as later expressed in *Le Temps retrouvé*: the importance of instinct and inspiration in art; the emphasis on reading as deciphering of signs; and the central focus on involuntary memory in the process of literary creation. But the undeniable parallels that exist between the two authors on the level of explicit statement should not cause us to see in "John Ruskin" a mere rewriting of "Journées de pèlerinage" on a more sophisticated analytical plane, where once again the disciple is willing to pay tribute without question or critical confrontation. Throughout the initial laudatory section of his essay, Proust continually returns to the problematic coexistence with

Proust postulates that religious thoughts *determined* esthetic sentiments for Ruskin ("C'est ainsi que son sentiment religieux a dirigé son sentiment esthétique"), but in stating this so dogmatically, he must defend against the possibility that Ruskin's religion may have interfered with and falsified his esthetics. Rhetorically, this defense is accomplished by a subtle twist of reasoning whereby Proust equates religious beliefs with the "force" of genius. Since we are students of Ruskin's genius, since we as readers stand beneath the shadow of its energy, it matters little whether any given belief is true or demonstrably false, as long as the Ruskinian process of interpretation is productive of new meanings:

> Tous ceux qui ont quelque notion des lois de développement du génie savent que sa force se mesure plus à la force de ses croyances qu'à ce que l'objet de ces croyances peut avoir de satisfaisant pour le sens commun. Mais, puisque le christianisme de Ruskin tenait à l'essence même de sa nature intellectuelle, ses préférences artistiques, aussi profondes, devaient avoir avec lui quelque parenté.

In expressing his unqualified admiration for the properly creative power of Ruskin, Proust makes it possible to "excuse" his predecessor for whatever interpretive errors he may have perpetrated, thus *de facto* liberating Ruskin's work from the purview of critical scrutiny. Indeed, if we find in Ruskin's argumentation traces of logical fallacies or in the detail of his highly imagistic prose a tendency to enchant the reader and influence him to adopt given opinions, Proust is saying that we should not therefore find fault with the writer, but rather, consider these factors as a part of the force of genius, which is beyond analysis or dissection.

According to the first section of "John Ruskin," the analytical act, which consists of uncovering and exploiting contradictions in an author's work, is condemned as a sign of unproductive disrespect, while the process of reading is equated with original creativity. Whether Ruskin was correct in stating that Le Beau Dieu, Amiens's Christ-figure, "dépassait en tendresse sculptée ce qui avait été atteint jusqu'alors" or whether Huysmans was right in mocking it as a "bellâtre à figure ovine," the important fact is that the same statue fascinated two minds and engendered two interpretations. Proust's conclusion is, therefore, that reading is a cycle of errors, but that these errors are the unessential by-product of a higher power called *enthusiasm*:

> Les grandes beautés littéraires correspondent à quelque chose, et c'est peut-être l'enthousiasme en art qui est le critérium de la vérité. A supposer que Ruskin se soit quelquefois trompé, comme critique, dans l'exacte appréciation de la valeur d'une oeuvre, la beauté de son jugement erroné est souvent plus intéressante que celle de l'oeuvre jugée et correspond à quelque chose qui, pour être autre qu'elle, n'est pas moins précieux.

The question that inevitably arises is whether Proust's critical practice truly corresponds with this theory, whether his reservations concerning Ruskinian style and esthetics are easily subsumed within the transcendence of an "enthusiastic" discipleship. Does Proust seem willing to become an initiator of "beautiful" erroneous judgments like his precursors, thus integrating himself into the cycle of creative reading as the equal of Ruskin and Huysmans? Or is there a level of his critical discourse which resists assimilation to the creative impulse, which remains independent, analytical, detached, disapproving, which, embedded in the complexity of forms, remains separated from the primacy of force and genius? To answer these questions, we will examine those elements of "John Ruskin" that might have gone undeveloped if Proust had not reread himself in an admirably lucid "postscript."

From a psychological point of view, the last twelve pages of "John Ruskin" represent a successful overcoming of the repression that had caused Proust to adopt an attitude of pure admiration toward the author of *The Bible of Amiens*. The major reservation that had been cautiously expressed in the earlier development becomes the center of Proust's reflections: namely, Ruskin's tendency to "adore" the surface of signs, to worship the external trappings of stylistic effect at the expense of logical coherence and intellectual sincerity. In the first stages of his article, Proust had qualified his criticism with the kind of elegant politeness characteristic of his social self. Describing the intellectual affinities between Gustave Moreau and Ruskin, Proust had observed that both men condemned the depiction of violence in art, especially insofar as this violence could arise from a superficial formal virtuosity appealing excessively to the senses. But this having been observed, Ruskin and Moreau are said to be immune from such "fetishism" themselves ("fétichisme peu dangereux d'ailleurs pour des esprits si attachés au fond au sentiment symbolique qu'ils pouvaient passer d'un symbole à l'autre, sans être arrêtés par les diversités de pure surface"). When we arrive at the second part of the essay, we discover what Proust had wished to elaborate all along: that Ruskin was constantly guilty of this sin of idolatry, that his prose is an impure mixture of rhetorically devious statements and counterstatements, that he often forced his thoughts to fit the mold of his ornamental style. Here, Proust sheds the mantle of respect and assumes the more difficult, for him more painful, function of demystifying critic.

Since all of Proust's argument derives from the central accusation of *idolatry*, we need to define the term, or, more modestly, reconstruct its semantic field. The denotative meaning of the word is, of course, religious. In Pascalian terms, idolatry is a *divertissement* of the mind from the true object of worship (in the Christian context, the risen Christ) to a false substitute, whereby the energies of our spiritual nature are misdirected and misapplied. It is in this religious sense that Proust introduces "idolatry" into his analysis. He quotes from Ruskin's *Lectures on Art:*

Ç'a été, je crois, non sans mélange de bien, sans doute, car les plus grands maux apportent quelques biens dans leur reflux, ç'a été, je crois, le rôle vraiment néfaste de l'art, d'aider à ce qui, chez les païens comme chez les chrétiens—qu'il s'agisse du mirage des mots, des couleurs ou des belles formes,—doit vraiment, dans le sens profond du mot, s'appeler idolâtrie, c'est-à-dire le fait de servir avec le meilleur de nos coeurs et de nos esprits quelque chère ou triste image que nous nous sommes créée, pendant que nous désobéissons à l'appel présent du Maître, qui n'est pas mort, qui ne défaille pas en ce moment sous sa croix, mais nous ordonne de porter la nôtre.

As Proust indicates in a footnote to his translation, this passage is the conclusion of a development on "realistic" religious art in Europe, where Ruskin takes exception to the "morbid" representations of the suffering and death of Jesus that are so prevalent in the cathedrals of the Southern countries. To worship the dying Christ is to misunderstand the very reason for his death, which is not death for the believer, but eternal life. The artists who concentrate their creative powers on the symbolization of such violence themselves commit idolatry and are to be held responsible for the fallaciously constituted faith of the semiologically unsophisticated multitudes.

When Proust applies the word "idolatry" to Ruskin's writing, he does not adhere to the strict denotational sense of the definition, but refers to a stylistic manipulation in which unconsciously chosen esthetic preferences undermine the integrity of consciously stated moral ideas. In a nutshell: "Les doctrines qu'il [Ruskin] professait étaient des doctrines morales et non des doctrines esthétiques, et pourtant il les choisissait pour leur beauté. Et comme il ne voulait pas les présenter pour belles, mais comme vraies, il était obligé de se mentir à lui-même sur la nature des raisons qui les lui faisaient adopter." To illustrate his criticism, Proust quotes from a passage of *The Stones of Venice* that describes the reasons for the great city's fall. Ruskin's logic of condemnation can be resumed as follows: Venice was privileged over other places because it had, in the cathedral of St. Mark, an illuminated Bible of stone; its decadence is the less excusable since it took place within proximity of God's concretely depicted message:

Pour les nations du Nord, une rude et sombre sculpture remplissait leurs temples d'images confuses, à peine lisibles; mais pour elle [Venise], l'art et les trésors de l'Orient avaient doré chaque lettre, illuminé chaque page, jusqu'à ce que le Temple-Livre brillât au loin comme l'étoile des Mages. Dans d'autres villes, souvent les assemblées du peuple se tenaient dans des lieux éloignés de toute association religieuse, théâtre de la violence et des bouleversements; sur l'herbe du dangereux rempart, dans la poussière de la rue troublée, il y eut des actes accomplis, des conseils tenus à qui nous ne pouvons pas trouver de justification, mais à qui nous pouvons quelquefois donner notre pardon. Mais les péchés de Venise, commis dans son palais ou sur sa piazza, furent accomplis en présence de la Bible qui était à sa droite.

Here, Proust protests that the Ruskinian confusion of *forme* and *fond*, of attention to artistic detail and elaboration of prophetic discourse, causes the reader to be falsely persuaded that the Venetians were *more* guilty of their faithlessness than other corrupted Christians. In other words, the difference between a multicolored marble cathedral inlaid with golden mosaics and a more soberly decorated Northern church should have nothing to do with our judgment of the worshippers themselves. In rhetorical terms, Ruskin has manipulated what is in fact a strict metonymical relationship (spatial copresence of people and a cathedral) into the fluid appearance of a metaphorical synecdoche (the people are part of a whole represented by, incarnated in, the cathedral). Seventy years before "Métonymie chez Proust," the author of the *Recherche*, in laying bare the mechanism of Ruskin's rhetoric, has anticipated the deconstructive rigor of modern textual analyses.

But Proust is not content to separate himself from Ruskin in the Olympian detachment of the lucid interpreter: he is just as interested in the complex reasons for the charm and persuasion of this passage as he is in the demonstrable deviousness of its tropological play. In a description reminiscent of Ruskin's evocative prose, Proust relates the "mixed joy" (*joie mêlée*) he felt while reading the paragraph about Venice's decline and fall and emphasizes the contagious magic of the text and the cathedral, the strange power of mutual attraction that made of his idolatrous pilgrimage a moment of unexplainable beauty:

A quel ordre de vérité peut correspondre le plaisir esthétique très vif que l'on prend à lire une telle page, c'est ce qu'il est assez difficile de dire. Elle est elle-même mystérieuse, pleine d'images à la fois de beauté et de religion comme cette même église de Saint-Marc où toutes les figures de l'*Ancien* et du *Nouveau Testament* apparaissent sur le fond d'une sort d'obscurité splendide et d'éclat changeant. Je me souviens de l'avoir lue pour la première fois dans Saint-Marc même, pendant une heure d'orage et d'obscurité où les mosaïques ne brillaient plus que de leur propre et matérielle lumière et d'un or interne, terrestre et ancien, auquel le soleil vénitien, qui enflamme jusqu'aux anges des campaniles, ne mêlait plus rien de lui; l'émotion que j'éprouvais à lire là cette page, parmi tous ces anges qui s'illuminaient des ténèbres environnantes, était très grande et n'était pourtant peut-être pas très pure. Comme la joie de voir les belles figures mystérieuses s'augmentait, mais s'altérait du plaisir en quelque sorte d'érudition que j'éprouvais à comprendre les textes apparus en lettres byzantines à côté de leurs fronts nimbés, de même la beauté des images de Ruskin était

avivée et corrompue par l'orgueil de se référer au texte sacré. Une
sorte de retour égoïste sur soi-même est inévitable dans ces joies
mêlées d'érudition et d'art où le plaisir esthétique peut devenir
plus aigu, mais non rester aussi pur. Et peut-être cette pages des
Stones of Venice était-elle belle surtout de me donner précisément
ces joies mêlées que j'éprouvais dans Saint-Marc, elle qui, comme
l'église byzantine, avait aussi dans la mosaïque de son style
éblouissant dans l'ombre, à côté de ses images sa citation biblique
inscrite auprès.

Underlying Proust's analysis of Ruskinian imagery is the hypothesis that
some form of truth must reside in the experience of esthetic pleasure:
otherwise we would not be motivated to read Ruskin in the first place. Yet
the farther one penetrates the mixed mode of poetic discourse, the more
difficult it becomes to distinguish what is presumed to be artistically revealed truth from the rhetorical lie in which it is enveloped. When Proust
opens *The Stones of Venice* and reads its descriptions of St. Mark's while he
stands in the darkly illuminated cathedral, the knowledge he gains from a
comparison of literary text and iconic representations is not a pure knowledge, but the "proud" understanding of an egotistical *retour sur soi–même,*
where the pleasure of an erudite mastery substitutes itself for rigorous,
unprejudiced contemplation. The depth, complexity, and originality of
Proust's paragraph derive from the fact that this substitution of narcissistic
gratification for analytic sobriety is not condemned or otherwise neutral-
ized: it is viewed as a constitutive part of the process of reading, as a logically
necessary step in the temporal deployment of the text's interpretation.
Ultimately, although his conscious purpose was not so formulated, Proust
questions the theoretical possibility of a pure or unmixed method of writing
which would, in fact, "tell the truth." If we say that we search for the
manifestation of truth in the form of an esthetic object, we tend to forget
that this search is really a desire, that this desire is the effort to possess,
incorporate, interiorize the object in an act of anxious imprisonment. This
pattern holds not only for the reader but for the writer before him, who is
principally a reader and reinterpreter of earlier texts, and for the writer
before him, *en abyme.* Hence the parallel mirror-sequence of referential
idolatry that opens the Proustian description, causing it to trail outward
from the impossible truth it seeks to unveil. In attempting to understand
the hieroglyphics of St. Mark's, Ruskin imitates the cathedral's surface and
falls prey to a formal fetishism; in attempting to probe the origins of the
esthetic pleasure he feels in reading Ruskin, Proust reproduces the impure
beauty of Ruskinian rhetoric which, in turn, charms us as readers, causing
us to remain within the infinitely repeatable cycle of desire.

    At its deepest textual level, "John Ruskin" is a reflection on the rela-
tionship of criticism to creation, reading to writing. In his conclusion, Proust
emphasizes the unbridgeable distance separating us as readers from the

originality of the text we seek to decipher by comparing the translator or critic to the restorer of a tomb: like Antigone, we cannot hope to conquer death, but we can assume the task of preserving the remnants of what once lived and breathed. In a foreshadowing of the vocabulary of *Contre Sainte-Beuve*, Proust associates creation with involuntary memory, and criticism with its purely voluntary, rational counterpart:

> Ne pouvant réveiller les flammes du passé, nous voulons du moins recueillir sa cendre. A défaut d'une résurrection dont nous n'avons plus le pouvoir, avec la mémoire glacée que nous avons gardée de ces choses,—la mémoire des faits qui nous dit: "tu étais tel" sans nous permettre de le redevenir, qui nous affirme la réalité d'un paradis perdu au lieu de nous le rendre dans le souvenir, nous voulons du moins le décrire et en constituer la science. C'est quand Ruskin est bien loin de nous que nous traduisons ses livres et tâchons de fixer dans une image ressemblante les traits de sa pensée. Aussi ne connaîtrez-vous pas les accents de notre foi ou de notre amour, et c'est notre piété seule que vous apercevrez ça et là, froide et furtive, occupée, comme la Vierge Thébaine, à restaurer un tombeau.

According to this categorical description, criticism and creation relate to each other as polar opposites. Criticism is a "cold" act of the fancy: it can only restate facts abstractly; it remains separate from its object; it adheres to the surface of things and is forever "too late" with respect to the creative source it cannot reach. Creation takes place through the "warm" imaginative process of a memory that descends into the inner essence of phenomena and reveals them in their atemporal, universal significance. By formulating this distinction, Proust announces his desire to cease working at the outside of Ruskin's domain and to begin elaborating the remembered world of Combray from the inside, from the storehouse of his guarded impressions. If we take this argument seriously, we then conclude that the novel *A la recherche du temps perdu* becomes possible once the critical act as such is negated and overcome definitively. But as was apparent in the convoluted cycle of idolatry, the Proustian praxis of reading combines the two intellectual elements that the end of "John Ruskin" separates: the moment in which we recognize the fetishistic rhetoric of the creator, thereby affirming our own critical distance, is followed by our *engagement* into this rhetoric as we also succumb to the persuasive seductiveness of forms.

Reading, then, is neither properly critical nor creative: it is that which renders the discriminatory rigor of analysis incapable of accounting for textual complexity, that which deconstructs the pretensions of a precisely limited genre, such as what we call the "novel," to develop on the far side of rhetoric, in the supposedly self-sufficient isolation of memory's re-created paradise. We need to leave open the possibility that what we call a novel is able to inaugurate itself only by forgetting its dependency on the texts it refuses to read. But this means that the *Recherche*, as texture of memory and forgetfulness, will alternately weave and unweave the reading of its writing, thus reproducing in fictional shape the alternations of lucidity and blindness that constitute literary idolatry.

When Proust tells the story of his successive reactions to Ruskin's work, the mechanism of passion and indifference sounds familiar to the reader of the *Recherche*. This is because what we have been calling "reading" is given the name of "love" in "Un Amour de Swann," where the purely rhetorical substitutions and exchanges of an argument are clothed in the color of fiction. I quote now from "John Ruskin" a passage in which Swann and Odette appear as disincarnated shadows of a plot résumé:

> Cette idolâtrie et ce qu'elle mêle parfois d'un peu factice aux plaisirs littéraires les plus vifs qu'il nous donne, il me faut descendre jusqu'au fond de moi-même pour en saisir la trace, pour en étudier le caractère, tant je suis aujourd'hui "habitué" à Ruskin. Mais elle a dû me choquer souvent quand j'ai commencé à aimer ses livres, avant de fermer peu à peu les yeux sur leurs défauts, *comme il arrive dans tout amour. Les amours pour les créatures vivantes ont quelquefois une origine vile qu'ils épurent ensuite. Un homme fait la connaissance d'une femme parce qu'elle peut l'aider à atteindre un but étranger à elle-même. Puis une fois qu'il la connaît il l'aime pour elle-même, et lui sacrifie sans hésiter ce but qu'elle devait seulement l'aider à atteindre.* A mon amour pour les livres de Ruskin se mêla ainsi à l'origine quelque chose d'intéressé, la joie du bénéfice intellectuel que j'allais en retirer. (my emphasis)

Here, a series of rhetorical transfers foreshadows the organization of a novella. The stages of Swann's love for Odette are rigorously parallel to the dialectics of "idolatrous" reading in which interest and disinterest contend for mastery in the mind of the subject. Reading is "like" love ("*comme il arrive dans tout amour*") and love is "like" reading, insofar as they both evolve in the mixed mode of fetishism and intellectual sincerity. "Un Amour de Swann" is thus a rewriting of "John Ruskin" and a repetition, in fictional terms, of a critical argument. But how is it that the *mise en scène* of an analytical act—be it called "love" or "reading"—generates a narrative structure? To develop this question, we must turn to Proust's later study of Ruskin.

SESAME AND LILIES AND "JOURNEES DE LECTURE"

In 1906, two years after the publication of *La Bible d'Amiens*, Proust's translation of *Sesame and Lilies* was completed. Soon afterward Proust was to abandon his interpretation of Ruskin and begin the project of *Contre Sainte-Beuve* that led to the first drafts of the *Recherche*. From the standpoint of intellectual biography, *Sésame et les lys* represents a transition and a change in attitude: Proust's impatience with the ideas of Ruskin is evident in the footnotes of his translation, which, unlike those of *La Bible d'Amiens*, are no longer basically informational but openly critical; these notes, in turn, reflect the preoccupations that are developed with admirable coherence in the prefatory essay "Journées de lecture."

Sesame and Lilies (1865) is composed of three essays, each of which is a transcription of an oral address. The thematic unity of the volume is questionable, especially the relationship of the final talk, "The Mystery of Life and Its Arts," to the first two, "Sesame" and "Lilies," both of which deal with the subject of reading. For understandable logical reasons, Proust did not translate the third article. This editorial decision has the interesting result of rendering Ruskin's translated work more rationally appealing than it was in 1865. Yet even the reduction of the text to a diptych does not eliminate one central problem: that Ruskin's essay merely begins to treat its theme and soon digresses to include a catalogue of concerns that have little to do with reading itself. One can restate the fundamental line of argumentation in "Sesame" as follows: unlike the laws of social life, which are based upon "advancement" and competition, the essence of reading is nobler, in that it engages the best part of a person and makes it possible for him to enjoy the higher "friendship" of books. Unlike human beings, who are fickle and often unavailable for communication, books are our constant companions, the pure colleagues of the philosophical life. But reading is not to be confused with solipsistic enjoyment: on the contrary, our duty as faithful interpreters is to adhere painstakingly to the text, thereby "annihilating our own personality."

Immediately after these remarks directly concerned with books and their human significance, Ruskin becomes involved in a somewhat tedious discussion of the vulgarity of modern English life, then passionately condemns capitalist exploitation and the violence inherent in the hierarchies of social nobility. Ruskin's conclusion: "I do not know why any of us should talk about reading when our lives need mending" (*Sesame and Lilies*). After this point, the author heeds his own advice and does very little talking about reading. During this period of his career, Ruskin's consciousness of economic inequalities and social injustice caused him to adopt the attitude of "first things first"; intellectual pursuits such as reading had to wait until the primary necessities of life were achieved for all citizens. Although he returns briefly to his theme in an association of reading with the "Open Sesame" of magical possession-taking, most of "Sesame"'s second section is about "money-making mobs" and the excesses of so-called free trade.

In "Lilies" books are discussed in their relationship to the education of women: the emphasis is not on the act of reading as psychological or intellectual process but rather on its beneficial or nefarious moral effects. The sudden diminution of translator's footnotes is an obvious indication that Proust has little interest in or sympathy for Ruskin's overly protective and delicate paternalism. "Journées de lecture" will criticize, complicate, and invert Ruskin's "Sesame" and virtually ignore "Lilies."

Proust's ambivalently admiring and critical attitude toward Ruskin's theory of reading is evident not only in his prefatory essay but also in the

running commentary furnished by his copious notes, which, when combined in sequence, form a second essay worth examining in itself. Indeed,
the printed page of *Sésame et les lys* is a double text, with Ruskin and Proust
alternately speaking and exchanging opinions: commentary and original
work merge in what might be called a "conversational" unity. The extent
of Proust's ambivalence is immediately clear from the first note, in which
he both praises Ruskin for the latter's polysemic variations on the word
"Sesame" and also warns against the tendency to fetishistic adoration that
resides in such a love of words in themselves. In literary terms, the praise
amounts to an eloquent defense of thematic structure and, by anticipation,
a justification of the thematic/symphonic harmonies of the *Recherche*.

Within the word "Sesame" Proust finds three principal meanings: the
literal sense of the sesame seed, the metaphorical sense of a magical opening
(*Arabian Nights*), and the allegorical level that derives from the metaphorical:
"La parole magique qui ouvre la porte de la caverne des voleurs . . . étant
l'allégorie de la lecture qui nous ouvre la porte de ces trésors où est enfermée
la plus précieuse sagesse des hommes: les livres" (*Sésame et les lys*; my
emphasis). Later variations split the three themes apart and add connotative
nuances, so that in the end Proust thinks he can recognize as many as
seven themes inextricably mixed, illuminating each other in a mutually
reflective radiance. Yet this apparent total identification of critic and author
in shared esthetic beliefs is accompanied by the warning against idolatry
which, throughout the notes of *Sésame et les lys*, becomes a veritable obsession for Proust. On the one hand, the author of the *Recherche* excuses
the disorderly appearance of Ruskin's argument by postulating that the
thematic richness of the word "Sesame" imposes retrospectively on the
essay a "logique supérieure"; yet at the same time the reiterated accusation
of idolatry constitutes an analytical dissection of Ruskin's logical/rhetorical
fallacies. As in "John Ruskin," the notes to *Sésame et les lys* express a
certain theoretical discomfort, because the critic finds it impossible to choose
definitively between the attitudes of polite respect and negative judgment.

On the whole, the scale is tipped toward criticism and judgment, and
the general mechanism of fetishism or idolatry allows Proust to unveil
contradictions at every step of his master's path. When Ruskin equates
reading with a higher form of friendship, he distinguishes between the
fortuitousness of human encounters and the "necessary" relationship that
links a reader to his books. Our friends in life are simply there, present,
whether we like it or not: books are the instruments of conscious choice,
they come to us only on command and leave us when we tire of their
momentary charm. According to Proust, this line of argument is based
upon a "raisonnement spécieux." The true difference between what Montaigne called two forms of *commerce* is, in Proust's words, "la manière dont
nous communiquons avec eux [les amis et les livres]." By revealing the
logical fallacy on which Ruskin's thought is constructed (i.e., it is not really
true that we cannot choose our friends; and furthermore, even if we can

choose them freely, they are really not comparable to books, being of a different "essence"), Proust then can introduce his own theory: reading is to friendship what reflective solitude is to conversation—that is, a superior form of communication in which we reach the inner heart of things:

> Notre mode de communication avec les personnes implique une déperdition des forces actives de l'âme que concentrent et exaltent au contraire ce merveilleux miracle de la lecture qui est la communication au sein de la solitude . . . on peut dire qu'en général la conversation nous met sur le chemin des expressions brillantes ou de purs raisonnements, presque jamais d'une impression profonde. Donc la gracieuse raison donnée par Ruskin (l'impossibilité de choisir ses amis, la possibilité de choisir ses livres) n'est pas la vraie . . . une conversation avec Platon serait encore une conversation, c'est-à-dire un exercice infiniment plus superficiel que la lecture, la valeur des choses écoutées ou lues étant de moindre importance que l'état spirituel qu'elles peuvent créer en nous et qui ne peut être profond que dans la solitude ou dans cette solitude peuplée qu'est la lecture.

Proust's conception of reading as an exercise of innerness can be linked to the penetrative power of the Romantic imagination, whereas Ruskin's conversational bias is a product of the fancy, a worship of formal decoration, of brilliance for the sake of brilliance, an idolatry.

In examining the deviousness of Ruskin's rhetoric, Proust isolates one constantly recurring feature: the presence, on a metaphorical level, of the themes of "advancement" and "noble superiority" that had been condemned in the literal explicitness of declarative statement. In "Sesame," books were said to be incompatible with the competitiveness of capitalism on the one hand and with the superficial concerns of aristocratic snobbery on the other. Yet when Ruskin attempts to persuade his audience that reading is inherently more worthwhile and more ethically admirable than all necessarily impure social motivations, he resorts to such comparisons as: "Will you go and gossip with your housemaid, or your stable-boy, when you may talk with queens and kings?" (here, the queens and kings stand for the "noble" company of books). And later, describing the "kingdom" of books, he comments: "By your aristocracy of companionship there, your own inherent aristocracy will be assuredly tested, and the motives with which you strive to take high place in the society of the living, measured, as to all the truth and sincerity that are in them, by the place you desire to take in this company of the Dead." Referring to the first of these passages, Proust writes: "Quelle vanité que la métaphore quand elle donne de la dignité à l'idée précisément à l'aide des fausses grandeurs dont nous nions la dignité." And in the second case, his demolition of Ruskinian logic foreshadows the social criticism of the *Recherche*. In the following paragraph we see how *snobisme* relates to *sophisme*:

En réalité la place que nous désirons occuper dans la société des morts ne nous donne nullement le droit de désirer en occuper une dans la société des vivants. La vertu de ceci devrait nous détacher de cela. Et si la lecture et l'admiration ne nous détachent pas de l'ambition . . . c'est un sophisme de dire que nous nous sommes acquis par les premières le droit de sacrifier à la seconde. Un homme n'a pas plus de titres à être "reçu dans la bonne société" ou du moins à désirer de l'être, parce qu'il est plus intelligent et plus cultivé. C'est là un de ces sophismes que la vanité des gens intelligents va chercher dans l'arsenal de leur intelligence pour justifier leurs penchants les plus vils. Cela reviendrait à dire que d'être devenu plus intelligent, crée des droits à l'être moins. Tout simplement diverses personnes se côtoient au sein de chacun de nous, et la vie de plus d'un homme supérieur n'est souvent que la coexistence d'un philosophe et d'un snob.

An examination of the notes to *Sésame et les lys* reveals the semiological coherence of Proust's theoretical reflections and tends to confirm that the *Recherche* is, at its deepest level, a fictional working-out of the deconstruction of idolatry. As we have seen in the juxtaposition of "Journées de pèlerinage" to the Balbec-en-terre episode, the central Proustian experience is the discovery of the constitutive cleavage that splits the sign into a liberated, irresponsible *signifiant* and a referentially determined meaning (the *signifié* cannot remain "pure," but is imprisoned in the referent, caught up in an incestuous metonymical bond with the constraints of reality). The error demonstrated in the passage from "Noms de pays: le nom" to "Noms de pays: le pays" is that of an excessive adherence to the surface of the *signifiant*. This is precisely the mistake of the idolater or snob, who attaches too much value to the outside of forms, at the expense of the significant core that these forms hide. The intellectual insincerity that Proust discovers in the metaphorical fabric of Ruskin's writing is the purely intellectual equivalent of the narrator's naïve admiration of the name and symbolic attributes of the Guermantes family, the only difference being that of a structural reversal: whereas Ruskin believes he speaks in the mode of truth, he in fact lies to himself and undermines his credibility; the narrator of the *Recherche*, beginning in a state of idolatrous adoration of the nobility, must learn to recognize his self-deception in order to achieve the gift of revealed truth from which his future work will emanate. This ideal pattern composes the outward narrative progression of the novel, but the extent to which a language of truth is possible is made questionable by the ironical presence of idolatry within all discourse, especially within that discourse which presumes to tell the truth. As we turn now to "Journées de lecture," we will proceed further in an analysis of the interaction between reading as semiological process (discovery and understanding of the truth embedded in signs) and reading as rhetorical articulation (exploitation of "idolatrous" poetic effects).

To read "Journées de lecture" analytically is to enter a magic world of *correspondances* and break its charm: one hesitates at the threshold, as might any perpetrator of sacrilege aware of the destruction he is about to cause. Doubtless, Proust's preface to *Sésame et les lys* is one of the most beautiful, sensually appealing, and intellectually rigorous accounts of "l'acte psychologique original appelé *Lecture*" ("Journées de lecture") in French literature. It is divided into two parts, the first being essentially an evocation of the protective atmosphere enveloping a young reader whose resemblance to the "Marcel" of Combray is obvious, the second being an elaboration of Proust's theory of reading as compared and contrasted to that of Ruskin, with special emphasis on the values of reflection, innerness, and solitude. The problem which the present interpretation addresses is that of the logical relationship between the first twelve pages and the last twenty-two. How is it that the prefigurative sketch of Combray's charms, in which the act of reading is depicted not for itself, but in a labyrinth of metaphorical associations, coexists with a far more rational discourse of theoretical distinction and discrimination? On the level of direct declaration, Proust provides an answer to this question himself at the close of the first section, when he says: "Avant d'essayer de montrer au seuil des 'Trésors des Rois' pourquoi à mon avis la lecture ne doit pas jouer dans la vie le rôle prépondérant que lui assigne Ruskin dans ce petit ouvrage, je devais mettre hors de cause les charmantes lectures de l'enfance dont le souvenir doit rester pour chacun de nous une bénédiction." Proust's initial appeal to what, in Ruskinian terms, might be called the "common treasury" of all readers—those never-to-be-forgotten days in which we entered the pages of a book and lost contact with the vicissitudes of reality—is a necessary catharsis which, once accomplished, allows us to speak seriously of reading in the purer context of theoretical discernment. Proust admits, in the succeeding sentences, that the very length and tone of the first part indicate his own vulnerability to the "sortilège" of which he must rid himself before assuming a properly critical stance; but the assumption remains that we can walk the straight path of analytical clarity and systematic theoretical exposition only when the "chemins fleuris et détournés" of childhood sensations in the re-created paradise of memory have been interiorized and subordinated to the higher purpose of rational understanding.

If, by an act of critical incursion, we penetrate the flowery and devious web of Proust's rhetoric at the beginning of "Journées de lecture," we find that the unquestionably seductive beauty of the passage derives from the "association of ideas" that Ruskin condemned in *Modern Painters II*. More precisely, we see that the reason for the passage's powerful psychological effect upon us is that it does not limit itself to a discussion of books as such, but, in developing a network of physical impressions that "surround" the process of reading in the mind of the young writer/narrator, it entices us to abandon our own posture of theoretical vigilance and allow ourselves to be bathed in the sunlight of a spring afternoon in the country. Proust begins his essay with the sentence: "Il n'y a pas de jours de notre enfance que nous ayons si pleinement vécus que ceux que nous avons cru laisser sans les vivre, ceux que nous avons passés avec un livre préféré." The remainder of the first paragraph and, in a sense, the entirety of the first twelve pages constitute a sophisticated persuasive argument which demonstrates that the time we thought to have wasted in reading is in fact recuperable on the level of deep inner experience. In other words, although the mature Marcel Proust may no longer be enchanted by the content of the books he read as a child, his remembrance of "le jeu pour lequel un ami venait nous chercher au passage le plus intéressant, l'abeille ou le rayon de soleil gênants qui nous forçaient à lever les yeux de la page ou à changer de place, les provisions de goûter qu'on nous avait fait emporter et que nous laissions à côté de nous sur le banc" is closely (metonymically) linked to the printed page. It is this remembrance—of what for the young boy was mere contingent distraction—that now becomes the necessary chain of associative phenomena granting access to the essence of past time: "S'il nous arrive encore aujourd'hui de feuilleter ces livres d'autrefois, ce n'est plus que comme les seuls calendriers que nous ayons gardés des jours enfuis, et avec l'espoir de voir reflétés sur leurs pages les demeures et les étangs qui n'existent plus." The resurrection of involuntary memory on which Proust's novel will be based has its origin here, in the reflected, recoverable beauty of youth. But we must not lose sight of the paragraph's rhetorical *glissements*, which ground the poetry of remembrance in a nonreading. We "live" and relive our former existence only because the actual act of reading as enjoyed by the child has been forgotten and is now replaced by the pleasurable fabric of a unified fictional world.

But what is the essential of reading as concrete intellectual activity? Although it is only in the second part of "Journées de lecture" that Proust attempts to answer this question explicitly and in theoretical terms, one can find in the initial pages of the essay a coherent series of remarks pointing to a psychological solution. If we accept that the term "essence" here implies an inner constitutive core without which the process of reading cannot come into being, then we can define the essence of reading as the desire of the self to possess the other while remaining protected from the other's actual embrace. The theme of protectiveness, everywhere present in "Journées de lecture," is tied closely to the idea of hiding and to the delightful posssibility of an unobservable observation point or inviolable sanctuary. Some examples:

> Qui ne se souvient comme moi de ces lectures faites au temps des vacances, qu'on allait *cacher* successivement dans toutes celles des heures du jour qui étaient assez paisibles et assez *inviolables* pour pouvoir leur *donner asile.*

> Je montais en courant *dans le labyrinthe* jusqu'à telle charmille, où je m'asseyais, *introuvable* . . . Dans cette charmille, le silence était

profond, *le risque d'être découvert presque nul*, la *sécurité* rendue plus douce par les cris éloignés qui, d'en bas, *m'appelaient en vain*.

Et quelquefois à la maison, *dans mon lit*, longtemps après le diner, les dernières heures de la soirée *abritaient* aussi ma lecture. . . . Alors, *risquant d'être puni si j'étais découvert* et l'insomnie qui, le livre fini, se prolongerait peut-être toute la nuit, dès que mes parents étaient couchés je rallumais ma bougie. (my emphasis)

The scene of reading has a constant structure which is infinitely repeatable. Whether the writer imagines his mental adventures as being hidden within the "hours of the day" or, more concretely, as taking place inside the refuge of a thicket or the dark silence of a room, in each case the experience of reading is a threat to the stable bourgeois virtues of the family context and is also itself threatened by the constraints of real life. The protective cocoon in which the young Proust is sheltered is an artistic representation of the womb. The proliferation of rooms that the narrator of the *Recherche* evokes at the beginning of the novel derives from the impossible, exasperated desire to recover the fragile isolation of the original matrix. Proust's novel is thus the progression of a regression: the changes of location and evolution of characters, the protagonist's obstinate search for artistic truth and his successful discovery of a vocation, serve to mask the fact that with each positive step "forward," there is an increasingly violent effort to return to the defensive status of a quasi-embryonic tactile consciousness. Reading is what Kierkegaard would have called an "absolute paradox," since its mode of existence is passive, hidden, enclosed, involuted, but its intent is active, oriented toward discovery, based upon the presumed capacity of the reader to "annihilate himself" and open himself to the creative power of the *other*.

Proust's response to this paradoxical situation is to simulate openness to exterior reality and receptiveness to that which menaces the integrity of his ego while he forges a logic of domination and control that allows for no real communication with the outside. Thus, in a digressive discussion of the decoration of rooms, Proust initiates his argument polemically, by taking exception to those people who surround themselves with familiar objects and works: "Je laisse les gens de goût faire de leur chambre l'image même de leur goût et la remplir seulement de choses qu'il puisse approuver. Pour moi, je ne me sens vivre et penser que dans une chambre où tout est la création et le langage de vies profondément différentes de la mienne, d'un goût opposé au mien, où je ne retrouve rien de ma pensée consciente, où mon imagination s'exalte en se sentant plongée au sein du non-moi." But this plunge into the heart of the *other*, which carries with it the force of alienation and subjective dispossession, soon gives way to its opposite: the violent appropriation of the room's identity in an act of mastery or imprisonment whose closest psychological equivalent is a phantasmic rape. I now quote the conclusion of the paragraph on room decoration, in which the original rationale of the polemical discussion is overshadowed by a coherent sexual metaphorics. Here, Proust describes a hypothetical impersonal hotel somewhere in the province—its noises, smells, and cold atmosphere. We enter the room:

> Le soir, quand on ouvre la porte de sa chambre, on a le sentiment de *violer* toute la vie qui y est restée éparse, de la prendre hardiment par la main quand, la porte refermée, on entre plus avant, jusqu'à la table ou jusqu'à la fenêtre; de s'asseoir dans une sorte de *libre promiscuité* avec elle sur le canapé exécuté par le tapissier du chef-lieu dans ce qu'il croyait le goût de Paris; de *toucher partout la nudité* de cette vie dans le dessein de *se troubler soi-même* par sa propre familiarité, en posant ici et là ses affaires, *en jouant le maître* dans cette chambre pleine jusqu'aux bords de l'âme des autres et qui garde jusque dans la forme des chenêts et le dessin des rideaux l'empreinte de leur rêve, en marchant pieds nus sur son tapis inconnu; alors, *cette vie secrète, on a le sentiment de l'enfermer avec soi* quand on va, tout tremblant, tirer le verrou; de *la pousser devant soi dans le lit et de couchewr enfin avec elle* dans les grands draps blancs qui vous montent par-dessus la figure, tandis que, tout près, l'église sonne pour toute la ville les heures d'insomnie des mourants et des amoureux. (my emphasis)

For the reader of the *Recherche* this passage has a prophetic ring: it foreshadows the nature of the relationship between Marcel and Albertine. In *La Prisonnière* and *La Fugitive* the efforts of the protagonist are directed toward the impossible possession of a creature who fictively incorporates the *non-moi* of the provincial hotel room: Albertine also contains a "soul" and "dreams" that are the target of jealous investigations. Just as the desired mastery of the room is accomplished by an act of violence, in the same way Albertine can be possessed only through force, only by the kind of domination that betrays a fundamental insecurity in the hero's psychological constitution. If we read the above paragraph allegorically, keeping in mind its prefigurative status for the novel, we find that the process of reading vacillates between the unhappy consciousness of a fall into alterity (in opening a book, we plunge into the enigmatic otherness of signs) and the rhetorically fallacious but inevitable gesture by which we deny the existence of the *other* as such. In the latter volumes of the *Recherche* this pattern emerges as the alternation between anxiety and repose within the protagonist's imagination. When Albertine is correctly deciphered as elusive figure of ambivalence, Marcel loses his sense of self and gives in to a profound depression; when he naïvely assumes that he can empty her of her meanings and render her semiologically inactive, he enjoys a short-lived, illusory triumph. Thus, that which reading seems to promise as the logical result of its unfolding—the unveiling of truth in the luminosity of a successful hermeneutics—is in fact the hopeful projection of a subjectivity that prefers not to abdicate its control over the complexity of the sign or become overwhelmed by the rhetoric of lying.

If we turn now to the second part of "Journées de lecture," in which Proust elaborates a theory of reading grounded in "ce miracle fécond d'une communication au sein de la solitude," we bring to the text an ironic awareness of the considerable price one has to pay to remain happily ensconced in the fragility of a protective solitude. On the one hand, it is impossible not to agree with Proust that the silent atmosphere of meditation is inherently and objectively more conducive to the exercise of reading than is the superficial context of conversation. We can also agree, on a pragmatic level, that it is a mistake to expect too much of reading, a mistake to confuse the book learning of the dilettante with the more profound efforts of an artist to find his own language, to make the transition from what he has learned of another author to what he now must discover within himself. On the other hand, however, we must not forget that the choice of solitude as opposed to conversation is in fact the expression of a deeper desire: that of a pure narcissism which would constitute itself in the transparency of self-contemplation. Psychologically, conversation represents a major threat to the author of "Journées de lecture," since it implies an actual encounter with opinions which the self might not master easily. Hence, the scientifically objective presentation of the final pages of the essay acts as a mask hiding the "chemins fleuris et détournés" of the self's (hidden) rhetoric. But the masking effect is only partially successful, and at every twist and turn of his discourse, Proust returns to his obsessive metaphorics of possession and penetration. Indeed, it seems impossible to describe the process of reading without resorting to the figuration of sexual desire. When we read an isolated phrase of a writer, we see a small corner of a domain whose entirety we wish to visit and appropriate: "Dans chaque tableau qu'ils [les poètes] nous montrent, ils ne semblent nous donner qu'un léger aperçu d'un site merveilleux, différent du reste du monde, *et au coeur duquel nous voudrions qu'ils nous fissent pénétrer*." Later in the same passage, Proust characterizes artistic "vision" as an essentially erotic relationship linking the reader to the beckoning surface of esthetic objects: "Cette apparence avec laquelle *ils nous charment et nous déçoivent et au-delà de laquelle nous voudrions aller*, c'est l'essence même de cette chose en quelque sorte sans épaisseur—mirage arrêté sur une toile—qu'est une vision. Et cette brume que nos yeux avides *voudraient percer*, c'est le dernier mot de l'art du peintre" (my emphasis). The basis of rhetorical discourse is its charm, which is always a charm of deception. We are made to believe the unbelievable—for example, that reading can be accounted for in theoretically neutral terms—whereas we will always "go beyond" the sense of the poetic structure itself, constructing our own subjectively rooted meanings, in an effort to impregnate the already-filled text—with ourselves.

The subversion of theoretical clarity by rhetorical association through which "Journées de lecture" deconstructs itself demonstrates that literary language cannot originate in a "pure" inwardness. The ideal of solitary communication is a desire, and the ideal of a prose free from referential imprisonment is ironized by the erotic/culpable relationship of the self to the reality from which it seeks to hide. If, in studying Proust's intellectual debt to Ruskin, we adopt the historical-psychological scheme proposed by Bloom and Terdiman for the evolution of modern literature, according to which an increased inwardness and loss of reciprocity with the world separates the unhappy son from his happier father, we must add a restriction: it is only on the conscious and declarative theoretical level that the son seems to succeed in eliminating the father's influence—in Proust's case by an intelligent equation of idolatry with the superficial outwardness of conversation. But in the act of writing, in the very movement of turning inside, Proust becomes engaged in the rhetoric of idolatry and can only repeat Ruskin's pattern of possession-taking. From the standpoint of theory, Proust creates a metaphorics of depth as the logical expression of a clear conceptual scheme; in Ricardou's terminology, "depth" is used as a mere ornament. But in fact, as was evident in the paragraph on the provincial hotel room, underlying the rational argument of Proust's discourse is a deeper depth, *la profondeur en tant que schème ordinal*. There is, first of all, at the most fundamental generative level, a desire of depth from which the coherent eroticism of the passage derives. If Proust "goes beyond" Ruskin, it is not because he has a better theory, but because he sinks into the abyss of possession/dispossession and assumes the desperate task of imprisoning a forever escaping sign. "Journées de lecture" is an especially important early text because, in describing the central scene of reading, it also demonstrates the apparently effortless transition from an isolated, self-centered privileged moment to the narration of that moment as an "allegory of reading," wherein the alternative recognition of and fall into idolatrous rhetoric takes on the temporal progression of a fiction. Within the scene of reading are the seeds from which the *Recherche* as a novelistic structure takes form.

Qual Quelle: Valéry's Sources

Jacques Derrida

I—mark(s) first of all a division in what will have been able to appear in the beginning.

"Valéry's Sources," here, do not entitle those sources on which these are written. What historians might name "influences" will not be followed upstream toward their hidden "sources," the near or distant, presumed or verified, origins of a "work," that is of a "thought" whose card in the catalogue thereby could be manipulated. Valéry himself warned of this in advance: concerning what is written here, the "discourse of history" would chatter on about heritages, readings, borrowings, biographical inner springs. The sources could multiply themselves infinitely, but as so many "sources of error and powers of falsifications" (*Discours de l'histoire*). We will not, as do positive historians, account for all that could have flowed into this text *from the outside*.

But—I mark(s) the division—by taking a different turn, by observing from an excentric place the logic of Valéry's aversions, why not ask ourselves about another outside, about the *sources set aside*, the sources that Valéry could get a glimpse of only on the bias, as in a brief, or rather foreshortened, mirroring, just the time to recognize or reflect himself and immediately to turn away—quickly, decidedly, furtively too, like an about-face to be described according to the gesture of Narcissus. We will analyze this turning away only where it has left marks *within* Valéry's textual system, as a regular crinkling of every page. Here, for example, the names would be those of Nietzsche and Freud.

Further, under this heading one might also have expected a reading

From *Margins of Philosophy*, translated by Alan Bass. © 1982 by The University of Chicago. University of Chicago Press, 1982.

of "In Praise of Water," with which Valéry, in 1935, prefaced a collection of tributes to the *Source Perrier*. (This booklet, published by the *Source Perrier* contains "The History of a Source," by P. Reboux, "The Therapeutic Benefits of the Perrier Source," by Dr. Gervais, "How, and In What Circumstances, To Serve Perrier Water," by Baron Fouquier. In 1919 Gide had written to Valéry: "I cannot for an instant believe in the exhaustion of your resources or the drying up of your source: what is difficult is to bottle it, but there is nothing surprising about the fact that you find yourself worn out after the efforts of the winter," thereby describing everything at stake in the question that concerns us here. Without taking into account that by itself the name of the source in question, in a single word, reassembles the extensible length of a sentence. [*Perrier* in French is pronounced the same way as the sentence "Père y est"—"Father is there."]) Will academic accusations be made of the resources that Valéry more than once found for his talent? No moral or political lesson could be elaborated whose premises had not already infallibly been recognized by Valéry. In Mallarmé's wake, quite early on, he had analyzed the law that administers the exchanges between the values of language, philosophy, or literature, for example, and those of political economy. The *Memoirs of the Poet* had compared the febrile agitation of Literature to that of the stock market. And the trials to which he would be subjected still would derive from those "convictions . . . (that are) naively and secretly murderous," and which he knew always explain "the deep meaning of speculative quarrels and even literary polemics" (*Discours de l'histoire*).

But—again I mark(s) and multiply (multiplies) the division—we will not forget "In Praise of Water." Rather, in pretending that we abandon its subterranean discourse, perhaps we will see it reemerge, both itself and totally other, after several meanders. This discourse already entails that the "nymph and the spring stand at that holy place where life sits down and looks around her." Further, it announces that the water of the source holds up the tree on its own course. "Consider a plant, regard a mighty tree, and you will discern that it is none other than an upright river pouring into the air of the sky. By the tree WATER climbs to meet light." The "amorous form" of the source traverses and divides the tree in its ascent. In the course of his innumerable statements on the tree, the "supreme beech" [*hêtre suprême*], Valéry will have taken into account a "blind tree," and then a tree trembling in that "there are two *trees* within it." This is a moment at which the erect, and thus divided, tree, separated from itself within itself, lets itself be cut off from the simple source. This is where we find the incision into the dream of the source. To be cut off from the source, as predicted finally by "In Praise of Water," is to let oneself be multiplied or divided by the difference of the other: to cease to be (a) self. The lure of the source ("Now comes the HOUR, the thirst, the spring [*la source*] and the siren" *Hour*): to become again present to oneself, to come back to oneself, to find again, along with the pure limpidity of water, the always efficient mirage of the point of emergence, the instant of welling up, the fountain or well surnamed Truth, which always speaks in order to say I: "Well one knows that pure thirst is quenched only in pure water. There is something exact and satisfactory in this matching of the real desire of the organism with the element of its origin. To thirst is to lack a part of oneself, and thus to dwindle into another. Then one must make good that lack, complete oneself again, by repairing to what all life demands. [*Etre altéré c'est devenir autre: se corrompre. Il faut donc se desaltérer, redevenir, avoir recours à ce qu'exige tout ce qui vit.*] The very language is filled with the praise of WATER. We say that we THIRST FOR TRUTH. We speak of a LIMPID discourse." And when Valéry ends with an "I adore WATER," which resembles, for whoever would be taken in by it, an advertiser's platitude, he is speaking only of speech, insisting on the transition which puts water into the mouth, engenders discourse, oration, incantation.

What does the course of the source become when the course is made into discourse? What, then, of this turning away?

In letting oneself be carried along by the flow, one would rush, under the rubric of sources, toward a thematics of water, a semantics in "phenomenological" style or a psychoanalysis of material imagination, both spellbound by the unity, which is precisely originary, of a meaning or a theme flowing from the source and affecting itself with forms, modulations, and variations in a discourse. There would be no lack of material for such an inventory, which would filter almost the entirety of Valéry's text, ingenuously following the trail of the "MULTIFORM WATER" which from the source goes "down unconquerably to the ocean where she most abides." At the mouth again one would come back to the source of Paul Valéry himself, who often explained himself thus: "I was born in a port."

Without pretense of going any further than this thematic or semantic reading, rather let us attempt abstractly to complicate the question of meaning or of the theme; and of what happens to a text—as text—when the source is divided within it, and altered to the point of no longer rejoining the unity of the resources (the *s* divides itself again) that moreover it never will have been. In sum, repeating the critical question, Valéry's very insistent and very necessary question about *meaning* (theme, subject, content, etc.), we will bring the question to a certain heterogeneity of the source: and first, there are sources, the source is other and plural. But by means of this repetition we may be prepared to poison the question of meaning and to calculate the price that Valéry had to pay for the discredit that, to a certain extent and in a certain way, he justifiably threw on the value and authority of meaning. A repetition of Valéry's, doubtless, but perhaps we will not close this reflection in ring form. Or at least it will not return to where it was expected, to its origin, before leaving behind, thereby affecting and infecting itself, some hardly philosophical venom: thus giving us the sketch of a snake, amongst the tree, hissing with its double-edged tongue whose venom, however vile, leaves far behind the well-tempered hemlock!

Rebound

I had not reread Valéry for a long time. And even long ago, I was far from having read all of Valéry. This is still true today. But in going back to the texts that I thought I knew, and in discovering others, especially in the *Notebooks*, naturally I asked myself in what ways a certain relationship had changed. Where had the displacement, which in a way prevented me from taking my bearings, been effected? What does this signify here, now? A banal question, a ring once more in the form of the return to the sources which always afflicts the rhetoric of the anniversaries of a birth: Valéry one hundred years later, Valéry for us, Valéry now, Valéry today, Valéry alive, Valéry dead—always the same code. What laws do these rebirths, redis-coveries, and occultations too, obey, the distancing or reevaluation of a text that one naively would like to believe, having put one's faith in a signature or an institution, always remains the same, constantly identical to itself? In sum a "corpus," and one whose self identity would be even less threat-ened than one's own body [*corps propre*]? What must a text be if it can, by itself in a way, turn itself in order to shine again, after an eclipse, with a different light, in a time that is no longer that of its productive source (and was it ever contemporaneous with it?), and then again repeat this resur-gence after several deaths, counting, among several others, those of the author, and the simulacrum of a multiple extinction? Valéry also was in-terested in this power of regeneration. He thought that it—the possibility for a text to yield (itself) several times and several lives—calculates (itself). I am saying *it calculates itself:* such a ruse cannot be machinated in the brain of an author, quite simply, except if he is situated like a spider who is somewhat lost in a corner of its web, off to the side. The web very quickly becomes indifferent to the animal-source, who might very well die without even having understood what had happened. Long afterward, other ani-mals again will come to be caught in its threads, speculating, in order to get out, on the first meaning of a weave, that is of a textual trap whose economy can always be abandoned to itself. This is called writing. It cal-culates itself, Valéry knew, and coming back to him, to the enormous cardboard web that literally bears his signature, I said to myself that it had, and not only in the form of the *Notebooks*, more than one certain return. Supposing, of course, that a return can ever be certain, which is precisely what is in question, as will be seen. In the calculation of this economy, for it to "work" (this is Valéry's expression), the price to be paid negotiates with death; with what cuts the *oeuvre* from its source ("thus there is no author"), henceforth imprinting on it a survival duration that is necessarily *discrete* and *discontinuous*. I am borrowing these qualifications from Valéry. When he analyzes what programs the duration and return of a writing, he never does so in terms of genius, meaning, or force, but in terms of "ap-plication of force."

How does the return *of* the source negotiate—and dissociate—itself?

Let us repeat the question. Was the source a theme for Valéry? A great number of poems, analyses, meditations, and notes regularly seem to come back to the source as to their object or principal subject. There is here something like an overflow. And already, this thematic overabundance, in making the demonstration all too easy, makes us suspect confusion somewhere else. Here, the recurrence announces, as perhaps it always does, that one does not touch a theme, especially a principal theme. The compulsive obstinacy that always leads back toward a place, a locus, signifies that this topos cannot become a theme or the dwelling place of a rhetoric: it rejects any presentation, any representation. It can never be there, present, *posed* before a glance, facing it; it never constitutes a present or hidden unity, an object or a subject supporting, according to the occurrence or position of the theme, a system of variations, of modulations, of transformations whose meaning or substantial content at heart would remain identical to themselves.

The source for Valéry, then, must be that which never could become a theme. If we persist in considering it in this way, then at least we must specify from some angle or fold that this was the theme of that which cannot be thematized.

It is that the source cannot be reassembled into its originary unity. Because—first of all—it has no proper, literal meaning.

And yet if there is a word with a proper, literal meaning, is it not this one?

We are indeed certain that we know what the word *source* means before the intervention of all these metaphors, whose work was always remarked by Valéry.

Is not the source the origin, the point of formation, or rather emergence, of a flowing body of water, brook, stream, river? Nothing is more familiar to us than water, and than the very familiarity of the earth with water, which is sealed here and there, and unsealed in the *point d'eau*— incalculable syntagm—that is called source: *origo fontium*. [*Point d'eau* is an incalculable—and untranslatable—syntagm because it means both a "source of water" and "no water at all." Derrida plays on this double meaning throughout this essay. Whenever he does so, *point* is left untranslated. —*Translator's Note.*]

But this meaning denominated as proper can appear for us within the element of familiarity only if we already know, or believe that we already know, what we are thinking when we say the source is the *origin* of a body of water. If there were not an immemorial complicity with the meaning of the word *origin*, with the naked meaning of the word origin in general, could we ever come close to the determined origin that is a source (*origo fontium*), the birth of a body of water, its *nature,* that is the so-called *proper* and unique meaning of the word *source*? Therefore, we *already* would have to understand the meaning of the word *origin* when it designates something totally other than the welling up of a body of water, in order to gain access to that which nevertheless was proposed as the proper meaning of the source. One first would have to fix what *origo* means, the status of the origin or of the "source" in general, of the *departure* or beginning of anything at all, that is of the departure as ab-solute, of emergence unloosed from any determination, before coming back to what nevertheless would remain the proper meaning of the word *source:* the origin of a body of water, departure and *point d'eau;* locutions which are all very near to veering off, in a way that is not fortuitous, toward the figures of drought, the negative, and separation.

Therefore, we should not be surprised if generality (the origin in general) becomes the accomplice of metaphoricity, and if we learn from the trope about the status of literal, proper meaning, the status of that which *gives itself as* proper meaning.

But what is *to give itself,* what is the *as* when the issue is one of the proper (meaning)?

Proper meaning derives from derivation. The proper meaning or the primal meaning (of the word *source,* for example) is no longer simply the source, but the deported effect of a turn of speech, a return or detour. It is secondary in relation to that to which it seems to give birth, measuring a separation and a departure from it. The source itself is the effect of that (for) whose origin it passes. One no longer has the right to assimilate, as I have just pretended to do, the proper meaning and the primal meaning. That the proper is not the primal, that it is not at the source, is what Valéry gives us to read, thereby reawakening en route the debate to which this confusion of the proper and the primal gave rise in the history of classical rhetoric.

Therefore we will not listen to the source *itself* in order to learn what it is or what it means, but rather to the turns of speech, the allegories, figures, metaphors, as you will, into which the source has deviated, in order to lose it or rediscover it—which always amounts to the same.

Often designated as *source,* for Valéry the absolute origin first has the form of the *ego,* the I, the "most naked I," of "the pure *I,* that unique and monotonous element of each being, [that] is lost and recovered by itself, but inhabits our senses eternally" as "the fundamental permanence of a consciousness that depends on nothing" (*Note and Digression*). Nothing in the world, or at least nothing that is presented within it, appears as phenomenon, theme, or object, without first being for me, for (an) ego, and without coming back to me as to the opening, the very origin of the world: not as the cause of its existence, but as the origin of its presence, the point of source on whose basis *everything* takes on meaning, appears, delineates, and measures itself. Everything, that is to say everything that is not I. The non-I is *for* the I, appears as non-I for an I and on the basis of an I. Everything: which is to say that the I, the exception to and condition for everything that appears, does not appear. Never being present to itself, the source hardly exists. It is there for no one. For what Valéry here calls the pure I, and what philosophers usually name the transcendental *ego,* is not the "person," the ego or empirical consciousness of the psychologists. An unnamable, "unqualifiable" source, in effect it has no determinable character since it is not in the world and never presents itself.

Valéry encircles, or rather tracks down, this incessant disappearance, among other places, in the *Note and Digression* to the *Leonardo:* "But what he raises to this high degree is not his precious personal *self,* since he has renounced his personality by making it the object of his thought, and since he has given the place of *subject* to that unqualifiable *I* which has no name or history, which is neither more tangible nor less real than the center of gravity of a ring or that of a planetary system—but which results from the whole, whatever that whole may be" (Valéry's italics).

The source results here. Valéry would probably have been *irritated* (I am borrowing this word from him for reasons to be given later) if he had been reminded that this proposition—the origin as result—is literally Hegelian, that it reassembles the essence of speculative dialectics whose proposition it properly is. Hegel does not by chance write it in Latin (*Der Anfang ist das Resultat*) at the beginning of the Greater Logic. In *Identity and Difference,* taking his departure from Hegel, Heidegger also analyzes this *ressaut* (*resultare, resilire, resalire*) of the origin in the result, of the founding proposition in the rebound or reflexive counter-motion (*Rückprall*).

The pure I, the source of all presence, thus is reduced to an abstract point, to a pure form, stripped of all thickness, of all depth, without character, without quality, without property, without an assignable duration. This source therefore has no proper meaning. Nothing of that which proceeds from it belongs to it. *Point d'eau*—that is of it. Thus it has no proper name. It is so universal and so abstract a pronoun (*me, I*) that it *replaces, stands for* no proper name of a person in particular: A universal pronoun, but of so singular a universality that it always remains, precisely, singular. The function of this source which *names itself I* is indeed, within and without language, that of a singular universal. In the same text, Valéry describes "the plurality of the singular, in the contradictory coexistence of mutually independent durations—as many of these as there are persons, *tot capita, tot tempora*—a problem comparable with that of *relativity* in physics, though incomparably more difficult." He also names, as if in resonance with the *Phenomenology of Spirit,* "the I, the universal pronoun, the appellation of which has no connection with a face."

That has no relation with a *face:* let us understand this equally as with a particular subject, empirically determined, and with the system which defines the face, to be reconsidered further on as a source which can also receive: the eyes, the mouth, the ears which yield (themselves to) sight, speech, hearing. This pure I which is the source, this singular universal above all does not amount to the individual. A pure consciousness, without the least psychic or physical determination, it "in an instant immolates its individuality." Like the transcendental consciousness described by Husserl, it is constituted, not being *in* the world, neither by a body, which goes without saying, nor even by a soul. The *psyche*, in effect, is a region of that which is in the world (the totality of that which is). But inversely, not being in the world, not belonging to the totality of the things which exist, which are maintained for and before it, this source is nothing, almost nothing. It would be experienced, if it were experienced, as the excess of everything that can be related to it. A relation of nothing to nothing, this relationship is barely a relation. Imagine the God of a negative theology attempting by himself to describe himself, to catch himself in the grid of a determining discourse: he will almost annihilate himself. "It [this consciousness] feels compelled to define itself by the sum total of things, as the *excess* over that totality of its own power of perception. In order to affirm itself, it had to begin by denying an infinite number of elements an infinite number of times, and by exhausting the objects of its power without exhausting that power—with the result that it differs from nothingness by the smallest possible margin."

Incapable of receiving the imprint of any characteristic, evading all predication, not permitting itself to be attributed any property, this source also will be able to lend itself without resistance to the most contradictory determinations. Valéry grants it, for example, a certain Being, but this is only to deny it all presence. Or almost, the *almost* imprinting with its regular cadence the play which disqualifies, and does so by arbitrating disqualification, confusing oppositions, and dissolving any ontological pertinence. In question is that which in "blending all the categories is something *that exists and does not exist*." Thus, this I is not an individual, is almost impersonal, very close to being a non-I. Of this consciousness which itself cannot posit itself, itself come before itself, become for itself a thesis or a theme, we cannot even say that it is present for-itself, become for itself a thesis or a theme, we cannot even say that it is present for-itself. This source which cannot be made a theme therefore is not a self consciousness, is hardly a consciousness. Is it not unconscious in a certain way or, barely to displace the citation, different from the unconscious by the smallest possible margin?

The analysis of consciousness, therefore, is not a sure thing. Let us not hasten to reproach Valéry for having limited himself to an analysis of consciousness. We are far from having finished with it. Freud says somewhere that what is most enigmatic, finally, is consciousness.

This I which is not an I, this unconscious consciousness, this X which properly has or is nothing, which is not what it is because it is pure, and which therefore is impure because it is pure—will it still be called a source? The source is, and it is in the world. Therefore, it is *for* the I that is called source. Therefore, it remains the deported metaphor of the I. But the I of which it would be the metaphor being intrinsically, properly, improper, that is, non-proper, impure to the extent that it is pure, it is nothing outside its metaphors, nothing except that which transports it outside itself and throws it outside itself at the instant of its birth, as the irruptive welling up, the sometimes discreet, but always violent effraction of the emerging source. As such, this source, in the purity of its waters, is always disseminated far from itself, and has no relation to itself as source. If pure consciousness and the pure I are *like* the source, it is in not being able to come back to it. In their perpetual and instantaneous loss of consciousness, they cannot become themes or give rise to proper or improper definitions, not even, if one might put it thus, to true tropes. Perhaps to the violence of catachreses, which Fontanier says are "not true figures."

And yet *there are* effects of theme, of meaning, of figure. The impossible is possible, by means of the abuse of the twisting which is not yet rhetoric in that it opens and furrows the space of rhetoric. The impossible is possible: the "source," for example, but equally everything that will place it in the position of a secondary proper meaning in order to bring back into it divisions and turns.

Der sich aufhebende Ursprung or La Coupe de Source

But how is the impossible possible? How can the source divide itself—the sources germinal from the title onward—and thus by itself separate from itself in order to be related to itself—which is, as a pure origin, the irreference to itself. And from as soon as the source begins its process, incising itself and escaping itself, is there a *first* metaphor of the origin? A properly originary metaphor? A metaphor in which the source loses itself less than in another metaphor? Or in which, losing itself *even more* it comes back to itself more certainly? In this procession—Plotinus's language imposes itself here—is there a first metaphoric emanation of the One which is the source?

The I has "no relation with a face." That which sees and is seen first of all, that which yields (itself to) seeing, the face, then, elevates the source into an initial displacement. In this figure an initial metaphoricity perhaps places on view that which has no *figure*.[*Figure* here has the double meaning of (1) figure of speech, and (2) face, visage. —*Translator's Note*.] Perhaps, but let us wait.

In the text to which I have referred, as in many others, the source (of the)—I is often described *as* a glance, as the site of the glance. The eye becomes simultaneously the division that opens and the substance of the source, the point of departure and the *point d'eau*. The allegory immediately becomes theatrical. Everything that separates itself from the source comes to be placed before it, a visible object on a stage. Facing the source in the light is everything that is presented to it which is not present to itself. Presence is objectivity. And if the source has no profile for itself, it is like an absolute glance which being always opened wide and thrown toward the visible, cannot itself perceive itself, never emerging from its night.

Incapable of putting itself onstage, pure consciousness therefore cannot give itself any image of itself; but this itself can be said only if, by means of an ancient and unperceived image, one already has made this consciousness into an eye and the source into a spectator. In order to speak of the source, which remains interdicted, first it has had to be *turned:* by means of a trope, it must yield to being seen and yield to seeing. The trope does not first consist of speaking, but of seeing. And more precisely, of seeing the invisible, that which only is said, in order blindly to say the interdicted.

Such is the reverie: "The image it brings to mind spontaneously is that of an invisible audience seated in a darkened theater—a presence that cannot observe itself and is condemned to watch the scene confronting it, yet can feel nevertheless how it creates all that breathless and invincibly oriented darkness."

The invincible orient, always apprehended as such from its occidental other (*Orientem Versus*), is the source in that it can have but a single meaning. The eye is always turned in the same direction, toward the outside, and everything is related to this orient. Therefore, the misfortune is to have a meaning, a single invincible meaning. It is because it has a meaning that the source has nothing proper to it, a proper meaning permitting it to come back to and be equal to itself, to belong to itself. It is a kind of nature, or rather a threatened God, impoverished and impotent by virtue of its very originality and its independence from the source. As for this negativity which works upon and anguishes the generative god from within, a certain president, whom we are still leaving in the margin, may have shared knowledge of it with an entire mysticism, a theology, and a certain Hegelianism. ([The "certain president" referred to is Schreber, whose memoirs of his mental illness were analyzed by Freud.] Hegel: "And this negativity, subjectivity, ego, freedom are the principles of evil and pain. Jacob Boehme viewed egoity (selfhood) as pain and torment (*Qual*), and as the fountain (*Quelle*, source) of nature and of spirit." *Hegel's Philosophy of Mind* (part 3 of the *Encyclopedia*). In the *Lectures on the History of Philosophy*, after recalling that, for Boehme, negativity works upon and constitutes the source, and that in principle "God *is also* the Devil, each for itself," etc., Hegel writes this, which I don't attempt to translate: "*Ein Hauptbegriff ist die* Qualität. *Böhme fängt in der* Aurora (Morgenröte im Aufgang) *von den Qualitäten an. Die erste Bestimmung Böhmes, die der Qualität, ist Inqualieren, Qual, Quelle. In der* Aurora *sagt er: 'Qualität ist die Beweglichkeit, Quallen (Quellen) oder Treiben eines Dinges'* " (part 3, sec. 1, B. Jakob Böhme). It is within this context (negativity and division in the principle of things, in the mind or in God) that Hegel's well-known *ein sich Entzweiendes* (one dividing itself in two) also must be read. (See, for example, *Die Philosophie der Weltgeschichte, Allgemeine Einleitung*, II, 1 b.) The law-of-the-proper, the *economy* of the source: the source is produced only in being cut off (*à se couper*) from itself, only in taking off in its *own* negativity, but equally, *and by the same token*, in reappropriating itself, in order to amortize its own, proper death, to rebound, *se relever*. Reckoning with absolute loss, that is, no longer reckoning, general economy does not cease to pass into the restricted economy of the source in order to permit itself to be encircled. Once more, here, we are reduced to the inexhaustible ruse of the *Aufhebung*, which is unceasingly examined, in these margins, along with Hegel, according to his text, against his text, within his boundary or interior limit: the absolute exterior which no longer permits itself to be internalized. We are led back to the question of dissemination: does semen permit itself to be *relevé*? Does the separation which cuts off the source permit itself to be thought as the *relève* of oneself? And how is what Hegel says of the child to be read in general: "Der sich aufhebende Ursprung" (*Realphilosophie d'Iena*) or "Trennung von dem Ursprung" (*Phenomenology of Spirit*)? [For our system of notes on *relève*, see "La différance."]) The text on the originary scene continues: "Nothing can be born or perish, exist in some degree, possess a time, a place, a meaning, a figure—except on this definite *stage*, which the fates have circumscribed, and which, having separated it from who knows what primordial chaos, as light was separated from darkness on the first day, they have opposed and subordinated to the condition of *being seen*" (Valéry's italics).

For the source to become in turn an image, for it to become engaged in a tropic or fantastic system as well as to appear and to receive, for it to see itself as the glance of the origin, it must divide itself. Wherever the mirror intervenes, each time that Narcissus comes on stage in Valéry's text, the source can be found again as an effect of the mirror only by losing itself twice. The mirror, another unfindable theme (but it propagates itself like a theme that does not exist), manifests in this double loss the singular operation of a multiplying division which transforms the origin into effect, and the whole into a part. Valéry has recognized that the specular agency, far from constituting the I in its properness, immediately expropriates it in order not to halt its march. The imaginary is broken up rather than formed here. [The reference is to Lacan's theory linking the agency he calls the imaginary to the formation of the ego in the mirror stage. —*Translator's Note*.]

Glance of the figure, figure of the glance, the source is always divided, carried away outside itself: before the mirror it does not come back to itself, its consciousness is still a kind of unconscious. As soon as it performs Narcissus' turn, it no longer knows itself. It no longer belongs to itself. Narcissus defends himself from death only by living it, whether he distances himself from the "venerable fountain" ("Fountain, my fountain, water coldly present"), or whether within it he unites himself to his own body in the moment of "extreme existence" in which the I loves itself to death:

> *I love, I love.* And who can love any other
> Than himself? . . .
> > You only, body mine, my dear body
> I love, the one alone who shields me from the dead!
> . . . .
> > And soon let me break, kiss
> This frail defense against extreme existence
> This quivering, fragile and holy distance
> Between me and the surface . . .
> > *(Fragments of the Narcissus)*

Confronted with this menacing turn of the source, subjected to the contradiction of the apotropaic, desire cannot be simple. Implacable when he analyzes mortal division, Valéry is equally unalterable in his thirst for the origin: into which the analysis itself empties, if it decomposes only in going back toward the principle.

If the source cannot maintain itself, look at itself, present itself to itself in daylight, perhaps it lends itself to being heard. If one displaces the metaphor in order to write it according to other characteristics of the face, shutting the eye and the stage, perhaps the source will be permitted to return to itself: following another turn, another allegory of the origin, another *mythical* circuit from self to self. "In the Beginning Was the Fable."

Narcissus speaks. The poem that bears this title also says "the voice of the springs (*sources*)" and the shout "to the echoes." I do not see myself, said the source. But it says so at least, and thus hears itself. I say to myself that I do not see myself. I say to myself . . . perhaps again becoming myself between my direct and my indirect object, reassembling in this operation, virtually perfected, the subject, the object, the interlocutor—I, him, you. I—mark(s) the division.

Less well known, because Valéry devoted himself to them above all in the *Notebooks*, are the analyses reserved for the voice, the voice of the origin, the origin of the voice. The latter is heard as close as possible to the place where it sounds; it seems to do without the detour through the exteriority of the mirror or the water, the world, in order immediately to reflect itself in the intimate instantaneousness of resonance. Does not this echo without delay lift Narcissus from the death to which he was exposing himself? If the eye fails to institute itself as origin, perhaps the voice can produce itself, emerge from itself, all the while remaining or coming back to itself, without detour or organ, in the inner instance of what I propose to call "hearing oneself speak." Speech, then, would be the authentic exchange of the source with itself. Will it be said that the voice is finally the source? That it says the source? That it lets the source say itself? Or inversely that it produces only an effect of the source? And what does such an *effect* mean? We still must wait.

It belongs to the very structure of speech that it may be, or seem to be, immediately sensible from the source. What appears to be is not an accident here. It belongs to the very production of speech. Between what I say and what I hear myself say, no exteriority, no alterity, not even that of a mirror, seems to interpose itself. Mutism and deafness go hand in hand, and there is nothing less fortuitous. Hence, the interior speech that is not proffered, no longer would be a contingent event, occasionally occurring here or there: it is the condition for speech itself. The voice, it appears, therefore can accomplish the circular return of the origin to itself. In the circle the voice steps beyond the interdiction which made the eye blind to the eye. The true circle, the circle of the truth is therefore always an effect of speech. And Valéry recognized the immense bearing of this

autonomous circuit of "hearing-oneself-speak," an apparently highly factual phenomenon, which always might be explained by the anatomical
configuration of an animal in the world (but which produces, if one wishes
to pursue its consequences, even the concept of an origin of the world,
thereby disqualifying the alleged regional empiricity of the "physiological"
explanation), and he did so better, without a doubt, than any traditional
philosopher, better than Husserl, and better than Hegel, who nevertheless
had described phonic vibration as the element of temporality, of subjectivity, of interiorization, and of idealization in general, along with everything
which thereby systemically lets itself be carried along in the circle of speculative dialectics.

But, like the lucid source, the sonorous source attempts to rejoin itself
only by differentiating itself, dividing, differing, deferring without end.
Quite simply, the lure of reappropriation this time becomes more interior,
more twisted, more fatal. Valéry, as we will verify in an instant, did describe
this movement which goes back to the source and which separates from
the source or simultaneously interdicts the source. Which then occupies
another position; it is no longer only that approaching which movement
exhausts itself, but also that which somewhere eludes, always a bit further
on, our grasp. It is born of this very eluding, like a situated mirage, a site
inscribed in a directionless field. It is nothing before being sought, only an
effect produced by the structure of movement. The source therefore is not
the origin, it is neither at the departure or the arrival. Valéry marks in
speech both the circle of hearing-oneself-speak, the lure of the source re-
joined, and the law which makes such a return to itself an effect. An effect:
simultaneously the derivation of that which is not *causa sui*, and the illusion,
the trap, or the play of appearance.

Among many others, here are three fragments from the *Notebooks*:

"Linguistics
I is an element of language linked to speech itself. All speech has its source
which is an I. This *I* is mine if that of *X* if *X* hears it gives and receives this
speech, and in receiving it recognizes himself as source, i.e. simultaneously
an object among objects and a non-object, a space or world of objects.

"I, You, Him, this triangle—Trinity! The three roles of the same in
relation to the verb, Mouth, ear, thing" (1926). A very enigmatic sequence
from 1910, in examining the "believer" who "believes he believes," proposed what is doubtless the most efficacious formula for every deviation
of the source: "Thereby, change 3 to 4 in the Trinity."

In the return of the phonic circle, the source appears as such only at
the moment, which is no longer a moment, the barely second second, of
the instant emission in which the origin yields itself to receive what it
produces. The source receives, receives itself, interrupts circulation only in
order to saturate it. Would the circle disjoin itself only in the separation
which is in sum undefinable, and hardly probable, between a voice of the

interior and an effectively proffered voice? Such a separation in effect remains ungraspable in linguistic, poetic, or phenomenological terms. Neither in the form nor the content of a statement could we assign an intrinsic difference between the sentence I am pronouncing here, now, in my so-called speaking voice, which soon will return to the silence from which it proceeds, very low in my voice or on my page, and the *same* sentence retained in an inner instance, mine or yours. The two events are as different as possible as events, but in the qualitative description of events, in the determination of predicative traits, form or content, the principle of discernibility, the concept of difference evades us. Like the separation that disjoints the circle, a certain tangency here appears to be both nul and infinite. Another note from the *Notebooks*, concerning the *point de source:* "no (*point de*) 'me' without 'you.' To each his Other, which is his Same. Or the *I is two*—by definition. If there is *voice*, there is ear. Internally there is voice, there is no sight of who is speaking, And who will describe, will define the *difference between the same sentence which is said* and *not pronounced*, and the *same sentence sounding in the air*. This identity and this difference are one of the essential secrets of the nature of the mind—and who has pointed it out? Who has 'exhibited' it? The same for sight. I believe that the relationship of these possibilities of double effect is in the power of motility, which will never sufficiently be thought about. Within it lies the mystery of time, i.e. the existence of that which is not. Potential and unactual" (1939; Valéry's italics).

Not long after, still as a displacement but from whence the snake again is sketched in the form of circles drawn in the margin, we have from Valéry's hand: "There is nothing more astonishing than this 'interior' speech, which is heard without any noise and is articulated without movement. Like a closed circuit. Everything comes to be explained and thrashed out in this circle similar to the snake biting its tail. Sometimes the ring is broken and emits the internal speech. Sometimes the communication between what is being born and the born is regular, regimented, and the distinction can no longer be felt. Sometimes the communication is only delayed, and the internal circuit serves as a preparation for a circuit of *external intention:* then there is emission to choice" (1940).

The difference between internal speech and external speech therefore passes understanding. No concept can make it its own. Its reserve is almost unheard—with what ear could it be heard?—or in any event undescribable. Thirty years earlier: "How to *write* this singular difference rationally?" (1905). How to write it, in effect, if writing, phonetic writing above all, precisely has as its function the restitution of speech to the internal regime, and to act such that in its event effectively proffered speech is but an accident lost for reading? The regime, being regimented, in effect seems to insure the "normal" communication of the source with itself, thereby regularly circulating between the external event and the internal event, conferring upon the origin the invisible appearing, the calm being near to itself that the glance saw itself refused.

Now here, again, Valéry remarks a cutting difference: not the external prolation which accidentally would come to interrupt the circle, but already the circuit's return to itself: "Who speaks, who listens [in the interior speech]? It is not exactly the same. . . . The existence of the speech from self to self is the sign of a *cut*" (1920). The circle turns in order to annul the cut, and therefore, by the same token, unwittingly signifies it. The snake bites its tail, from which above all it does not follow that it finally rejoins itself without harm in this successful auto-fellatio of which we have been speaking all along, in truth.

Cut off from the end as from the origin, the source is no longer anything but an effect of "reaction" or, if you will, of revolution, in a system that never will have obeyed it. "I speak *to myself*. The action formulated this way suggests a distinction. And in effect what one says (or shows) to the other *I* teaches the latter something—or rather excites a reaction—, which becomes an origin" (1931). Earlier: "On the relations of the I and the me. If I *say* something *to myself*, what I say acts on what follows and modifies what I will say to myself—becomes an origin" (1928).

The source having *become*—which is the unintelligible itself—time opens itself as the delay of the origin in relation to itself. Time is nothing other. "What comes to 'mind'—to the lips—modifies you yourself in return. What you have just emitted, emits toward you, and what you have produced fecundates you. In saying something without having foreseen it, you see it like a foreign fact, an *origin*—something you had not known. Thus you were delayed in relation to yourself" (1926). And elsewhere: "We are made of two moments, and as if of the *delay* of a 'thing' for itself" (*Mauvaises Pensées et autres*; Valéry's italics).

Thus, we have at our disposition, as a paradigm, all the movements by means of which Valéry could *track down* the source. And, for the very reason we have just analyzed, we no longer have to decide if this paradigm is an origin and a model or one example among others. To track down, to set out on the path on which the living signals death, is indeed to repeat without end the indestructible desire which comes back to the source as to the complicity or implicity of life and death. In the purity of the source the living is the dead. But to track down is also to disspell the illusion, to flush out all the questions and concepts of the origin. It is to unseal at the source the separation of an altering difference.

Among others, three fragments from the *Notebooks:* "Heaven preserve you from questions of origin" (1938). "We are not origins, but the illusion of being so is with us" (1922). "Some go to the furthest reach of the *origin*— which is the coincidence of *presence* and of the initial event—and attempt to go to find in this separation *gold, diamonds*" (1931–32; Valéry's italics).

Point de philosophie—Writing

The origin—coincidence of presence and the initial event. Perhaps I will let myself be guided now by the question put this way: can one dissociate the "initial event" from presence? Can one conceive of an initial event without presence, the value of a *first time* that cannot be thought in the form or category of presence? Would this be the impossible itself? And if so, impossible for whom, for what, according to what space?

Here we come to *philosophy*.

Valéry lays out his entire reading of the history of philosophy according to this snare. The philosopher—it is he of whom Valéry speaks, and whom Valéry summons to appear, rather than philosophy itself—is the person who wears himself out over vain questions of origin: an illusion both transcendental and natural, natural since it invincibly returns to the orient, to "nature," to birth, to the source. Everywhere that "nature" intervenes in philosophical discourse, that is everywhere, Valéry pursues it with ironic apostrophes that never aim at nature alone, but also the entire cortege of distinctions and oppositions that nature activates and regulates.

Let us sketch out the scheme of this critical solicitation of philosophical discourse. It always insists upon a crisis of the origin.

Valéry reminds the philosopher that philosophy is written. And that the philosopher is a philosopher to the extent that he forgets this.

Philosophy is written—producing at least three consequences.

First of all, a break with the regime of hearing-oneself-speak, with self-presence in the meaning of a source whose truth continuously resources itself. Irreversibly, something of this presence of meaning, of this truth which nonetheless is the philosopher's great and only theme, is lost in writing. Hence the philosopher writes against writing, writes in order to make good the loss of writing, and by this very gesture forgets and denies what occurs by his hand. These two gestures must be kept together. As if unknown to each other, they cooperate as soon as one interprets writing as does Valéry in this context. The philosopher writes in order to keep himself within the logocentric circle. But also in order to reconstitute the circle, to interiorize a continuous and ideal presence which he knows, consciously or unconsciously—which does not matter since in any event he feels the effect—*already* to have been dispelled within the voice itself. Discontinuity, delay, heterogeneity, and alterity already were working upon the voice, producing it from its first breath as a system of differential traces, that is as writing before the letter. Philosophical writing, then, literally comes to bridge this gap, to close the dike, and to dream of virgin continuity.

Whence Valéry's apparently paradoxical argument, which opposes the continuousness of writing, or rather of the graphic, to the discontinuousness of speech. The philosopher intends to come back to the proximity of the speaking source, or rather to the source murmuring its interior speech, and to deny that he is writing. Terrified by the difference within hearing-oneself-speak, by the writing within speech, the philosopher writes—on the page—in order to erase and to forget that when he speaks the evil of the cipher is already there in germ. "But the nature of language is quite opposed to the happy outcome of this great endeavor to which all the philosophers have devoted themselves. The strongest of them have worn themselves out in the effort to *make their thoughts speak*. In vain have they created or transfigured certain words; they could not succeed in transmitting their inner reality. Whatever the words may be—Ideas or Dynamis or Being or Noumenon or Cogito or Ego—they are all *ciphers*, the meaning of which is determined solely by the context; and so it is finally by a sort of personal creation that their reader—as also happens with readers of poetry—gives the force of life to writings in which ordinary speech is contorted into expressing values that men cannot exchange and that do not exist in the realm of spoken words" ("Leonardo and the Philosophers," in *Leonardo, Poe, Mallarmé;* Valéry's italics).

These philosophical ciphers formalize natural language and tend to forge, by means of the contract of their conventional formality, a kind of chain of security, of quasi-continuous plenitude which occasionally makes these ciphers resemble the thing itself. They tend to erase the breaks, the tremors working within speech and writing in what is called "natural language," which is also, from the start, a diastemic organization, a system of "arbitrary" signs, or in any event of discrete and diacritical signs. Now the paradoxical law that Valéry was able to recognize is that the more the graphic is formalized the more it is naturalized. As an artist of form, which is what he is from Valéry's point of view, the philosopher is still dreaming of nature. Here we might elaborate the motif of a critique of formalist illusion which would complicate what is often considered to be Valéry's formalism somewhat. The complication is due to the fact that formality, far from simply being *opposed* to it, *simultaneously* produces and destroys the naturalist, "originarist" illusion. Always insufficiently formalized, still too embroiled in natural langauge, in natural langauge's vagueness, equivocalness, and metaphoricity, philosophical writing does not support comparison with its model: the rigor and exactitude of a purely formal language. Valéry has just recalled the effort of the philosopher wearing himself out in *making his thoughts speak:* "Today, in a number of truly remarkable cases, even the expression of things by means of discrete signs, arbitrarily chosen, has given way to lines traced by the things themselves, or to transpositions or inscriptions directly derived from them. The great invention that consists in making the laws of science visible to the eyes and, as it were, readable on sight has been incorporated into knowledge; and it has in some sort *doubled* the world of experience with a visible world of curves, surfaces, and diagrams that translate properties into forms whose inflexions we can follow with our eyes, thus by our consciousness of this movement gaining an impression of values in transition. The *graphic* has a continuity of movement that cannot be rendered in speech, and it is superior to speech in immediacy and precision. Doubtless it was speech that commanded the method to exist; doubtless it is now speech that assigns a meaning to the graphisms and interprets them; but it is no longer by speech that the act of mental possession is consummated. Something new is little by little taking shape under our eyes; a sort of ideography of plotted and dia-grammed relations between qualities and quantities, a language that has for grammar a body of preliminary conventions (scales, axes, grids, etc.).''

Philosophy is written—second consequence—so that it must reckon with a formal instance, reckon with form, is unable to get away from it: ''I said one day before philosophers: philosophy is an affair of form.''

A task is then prescribed: to study the philosophical text in its formal structure, in its rhetorical organization, in the specificity and diversity of its textual types, in its models of exposition and production—beyond what previously were called genres—and also in the space of its mises en scène, in a syntax which would be not only the articulation of its signifieds, its references to Being or to truth, but also the handling of its proceedings, and of everything invested in them. In a word, the task is to consider philosophy also as a ''particular literary genre,'' drawing upon the reserves of a language, cultivating, forcing, or making deviate a set of tropic re-sources older than philosophy itself. Here we are quite close to Nietzsche, but let us not hasten to compare: ''What becomes of it (philosophy) when—in addition to feeling beset, overrun, and dismayed at every turn by the furious activity of the physical sciences—it is also disturbed and menaced in its most ancient, most tenacious (and perhaps least regrettable) habits by the slow and meticulous work of the philologists and semanticists? What becomes of the philosopher's *I think,* and what becomes of his *I am*? What becomes, or rebecomes, of that neutral and mysterious verb TO BE, which has had such a grand career in the void? From those modest syllables, released to a peculiar fortune by the loss or attrition of their original mean-ing, artists of great subtlety have drawn an infinite number of answers.

''*If, then, we take no account of our habitual thinking* and confine ourselves to what is revealed by a glance at the present state of intellectual affairs, we can easily observe that philosophy as defined by its product, which is *in writing,* is objectively a particular branch of literature . . . we are forced to assign it a place not far from poetry. . . .

''But the artists of whom I was speaking fail to recognize themselves as artists and do not to be such. Doubtless their art, unlike that of the poets, is not the art of exploiting the sound values of words; it speculates on a certain faith in the existence of an absolute value that can be isolated from their meaning. 'What is reality?' the philosopher asks, or likewise, 'What is liberty?' Setting aside and ignoring the partly metaphorical, partly social, and partly statistical origin of these nouns, his mind, by taking advantage of their tendency to slip into indefinable meanings, will be able to produce combinations of extreme depth and delicacy.''

Perhaps I will be able to state further on how the critical necessity of this aesthetics, of this formalism or conventionalism, if adhered to other-wise than with controlled insistence and calculated stategic reaction, would risk just as surely leading us back to the places in question.

Philosophy is written—third consequence—as soon as its forms and operations are not only oriented and watched over by the law of meaning, thought, and Being, which speaks in order to say I, and does so as close as possible to the source or the well.

Of this proposition, as of its simulacrum, Descartes here is exemplary. Valéry does not cease to question him, never leaves him; and if his reading of Descartes at the very least might appear uneven to the historians of philosophy, the fact was not unforeseen by Valéry, who interpreted it in advance. We will concern ourselves with this for a while.

What is the operation of the I in the Cogito? To assure itself of the source in the certitude of an invincible self presence, even in the figure— always paternal, Freud tells us—of the devil. This time a *power* is gained in the course of a movement in grand style which takes the risk of enunciating and writing itself. Valéry very quickly suggests that truth is Descartes's last concern. The words "truth" and "reality" are once again in quotation marks, advanced as effects of language and as simple citations. But if the "I think therefore I am" "has no meaning whatever," and a fortiori no truth, it has "a very great value," and like the style is "entirely characteristic of the man himself." This value is that of a shattering blow, a quasi-arbitrary affirmation of mastery by means of the exercise of a style, the egotistic impression of a form, the strategem of a mise en scène powerful enough to do without truth, a mise en scène keeping that much less to truth in its laying of truth as a trap, a trap into which generations of servile fetishists will come to be caught, thereby acknowledging the law of the master, of I, René Descartes.

Valéry insists upon the style: "It is precisely this that I think I see in the *Cogito*. Neither a syllogism nor even meaning in the literal sense; but a reflex action of the man, or more accurately, the explosion of an act, a shattering blow. There is, in any thinker of such intellectual power, what might be described as a home policy and a foreign policy of thought; he sets up certain 'reasons of state' against which nothing can prevail. . . . Never, until he came, had a philosopher so deliberately exhibited himself on the stage of his own thought, risking his own neck, daring to write 'I' for whole pages on end; he does it above all, and in an admirable style, when writing the *Meditations*. . . . I have called his style admirable" ("A View of Descartes").

Further on, and elsewhere, Valéry associates style with the "timbre" of the voice. Descartes could assert himself, posit his mastery, only by "paying with his person," exposing himself in a theater, putting himself on stage and into play "by risking the I." And henceforth at issue are the *style* of his writing and the *timbre* of his voice.

How are we to reassemble these propositions? Will it be said that Descartes, by means of what is inimitable in his text (timbre and style), has succeeded in imposing the source, in restoring the presence of the origin that is so implacably set aside by the play of signification?

Not at all, and such is the risk of what is at stake. In order to understand this, we must recall that the concepts of style and timbre have a rigorous definition in Valéry's analyses. In its irreplaceable quality, the timbre of the voice marks the event of language. By virtue of this fact, timbre has greater import than the *form* of signs and the *content* of meaning. In any event, timbre cannot be summarized by form and content, since at the very least they share the capacity to be repeated, to be imitated in their identity as objects, that is, in their ideality. ("Now, as far as you are concerned, all I need do is watch you talk, listen to your timbre, the excitement in your voice. The way people talk tells you more than what they say. . . . The content in itself has no . . . essential importance—Odd. That's one theory of poetry" [*Idée fixe*].) Numerous notes in the *Notebooks* confirm this point. Not lending itself to substitution, is not timbre on the order of a pure event, a singular presence, the very upsurge [*sourdre*] of the source? And is not style the equivalent of this unique vibration in writing? *If there is* one poetic event, it sounds in timbre; *if there is* one literary event, it is inscribed by style. "Literature, style—it is to write that which will supplement for the absence of the author, for the silence of the absent, for the inertia of the written thing" (1926). This proposition, and others along the same lines, appear to be quite classical, and doubtless are so up to a certain point: style, supplementing timbre, tends to repeat the event of pure presence, the singularity of the source present in what it produces, supposing again that the unity of a timbre—immediately it is identifiable—ever has the purity of an event. But, if style supplements timbre, nothing, it appears, can supplement their unique exchange, nothing can repeat the pure event (if at least there is something like the purity of a style and a timbre, which for me remains quite a hypothesis) that style and timbre constitute.

But, if there is a timbre and a style, will it be concluded that here the source *presents itself?*

Point. And this is why *I* loses itself here, or in any event exposes itself in the operation of mastery. The timbre of my voice, the style of my writing are that which for (a) me never will have been present. I neither hear nor recognize the timbre of my voice. If my style marks itself, it is only on a surface which remains invisible and illegible for me. *Point* of *speculum:* here I am blind to my style, deaf to what is most spontaneous in my voice. It is, to take up again the formulation from above, and to make it deviate toward a lexicographical monstrosity, the *sourdre* of the source. The spontaneous can emerge as the pure initiality of the event only on the condition that it does not itself *present itself,* on the condition of this inconceivable and *irrelevable* [*irrelevable,* i.e. that which cannot be *relevé,* subjected to the Hegelian operation of the *Aufhebung —Translator's Note*] passivity in which nothing can present itself to itself. Here we are in need of a paradoxical logic of the event as a *source which cannot present itself, happen to itself.* The value of the event is perhaps indissociable from that of presence; it remains rigorously incompatible with that of self-presence.

The Event and the Regime of the Other: Timbre

To hear oneself is the most normal and the most impossible experience. One might conclude from this, first, that the source is always other, and that whatever hears itself, not itself hearing itself, always comes from elsewhere, from outside and afar. The lure of the I, of consciousness as hearing-oneself-speak would consist in dreaming of an operation of ideal and idealizing mastery, transforming hetero-affection into auto-affection, heteronomy into autonomy. Within this process of appropriation somehow would be lodged a "regime" of normal hallucination. When I speak (to myself) without moving tongue and lips, I believe that I hear myself, although the source is other; or I believe that we are two, although everything is happening "in me." Supported by a very ancient history, traversing all the stations of the relation to the self (sucking, masturbation, touching/ touched, etc.), this possibility of a "normal" double hallucination permits me to give myself to hear what I desire to hear, to believe in the spontaneity of the power which needs no one in order to give pleasure to itself. Valéry perhaps has read into this the essence of poetic power. "A Poet's Notebook" opens with these words: "Poetry. Is it impossible, given time, care, skill, and desire, to proceed in an orderly way to arrive at poetry? To end by *hearing* exactly what one wished to hear by means of a skillful and patient management of that same desire?"

At a certain moment in history, for reasons to be analyzed, the poet ceased being considered the prey of a foreign voice, in mania, delirium, enthusiasm, or inspiration. Poetic "hallucination" is then accommodated under the rubric of the "regime": a simple elaboration of hearing-oneself-speak, a regulated, normed exchange of the same and the other, within the limits tolerated by a kind of general organization, that is, an individual, social, historical system, etc.

But what happens when this organization, still intolerant somewhere, incriminates "literally" abnormal hallucination? What happens, for example, when someone hears voices that he *remains alone* to hear, and that he perceives as a foreign source, which proceeds, as is said, from his own interior? Can one settle this problem as being the poet's? Can one content oneself with saying that since the source is transcendentally other, in sum, this hallucination too is normal, more or less, i.e. an exaggeration hardly baring the truth that would be the essential heterogeneity of the source?

Here is announced the question of psychoanalysis. In one of the *Notebooks* of 1918–21, concerning silent discourse, Valéry noted: "This voice (morbidly) might become entirely foreign" (1920). And, during the course of an analysis that is systematically, in detail, to be collated with Freud's analysis of Schreber's *Memoirs*, Valéry slips in, without pausing, an allusion to Swedenborg's father. Then, like Freud, setting aside the hypothesis of a purely delirious disorder, Valéry wonders: *"How is a Swedenborg possible?"*

analyses, which moreover are reproached for being too "significant": "No! no! I do not at all like to find myself once more in mind of the ancient pathways of my life. I will not track down Things Past! And even less would I approve of those absurd analyses which inculcate in people the most obscene rebuses, that they are already to have composed at their mothers' breasts." And in the *Notebooks,* concerning love: "What is more stupid than Freud's inventions on these matters?"

Here I am setting aside two questions. Not that I judge them to be without interest or without pertinence, but in the small amount of time given us here, they might distract us from reading which appears more urgent. In the first place, the issue will not be to improvise by tinkering with something which might resemble a psychoanalysis of Valéry's resistance to psychoanalysis. In the conditions under which this might be done, it would be very naive, and would fall well within Valéry's text, and the problems it elaborates, the questions it puts to a psychoanalysis of the text, to a psychoanalysis in the text, neither of which have come close to being articulated, or could not be, except by means of major transformations. Second, the issue will not be of a historical analysis explaining why Valéry, at a given date, could not read Freud, read him as we read him now, or will read him henceforth. One would have to take into account a large number of elements—the state of the translation and introduction of Freud in France and elsewhere, a general weave of resistances, and their relation to a certain state of Freudian theory, the heterogeneity of the psychoanalytic text in general, etc. It is not certain that Valéry simply participated in this closing off, that is, that he simply consolidated it. Valéry's work, his attention to language, to rhetoric, to formal agencies, to the paradoxes of narcissism, his distrust concerning naive semanticism, etc. all have probably contributed, or in any event belonged, to an entire groundswell which, after the war, carried along a particular rereading of Freud. As for the irony directed against the psychoanalytic "fashion," the ingenuous rush toward a mono- or pansexual semanticism for Parisian parlor games or literary futilities (Valéry at the time was thinking primarily of the Surrealists), nothing could appear less anti-Freudian, whatever Valéry may have thought himself, and nothing could be more needed.

Having reserved these two questions, we will ask, then, which concepts and which internal marks are the means with which to recognize, in Valéry's textual system, a certain division and a certain conflict of forces between two critical operations, at the sharpest and most novel point of two necessarily heterogeneous discourses: Valéry's and Freud's.

Here we must content ourselves with the most schematic reading. Thus, without pretending to determine any center in Valéry's text, without defining some closed fist that everything in a powerful, open, and ceaselessly questioning work renders improbable, I nevertheless will venture to localize a concept, and even a word, that nothing in what I have read seems to contradict. In question is a focal point of great economic density, the intersection of a great circulation, rather than some theological principle. Implied everywhere, never surprised or exceeded, this focal point seems to bring everything back to itself as if to a source. Thus, you will very quickly be tempted to object: aren't you going to reduce a text to its thematic or semantic center, to its final truth, etc.? I will adduce the singular form of this word-concept, which precisely marks an implication that is not one, an implication that cannot be reduced to anything simple, an implication and complication of the source that in a certain way cannot be disimplicated: thus, the IMPLEX.

The implex: that which cannot be simplex. It marks the limit of every analytic reduction to the simple element of the point. An implication-complication, a complication of the same and the other which never permits itself to be undone, it divides or equally multiplies infinitely the simplicity of every source, every origin, every presence. Throughout the numerous variations and contextual transpositions to which Valéry submits this concept, the same structure is always sketched out: the impossibility for a present, for the presence of a present, to *present itself* as *a source*: simple, actual, punctual, instantaneous. The implex is a complex of the present always enveloping the nonpresent and the other present in the simple appearance of its pointed identity. It is the potentiality or rather the power, the dynamis and mathematical exponentiality of the value of presence, of everything the value of presence supports, that is of everything—that *is*. Among many possible citations, let us focus upon *Idée fixe*. In question is the present and that which the "popular conception," that is philosophy, discerns as past, present, future: "Thus if you stick the point of the *present* into the actual moment . . . You create the present tense of the present, which you express as: *I am in the process of* . . . You create the future tense of the present: *I am just about to* . . . And so on. The present tense of the present of the present tense, the present tense of the future of the past pluperfect, and so on . . . You could refine on that. A mathematician could . . . You've started exponentiating all by yourself . . . To sum up, what I signify by *Implex* is that by which, and in virtue of which we remain contingent, conditional."

This value of contingency, eventuality, describes what is at stake in the concept. The implex, a nonpresence, nonconsciousness, an alterity folded over in the *sourdre* of the source, envelops the possible of what it is not yet, the virtual capacity of that which presently it is not in act. ". . . Now what about that word, that name? . . . —My name for all that inner potentiality that we were talking about is: the IMPLEX . . . No, the Implex is not an activity. Quite the contrary. It's a *capacity*."

This nonconsciousness or nonpresence, this nonsimplicity is *the same as* that which it actually is not; it is homogenous with present consciousness, that is with the self presence whose dynamic virtuality it opens. Even if, at the limit, it were impossible to make it explicit, it relates perception to self-consciousness as potentiality to act. It belongs to the same system as that which would remain, at the limit, always doubled over within it. Such a system covers that of the classical philosopheme of *dynamis*.

This limit is precisely the one which seems to pass between Valéry's critique of consciousness and Freudian psychoanalysis. The unconscious, that which Freud names in this way, is not a virtual consciousness; its alterity is not homogenous with the alterity lodged in the implex. Here the *sourdre* is entirely other. And the operation that Freud calls repression, which seems to have no specific place in Valéry's analysis, would introduce, if some such thing exists, a difference irreducible to the difference between the virtual and the actual; even if this virtuality must remain an undecomposable implex. This is what, from the outset, would separate the analysis of Swedenborg from the analysis of Schreber.

But would this be teaching Valéry anything? He indeed knew that such was the site of his resistance to psychoanalysis. If I have chosen to remain within *Idée fixe*, it is that in this text everything seems to be edified around this center, like a system of fortifications impenetrable by psychoanalysis. The implex represents the major device here. From this strong point, one can throw psychoanalysis back where it comes from, that is, from the sea, into the sea, a movement which could not have been simple for Valéry— such occasionally seems to be the obsidional operation of the *Idée fixe* itself. When the interlocutor, imprudent soul, proposes to "open up the Implex," even risking a rapprochement between the implex and the unconscious, he is simply threatened with being thrown into the sea. All the criticisms that have been addressed to psychoanalysis in France for fifty years, find their resources here: "We'll have to open up the *Implex.* But wait a moment. Does this Implex of yours amount to any more than what vulgar, common mortals, the masses, philosophers, psychologists, psychopaths, the non-Crusoes—the herd, in fact—call quite simply and crudely the 'unconscious' or the 'subconscious.'?

"—Do you want me to pitch you into the sea? . . . Don't you know I detest such dirty words? . . . And anyhow, it isn't the same thing at all. They are meant to signify some inconceivable hidden springs of action— at times they stand for sly little inner goblins, marvelous tricksters, who can guess riddles, read the future, see through brick walls, and carry on the most amazing industry inside our hidden workings."

Immediately afterward defining the implex as virtuality and general *capacity* ("for feeling, reacting, doing, and understanding"), it is true that Valéry adds to the end of the list the "capacity for resistance": "To all that we must add our capacity for resistance."

We will not ask what the *meaning* of this resistance is before pointing out that what Valéry intends to resist is meaning itself. What he reproaches psychoanalysis for is not that it interprets in such a fashion, but quite simply that it interprets at all, that it is an interpretation, that it is interested above all in signification, in meaning, and in some principal unity—here, a sexual unity—of meaning. He reproaches psychoanalysis for being a "symbol-ics"—this is what he names it—a hermeneutism, a semanticism. Is there not, henceforth, a place where all of Valéry's poetic and linguistic formalism, his very necessary critique of thematicist or semanticist spontaneity, in literature and elsewhere, all the irony with which he paralyzed the prejudices of meaning, theme, subject, content, etc., a place, then, where all of these come to be articulated systematically with his compulsive and obstinate rejection of psychoanalysis, a rejection operating as close as possible to psychoanalysis, and completely opposed to it? Was there not in meaning, to the extent that it is worked upon and afterward constituted by repression, something which above all had not to be dealt with? Something which formally had to be thrown back into the sea?

Above all I will not conclude that this hypothesis disqualifies Valéry's critical formalism. Something within it remains necessary and must be maintained, it seems to me, in opposition to all precritical semanticisms. The psychoanalytic discourses known to us are far from being exempt from this semanticism. Perhaps we here are touching upon a limit at which the opposition of form and meaning, along with all the divisions coordinated to it, loses its pertinence, and calls for an entirely other elaboration.

This elaboration would pass through the rereading of all these texts, of course, and of several others. It demands that one become engaged in it without endlessly circling around the form of these texts, that one decipher the law of their internal conflicts, of their heterogeneity, of their contradictions, and that one not simply cast an aesthete's glance over the philosophical discourse which carries within it the history of the oppositions in which arc displaced, although often under cover, both critical formalism and psychoanalytic hermeneutics.

Like Nietzsche, reinterpret interpretation.

I proposed that Nietzsche may have been Valéry's other set-aside source. Everything should have led Valéry back to him: the systematic mistrust as concerns the entirety of metaphysics, the formal vision of philosophical discourse, the concept of the philosopher-artist, the rhetorical and philological questions put to the history of philosophy, the suspiciousness concerning the values of truth ("a well applied convention"), of meaning and of Being, of the "meaning of Being," the attention to the economic phenomena of force and of the difference of forces, etc.

Valéry no doubt sensed this perhaps excessive proximity. He was ready to associate Nietzsche with Poe. And yet, in certain letters, after having rendered homage to Nietzsche, he explains why Nietzsche "shocked" him, "irritated" him (this is often his reaction to philosophy). In the course of a rather summary argumentation, he accuses Nietzsche of being "contradictory," of being a "metaphysician," and of "seeking to create a philosophy of violence." Elsewhere, in the form of a parody, he composes a false letter by Nietzsche, marked, if one may put it thus, by a Teutonic accent, in which the stiffest, and also most ardent, seriousness seems to be more on Valéry's side.

Why does M. Teste again permit himself to be irritated here? Why did Valéry not want, not want to be able, to read Nietzsche? Did he consider him threatening? And why? Too close? And in what way? These two hypotheses are not any more mutually exclusive than the for or the against. Did not Valéry push away Nietzsche for the same reason that made him push away Freud?

This is what Freud thought, and he was well placed to know so. Freud in advance knew that if Valéry could not acknowledge Nietzsche, it is because Nietzsche resembled Freud too much. And he had said so around 1925, or rather whispered it, with an imperturbable confidence.

For one to admire the wicked ruse of a certain *igitur* (*ja*), it suffices to make psychoanalysis probable from the very fact of its own *mise en scène* (*Selbstdarstellung*): "Nietzsche, another philosopher whose guesses and intuitions often agree in the most astonishing way with the laborious findings of psycho-analysis, was for a long time avoided by me on that very account; I was less concerned with the question of priority than with keeping my mind unembarrassed" (*An Autobiographical Study*).

Bachelard and the
Romantic Imagination

Margaret R. Higonnet

The coherence of Gaston Bachelard's ideas about imagination has long eluded students of his work. Because of his shifts in critical approach, a debate has arisen over what system, if any, governs his meditations on poetic imagery.

The problem requires a comparative approach, since Bachelard's work is rooted in the poetics and poetry of English and German Romanticism, a period for which he declared his affinity. The purpose of comparing Bachelard's thought to that of his Romantic predecesors is not, however, to demonstrate his intellectual dependence. Many students of Bachelard have noted in passing his interest in writers like Novalis. Since none explores this interest in detail, it has not been recognized that his thought is closer to Romantic theories than to later aesthetic systems. The key point is that Bachelard turned to Romantic precedents not only for isolated ideas but also for his most characteristic and problematic critical procedures: his reliance on metaphoric associations, disjunctive maxims, and apparently contradictory assertions. These methods are part of his message, which in its dialectical and symbolic character closely resembles Romantic idealism.

Two kinds of contradiction are evident in Bachelard's statements about imagination. First, his values appear to change: the essays on philosophy of science and to some extent *Psychanalyse du feu* (1938) set poetic imagery against reason and science, whereas *L'Eau et les rêves* (1942) and later works explore imagery with great sympathy. He strives originally to unmask, then to recover "l'esprit préscientifique" [*L'Eau et les rêves: Essai sur l'imagination de la matière*; all further references to this text will be abbreviated as *ER*]. Second, his method shifts from psychoanalysis of images in their genesis (1938–48) to phenomenological evocation of their effects (1957–62).

From *Comparative Literature* 33, no. 1 (Winter 1981). © 1981 by the University of Oregon.

Critics have responded to these shifts in various ways. Many divide his work into periods, a reflection perhaps of Bachelard's own principle of the *rupture*; in the words of Jean Starobinski, "Il y a au moins deux styles (ou époques) de la critique chez Gaston Bachelard" ("La Stylistique et ses méthodes: Leo Spitzer," in *Critique* 20 [1964]). Others elaborate an exceedingly complicated theoretical scaffolding whose connections resemble those of a Rube Goldberg cartoon. Some, like Sartre, claim a consistency in method only: "Sa psychanalyse semble plus sûre de sa méthode que de ses principes et sans doute compte-t-elle sur ses résultats pour éclairer sur le but précis de sa recherche. Mais c'est mettre la charrue devant les boeufs (*L'Etre et le néant*). More recently, critics have questioned whether Bachelard has either the method attributed to him by Sartre or a system of aesthetic principles. While there is a consensus that Bachelard adheres to certain general values (such as dynamism, liberation, or idealism), even the clearest expositions of his aesthetic theories tend to view his specific ideas as a grab-bag assortment.

Bachelard himself occasionally lends support to the assumption that his work has no systematic underpinning. In *La Poétiques de la rêverie* (1960), he takes as his motto Jules Laforgue's *légende morale*, "Méthode, Méthode, que me veux-tu? Tu sais bien que j'ai mangé du fruit de l'inconscient." In both *La Poétique de la rêverie* and *La Poétique de l'espace* he calls attention to his own drastic shifts in approach and argues that one must "se déphilosopher." The preface to *La Flamme d'une chandelle* (1961) tells us that Bachelard wishes to write "sans nous emprisonner dans l'unité d'une méthode d'enquête." According to Colette Gaudin, he began one of his lectures by declaring, "I would like to develop a philosophy that would have no point of departure" (Introduction to *Our Poetic Imagination and Reverie*). Bachelard's evident resistance to systematic theories reflects in part his quite conventional belief that analytic comprehension of the process of imagination is equivalent to loss of imagination: "La moindre réflexion critique . . . détruit la primitivité de l'imagination" [*La Poétique de l'espace*; all further references to this text will be abbreviated as *PE*]. "Quand on saurait dire comment on imagine, on n'imagine plus" (*PE*).

At the same time, it must be seen that Bachelard recognizes the value of schematization, in spite of its reductive tendency: "Certes, toute schématisation risque de mutiler la réalité, mais elle aide à fixer des perspectives" [*La Poétique de la rêverie*; all further references to this text will be abbreviated as *PR*]. The manuscript left at his death, *La Poétique du phénix*, quotes Rimbaud: "Nous t'affirmons, méthode!" Indeed, he repeatedly voices theoretical ambitions which imply a unified philosophy. At the beginning of the *Poétique de l'espace* he indicates that he intends to found "une phénoménologie de l'imagination" or even "une métaphysique de l'imagination." This intention can be traced through his earlier works as well. Already in *L'Air et les songes* (1943), he declares, "La métaphysique de l'imagination . . . reste partout notre but avoué." In *La Terre et les rêveries du repos* (1948), he again claims, "Dans cet ouvrage, ainsi que dans tous ceux que nous avons consacrés à l'imagination, nous ne voulons que préparer une doctrine de l'imagination littéraire." And in the companion volume *La Terre et les rêveries de la volonté* (1948) he describes his books as "essais qui devraient constituer peu à peu les éléments d'une philosophie de l'image littéraire."

Bachelard's thought, then, may be seen as both unsystematic and coherent. He claims that his works progress toward a coherent theory of the imagination despite the obvious fact that the early works propose a psychological system of four materially determined creative mentalities,"une doctrine tétravalente des tempéraments poétiques" [*Psychanalyse du feu*; all further references to this text will be abbreviated as *PF*], which the later *Poétiques* abandon for a phenomenological approach. In what theoretical direction, then, does this sequence of works point?

To locate the source of Bachelard's inspiration and the direction of his thought, some critics have connected him to Henri Bergson, C.G. Jung, and André Breton. The seed of his thought, however, lies further in the past, in the idealist poetics of the imagination which became established during the Romantic period. In this essay I will study the specific theses and strategies of presentation and organization shared by Bachelard and Romantic literary theorists. I do not propose to offer an influence study tracing the course of Bachelard's omnivorous readings but rather to consider the striking number of affinities between his poetics and the theories of the Romantic writers to whom he himself calls our attention. (One cautionary note should be sounded. Although Bachelard not infrequently cites German and English Romantic writers like the Schegels and Shelley, his actual quotations often come in translation, through secondary sources like Albert Béguin's *L'Ame romantique et le rêve*, Paul de Reul's *De Wordsworth à Keats*, or Ricarda Huch's *Les Romantiques allemands*, which he read in French. As Claude Pichois points out in his study of Jean Paul's impact in France, Bachelard sometimes uses unreliable French versions [*L'Image de Jean-Paul Richter dans les lettres françaises*]. Passages or phrases important to Bachelard may be of minor importance in the original text. In general, however, these deformations and mediations are of little significance here, since it is ultimately a systematic parallel to the broad tradition of Romantic poetics with which I am concerned, rather than a study of influences.) Unlike much recent work on Bachelard, this essay will focus on theory rather than on interpretative methods. The *Poétiques*, which appeared long after Sartre's critique, allow us to perceive the *boeuf* that draws the *charrue*. I emphasize the *Poétiques* because they represent in many ways a culmination of Bachelard's earlier work. The themes central to these highly self-conscious and reflexive texts are already implicit in the preceding works, as the examples in this study demonstrate.

Since Bachelard draws upon a range of elements in Romantic poetics, it may help to sketch first some key ideas that emerged at the end of the eighteenth century from the writings of Rousseau, Diderot, Young, Herder, and others. In this Romantic poetics the most important feature is the focus on the creative imagination. Allied with the genetic concern for imagination is the more cognitive concern for the element of imagery or symbolism in poetry, seen not only as an instrument for expression but as one of the means by which poetry transfigures and translates nature. Concomitant with imagination and imagery, we find such related topics as novelty, liberation from norms or clichés, and primitivism of various kinds. These are the main Romantic themes whose importance for Bachelard constitutes the first part of my argument, leading up to an examination of the ways in which these themes are organized and presented.

The most characteristically Romantic aspect of Bachelard's poetics is the central ontological function assigned to the imagination. He locates the imagination at the center of being as that which defines man "la faculté hominisante par excellence" [*L'Air et les songes: Essai sur l'imagination du mouvement*; all further reference to this text will be abbreviated as *AS*]. It is the source not merely of all artistic creativity but of all vitality. The *Poétique de l'espace* proposes to consider the imagination as "une puissance majeure de la nature humaine." In the *Poétique de la rêverie* Bachelard proclaims his goal to be "une phénoménologie de l'imaginaire où l'imagination est mise à sa place, à la première place, comme principe d'excitation directe du devenir psychique." It is this thesis which most clearly unites Bachelard's essays in poetics and which emerges as the dominant theme of his later works.

The ontological significance of the imagination is a tenet which Bachelard links regularly to Romantic writers like Blake: "Plus que toute autre puissance, elle spécifie le psychisme humain. Comme le proclame Blake: 'L'imagination n'est pas un état, c'est l'existence humaine elle-même.' " He finds a similar view of imagination in Novalis, for whom poetry if "Gemütserregungskunst," translated by Bachelard as "l'art du dynamisme psychique,"and imagination "das würckende Princip." If we follow Novalis, he claims, "alors on s'établit dans *une philosophie de l'imagination* pour laquelle l'imagination est l'être même, l'être producteur de ses images et de ses pensées."

In these passages Bachelard turns consciously to English and German Romantic models for the ontological view of creative imagination which he repeatedly contrasts to Bergson's philosophy (ironically so, given Bergson's own connections to German Romanticism). One reason may be the emphasis on poetry in the aesthetics of writers like Novalis and Schelling, which apparently provides a more useful precedent for Bachelard's theory of verbal imagination than does Bergson's alingual intuition. Already in *Psychanalyse du feu*, he distinguishes creative imagination from Bergson's *élan vital* and from Schopenhauer's "will": "Plus que la volonté, plus que l'élan vital, l'Imagination est la force même de la production psychique." He thus affirms a return to the Romantic cult of the poetic imagination as first principle.

The ontological conception of imagination as life force finds its epistemological corollary in Bachelard's value-laden distinction between imagination and either perception or memory. *La Terre et les rêveries de la volonté,* for example, aims to show "comment ce qu'on imagine commande ce qu'on perçoit, pour donner ainsi à l'imagination la place qui lui revient dans l'activité humaine: la place première." The imagination creates, it does not reproduce images of reality: "L'imagination créatrice a de tout autres fonctions que celles de l'imagination reproductrice."

Bachelard appears to contradict himself about the relative priorities of imagination and perception. At the beginning of *L'Air et les songes,* he describes the imagination as a power that transforms the images of perception: "On veut toujours que l'imagination soit la faculté de *former* des images. Or elle est plutòt la faculté de *déformer* les images fournies par la perception, elle est surtout la faculté de nous libérer des images premières, de *changer* les images." Near the end of the same work, he emphasizes by contrast the creative novelty of the literary image, arguing that it precedes and does not cloak external perception: "Il n'y pas de réalité antécédente à l'image littéraire." At times he slides from an objective to a subjective definition of reality: "s'ouvrir au Monde objectif, entrer dans le Monde objectif, constituer un Monde que nous tenons pour objectif (*PR*). Clearly there is a dialectic between the two positions, but Bachelard generally subordinates external to internal reality: "Le *fait imaginé* est plus important que le *fait réel*" (*ER*). As an idealist, he playfully undermines the value of *réalité* when he attributes to the imagination "une fonction de l'irréel" whose utility is superior. As early as 1933 Bachelard could write, "Le monde est ma miniature," a position which he echoes in *La Terre et les rêveries du repos:* "Quand la Nature imite l'humain, elle imite l'*humain imaginé.*

Among the works on the imagination, only in *Psychanalyse du feu* does Bachelard warn of the dangers of poetry or revery as opposed to reality and promise to cure man of the happy infection of the imagination: "guérir l'esprit de ses bonheurs." His language reveals, however, that his proposal is ironic—"un exercice où nous sommes maître: se moquer de soi-même." In any case, even here he asserts the priority of the imaginative vision, which mathematical reason merely follows and corrects. On the relationship between imagination and perception, then Bachelard is consistent, even in *Psychanalyse du feu.*

That Bachelard celebrates "la victoire de l'imagination créatrice sur le réalisme" (*ER*) is too obvious a point to belabor here. What is important for our purposes is that he repeatedly identifies this thesis with his favorite Romantic writers, from Blake and Shelley to Richter and Novalis, and that he chooses to express it in their words. The distinction between imagination and perception or memory is not an exclusively Romantic phenomenon, of course. For Bachelard, however, it is unquestionably a distinction identified with English and German Romanticism.

For each aspect of this idealist epistemology we find a reference to a

Romantic precedent. In a key passage of the introduction to *La Poétique de l'espace*, Bachelard attacks Bergson's treatment on imagination as "la mémoire poétisée in *Matière et mémoire* and turns to Jean Paul Richter for a more satisfactorily creative view: "Jean-Paul Richter n'a-t-il pas écrit: 'L'imagination reproductrice est la prose de l'imagination productrice.' " Another Romantic to whom Bachelard links the distinction between imagination and perception is Shelley: "Le monde réel est absorbé par le monde imaginaire. Shelley nous livre un véritable théorème de la phénoménologie quand il dit que l'imagination est capable 'de nous faire créer ce que nous voyons.' (While no passage in "A Defence of Poetry" directly corresponds to this quotation, two are closely allied: "All things exist as they are perceived" and "[Poetry] compels us to feel that which we perceive and to imagine that which we know. It creates anew the universe.") En suivant Shelley, en suivant les poètes, la phénoménologie de la perception elle-même doit céder la place à la phénoménologie de l'imagination créatice" (*PR*). Perhaps the most extreme formulation of Bachelard's position comes in a passage of *L'Air et les songes* where he quotes Blake: "Or, on n'imagine pas bien ce que l'on connaît. Blake a justement écrit: 'Les objets naturels n'ont jamais cessé d'affaiblir, d'abrutir et d'effacer l'imagination en moi' . . . L'*irréel* commande le *réalisme de l'imagination*." But his favorite spokesman for epistemological idealism is Novalis. He quotes him as saying that nature is "une fixation de l'Imagination," and that "l'univers est en quelque sorte un précipité de la nature humaine." He also finds in him a source for his *pancalisme*, his theory that the imagination animates and "valorizes" the materials of perception: "Ainsi, pour l'idéalisme magique de Novalis, c'est l'être humain qui éveille la matière" [*La Terre et les rêveries de la volonté*; all further references to this text will be abbreviated as *TRV*]. Such statements make clear the importance of idealist Romantic precedents in Bachelard's formulation of his ideas about the place and function of the imagination.

The priority of the imagination over perception or memory reflects Bachelard's reliance on a hierachy of mental faculties. This assumption is again common among Romantic writers such as Jean Paul and Coleridge, though it is rarely presented with rigorous consistency. Bachelard attributes it to Novalis: "Nous dirons donc avec Novalis: 'De l'imagination productrice doivent être déduites toutes les facultés, toutes les activités du monde intérieur et du monde extérieur.' " Not surprisingly, he also refers to Baudelaire's thesis that the imagination is the queen of the faculties: "L'être entier est mobilisé par l'imagination, comme l'a reconnu Baudelaire: 'Toutes les facultés de l'âme humaine doivent être subordonnées à l'imagination qui les met en réquisition toute à la fois' " (*TRV*). In drawing thus on the traditional language of faculty psychology to describe poetic creativity, Bachelard sets himself apart from most modern speculation like that of the French phenomenologists.

The cult of the imagination is the main currency of Romantic poetics; the obverse of the coin is a cult of the image or symbol. Bachelard, like the

Romantics, emphasizes the psychology of the artist in his definition of the work of art, and like them he also connects the theory of the imagination to the theory of the image. Together with Coleridge, Bachelard believes that "What is poetry? is so nearly the same question with, what is a poet? that the answer to the one is involved in the solution of the other" (*Biographia Literaria*, chap. 14). Among the major assumptions he shares with writers like Novalis, Schlegel, Wordsworth, and Coleridge is the association of poetry with image or metaphor, with dreams and the sources of conscious life, with various kinds of literary primitivism, with alchemy, and with metamorphosis.

Bachelard gives the image the very highest importance in poetry (a term which for him as for the romantics, includes prose). The *Poétique de l'espace* affirms that the creation and association of images are the main tasks of the poet: "s'il y a métier chez le poète c'est dans la tâche subalterne d'associer des images." This primacy of the image can be traced back through all his earlier works on poetics. In *Psychanalyse du feu*, for example, we find one of his best-known phrases: "Les métaphores s'appellent et se coordonnent plus que les sensations, au point qu'un esprit poétique est purement et simplement une syntaxe de métaphores." In *L'Eau et les rêves* he declares, "La métaphore est le phénomène de l'âme poétique." And in a brief "Message" Bachelard describes the symbol as "une force créatrice": "Le symbole centralise des forces qui sont en l'homme et des forces dispersées dans tous les êtres du monde." While his terms change (image, metaphor, symbol, and archetype acquire different relative significance as his work progresses), the ontological value attached to the image parallels that attributed to the imagination. Poetic images are "des miniatures de l'élan vital" (*PE*).

Hence whether his subject is fire, water, air, earth, space, or revery itself, the focus of Bachelard's literary interpretation is always the image. Indeed, this constitutes one of the major charges brought against his method, namely that it is concerned with an element of poetry, not with poems as aesthetic wholes. Bachelard himself comments on his pointilliste method, which has met so much opposition. In *La Terre et les rêveries du repos* he explains, "Pour nous, les 'cas' sont de toutes petites images trouvées au coin d'une page," a limitation which he claims enables him to isolate the problem of expression. As he repeats in the late *Poétiques*, the poetic image is important to him because it lies at the origin of consciousness and of language. In his emphasis on the image, Bachelard resembles the Romantics, but in this neglect of context, he distances himself from the preoccupation of Romantic writers with what they considered to be the organic whole.

Inevitably, since Bachelard locates the image at the origin of consciousness, he is interested in the connections among dream, revery, and imaginative literature, and his interest in dreams leads him to cite several Romantic writers as masters of dream-literature, such as Novalis, Richter, and E.T.A. Hoffmann. For example, referring to Novalis, he argues that the full subjective value of an image can be grasped only by recovering its primitive dream-function: "Mais allez au fond de l'inconscient; retrouvez, avec le poète, le rêve primitif et vous verrez clairement la vérité" (*PF*). It is important to note that he is interested in the dream image or scene, not in sequences, not in the violations of connection which are the subject of Novalis' famous fragment on the *Märchen*, although Bachelard does postulate a "rupture" as the hallmark of the creatively vital image.

Daydreams and verbal reveries interest Bachelard more than dreams. Already in *Psychanalyse du feu*, he distinguishes his own imaginative study of conscious daydreams and reveries centered on an object or image from the psychoanalysis of involuntary, nocturnal dreams. In general, Bachelard identifies the literary imagination with poetic revery: both are expressed in images and both react to images with profound associations. For Bachelard to dream about images means to give them value by amplifying or concentrating their essential oneiric features, "une analyse des valeurs oniriques." One should, therefore, "expliquer les rêves par les rêves" [*La Terre et les rêveries du repos*; all further references to this text will be abbreviated as *TRR*], a maxim with the same reflexive ring as Friedrich Schlegel's *Lyceum* fragment 117: "Poesie kann nur durch Poesie kritisiert werden." *La Poétique de l'espace* returns to this definition of Bachelard's interpretative goals: "La lecture des poètes est essentiellement rêverie." Such associative responsiveness fosters a return to primitive themes: "La rêverie reprend sans cesse les thèmes primitifs."

The identification of revery with primitive values introduces another feature of Bachelard's theory of images: primitivism. Bachelard's thesis of the expressive primacy of the image is very closely allied to the Vichian linguistic primitivism of the late eighteenth and early nineteenth centuries, according to which man first expresses himself in figurative language. Bachelard links the idea to Novalis: "Le psychisme humain se formule primitivement en images . . . cette pensée de Novalis . . . est une dominante de *l'idéalism magique*" (*TRV*). The idea is one which Novalis shares with many others of the Romantics Bachelard read; Shelley, for example, says that the language of the first men is "vitally metaphorical." Discussing the power of a novel image to renovate language, Bachelard refers to Jacobi, who read Vico at Goethe's suggestion: "Réanimer un language en créant de nouvelles images, voilà la fonction de la littérature et de la poésie. Jacobi a écrit: 'Philosopher, ce n'est jamais que découvrir les origines du langage' " (*TRV*).

Bachelard, of course, recognizes the Romantics' interest in primal myths, as well as images and *Ursprache*. He argues, following Albert Béguin, that "les romantiques, en revenant à des expériences plus ou moins durables de la primitivité," were able to recover the essential values of images like fire, and he describes the poetry of Novalis as "un effort pour revivre la *primitivité*. Pour Novalis, le conte est toujours plus ou moins une cosmogonie" (*PF*).

The primitivism implicit in Bachelard's cult of the image is thus one of its most strikingly Romantic features. The image is primary and primal as much as primordial, a conflation of concepts as common to Romantic writers as it is to Bachelard. This cluster of different connotations is woven together constantly by Bachelard: "L'image, dans sa simplicitè, n'a pas besoin d'un savoir. Elle est le bien d'une conscience naïve. En son expression, elle est jeune language. Le poête, en la nouveauté de ses images, est toujours origine de langage" (*PE*). At the psychological level, the verbal image as the spontaneous autonomous product of the imagination precedes the verbal expression of other faculties: "Les images sont les réalités psychiques premières. Tout commence, dans l'expérience même, par des images" (*TRR*).

An important ambiguity emerges when the image is seen as primary, for it is both novel and eternal, both youthfully fresh and ancestrally primordial. From *L'Eau et les rêves* to *La Poétique de la rêverie*, Bachelard repeats that the two somehow go together, "l'image nouvelle greffée sur une image ancienne" (*ER*), the new verbal act reviving and reverberating against the fundamental archetype. "Cette exigence, pour une image poétique, d'être une origine psychique, aurait cependant une dureté excessive si nous ne pouvions trouver une vertu d'originalité aux variations mêmes qui jouent sur les archétypes les plus fortement enracinés" (*PR*). As important as Jung inevitably is for Bachelard's theories of archetypes and imaginative alchemy, he does not find it necessary to accept Jung's postulate of a collective unconscious which would explain the image causally. Unlike the analyst, who wishes to explain the poetic flower by the fertilizer, Bachelard asserts, "Une image poétique, rien ne la prépare, surtout pas la culture, dans le mode littéraire, surtout pas la perception, dans le mode psychologique" (*PE*). Bachelard therefore has more sympathy with a Romantic emphasis on the novelty, the metamorphic and liberating powers of the image, than with a modern theory of eternal archetypes. It may be worth noting that it is not just the later works like *La Poétique de l'espace* which assert: "L'acte poétique n'a pas de passé." Earlier works like *L'Air et les songes* also stress the idea the "il n'y a pas de *poésie* antécédente à l'acte du verbe poétique." Each archetypal image "doit avoir sa différentielle de nouveauté" (*TRV*), as a token of its creative power. An affective version of primitivism can be uncovered in what Bachelard says about the impact of this novelty on the reader. In part, the implication is Rousseauistic. Bachelard wishes to liberate man from the burden of tradition, "à écarter tous les entraînements de la culture," and to recover the wonder of childhood, "retrouver notre naïf émerveillement" (*PE*). The imagination cleanses the doors of perception, as Blake would put it; it restores "the sparkle and the dew drops" which have dried up with custom, according to Coleridge; Novalis' term is *dephlegmatisiren*. Perhaps even closer to Bachelard's attitude is Shelley's description of poetry: "It purges from our inward sight the film of familiarity which obscures from us the wonder of our being. It compels us to feel that which we perceive, and to imagine that which we know. It creates anew the universe after it has been annihilated in our minds by the recurrence

Within the tradition of French aesthetics, Bergson's creative joy would be the closest analogy.

Each of these individual ideas links Bachelard to Romantic thought. More important, the ways in which these ideas come together in Romantic thought help us to understand how they can coexist in Bachelard's work. The second part of my argument, then, is that we can recognize the coherence of Bachelard's thought once we identify the argumentative structures he also drew from Romantic poetics.

As René Wellek has noted, most romantic literary theories operate within a dialectical framework, opposing imagination and reason, poetry and science, or self and reality. At times, the result appears contradictory: the poet strives, for example, to achieve both originality and the eternal values of myth and primitive expression. Novalis and Friedrich Schlegel rely heavily on the speculative devices of ironic juxtaposition and paradox; Schlegel gives the name "parabolic form" to this philosophic procedure. Romantic poetics are also organized on the principle of the associative clustering of ideas, linked often by puns and metaphors. Yet another heuristic strategy of Schlegel, Novalis, and Blake is the fragmentary or aphoristic formulation of ideas, striving for a combination of formal closure and intellectual open-endedness. These various rhetorical devices are used by the Romantics both to engage the imagination of the reader and to express the qualities of originality, dynamism, and synthesis they attribute to the imagination.

Bachelard takes over these patterns of aphoristic formulation, metaphoric association, and dialectical opposition from the Romantics, along with their basic tenets about imagination and poetry. A failure to recognize the expressive function that unites these seemingly discontinuous patterns is partly responsible for the controversy over the unity of his thought.

Bachelard habitually elaborates his theses not through logic but through analogy, allusion, and witty aphorism. As a result, his ideas appear to scatter rather than proceed toward a single goal. Typical aphorisms would be his Kantian defense of "l'utilité de l'inutile" or the Schlegelian recommendation, "expliquer les rêves par les rêves." His love of paradox joins with his penchant for associative thinking to explain the contradictory usage of the term "primitif" to mean both the novel and the eternal. The connection between these devices and Romantic poetics is one Bachelard understood. In *La Flamme d'une chandelle,* for example, he confesses that he is drawn to Romantic writers like Novalis by their use of fragments: "Nous avons bien souvent été attiré par des pensées en fragments, par des pensées qui ne prouvent pas, mais qui, en des affirmations rapides, donnent à la rêverie des impulsions sans pareille." The rhetoric thus supports his identification of poetry—and poetics—with imagination and revery.

His theoretical focus on imagery leads Bachelard to use imagery rather than expository prose, a method which constitutes one of the beauties and difficulties of his work. The images he selects frequently remind us of those figures of speech characteristic of Romantic poetics. The most common may be the images of inner light, inner vision, and inner form (*ER*) which echo the Romantic substitution of the lamp for the mirror as emblem of creativity, some of which I have already quoted. Bachelard speaks in *La Poétique de l'espace* of "une lumière intérieure, celle qu'une 'vision intérieure' connaît." The lamp is implicit in his description of active vision; "Pour la vision active, il semble que l'œil projette de la lumière" (*ER*).

In addition to these persistent images of light we find the Aeolian harp, "cette petite harpe éolienne, délicate entre toutes, placée par la nature à la porte de notre souffle" (*PE*). Bachelard also associates the breeze, like a romantic, with inspiration, and the image with a seed or plant, "une image-germe, un germe-image" [*La Flamme d'une chandelle*; all further references to this text will be abbreviated as *FC*]. Organic figures recur to explain the creative process: "L'image est une plante qui a besoin de terre et de ciel, de substance et de forme" (*ER*). In short, Bachelard seems so imbued with Romantic thought about the imagination and imagery that he returns constantly to the figures most closely identified with that thought.

Above all, the pattern which emerges to unify these features of Bachelard's writing is dialectical. He defines poetry in terms of a series of oppositions, for the most part derived from the polarities of imagination and reason or imagination and perception. Imagination operates at two levels, an ambiguity that lies at the heart of the confusion about Bachelard's thought. At the lower level, imagination is opposed to reason, as thesis to antithesis. At the higher level, imagination is the power of synthesis.

Logically, the queen of faculties rules and integrates the other faculties: "L'imagination met en effet une pointe à tous nos sens" (*PE*). "Tous les sens s'éveillent et s'harmonisent dans la rêverie poétique" (*PR*). In the terminology of his early works on the material imagination, "dans l'aperception imaginaire totale (forme et matière), la synthèse est première" (*TRR*). That the imagination should represent the highest, synthesizing power will come as no surprise to students of Romanticism. Bachelard himself refers to the late German Romantic K.W.F. Solger to support his argument that in its proper role the imagination reintegrates the powers of thought and feeling: "Il suffit de rendre son rôle premier à l'imagination, au seuil de la parole et de la pensée . . . Ainsi est réintégré le sentir dans le penser, comme le voulait Solger." Bachelard's belief in "l'action synthétique de l'imagination" (*TRR*) could also be compared to Coleridge's "magical and synthesizing power," Shelley's "principle of synthesis," or Richter's harmonizing and totalizing *Phantasie*.

While the synthesizing imagination is ultimately supreme, at a lower level imagination is paired with reason or perception as opposite but equal; the value of reason and reality relative to imagination therefore depends upon the context. A point often overlooked is that, for Bachelard, poetry requires the collaboration of both imagination and reason, of *l'âme et l'esprit*, or *anima* and *animus*. The poetic image arises through a simple movement of *l'âme*, but to complete and structure a poem requires *l'esprit:* "Il faut l'union d'une activité rêveuse et d'une activité idéative pour produire une œuvre poétique. L'art est de la nature greffée" (*ER*). This basic antinomy takes many forms in his work: besides the pairs already cited, we find *l'image* and *le concept*, unconscious and conscious imagination, material and formal imagination. In *La Poétique de l'espace* he indicates a preference for the German terms *der Geist* and *die Seele* as more clearly distinct than the French equivalents.

The way Bachelard sets up these oppositions echoes the pattern of Romantic poetics. For Bachelard, imagination is at once voluntary and involuntary: "L'image littéraire, si spontanée qu'elle prétend être, est tout de même une image réefléchie, une image surveillée (*TRR*). This balance is essential to his distinction between active revery and passive dream: "L'imagination dynamique est . . . la *volonté qui rêve*" (*AS*). Very similar pairings occur in the theories of Bachelard's favorite writers. Richter in the *Vorschule* attributes both *Besonnenheit* and *Instinkt* to genius; A.W. Schlegel argues that Shakespeare was both conscious and inspired; and Coleridge in *Biographia Literaria* stresses the poetic "balance or reconciliation" of idea with image, judgement with enthusiasm, and thought with feeling. These are not isolated examples of dialectic in Romantic aesthetic psychology. Furthermore, Bachelard's self-conscious references to the division in his work between poetics of revery and philosophy of science may be compared to the Romantic contrast between poetry and science (rather than history).

The form of dialectic that Bachelard derives most explicitly from Romantic thought is that of subject and object. His early version, the distinction between the material and formal imaginations, should perhaps be traced to Schiller's *Stofftrieb* and *Formtrieb*. Yet he is more prone to link the dialectic of subject and object or of man and nature, implicit in the notion of formal and material drives, to somewhat later writers. He praises Coleridge for recognizing the union of sentiment and sight in "l'*Einfühlung* aérienne" (*AS*), and he cites at length Book IV of Wordsworth's *Prelude* for the interplay of reality and reflection (*ER*). *La Poétique de la rêverie* finds the dialectic of external and internal worlds in Richter: "Jean-Paul pousse jusqu'a l'absolu la dialectique de monde contemplé et du monde reréé par la rêverie." Novalis, however, is the name with which he most often associates this "union pancaliste du visible et de la vision" (*ER*). Novalis's theory of magical idealism as expounded in the *Athenaeum* fragments explains for him the interaction of subject and object: "L'image a une double réalité: une réalité psychique et une réalité physique. C'est par l'image que l'être imaginant et l'être imaginé sont au plus proche" (*TRV*).

Some of the ideas Bachelard shares with his romantic predecessors can, of course, also be attributed to Bergson or to phenomenological predecessors such as Husserl and Heidegger: for example, the cult of creativity, the emphasis on the moment of aesthetic experience as "une prise de conscience," and the intensity of the feeling–experience. Although Bachelard neglects key features of Husserlian aesthetics such as intentionality and self-consciousness, his emphatic approach is in many ways characteristic of French phenomenology: images are lived, reimagined, renovated through conscious revery. The reader "tente de répéter pour lui la création, de continuer, s'il se peut, l'exagération" (*PE*). The dialectical movement (*retentissement*) between reader and poet is the tenet which brings him closest to the phenomenological approach.

Perhaps because of some anxiety of influence, however, Bachelard carefully distinguishes himself from these models. He prefers Jean-Paul's description of the imagination to Bergson's, as we have seen. Not Sartre but a character in Jean-Paul's *Titan* provides an example of "l'adhésion phénoménologique totale" or sympathetic creativity. He turns not to Heidegger but to Novalis for a discussion of *ecsistence*, "*l'art de sauter au-delà de soi-même*" (*FC*), and for a description of man as the meaning-giver.

Furthermore, comparison of Bachelard's thought with that of the Romantics helps illuminate the presence in his work of elements not generally associated with phenomenology. As already noted, his reliance upon the terminology of faculty psychology, characteristic of romantic theorists, would be quite unusual in strict phenomenology. Another element of Bachelard's thought which falls into place once one approaches him from a Romantic perspective is his insistence on poetic autonomy, which follows from his assumptions about the priority of the imagination. His distinction between vital, polysemous images and dead, monovalent metaphors (where Bergson again lands ironically on the wrong side of the fence) parallels the old distinction between symbol and allegory.

Finally, Bachelard's combination of idealism and an emphasis on the material sources of imaginative power may be compared profitably to the affirmation in Romantic poetics of both the metamorphic imagination and the return to nature. As Paul de Man has shown, this conjunction creates a problematic tension in Romantic thought ["Intentional Structure of the Romantic Image," in *The Rhetoric of Romanticism*]. Bachelard appears deliberately to exploit this tension, refusing either to expound a synthesis or to analyze ironic distances and discontinuities. His rhetoric is, as it were, a rhetoric of atemporality.

Of all the Romantics the most important for him is Novalis, whose work has served him as a kind of Bible: "Nous avons lu et relu l'œuvre d'un Novalis. Nous en avons reçu de grandes leçons" (*FC*). If we apply Bachelard's categories of analysis to his own work, we find that his critical method from *Psychanalyse du feu* onward exemplifies what he calls the Novalis complex, "ce besoin de *pénétrer*, d'aller à l'*intérieur* des choses, à l'*intérieur* des êtres" (*PF*). There are many verbal echoes of Novalis; the title *La Flamme d'une chandelle*, for example, comes from one of Novalis's fragments. Bachelard's main themes are consistently identified with Novalis, especially the belief in a dynamic imagination that transfigures the natural world, "la thèse de Novalis d'un pancalisme actif" (*PR*). Given his emphasis on the material imagination, it is perhaps somewhat surprising that Bachelard should show so much interest in the idealism of Novalis. Yet recognition of this affinity is essential to any understanding of Bachelard's work as a whole. We must remember that Bachelard's materialism operates dialectically within an idealist context: "Dans le règne de l'imagination, à toute immanence s'adjoint une transcendance." Bachelard wishes to provide in a modest way the transcendental theory of the imagination that Novalis hoped from Fichte, "une 'Fantastique transcendantale' " (*TRV*). The highest philosophic accomplishment for him is transcendental irony: "L'art de sauter au-delà de soi-même est partout l'acte le plus haut. . . . Ainsi la philosophie commence là où le philosophant se philosophise luimême" (*FC*). It is an idea he takes from Novalis, one whose reflexiveness proves him even more closely related to German romanticism—to Novalis, Schlegel, and Solger—than to English or French Romanticism.

If we recognize the affinities of Bachelard to the Romantic past, we can better locate him in the topography of modern poetics. As Gillo Dorfles has shown, Vichian theories of myth, metaphor, and primitive ("heroic") language have played a considerable role in twentieth–century theories, from Ernst Cassirer and Susanne Langer to Herbert Read and Owen Barfield ["Myth and Metaphor in Vico and in Contemporary Aesthetics," in *Giambattista Vico: An International Symposium* (1969)]. Phenomenology offers the best parallel to Bachelard's *retentissement* between author and reader, his affective orientation, but his focus on the image finds a closer parallel in American New Criticism. Set into the context of New Criticism, his love for the verbal detail, for paradox, and for ambivalent or multivalent structures comes to the fore.

It could well be argued that Bachelard's alignment is comparative, since his literary perspective is never confined by national borders. The cultural context within which his mind operates differs sharply from the traditional context of seventeenth-century French literature which dominates in the critics associated with the Ecole Normale Supérieure, ranging over European literature from Romanticism to Surrealism. Certain names recur— Novalis, Shelley, and among later writers Nietzsche, Rilke, Valéry, Breton, Bosco—and these reveal special affinities that help us to understand his thought.

Beneath Bachelard's wide-ranging, apparently eclectic sampling of Europeon and American literature lies a consistently Romantic poetics for which Novalis provides the main model. The coherence of Bachelard's theory goes beyond the central idealist theses about the nature of imagery and of the imagination. Comparison to Romantic poetics brings to light the interconnections among secondary themes such as primitivism or literary autonomy, and, most important, it reveals the dialectic structure of Bachelard's thought. For Bachelard finds this structure to be one which enables him to affirm paradoxes and to read expansively, in a literary quest that resembles the romantic "Sehnsucht nach dem Unendlichen."

Breton and Freud

Jean-Pierre Morel

From at least three viewpoints, quite as inseparable as art and life usually are for the surrealists, Breton affirms the importance of dreams: to the poet, painter, or sculptor, dreams furnish the models—procedures and products—of an activity which is unencumbered by the constraints of realist representation; to the explorer of daily life, they indicate by analogy how spaces and events which initially appear disconcerting are organized among themselves; to man in general, that "definitive dreamer," the analysis of dreams provides the most vivid sense of all the possibilities which existence offers him. Apprehending his dreams, man would in the same breath apprehend the "natural necessity" which governs all life.

Appearing ten years after the beginning of the surrealist experiments, *Les Vases communicants* returns to and develops all of these intuitions. Yet the interest of this text, though it does not stop there, lies in the way in which Breton compares his views to the theory and method of psychoanalysis. Almost from the opening page, Breton accords considerable historical import to Freud's work: "Until 1900, the publication date of Freud's *Interpretation of Dreams*, there was a succession of the least convincing and most contradictory theses." Despite important reservations, Breton borrows from Freud the essential elements of the notions presented in *The Interpretation of Dreams*: wish-fulfillment, manifest and latent content, the mechanisms and the processes of dream-work, the method of "free association" ("by far the most original find of this author"). He sends his text to Vienna and Freud's answer is not slow in coming.

Moreover, if we compare *Les Vases communicants* to certain passages of the 1924 *Manifesto* or *Nadja* (1928) which question the validity of psychoanalysis when it claims to provide a full explanation of dreams, or to the

From *Diacritics* 2, no. 2 (Summer 1972). © 1972 by Diacritics, Inc.

pages of the second *Manifesto* (1929) which Breton devotes to disputing the theory of sublimation, one fact stands out: the method of interpreting dreams opens a considerable breach in the defensive system of surrealism. Breton recognizes that the method is valid and necessary not only for understanding night-dreams and certain phenomena of the wakeful state but also for explaining the activity, in literature or the plastic arts, of the surrealist. The 1924 *Manifesto* kept open, in the domain of dreams, the possibility of several investigations that would be neither competitive nor dependent on one another, including those of the analyst and the poet. *Les Vases communicants*, however, would at least appear to support a very different hypothesis: the poet has followed in the footsteps of the scientist, has borrowed from him the tools, if not the spirit, (but is such a division possible?) of his research. It has even been possible to write that after spending ten years producing "material" (texts, paintings, collages, diverse games and experiences) surrealism inaugurated a new period with *Les Vases communicants:* that of the interpretation of this material. Thus we are led to ask whether this text indicates that Breton is abandoning the ideas which have governed the organized activity of surrealism since 1922 in favor of recognizing the results achieved by the science of psychoanalysis, still in its formative stages, or whether he is trying to develop the earlier intuitions of surrealism in another way. And in the latter case, what would be the import of the borrowings from Freud? We cannot attempt to answer these questions without recalling, if only in a very summary fashion, the focal points of André Breton's undertaking.

First of all, a fundamental relationship unites man with the universe which surrounds him. Thus the knowledge of subjectivity is the best preparation for apprehending the world through human understanding. Inversely, all dogmatism and all oppression are based on the refusal to consider the individual being in his subjectivity. Now, in this area, there is no phenomenon so important, and until now so poorly understood, as "the constant exchange which must take place in thought between the external and the internal world, an exchange which requires the continuous interpenetration of the activity of wakefulness and of the activity of sleep." On this point, the discoveries of psychoanalysis seem fundamental, for they will make it possible to answer several questions which, as is usual with Breton, have been raised "by life" itself: what is the relationship of dreaming to external reality? what criterion makes it possible to distinguish between the former and the latter? in what way does this relationship affect the emotional life of all men? Following the example of Freud, Breton analyzes, in the first part of *Les Vases communicants*, two of his dreams, and in the second part, a period of his life (three weeks of April 1931) that he likens to a daydream (*rêve éveillé*). The results of this self-analysis can be restated under three headings:

(a) All the elements which compose the night-dream come from lived experience: memories of datable events spread out over a period running from the dreamer's childhood up to the day before the dream; worries, projects, or preoccupations which occupied Breton's mind in the wakeful state; finally, physical stimuli. Thus we find nothing which can, in the dream, "constitute an appreciable *residue* which one might try to represent as irreducible. From the point of view of the poetic supernatural, perhaps something; from the point of view of the religious supernatural, absolutely nothing. Of course these formative elements are subject to the action of the transformational proceses which Freud noted and described, and in which he saw the essential aspect of dreaming itself, dream-work.

The self-analysis shows, on the other hand, that these mechanisms of elaboration are not peculiar to dreaming. In certain circumstances, they can even completely supplant conscious thought. Summarizing his emotional and moral crisis of April 1931, Breton writes; "It must be impossible, considering the foregoing not to be struck by the analogy which exists between the state that I have just described as having been mine at that time and the dream-state as it is usually conceived. The two succeeding analyses lead therefore to complementary conclusions: the dream is formed solely with the elements of wakeful life; but also in the state of wakefulness it can happen that the human mind functions no differently than it does in dreaming. Whence the metaphor of the "communicating vases": the fluid which runs through them is desire.

(b) This force of desire, and the identity of the transformational processes to which it subjects its raw material, "whether in reality or in dreams," do not act at the expense of external reality. Dreaming never abolishes in man the faculty which recognizes that the external world exists outside of him and independently of him. Only madness, idealist philosophy, or religion allow and keep alive such a confusion. As a consistent materialist, Breton tries to show that space, time, and the principle of causality are identical in dreams to what they are in reality, i.e., laws or objective forms of existence, and not properties of our mind. (Breton's discussion of this point stems from his reading of Lenin). In dreams, the wish transforms reality without investing it with new properties which might change its nature.

(c) This conclusion is crucial because of its practical consequences. For according to whether man recognizes or not the existence of external reality and its preponderance over the human mind, the function of dreaming changes completely. The example of the first attitude is given by Breton himself: he never loses sight of reality, never claims that it is merely dependent upon his freedom or his wishes. In these conditons, dreaming or daydreaming has a positive influence; better than conscious thought, they help man resolve problems, calm worries, make decisions. Thus his daydreaming in April 1931 helps Breton reinforce his "ego," cruelly damaged by the departure of the woman he loved; the dream of August 1931 completes the action of the preceding dreams by pressing the author to return toward a life of love and political action. Breton hails his dream as "the salutary principle, . . . the unknown source of light intended to make us remember that, at the beginning of the day as at the beginning of human life on earth, we can have only one resource, which is *action*.''

Inversely, the price of ignoring or disdaining external reality is the renunciation of action. For dreaming (while one is awake or asleep), when it is cut off from its origin, is henceforth considered as a degraded or larval form of the mind's activity, or as the gratuitous play of an illusion, or as the mark of a providence or divinity. Each of these interpretations precludes the possibility of a human activity that would transform the world: ''Just as underneath the dream we discover in the last analysis only a real substance borrowed from events already experienced, the extreme impoverishment of this substance condemns the mind to seek refuge in dream-life. . . . The dream, which has been lacking in nutriment for a while, here plays the part of a destroyer. Thus for Breton the historical solidarity of social conservatism and idealism appears clearly in the idea of the dream conceived as a refuge or as a sign of suprahuman action. The three apparently opposing solutions of the worldly life, religious retreat, and suicide are, in his eyes, only three ways of giving in to the ascendancy of negative dreaming and institutionalizing it. In the ''idealist subjective system carried to the extreme,'' the ''system grounded in unhappiness,'' to live or to cease to live is only to pursue the Bad Dream, a dream which is based upon the perpetual denial of a truth that Breton takes to be fundamental: ''the world of dreams and the real world are but one.''

''A double play of mirrors.'' In *Nadja* Breton gave this definition of the relations between dream and lived reality. This optical construction returns in 1932 in a more systematized form. Thus, in the first part of *Les Vases communicants*, the coexistence of opposites in the unconscious is supposed to reflect the dialectic of nature within man. In the second part, the nocturnal dream-work is echoed by that of the daydream. But now this construct is based less on intuition than on a critical reading of the work of Freud. Can we say, however, that Breton showed himself to be faithful to the ''illustrious master''?

The first difference between them concerns precisely the relations of reality and the night-dream. All the elements which Breton observes and identifies in his personal experience in order to show, after a scrupulous inventory, that they are the driving forces of his dream, are, in Freud's theory, ''day's residues,'' i.e., thoughts, worries or problems which, in a conscious or latent fashion, occupy the mind of the wakeful subject. Localized in the preconscious system, these residues, despite their importance, cannot on their own motivate the formation of a dream:

> The position may be explained by an analogy. A daytime thought may very well play the part of *entrepreneur* for a dream: but the *entrepreneur*, who, as people say, has the idea and the initiative to carry it out, can do nothing without capital; he needs a *capitalist*

who can afford the outlay, and the capitalist who provides the physical outlay for the dream is invariably and indisputably, whatever may be the thoughts of the previous day, a wish from the *unconscious*.

(The Interpretation of Dreams, trans. James Strachey)

In other words, it is probable that the emotional, political or intellectual concerns which Breton writes about would be, for the psychoanalyst, only the pretexts of unconscious desire. Should there be any surprise that Breton's analysis remains silent, or very reticent, with respect to the nature of this desire, the supplier of instinctual energy, without which there would be no dreaming? Probably not. But it is more surprising to see Breton limit the origin of dreaming to what is only, in fact, the prolongation, in sleep, of a part of a wakeful thought and write at the end of this interpretation: "I insist very strongly on the fact that it *exhausts*, according to me, the content of the dream."

The second difference between Breton and Freud concerns the daydream and seems to be a counterpart of the first. If, in the first case, the night-dream is markedly simplified, in the second the notion of daydreaming undergoes a notable extension. Of course, it was Freud himself who discovered the resemblances which link the dream and the series of "fantasies, castles in Spain or daydreams": the common element is the fantasy, an imaginary scenario, always centered upon a wish, possessing a single structure, but open to diverse manifestations. (See *Der Dichter und das Phantasieren* [1908].)

Now the fantasy is not even evoked by Breton. In the case of the night-dream, he shows no further interest in it, as we can see in his analysis of Maury's "dream of the guillotine." Freud's explanation of this dream, based on the presence of a fantasy of ambition, remains unknown to him. In the case of the relationship of the night-dream to the daydream, neither is it a question of this structural identity, which is nevertheless essential, but of an analogy between manifestations: "The manifest content of this daydream, lasting for several days, was at first glance hardly more explicit than that of a night-dream." Here Breton is dealing with a daydream that is largely conscious. Once again he is less concerned with the nature of the unconscious wish, the driving force of daydreaming or dreaming, than with the way in which it transforms certain representations of external reality.

A common reason underlies these differences: Breton refuses to consider, except in his criticisms, Freud's fundamental hypothesis concerning the existence of unconscious psychic processes. But if it is true that "dreams are always wish-fulfillments [because] they are products of the system *Unconscious* whose activity knows no other aim than the fulfillment of wishes and which has at its command no other forces than wishful impulses" (*The Interpretation of Dreams*), it becomes difficult to combat the idea of the unconscious, or to manage without it, and to insist on maintaining at the same time, as Breton does, the relationship of dreaming and wishing. Then there is the well-known notion of *The Interpretation of Dreams* according to which the wish that is fulfilled by the dream, under the cover of latent thoughts, is a sexual wish dating from childhood; the representions which are connected to it have been attracted by other wishes and, like them, held at a distance from the preconscious by an anti-cathexis of psychic energy, a "repression." Like the word fantasy, the term repression, in its theoretical sense, has no place in Breton; it is another cornerstone of psychoanalysis which has been discarded.

Breton constructs an idea of the theory of sexuality which is paradoxical. For on the one hand, he reproaches Freud for his pusillanimity: never, in the *Traumdeutung,* did Freud dare to take up directly his own sex life. On the other hand, Breton holds ideas that are common to the detractors of Freudian "pansexualism." For example, he criticizes Freud for basing his conclusions on the analysis of hysterics: either Freud made them say what he wanted, or, as Babinski, another of Breton's masters, taught, he allowed himself to be taken in by the states that they simulated or the revelations that they pretended to make. Without going so far as to wonder whether the very choice of self-analysis is not dictated by a considerable distrust in regard to psychoanalysts and their "virtuoso tricks," which are mentioned in *Nadja,* it is necessary to observe that Breton grants but very little importance to the repressed elements this his own analysis could bring out. His dreams, he says, "very plausibly derives in part" from a childhood scene, but the recall of this scene "offers only a secondary interest here." And he says this although he wishes to be, better than Freud, "an imprudent and spotless observer."

By putting aside the theory of the unconscious and the process of repression, and by pursuing the consequences, Breton succeeds in supporting more solidly his theory of the "communicating vases." In Freud, it is the presence of repressed and unconscious desire, acting from a distance upon preconscious representations, which allows us to explain the form of visual hallucination that the dream most often takes. Breton retains without explaining it the fact that the dream very often puts thoughts into images. Likewise, he takes the processes of condensation and displacement from Freud without linking them to the "primary" process. For Freud again, the state of sleep is primordial: by weakening certain anti-cathexes which would limit the "return of the repressed," sleep allows wish-fulfillment to occur. For Breton, this condition is not indispensable: "The fundamental difference which depends on the fact that here I am lying down asleep and that there I am really moving about in Paris does not succeed in inducing for me, on the one hand and on the other, representations which are really distinct."

Finally, sleep provisionally suspends the ability of every normal man to differentiate between material reality and a hallucination. The perception of an external reality is one that an action can cause to disappear; in sleep, which shuts the door leading to motility, man is incapable of action and his wish-fantasies assume the value of an undisputed reality. In Breton, the facts are presented in a way that is both more simple and more paradoxical. On the one hand, there is no difference between dreamed representations and real perceptions. In a dream it is possible to give the same status to the image of a composite person and the abstract idea of woman which develops out of ongoing encounters, in the wakeful state, with real women. On the other hand, neither in the night-dream nor in daydreaming is reality-testing entirely suspended: at every moment the external world is incapable of reaffirming its rights.

In reviewing the divergences that we have just observed, we notice that Freud and Breton situate the problem of dreaming on different ground. The discovery of unconscious processes allows Freud to leave aside the debate concerning dream and reality. The dream no longer has as much to do with external reality as with a series of particular psychic formations (compromises, substitutes, reaction formations) which are re-discovered in diverse degrees in the "slips" of everyday life or the symptoms of neuroses or psychoses and which are produced, according to specific modes which allow them to be classified, from the raw material of unconscious wishes and fantasies. In each of these formations and in their various combinations, there is a notable variation of the relation of "psychic reality" to "material reality." They can merge, be opposites, or substitute for one another. For his part, Breton undertakes to overthrow a philosophic and literary tradition which treats dreaming and the wakeful state as a pair of opposites, indeed antagonists. In place of this struggle, which is resolved sometimes to the benefit of dreaming and sometimes to the benefit of wakefulness (according to the prevalent doctrines), surrealism wants to substitute "universal reciprocal action." This means that if it changes the relationship, it needs to conserve the two terms: dream and reality, dreaming and the wakeful state; and in order to establish continuity between them, Breton must indeed neglect the distinctions which psychoanalysis introduces between the unconscious and the preconscious, on the one hand, and between dream-work and wakeful thought on the other. He must also give the same status, as the second part of the book demonstrates, to the night-dreams, demented ideas, confusions, misunderstandings and superstitious ideas. Not only are their mechanisms analogous to those of the dream, but their effects are entirely identical to those that the dream produces.

Yet dreaming cannot reveal the "real functioning of thought," discussed in the 1924 *Manifesto*, unless, as we have seen, it loses some of the characteristics that derive from sleep: suspension of reality-testing and "regression." Now in Freud these particularities of dreaming lead to this famous hypothesis: *"The scene of action of dreams is different from that of waking ideational life. This is the only hypothesis that makes the special peculiarities of dream-life intelligible"* (*The Interpretation of Dreams*). But no supposition could be more vigorously fought by Breton. If the dream serves as a model for imaginary productions such as poetry or play, it cannot be detached from the one and only sphere. i.e., from the world in which man lives, loves, and struggles. The imaginary and the real are one and the same thing. Or at least this should be the case. From the beginning of *Les Vases communicants*, Breton, echoing the 1924 texts, insists on "the increasingly necessary conversion . . . of imagined experience into lived experience, or more precisely into experience that should live [*devoir-vivre*], and on the necessity of showing the continuity between dream and reality, "a door already ajar beyond which there is but a single step to make, upon leaving the wobbly house of the poets, in order to stand securely in life." Thus any attempt to locate dreaming on another scene of action, as in Fechner or Freud, can only be, for Breton, the product of a terrible "misunderstanding."

Thus it is less Marxist criticism than the intuitions and basic requirements of surrealism—the desire to promote the "triumph of a monism which is both magical and materialist, in which energy of desire can be mobilized in every sense," as Starobinski writes ("Freud, Breton, Meyers")—which forced Breton to refuse, in 1932, to distinguish between the unconscious wish and latent thoughts, wish-fulfillment and the search for the last woman, Freud's analysis and the experiments of Hervey, the "other scene" and the real world. For Freud, "dreams do not differentiate between what is wished and what is real." Breton transforms the phrase: it is the wish which does not differentiate between dream and reality.

If Freud's theoretical conclusions are vitiated by idealism, the method for interpreting dreams continues, according to Breton, to merit interest: "it is not at all necessary, in order to recognize its value, to adopt for oneself the hasty generalizations to which the author, a fairly crude mind when it comes to philosophy has subsequently habituated us." We shall now examine, on just a few points, the revival of this method.

First of all, Breton's self-analysis is not lacking in references to the author's sex life. But these are always introduced in terms of symbolism, i.e., through the process of visual figuration which plays upon an almost constant relationship between certain manifest representations and a very small number of latent elements. For example, in Breton's text, the table, the tie, the money machines, the bridge or the giraffe's neck refer to the sexual act or organs. Of course the use of this type of "code," when it replaces, as it does here, the method of free associations, generally causes the analysis to deviate toward a mechnical translation, and we can suppose that, if Breton takes recourse to it, it is precisely because of the resistance that is met by the representations of repressed desires that his analysis should uncover.

However, another point seems crucial to Breton. Freud himself admits that symbolic figuration is neither an exclusive property of dreams nor a discovery of psychoanalysis. "This symbolism is not peculiar to dreams, but is characteristic of unconscious ideation, in particuar among the people, and it is to be found in folklore, and in popular myths, legends, linguistic idioms, proverbial wisdom and current jokes, to a more complete extent than in dreams." Consequently, if all the sexual representations which compose a dream are reduced to the code of symbolic figuration, and if the use of this code in numerous and varied cultural or artistic formations is clearly understood, then the explanation of the dream on the basis of the fulfillment of unconscious and repressed wishes becomes a matter of secondary importance. Psychoanalysis is less a scientific discovery than the pursuit of a literary and philosophic tradition which accords its full value to the faculty of imagination. This suggests an explanation of Breton's accusation that, "on the subject of the symbolic interpretation of dreams," Freud plagiarized the philosopher Volkelt. On this point, Freud answered Breton quite sharply. In Jean Starobinski's judgement this argument is absurd. This is doubtless true for Freud, who is not responsible for the omission of Volkelt's name in the bibliography of his book. Volkelt himself is not in question since he simply organized the intuitions of another author to whom Freud had paid homage in public several times, K.A. Scherner. But is it absurd for Breton? It is the only by the résumé that Freud provides at the beginning of *The Interpretation of Dreams* that he knows the ideas of Scherner and Volkelt. The author matters little in any case, the ideas are apt to win Breton over:

> The mental activity which may be described as "imagination," liberated from the domination of reason and from any moderating control, leaps into a position of unlimited sovereignty. Though dream-imagination makes use of recent waking memories for its building material, it erects them into structures bearing not the remotest resemblance to those of waking life; it reveals itself in dreams as possessing not merely reproductive but *productive* powers. . . . Being freed from the hindrances of the categories of thought, it gains in pliancy, agility and versatility. . . . It is obliged to paint what it has to say pictorially and prefers some extraneous image which will express only that particular one of the object's attributes which it is seeking to represent. Here we have the "symbolizing activity' of the imagination.
>
> (*The Interpretation of Dreams*)

This praise of a creative imagination, freed from the control of reason and avid in its use of metaphor, is quite close to surrealist inspiration in its beginnings. And were we to re-establish the true lineage which, according to Breton, Freud would wish to hide, we would put the poets first, then Scherner, whose merit was to distinguish "the sexual character" of the imagination "sensed long ago by the poets," and finally Freud, "the idea of constructing a system . . . which would give birth to psychoanalysis" having been voiced before him. It would seem that, by putting the discoveries of psychoanalysis and its own experiments on common ground, surrealism quickly secures its claims to scientific legitimacy.

Whereas in Freud the representations which compose the "reserve" of the human imagination are at first wish-fantasies, Breton considers sexuality to be only one of the provinces, so to speak, of the imagination. And as the imagination itself is life's capacity to translate itself into images, the representations linked to repressed desires make up only a part of the material issuing from the vital drives as a whole. Aside from sexual desires, this category of ideas includes the force of feelings, the necessities of knowledge, the demands of practical action—a conception much closer to the notion of "infinity" which allows Hegel to relate the problem of knowledge to that of life, than to the notion of desire in Freud. Far from connecting, in a complex way, latent and transient thoughts of unequal importance to an unconscious and indestructible desire, the dream relates, in Breton, thoughts which are equal in force and in dignity. No wish can be fulfilled without the active assistance of the others and without a perpetual "recreation." However, this fulfillment has no value unless practical life provides a sanction for it. Thus the choice that imagination makes among the thoughts of conscious life and the visual figuration that it gives to these elements not only have a meaning, but also an end. The imagination chooses what is essential and enacts it so as to obtain a tripartite result: a "reparation," because the dream compensates for the loss of substance caused by real life; an understanding, since it shows the close connection of feeling, knowledge and involvement, a connection that daily life usually conceals; an incitement to action, because, showing how the contradictions are bound together, it reveals to the dreamer the way to resolve them. In Breton's eyes, the hypotheses which see in dreaming a hallucinatory satisfaction, made possible by a regression to repressed perceptions (an entirely asocial satisfaction which is even, most of the time, incomprehensible for the dreamer), can only show Freud's own "almost complete lack of a dialectical conception." Breton is less interested in the meaning and elaboration of dreams than in their utility and function. He studies the dream less than he points to its value. And on this point he shows many more affinities with Jung than with Freud.

Thus the imagination carries into the dream what is essential in the representations of conscious life, but it arranges these representations so as to obtain an effect of understanding. The dream-work can then no longer consist simply in a transformation of the latent content. When it, too, is "dialectized," it becomes unlike what it is in Freud, capable of thinking and creating. For instead of displacing the object of desire or inventing substitutes for it, the principal processes of dream-work strive to bring out the essential, what lies beyond immediate appearances: "this persistent will of the dream continuing in other respects, of course, to convince me of the necessity of freeing myself of scruples in order to live." Moreover, Breton does not limit himself to interpreting dream-work; he changes certain of its processes when they chance not to fit in with the rhetoric of persuasion that constitutes for him the dream. Thus he rejects the rule according to which "the dream-work produces absurd dreams and dreams containing individual absurd elements if it is faced with the necessity of representing any criticism, ridicule or derision which may be present in the dream-thoughts" (*The Interpretation of Dreams*). Certain latent jokes at the expense of various persons are found unaltered in the manifest contact of his first dream. Elsewhere, he turns a conclusion of Stekel, adopted by Freud, into its inverse: if a fragment of a dream is perceived as such by the dreamer, it is "equivalent to wishing that the thing described as a dream had never happened" (*The Interpretation of Dreams*). For Breton, it is the wish that the event, conceived as possible, had really occurred, "a real *dialectization* of the thinking of the dream which, in a hurry to reach its ends, is free to break down the last logical frameworks."

Silberer, one of Freud's disciples, had noted that at the boundary of sleep thought is often transformed into images which represent its own functioning. This "auto-symbolic" phenomenon, which would be fairly well developed in dreams containing intellectual activities or emotional processes, is accepted by Freud on the condition that it should not reinforce the tendency toward abstract symbolic interpretation. Without quoting Silberer, Breton notes that his dream of August 1931, which aims at pushing him toward making a decision, is marked by the regular reappearance of the image of a bridge, which is itself symbolic of the passage and of the choice. This detail is characteristic, on the one hand of the anagogical tendency of his interpretation, and on the other hand of the permanence of an intuition developed in the *Manifesto:* certain activities allow us to intercept pure thought, expressing at once both something other than itself and its own operation. Therefore one can wonder to what extent the transformations that Breton imposed upon dream-work, as Freud conceived of it, result in making this work the equivalent of literary activity: staging, representation, probationary speech, a self-reflexiveness, the dream is all that simultaneously. Is it simply a matter of chance that Breton substitutes for the expression "dream-work" another formula, "the poetry of the dream"? Does not desire, which deliberately ignores the limits of dream and reality, neglect just as much those of lived experience and literary fiction?

In this respect, no technique of the "poetry of dreaming" holds greater interest than that of condensation. Initially it consists in a salutary simplification: Intervening when the representations borrowed from reality are too numerous, it skims off only the essential. Then it puts this essential into play, "bearing witness to the need inherent in dreaming to *magnify* and *dramatize,* in other words to present in an extremely interesting and striking theatrical form, what is conceived and developed rather slowly in reality, which no inordinate shocks, so that organic life can carry on." Let us recall that, for Breton, there is no "other scene of action." The life of a man in time can simply be apprehended at very different levels: that of organic life, that of the "empty moments" of habit, of "the most telling episodes" (*Nadja*), finally that of the essential moments which structure a whole life and of which condensation, in dreaming or daydreaming, gives the clearest image. The most dramatic one, too, for this theatrical staging is also a vital entry into action. To use a word that Breton cherished, the "sanction" of this staging can be, from case to case, the renunciation of hope, suicide, madness, or to the contrary, the renewal of hope and of the taste for life and action.

In *Les Vases communicants*, condensation sets in motion a debate to which Breton's whole life is tied: is it possible to pass from loving one woman to loving another? Can love be repeated? The question appears to be simple, but we quickly run into a seeming paradox: at this most condensed level of a poet's life, where the movement from a lost love to a new possibility of loving is repeated (rehearsed), repetition is an extremely complicated phenomenon. In the second part of the book, Breton seems to foresee the objection of some readers:

> So there is a narrative which changes suddenly! A character is no sooner presented than he is abandoned for another—and who knows if it is even for another? So from here on, what good is the effort expended on exposition? But the author, who seemed to have undertaken to reveal to us some part of his life, speaks as if he were in a dream!—*As in a dream.*

What is underscored here, aside from the indecision concerning the real or dream-like character of the events which are related, is the essentially repetitive shape of these events: Breton's encounters possess enough traits in common to give the impression that they reiterate, except for a few variants, the same sequence. On the other hand, some transitions are always going on in the narration: the characters are substituted for one another, the narrative loses sight of its initial goal. Moreover, Breton's reader also finds these traits, concentrated or scattered, in *Nadja* and *L'Amour fou*, the two prose texts which provide the framework for *Les Vases communicants*. Also appearing in these texts is the character X, the woman who is loved and lost, who is never presented directly to the reader despite the important role that she plays.

An "emotional, sexual automatism" forces man, after breaking off a love relationship, to begin loving another woman. But the repetition of love hardly follows a simple pattern. Not one of the women evoked here makes a lasting appearance. Thus the role in which, one after another, they replace each other is ambiguous: they are no longer the lost woman, they are not yet the rediscovered woman. In addition, each appearance of the new woman brings with it the memory of people whom Breton had known before, or of beings created by artists. The girl with the kherkins and the girl in the Batifol care are inseparable from Gustave Moreau's Delila and Sade's Justine. And with these memories, all sorts of questions come back and crowd together in the poet's consiousness. Sometimes, due to the incomprehensible ordering of events, the necessity of this return even seemed to be recorded in texts which Breton had written in an earlier period of his life: the encounter with the girl named "Parisette" echoes some lines written in 1922. With the return in dreams of the image of Nadja, both a real person and a character in the novel, the relation of the past to the present and even the future is situated at the heart of repetition. Nadja emerges from a past whose threat must be averted; however, she is also, for the future, the image of an ideal which surrealism must strive to attain. Finally, all the elements which come back are, in the image of X and Nadja, beings in flight: "the books—just, so it seems, as the woman—tended to substitute for another."

If the books can be substituted for one another, *Les Vases communicants* should not escape from the rule. The epigraph of the first two parts, as well as quotations, indeed literary borrowings, and rather frequent allusions tell us what particular texts are revived and "condensed": Nerval's *Aurélia* and Jensen's *Gradiva*. The two principal references attest that Breton's personal situation in 1931 can recall the distress of the narrator of *Aurélia*, that his "wakeful dream" can reproduce in some respects the frustrations of Jensen's hero: likewise, they point clearly, after the very serious crisis, to the possibility of a favorable outcome in the long run. The essential point is that, at a certain distance from these two works, *Les Vases communicants* replays the question which is peculiar to their characters, i.e., the question of repetition, as Gilles Deleuze observes in the admirable pages which he devotes to the problem of time: "Nerval's *Sylvie* already brought us into this theater and *Gradiva*, so nearly Nervalian in inspiration, shows us a hero who simultaneously experiences repetition as such and what is repeated as always disguised in repetition" (*Différence et Répétition*). *Aurélia* and *Gradiva* also present the repetition of a fairly small number of fundamental sequences in which the love and life of the principal character are at stake. The variety of psychic registers—dream, reality, madness, or momentary delirium—which makes these texts extraordinary (and has been largely responsible for their celebrity) allows for the reconsideration of the same destiny on different levels, far removed from each other in appearance. In Jensen, real life and the *idée fixe* seem to be at opposite poles from each other. In Nerval, recourse to the split personality and metempsychosis allows one life to assume and re-orient others at its own level; moreover, for the same man, dreaming is viewed as a "second life." The relation to the individual past and to every poetic, philosophic or religious tradition is affirmed in Nerval, as in Jensen the relation to the historical and mythic past. But the bonds of love and the past are such that memory, in these two texts, is "no less inventive than memorative" (*Différence et répétition*). The narrator of *Aurélia* and Norbert Harrold alike are able to relive a past which they have not lived: for the former, the past of his ancestors, but also all the history of the earth, of races and religions; for the latter, the life and destruction of Pompeii, even though nearly two thousand years separate him from it. And in each case, the simple memory and reminiscence are ordered around the lover's pursuit of a woman who is never identical to herself. For Zoé Bertgang is and is not this Gradiva whom Harrold seeks and whom he treats "both as a stranger and at the same time as known, as already experienced" (Wilhelm Jensen, *Gradiva*). Similarly, Aurélia, beneath "the furtive marks of her diverse incarnations," takes on the identity of the beloved woman and the mother whom Nerval knew, but she is also the one whom he was never able to know, the goddess who guides the evolution of humans "in the mystic splendors of the Asian sky" and the mother of the Christian God: "I am the same as Mary, the same as your mother, the same one whom in every form you have always loved. In each of your trials, I have taken off one of the masks with which I veil my traits, and soon you will see me as I am."

In these texts as in the text of André Breton, dreaming has a central function. It is the dream which seems to act out most clearly the relationship of all human life to a founding repetition, disguised and elusive, which is itself founded on the bond of love to memory. The bond does not appear in Breton, as in Nerval or Proust, in the form of reminiscence, of access to the pure past. However, it comes into view in the case of certain texts which seem, retrospectively, to have prefigured life when they were written. As we have already noted, if we do not wish to record simple coincidence, we have to interpret the encounter with "Parisette" in 1931 as an echo or confirmation of the allusion to Parisette nine years before, or else interpret the earlier allusion as an announcement of the subsequent encounter. Ultimately, we can no longer tell which is the first term. In 1936, after the analysis of a much more convincing example, Breton will write:

> I insisted, especially in *Les Vases communicants*, on the fact that self-analysis is, by itself in many cases, able to exhaust the content of dreams. . . . On the other hand, I may have side-stepped too quickly when it was, for me, a question of showing that, similarly, self-analysis could sometimes exhaust the content of real events, to the point of making them entirely dependent on the least directed previous activity of the mind.
>
> (*L'Amour fou*)

In other words, if the dreams do depend on life, the latter can, in certain cases, depend on the texts. What the dream repeats and plays out—the life of a man at its essential level—can also be played out and repeated by the text. If it is not the text of the poet himself, as in *L'Amour fou*, it can very well be texts written by others. They will then have the value of a model. The recourse to Nerval and Jensen shows that in *Les Vases communicants* Breton knows that fiction or poetry are the instruments most apt to set man on the path of his wish.

The wish, working in the dream, refers back to the text, by an identity of techniques, and to the repetition of the texts. But the text refers to the wish, to its repetition, and to its always deferred and disguised fulfillment. The name of this wish can be Aurélia, Gradiva or X. It can also be Tournesol. Despite the name, it would be wrong to liken the object of this wish too quickly to a real person or to a real object, which it would be necessary to rediscover or replace. Surrealism, says Breton, has always disdained the prey and the shadow "in favor of what is already no longer the shadow and not yet the prey: the shadow and the prey combined in a single flash" (*L'Amour fou*). What is essential in this movement is not to be found in the passage from wish to fulfillment, nor in the relation, deceptive or advantageous, to an object. It is in the incessant, masked sliding which animates the movement from one series of real events to another: a dream, an encounter, a text. Reality, daydreaming, and poetry are the way-stations of desire (wish). It is perhaps in contemporary psychoanalysis, which shows man subjected to desire and desire itself imposed upon the subject by the existence and demands of discourse, that we should seek the explanation of this affinity, observed by Breton, between the movement of desire—for example, in dreams—and poetic writing: "Once again, nothing could be more necessary, in this respect, than making a thorough study of the process of forming images in dreams, making use of what can be known in addition about its poetic elaboration."

To the questions that Breton asks about dreaming and desire in *Les Vases communicants*, Freud's work could only offer partial answers. In skimming through *The Interpretation of Dreams*, Breton retraces an earlier route: and his paths are neither those of the scientists nor of the poet, rather those of a certain practice of poetry or fiction.

Appearing half a century ago in the Parisian literary avant-garde, psychoanalysis probably inflicted there as elsewhere a deep "narcissistic wound" upon those who welcomed it. In a society in which literature was, by tradition, the instrument of a representation of the world or an expression of individuals or groups, Freud taught that the act of writing works in conjunction with unconscious desire. The way in which literature puts desire into play, if only in relation to speech (but the exercise of speech was not then so clearly distinguished from the work of writing as it is today), is less important here than this observation: taking a familiar activity, close to its producer and usually close to the reading public as well, psychoanalysis treated it as an "uncanny" (Freud: *unheimlich*) practice. A social figure, recognized or despised, the writer saw the emergence of his double: a being of desire. The individual and collective complicities which went into the literary game turned into a disquietude which has, for the most part, continued unabated.

André Breton is doubtless one of those who wished to maintain this strangeness which the discovery of its relationship to desire conferred upon poetry. Moreover, it is plausible that his experience of strangeness, felt in automatic diction or in the confrontation of the powers of others, Desnos or Nadja, led him to draw closer to Freud. In the face of the enemies of psychoanalysis or its overly hasty inveiglers, he thus maintains that strangeness for a time, without carrying too far his questioning in regard to its source, which are recognized today in the forms of the body, pleasure, and death. He inserts it in an order and, soon, in a tradition. As early as March 1922 the first dream narratives are accompanied, in *Littérature*, by the account of a series of encounters; here already are the outlines of *Les Vases communicants*. The strangeness of writing is thus linked to, and justified by, the order of lived strangeness, of the fantastic aspects of everyday life (premonitions, coincidences, lucky finds, encounters, returns of places, names, or identical numbers), but also justified by the strangeness of fiction (itself, according to Freud, often more rich and intense than the strangeness of experience and serving as its model, surety, and protective restraint). It is within a certain literary tradition of the Strange that Breton will not stop, at least until the war, looking for predecessors of surrealism: after Nerval, he finds Jensen, and soon Achim von Arnim. In this, moreover, he was faithful to the *Manifesto* of 1924: "What is admirable about the fantastic is that there is no longer anything fantastic, there is only the real." Today psychoanalysis would see in this sentence a pre-eminent example of delusion, the real to which Breton refers being one of the unconscious masks of that inadmissible reality with which psychoanalysis is concerned.

It is through the renewal of writing within an order and a tradition of strangeness that Breton preserves for poetry its status as an autonomous and exemplary activity. Thus he can treat dreaming in turn as the model of the text and the copy of poetic reconciliation. Communicating vases, but still more, perhaps, a circle from which it is hard to escape. As he writes: "we are dealing with a *poetic* object, which does or does not have value on the level of *poetic* images, and with nothing else. The whole question comes down to knowing what this level is."

Doors: Simone Weil with Kafka

A. Smock

Simone Weil appears to have started out on the left and ended up on the right. "La femme enseignante révolutionnaire qui, en 1931, portait le drapeau rouge en tête des manifestations des chômeurs du Puy, la collaboratrice de "L'Ecole émancipée" et de la "Révolution prolétarienne," en vient à exposer, onze ans plus tard, dans ses "Ecrits de Londres," la conception d'un Etat dont le chef serait nommé à vie, où le droit de grève serait limité, la laïcité supprimée, les partis politiques interdits et où les infractions à la censure pourraient conduire le délinquant au bagne," writes Colette Aubry in her preface to Philippe Dujardin's *Simone Weil, idéologie et politique*. Much could certainly be said to explain this apparent reversal. On the one hand it could be argued that even her early positions are fundamentally reactionary (this is Dujardin's thesis). On the other hand, there are obvious and profound differences between her last writings and the Vichy ideology which they often seem to echo. The present essay, however, does not pretend to evaluate Simone Weil's political itinerary; it is a somewhat fanciful consideration of what it means to take sides. Hence the importance of the door as a figure. Often it seems to split two sides by forming a peculiar equation: each could be the other, or rather each is the other instead. Perhaps certain barricades are erected by a premature confusion as to which side is which. Error, in fact, is a particularly important motif in Simone Weil's thought. As is love, that saves the world. So alongside the difference/identity maintained by the door, I want to put another paradox: what is undifferentiated, and therefore very different—for example, the Virgin, blessed among women.

The world is a barrier, Simone Weil writes. We ask that this door be opened, that we might walk in the orchards and drink the cool water where

From *MLN* 95, no. 4 (May 1980). © 1980 by The John Hopkins University Press.

the moon leaves its trace. Here, in the desert, we thirst and in this emptiness find no rest. We wait and ask, and knock and beat upon the barrier so long that finally desire is exhausted and we turn away. Then the door opens, revealing no orchards, but this selfsame desert, just as it is and has always been, in the pure light of *no other side* which fills the heart, with emptiness. Transfiguration: absolutely nothing changed.

> La porte est devant nous; que nous sert-il de vouloir?
> Il vaut mieux s'en aller abandonnant l'espérance.
> Nous n'entrerons jamais. Nous sommes las de la voir.
> La porte en s'ouvrant laissa passer tant de silence
>
> Que ni les vergers ne sont parus ni nulle fleur;
> Seul l'espace immense où sont le vide at la lumière
> Fut soudain présent de part en part, combla le coeur,
> Et lava les yeux presque aveugles sous la poussière
> *La Porte (Poèmes, suivis de Venise sauvée)*

"Dieu ne change rien à rien" (*La Pesanteur at la grâce*). The world is full of noises, Simone Weil writes, which signify nothing. Desperate for a voice that really speaks, men cry out to God and this cry tears them apart. "Il ne dit rien" (*La Pesanteur at la grace*). That makes all the difference. The kingdom of heaven opens as the door falls shut forever; there is without the slightest doubt a far side, because it is the near, incontrovertible.

"Le monde en tant que tout à fait vide de Dieu est Dieu lui-même" (*La Pesanteur*). Creation, this world, this miracle, is not the glory of God, divine omnipotence manifest. What clear eyes see here—eyes, that is, that just give up, turn away and close—is not more but less, miraculously less than there might have been by a miracle: a sun left to shine and rain left to fall on the righteous and the wicked alike, tides left to ebb and flow, waves left to curl and crash over broken ships, left to their unhesitating, shapely movement by a weak and bleeding God who leaves himself to die under the sun, under the sun which that very day causes crowns and scepters to glitter beautifully just as on the day before. Likewise, the world transfigured by grace is the world minus this very marvel. For Simone Weil, God is his subtraction, the absolute purity of his love its desperate lack. She is adamant in her refusal to receive the consolations of religion. She could not accept baptism, she would not pass through the open door of the Church. She had, she said, to stick to this side, the outside. "Je sens qu'il m'est nécessaire, qu'il m'est préscrit de me trouver seule, étrangère et en exil" (*Attente de Dieu*). She would not put out a hand for her salvation, not even, she insisted, if it lay before her on the table. She knew she had to wait: to wait till, in spite of her, necessity moved her hand, till, that is, the force of time, as it would anyway, froze it. Just as the existence of evil could be explained as a benefaction—as the one thing which cannot be desired, upon which love cannot sustain itself but must at length be bro-ken—so our bit of life, our semblance of importance is sometimes explained by Simone Weil as that which is granted so that something can fail, can simply fall short. So that far from anyone's dying of love or dying for love, love just dies. Leaving not a trace. Then it is perfect, then it is divine.

But if failure is perfection, how can one fail—or should we say, how can one not: not fail to fail? How can the pure mark of not a single trace not leave a blank? If perfection were failure, how, on the other hand, could it be perfect—or should we say, how could it not: not be perfect failure, simply failure, failure itself, a stain?

In Simone Weil's tragedy, *Venise sauvée*, the sun that rises every day, perfectly indifferent to the city's fortunes, bathes with its lovely light a city which has come through the night miraculously unscathed. In the bright morning Venice awakens exactly as it does every morning: not only unmoved by grief but untouched by gratitude. Unenlightened. The miracle does not make the slightest difference. The city is perfectly innocent—of its salvation, which just leaves it alone, all its polished hardness intact, its worldly splendor immaculate. Its proud people do not know how utterly defenseless is their indefensible love for a cruel and inviolate city. They do not perceive beauty in the desperate fragility of the stone facades which all the day before, while festival garlands were being prepared, stood completely exposed to the brutality of men, men made desperate by this haughty elegance. They are unaware that the beauty of the sunlight is the beauty that shines on ashes, and that indeed it is shining upon the corpses of the defeated, their miserable enemies, whom they do not recognize. They do not know that Venice's festival day is another perfect day on which the surest successes prove dreadful failures and the strongest men die, the just are condemned. They do not know that their happiness intact is—just like the despair of their enemies abandoned by God—godlessness which the touch of grace leaves untouched, pure. Violetta, the flower of Venice, who was surely to have been pitilessly trampled by the unhappy men whom she and her beloved city have never pitied, turns her unsuspecting face to the sun, like a tender shoot turning all unthinking to the light, or a jaded woman turning thoughtlessly from a beggar. In the dark while she slept her father has liquidated his enemies and exterminated the city's savior as well. She lifts with unguarded simplicity her perfectly innocent voice and, guarded by the red and glistening swords of her father's sagacious men, praises the clear light of day upon the sea.

> Sur la mer s'étend lentement la clarté.
> La fête bientôt va combler nos désirs.
> La mer calme attend. Qu'ils sont beaux sur la mer,
>   Les rayons du jour!
>   (*Poèmes, suivis de Venise sauvée*)

The light: nothing changed. Not a sign. Salvation spares the world grace. Thus creation is more pure than possible and, left for sheer love to error, more innocent than anything can be.

Mercenaries—oppressed and unhappy Venetians in the service of

Spain—plot to pillage the city by night. Having conquered Venice they will take over the world. They speak of the grand dream they will impose upon Creation, and of the nightmare into which their oppressors will awaken. Their plot is foolproof. The magnificent city, exulting in its beauty, assuredly preparing its festival day, lies in fact at their feet. In the eyes of one of them, however, there is pity. Jaffier, this weak spot, this gap in the clouds of dreams, must die, otherwise the plot might be betrayed. But Pierre, chief of the adventurers, forbids the murder and, to prove that compassion is not a flaw but a strength, hands over all his authority to Jaffier. No triumph could afford Pierre more joy than the brilliant success of his dearest friend. Out of pity for the vulnerable beauty of Venice, and for love of Violetta's frail innocence, Jaffier discloses the plot to Venice's Council of Ten in exchange for the safety of twenty of his men, including Pierre. The Ten send these twenty to the torture chamber. Paying the traitor in gold, they banish him from the city. No longer having any life to lose, Jaffier departs for his death, the sun rises on the calm sea and Violetta sings.

Each scene, each expression of love is, one might say, divine. And divinity does not lie behind the X that marks it out, shining through nevertheless; on the contrary, it is the cross. That which consistently bars purity from the play, the human weakness which is allowed, undiluted, to dilute every word and every action, endows everything with a supernatural beauty. The absence of grace, the impossibility of the good—the weight, so to speak, that inevitably causes each gesture to falter, the gravity which never stops pulling and guarantees that nothing soar beyond a certain limit—transfigures every scene. Violetta fondly praises, in the beginning, the little she knows how to love: her proud, secure, magnificent home. And thus one hears an ironic echo: words of love for everything she cannot love, for the inexpressible beauty of all that cannot endure. Her hymn of praise, at the end, to the clear light on her cruel and monumental city's festival day likewise honors the dead who never will be mourned, to whom no monument will ever be erected, whom no one knows how to love. And Pierre, who does not know whom he loves more than himself, who therfore offers in friendship an ignoble gift—all the treasure, all the women of a pillaged city—offers what he is incapable of surrendering, his very life; Jaffier, who sells this gift for money, dies as none ever can, for love. If Violetta is like the sweetest flower because she is like the coldest stone, Jaffier is like Christ because he is like Judas. And if Venice is saved by love, it is because Jaffier's death is the same as it would have been were it not for love, had Pierre never saved him.

Such perceptions, however, are possible only from some Olympian point of view outside—in front of—the play. There is no such vantage point in Simone Weil's universe. God himself dies, in compromising circumstances, between a pair of thieves, but a little more absurd ("le malheur est ridicule"). As a matter of fact *Venise sauvée* never had an audience. It was never finished, much less performed. Doubtless the incompleted text is touching in part because there is no one at all to understand and embrace the totality, no whole available for omniscience. One is moved by an emotion there isn't, or by its impossibility. The beauty of the play—of the world washed in purity so perfect that it not being there at all is its presence—requires blindness. It requires the unconsciousness of characters in a fragmented text down at the literal level of the torn plot where the sole choice is among witless betrayals. The sense of *Venise sauvée*—that the meaning is the meaning of none whatever—demands failure to understand it. It must be mistaken, otherwise it surely will be. "Le vide est la plénitude suprême, mais l'homme n'a pas le droit de la savoir. Le seul fait d'y songer constitue une violation" (cited by M. Blanchot in "L'Affirmation [le désir, le malheur]," in *L'Entretien infini*). If you know that God's absence is God himself, it is not God at all that you know, and you do not even know this; you are godless like the too-ignorant-to-be-ignorant Violetta, innocent of nothing except her very innocence. Those who, unlike Violetta, *hear* the silence and are touched by the absence of any touch, do not know that God has spoken, has approached and even entered them. They hear, like Jaffier, utter rejection. They feel the blow of an unappealable condemnation. Unless, of course, unable to bear the silence, they set to talking to themselves, filling up the stillness with imaginary noise, crowding from their heart the emptiness which alone can fill it, like the wretched mercenaries who dream of revenge.

Two mistakes: where what is required is a failure of understanding—where the threshold to be crossed is the outer, impassable edge of wisdom (just as the truth to be reached is the point where true love of it wears out and surrenders)—one can *mis*understand, or not even not get it. By pure love that leaves no trace one can remain untouched like Violetta, or be abandoned as an untouchable, like Jaffier. Of these two errors, these two fates, Simone Weil, for her own part, uncompromisingly chooses one. She chooses the near side of the door, the outside just as it is. She keeps among the literal-minded upon whom the meaning(-lessness) is literally lost. Among the unbelievers, for whom that which inasmuch as it makes no difference at all makes all the difference, remains *horrendously* inconsequential. For whom everything is exactly as hopeless as it would have been in any case. "Aucune pensée ne me fait plus de peine que celle de quitter la masse malheureuse des incroyants" (*Attente de Dieu*). Thus she thinks of love that leaves the beloved immaculate strictly as if she had definitely been refused it, lest for lack of this misapprehension she misconstrue it, and it, deprived of its capacity to make all the difference, leave her a spinster—like Violetta, innocent of innocence. "Il entra dans ma chambre," she writes. He came to find her, he led her to an attic room where they stayed together, sharing bread and wine that had the true taste of real bread, of real wine, and one day he told her: "Now go away." "Je n'ai jamais essayé de retrouver cette maison. . . . Ma place n'est pas dans cette mansarde. Elle est n'importe où, dans un de ces salons bourgeois plein de bibelots et de peluche rouge, dans une salle d'attente de gare, n'importe où, mais non dans cette mansarde." (cited by Simone Pétrement in *La Vie de Simone Weil*). The mark of love, of invisible love so pure it leaves no trace—which she considers hers to bear—is the unsightly one which sets apart the utterly indistinguished: "la marque au fer rouge que les Romains mettaient au front de leurs esclaves les plus méprisés" (*Attente de Dieu*).

But what is the difference between Jaffier's misunderstanding, his stigmatizing ignorance, and Violetta's failure not to understand, her innocence which isn't there? What is the difference between the near side of the door, the side of the outcast unworthy of any sign of favor, and the other side, where one is not even barred, where the exclusion is omitted and beatitude, left intact, thus ruled out? What is the difference, in Kafka's story, *Das Schloss* [*The Castle*], between Frieda and Amalia?

If we evoke Kafka, it is because the mark of true love was his concern also—the touch that traces this sign: intact, not a trace, no sign— and the real meaning which only none bears, the perfect sense unique to insignificance. We recall Kafka because for him as well these questions arise: if insignificance alone were meaningful how could there ever be any? How could meaning fail, how could its failure fail too? His tales confirm that love requires a mistake, that salvation demands an error, not to say a crime. And that all depends upon not mistaking this mistake. But also that the error made with no mistake and the error missed are doubles. While no one is ever refused a mistake, no one ever makes his own, each mistakes it (for the other) and each pays the price of *this* mistake, the one all make regardless. Each receives the wages of another's sin. The mark of pure love disfigures virginity which is no one's but the bride's whose perfect marriage is just endless celibacy. And it is this disconsolate woman, still up and waiting through night after night—it is this one, impure at heart, who shall have the branded virgin's peace, while her own sad restlessness shall be the lot of her pure black twin, barred from the night in which she is laid to rest forever.

K. falls in love falling from this fall, He loves Klamm's chosen, the woman distinguished by this Herr, this Lord, as his own: He loves the significance, that is to say, of Frieda's drab, meager, unremarkable presence, the incomparable beauty of *this* side of the door, the privileged sense of this senseless near side, the perfect loveliness of no other side. And thus he fails to notice Frieda. He overlooks this senseless near side (disdains the humble village beneath the Castle); he mistakes his dim and tattered fiancée—the girl who despite her reputation as Klamm's mistress seems still to have no name of any account—for the bright clarity with which she would have shone, for the clear meaning, the prestigious name she would have borne only if he had overlooked her—only had he missed that (in)distinguishing mark and never loved her, which, in fact, he never has, never having so neglected to.

Sortini does—neglect to—love Amalia, Amalia who, unlike Frieda is clearly gorgeous, whose name is the name of the loveliest, the most respected young girl in the village, the maiden to whom, so to speak, everything points. He sends her a vile letter, ordering her to his Castle bedroom as if she were just any girl of no account, somebody or other to sleep with. His missive, we suppose [*we suppose*: for we never get to read the letter; doubtless, like the text of the law in *In der Strafkolonie*, it is legible only by the flesh], addresses her flesh exclusively: the nameless, impersonal dark, void of meaning. The Lord's word greets the reknowned unknown of the maiden's body to inscribe there what all admire and even kneel before as if it were *there* and they could know of it, the absence of any mark, the very innocence. Sortini's letter arrives to know at last what none has ever known: the unknown and pure. To conceive: immaculate. To cross out, with this unknown's this insignificance's meaning, its meaning.

Sortini mistakes Amalia for a whore—to which status, because she does not take the letter and makes no answer (who could receive, who could respond to a message in which *nothing* is conveyed?), she falls.

Amalia has been *correctly* mistaken. K. missed Sortini's mistake when, failing his fall, he fell for Frieda. He missed her namelessness. He mistook her for what she could only have been had he mistaken her otherwise, for a common slut, beneath notice. Granted, K. *made* this latter mistake: Frieda never becomes his bride. He keeps her like a concubine, and never is her loveable significance of any account to him. But he errs thus *because* he errs otherwise, by mistake (which?).

The error, which K. makes by mistake (makes, then, really?)—which consists in not noticing the nameless unremarkableness, not (re)marking (upon) it—is Klamm's with respect to Frieda. Klamm and Frieda, Sortini and Amalia: two errors each of which is always the other by mistake.

Unlike Amalia, Frieda regularly obeyed the summons from the Castle. For if Sortini treated Amalia, Amalia in particular, no one else, like any prostitute, Klamm sent for Frieda by her very own name—which, however, might just as well have been anyone's or no one's. Nobody, in fact, knows whether he associated this name with anyone in particular, whether he remembered Frieda from one occasion to the next or whether he was ever even awake when she came to him. And she herself says of this period, disconsolately, that it was as if it had all happened long ago, to someone else, and she had only heard tell of it, or as if she had already forgotten all about it. While Sortini marks Amalia, Amalia alone, undistinguished—while he stains her with very immaculateness, with this proper name: no name whatever—Klamm leaves Frieda, Frieda like no matter who, pure as the driven snow, blank. The lack of his perfect meaning leaves her, who nameless listens anxiously for the significance she lacks or rather for the significance *of* this lack, at a loss, casting about restlessly. Frieda is talkative, agitated, an inexhaustible source of pious advice, fussy interpretations, tirelessly energetic. Yet her name is Peace. And Amalia, the name of the silent woman, who made no answer when the Lord's word came, who henceforth lie unmoved, venturing nothing, means labor, ceaseless activity.

Of God, Simone Weil says, "nous ne pouvons pas prendre un seul pas vers lui" (*Attente de Dieu*). We must not budge, we are not to take a single step from the position of unbelievers, exiles, outcasts—except the step we take in spite of ourselves by the force that ultimately and inevitably makes us lie still, here on the near side. But Blanchot, among others, remarks uppon her disquietude and her agitated loquaciousness—especially when she warms to her favorite subject, her Lord of whom she speaks so familiarly, saying he is absolutely secret and silent—as if she had committed the error (Frieda's) which, keeping steadfastly to error (Amalia's), she was to avoid. And the brand of slavery, her cross, the marking out of every mark of love: it was this sign, of love, that passed her by. It was for someone else: for her, "un détail presque indifférent." ". . . même au moment où véritablement je n'en peux plus, ces souffrances, je ne les ressens pas comme les miennes, je les ressens en tant que souffrances des ouvriers, et que moi, je les subisse ou non, cela m'apparaît comme un détail presque indifférent" ("Lettre à Boris Souvarine," in *La Condition ouvrière*). This branding pain was, we want to suggest, for someone who made, by eschewing it, the error she missed by cleaving to it. And yet, did it not come to her after all ("J'ai reçu pour toujours la marque de l'esclavage . . . ")—the way the wages of another's failing come to each—did it not come to her who, safe on the other shore, starved in London in '43 for want of Frenchmen's hunger?

"Nous ne pouvons pas prendre un seul pas. . . . " Light streams from the door in *Vor dem Gesetz* [*Before the Law*] as it does in Simone Weil's poem, *La Porte*, bathing the sightless eyes of him just now shut out. Kafka's man from the country had waited, like the seekers in Simone Weil's poem who long for the orchards on the other side, all his life before the door, never ceasing: never ceasing persistentlly not to budge. All that time standing ajar, but attended by a guard who says not yet, you may not enter yet, the door held open for him, for him alone, access to his side, the near side where he dies—where he stops stopping, where Simone Weil's pilgrims turn back, their desire and all their will, all their strength exhausted. With his last breath the man from the country asks: Why has no one else ever sought to enter the law? and the guard replies, "No one elso could enter here, for this door was made only for you. Now I am going to shut it."

To enter one need only die, be left out, take at last the step which is: no step. Stillness. "Je reste aux côtés de toutes les choses qui ne peuvent pas entrer," writes Simone Weil (*Attente de Dieu*). But this near side, this outside—suffused in the pure light of no other side, in the radiance that pours from the closed door in Kafka: it is not the place we are and have been always and would in any event necessarily have found ourselves. It is not a place where any abide (though to be sure there is no place else)— but the place with no entrance except the exit, from which all depart before arriving. It has no access except *no step,* which all the while not taken is not even that step, and which when at last it is taken is one step too many. Or rather, which all the while not taken is too much anxious anticipation and which when at last it is taken is just negligence, too little perseverence. And just as you cannot be left out until you cross over which you cannot do until you are left out, so you cannot be too anxious except by being neglectful. You cannot make one mistake except by making the other. To die is unavoidable and this false step which guarantees: no other side, is the one all take in any case. But no one ever manages not to avoid it—not, in taking the required false step, to overstep it, thus falling fatally short. No one is immortal. This side of the door, Simone Weil's side, where we die, is like the error which is necessarily always missed. This side is the other, the near side the far, only in the sense that one error is always only the other, and all mistakes come to the same.

"Hier fehlt es an Liebe nie." Thus Olga explains to K. that the two women who mistake and are mistaken by love, to all appearances in opposite ways, are identical (*Das Schloss*). Frieda and Amalia, who show K. the error he made by mistake, as well as the opposite error, that mistake— these two women are alike. The two between whom K. vacillates as if he couldn't tell black from white, pure shadow from the blank light of complete clarity—as if he couldn't decide for which he has a weakness, where his failing lies—are no different. Just as each one bears the other's name, each represents the same mistake: the other's. Amalia hears the meaning which could only have rung true to Frieda's particular degree of tone deafness; Frieda hears the insignificance which only hearing tuned to the special falseness of Amalia's could fall for. Neither woman commits her error, neither fails in love. "Hier fehlt es an Liebe nie." Love never fails, the failure always does.

Whenever it appears not to, whenever persistent love seems simply to run out, as though in the way that everything eventually must run down and necessarily comes to an end, this necessary end has had to be elaborately arranged. Merely to explain that a person comes to the end of his life there apparently has to be an inexplicable parable, *Vor dem Gesetz,* surrounded by authoritative but contradictory glosses. Likewise, merely to allow for the inevitable in human affairs a cumbersome and unjustifiable political apparatus must inevitably be constructed. Things just as they are, as they would be necessarily without the marvelous absence of the marvel of love, are the outcome, so to speak, of a critical intervention. All such interpretations, as Joseph K. remarks about *Vor dem Gesetz* when this tale is recounted to him in *Der Prozess* [*The Trial*] (and the priest who tells him the tale concurs), begin necessarily from a false premise. Hence, perhaps, the disagreeable impression provoked by *L'Enracinement.* In this book Simone Weil, champion of the weak and oppressed—and *because,* precisely, of this commitment (because in "true socialism" the weak are first and the triumphant last, while socialism that aims to win is the same as imperial-

Biographical Notes

Antoine-Louis-Claude Destutt de Tracy (1754–1836) was born in Paris and educated at the University of Strasbourg. He served in the army before representing the Bourbon nobility at the Estates General, where he was in favor of reform of the monarchical government. In 1792, at odds with the extremism of the revolutionaries, he joined the group of philosopher-scientists (which included Cabanis, Condorcet, and Volney) and which met at Auteuil in the home of Mme Helvétius. While emprisoned for a year during the Terror, he read Locke and Condillac, who determined his elaboration of what he called *idéologie*, the analysis of ideas into the sensory elements of which they are composed. The group associated with him, the *Idéologues*, became influential from 1795 on in the two new educational institutions of the Ecole Normale and the Institut National, especially the latter's Second Class. In 1801 Destutt de Tracy published the *Observations sur le système d'instruction publique*. Although the *Idéologues* had supported Napoleon's rise to political power in 1799, they soon opposed him, and in 1803 the soon-to-be emperor abolished the Second Class. Napoleon could not tolerate Destutt's view that each man was able to determine the truth or falsity of his ideas without recourse to authority. Destutt's major work, *Eléments d'idéologie*, was written and published in four volumes between 1801 and 1815, during which time he also served as a senator under Napoleon, and entered the Académie française in 1808. Destutt corresponded with Thomas Jefferson, who was the first to translate and publish his *Commentary and Review of Montesquieu's Spirit of Laws* in 1811. Other works by Destutt de Tracy include *Quels sont les moyens de fonder la morale chez un peuple?* (1798), *Grammaire générale* (1803), *Logique* (1805), and *Traité de la volonté et de ses effets* (1805).

Anne-Louise-Germaine Necker, Madame de Staël (1766–1817) was born in Paris, the daughter of Jacques Necker, a Minister of the Republic of Geneva to the court of Louis XVI, whose Minister of Finance he was to become (1778–81). In the salon of her mother she met with such thinkers as d'Alembert, Diderot, and Buffon, and in 1788 she published successfully *Lettres sur les ouvrages et le caractère de J. J. Rousseau*. In 1786, she married Eric de Staël-Holstein, the Swedish ambassador in Paris from whom she was to separate in 1800. She supported the French Revolution, but her salon, the meeting place of liberal aristocrats and politicians as well as artists, soon became suspect by the government. In 1792 and 1793 she traveled to England and Coppet, in Switzerland, while helping to rescue friends from the Terror. In 1794 she met Benjamin Constant with whom she was to have a stormy affair. While in exile, she published *Réflexions sur la paix, Essai sur les fictions* (1795), and *De l'influence des passions sur le bonheur des individus et des nations* (1796). Her *De la littérature considérée dans ses rapports avec les institutions sociales* (1800) argues the superiority of northern cultures over those of the south, that literature is the expression of a nation's ethos, and offers England and Germany as models to be followed. Her opposition to Napoleon led to her banishment from Paris (1803–14). During that time, Coppet became the displaced center of political and artistic activities. She also traveled to Germany, where she met with Goethe, Schiller, A. W. Schlegel, and other writers, and to Italy. In 1810 she published *De l'Allemagne*, which introduced a wide-ranging discussion of German literature and philosophy, although a distorted one. Germaine de Staël also wrote two novels: *Delphine* (1802) and *Corinne ou l'Italie* (1807), which argue the independence of women. Her other works include *Réflexions sur le suicide* (1813), *Considérations sur la Révolution française* (1818), and *Dix années d'exil* (1821).

Henri-Benjamin Constant de Rebecque (1767–1830) was born of French Huguenot ancestry at Lausanne. He was educated privately and at the universities of Oxford, Erlangen, and Edinburgh. At the last of these (1783–85), he was an active member of the Speculative Society where he encountered many of the ideas he was to develop in his subsequent political activities. In 1794, following his first meeting with Germaine de Staël, with whom he had an affair until 1806, he settled in Paris, published his first political pamphlet, *De la force du gouvernement actuel et de la nécessité de s'y rallier* (1796), and helped found the Cercle Constitutionnel. A year after gaining French citizenship, he became a member of the Tribunate where he represented the liberals until his expulsion in 1802. Upon Napoleon's fall in 1814, he resumed his political activities, publishing the anti-Napoleonic *De l'esprit de conquête et de l'usurpation*, *Réflexions sur les constitutions* and *De la liberté des brochures*. However, during the Cent-Jours of Napoleon's return, he became a member of the Council of State, was involved in drafting constitutional amendments, and was accused of political opportunism, which he tried to deny in his *Mémoires sur les Cent-Jours* (1820–22). Under the Restoration, he published *Principes de politique* (1815), which defends individual freedoms; the *Cours de politique constitutionnelle* (1818–20), which established him as a founder of liberalism; and several essays for *Le Mercure de France* and *La Minerve française*. In 1819 he was elected to the Chamber of Deputies where he was an outspoken defender of liberal ideals. He was instrumental in bringing about the constitutional monarchy of 1830 and became president of the Council of State, a post he maintained until his death. He also wrote a psychological and autobiographical novel, *Adolphe* (1816); *Mélanges de littérature et de politique* (1829); and a comparative study of religions in five volumes, *De la religion considérée dans sa source, ses formes et ses développements* (1824–31). His autobiographical writings, *Le Cahier rouge* and *Journaux intimes*, were published posthumously.

François-René, Vicomte de Chateaubriand (1768–1848) was born in Saint-Malo in a family of Breton aristocrats, and raised at the château of Combourg. He entered the army in 1786 and was presented at the court the following year. He watched the beginning of the Revolution before sailing for America in 1791. This voyage provided him with the fictional background and themes of *Atala* (1801), *René* (1802), *Les Natchez* (1827), and a volume of memoirs, *Voyage en Amérique* (1827). Upon his return in 1792, he joined the royalist army of *émigrés* and participated in the Thionville campaign during which he was wounded. That same year he married Céleste Amable Buisson de la Vigne. In 1793 he emigrated to England where he stayed until 1800 and supported himself by teaching and translating. In 1797 he published his *Essai sur les révolutions* in which he judged himself and his period. He returned to France to contribute to the restoration of the moral order and to announce "le mal du siècle" in *Atala* and *René*. The appearance of *Le Génie du christianisme* (1802) drew to him the attention of Napoleon, but, although an admirer of the latter and eager for a political career, he was only appointed to the unpromising post of embassy secretary in Rome. Following the assassination of the duc d'Enghien in 1804, Chateaubriand broke all ties with Napoleon to become a most vocal opponent—opposition Napoleon chose not to act upon.

From 1806 to 1807 he traveled through Greece, Palestine, and Egypt, following which he wrote *Les Martyrs*, a historical romance and an illustration of his conception of the Christian odyssey, and his *Itinéraire de Paris à Jérusalem* (1811). In 1811 he was elected to the Académie française. Three years later he published *De Buonaparte et des Bourbons*. Upon the return of the Bourbons in 1814 and until 1824, he hoped to cash in on his opposition to Napoleon and be appointed prime minister, but his apparent inability to commit himself to the class to which he belonged, and a series of political misjudgments, only saw him named Peer of France (1815), minister to Berlin (1821), ambassador to London and foreign minister (1822), a post from which he was relieved in 1824. From that time until the reign of Louis-Philippe (1830) he figured in the liberal opposition. In 1832, he retired from political life, preferring instead the salon of his lifelong friend Madame Récamier, and writing his masterpiece, *Mémoires d'outre-tombe*. He also published *Essai sur la littérature anglaise*, a translation of Milton's *Paradise Lost* (1836), and *Vie de Rancé* (1844), the latter a task assigned to him by his confessor.

Charles Fourier (1772–1837) was born in Besançon, the son of a cloth merchant, and educated at the local Jesuit academy. Although a promising student, he abandoned his studies for a business career. As a commercial traveler he went to Holland and Germany, noting the differences in climate, production, and manners. The beginning of the Revolution saw him in Lyon, and during the Terror (1793) he lost nearly all he had, was imprisoned, and almost guillotined. From 1794 to 1796 he served as a conscript in the army. Between 1796 and 1826, while holding diverse commercial jobs in the Besançon and Lyon areas, he spent his spare time studying and writing. Obsessed by the abuses of commerce, he set out to create a social utopia composed of "phalanxes," human groups of 1,600, in which the miseries stemming from the restraints of civilization would be alleviated through an unfettering of the passions—thus bringing about universal "harmony." He expounded his theory in his *Théorie des quatre mouvements et des destinées générales* (1808), *Traité de l'association domestique agricole* (1822), *Le Nouveau Monde industriel et sociétaire* (1829), *Pièges et charlatanisme des deux sectes Saint-Simon et Owen* (1831), and *La fausse industrie morcelée* (1835–36). In 1826, supported by a small family legacy, he moved to Paris. In the early 1830s Fourier won over a number of disciples, the foremost of whom was Victor Considérant, who founded the journal *La Réforme industrielle ou le Phalanstère* in order to propagate "fouriérisme." Fourier's theory was experimented with at Brook Farm in Massachusetts (1841–46), thereby attracting the attention of such American writers as Hawthorne and Emerson. He is also said to have helped Marx develop his notion of "alienation" and to have been a forerunner of Freud.

Claude-Henri de Rouvroy, Comte de Saint-Simon (1760–1825) was born in Paris, the eldest son of an impoverished aristocratic family, related to the family of the chronicler of Louis XIV's court life at Versailles. He was educated privately by tutors, among whom was the encyclopedist d'Alembert. Saint-Simon began a military career at seventeen and took part in the American War of Independence during which he was wounded in 1782. A supporter of the French Revolution, he renounced his title, but was jailed by mistake in 1793. Under the Directory (1795–99) he made a small fortune speculating on land confiscated from the *émigrés* and the Church, which allowed him to finance a salon for politicians, men of letters, and scientists, particularly from the new Ecole polytechnique. In 1802 he published the *Lettres d'un habitant de Genève à ses contemporains*. By 1804 his short marriage had ended and, finding himself destitute, he had to depend on the generosity of friends and a small allowance from his family to continue his career as a writer on social reform. He was the first to see that the vacuum left by the destruction of the old structures was to be filled by science and industry (*Introduction aux travaux scientifiques du XIXe siècle* [1807], *Mémoire sur la science de l'homme* [1813], *De la réorganisation de la sociétée europénne* [1814]) and was noted for the breadth of his treatment of the transformation from feudal to bourgeois society. After meeting the future historian Augustin Thierry, an enthusiastic disciple, his writings began to reach a wider public. Saint-Simon then began publishing under his own editorship a series of periodicals such as *L'Industrie*, *L'Organisateur*, and *Du Système industriel* (1816–22), which addressed themselves to industrialists and bankers. From 1817 to 1824, Auguste Comte served as his secretary. Saint-Simon's last book, *Le Nouveau christianisme* (1825), studies the function that religion should have in future society.

Auguste Comte (1798–1857), the founder of sociology, was born in Montpellier, the son of a tax collector, and was educated there at the Lycée impérial. His relations with his family were strained when, at the age of fourteen, he rejected the Catholic faith and became a republican. In 1814 he was admitted to the Ecole polytechnique where he spent two years studying Carnot, Lagrange, and Laplace before his expulsion during the royalist reorganization of the school. In 1817 Comte began his crucial association with Saint-Simon, which was to last for seven years and end in a bitter quarrel over Comte's publication in 1822 of "Prospectus des travaux scientifiques nécessaires pour réorganiser la société." In 1825 he contracted a civil marriage with Caroline Massin. The following year he began to teach his course in positive philosophy privately at his home, but his lectures were soon interrupted by a severe mental breakdown. In 1827 he attempted suicide and did not resume his teaching until 1829. In 1830 the first volume of his *Cours de philosophie positive* appeared, publication of which was to continue in five more installments until 1842. While he acknowledged the influence of Montesquieu and Condorcet, he denied that of Saint-Simon, although it was from Saint-Simon that he borrowed "the law of three stages," which he systematized. In 1832 Comte was appointed Assistant Lecturer in Analysis and Mechanics at the Ecole polytechnique, and in 1836, admission examiner. The end of his marriage and the beginning of his financial troubles began in 1842, as the last volume of his *Cours* had offended his patrons. He was not reappointed admission examiner in 1844. John Stuart Mill, with whom he had started a correspondence in 1841, raised funds to make up for Comte's loss of income. In 1848 the Positivist Society was founded, followed the next year by the Universal Church of the Religion of Humanity. Comte established a positivist calendar of saints to which was added in 1852 his *Catéchisme positiviste ou sommaire exposition de la religion universelle*. In 1851 Comte lost not only his position as assistant lecturer at the Ecole but also a number of friends who resigned from the society when he endorsed the coup d'état of Louis-Napoléon. That same year he published the first of four volumes of his *Système de politique positive ou Traité de sociologie instituant la religion de l'humanité*. Subsequent volumes appeared in 1852, 1853, and 1854. Other works by Comte include *Appel aux conservateurs* (1855) and *Synthèse subjective ou système universel des conceptions propres à l'état normal de l'humanité* (1856).

Jules Michelet (1798–1874) was born in Paris, the son of a printer. The poverty of his parents did not permit the start of his education until he was twelve. He entered the Mélot Latin School in 1810 and the Collège Charlemagne in 1812 where he became a *bachelier* in 1817. After obtaining his *agrégation* in 1821 he was appointed Professor of History successively at the Collège Sainte-Barbe (1822–27), the Ecole normale supérieure (1827–36), and the Collège de France (1838–51). In 1824 he married Pauline Rousseau, a marriage that lasted until her death in 1839, and in 1849, Athénaïs Mialaret, who collaborated in the composition of some of his works. During much of this time Michelet was head of the historical section of the National Archives (1830–52), traveled extensively and continuously throughout Europe, and published a prodigious number of books, including his two editions of *L'Histoire de France*, the first in six volumes (1833–44) and its revision in seventeen volumes (1852–67), and *La Révolution française* in seven volumes (1847–53). The more topical books of this period include *Des Jésuites* (1843, written with Edgar Quinet with whom he had a lifelong friendship), *Du Prêtre, de la femme et de la famille* (1845), *Le Peuple* (1846), *Les Femmes de la Révolution* (1854), *La Femme* (1859), *La Sorcière* (1862), and several volumes of natural history, including *L'Oiseau* (1856), *L'Insecte* (1857), and *La Mer* (1861). Michelet was instrumental in altering the course of the French conception of history, not only by introducing the thought of Vico, through his translation of *La Scienza Nuova* in 1827, but by shifting his focus from individual figures to collective movements and taking into account material phenomena such as climate, working conditions, and food. He was also father of the Annales school. His vocal, anticlerical republicanism and his refusal to take the oath of allegiance to Napoleon III cost him his chair at the Collège de France (1851) and his position at the National Archives (1852). His last work, the three-volume *Histoire du dix-neuvième siècle* (1872–74) is also an attack on both Napoleons.

Edgar Quinet (1803–75) was born in Bourg-en-Bresse, the son of a commissioner of war. His mother was in charge of his early education and inculcated in him her deep but nondogmatic religious spirit. He started formal schooling in 1811 and was enrolled at the colleges of Bourg (1815) and Lyon (1817). Although more interested in literature and philosophy, he studied law in Paris in 1821. His first work, *Tablettes du Juif errant*, a satire of current philosophical and literary systems, was published in 1823. His introduction to his own translation of Herder's *Philosophy of History* (1825) brought him recognition and the friendship of Michelet. Like Michelet, Quinet traveled extensively: to Germany, where he tried to reconcile the opposite geniuses of France and Germany (he married a German woman in 1834), and predominantly to the Mediterranean countries of Greece, Italy, Spain, and Portugal, investigating the influence of Catholicism and the Catholic Church on the mores of the people and on political institutions. Following his return from Greece in 1830, he published *La Grèce moderne* and a series of brochures including *De la philosophie dans ses rapports avec l'histoire politique*, *L'Allemagne et la Révolution*, and *Avertissement à la monarchie de 1830*. Parallel to his political and religious studies, he pursued literary interests, publishing *Des épopées françaises du douzième siècle* (1831), and a prose poem, *Ahasuérus* (1833). *Allemagne et Italie* appeared in 1836 and *L'Examen de la vie de Jésus-Christ* was published in 1838. Although Quinet had not received any traditional academic training, he was appointed Professor of Foreign Literatures at the University of Lyon in 1838 (he defended his theses in Strasbourg in January 1839). There he gave a series of lectures (published as *Le Génie des religions* in 1842) that brought him the chair of Meridional Literatures and Institutions, created for him at the Collège de France in 1841. It was also at the Collège that he joined Jules Michelet in his attack against the Jesuits (*Les Jésuites* [1843]). Quinet's lectures caused so much commotion that the government suppressed them in 1846. He took an active part in the Revolution of 1848, and was deputy in the National Assembly until the coup d'état of 1851. He spent the years of Napoleon III's dictatorship in exile in Brussels and Switzerland publishing *Les Révolutions d'Italie* (1848–52), *Les Esclaves* (1853), *Merlin l'enchanteur* (1860), *La Révolution religieuse au XIXᵉ siècle* (1857), *Histoire de mes idées* (1858), and *Histoire de la Révolution* (1865), among other works. After Napoleon's downfall in 1870, he held seats in the national assemblies at Bordeaux and Versailles. Among his last books were *La Création* (1870), *La République* (1872), and *L'Esprit nouveau* (1874).

Charles-Augustin Sainte-Beuve (1804–69) was born in Boulogne-sur-Mer, the son of a tax superintendent who died before his birth. In 1818 he went to Paris to complete his studies at the Collège Charlemagne and later enrolled as a medical student (1823–27). From 1824 to 1827 he wrote short articles for *Le Globe*. A positive review of Victor Hugo's *Odes et Ballades* (1827) led to a friendship that was to last until 1834 (Sainte-Beuve had an affair with Adèle Hugo from 1832 to 1837) and to his defense of the romantic movement in his *Tableau historique et critique de la poésie française et du théâtre français au XVIᵉ siècle* (1828), which related romanticism to the tradition of Ronsard and the Pléiade. Between 1829 and 1837, Sainte-Beuve published volumes of verse, *Vie, poésies et pensées de Joseph Delorme* (1829), *Les Consolations* (1830), *Pensées d'Août* (1837) and a semiautobiographical novel, *Volupté* (1834), and established his reputation as a critic, writing for *La Revue des Deux Mondes* and the collection of *Critiques et portraits littéraires* (1832). From 1837 to 1838 he taught a course on Jansenism in

Lausanne, which was published as *Port-Royal* (5 vols., 1840–59). In 1840 he was appointed *conservateur* at the Bibliothèque Mazarine, and in 1844, elected to the *Académie française*. In 1848 he resigned his post from the Bibliothèque to teach a course, the lectures of which were later published as *Chateaubriand et son groupe littéraire* (1860), at the University of Liège, Belgium. In 1854 he was appointed to the chair of Latin poetry at the Collège de France (his lectures published as *Etude sur Virgile* [1857]), but he resigned, prevented from lecturing by student hostility. He also taught a course on French literature at the Ecole normale supérieure between 1857 and 1861. In 1865 he was named senator by Napoleon III, but defended Renan, and the freedom of education and of thought, in his senate speeches. Concurrently, Sainte-Beuve was contributing critical articles to *La Revue suisse, Le Constitutionnel, Le Moniteur, La Revue contemporaine,* and *Le Temps,* which were collected in *Portraits de femmes* (1844), *Portraits contemporains* (1846), *Causeries du lundi* (1851–62), and *Nouveaux lundis* (1863–70).

Alexis-Henri-Charles-Maurice Cleriel, Comte de Tocqueville (1805–59) was born in Paris of an aristocratic family. He was tutored by the abbé Lesueur, the family priest, and at age fifteen began his formal studies at the college in Metz. He studied law in Paris (1823–27) and served as *juge auditeur* in the Court of First Instance at Versailles (1827–30). Following the July Revolution of 1830, with his friend Gustave de Beaumont, he accepted a commission from the government to visit the United States (1831–32) and report on its prison system, which was presumed a model to be imitated by the French (*Du système pénitentiaire aux Etats-Unis et de son application en France* [1833]). From this voyage Tocqueville also brought back observations that led to the writing of *De la démocratie en Amérique* (2 vols., 1835 and 1840). Between 1833 and 1835 Tocqueville also traveled to England where he met Mary Motley, whom he married in 1836. In 1839 he was elected to the Chamber of Deputies from Valogne (Normandy), where in his first speech he debated the necessity of a French presence in the conflict of the Near East (in 1841 he traveled to Algeria, which France had begun to colonize in 1830), and where he fought for the abolition of slavery, prison reforms, and the freedom of education. After the February Revolution of 1848, he was elected to the National Assembly, appointed member of the Committee for the Constitution of 1848, and in 1849 (from June 2 to October 31) Minister of Foreign Affairs. After Louis-Napoléon's coup in 1851, he retired from politics to his Château de Tocqueville (Normandy) to write his *Souvenirs* (1893) of the Second Republic and *L'Ancien Régime et la Révolution* (1856).

Pierre-Joseph Proudhon (1809–65) was born in Besançon, the son of a brewer whose refusal to make a profit made for an impoverished upbringing. He attended the Collège de Besançon for a brief period but was largely self-educated in the public library and in his work as a printer, through which he encountered Fourier's *Le Nouveau Monde industriel et sociétaire* (1829). He taught himself Greek and Hebrew and contributed notes on the Hebrew language to an edition of the Bible. In 1838 he published *Essai de grammaire générale* and won a scholarship from the Besançon Academy, which allowed him to go to Paris and gave him the time to write *Qu'est-ce que la propriété?* (1840). In 1842 he was tried for his revolutionary ideas but was acquitted. In 1846 he published his *Système des contradictions économiques ou Philosophie de la misère,* which prompted Marx (who earlier had praised Proudhon's book on property) to write *Misère de la philosophie* (1847), a harsh attack of Proudhon. In 1848 Proudhon was elected to the National Assembly, but his opposition to Louis-Napoléon—he anticipated that the latter would become president and emperor—led to his imprisonment (1849–52). While in prison he wrote for and edited several Paris newspapers and published *Confessions d'un révolutionnaire; Actes de la Révolution* (1849); *Gratuité du crédit* (1850); *Idée générale de la Révolution au XIXe siècle* (1851), in which he criticized representative democracy contending that actual political authority is exercised by only a small number of people; and *La Révolution social démontrée par le coup d'état* (1852). During the early years of the Second Empire, Proudhon was under constant police surveillance, and in 1858, when again sentenced to three years in jail, he fled to Belgium, where he remained until 1862. During his final years in Paris he gained a considerable following, and when the First International was founded (1864), his followers were Marx's most powerful opponents. Proudhon's later works include *De la Justice dans la Révolution et dans l'Eglise* (1858), *Du principe fédératif* (1863), *De la capacité politique des classes ouvrières* (1863), and *La Pornocratie, ou Les Femmes dans les temps modernes* (1865).

Charles-Pierre Baudelaire (1821–67) was born in Paris, the son of Caroline Dufaÿs and François Baudelaire. His father, who died in 1827, left him a legacy he was to inherit (and squander rapidly) upon turning twenty-one. He was educated at the Collège Royal in Lyon (where he lived for a time following his mother's marriage to the Colonel Aupick), and at Louis-le-Grand in Paris. He made his literary debut in 1843 in a collection of poetry entitled *Vers*, and joined Théophile Gautier at Madame Sabatier's for the Club des Haschichins. Until 1855, when eighteen poems under the title *Les Fleurs du mal* were published in *La Revue des deux mondes*, he wrote numerous articles of criticism on literature and painting including his *Salons; De la peinture moderne*, translated into English by Edgar Allan Poe; *Les Paradis artificiels* (1851, part 1); *Edgar Allan Poë, sa vie, son oeuvre* (1852); and *Morale du joujou* (1853). In 1857, as a result of the publication of *Les Fleurs du mal*, Baudelaire stood trial for charges of outrage to morality. Six poems were suppressed and in 1860 a new, amended version was brought out. Continuously plagued by financial problems and ill health, Baudelaire went on with his literary output, both poetic and critical. In 1861 he tried unsuccessfully to be elected to the Académie française and published his essay on Richard Wagner. In September 1862 twenty prose poems were published in *La Presse*, followed the next year by other prose poems in *Le Figaro* and in *La Revue des deux mondes* as *Le Spleen de Paris*. Between 1864 and 1866, he traveled to Belgium to deliver lectures and negotiate the sale of his works, but, feeling ill-treated, he developed a hatred for the Belgians and wrote epigrams and pamphlets against them (*Pauvre Belgique!*) The first edition of Baudelaire's complete works was published between 1868 and 1870 in seven volumes.

Joseph-Ernest Renan (1823–92) was born in Tréguier (Brittany), the son of a merchant-mariner. After his father's death, his mother and sister sent him to the seminary, first in Tréguier (1832–38) then to Paris (1841–45). Instead of the priesthood, however, Renan decided upon a lay career. In 1847 he won the Volney Prize for an essay on Semitic languages. In 1848 he received the *agrégation* in philosophy and published *De l'origine du langage*. In 1851 he began writing for *La Revue des deux mondes* and, in 1853, for *Le Journal des débats*. Before his departure on a learned mission to Syria and the Holy Land in 1861, he published *Histoire générale et système comparé des langues sémitiques* (1855), *Etudes d'histoire religieuse* (1857), and *Essais de morale et de critique* (1859). He also translated *The Book of Job* and *The Song of Songs*, and was appointed to the committee assigned to write the literary history of France. In 1863, following the controversy over his *Vie de Jésus* (volume 1 of *Les Origines du christianisme* [1862–83]), Renan was expelled from the chair he had held for one year at the Collège de France and was not reinstated until the fall of the Second Empire in 1870. In 1869 he ran unsuccessfully for the National Assembly on a program for constitutional monarchy. Until the end of his life he traveled extensively, taught, and primarily wrote and published, while holding seats at the Académie française and the Société asiatique. Some of his other works include *La Réforme intellectuelle et morale* (1871), *Dialogues et fragments philosophiques* (1876), *Histoire de la science* (1890, written in 1849), and the five volumes of *Histoire du peuple d'Israël*.

Hippolyte-Adolphe Taine (1828–93) was born in Vouziers (Ardennes), the son of a country lawyer who died when Taine was twelve. He was first educated privately by a priest and then sent to Paris in 1841 to the Lycée Bourbon. In 1848 he entered the Ecole normale supérieure but three years later failed the examination for the *agrégation* in philosophy. After a brief period of teaching in provincial schools, he abandoned this career (he refused to take the oath of allegiance to the emperor) and settled in Paris. In 1853 he obtained his doctorate in letters and published his thesis on La Fontaine. In 1855 his essay on Livy received the prize of the Académie française. During this period he also published articles of literary criticism for magazines, later collected in *Philosophes français du XIXe siècle* (1857, an attack on the reigning philosophers) and in *Essais de critique et d'histoire* (1858). In 1863 he was appointed admission examiner at the Military Academy of Saint-Cyr, and in 1864 he published *Histoire de la littérature anglaise,* an attempt to understand the English character through literature. That same year he began a series of lectures as Professor of Aesthetics and Art History at the Ecole des Beaux-Arts (*La Philosophie de l'art* [1880]). His important essays on Racine, Balzac, and Stendhal appeared in *Nouveaux essais* (1865). After a liaison with the novelist Camille Selden, he married Melle Deruelle in 1868 and traveled to Germany, Switzerland, and Italy. After the publication of *De l'intelligence* (a treatise on psychology [1870]), Taine lectured on Corneille and Racine at Oxford University, where he received an honorary doctorate. In 1872 he began work on *Les Origines de la France contemporaine* (1875–93), a narrative and philosophical history which occupied him until his death.

Etienne (Stéphane) Mallarmé (1842–98) was born in Paris, the son of a clerk in the Registry and Public Property Office. His mother died when he was five, his younger sister when he was fifteen. He wrote his first poems, strongly influenced by Baudelaire, in 1861. In 1862 Mallarmé's first poems were published, and he traveled to England with Maria-Christina Gerhard, later his wife, to learn English. The following year, after the death of his father, Mallarmé married Maria and took a job teaching English at Tournon. He published his first prose poems in 1864, the year his daughter Geneviève was born. In 1866 he published ten poems in *Le Parnasse contemporain.* ''Hérodiade'' appeared in the next issue in 1871. His son Anatole was also born in 1871, and Mallarmé received a teaching appointment in Paris at the Lycée Fontanes. He began his ''Tuesday evening'' poetry sessions in 1872 and published a number of prose poems and translations of Poe. In 1874 he published eight issues of *La Dernière Mode,* a fashion magazine, and in 1878 and 1880, two textbooks: *Les Mots anglais* and *Les Dieux antiques.* His son Anatole died in 1879, inspiring the never-completed *Un Tombeau pour Anatole. Les Poésies de Stéphane Mallarmé* and *Album de vers et de prose* were published in 1887, Mallarmé's first book-length collections. Elected Prince of Poets in 1896, Mallarmé died two years later at Valvins, his summer home.

Ferdinand de Saussure (1857–1913) was born in Geneva, the son of a scientist. Early on he was introduced to linguistic studies by Adolphe Pictet, a philologist and family friend. In 1875 he entered the University of Geneva and took courses in physics and chemistry, as well as in Greek and Latin grammar. At the end of the first year he left to study Indo-European languages at the University of Leipzig, which was the center for a school of young historical linguists, the *Junggrammatiker.* He also spent eighteen months in Berlin and in 1878 published his *Mémoire sur le système primitif des voyelles dans les langues indo-européennes.* After defending his thesis on the use of the genetive case in Sanskrit, he left for Paris where he lectured at the Ecole pratiques des hautes etudes (1881–91), later to return to a chair in Geneva where he spent the rest of his life. In Geneva he taught Sanskrit and historical linguistics, wrote on Indo-European philology, studied Lithuanian and medieval German legends, and worked on his theory that Latin poets had hidden anagrams of proper names in their verses. Although he had refused requests to expound his ideas on the theoretical foundations of linguistics, the retirement of a professor in 1906 forced him to teach a course of general linguistics, which was edited posthumously from students' lecture notes as *Cours de linguistique générale* (1916), a book which became the foundation of modern linguistics.

Emile Durkheim (1858–1917) was born in Epinal (Vosges) to a family of rabbis. In 1879 he entered the Ecole normale supérieure to study philosophy, and in 1882 received his *agrégation*. Between 1882 and 1885 he taught philosophy in provincial cities and then took a year's leave to go to Germany where he studied under the psychologist Wilhelm Wundt. In 1887 he married Louise Dreyfus. That same year he was appointed Lecturer in Education and Sociology at the University of Bordeaux, and in 1896 Professor of Sociology, the first professorship in sociology in France. While in Bordeaux, he defended his thesis, *De la division du travail social: étude sur l'organisation des sociétés supérieures* (1893), and published *Les Règles de la méthode sociologigue* (1895) and *Le Suicide: étude de sociologie* (1897). In 1897 he founded the journal *L'Année sociologique* to promote specialization and collective work in the field of sociology. In 1902 he was appointed at the Sorbonne where he remained until his death, dividing his time between his teaching and the direction of the journal. In 1912 he published *Les Formes élémentaires de la vie religieuse: Le système totémique en Australie*, and, in 1915, two nationalist booklets, *Qui a voulu la guerre? Les Origines de la guerre d'après les documents diplomatiques* and *"L'Allemagne au-dessus de tout": La mentalité allemande et la guerre*. After his death his students published his lectures and articles in such collected volumes as *Le Socialisme: Sa définition, ses débuts, la doctrine Saint-Simonienne* (1928), *L'Evolution pédagogique en France* (2 vols., 1938), and *Montesquieu et Rousseau, précurseurs de la sociologie* (1953).

Henri-Louis Bergson (1859–1941) was born in Paris of Jewish parents. His mother was English, and his father, a music teacher and composer, was Polish. After graduating from the Lycée Condorcet, Bergson entered the Ecole normale supérieure in 1878. After receiving his *agrégation* in 1881, he taught philosophy in Angers and Clermont-Ferrand until his return to Paris (1888) where he taught at the Lycée Henri IV and at the Ecole normale supérieure until his appointment to the Collège de France in 1900. His doctoral thesis, *Essai sur les données immédiates de la conscience*, was published in 1889. In 1891 he married Louise Neuberger with whom he had a daughter, born deaf, who became a painter. In 1896 his *Matière et mémoire* appeared, and, in 1900, *Le Rire*. In 1901 Bergson was elected to the Académie des Sciences Morales et Politiques. *L'Evolution créatrice* (1907) established his international reputation, and in 1911 he lectured at Oxford and Birmingham and, in 1913, in New York. In 1914 Bergson's works were put on the Catholic Church's Index of prohibited books because of his influence on the advocates of Catholic modernism. That same year he was elected to the Académie française. In 1917 he was sent on a diplomatic mission to the United States to convince the American government to join the war. After the war he was elected president of the Commission Internationale de Coopération Intellectuelle (1919–25). In 1919 he published *L'Energie spirituelle* and later, *Durée et simultanéité* (1922). In 1927 he was awarded the Nobel Prize for Literature. In 1932 *Deux sources de la morale et de la religion* appeared, followed by *La Pensée et le mouvant* (1934). In 1937 Bergson prepared a will in which he stated that he would have joined the Catholic Church had not the growth of anti-Semitism convinced him to remain on the side of the persecuted. In this same will he forbade the publication of any of his unpublished manuscripts, letters, and notes.

Charles Maurras (1868–1952), writer, critic, and political theorist, was born in Martigues, near Marseilles, the son of a tax collector. He studied classics at a Roman Catholic collège in Aix-en-Provence, but his formal education ended with his baccalaureate in 1885. During his childhood he was suddenly struck deaf, a trauma that triggered his interest in the problem of evil and later caused him to lose his faith. In 1886 he went to Paris and began a career as a journalist. In 1891, with Jean Moréas, he helped found the Ecole romane, and in 1893, with François Amonet, took over the *Félibrige*—two movements dedicated to the purification of French language and culture. In 1895 he published the first of his political writings, *Le Chemin de paradis*. A voyage to Greece that same year convinced him of the superiority of classicism over romanticism (*Le Voyage d'Athènes* [1896–98], *Anthinéa* [1901], *Les Amants de Venise: George Sand et Alfred de Musset* [1902], *Barbarie et poésie*, [1926]). An opponent of Dreyfus, Maurras advocated the exclusion of everything and everyone "non-

French," the end of democracy, and the return of monarchism. His most influential political writings were *Trois idées politiques* (1898), *Enquête sur la monarchie* (1901–9), and *L'Avenir de l'intelligence* (1905). In 1908, with Léon Daudet and others, he founded the daily paper *L'Action française*, in which he virulently polemicized against the republican government of Briand and later Blum, and advocated relations with fascist Italy and support for Franco and the Munich accords. Seeing the Church as a possible ally, he tried to rally it to his cause; in 1926, however, five of his books were put on the Church's Index of prohibited books, and *L'Action française* was condemned. In 1936 Maurras was imprisoned for his attack against Blum's government. His election to the Académie française in 1938 caused an uproar, and he was stricken from its roster in 1945. Although he opposed collaboration during the German occupation, he was sentenced to life imprisonment in 1945 for his support of Marshal Pétain.

André Gide (1869–1951) was born in Paris of a Catholic mother and a Protestant father, a professor in the law school of the University of Paris. Until 1887 his schooling was irregular due to ill health, but in 1889 he finally passed the baccalaureate examinations and began to publish his writings in the journals of the Symbolist school. In 1891 he met Valéry, Mallarmé, and Oscar Wilde and published *Les Cahiers d'André Walter* (anonymously) and *Le Traité du Narcisse*. In 1893 he traveled to north Africa where he had his first homosexual experience. In 1895 he published *Paludes*, returned to North Africa, and married his cousin Madeleine Rondeaux. The hedonism of *Les Nourritures terrestres* (1897) attracted many disciples, and until 1910 Gide's works seemed to alternate between sensualism and puritanism: *Le Prométhée mal enchaîné* (1899), *L'Immoraliste* (1902), *Saül* (1903), *Le Retour de l'enfant prodigue* (1907), and *La Porte étroite* (1909). In 1909 he participated in the founding of *La Nouvelle Revue française* on which he collaborated, except for the period of the German occupation, until his death. In 1914 he published the reflections on his experience as a juror in *Souvenirs de la Cour d'Assises*, and *Les Caves du Vatican*, which eventually caused a break with his Catholic friends who had tried to convert him. During World War I he devoted himself to the care of refugees and gave his moral backing to *L'Action française*. Later he published *La Symphonie pastorale* (1919), *Si le grain ne meurt* (1921), and *Dostoïevsky* (1923), among other works. The publication of his *Voyage au Congo* and *Le Retour de Tchad* (1927) led to parliamentary inquiries into the activities of holding companies in equatorial Africa. Meanwhile, he also wrote *Les Faux monnayeurs* (1925), *Essai sur Montaigne* (1929), and *Oedipe* (1931). His political activism began in 1932 and lasted until his return from the USSR in 1937 when his intellectual integrity and anti-Stalinism forced him to denouce the regime he had earlier supported (*Retour de l'URSS* [1936]). Gide spent World War II in the south of France. In 1947 he received the Nobel Prize for Literature. The publication of his complete works, begun in 1932, includes *Les Nouvelles Nourritures* (1935) and his *Journal*.

Marcel Proust (1871–1922) was born in Auteuil, near Paris, the son of an eminent physician. At the age of nine he suffered his first attack of asthma, an illness around which he would organize his life. He studied at the Lycée Condorcet until his graduation in 1889. Between 1890 and 1895 he studied law at the Ecole des Sciences Politiques, attended Bergson's lectures at the Sorbonne, and began to frequent the salons. At the same time he wrote articles for *Le Banquet* and *La Revue blanche*, and in 1896 published *Les Plaisirs et les jours*. During the following years he folowed the *Affaire* in the Dreyfus camp and wrote a novel (*Jean Santeuil*, unpublished until 1952) and articles on aesthetic subjects and society life. After Ruskin's death in 1900 Proust published "Pélerinages ruskiniens en France" in *Le Figaro*, which he followed with more articles in other papers. He then began to translate Ruskin's *The Bible of Amiens* and *Sesame and Lilies* (1906) while traveling to Venice, Holland, and around France. After his mother's death in 1905 he had his bedroom lined with cork and began to write *A la recherche du temps perdu*. At the same time he continued to write articles and pastiches for *Le Figaro* (*Pastiches et mélanges* [1919]) and his *Contre Sainte-Beuve*, completed in 1910. In

1913 he published at his own expense the first volume of *A la recherche, Du côté de chez Swann*. The remaining volumes were published by *La Nouvelle Revue française*. *A l'ombre des jeunes filles en fleurs* (1918) won the Goncourt Prize in 1919 and was followed by *Du côté de Guermantes* (1920) and *Sodome et Gomorrhe* (1920 and 1922). The remaining three volumes were published posthumously: *La Prisonnière* (1923), *Albertine disparue* (1925), and *Le Temps retrouvé* (1927).

Paul-Ambroise Valéry (1871–1945) was born in Sète of an Italian mother and Corsican father. He studied at the college in Sète and the lycée in Montpellier before entering the law school of the University of Montpellier. When he started to publish poems in 1890, he met André Gide, who became a lifelong friend; he later met Mallarmé during his first trip to Paris. In 1892 Valéry received his law degree. That same year, although he had written hundreds of poems, he decided to renounce literature and devote himself to abstract speculation and study. In 1894 he settled in Paris and started the notebooks (*Cahiers*), which were to number 250. In 1895 he published his *Introduction à la méthode de Léonard de Vinci*, and the following year, *La Soirée avec Monsieur Teste*. In 1900 he married Jeanne Gobillard, and a selection of his early poems were included in the anthology *Poètes d'aujourd'hui*. Later, André Gide and the staff of *Nouvelle Revue française* convinced him to let them publish some of his earlier poetry and prose. While revising his work, Valéry also started to write *La Jeune Parque* (1917). During that time, with his reputation as a poet established, he continued to publish poems in various reviews, later collected in *Charmes* (1922), and in 1920 *Le Cimetière marin* and the *Album de vers anciens* appeared. In 1922, finding himself without a job, Valéry decided to capitalize on his still-growing fame and to make a living by writing and lecturing throughout Europe. In 1924 he helped found the literary review *Commerce* and published the first volume of a collection of essays, *Variétés*; excerpts from his *Cahiers, Fragments sur Mallarmé*; and *Situations de Baudelaire*. In 1925 he was elected to the Académie française. Until his appointment to the chair of poetics created for him at the Collège de France (1937), he wrote *Littérature* (1930), *Discours en l'honneur de Goethe, Discours sur l'histoire* (1932), and essays on Villon, Verlaine, and Stendhal, among other works. During World War II he wrote *Mon Faust* (1941) and continued to give lectures, the last of which was on Voltaire in 1944.

Gaston Bachelard (1884–1962) was born in Bar-sur-Aube (Champagne) of a family of shopkeepers. He was educated at the colleges of his home town and of Sézanne. Beginning in 1903, he worked for six years in the local post office, until his enrollment as a mathematics student in the Lycée Saint-Louis in 1909. After obtaining his degree in mathematical science (1912), he received a scholarship from the Lycée. In 1914, shortly after marrying a school-teacher, he was drafted and forced to spend most of the war at the front. After the war, while teaching at the Collège de Bar-sur-Aube, he received his *agrégation* in philosophy (1922) as well as a doctorate in letters from the Sorbonne (1927) upon the successful defense of his thesis, *Essai sur la connaissance approchée* (1928). He also published his two doctoral dissertations, *Etude sur l'évolution d'un problème de physique* (1928) and *La Valeur inductive de la relativité* (1929), before being appointed to the chair of philosophy at the University of Dijon. His most important works published during this period are *L'Intuition de l'instant* (1932), *Le Nouvel esprit scientifique* (1934), *La Formation de l'esprit scientifique, La Psychanalyse du feu* (1938) and *Lautréamont* (1939). In 1940 he was appointed to the chair of history and philosophy of science at the Sorbonne, and became the director of the Institute of the History of Science. *La Philosophie du non* appeared that same year, followed by *L'Eau et les rêves* (1942), *L'Air et les songes* (1943), *Le Rationalisme appliqué* (1949), and *Le Matérialisme rationel* (1953). In 1955, a year after he relinquished his chair at the Sorbonne, Bachelard was elected to the Academy of Moral and Political Sciences, and in 1961 he was awarded the Grand Prix National des Lettres. His other works include *La Poétique de l'espace* (1957) and *La Poétique de la rêverie* (1960).

André Breton (1896–1966) was born in Tinchebray (Normandy) and led a life that was inextricably linked with the history of the Surrealist movement. After medical studies, he was drafted in 1915 and assigned to the neuropsychiatric corps where he met Jacques Vaché. He also had contact with Tzara and the Dadaist movement, and in 1919, with Aragon and Soupault, he founded the review *Littérature*, in which "Les Champs magnétiques," the first text of automatic writing, reflected the growing importance of psychoanalysis to literature. In 1922 Breton became the editor of *La Révolution surréaliste*. In 1924 he published the first *Manifeste du surréalisme*, followed by *Nadja* (1928) and the creation of the review *Le Surréalisme au service de la révolution*. In 1926 Breton joined the Communist party from which he would withdraw in 1935. *Les Vases communicants* was published in 1932 and *Position politique du surréalisme* in 1935. He traveled to Prague and the Canary Islands in 1935, and the following year he organized the International Surrealist Exhibition in London (the first of many which were to take place in Paris as well as in New York). *L'Amour fou* appeared in 1937, and in 1938 Breton traveled to Mexico where he met with Trotsky. He spent World War II in New York where he worked for the Voice of America and founded the review *VVV* with Marcel Duchamp and Max Ernst. Returning to Paris in 1947, Breton promptly published his *Ode à Charles Fourier* and *Arcane 17*. From then until his death, and with the new Surrealist group which had formed around him, Breton was active in politics as well as in literature (in reviews such as *Médium* [1952], *Le Surréalisme même* [1956], and *La Brèche, action surréaliste* [1961]) and art (organizing exhibitions in 1947, 1959, and 1965). Breton's other important works are *Anthologie de l'humour noir* and *Fata Morgana* (1940), *La Clé des champs* (1953), *Prolégomènes à un troisième manifeste ou non* (1955), and two collections of poems, *Claire de Terre* (1966) and *Signe Ascendant* (1968).

Simone Weil (1909–43) was born in Paris, the daughter of Jewish parents. A very precocious child, she studied at the Lycée Victor Dupuy where she obtained her baccalaureate at the age of fifteen. She attended the Lycée Henri IV to prepare for her admission to the Ecole normale supérieure (1927). After obtaining here *agrégation* in philosophy in 1931, she taught in the lycées of Le Puy and elsewhere (1931–37). By this time she was quite interested in politics and joined in the activities of the Trotskyists and of the militants of *La Révolution prolétarienne*. She studied Marx and published her first article in 1931 in *Libres propos*, the review of her teacher Alain. While in Le Puy, she picketed for *La Révolution prolétarienne* and gave away most of her salary, refusing to live on more than the unemployed workers. She maintained this habit of voluntary poverty even though it eventually ruined her health and led to her premature death. In 1934 she took a leave of absence from teaching to experience the life of workers in the Renault factory in Paris, and in 1936 she went to Barcelona to join the ranks of the anarchists fighting Franco. In Spain she realized that on either ideological side man was crushed by the social and war machines and reduced to a state of anonymous function. Following a mystical experience she embraced the New Testament as a source of guidance, although she never joined the Catholic Church, which in her opinion was bound to the capitalist system (she had never embraced Judaism either). After the German invasion she went to Marseilles, and, unable to work because of the racial laws, she began to write her *Cahiers* (3 vols., 1951–56; also published in excerpts as *La Pesanteur et la Grâce*, 1949). She wrote articles for the *Cahiers du Sud* under the pseudonym Emile Noris. When she was able to leave France in 1942, she traveled to the United States and then, several months later, to England, where she died in the sanatorium of Ashford. Simone Weil's writings were published posthumously and include *L'Enracinement* (1949), *L'Attente de Dieu* (1950), *La Condition ouvrière* (1951), *La Source grecque* (1953), *Oppression et liberté* (1955), and *Ecrits historiques et politiques* (1960).

Contributors

Harold Bloom, Sterling Professor of the Humanities at Yale University, is the author of *The Anxiety of Influence, Poetry and Repression*, and many other volumes of literary criticism. A MacArthur Prize Fellow, he is general editor of five series of literary criticism published by Chelsea House. During 1987–88, he served as Charles Eliot Norton Professor of Poetry at Harvard University.

Brian William Head has written on the origins of *"la science sociale"* and of *"idéologue"* and *"idéologie."* He is the author of *Ideology and Social Science: Destutt de Tracy and French Liberalism*.

Lilian R. Furst holds the Marcel Bataillon Chair of Comparative Literature at the University of North Carolina, Chapel Hill, and is Kenan Professor of Humanities at the College of William and Mary, Williamsburg. She is the author of *Romanticism in Perspective, The Contours of European Romanticism*, and *Fictions of Romantic Irony*, among others.

Stephen Holmes is Associate Professor of Political Science at the University of Chicago. He is the author of *Benjamin Constant and the Making of Modern Liberalism* and is currently working on a book concerning the history of public-private distinction in eighteenth-century French thought.

Andrew Martin is Fellow of King's College at Cambridge, England. He is the author of *The Knowledge of Ignorance: From Genesis to Jules Verne*.

Roland Barthes was Professor at the Collège de France at the time of his death in 1980. One of the most influential intellectuals of the structuralist and postmodern scene, he was a prolific writer, the author of *Writing Degree Zero, S/Z, The Pleasure of the Text, Camera Lucida, The Lover's Discourse*, and of collections of critical essays such as *The Responsibility of Forms* and *The Rustle of Language*.

Herbert Marcuse was a founder of the Frankfurt Institute for Social Research in the 1920s. A refugee from Nazi Germany to the United States, where he taught political philosophy for many years, he became a crucial theorist for the American New Left of the 1960s and 1970s. His legacy continues in such books as *Reason and Revolution, Eros and Civilization,* and *One-Dimensional Man.*

Linda Orr is Professor of Romance Languages at Duke University. She has written on Bataille and Tocqueville, and is the author of *Jules Michelet, History, and Language.*

Ceri Crossley is Lecturer in the Department of French Language and Literature at the University of Birmingham, England. He is the author of *Edgar Quinet (1803–1875): A Study in Romantic Thought.*

Emerson R. Marks teaches in the Department of English at the University of Massachusetts, Boston. He is the translator and editor of the *Literary Criticism of Sainte-Beuve* and the author of *Relativist & Absolutist: The Early Neoclassical Debate in England.*

Francois Furet is a prominent figure of *"la nouvelle histoire."* He has been director of the Ecole des Hautes Etudes en Sciences Sociales in Paris and is currently the president of Fondation Saint-Simon and the director of the Institut Raymond Aron. He has coauthored a history of alphabetization, *Lire et écrire,* and written *L'Atelier de l'histoire, Marx dans la Révolution française, La Gauche et la Révolution française,* and *Penser la Révolution française.*

Aaron Noland is the author of *The Founding of the French Socialist Party (1893–1905)* and joint editor of *Ideas in Cultural Perspectives* and *Roots of Scientific Thought: A Cultural Perspective.*

Susan Blood is a lecturer in the French department at Yale University. She has written on Ampère and is currently working on the ethical imperative in Baudelaire's aesthetics.

Edward W. Said is Parr Professor of English and Comparative Literature at Columbia University. He is the author of *Beginnings: Intention and Method, The Question of Palestine, Orientalism,* and *The World, the Text, and the Critic.*

Hans Aarsleff is Professor of English at Princeton University. He is the author of *The Study of Language in England, 1780–1860* and of *From Locke to Saussure: Essays on the Study of Language and Intellectual History.*

Maurice Blanchot has published hundreds of essays and some two-dozen books. Those available in English range from novels and shorter fictions (*Thomas the Obscure, Death Sentence, The Madness of the Day,* and *Time Comes*) to works in literary criticism and theory, political theory and analysis, and philosophy (*The Siren's Song, The Space of Literature, The Writing of the Disaster,* and *The Gaze of Orpheus*).

Barbara Johnson is Professor of Romance Languages and Literature at Harvard University. She is the author of *Défiguration du language poétique, The Critical Difference,* and *A World of Difference.* She is also editor of *The Pedagogical Imperative: Teaching as a Literary Genre* and the translator of Jacques Derrida's *Dissemination.*

Sylvère Lotringer is a professor in the French department at Columbia University. He has written on Saussure, Benveniste, Artaud, Bataille, and Deleuze, and is the editor of *Semiotexte* (special editor of the issue *Schizo-Culture*) and of the Foreign Agents Series.

Terry F. Godlove, Jr., is Assistant Professor of Philosophy at Hofstra University. He is the author of *Interpretation, Religion, and Diversity of Belief,* forthcoming from Cambridge University Press. His areas of research include epistemology, philosophy of religion, and the work of Immanuel Kant.

Gilles Deleuze teaches philosophy at the University of Paris and has written two books on Nietzsche, as well as texts on Bergson, Hume, Sacher-Masoch, Spinoza, and Kafka. His *Nietzsche and Philosophy* has been translated into English, as have *Proust and Signs, Kant's Critical Philosophy,* and two books written with Felix Guattari, *Anti-Oedipus* and *A Thousand Plateaus.*

Michael Sutton is the author of *Nationalism, Positivism and Catholicism: The Politics of Charles Maurras and French Catholics 1890–1914.*

Kevin Newmark is Assistant Professor of French at Yale University. He has written on Kierkegaard and French Symbolism.

David R. Ellison is Dean of Studies at Mount Holyoke College. *The Reading of Proust* is his first book.

Jacques Derrida is Directeur d'Etudes at the Ecole des Hautes Etudes en Sciences Sociales in Paris, and is Visiting Professor at the City University of New York and at the University of California, Irvine. He has written two books on Nietzsche, *Otobiographies* and *Spurs/Eperons,* and is the author of many articles and books, including *Of Grammatology, Speech and Phenomena, Dissemination, Margins of Philosophy, Glas, The Post-Card, Truth in Painting, Parages* (a collection of essays on Blanchot), and *Schibboleth pour Paul Celan.*

Margaret R. Higonnet is a professor in the History department at Harvard University. She has written on Madame de Staël and German romanticism.

Jean-Pierre Morel teaches comparative literature in France. He is the author of a novel, *Le Mural,* and of *Le Roman insupportable.*

A. Smock is a professor in the French Department at the University of California, Berkeley. She is the translator of Blanchot's *L'Espace littéraire* (*The Space of Literature*) and *L'Ecriture du désastre* (*The Writing of the Disaster*), and is the author of *Double Dealing.*

Bibliography

GENERAL

Alexander, Jean. *Affidavits of Genius: Edgar Allan Poe and the French Critics, 1847–1924.* Port Washington, N.Y.: National University Publications/Kennikat Press, 1971.

Aron, Raymond. *Main Currents in Sociological Thought.* 2 vols. London: Weidenfeld & Nicolson, 1965.

Barlow, Norman H. *Sainte-Beuve to Baudelaire: A Poetic Legacy.* Durham, N.C.: Duke University Press, 1964.

Brée, Germaine. *Twentieth-Century French Literature 1920–1970.* Chicago: University of Chicago Press, 1984.

Bryant, Christopher G. A. *Positivism in Social Theory and Research.* London: Macmillan, 1985.

Burns, C. A., ed. *Literature and Society: Studies in Nineteenth and Twentieth Century French Literature Presented to R. J. North.* Birmingham: University of Birmingham, 1980.

Caute, David. *Communism and the French Intellectuals 1914–1960.* New York: Macmillan, 1964.

Caws, Mary Ann, ed. *Writing in a Modern Temper: Essays on French Literature and Thought, in Honor of Henri Peyre.* Stanford French and Italian Studies 33. Saratoga, Calif.: ANMA Libri, 1984.

Charlton, D. G., ed. *The French Romantics.* 2 vols. Cambridge: Cambridge University Press, 1984.

Chiari, Joseph. *Twentieth Century French Thought: From Bergson to Lévi-Strauss.* London: Paul Elek, 1975.

Cobb, Richard. *French and Germans, Germans and French.* Hanover: University Press of New England, 1983.

Collectif. *Préromantisme: Hypothèque ou hypothèse?* Paris: Klincksiek, 1975.

Compagnon, Antoine. *La Troisième République des lettres de Flaubert à Proust.* Paris: Éditions du Seuil, 1983.

Cruickshank, John. *Variations on Catastrophe: Some French Responses to the Great War.* Oxford: Clarendon Press, 1982.

Dakyns, Janine R. *The Middle Ages in French Literature 1851–1900.* New York: Oxford University Press, 1973.

Finke, Ulrich, ed. *French Nineteenth Century Painting and Literature, with Special Reference to the Relevance of Literary Subject-Matter to French Painting.* Manchester: Manchester University Press, 1972.

Furst, Lilian R. *Counterparts: The Dynamics of Franco-German Literary Relationships 1770–1895.* London: Methuen, 1977.

Hamilton, Alistair. *The Appeal of Fascism: A Study of Intellectuals and Fascism 1919–1945.* New York: Macmillan, 1971.

Haskell, Francis; Anthony Levi; and Robert Shakleton, eds. *The Artist and the Writer in France.* Oxford: Clarendon Press, 1974.

Hughes, H. Stuart. *The Obstructed Path: French Social Thought in the Years of Desperation 1930–1960.* New York: Harper & Row, 1966.

Iknayan, Marguerite. *The Concave Mirror: From Imitation to Expression in French Aesthetic Theory 1800–1830.* Saratoga, Calif.: ANMA Libri, 1983.

Juden, Brian. *Traditions orphiques et tendances mystiques dans le romantisme français 1800–1855.* Paris: Klincksieck, 1971.

Keller, Luzius. *Piranesi et les romantiques français.* Paris: José Corti, 1966.

Kolakowski, Leszek. *Positivist Philosophy: From Hume to the Vienna Circle.* Harmondsworth: Penguin, 1972.

Martin, Andrew. *The Knowledge of Ignorance: From Genesis to Jules Verne.* Cambridge: Cambridge University Press, 1985.

MLN 95 (May 1980). Special issue, "Les Années 30."

Mouchoux, André. *L'Allemagne devant les lettres françaises 1814–1835.* Toulouse: Colin, 1953.

Peyre, Henri. "History as Prophecy: French Predictions of Russian-American Antagonism." *Journal of the History of Ideas* 44 (1983): 277–92.

Poulet, Georges. *La Conscience Critique.* Paris: José Corti, 1971.

———. *La Mesure de l'instant: Etudes sur le temps humain—IV.* Paris: Plon, 1968.

Proust, Marcel. *Contre Sainte-Beuve.* Paris: Gallimard (Pléiade), 1971, 1978.

Quinn, Patrick F. *The French Face of Edgar Poe.* Carbondale: Southern Illinois University Press, 1957.

Sabin, Margery. *English Romanticism and the French Tradition.* Cambridge, Mass.: Harvard University Press, 1976.

Simon, John K., ed. *Modern French Criticism: From Proust and Valéry to Structuralism.* Chicago: University of Chicago Press, 1972.

Simon, Walter M. *European Positivism in the Nineteenth Century.* Ithaca: Cornell University Press, 1963.

Soucy, Robert. "French Fascist Intellectuals in the 1930's: An Old Left?" *French Historical Studies* 8 (1974): 445–58.

Sternhell, Zeev. *La Droite révolutionnaire 1885–1914: Les Origines françaises du fascisme.* Paris: Seuil, 1978.

———. *Ni droite ni gauche: Idéologies fascistes en France.* Paris: Editions du Seuil, 1983.

Tannenbaum, Edward R. *The Action française: Die-hard Reactionaries in Twentieth-Century France.* New York: John Wiley, 1962.

Tardiman, Richard. *Discourse/Counter-Discourse: The Theory and Practice of Symbolic Resistance in Nineteenth-Century France.* Ithaca: Cornell University Press, 1985.

Tison-Braun, Micheline. *L'Introuvable Origine: Le Problème de la personalité au seuil du XXe siècle: Flaubert, Mallarmé, Rimbaud, Valéry, Bergson, Claudel, Gide, Proust.* Geneva: Droz, 1981.

Virtanen, Reino. "Poe's *Eureka* in France from Baudelaire to Valéry." *Kentucky Romance Quarterly* 29 (1982): 223–34.

Wilson, Edmund. *To the Finland Station: A Study in the Writing and Acting of History.* New York: Farrar, Straus & Giroux, 1972.

Wohl, Robert. *The Generation of 1914*. Cambridge, Mass.: Harvard University Press, 1979.

ANTOINE-LOUIS-CLAUDE DESTUTT DE TRACY

Alciatore, Jules C. "Stendhal, Destutt de Tracy et le précepte *Nosce te ipsum*." *Modern Language Quarterly* 14 (1953): 112–19.

———. "Stendhal et Destutt de Tracy: *La Vie de Napoléon* et le *Commentaire sur 'L'Esprit des lois.'* " *Modern Philology* 47 (1949): 98–107.

———. "Stendhal et Destutt de Tracy sur la cause première de toute erreur." *Symposium* 4 (1950): 358–65.

Caillet, Emile. *La Tradition littéraire des idéologues*. Philadelphia: American Philosophical Society, 1943.

Canivez, A. "Les Idéologues." In *Histoire de la Philosophie*, vol. 3. *Encyclopédie de la Pléiade*, vol. 38. Paris: Gallimard, 1974.

Chinard, Gilbert. *Jefferson et les idéologues, d'après sa correspondance inédite avec Destutt de Tracy, Cabanis, J. B. Say et Auguste Comte*. Baltimore: Johns Hopkins University Press, 1925.

Foucault, Michel. "The Limits of Representation." In *The Order of Things: An Archeology of the Human Sciences*, 217–49. New York: Random House, 1970.

Gusdorf, Georges. *La Conscience révolutionnaire: Les Idéologues*. Paris: Payot, 1978.

Head, Brian W. "The Origins of 'Idéologue' and 'Idéologie.' " *Studies on Voltaire and the Eighteenth Century* 183 (1980): 257–64.

———. "The Political and Philosophical Thought of Destutt de Tracy." Ph.D. diss.: London School of Economics, 1979.

———. *Ideology and Social Science: Destutt de Tracy and French Liberalism*. The Hague: Martinus Nijhoff, 1985.

Imbert, Pierre Henri. *Destutt de Tracy, critique de Montesquieu ou de la liberté en matière de politique*. Paris: Nizet, 1974.

Kaplan, Lawrence S. *Jefferson and France: An Essay on Politics and Political Ideas*. New Haven: Yale University Press, 1967.

Kennedy, Emmet. "Destutt de Tracy and the Unity of the Sciences." *Studies on Voltaire and the Eighteenth Century* 171 (1977): 223–39.

———. *A 'Philosophe' in the Age of Revolution: Destutt de Tracy and the Origins of 'Ideology.'* Philadelphia: American Philosophical Society, 1978.

Lichteim, George. "The Concept of Ideology." *History and Theory* 4 (1965): 165–95.

Moravia, Sergio. *Gli Ideologues: Scienza e filosofia in Francia (1780–1810)*. Bari: Laterza, 1974.

Parc, Yves du. "Destutt de Tracy, Stendhal et *De l'amour*." *Stendhal Club* 8 (1960): 335–40.

Rastier, François. *Idéologie et théorie des signes: Analyse structurale des* Eléments d'idéologie *d'Antoine-Louis-Claude Destutt de Tracy*. The Hague: Mouton, 1972.

Smith, Colin. "Aspects of Destutt de Tracy's Linguistic Analysis as Adopted by Stendhal." *Modern Language Review* 51 (1956): 512–21.

———. "Destutt de Tracy's Analysis of the Proposition." *Revue Internationale de Philosophie* 21 (1967): 475–85.

———. "Destutt de Tracy and the Bankruptcy of Sensationalism." In *Balzac and the Nineteenth Century: Studies in French Literature Presented to Herbert J. Hunt by His Pupils, Colleagues and Friends*, edited by D. G. Charlton et al., 195–207. New York: Humanities Press, 1972.

Van Duzer, Charles H. *Contribution of the Idéologues to French Revolutionary Thought*. Baltimore: Johns Hopkins University Press, 1935.

Welch, Cheryl. *Liberty and Utility: The Ideologues and the Transformation of Revolutionary Liberal Theory.* New York: Columbia University Press, 1984.

MADAME DE STAËL

Andrews, Wayne. *Germaine: A Portrait of Mme de Staël.* New York: Atheneum, 1963.

Aulau, Bestia. *La Jeunesse de Mme de Staël.* Geneva: Droz, 1970.

Balaye, Simone. *Madame De Staël: Lumières et liberté.* Paris: Klincksieck, 1979.

Bede, Jean-Albert. "Madame de Staël, Rousseau et le suicide." *Revue d'Histoire Littéraire de la France* 66, no. 1 (1966): 52–70.

Berger, Morroe, ed. *Madame de Staël on Politics, Literature, and National Character.* Garden City, N.Y.: Doubleday, 1965.

Bonnet, Jean-Claude. "Le Musée Staëlien." *Littérature* 42 (May 1981): 4–19.

Cahiers Staëliens. Société des Etudes Staëliennes, 1962.

Caramaschi, Enzo. *Voltaire, Mme de Staël, Balzac.* Padova: Liviana, 1977.

Cleary, John. "Mme de Staël, Rousseau, and Mary Wollstonecraft." *Romance Notes* 21 (1981): 329–33.

Collectif. *Madame de Staël et l'Europe: Colloque de Copet.* Paris: Klincksieck, 1970.

———. *Le Groupe de Copet—Actes du colloque de juillet 1974.* Paris: Champion, 1977.

de Man, Paul. "Madame de Staël et Jean-Jacques Rousseau." *Preuves* 190 (December 1966): 35–40.

Diesbach, Christain de. *Madame de Staël.* Paris: Perrin, 1983.

Forsberg, Roberta J. *Mme de Staël and the English.* New York: Astra Books, 1967.

Frank, Frederick S. "The Dawn and the Thunderstorm: Byron and Mme de Staël." *Revue de Littérature Comparée* 43 (1969): 320–43.

Gibelin, Jean. *L'Esthétique de Schelling et l'Allemagne de Mme de Staël.* Paris: Champion, 1934.

Gutwirth, Madelyn. *Mme de Staël, Novelist: The Emergence of the Artist as a Woman.* Urbana: University of Illinois Press, 1978.

———. "Mme de Staël, Rousseau and the Woman Question." *PMLA* 86 (1971): 100–109.

Gwynne, Gruffed E. *Madame de Staël et la Révolution française.* Paris: Nizet, 1969.

Hamilton, James F. "Structural Polarity in Mme de Staël's *De la littérature.*" *French Review* 50 (1977): 706–12.

Hartman, Elwood. "Mme de Staël, the Continuing Quarrel of the Ancients and Moderns, and the Idea of Progress." *Research Studies* 50 (1982): 33–45.

Herold, J. Christopher. *Mistress to an Age: A Life of Madame de Staël.* Indianapolis: Bobbs-Merrill, 1958.

Higonnet, Margaret R. "Madame de Staël and Schelling." *Comparative Literature* 38 (1986): 159–80.

Holmann, Etienne, ed. *Benjamin Constant, Madame de Staël et le Groupe de Copet.* Oxford: The Voltaire Foundation, 1982.

Hopsett, Charlott. *The Literary Existence of Germaine de Staël.* Carbondale: Southern Illinois University Press, 1987.

Lonchamp, Frederic. *L'Oeuvre imprimée de Mme de Staël.* Geneva: P. Ceiller, 1949.

Luppe, Robert de. *Les Idées littéraires de Madame de Staël et l'héritage des lumières—1795–1800.* Paris: Vrin, 1969.

Mercken-Spaas, Godelieve. "Death and the Romantic Heroine: Chateaubriand and de Staël." In *Pre-text, Text, Context: Essays on Nineteenth-Century French Literature,* edited by Robert L. Mitchell, 79–86. Columbus: Ohio State University Press, 1980.

Moers, Ellen. "Mme de Staël and the Woman of Genius." *American Scholar* 44 (1975): 225–41.

Monchoux, André. "La Place de Madame de Staël parmi les théoriciens du romantisme français." In *Madame de Staël et l'Europe,* 261–376. Paris: Klincksieck, 1970.

Mortier, Roland. "Madame de Staël et l'héritage des lumières." In *Madame de Staël et l'Europe,* 129–39. Paris: Klincksieck, 1970.

Occident et cahiers Staëliens. Société des Etudes Staëliennes, 1930–1939.

Pange, Jean de. *Auguste Guillaume Schlegel et Madame de Staël.* Paris: Albert, 1938.

Pange, Victor de. *Le Plus Beau de toutes les fêtes: Mme de Staël et Elisabeth Harvey, duchesse de Devonshire d'après leur correspondance inédite, 1804–1817.* Paris: Klincksieck, 1980.

Porter, Laurence M. "The Emergence of a Romantic Style: From *De la littérature* to *De l'Allemagne.*" In *Authors and Their Centuries.* French Literature Series vol.1, edited by Phillip Crant, 129–42. Columbia: University of South Carolina Press, 1973.

Postgate, Helen B. *Madame de Staël.* New York: Twayne, 1968.

Poulet, Georges. "La pensée critique de Mme de Staël." *Preuves* 190 (December 1966): 27–35.

Solovieff, Georges. "A propos des choix, omissions et repentirs dans *De l'Allemagne* de Mme de Staël." *Studi Francesi* 28 (1984): 53–74.

Souriau, Eve. *Mme de Staël et Henri Heine: Les Deux Allemagnes.* Paris: Didier, 1974.

Starobinski, Jean. "Suicide et mélancolie chez Mme de Staël." *Preuves* 190 (December 1966): 41–48. Reprinted in *Madame de Staël et l'Europe.* Paris: Klincksieck, 1970.

Tenenbaum, Susan. *The Social and Political Thought of Mme de Staël.* Ph.D. diss.: City University of New York, 1976.

Tournier, Michel. Preface to *L'Essai sur la fiction.* Paris: Ramsey, 1979.

Vallois, M. "Les Voi(es) de la Sibylle: Aphasie et discours féminin chez Mme de Staël." *Stanford French Review* 6 (1982): 35–48.

Weightman, John. "Madame de Staël." *Encounter* 41 (October 1973): 45–54.

West, Anthony. *Mortal Wounds.* New York: McGraw-Hill, 1973.

Winegarten, Renée. *Mme de Staël.* Leamington Spa, U.K.: Berg Publishers, 1985.

BENJAMIN CONSTANT

Actes du Congrès Benjamin Constant à Lausanne, octobre 1967. Geneva: Droz, 1968.

Barrès, Maurice. "Méditation spirituelle sur Benjamin Constant." In *Un homme libre,* 2d ed., 92–107. Paris: Émile Paul, 1912.

Barthou, Louis. "Benjamin Constant contre les discours écrits." *Revue de France* 1 (January 1933): 39–51.

Bastid, Paul. *Benjamin Constant et sa doctrine.* 2 vols. Paris: Armand Colin, 1966.

Berlin, Isaiah. "Two Concepts of Liberty." In *Four Essays on Liberty,* 118–72. Oxford: Oxford University Press, 1969.

Bressler, Henri. *Benjamin Constant et les femmes.* Geneva: Droz, 1973.

Cruickshank, John. *Benjamin Constant.* New York: Twayne, 1974.

Deguise, Pierre. *Benjamin Constant: De la perfectibilité de l'espèce humaine.* Lausanne: Editions de l'Age d'homme, 1968.

———. *Benjamin Constant méconnu: Le livre de la religion.* Geneva: Droz, 1966.

Dodge, Guy H. *Benjamin Constant's Philosophy of Liberalism: A Study in Politics and Religion.* Chapel Hill: University of North Carolina Press, 1980.

Europe no. 467 (1968). Special Constant issue.

Fink, Beatrice C. "Benjamin Constant and the Enlightenment." *Studies in Eighteenth-Century Culture* 3 (1973): 67–81.

————. "Benjamin Constant on Equality." *Journal of the History of Ideas* 33 (1972): 307–14.

Franck, Adolphe. "Idées de Benjamin Constant sur la religion." *Revue Politique et Littéraire* 5 (1968): 170–78, 434–38, 442–45.

Gauchet, Marcel. "L'Illusion lucide du libéralisme." Preface to *De la liberté chez les modernes*, 11–91. Paris: Pluriel, 1980.

Gouhier, Henri. *Benjamin Constant.* Paris: Desclée de Brouwer, 1967.

Harpaz, Ephraim. *Benjamin Constant: Recueil d'articles 1817–1820. Le Mercure, La Minerve et La Renommée.* 2 vols. Geneva: Droz, 1972.

————. *Benjamin Constant: Recueil d'articles 1795–1817.* Geneva: Droz, 1978.

————. *Benjamin Constant: Recueil d'articles 1820–1824.* Geneva: Droz, 1981.

Hartman, Mary S. "Benjamin Constant and the Question of Ministerial Responsibility in France 1814–1815." *Journal of European Studies* 6 (1976): 248–61.

Hofmann, Etienne. *Les "Principes de politique" de Benjamin Constant: La Génèse d'une oeuvre et l'évolution de la pensée de leur auteur (1789–1806).* Geneva: Droz, 1980.

————, ed. *Bibliographie analytique des écrits sur Benjamin Constant (1796–1980).* Oxford: The Voltaire Foundation, 1980.

Holdheim, William W. *Benjamin Constant.* London: Bowes & Bowes, 1961.

Holmes, Stephen. *Benjamin Constant and the Making of Modern Liberalism.* New Haven: Yale University Press, 1984.

Jasinski, Béatrice W. *L'Engagement de Benjamin Constant: Amour et politique 1794–1796.* Paris: Minard, 1971.

Kelly, George. "Constant Commotion: Avatars of a Pure Liberal." *Journal of Modern History* 54 (1982): 497–518.

Kloocke, Kurt. "Benjamin Constant et les débuts de la pensée nihiliste en Europe." In *Benjamin Constant, Madame de Staël et le Groupe de Coppet,* edited by Etienne Hofmann, 182–220. Oxford: The Voltaire Foundation, 1982.

Lowe, David K. *Benjamin Constant: An Annotated Bibliography of Critical Editions and Studies 1946–1978.* London: Grant & Cutler, 1979.

Oliver, Andrew. *Benjamin Constant écriture et conquête de moi.* Paris: Minard, 1970.

Poulet, Georges. *Benjamin Constant par lui-même.* Paris: Editions du Seuil, 1968.

Sainte-Beuve, Charles-Augustin. "Benjamin Constant: Son Cours de politique constitutionnel." In *Nouveaux lundis,* vol. 9, 135–60. Paris: Celman-Lévy, 1871.

Todorov, Tzvetan. "Benjamin Constant, politique et amour." *Poétique* 56 (1983): 485–510.

FRANÇOIS-RENÉ, VICOMTE DE CHATEAUBRIAND

Aynesworth, Donald. "Autobiography and Anonymity." *French Review* 52 (1979): 401–9.

Barbéris, Pierre. *A la recherche d'une écriture: Chateaubriand.* Paris: Marne, 1974.

————. *Chateaubriand: Une Réaction au monde moderne.* Paris: Larousse, 1977.

Barthes, Roland. "Chateaubriand: *Life of Rancé.*" In *New Critical Essays,* translated by Richard Howard, 41–54. New York: Hill & Wang, 1980.

Bassan, Fernande. *Chateaubriand et la Terre Sainte.* Paris: Presses Universitaires de France, 1959.

Bazin, Christian. *Chateaubriand en Amérique.* Paris: Table Ronde, 1969.

Berchet, Jean-Claude. "Un Voyage vers soi." *Poétique* 53 (1983): 91–108.

Butor, Michel. "Chateaubriand et l'ancienne Amérique." *Nouvelle Revue Française* 11 (1963): 1015–31.

Dalmas, André. "Dialectica. Ici, proche de Rancé . . . Maurice Blanchot." *Le Nouveau Commerce* 61 (1985): 6–12.

Doran, Eva. "Two Men and a Forest: Chateaubriand, Tocqueville and the American Wilderness." *Essays in French Literature* 13 (November 1976): 44–61.

Evans, Joan. *Chateaubriand: A Biography.* London: Macmillan, 1939.

Gracq, Julien. "Réflexions sur Chateaubriand." *Cahiers du Sud* 50 (1960): 163–72.

Grevlund, M. *Paysage intérieur et paysage extérieur dans* Les Mémoires d'outre-tombe. Paris: Nizet, 1968.

Guillemin, Henri. *L'Homme des* Mémoires d'outre-tombe. Paris: Gallimard, 1964.

Lynes, Carlos. *Chateaubriand as a Critic of French Literature.* Baltimore: Johns Hopkins University Press, 1946.

Main, Margaret. "Chateaubriand, a Precursor of Proust." *French Review* 45 (1971): 388–400.

Maréchal-Trudel, Michèle. *Chateaubriand, Byron et Venise: Un Mythe contesté.* Paris: Nizet, 1978.

Milner, Max. "Les Possibles inaccomplis dans la première partie des *Mémoires d'outre-tombe.*" In *Le Lieu et la formule: Hommage à Marc Eideldinger*, 60–70. Neuchâtel: La Baconnière, 1978.

Moreau, Pierre. *Chateaubriand, l'homme et l'oeuvre.* Paris: Hatier, 1956.

Painter, George D. *Chateaubriand: A Biography.* Vol. 1, *The Longed-for Tempests (1768–93).* London: Chatto & Windus, 1977.

Porter, Charles A. *Chateaubriand: Composition, Imagination, and Poetry.* Stanford French and Italian Studies 9. Saratoga, Calif.: ANMA Libri, 1978.

———. "Chateaubriand's Revenge on History in the *Mémoires d'outre-tombe.*" *Symposium* 35 (1981): 267–80.

———. "Chateaubriand's Classicism." *Yale French Studies* 38 (1967): 156–71.

Reboul, Pierre. *Chateaubriand et le conservateur.* Lille: Université de Lille III, 1973.

Redman, Harry, Jr. "Chateaubriand's Rancé and Cardinal de Retz." *Nineteenth Century French Studies* 14 (1985–86): 28–36.

Richard, Jean-Pierre. *Paysage de Chateaubriand.* Paris: Editions du Seuil, 1967.

Riffaterre, Michael. "Comment décrire le style de Chateaubriand?" *Romanic Review* 53 (1962): 128–38.

———. "Descriptive Imagery." *Yale French Studies* 61 (1981): 107–25.

———. "From Structure to Code: Chateaubriand and the Imaginary Monument." In *Text Production*, 125–56. New York: Columbia University Press, 1983.

Sainte-Beuve, Charles-Augustin. *Chateaubriand et son groupe littéraire sous l'empire.* 2 vols. Paris: Garnier, 1948.

Sieburg, Friedrich. *Chateaubriand.* Translated by Violet M. MacDonald. London: Allen & Unwin, 1961.

Switzer, Richard, ed. *Chateaubriand Today.* Madison: University of Wisconsin Press, 1970.

———. *Chateaubriand.* New York: Twayne, 1971.

Vollrath, Robert A. *Chateaubriand: A Study of his Aesthetics.* Baltimore: Johns Hopkins University Thesis, 1981.

CHARLES FOURIER

Actualité de Fourier: colloque d'Arc-et-Senans—sous la direction d'Henri Lefebvre. Paris: Anthropos, 1975.

Beecher, Jonathan F. *Charles Fourier: The Visionary and His World.* Berkeley: University of California Press, 1987.

Breton, André. *Ode to Charles to Charles Fourier.* Translated by Kenneth White. London: Cape Goliard Press, 1969.

Corcoran, P. E. "Early French Socialism Reconsidered. 1. The Propaganda of Fourier and Cabet." *History of European Ideas* 7 (1986): 469–88.

Debout, Simone. *"Griffe au nez"; ou, Donner "have ou art": Ecriture inconnue de Charles Fourier*. Paris: Anthropos, 1974.

―――. *L'Utopie de Charles Fourier: L'illusion réele*. Paris: Payot, 1978.

Debû-Bridel, Jacques. *L'Actualité de Fourier: De l'utopie au fouriérisme appliqué*. Paris: France-Empire, 1978.

Descroche, Henri. *La Société festive: Du fouriérisme écrit aux fouriérismes pratiques*. Paris: Editions du Seuil, 1975.

Goldstein, Leslie F. "Early Feminist Themes in French Utopian Socialism: The St. Simonians and Fourier." *Journal of the History of Ideas* 43 (1982): 91–108.

Goret, Jean. *La Pensée de Fourier*. Paris: Presses Universitaires de France, 1974.

Klossowski, Pierre. *Les Derniers Travaux de Gulliver suivi de Sade et Fourier*. Montpellier: Fata Morgana, 1974.

Lehouck, Emile. *Fourier aujourd'hui*. Paris: Denoël, 1966.

―――. *Vie de Charles Fourier*. Paris: Denoël-Gonthier, 1978.

―――. "La Lecture surréaliste de Charles Fourier." *Australian Journal of French Studies* 20 (1983): 26–36.

Revue internationale de philosophie 60 (1962). Special Fourier issue.

Riasanovsky, Nicholas V. *The Teaching of Charles Fourier*. Berkeley: University of California Press, 1969.

Schérer, René. *Charles Fourier; ou, La Contestation globale*. Paris: Seghers, 1970.

Vergez, André. *Fourier*. Paris: Presses Universitaires de France, 1969.

Zeldin, David. *The Educational Ideas of Charles Fourier (1772–1837)*. London: Cass, 1969.

CLAUDE-HENRI DE SAINT-SIMON

Dumas, Georges. *Psychologie de deux messies positivistes: Saint-Simon et Auguste Comte*. Paris: Alcan, 1905.

Durkheim, Emile. *Socialism and Saint-Simon*. Translated by C. Sandler, and edited by A. W. Gouldner. Yellow Springs, Ohio: Antioch, 1958.

Fehlbaum, Rolf Peter. *Saint-Simon und die Saint-Simonisten: Vom Laissez-faire zur Wirtschaftsplanung*. Tübingen: J. C. B. Mohr, 1970.

Manuel, Frank. *The New World of Henri Saint-Simon*. Cambridge, Mass.: Harvard University Press, 1956.

Markham, Felix M. H., ed. Introduction to *Henri Comte de Saint-Simon: Selected Writings*, 11–49. Oxford: Blackwell, 1952.

Pankhurst, Richard K. P. *The Saint-Simonians, Mill and Carlyle: A Preface to Modern Thought*. London: Sidgwick & Jackson, 1957.

Revue internationale de philosophie 53–54 (1960). Special Saint-Simon issue.

Saint-Simon, Henri. *The Doctrine of Saint-Simon: An Exposition; First Year 1828–29*. Translated and edited by George G. Iggers. New York: Schocken Books, 1972.

―――. *Henri Saint-Simon 1760–1825: Selected Writings on Science, Industry and Social Organizations*. Translated and edited by Keith Taylor. London: Croom Helm, 1975.

Wokler, Robert. "Saint-Simon and the Passage from Political to Social Sciences." In *The Languages of Political Theory in Early-Modern Europe*, edited by Anthony Pagden, 325–38. New York: Cambridge University Press, 1987.

AUGUSTE COMTE

Arnaud, Pierre. *Politique d'Auguste Comte*. Paris: Armand Colin, 1965.

―――. *Sociologie de Comte*. Paris: Presses Universitaires de France, 1969.

————. *Le 'Nouveau Dieu': Préliminaires à la politique positive.* Paris: Vrin, 1973.

Bryant, Christopher G. A. *Positivism in Social Theory and Research.* London: Macmillan, 1985.

Bulletin de la Société française de philosophie, 1958. Célébration du centenaire de la mort d'Auguste Comte.

Canguilhem, Georges. "Histoire des religions et histoire des sciences dans la théorie du fétichisme chez Auguste Comte." In *Etudes d'histoire et de philosophie des sciences.* Paris: Vrin, 1968.

————. "La Philosophie biologique d'Auguste Comte et son influence en France au XIXᵉ siècle." In *Etudes d'histoire et de philosophie des sciences.* Paris: Vrin, 1979.

Cashdollar, Charles D. "Auguste Comte and the American Reformed Theologians." *Journal of the History of Ideas* 39 (1978): 61–79.

Charlton, D. G. *Positivist Thought in France during the Second Empire (1852–1870).* Oxford: Clarendon Press, 1959.

Coser, Lewis. "Comte." In *Masters of Sociological Thought,* 2–41. New York: Harcourt Brace Jovanovich, 1971.

Eisen, S. "Herbert Spencer and the Specter of Comte." *Journal of British Studies* 7 (1967): 48–67.

Evans-Pritchard, E. E. *The Sociology of Comte: An Appreciation.* Manchester: Manchester University Press, 1970.

Fletcher, Ronald. *Auguste Comte and the Making of Sociology.* London: Athlone Press, 1966.

————. *The Crisis of Industrial Civilization: The Early Essays of Auguste Comte.* London: Heinemann Educational Books, 1974.

Fulcher, Jane. "Wagner, Comte and Proudhon: The Aesthetics of Positivism in France." *Symposium* 33 (1979): 142–52.

Gouhier, Henri. *La Jeunesse d'Auguste Comte et la formation du positivisme.* 3 vols. Paris: Vrin, 1933–41.

Habermas, Jürgen. "Comte and Mach: The Intention of Early Positivism." In *Knowledge and Human Interests,* translated by Jeremy L. Shapiro, 71–90. Boston: Beacon Press, 1971.

Kofman, Sarah. *Aberration, le devenir-femme d'Auguste Comte.* Paris: Aubier-Flammarion, 1978.

Kremer-Marietti, Angèle. *Le Projet anthropologique d'Auguste Comte.* Paris: Société d'Edition d'Enseignement Supérieur Réunis, 1981.

Laudan, L. "Towards a Reassessment of Comte's 'Methode Positive.' " *Philosophy of Science* 38 (1971): 35–53.

Leuzer, Gertrud, ed. *Auguste Comte and Positivism: The Essential Writings.* New York: Harper & Row, 1975.

Lévy-Bruhl, Lucien. *The Philosophy of Auguste Comte.* Translated by Kathleen de Beaumont-Klein. New York: Putnam's, 1903.

Löwith, Karl. "Comte." In *Meaning in History,* 67–91. Chicago: University of Chicago Press, 1949.

Manuel, Frank. *The Prophets of Paris.* Cambridge, Mass.: Harvard University Press, 1962.

Mill, John Stuart. *Auguste Comte and Positivism.* London: N. Trübner, 1865. Ann Arbor: University of Michigan Press, 1961.

Popper, Karl. *The Poverty of Historicism.* Boston: Beacon Press, 1957.

Pouillon, Jean. "Fétiches sans fétichisme." *Nouvelle Revue de Psychanalyse* 2 (1970): 135–47.

Schmaus, Warren. "A Reappraisal of Comte's Three State Law." *History and Theory* 21 (1982): 248–66.

Simon, W. M. *European Positivism in the Nineteenth Century*. Ithaca: Cornell University Press, 1963.

Spencer, Herbert. *The Classification of the Sciences; to Which Are Added Reasons for Dissenting from the Philosophy of M. Comte*. New York: Appleton, 1864.

Thompson, Kenneth. "Introductory Essay. Auguste Comte: Founder of Sociology." In *Auguste Comte: The Foundation of Sociology*, 1–35. New York: John Wiley, 1975.

Vernon, Richard. "Auguste Comte and the Withering-Away of the State." *Journal of the History of Ideas* 45 (1984): 549–66.

JULES MICHELET

L'Arc 52 (1973). Special Michelet issue.

Atherton, Jorn. "Michelet: Three Conceptions of Historical Becoming." *Studies in Romanticism* 4 (1965): 220–39.

Bann, Stephen. "A Cycle in Historical Discourse: Barante, Thierry, Michelet." *Twentieth-Century Studies* 3 (1970): 110–30.

Barthes, Roland. *Michelet par lui-même*. Paris: Editions du Seuil, 1954.

———. "La Sorcière." In *Critical Essays*, translated by Richard Howard. Evanston, Ill.: Northwestern University Press, 1972.

Bataille, Georges. "Michelet." In *Literature and Evil*, translated by Alastair Hamilton, 45–57. London: Calder & Boyars, 1973.

Burrows, Toby. "Jules Michelet and *Annales* School." *Clio* 12 (1982): 67–82.

Calo, Jeanne. *La Création de la femme chez Michelet*. Paris: Nizet, 1975.

Crouzet, Michel. "Michelet, les morts et l'année 1842." *Annales, Economies, Sociétés, Civilisations* 31 (1976): 182–96.

Europe nos. 535–36 (1973). Special Michelet issue.

Febvre, Lucien. *Michelet*. Geneva: Editions des Trois Collines, 1946.

Gossman, Lionel. "The Go-Between, Jules Michelet, 1798–1874." *MLN* 89 (1974): 503–41.

Haac, Oscar A. "The Literature of History: Michelet's Middle Ages." *Nineteenth Century French Studies* 4 (1976): 162–68.

———. *Jules Michelet*. Boston: Twayne, 1982.

Kaplan, Edward K. *Michelet's Poetic Vision: A Romantic Philosophy of Nature, Man, & Woman*. Amherst: University of Massachusetts Press, 1977.

Kippur, Stephen A. *Jules Michelet: A Study of Mind and Sensibility*. Albany: State University of New York Press, 1981.

Le Goff, Jacques. "Le Moyen-Age de Michelet." In *Pour un autre Moyen-Age: Temps, travail et culture en Occident*, 19–45. Paris: Gallimard, 1977.

McCallum, Pamela. "Michelet's Narrative Practice: Naturality, Populism, and the Intellectual." *Cultural Critique* 1 (1985): 141–58.

Michelet, Jules. *Mother Death: The Journal of Jules Michelet 1815–1850*. Translated and edited by Edward K. Kaplan. Amherst: University of Massachusetts Press, 1984.

Orr, Linda. *Jules Michelet: Nature, History, and Language*. Ithaca: Cornell University Press, 1976.

———. *Michelet: Sa vie, son oeuvre 1798–1874*. Paris: Archives de France, 1961.

Picon, Gaëtan. "Michelet et la parole historienne." Introduction à *L'Étudiant*. Paris: Editions du Seuil, 1970.

Poulet, Georges. "Michelet et le moment d'Eros." *Nouvelle Revue Française* 30 (1967): 610–35.

Revue d'Histoire Littéraire de la France (September–October 1974). Special Michelet issue.

Richard, Jean-Pierre. " 'La Fiancée du vent': Commentaire d'une page de Michelet." *Poétique* 20 (1974): 416–36.

Richer, Jean. "Jules Michelet et Albert Dürer." In *La Gloire de Dürer*, edited by Jean Richer, 183–203. Paris: Klincksieck, 1974.

Seebacher, J. "Le Côté de la mort, ou L'Histoire comme clinique." *Revue d'Histoire Littéraire de la France* 74 (1974): 810–23.

Serres, Michel. "Le Tricorne et l'amour sorcier." *Critique* 24 (1968): 57–69.

———. "Traduction thèse à thèse: *La Sorcière*." In *La Communication. Hermès I*, 219–32. Paris: Editions de Minuit, 1968.

Viallaneix, Paul. *La Voie royale: Essai sur l'idée du peuple dans l'oeuvre de Michelet*. 2d ed. Paris: Flammarion, 1971.

———, ed. *Michelet cent ans après*. Grenoble: Presses Universitaires de Grenoble, 1975.

Ward, Patricia A. "Encoding in Romantic Descriptions of the Renaissance: Hugo and Michelet on the Sixteenth-Century." *French Forum* 3 (1978): 132–46.

White, Hayden. "Michelet: Historical Realism as Romance." In *Metahistory: The Historical Imagination in Nineteenth-Century Europe*, 135–62. Baltimore: Johns Hopkins University Press, 1973.

Wilson, Edmund. "Michelet . . . " In *To The Finland Station: A Study in the Writing and Acting of History*, 2–41. New York: Farrar, Straus & Giroux, 1972.

EDGAR QUINET

Bernard-Griffiths, Simone. "Le Dossier Quinet." *Romantisme* 5 (1975): 126–35.

———. "Edgar Quinet pèlerin romantique." *Revue des Lettres* (April–June 1975): 16–31.

———. "Rupture entre Michelet et Quinet." In *Michelet cent ans après*, edited by Paul Viallaneix, 145–65. Grenoble: Presses Universitaires de Grenoble, 1975.

———. "La Fête révolutionnaire vue par Edgar Quinet ou L'Illusion tragique." *Les Fêtes de la révolution*, edited by J. Ehrard and P. Viallaneix, 605–19. Paris: Société des Etudes Robespierristes, 1977.

———, and P. Viallaneix, eds. *Edgar Quinet. Ce Juif errant. Actes du colloque international de Clermont-Ferrand, 1975*. Clermont-Ferrand: Faculté des Lettres, 1978.

Charlton, D. G. *Secular Religions in France: 1815–1870*. London: Oxford University Press, 1963.

Chassin, Charles L. *Edgar Quinet: Sa vie, son oeuvre*. Geneva: Slatkine Reprints, 1970.

Chazin, M. "Extracts from Emerson by Edgar Quinet." *Revue de Littérature Comparée* 14 (1935): 136–49, 310–26.

———. "Quinet: An Early Discoverer of Emerson." *PMLA* 48 (1933): 147–63.

Clarke, M. A. *Rimbaud and Quinet*. Sydney: Simmons, 1945.

Crossley, Ceri. "Edgar Quinet and Messianic Nationalism in the Years Preceding 1848." In *1848: The Sociology of Literature*, edited by Francis Barker et al., 265–76. Essex: University of Essex Press, 1978.

———. "Edgar Quinet: Conscience de soi et mal du siècle." *Romantisme* 10 (1980): 47–58.

———. "Idée de Dieu et nature chez Quinet jusqu'en 1842." In *Romantisme et religion*, edited by Michel Baude and Marc-Matthieu Münch, 283–90. Paris: Presses Universitaires de France, 1980.

———. *Edgar Quinet (1803–1875): A Study in Romantic Thought*. Lexington, Ky.: French Forum, 1983.

Domino, M. "Edgar Quinet: Être dans l'histoire, écrire l'histoire." In *Les Genres et l'histoire*, 345–71. Paris: Les Belles Lettres, 1977.

————. "Religion et révolution chez Quinet." In *Romantisme et religion*, edited by Michel Baude et Marc-Matthieu Münch, 291–306. Paris: Presses Universitaires de France, 1980.

Dumas, J.-L. "Quinet et la philosophie allemande de l'histoire." *Revue de Littéraire Comparée* 52 (1973): 384–98.

Du Pasquier, Marcel. *Edgar Quinet en Suisse: Douze Années d'exil, 1858–1870*. Neuchâtel: La Baconnière, 1959.

Mouchoux, André. "L'Aventure allemande d'Edgar Quinet." *Revue de Littérature Comparée* 39 (1960): 81–107.

Powers, R. H. *Edgar Quinet: A Study in French Patriotism*. Dallas: Southern Methodist University Press, 1957.

Quinet, Edgar. *Histoire de mes idées: Autobiographie*. Introduction, bibliography, and notes by Simone Bernard-Griffiths. Paris: Flammarion, 1972.

Trouchon, H. *Le Jeune Edgar Quinet ou l'aventure d'un enthousiaste*. Paris: Les Belles Lettres, 1937.

Vabre, Pradal, G. *La Dimension historique de l'homme, ou Le Mythe du Juif errant dans la pensée d'Edgar Quinet*. Paris: Nizet, 1961.

Viallaneix, Paul. "Michelet, Quinet et la légende protestante." In *Les Protestants dans les débuts de la troisième république (1871–1885)*, edited by A. Encrevé and M. Richard, 79–89. Paris: Société de l'Histoire du Protestantisme Français, 1979.

CHARLES-AUGUSTIN SAINTE-BEUVE

Antoine, Gérald, ed. *Sainte-Beuve: Vie, poésies et pensées de Joseph Delorme*. Paris: Nouvelles Editions Latines, 1956.

Barlow, Norman H. *Sainte-Beuve to Baudelaire: A Poetic Legacy*. Durham, N.C.: Duke University Press, 1964.

Billy, André. *Sainte-Beuve, sa vie, son temps*. Paris: Flammarion, 1952.

Bonnerot, Jean. *Un Demi-Siècle d'études sur Sainte-Beuve 1904–1954*. Paris: Les Belles Lettres, 1957.

Chadbourne, Richard M. *Charles-Augustin Sainte-Beuve*. Boston: Twayne, 1977.

Chinard, Gilbert. *Sainte-Beuve: Thomas Jefferson et Tocqueville, avec une introduction*. Princeton: Princeton University Press, 1943.

Decreus–Van Liefland, Juliette. *Sainte-Beuve et la critique des auteurs féminins*. Paris: Boivin, 1949.

Eliot, T. S. "Experiment in Criticism." In *Literary Opinion in America*, edited by M. D. Zabel. New York: Harper & Row, 1951.

L'Esprit Créateur 14, no. 1 (1974): Special Sainte-Beuve issue.

Fayolle, Roger. *Sainte-Beuve et le 18è siècle, ou Comment les révolutions arrivent*. Paris: Armand Colin, 1972.

James, Henry. "Charles-Augustin Sainte-Beuve." *Literary Criticism: French Writers; Other European Writers; The Prefaces to the New York Edition*, 664–95. New York: Library of America, 1984.

Lehmann, A. G. *Sainte-Beuve: A Portrait of the Critic 1804–1842*. Oxford: Clarendon Press, 1962.

Mahieu, R. G. *Sainte-Beuve aux Etats-Unis*. Princeton: Princeton University Press, 1945.

Molho, R. *L'Ordre et les ténèbres: Essai sur la formation d'une image du 17ᵉ siècle dans l'oeuvre de Sainte-Beuve*. Paris: Armand Colin, 1972.

Moreau, Pierre. *La Critique selon Sainte-Beuve*. Paris: Sociéte d'Edition d'Enseignement Superieur Réunis, 1964.

Nicolson, H. G. *Sainte-Beuve.* Garden City, N.Y.: Doubleday, 1957.

Pitwood, Michael. "Sainte-Beuve and Dante." *Modern Language Review* 77 (1982): 568–76.

Poulet, Georges. *La Conscience critique.* Paris: José Corti, 1971.

Proust, Marcel. *Contre Sainte-Beuve.* Paris: Gallimard (Pléiade), 1971.

Richard, Jean-Pierre. *Essais sur le romantisme.* Paris: Editions du Seuil, 1971.

Rigolot, François. *Le Texte de la Renaissance: Des Rhétoriqueurs à Montaigne.* Geneva: Droz, 1983.

Romantisme 3 (1972). Special Sainte-Beuve issue.

Sainte-Beuve et la critique littéraire contemporaine: Actes du colloque tenu à Liège du 6 au 8 octobre 1969. Paris: Les Belles Lettres, 1972.

Welleck, René. "Sainte-Beuve." In *A History of Modern Criticism, 1750–1950.* Vol. 3, *The Age of Transition,* 34–72. New Haven: Yale University Press, 1965.

ALEXIS DE TOCQUEVLLE

Alexis de Tocqueville: Livre du centenaire, 1859–1959. Paris: Editions du Centre National de la Recherche Scientifique, 1960.

Aron, Raymond. "La Définition libérale, Alexis de Tocqueville et Karl Marx." *European Journal of Sociology* 15 (1964): 159–89.

———. *Auguste Comte et Alexis de Tocqueville: Juges de l'Angleterre.* Oxford: Clarendon Press, 1965.

Birnbaum, Pierre. *Sociologie de Tocqueville.* Paris: Presses Universitaires de France, 1970.

Boesche, Roger. "Tocqueville and *Le Commerce*: A Newspaper Expressing his Unusual Liberalism." *Journal of the History of Ideas* 44 (1983): 277–92.

Brogan, Hugh. *Tocqueville.* Fontana, Calif.: Collins, 1973.

———. "Tocqueville and the American Presidency." *Journal of American Studies* 15 (1981): 357–75.

Brunius, Teddy. *Alexis de Tocqueville, the Sociological Aesthetician.* Uppsala: Almqvist & Wiksells, 1960.

Cobb, Richard. *A Second Identity: Essays on France and French History.* Oxford: Oxford University Press, 1969.

Donohue, William A. "Tocqueville's Reflections on Safeguarding Freedom in a Democracy." *Tocqueville Review* 6 (1984): 389–99.

Drescher, Seymour. *Dilemmas of Democracy: Tocqueville and Modernization.* Pittsburgh: University of Pittsburgh Press, 1968.

———. *Tocqueville and England.* Cambridge, Mass.: Harvard University Press, 1964.

Furet, François. "The Young Tocqueville's Idea of the American Voyage (1825–1831)." *Proceedings of the Annual Meeting of the Western Society for French History* 11 (1984): 207–11.

Gargan, Edward T. *De Tocqueville.* New York: Hillary House Publishers, 1965.

———. *Alexis de Tocqueville: The Critical Years—1848–1851.* Washington, D.C.: Catholic University of America Press, 1955.

Gershman, Sally. "Alexis de Tocqueville and Slavery." *French Historical Studies* 9 (1976): 467–83.

Goldstein, Doris. *Trial of Faith: Religion and Politics in Tocqueville's Thought.* New York: Elsevier, 1975.

Hamburger, Joseph. "Mill and Tocqueville on Liberty." In *James and John Stuart Mill: Papers of the Centenary Conference,* edited by John M. Robson and Michael Laine, 111–25. Toronto: University of Toronto Press, 1976.

Hausen, Klaus J. "The Changing Fortunes of Tocqueville's *Democracy in America.*" *Queen's Quarterly* 89 (1982): 233–37.

Sainte-Beuve, C.-A. *P.-J. Proudhon, sa vie et sa correspondance 1838–1848*. Paris: Michel Lévy Frères, 1872.

Spear, Sr. Lois. "Pierre-Joseph Proudhon and the Myth of Universal Suffrage." *Canadian Journal of History* 10 (1975): 295–306.

———. "P.-J. Proudhon and the Revolution of 1848." Ph.D. diss.: Loyola University of Chicago, 1971.

Vernon, Richard. Introduction to *The Principle of Federation by P.-J. Proudhon*. Toronto: University of Toronto Press, 1979.

Vincent, K. Steven. *Pierre-Joseph Proudhon and the Rise of French Republican Socialism*. New York: Oxford University Press, 1984.

CHARLES-PIERRE BAUDELAIRE

Abel, Elizabeth. "Redefining the Sister Arts: Baudelaire's Response to the Art of Delacroix." *Critical Inquiry* 6 (1980): 363–84.

Abrams, M. H. "Coleridge, Baudelaire, and Modernist Poetics." In *New Perspectives in German Literary Criticism: A Collection of Essays*, edited by Richard E. Amacher and Victor Lange; translated by David Henry Wilson et al. Princeton: Princeton University Press, 1979.

Arnold, Paul. *Esoterisme de Baudelaire*. Paris: Vrin, 1972.

Auden, W. H. Introduction to *Intimate Journals*. Translated by Christopher Isherwood. Hollywood: Marcel Rodd, 1947.

Auerbach, Eric. "The Aesthetic Dignity of the *Fleurs du mal*." In *Scenes from the Drama of European Literature*. New York: Meridian Books, 1959.

Bataille, Georges. "Baudelaire." In *Literature and Evil*. Translated by Alastair Hamilton. London: Calder & Boyers, 1973.

Baudelaire, Charles. *The "Painter of Modern Life" and Other Essays by Charles Baudelaire*. Edited and translated by Jonathan Mayne. London: Phaidon Press, 1964.

Benjamin, Walter. *Charles Baudelaire, a Lyric Poet in the Era of High Capitalism*. Translated by Harry Zohn. London: Verso, 1983.

———. "Central Park." *New German Critique* 34 (Winter 1985): 32–58.

Bernard, Paul R., ed. *Essays on Baudelaire in Honor of Lois B. Hyslop*. Les Bonnes Feuilles 4, nos. 1–2. University Park: Pennsylvania State University Press, 1975.

Bersani, Leo. *Baudelaire and Freud*. Berkeley: University of California Press, 1977.

Blanchot, Maurice. "L'Echec de Baudelaire." In *La Part du feu*, 133–51. Paris: Gallimard, 1949.

Bloom, Harold, ed. *Modern Critical Views: Charles Baudelaire*. New Haven: Chelsea House, 1987.

Bowie, Malcolm, ed. *Imagination and Language: Collected Essays on Constant, Baudelaire, Nerval and Flaubert*. Cambridge: Cambridge University Press, 1981.

———, Alison Fairlie, and Alison Finch, eds. *Baudelaire, Mallarmé and Valéry: New Essays in Honour of Lloyd Austin*. Cambridge: Cambridge University Press, 1982.

Bowie, Theodore. *Baudelaire and the Graphic Arts*. Bloomington: Indiana University Press, 1957.

Buci-Glucksman, Christine. *La Raison baroque de Baudelaire à Benjamin*. Paris: Galilée, 1984.

Bulletin Baudelairien. Nashville, Tenn.: Centre d'Etudes Baudelairiennes, Vanderbilt University. W. T. Bendy, James Petty, Raymond Poggenburg, Claude Pichois, directors.

Bush, W., ed. *Regards sur Baudelaire. Actes du Colloque de London (Canada), 1970*. Paris: Les Lettres Modernes, 1974.

Butor, Michel. *Histoire extraordinaire: Essay on a Dream of Baudelaire's*. Translated by Richard Howard. London: Jonathan Cape, 1969.

Cargo, Robert T. *Baudelaire Criticism 1950–67: A Bibliography with Critical Commentary.* University: University of Alabama Press, 1968.

Castex, P. G. *Baudelaire Critique d'art.* Paris: Société d'Edition d'Enseignement Supérieur Réunis, 1969.

Chase, Cynthia. "Getting Versed / Reading Hegel with Baudelaire." In *Decomposing Figures: Rhetorical Readings in the Romantic Tradition,* 113–40. Baltimore: Johns Hopkins University Press, 1986.

———. "Paragon, Parergon: Baudelaire Translates Rousseau." In *Decomposing Figures: Rhetorical Readings in the Romantic Tradition,* 196–208. Baltimore: Johns Hopkins University Press, 1986.

Clemens, Patricia. *Baudelaire and the English Tradition—Canonization of the Subversive.* Princeton: Princeton University Press, 1985.

de Man, Paul. "Literary History and Literary Modernity." In *Blindness and Insight: Essays in the Rhetoric of Contemporary Criticism,* 142–65. Minneapolis: University of Minnesota Press, 1983.

———. "The Rhetoric of Temporality." In *Blindness and Insight: Essays in the Rhetoric of Contemporary Criticism,* 187–228. Minneapolis: University of Minnesota Press, 1983.

Eliot, T. S. "Baudelaire." In *Selected Essays,* 371–81. New York: Harcourt, Brace & World, 1950.

Emmanuel, Pierre. *Baudelaire: The Paradox of Redemptive Satanism.* Translated by Robert T. Cargo. University: The University of Alabama Press, 1970.

L'Esprit Createur 13, no. 2 (1973). Special Baudelaire issue.

Etudes Baudelairiennes. Neuchâtel: La Baconnière. Marc Eigeldinger, Robert Kopp, Claude Pichois, directors.

Evans, Martha Noel. "The Divine Grace of Cosmopolitanism: Baudelaire's Introduction to the Universal Exposition of 1855." *French Literature Series* 9 (1982): 43–52.

Fietkan, Wolfgang. *Schwanengesang auf 1848: Ein rendez-vous au Louvre: Baudelaire, Marx, Proudhon und Hugo.* Reinbeck bei Hamburg: Rowohlt, 1978.

Ford, Charles H., ed. *The Mirror of Baudelaire.* With a preface by Paul Eluard. Norfolk, Conn.: New Directions, 1942.

Fried, Michael. "Painting Memories: On the Containment of the Past in Baudelaire and Manet." *Critical Inquiry* 10 (1984): 510–43.

Galaud, R. *Baudelaire: Poétiques et Poésie.* Paris: Nizet, 1969.

Gilman, Margaret. *Baudelaire the Critic.* New York: Farrar, Straus & Giroux, 1971.

Gourmont, Remy de. "Marginalia in Edgar Poe and Baudelaire." In *Affidavits of Genius: E. A. Poe and the French Critics 1847–1924,* edited by Jean Alexander, 219–32. Port Washington, N.Y.: National University Publications/Kennikat Press, 1971.

Hemmings, F. W. J. *Baudelaire the Damned.* New York: Scribner's, 1982.

Hiddleston, J. A. "Baudelaire and 'la critique d'identification.' " *French Forum* 9 (1984): 33–41.

Howells, Bernard. "Baudelaire: A Portrait of the Artist in 1846." *French Studies* 37 (1983): 426–39.

Hyslop, Lois Boe, ed. *Baudelaire: Man of His Time.* New Haven: Yale University Press, 1980.

———. *Baudelaire as a Love Poet, and Other Essays Commemorating the Centenary of the Death of the Poet.* University Park: Pennsylvania State University Press, 1969.

———, and Francis E. Hyslop. "Baudelaire and Meryon: Painters of the Urban Landscape." *Symposium* 38 (1984): 196–220.

———, trans. *Baudelaire as a Literary Critic: Selected Essays.* University Park: Pennsylvania State University Press, 1964.

Johnson, Barbara. *Défigurations du langage poétique: La Seconde Révolution Baudelairienne.* Paris: Flammarion, 1979.

Kristeva, Julia. "De l'identification: Freud, Baudelaire, Stendhal." In *Travail de la Métaphore: Identification, Interpretation,* 53–86. Paris: Denoël, 1984.

Lacoue-Labarthe, Philippe. "Baudelaire contra Wagner." *Etudes Françaises* 17 (October 1981): 23–52.

Lloyd, Rosemary. *Baudelaire's Literary Criticism.* Cambridge: Cambridge University Press, 1981.

———. "Baudelaire's Creative Criticism." *French Studies* 36 (1982): 37–44.

Mayne, Jonathan, ed. and trans. *Art in Paris 1845–62: Salons and Other Exhibitions Reviewed by Charles Baudelaire.* New York: Phaidon Press, 1965.

McKenna, Andrew. "Baudelaire and Nietzsche: Squaring the Circle of Madness." *Pre-text/Text/Context: Essays on Nineteenth-Century French Literature,* edited by Robert L. Mitchell, 53–65. Columbus: Ohio State University Press, 1980.

McLees, Ainslie Armstrong. "Baudelaire and Caricature: Argot Plastique." *Symposium* 38 (1984): 221–33.

Mehlman, Jeffrey. "Baudelaire with Freud: Theory and Pain." *Diacritics* 4 (1974): 7–13.

Mickel, Emanuel J. "Baudelaire's 'Peintre de la vie moderne.'" *Symposium* 38 (1984): 234–43.

Moss, A. *Baudelaire et Delacroix.* Paris: Nizet, 1973.

Patty, James S. "Baudelaire and Dürer: Avatars of Melancholia." *Symposium* 38 (1984): 244–57.

Poulet, Georges. *Who Was Baudelaire?* Translated by Robert Allen and James Emmons. Cleveland: World Publications, 1969.

Preuves 207 (May 1968). "Baudelaire et la critique d'art."

Reed, Arden. "Abysmal Influence: Baudelaire, Coleridge, de Quincey, Piranesi, Wordsworth." *Glyph* 4 (1978): 189–206.

———. *Romantic Weather: The Climates of Coleridge and Baudelaire.* Hanover: University Press of New England, 1983.

Rees, Garnet. *Baudelaire, Sartre, Camus.* Cardiff: University of Wales Press, 1976.

Sartre, Jean-Paul. *Baudelaire.* Translated by Terese Lyons. New York: Columbia University Press, 1983.

JOSEPH-ERNEST RENAN

Barrès, Maurice. *Dante, Pascal et Renan.* Paris: Plon-Nourrit et Cie, 1923.

Cahiers renaniens 1 (1970–   ).

Chadbourne, Richard M. *Ernest Renan.* New York: Twayne, 1968.

———. *Ernest Renan as an Essayist.* Ithaca: Cornell University Press, 1957.

———. "Renan and Sainte-Beuve." *Romantic Review* 44 (1953): 126–35.

Cresson, André. *Ernest Renan, sa vie, son oeuvre, avec un exposé de sa philosophie.* Paris: Presses Universitaires de France, 1949.

Dumas, Jean-Louis. "La Philosophie de l'histoire de Renan." *Revue de Métaphysique et de Morale* 77 (1972): 100–128.

Dussaud, René. *L'Oeuvre scientifique d'Ernest Renan.* Paris: Guethner, 1951.

Galand, René. *L'Ame celtique de Renan.* New Haven: Yale University Press; Paris: Presses Universitaires de France, 1959.

Genette, Gérard. "Langue du désert." In *Mimologiques,* 241–55. Paris: Editions du Seuil, 1976.

Girard, Henri, and Henri Moncel. *Bibliographie des oeuvres d'Ernest Renan.* Paris: Presses Universitaires de France, 1954.

Guehenno, Jean. *Aventures de l'esprit*. Paris: Gallimard, 1954.

Guisan, Gilbert. *Ernest Renan et l'art d'écrire*. Geneva: Droz, 1962.

James, Henry. "Ernest Renan." In *Literary Criticism: French Writers; Other European Writers; The Prefaces to the New York Edition*, 628–45. New York: Library of America, 1984.

Lasserre, Pierre. *La Jeunesse d'Ernest Renan: Histoire de la crise religieuse au XIXᵉ siècle*. 3 vols. Paris: Garnier Frères, 1925.

Lee, D. C. J. "Renan's *Avenir de la science*: Dialogue for an Absent Christ." *Nineteenth-Century French Studies* 4 (1975–76): 67–88.

Lillie, Elisabeth. "Approaches to Symbolism in the Work of Ernest Renan." *Nineteenth Century French Studies* 14 (1985–86): 110–29.

Pommier, Jean. *La Jeunesse cléricale d'Ernest Renan*. Paris: Presses Modernes, 1933.

———. "Deux notes sur Ernest Renan: 1. Souffles d'Outre-Rhin." In *Connaissance de l'étranger*, 415–24. Paris: Didier, 1964.

———. "Aux sources de la pensée esthétique de Renan." *Humanisme Actif*. Vol. 1, 217–31. Paris: Hermann, 1968.

Psichari, Henriette. *Des jours et des hommes (1890–1961)*. Paris: Grasset, 1962.

———. *La Prière sur l'Acropole et ses mystères*. Paris: Editions du Centre national de la recherche scientifique, 1956.

———. *Renan et la guerre de 70*. Paris: Albin Michel, 1947.

———. *Renan d'après lui-même*. Paris: Plon, 1937.

Rétat, L. *Religion et imagination religieuse: Leurs formes et leurs rapports dans l'oeuvre d'Ernest Renan*. Paris: Klincksieck, 1977.

Said, Edward W. "Silvestre de Sacy and Ernest Renan: Rational Anthropology and Philological Laboratory." In *Orientalism*, 123–48. New York: Pantheon, 1978.

Smith, Colin. "The Fictionalist Element in Renan's Thought." *French Studies* 9 (1955): 30–41.

Wardman, H. W. *Ernest Renan: A Critical Biography*. London: Athlone Press, 1964.

———. " 'L'Esprit de finesse' and Style in Renan." *Modern Language Review* 54 (1964): 215–24.

HIPPOLYTE TAINE

Caramaschi, Enzo. "L'Image de la Renaissance italienne dans l'oeuvre d'Hippolyte Taine." In *Mélanges à la mémoire de Franco Simone: France et Italie dans la culture européenne*. Vol. 3, *XIXᵉ et XXᵉ siècles*, 485–536. Geneva: Slatkine, 1984.

Cassirer, Ernst. "Positivism and its Ideal of Historical Knowledge: Taine." In *The Problem of Knowledge: Philosophy, Science and History since Hegel*, 242–55. New Haven: Yale University Press, 1950.

Cresson, André. *Hippolyte Taine: Sa Vie, son oeuvre*. Paris: Presses Universitaires de France, 1951.

Daugherty, Sarah B. "Taine, James, and Balzac: Toward an Aesthetic of Romantic Realism." *Henry James Review* 2 (1980): 12–24.

Eustis, Alvin A. *Hippolyte Taine and the Classical Genius*. Berkeley: University of California Press, 1951.

Evans, Colin. "Taine and His Fate." *Nineteenth-Century French Studies* 6 (1977–78): 118–28.

———. *Taine: Essai de biographie intérieure*. Paris: Nizet, 1975.

Frank, Frederick S. "The Two Taines of Henry James." *Revue de Littérature Comparée* 45 (1971): 350–65.

Goetz, Thomas H. *Taine and the Fine Arts*. Madrid: Playor, 1973.

James, Henry. "Hippolyte Taine." In *Literary Criticism: French Writers; Other Eu-*

ropean Writers; The Prefaces to the New York Edition, 826–56. New York: Library of America, 1984.

Jeune, Simon. *Taine interprète de La Fontaine.* Paris: Didier, 1968.

———. "Taine, le romantisme et la nature." *Romantisme* 10 (1980): 39–48.

Kahn, Sholom J. *Science and Aesthetic Judgement: A Study in Taine's Critical Method.* London: Routledge & Kegan Paul, 1953.

Levin, Harry. "The Contribution of Taine." In *Literary Opinion in America*, edited by M. D. Zabel, 655–66. New York: Harper & Brothers, 1951.

Morawski, Stefan. "The Problem of Value and Criteria in Taine's Aesthetics." *Journal of Aesthetics and Art Criticism* 21 (1963): 407–21.

Nordmann, Jean-Thomas. "Taine et le positivisme." *Romantisme* 8 (1978): 21–33.

———. "Taine et la décadence." *Romantisme* 13 (1983): 35–46.

Romantisme 11 (1981). Special Taine issue.

Rosca, D. D. *L'Influence de Hegel sur Taine, théoricien de la connaissance et de l'art.* Paris: J. Gambert, 1928.

Schnack, Arne. "Positivisme et structuralisme." *Orbis Litterarum* 38 (1983): 1–12.

Sullivan, Jeremiah J. "Henry James and H. Taine: The Historical and Scientific Method in Literature." *Comparative Literature Studies* 10 (1973): 25–50.

Weinstein, Leo. *Hippolyte Taine.* New York: Twayne, 1972.

Wilson, Edmund. "Decline of the Revolutionary Tradition: Taine." In *To the Finland Station: A Study in the Writing and Acting of History*, 53–64. New York: Farrar, Straus & Giroux, 1972.

STÉPHANE MALLARMÉ

Austin, Lloyd James. "Mallarmé and the Visual Arts." In *French Nineteenth-Century Painting and Literature*, edited by Ulrich Finke, 232–57. Manchester: Manchester University Press, 1972.

Bersani, Leo. *The Death of Stéphane Mallarmé.* Cambridge: Cambridge University Press, 1982.

Blanchot, Maurice. "The Absence of the Book." In *The Gaze of Orpheus*, translated by Lydie Davis, 145–60. Barrytown, N.Y.: Station Hill Press, 1981.

———. "Approaching Literary Space: Mallarmé's Experience" and "The Igitur Experience." In *The Space of Literature*. Translated and with an introduction by Ann Smock, 37–48 and 108–19. Lincoln: University of Nebraska Press, 1982.

Bloom, Harold, ed. *Modern Critical Views: Stéphane Mallarmé.* New Haven: Chelsea House, 1987.

Brun, Gerald. "Mallarmé: The Transcendance of Language and the Aesthetics of the Book." In *Modern Poetry and the Idea of Language*. New Haven: Yale University Press, 1974.

Cassidy, Steven. "Mallarmé and Andrej Belyj: Mathematics and the Phenomenality of the Literary Object." *MLN* 96 (1981): 1066–83.

Colloque Mallarmé: Glasgow, November 1973. Paris: Nizet, 1975.

Derrida, Jacques. "The Double Session." In *Dissemination*. Translated by Barbara Johnson, 173–286. Chicago: University of Chicago Press, 1981.

Dornbush, Jean. "The Death of Penultimate: Paradox in Mallarmé's 'Le Démon de l'analogie.' " *French Forum* 5 (1980): 239–60.

Dragonetti, Roger. "Mallarmé ou le malaise divin de la Critique." In *Problèmes actuels de la lecture*, Colloque de Cerisy, 1979, 151–64. Paris: Clancier-Guénaud, 1982.

L'Esprit Créateur 1, no. 3 (1961). Special Mallarmé issue.

Genette, Gérard. "Au défaut des langues." In *Mimologiques*, 257–78. Paris: Editions du Seuil, 1976.

Gill, Austin. *The Early Mallarmé*. Vol. 1, *Parentage, Early Years, and Juvenilia*. Oxford: Clarendon Press, 1979.

Goux, Jean-Joseph. "La Monnaie de Mallarmé." In *Les Faux-Monnayeurs du langage*, 139–58. Paris: Galilée, 1984.

Greer-Cohn, Robert. "The Mallarmé Century." *Stanford French Review* 2 (1978): 431–49.

Hampton, Morris D. *Stéphane Mallarmé: Twentieth Century Criticism (1901–1971)*. Jackson: University Press of Mississippi, Romance Monographs, 1977.

Hayman, David. *Mallarmé et Joyce*. 2 vols. Paris: Les Lettres Modernes, 1956.

Hyppolite, Jean. "Le Coup de dés de Stéphane Mallarmé et le message." *Les Etudes Philosophiques* 4 (1958): 463–68.

Ireson, J. C. "Towards a Theory of the Symbolist Theater." In *Studies in French Literature Presented to H. W. Lawton*, edited by J. C. Ireson, I. D. McFarlane, and Garnet Rees, 135–56. Manchester: Manchester University Press, 1968.

Johnson, Barbara. "Les Fleurs du mal armé: Some Reflections on Intertextuality." In *Lyric Poetry: Beyond New Criticism*, edited by Chavira Hoosek and Patricia Parker, 264–280. Ithaca: Cornell University Press, 1985.

Kravis, Judy. *The Prose of Mallarmé: The Evolution of a Literary Language*. Cambridge: Cambridge University Press, 1976.

Kristeva, Julia. *La Révolution du langage poétique: l'Avant-garde à la fin du XIXe siècle, Lautréamont et Mallarmé*. Paris: Editions du Seuil, 1974. *Revolution in Poetic Language*. Translated by Margaret Waller. New York: Columbia University Press, 1984.

Mehlman, Jeffrey. "Mallarmé/Maxwell: Elements." *Romanic Review* 71 (1980): 374–80.

Meschonnic, Henri. "Mallarmé au-delà du silence." In *Mallarmé, écrits sur le livre*, edited by Christophe Romana and Michel Valensi. Paris: Editions de l'Eclat, 1986.

Olds, Marshall C. *Desire Seeking Expression: Mallarmé's "Prose pour des esseintes."* French Forum Monographs 42. Lexington, Ky: French Forum, 1983.

Oxenhandler, Neal. "The Quest for Pure Consciousness in Husserl and Mallarmé." In *The Quest for Imagination*, edited by O. B. Hardison, 149–66. Cleveland: Case Western Reserve University Press, 1971.

Paxton, Norman. *The Development of Mallarmé's Prose Style*. With the original text of twenty articles. Geneva: Droz, 1968.

Poulet, Georges. "Mallarmé." In *The Interior Distance*. Translated by Elliott Coleman, 235–83. Baltimore: Johns Hopkins University Press, 1959.

Richard, Jean-Pierre. *L'Univers imaginaire de Mallarmé*. Paris: Editions du Seuil, 1961.

Sartre, Jean-Paul. *Mallarmé*. Paris: Gallimard, 1986.

Sollers, Philippe. "Literature and Totality." In *Writing and the Experience of Limits*, 63–86. New York: Columbia University Press, 1983.

Valéry, Paul. *Ecrits divers sur Stéphane Mallarmé*. Paris: Gallimard, 1950.

Wolf, Mary Ellen. *Eros under Glass: Psychoanalysis and Mallarmé's Hérodiade*. Columbus: Ohio State University Press, 1987.

FERDINAND DE SAUSSURE

Avalle, d'Arco Silvio. "La sémiologie de la narrativité chez Saussure." In *Essais de la théorie du texte*, edited by Charles Bouazis, 17–50. Paris: Galilée, 1973.

Benveniste, Emile. "Saussure après un demi-siècle." In *Problèmes de linguistique générale*. Vol. 1, 32–48. Paris: Gallimard, Collection Tel, 1966.

Cahiers Ferdinand de Saussure (1941–   ).

Culler, Jonathan. *Ferdinand de Saussure.* Harmondsworth: Penguin, 1976.

Deguy, Michel. "La Folie de Saussure." *Critique* 25 (1969): 20–26.

de Man, Paul. "Hypogram and Inscription." In *The Resistance to Theory,* 27–53. Minneapolis: University of Minnesota Press, 1986.

Derossi, Giorgio. *Segno e struttura linguistici nel pensiero di F. de Saussure.* Udine: Del Bianco, 1965.

Derrida, Jacques. *Of Grammatology.* Translated by Gayatri C. Spivak. Baltimore: Johns Hopkins University Press, 1974.

Dupuis, M. "A propos des anagrammes saussuriennes." *Cahiers d'Analyse Textuelle* 19 (1977): 7–24.

Gardiner, A. M. "De Saussure's Analysis of the 'signe linguistique.' " *Acta Linguistica* 4 (1944): 107–10.

Godel, Robert. *Les Sources manuscrites du* Cours de linguistique générale *de Ferdinand de Saussure.* Geneva: Droz, 1957.

Hawkes, Terence. "Saussure." In *Structuralism and Semiotics,* 19–27. Berkeley: University of California Press, 1977.

Jakobson, Roman. "Réflections inédites de Saussure sur les phonèmes." *Essais de linguistique générale.* Vol. 2, 287–95. Paris: Editions de Minuit, 1973. "Saussure's Unpublished Reflexions on Phonemes." *Cahiers Ferdinand de Saussure* 26 (1970): 5–14.

———. "Sign and System of Language: A Reassessment of Saussure's Doctrine." *Poetics Today* 2, no. 1a (Autumn 1980): 33–38.

Kinser, Samuel. "Saussure's Anagrams: Ideological Work." *MLN* 94 (1979): 1105–29.

Koerner, E. F. K. *Bibliographia Saussureana 1870–1970: An Annotated, Classified Bibliography on the Background, Development, and Actual Relevance of Ferdinand de Saussure's General Theory of Language.* Metuchen, N.J.: Scarecrow Press, 1972.

———. *Contribution au débat post-saussurien sur le signe linguistique.* The Hague: Mouton, 1972.

———. *Ferdinand de Saussure: Origin and Development of his Linguistic Thought in Western Studies of Language, a Contribution to the History and Theory of Linguistics.* Braunschweig, W. Germ.: Vieweg, 1973.

Kristeva, Julia. "Pour une sémiologie des paragrammes." In *Sémiotiké: Recherches pour une sémanalyse,* 174–207. Paris: Editions du Seuil, 1969.

Lévi-Strauss, Claude. "Religion, langue et histoire: A propos d'un texte inédit de Ferdinand de Saussure." In *Méthodologie de l'histoire et des sciences humaines. Festschrift for Fernand Braudel.* Vol. 2. Toulouse: Presses de l'Institut d'Etudes Politiques de Toulouse, 1973.

Rastier, François. "A propos du Saturnien. Notes sur 'Le texte dans le texte,' . . . par Jean Starobinski." *Latomus* 29 (1970): 3–24.

Rey, Jean-Michel. "Saussure avec Freud." *Critique* 29 (1973): 136–67.

Semiotexte 1, no. 2 (1974) and 2, no. 1 (1975). Special Saussure issues.

Shepheard, David. "Saussure's Vedic Anagrams." *Modern Language Review* 77 (1982): 513–21.

Spence, N. C. W. "A Hardy Perennial: The Problem of 'la langue' and 'la parole.' " *Archivum Linguisticum* 9 (1957): 1–27.

Starobinski, Jean. *Words upon Words: The Anagrams of Ferdinand de Saussure.* Translated by Olivia Emmet. New Haven: Yale University Press, 1979.

Thiher, Allan. "Ferdinand de Saussure and Jacques Derrida." In *Words in Reflection: Modern Language Theory and Postmodern Fiction,* 63–90. Chicago: University of Chicago Press, 1984.

Weber, Samuel. "Saussure and the Apparition of Language: The Critical Perspective." *MLN* 91 (1976): 913–38.

Wells, Rulon. "De Saussure's System of Linguistics." *Word* 3 (1947): 1–31.
Wunderli, Peter. *Ferdinand de Saussure und die Anagramme.* Tübingen: Max Niemeyer, 1972.

EMILE DURKHEIM

Baxi, V. "Durkheim and Legal Evolution." *Law and Society Review* 8 (1974): 645–51.
Bloor, David. "Durkheim and Mauss Revisited: Classification and the Sociology of Knowledge." In *Sociology and Knowledge: Contemporary Perspectives on the Sociology of Knowledge,* edited by Nice Stehr and Volker Meja. New Brunswick, N.J.: Transaction Books, 1984.
Clark, Terry. "Emile Durkheim and the Institutionalization of Sociology in the French University System." *European Journal of Sociology* 1 (1968): 37–71.
Clarke, M. "Durkehim's sociology of Law." *British Journal of Law and Society* 3 (1976): 246–55.
Coser, Lewis. "Durkheim." In *Masters of Sociological Thought,* 128–74. New York: Harcourt Brace Jovanovich, 1971.
Davy, Georges. "Durkheim, Montesquieu and Rousseau." In *Montesquieu and Rousseau: Forerunners of Sociology,* 144–54. Ann Arbor: University of Michigan Press, 1965.
Etudes Durkheimiennes, 1975–.
Fenton, Steve, with Robert Reiner and Ian Hamnett. *Durkheim and Modern Sociology.* New York: Cambridge University Press, 1984.
Garland, D. "Durkheim's Theory of Punishment: A Critique." In *The Power to Punish,* edited by D. Garland and P. Young. London: Heinemann, 1983.
Giddens, Anthony. "Durkheim's Political Sociology." *Sociological Review* 19 (1971): 477–519.
Hearn, Frank. "Durkheim's Political Sociology: Corporatism, State Autonomy, and Democracy." *Social Research* 52 (1985): 151–77.
Huff, T. "Discovery and Explanation in Sociology: Durkheim on Suicide." *Philosophy of the Social Sciences* 5 (1975): 241–57.
Hynes, E. "Suicide and Homo Duplex: An Interpretation of Durkheim's Typology." *Sociological Quarterly* 16 (1975): 87–104.
Kaufman-Osborn, Timothy V. "Emile Durkheim and the Science of Corporation." *Political Theory* 14 (1986): 638–59.
Kuper, Adam. "Durkheim's Theory of Primitive Kinship." *British Journal of Sociology* 36 (1985): 224–37.
LaCapra, Domenick. *Emile Durkheim: Sociologist and Philosopher.* Ithaca: Cornell University Press, 1972.
Lukes, Steven. *Emile Durkheim, His Life and Work: A Historical and Critical Study.* London: Allen Lane, 1973.
———, and A. Scull. *Durkheim and the Law.* Oxford: Martin Robertson, 1983.
Mitchell, Marion M. "Emile Durkheim and the Philosophy of Nationalism." *Political Science Quarterly* 46 (1931): 87–106.
Nandan, Yash. *The Durkheimian School: A Systematic and Comprehensive Bibliography.* Westport, Conn.: Greenwood Press, 1977.
Nisbet, Robert, ed. *Emile Durkheim.* Englewood Cliffs, N.J.: Prentice Hall, 1965.
———. *The Sociology of Emile Durkheim.* London: Heinemann, 1975.
Orru, Marco. "The Ethics of Anomie: Jean-Marie Guyau and Emile Durkheim." *British Journal of Sociology* 34 (1983): 499–518.
Parson, Talcott. *The Structure of Social Action: A Study in Social Theory with Special Reference to a Group of Recent European Writers.* 2 vols. New York: Free Press, 1968.

Pickering, W. S. F. *Durkheim's Sociology of Religion: Themes and Theories.* London: Routledge & Kegan Paul, 1984.

Pope, Whitney. *Durkheim's Suicide: A Classic Analyzed.* Chicago: University of Chicago Press, 1976.

Scharf, B. "Durkheimian and Freudian Theories of Religion: The Case of Judaism." *British Journal of Sociology* 21 (1970): 151–63.

Schmaus, Warren. "Hypotheses and Historical Analysis in Durkheim's Sociological Methodology: A Comtean Tradition." *Studies in History and Philosophy of Science* 16 (1985): 1–30.

Spitzer, S. "Punishment and Social Organisation: A Study of Durkheim's Theory of Penal Evolution." *Law and Society Review* 9 (1975): 613–37.

Taylor, Steve. *Durkheim and the Study of Suicide.* London: Macmillan, 1982.

Tiryakin, Edward A. "Emile Durkheim." In *A History of Sociological Analysis,* edited by Tom Bottomore and Robert Nisbet, 187–236. London: Heinemann, 1978.

Turner, Stephen P. "Durkheim as Methodologist: Part I—Realism, Teleology, and Action." *Philosophy of Social Sciences* 13 (1983): 426–50.

———. "Durkheim as Methodologist: Part II—Collective Forces, Causation and Probability." *Philosophy of Social Sciences* 14 (1984): 51–72.

Verdon, Michel. "Durkheim and Aristotle: Of Some Incongruous Congruences." *Studies in History and Philosophy of Science* 13 (1982): 333–52.

Wellwork, Ernest. *Durkheim: Morality and Milieu.* Cambridge, Mass.: Harvard University Press, 1972.

HENRI BERGSON

Alexander, I. *Bergson: Philosopher of Reflection.* Cambridge: Bowes & Bowes, 1957.

Aut Aut no. 204 (November–December 1984): Special Bergson issue.

Barthélémy-Madaule, Madeleine. *Bergson et Teilhard de Chardin.* Paris: Presse Universitaires de Frances 1963.

———. *Bergson adversaire de Kant: Etude critique de la conception bergsonienne du kantisme, suivie d'une bibliographie kantienne.* Preface by V. Jankélévitch. Paris: Presses Universitaires de France, 1966.

———. *Bergson.* Paris: Editions du Seuil, 1967.

———. *L'Idéologie du hasard et de la nécessité.* Paris: Editions du Seuil, 1972.

Blanchot, Maurice. "Symbolism and Bergson." *Yale French Studies* no. 4 (1949): 63–66.

Buber, Martin. "In The Silent Question: On Henri Bergson and Simone Weil." In *The Writings of Martin Buber,* edited by Will Herberg, 306–14. New York: Meridian Books, 1958.

Campbell, Sue Ellen. "Equal Opposites: Wyndham Lewis, Henri Bergson, and their Philosophy of Time and Space." *Twentieth Century Literature* 29 (1983): 351–69.

Capek, Milic. *Bergson and Modern Physics: A Re-interpretation and Re-evaluation.* Dordrecht, Netherlands: D. Reidel, 1971.

Chevalier, Jacques. *Entretiens avec Bergson.* Paris: Plon, 1959.

Chiari, Joseph. "Bergson." In *Twentieth-Century French Thought: From Bergson to Lévi-Strauss,* 21–59. London: Paul Elek, 1975.

Delattre, Floris. *Ruskin et Bergson, de l'intuition esthétique á l'intuition métaphysique.* Oxford: Clarendon Press, 1947.

Deleuze, Gilles. *Le Bergsonisme.* Paris: Presses Universitaires de France, 1966.

Douglass, Paul. *Bergson, Eliot, and American Literature.* Lexington, Ky.: University Press of Kentucky, 1986.

Etudes Bergsoniennes (1948–).

Fressin, Augustin. *La Perception chez Bergson et chez Merleau-Ponty*. Paris: Société d'Edition d'Enseignement Supérieur Réunis, 1967.

Gilson, Bernard. *L'Individualité dans la philosophie de Bergson*. Paris: Vrin, 1985.

Griffiss, James E. *Proust and Bergson: An Approach to the Problem of Poetry and Philosophy*. Baltimore: Johns Hopkins University Thesis, 1951.

Gunter, Pete A. Y. "Bergson and Jung." *Journal of the History of Ideas* 43 (1982): 635–52.

———. *Henri Bergson: A Bibliography*. Bowling Green, Ohio: Philosophy Documentation Center, Bowling Green University, 1974.

———, ed. and trans. *Bergson and the Evolution of Physics*. Knoxville: University of Tennessee Press, 1969.

Hanna, Thomas. *The Bergsonian Heritage*. New York: Columbia University Press, 1962.

Herman, Daniel J. *The Philosophy of Bergson*. Washington, D.C.: University Press of America, 1980.

Ingarden, Roman. "Intuition und Intellekt bei Henri Bergson: Darstellung und Versuch einer Kritik." *Jahrbuch für Philosophie und Phänomenologie Forschung* 5 (1922): 285–461.

Janicaud, Dominique. *Une Généalogie du spiritualisme français: Aux sources du bergsonisme: Ravaisson et la métaphysique*. The Hague: Martinus Nijhoff, 1969.

Jankélévitch, Vladimir. *Henri Bergson*. Paris: Presses Universitaires de France, 1959.

Jones, Louisa. "The Comic as Poetry: Bergson Revisited." *Nineteenth-Century French Studies* 2 (1973–74): 75–85.

Kolakowski, Leszek. *Bergson*. New York: Oxford University Press, 1985.

Kumar, Shiv Kumar. *Bergson and the Stream of Consciousness Novel*. New York: New York University Press, 1963.

Maritain, Jacques. *Bergsonian Philosophy and Thomism*. Translated by Mabelle L. Audison, with J. Gordon Audison. New York: Philosophy Library, 1955.

Megay, Joyce N. *Bergson et Proust: Essai de mise au point de la question de l'influence de Bergson sur Proust*. Paris: Vrin, 1976.

Merleau-Ponty, Maurice. *L'Union de l'âme et du corps chez Malebranche, Biran et Bergson*. Paris: Vrin, 1978.

Mossé-Bastide, Rose Marie. *Bergson et Plotin*. Paris: Presses Universitaires de France, 1959.

Pilkington, A. E. *Bergson and His Influence: A Reassessment*. Cambridge: Cambridge University Press, 1976.

Revue Internationale de Philosophie 10 (1949). Special Bergson issue.

Roberts, James D. *Faith and Reason: A Comparative Study of Pascal, Bergson, and James*. Boston: Christopher Publishing House, 1962.

Robinet, André. *Péguy entre Jaurrès, Bergson et l'Eglise: métaphysique et politique*. Paris: Seghers, 1968.

Wagner, Helmut R. *A Bergsonian Bridge to Phenomenological Psychology*. Current Continental Research 204. Washington, D.C.: Center for Advanced Research in Phenomenology and University Press of America, 1984.

CHARLES MAURRAS

Barko, Ivan P. *L'Esthétique littéraire de Charles Maurras*. Geneva: Droz, 1961.

Barrès, Maurice. *La République ou le roi: Correspondance inédite (1888–1923) de Maurice Barrès et Charles Maurras*. Commentary by Henri Massis. Introduction and notes by Guy Dupré. Paris: Plon, 1970.

Boutang, Pierre. *Maurras: La destinée et l'oeuvre.* Paris: Plon, 1984.

Buthman, William C. *The Rise of Integral Nationalism in France—with Special Reference to the Ideas and Activities of Charles Maurras.* New York: Columbia University Press, 1939.

Capitan, C. *Charles Maurras et l'idéologie française.* Paris: Editions du Seuil, 1972.

Curtis, Michael. *Three against the Third Republic: Sorel, Barrès, and Maurras.* Princeton: Princeton University Press, 1959.

Dru, Alexander. "From the Action Française to the Second Vatican Council: Blondel's 'La Semaine Sociale de Bordeaux.'" *Downside Review* 81 (1963): 226–45.

Etudes Maurrassiennes 3 (1974). Actes du troisième colloque Maurras. April 4–6, 1972. Aix-en-Provence: Centre Charles Maurras.

Etudes Maurrassiennes 4 (1980). Actes du quatrième colloque Maurras. March 29–31, 1974. Aix-en-Provence: Centre Charles Maurras.

Massis, Henri. *Maurras et notre temps: Entretiens et souvenirs.* Paris: Plon, 1961.

McCearney, James. *Maurras et son temps.* Paris: A. Michel, 1977.

Nguyen, Victor. *Intelligence et politique autour des années 1900: Aux origines de l'Action française.* Thesis: University of Provence, 1982.

Osgood, Samuel. *French Royalism under the Third and Fourth Republics.* The Hague: Martinus Nijhoff, 1960.

Roche, A. V. *Les Idées traditionalistes en France de Rivarol à Charles Maurras.* Urbana: University of Illinois Press, 1937.

Sutton, Michael. *Nationalism, Positivism and Catholicism: The Politics of Charles Maurras and French Catholics, 1890–1914.* Cambridge: Cambridge University Press, 1983.

Thibaudet, Albert. *Les Idées de Charles Maurras.* Paris: Editions de la Nouvelle Revue Française, 1920.

Weber, Eugen. *Action française: Royalism and Reaction in Twentieth-Century France.* Stanford: Stanford University Press, 1962.

ANDRÉ GIDE

Apter, Emily S. "Writing without Style: The Role of Litotes in Gide's Concept of Modern Classicism." *French Review* 57 (1983): 28–36.

———. "Gide's *Traité du Narcisse*: A Theory of the Post-Symbolist Sign?" *Stanford French Review* 9 (1985): 189–200.

———. *André Gide: Strategies of Textual Negation.* Stanford French and Italian Studies. Saratoga, Calif.: ANMA Libri, 1986.

Barthes, Roland. "On Gide and His Journal." In *A Barthes Reader*, edited by Susan Sontag, 3–17. New York: Hill & Wang, 1982.

Benjamin, Walter. "André Gide et ses nouveaux adversaires." In *Essais II: 1935–40*, translated by Maurice de Gandillac, 127–42. Paris: Denoël, 1971, 1983.

Blanchot, Maurice. "Gide et la littérature d'expérience." In *La Part du feu*, 208–20. Paris: Gallimard, 1949.

———. "André Gide et Goethe." and "Au Sujet des *Nourritures Terrestres*." In *Faux pas*, 311–17 and 337–42. Paris: Gallimard, 1971.

Brachfeld, Georges I. *André Gide and the Communist Temptation.* Geneva: Droz, 1959.

Brée, Germaine. *Gide.* New Brunswick, N.J.: Rutgers University Press, 1963.

Brosman, Catherine S. "Gide, Translation, and 'Little Gidding.'" *French Review* 54 (1981): 690–98.

Bulletin des amis d'André Gide (1967–).

Cordle, Thomas. *André Gide.* New York: Twayne, 1969.

Delay, Jean. *La Jeunesse d'André Gide.* 2 vols. Paris: Gallimard, 1956–57.

de Man, Paul. "Whatever Happened to André Gide?" *New York Review of Books*, 6 May 1965: 15–17.

Fayer, Mischa H. *Gide, Freedom and Dostoevsky.* Burlington, Vt.: Lane Press, 1946.

Fillaudeau, Bertrand. *L'Univers ludique d'André Gide.* Paris: José Corti, 1986.

Fowlie, Wallace. *André Gide: His Life and Art.* New York: Macmillan, 1965.

Grover, Frederic J. "Les Années 30 dans la correspondance Gide-Paulhan." *MLN* 95 (1980): 830–49.

Harris, Frederick J. *André Gide and Romain Rolland: Two Men Divided.* New Brunswick, N.J.: Rutgers University Press, 1973.

Hytier, Jean. *André Gide.* New York: Frederic Ungar, 1967.

Klossowski, Pierre. "Gide, Du Bos et le démon" and "En Marge de la correspondance de Claudel et de Gide." In *Un Si funeste désir*, 37–54 and 55–58. Paris: Gallimard, 1963.

Lacan, Jacques. "Jeunesse de Gide, ou la lettre et le désir: Sur un livre de Jean Delay, et d'un autre de Jean Schlumberger." In *Ecrits*, 739–64. Paris: Editions du Seuil, 1966.

Lange, B. Renée. *André Gide et la pensée allemande.* Paris: Egloff, 1949.

Lottman, Herbert R. "André Gide's Return: A Case-Study in Left-Bank Politics." *Encounter* 58 (January 1982): 18–27.

Mann, Klaus. *André Gide and the Crisis of Modern Thought.* New York: Creative Age Press, 1943.

Marshall, W. J. "André Gide and the U.S.S.R.: A Re-Appraisal." *Australian Journal of French Studies* 20 (1983): 37–49.

Marty, Eric. *L'Ecriture du jour: Le journal d'André Gide.* Paris: Editions du Seuil, 1985.

Mauriac, Claude. *Conversations avec André Gide.* Paris: Albin Michel, 1951.

O'Brien, Justin. *Portrait of André Gide: A Critical Biography.* New York: Knopf, 1953.

Painter, George D. *André Gide.* New York: Atheneum, 1968.

Pasco, A. H., and Wilfrid J. Rollman, "The Artistry of Gide's Onomastics." *MLN* 86 (1971): 523–31.

Pierre-Quint, Léon. *André Gide: L'Homme, sa vie, son oeuvre.* Paris: Stock, 1952.

Rossi, Vinio. *André Gide: The Evolution of an Aesthetic.* New Brunswick, N.J.: Rutgers University Press, 1967.

Sahel, André P. "André Gide and North Africa: A Process of Liberation." *Aligarth Journal of English Studies* 8 (1983): 24–39.

Schlumberger, Jean. *Madeleine et André Gide.* Paris: Gallimard, 1956.

Segal, Naomi. " 'Parfois j'ai peur que ce que j'ai supprimé ne se venge,' Gide and Women." *Paragraph* 8 (October 1986): 62–74.

Thomas, Lawrence. *André Gide: The Ethic of the Artist.* London: Secker & Warburg, 1950.

MARCEL PROUST

Autret, Jean. *L'Influence de Ruskin sur la vie, les idées et l'oeuvre de Marcel Proust.* Geneva: Droz, 1955.

Bersani, Leo. *Marcel Proust: The Fictions of Life and of Art.* New York: Oxford University Press, 1965.

Blanchot, Maurice. "L'Expérience de Proust." In *Le Livre à venir*, 20–40. Paris: Gallimard, 1959.

Blumenthal, Gerda. *Thresholds: A Study of Proust.* Birmingham, Ala.: Summa Publications, 1987.

Brun, Bernard. "L'Edition d'un brouillon et son interprétation: Le problème du

Contre Sainte-Beuve." In *Essais de critique génétique,* 151–92. Paris: Flammarion, 1979.

Chantal, René de. *Marcel Proust: Critique littéraire.* 2 vols. Montréal: Presses Universitaires de l'Université de Montréal, 1967.

Cocking, J. M. *Proust: Collected Essays on the Writer and his Art.* New York: Cambridge University Press, 1982.

Deleuze, Gilles. *Proust and Signs.* Translated by Richard Howard. New York: George Braziller, 1972.

Doubrovsky, Serge. *La Place de la madeleine: Ecriture et fantasme chez Proust.* Paris: Mercure de France, 1974.

Ellison, David R. *The Reading of Proust.* Baltimore: Johns Hopkins University Press, 1984.

Erickson, John, and Irene Pagès, eds. *Proust et le texte producteur.* Baton Rouge: Louisiana State University Press, 1980.

Genette, Gérard. "Proust et le language indirect." In *Figures II,* 223–94. Paris: Editions du Seuil 1969.

——, and Tzvetan Todorov, eds. *Recherche de Proust.* Paris: Editions du Seuil, 1980.

Girard, René. "Narcissism: The Freudian Myth Demythified by Proust."In *Psychoanalysis, Creativity, and Literature,* edited by Alan Roland. New York: Columbia University Press, 1978.

Harlow, Barbara. "Sur la lecture." *MLN* 90 (1975): 849–71.

Henry, Anne. *Marcel Proust, théories pour une esthétique.* Paris: Klincksieck, 1981.

Hughes, Edward J. *Marcel Proust: A Study in the Quality of Awareness.* New York: Cambridge University Press, 1983.

Kasell, Walter. "Proust the Pilgrim: His Idolatrous Reading of Ruskin." *Revue de littérature comparée* 49 (1975): 547–60.

——. *Marcel Proust and the Strategy of Reading.* Philadelphia: J. Benjamin, 1980.

Keller, Luzins. "L'Autocitation chez Proust." *MLN* 95 (1980): 1,032–48.

Macksey, Richard. "Proust on the Margins of Ruskin." In *The Ruskin Polygon,* edited by J. D. Hunt and F. M. Holland, 172–97. Manchester: Manchester University Press, 1981.

Nattiez, J. J. *Proust musicien.* Paris: Christian Bourgois, 1984.

Painter, George D. *Marcel Proust: A Biography.* 2 vols. New York: Random House, 1959.

Richard, Jean Pierre. *Proust et le monde sensible.* Paris: Editions du Seuil, 1974.

Rivers, J. E. *Proust and the Art of Love.* New York: Columbia University Press, 1980.

Russell Taylor, Elisabeth. *Marcel Proust and His Contexts: A Critical Bibliography of English-Language Scholarship.* New York: Garland, 1981.

Strauss, Walter. *Proust and Literature: The Novelist as Critic.* Cambridge, Mass.: Harvard University Press, 1957.

Sussman, Henry. *The Hegelian Aftermath: Readings in Hegel, Kierkegaard, Freud, Proust and James.* Baltimore: Johns Hopkins University Press, 1982.

Yale French Studies no. 34 (1965). Special Proust issue.

Yoshida, Jo. "Proust contre Ruskin: La genèse de deux voyages dans *La Recherche* d'après des brouillons inédits." Diss.: Paris-Sorbonne, 1978.

PAUL VALÉRY

Adorno, Theodor W. "Les Ecarts de Valéry." In *Notes sur la littérature,* translated by Sibylle Müller, 101–40. Paris: Flammarion, 1984.

——. "Valéry Proust Museum." In *Prisms.* Translated by Samuel and Shierry Weber, 173–86. Cambridge, Mass.: MIT Press, 1981.

Bellemin-Noël, Jean, ed. *Les Critiques de notre temps et Valéry*. Paris: Garnier, 1971.

Bémol, Maurice. "Paul Valéry, *Cahiers* tomes I et II." *Revue d'Histoire Littéraire de la France* 58 (1958): 556–61.

———. "Paul Valéry, *Cahiers*, tomes III–X." *Revue d'Histoire Littéraire de la France* 60 (1960): 245–59.

Blanchot, Maurice. "Valéry et Faust." In *La Part du feu*, 263–77. Paris: Gallimard, 1949.

Bloom, Harold, ed. *Modern Critical Views: Paul Valéry*. New Haven: Chelsea House, 1987.

Bulletin des Études Valéryennes. Université Paul Valéry, Montpellier.

Celeyrette-Pietri, N. *Valéry et le moi*. Paris: Klincksieck, 1979.

Chapon, François, and Georges Karaïskakis, eds. *Paul Valéry: Bibliographie— 1889–1965*. Paris: Auguste Blaizot, 1976.

Combe, Dominique. "Lire la poésie, lire le roman, selon Valéry: Une phénoménologie de la lecture." *Littérature* 59 (October 1985): 57–70.

Crow, Christine. *Paul Valéry and the Poetry of Voice*. New York: Cambridge University Press, 1982.

Freedman, Ralph. "Valéry: Protean Critic." In *Modern French Criticism*, edited by John K. Simon, 1–40. Chicago: University of Chicago Press, 1972.

Gaède, E. *Nietzsche et Valéry*. Paris: Gallimard, 1962.

Genette, Gérard. "Valéry and the Poetics of Language." In *Textual Strategies: Perspectives in Post-Structuralist Criticism*, edited by Josué Harari, 359–73. Ithaca: Cornell University Press, 1979.

Ince, W. N. *Paul Valéry: Poetry and Abstract Thought*. Southampton: Camelot Press, 1973.

Jarrety, Michel. "La Voix de Descartes et la main de Pascal: Note sur Valéry et l'écriture philosophique." *Nouvelle Revue Française* 375 (1984): 62–71.

Jauss, Hans Robert. "Goethe and Valéry's *Faust*: On the Hermeneutics of Question and Answer." In *Toward an Aesthetic of Reception*. Translated by Timothy Bahti, 110–38. Minneapolis: University of Minnesota Press, 1982.

La Rochefoucauld, Édmée de. *En Lisant les Cahiers de Paul Valéry*. Paris: Editions Universitaires, 1964.

Laurenti, Hugette, ed. *Revue des Lettres Modernes*. Paris: Minard. Issues on Valéry: 3. *Approches du Système* (1979); 4. *Le Pouvoir de l'esprit* (1983).

Laurette, P. *The Theme of the Tree in Paul Valéry*. Paris: Klincksieck: 1967.

Lawler, James R. "Paul Valéry, *Cahiers*, tomes XXII–XXIX." *Revue d'Histoire Littéraire de la France* 63 (1963): 62–89.

Levaillant, Jean. "Inachèvement, invention, écriture, d'après les manuscrits de Paul Valéry." *Le Manuscrit inachevé*. Paris: Editions du Centre National de la Recherche Scientifique, 1986.

———, ed. *Ecriture et génétique textuelle: Valéry à l'oeuvre*. Lille: Presses Universitaires de Lille, 1982.

———, and Monique Parent, eds., *Paul Valéry contemporain*. Paris: Klincksieck, 1974.

Littérature 56 (1984). Special Valéry issue.

Mallet, Robert, ed. *Correspondance Gide-Valéry*. Paris: Gallimard, 1955.

Mehlman, Jeffrey. "On Tear-Work: L'art- de Valéry." *Yale French Studies* no. 52 (1975): 152–73.

———. "Cranometry and Criticism: Notes on a Valerian Criss-Cross." *Boundary 2* 11 (1982–83): 81–101.

MLN 87 (May 1972). Special Valéry issue.

Muller, Marcel. "La Dialectique de l'ouvert et du fermé chez Paul Valéry." *Michigan Romance Studies* 1 (1980): 163–85.

ANDRÉ BRETON

Antelme, Robert; Marguerite Bonnet; Michel Leiris; and Dionys Mascolo, "Sur un détournement de la pensée." *La Quinzaine littéraire* 114 (March 1971): 11–24.

Anzieu, D. *L'Auto-analys.* Paris: Presses Universitaires de France, 1958.

L'Arc 37 (1969). Special Surrealism issue.

Avni, Ora. "Breton et l'idéologie: Machine à coudre-parapluie." *Littérature* 51 (October 1983): 15–27.

Balakian, Anna. "Metaphor and Metamorphosis in André Breton's Poetics." *French Studies* 19 (1965): 34–41.

————. *André Breton, Magus of Surrealism.* New York: Oxford University Press, 1971.

Bataille, Georges. "André Breton: Le Révolver à cheveux blancs." *La Critique Sociale* 7 (January 1933): 47–50.

————. "Le Surréalisme et sa différence avec l'existentialisme." *Critique* 1 (1946): 99–100.

Benayoun, Robert. *Erotique du surréalisme.* Paris: Pauvert, 1965.

Benjamin, Walter. "Surrealism: The Last Snapshot of the European Intelligentsia." In *Reflections,* edited with an introduction by Peter Demetz, 177–92. New York: Harcourt Brace Jovanovich, 1978.

Blanchot, Maurice. "Réflexions sur le surréalisme." In *La Part du feu,* 90–102. Paris: Gallimard, 1949.

————. "Le Demain joueur." In *L'Entretien infini,* 597–619. Paris: Gallimard, 1969.

Bonnet, Marguerite. *André Breton: Naissance de l'aventure surréaliste.* Paris: José Corti, 1975.

————. *Les Critiques de notre temps et Breton.* Paris: Garnier, 1974.

Breton, André. *What Is Surrealism? Selected Writings.* Edited and introduced by Franklin Rosemont. New York: Pathfinder Press, 1978.

Browder, Clifford. *André Breton: Arbiter of Surrealism.* Geneva: Droz, 1967.

Caillois, Roger. "Intervention surréaliste (divergences et connivences)." In *Cases d'un échiquier,* 209–22. Paris: Gallimard, 1970.

Carrouges, Michel. *André Breton et les données fondamentales du surréalisme.* Paris: Gallimard, 1950.

Caws, Mary Ann. *A Metapoetics of the Passage: Architectures in Surrealism and After.* Hanover: University Press of New England, 1981.

————. *André Breton.* New York: Twayne, 1971.

————. *Surrealism and the Literary Imagination: A Study of Breton and Bachelard.* The Hague: Mouton, 1966.

Davis, Frederick B. "Three Letters from Sigmund Freud to André Breton." *Journal of the American Psychoanalytic Association* 21 (1973): 127–34.

Deguy, Michel. "En relisant les manifestes." *Nouvelle Revue Française* 20 (1962): 857–62.

Eigeldinger, Marc, ed. *André Breton: Essais et témoignages.* Neuchâtel: La Baconnière, 1970.

Ellenwood, Ray. *Breton and Freud.* Ph.D. diss.: Rutgers University, 1972.

Entretiens sur le surréalisme. Colloque de Cerisy-La-Salle. The Hague: Mouton, 1968.

Gersmann, H. S. "Valery and Breton." *Yale French Studies* no. 44 (1970): 199–206.

Halpern, Joseph. "Breton's Overheated Room." *French Forum* 4 (1982): 47–57.

Houdeline, Jean-Louis. "André Breton et la double ascendance du signe." *La Nouvelle Critique* 31 (1970): 43–45.

Ladimer, Bethany. "Madness and the Irrational in the Work of André Breton: A Feminist Perspective." *Feminist Studies* 6 (1980): 175–95.

Legrand, Gérard. *André Breton.* Paris: Belfond, 1977.

———. *André Breton en son temps.* Paris: Le Soleil Noir, 1976.

Matic, Dusan. *André Breton oblique.* Montepellier: Fata Morgana, 1976.

Matthews, J. H. *André Breton.* New York: Columbia University Press, 1967.

———. *Towards the Poetics of Surrealism.* Syracuse: Syracuse University Press, 1976.

———. *Surrealism, Insanity, and Poetry. Imagery of Surrealism.* Syracuse: Syracuse University Press, 1982

Nadeau, Maurice. *Histoire du surréalisme.* Paris: Seuil, 1964.

Nouvelle Revue Française 25 (April 1967). André Breton (1896–1966) et le mouvement surréaliste.

Parisier Plottel, Jeanine. "Surrealist Archives of Anxiety." *Yale French Studies* no. 66 (1984): 121–36.

Parmentier, Michel A. "André Breton et la question de l'unité du psychisme." *Australian Journal of French Studies* 20 (1983): 50–60.

Riese Hubert, Renée. "The Artbook as Poetic Code: Breton's *Yves Tanguy.*" *L'Esprit Créateur* 22 (Winter 1982): 56–66.

Robert, Bernard-Paul. "Breton, Hegel et le surréalisme." *Revue de l'Université d'Ottawa* 44 (July–September 1974): 281–301.

Schwarz, Arturo. *Breton/Trotsky.* Paris: U.G.E., 1977.

Sheringham Michael. *André Breton: A Bibliography.* London: Grant & Cutler, 1972.

Soupault, Philippe. *Le Vrai André Breton.* Liège: Dynamo, 1966.

———. *Profils perdus.* Paris: Mercure de France, 1963.

Starobinski, Jean. "Freud, Breton, Myers." *L'Arc* 34 (1968): 87–96. Reprinted in *La Relation critique.* Paris: Gallimard, 1970.

Waretime, Marja. "Beginning and Ending: The Utility of Dreams in *Les Vases communicants.*" *French Forum* 6 (1981): 163–71.

SIMONE WEIL

Allen, Diogenes. *Three Outsiders: Pascal, Kierkegaard, Simone Weil.* Cambridge, Mass: Cowley, 1983.

Anderson, David. *Simone Weil.* London: SCM Press, 1971.

Blanchot, Maurice. "L'Affirmation (le désir, le malheur)." In *L'Entretien infini,* 153–79. Paris: Gallimard, 1969.

Cabaud, Jacques. *Simone Weil: A Fellowship in Love.* New York: Channel Press, 1965.

Cahiers Simone Weil (1978–   ).

Chiari, Joseph. "Simone Weil and Pierre Teilhard de Chardin." *Twentieth-Century Thought: From Bergson to Lévi-Strauss,* 140–54. London: Paul Elek, 1975.

Coles, Robert. *Simone Weil: A Modern Pilgrimage.* Reading, Mass.: Addison-Wesley, 1987.

Debidour, Victor-Henry. *Simone Weil ou la transparence.* Paris: Plon, 1963.

Dujardin, Philippe. *Simone Weil, idéologie et politique.* Grenoble: Presses Universitaires de Grenoble, 1975.

Eliot, T. S. Preface to Simone Weil's *The Need for Roots: Prelude to a Declaration of Duties toward Mankind.* London: Routledge & Kegan Paul, 1952.

Fraisse, Simone. "La Représentation de Simone Weil dans *Le Bleu du ciel* de Bataille." *Cahiers Simone Weil* 5 (1982): 81–91.

Hellman, John. *Simone Weil: An Introduction to her Thought.* Philadelphia: Fortress Press, 1984.

Kahn, Gilbert, ed. *Simone Weil: Philosophe, historienne et mystique.* Paris: Aubier-Montaigne, 1978.

Little, Janet P. *Simone Weil: A Bibliography.* London: Grant & Cutler, 1973. Supplement, 1980.

————. "Society as Mediator in Simone Weil's *Venise sauvée*." *Modern Language Review* 65 (1970): 298–305.

Milosz, Czeslaw. "The Importance of Simone Weil." In *Emperor of the Earth*. Berkeley: University of California Press, 1977.

Murdoch, Iris. "On 'God' and 'Good.' " In *Revisions*, edited by Stanley Hawerwas and Alasdair MacIntyre. Notre Dame, Ind.: University of Notre Dame Press, 1983.

Panichas, George A. *Simone Weil Reader*. New York: Moyer Bell, 1977.

Pétrement, Simone. *Simone Weil: A Life*. Translated by Raymond Rosenthal. New York: Pantheon, 1976.

Rees, Richard. *Simone Weil: A Sketch for a Portrait*. Carbondale: Southern Illinois University Press, 1966.

Simonsuuri, Kirsti. "Simone Weil's Interpretation of Homer." *French Studies* 39 (1985): 166–77.

Sontag, Susan. "Simone Weil." In *Against Interpretation*, 49–51, New York: Farrar, Straus & Giroux, 1961.

Springsted, Eric. *Affliction and the Love of God: The Spirituality of Simone Weil*. Cambridge, Mass: Cowley, 1986.

Thibon, G., and J.-M. Perrin. *Simone Weil as We Knew Her*. London: Routledge & Kegan Paul, 1953.

White, George A., ed. *Simone Weil: Interpretations of a Life*. Amherst: University of Massachusetts Press, 1981.

Acknowledgments

"Destutt de Tracy: Ideology, Language, and the Critique of Metaphysics" (originally titled "Scientific Method and Ideology" and "Signs, Language and the Critique of Metaphysics") by Brian William Head from *Ideology and Social Science: Destutt de Tracy and French Liberalism* by Brian William Head, © 1985 by Martinus Nijhoff Publishers, Dordrecht. Reprinted by permission.

"Mme de Staël *De l'Allemagne:* A Misleading Intermediary" by Lilian R. Furst from *The Contours of European Romanticism* by Lilian R. Furst, © 1979 by Lilian R. Furst. Reprinted by permission of the University of Nebraska Press.

"Benjamin Constant: Ancient and Modern Freedom in Context" (originally titled "Freedom in Context") by Stephen Holmes from *Benjamin Constant and the Making of Modern Liberalism,* © 1984 by Yale University. Reprinted by permission of Yale University Press.

"The Occidental Orient: Chateaubriand" (originally titled "The Occidental Orient") by Andrew Martin from *The Knowledge of Ignorance: From Genesis to Jules Verne,* © 1985 by Cambridge University Press. Reprinted by permission.

"Fourier" by Roland Barthes from *Sade, Fourier, Loyola* by Roland Barthes, © 1976 by Farrar, Straus & Giroux, Inc. Reprinted by permission of Farrar, Straus & Giroux, Inc., and Jonathan Cape, Ltd.

"The Foundations of Positivism and the Rise of Sociology: Saint-Simon and Comte" (originally titled "The Foundations of Positivism and the Rise of Sociology") by Herbert Marcuse from *Reason and Revolution: Hegel and the Rise of Social Theory* by Herbert Marcuse, © 1954 by Humanities

Press Inc. Reprinted by permission of Humanities Press International, Inc.

"A Sort of History: Michelet's *La Sorcière*" by Linda Orr from *Yale French Studies*. no. 59 (1980), © 1985 by *Yale French Studies*. Reprinted by permission.

"The Treatment of Architecture in the Works of Edgar Quinet Published before 1851" by Ceri Crossley from *Literature and Society: Studies in Nineteenth and Twentieth Century French Literature,* edited by C. A. Burns, © 1980 by Ceri Crossley. Reprinted by permission.

"Sainte-Beuve's Literary Portraiture" by Emerson R. Marks from *L'Esprit Créateur* 14, no. 1 (Spring 1974), © 1974 by *L'Esprit Créateur*. Reprinted by permission.

"De Tocqueville and the Problem of the French Revolution" by François Furet from *Interpreting the French Revolution* by François Furet, translated by Elborg Forster, © 1981 by Maison des Sciences de l'Homme and Cambridge University Press. Reprinted by permission of Cambridge University Press and Elborg Forster.

"Proudhon and Rousseau" by Aaron Noland from *Journal of the History of Ideas* 28, no. 1 (January–March 1967), © 1967 by *Journal of the History of Ideas*, Inc. Reprinted by permission.

"Baudelaire against Photography: An Allegory of Old Age" by Susan Blood from *MLN* 101, no. 4 (September 1986), © 1986 by The Johns Hopkins University Press. Reprinted by permission.

"Islam, Philology, and French Culture: Renan and Massignon" by Edward W. Said from *The World, the Text, and the Critic* by Edward W. Said, © 1983 by Edward W. Said. Reprinted by permission of Harvard University Press and Faber & Faber, Ltd.

"Taine and Saussure" by Hans Aarsleff from *From Locke to Saussure: Essays on the Study of Language and Intellectual History* by Hans Aarsleff, © 1982 by the University of Minnesota. Reprinted by permission of the University of Minnesota Press.

"Mallarmé and Literary Space" by Maurice Blanchot from *The Sirens' Song: Selected Essays by Maurice Blanchot,* edited by Gabriel Josipovici and translated by Sacha Rabinovitch, © 1982 by The Harvester Press Ltd. Reprinted by permission of The Harvester Press, Ltd., and Indiana University Press.

"Mallarmé: Poetry and Syntax: What the Gypsy Knew" (originally titled "Poetry and Syntax: What the Gypsy Knew") by Barbara Johnson from *The Critical Difference: Essays in the Contemporary Rhetoric of Reading,* © 1981 by The Johns Hopkins University Press. Reprinted by permission.

"Saussure: The Game of the Name" (originally titled "The Game of the Name") by Sylvère Lotringer from *Diacritics* 3, no. 2 (Summer 1973), © 1973 by Diacritics, Inc. Reprinted by permission of The John Hopkins University Press.

"Epistemology in Durkheim's *Elementary Forms of Religious Life*" by Terry F. Godlove, Jr., from *Journal of the History of Philosophy* 24, no. 3 (July 1986), © 1986 by Journal of the History of Philosophy, Inc. Reprinted by permission.

"Movement-Image: Commentaries on Bergson" (originally titled "Theses on Movement: First Commentary on Bergson" and "The Movement-Image and Its Three Varieties: Second Commentary on Bergson") by Gilles Deleuze, from *Cinema 1: The Movement-Image,* translated by Hugh Tomlinson and Barbara Habberjam, © 1983 by Les Editions de Minuit, © 1986 by The Athlone Press. Reprinted by permission of The Athlone Press and University of Minnesota Press.

"Maurras's Genealogy of the Decline of France, and Proposed Remedies" (originally titled "Individualism, the Decline of France, and Maurras's Proposed Remedy") by Michael Sutton from *Nationalism, Positivism, and Catholicism: The Politics of Charles Maurras and French Catholics 1980–1914* by Michael Sutton, © 1982 by Cambridge University Press. Reprinted by permission.

"The Duplicitous Genre of André Gide" by Kevin Newmark, © 1987 by Kevin Newmark. Published for the first time in this volume.

"Proust Reads Ruskin" by David R. Ellison from *The Reading of Proust* by David R. Ellison, © 1984 by The Johns Hopkins University Press. Reprinted by permission.

"Qual Quelle: Valéry's Sources" by Jacques Derrida from *Margins of Philosophy* by Jacques Derrida, translated by Alan Bass, © 1982 by The University of Chicago. Reprinted by permission of the University of Chicago Press and The Harvester Press, Ltd.

"Bachelard and the Romantic Imagination" by Margaret R. Higonnet from *Comparative Literature* 33, no. 1 (Winter 1981), © 1981 by the University of Oregon. Reprinted by permission of the author.

"Breton and Freud" by Jean-Pierre Morel from *Diacritics* 2, no. 2 (Summer 1972), © 1972 by Diacritics, Inc. Reprinted by permission of The Johns Hopkins University Press.

"Doors: Simone Weil with Kafka" by A. Smock from *MLN* 95, no. 4 (May 1980), © 1980 by The Johns Hopkins University Press. Reprinted by permission.

Index